BUSINESS COMPUTER SYSTEMS
AN INTRODUCTION

THIRD EDITION

BUSINESS COMPUTER SYSTEMS
AN INTRODUCTION
THIRD EDITION

DAVID M. KROENKE

KATHLEEN A. DOLAN

M|**P** *Mitchell Publishing, Inc.*
Innovators in Computer Education
915 River Street • Santa Cruz, California 95060
(800) 435-2665 • In California (408) 425-3851

Dedication to Quality Publishing: All employees of Mitchell Publishing, Inc.
Sponsoring Editor: Erika Berg
Director of Product Development: Raleigh Wilson
Production Management: Richard Mason, Bookman Productions
Interior and Cover Design: Janet Bollow
Composition: Skillful Means Press
Printing: R.R. Donnelley and Sons Company

LIBRARY OF CONGRESS CATALOG NUMBER
86 - 82005

ISBN 0 - 394 - 39055 - 5

Printed in the United States of America

10 9 8 7 6 5 4 3 2

APPLICATION SOFTWARE   Application software is available from the publisher to supplement the text. Either limited-edition commercial software or popular shareware packages may be used, and both are accompanied by tutorial lab manuals.

SUPPLEMENTARY MICRO LAB MANUALS   Various tutorial lab manuals for the IBM PC and Apple are available to supplement the text. These popular lab manuals feature self-paced, step-by-step, hands-on introductions to the most popular software packages for word processing, spreadsheets, personal databases, and graphics.

COMPREHENSIVE INSTRUCTOR'S GUIDE   New to this edition is a special guide for new teachers, TAs, and part-timers that contains detailed lecture notes. Also included is a description of changes from the second edition. Retained are the sample course syllabi, lecture outlines, chapter objectives, teaching tips for part-time and TA instructors, and "emergency" lectures.

STUDY GUIDE/CASEBOOK (by Dee Stark)   This time-tested study guide is unique. It does not just routinely summarize the content of the text. Instead, it "drives" the reading of the text by requiring specific reading assignments necessary to answer questions and tests. Organized into one-hour lessons, the study guide includes objectives, highlights, reading assignments, questions, and alternatives to the cases in the text.

COMPUTERIZED TEST BANK   Class-tested for three years, the computerized test bank is not just a file of test questions. It is a test generator, with the ability to modify or delete the over 1,000 T/F, multiple choice, and fill-in-the-blank questions.

DYNAMIC SET OF TRANSPARENCY MASTERS   This material consists not of a fixed but a dynamic, ongoing set of transparencies. In addition to containing illustrations from the text, this set features new transparencies highlighting state-of-the-art topics, transparencies that will be updated on a semi-annual basis.

BASIC TUTORIAL (by Randy Johnston)   This brief, menu-driven BASIC tutorial, accompanied by documentation, comes in three versions — for the IBM PC, Apple II, and DEC Rainbow.

BROADCAST-QUALITY VIDEOTAPES   This documentary-style series of 17 half-hour tapes has been broadcast by PBS and numerous statewide consortia. The series, "Computers at Work," includes a Student Videocourse Manual that keys reading assignments in the text to each video lesson.

BRIEF TABLE OF CONTENTS

PHOTO ESSAY   HARDWARE: More and More for Less and Less

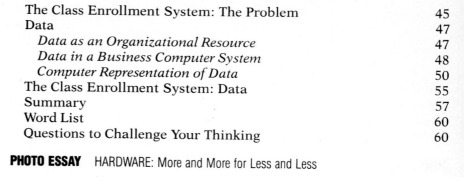

CHAPTER 3   INTRODUCTION TO BUSINESS COMPUTER SYSTEMS: HARDWARE, PROGRAMS, PROCEDURES, AND TRAINED PERSONNEL   61

CHAPTER 4   SURVEY OF BUSINESS COMPUTER SYSTEMS APPLICATIONS   95

PART TWO
FUNDAMENTAL BUSINESS COMPUTER SYSTEMS   **141**

CHAPTER 5   THE SYSTEMS DEVELOPMENT PROCESS   **143**

CHAPTER 6   A CASE APPLICATION   **171**

PHOTO ESSAY   MICROCOMPUTERS: How to Become a Smart Shopper

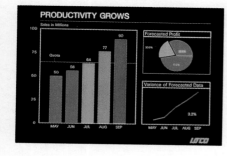

PART FOUR
SPECIAL COMPUTING TOPICS 411

PHOTO ESSAY   THE CHIP: The Heart of the Computer

PART FIVE
PROGRAMMING   **543**

The five color sections in this book are unique. Many computer textbooks today are full of color photographs. This new edition of Business Computer Systems also contains exciting color photos. However, what makes these photos unique is the way in which they are presented.

Each of the more than 200 color photos was carefully selected to illustrate the content of five essays — essays written on topics of special interest and importance for today's introductory computer student. The five photo essays are intended to be both instructional and entertaining. The photo essays conclude with review questions and enhance the content covered in the text. They may be used in any order or as optional assignments.

HARDWARE: More and More for Less and Less This photo essay presents today's computer hardware (input, processing, output, and storage) in an easily understandable format. The differences between microcomputers, minicomputers, and mainframes are emphasized with a wealth of examples and applications from the business world.

MICROCOMPUTERS: How to Be a Smart Shopper This extension of chapters 5 and 6 is not only interesting; it is practical. This photo essay introduces a small legal firm that is learning how best to select its own microcomputer hardware and software, and to develop a cost-effective system. Also featured are tips on how to select a printer, how to care for your disks and disk drives, how to select a service person, and how to choose a computer store.

THE CHIP: The Heart of the Computer The mystery surrounding the silicon chip is here imaginatively unraveled by a simple, straightforward explanation, accompanied by a wealth of colorful illustrations and photographs by award-winning National Geographic photographer, Chuck O'Rear.

COMPUTERS IN SOCIETY: More Uses, More Users, More Questions This photo essay examines many interesting computer applications and asks the reader to think about their impact — both good and bad — on society.

BUSINESS COMPUTER GRAPHICS: Persuasive Power at Your Fingertips Business computer graphics is one of the most exciting and explored areas in today's computer industry, and this photo essay illustrates why. Featured here are the reasons for the growing fascination for computer graphics, hardware and software requirements, color tips, objectives of presentation graphics, and practical applications.

In recent years many concerned educators have devoted considerable time to defining curriculum standards for the subject of information systems. Such standards are both very important and exceedingly difficult to keep current for a subject that is always changing with new technology. Several associations have done an outstanding job in formulating these standards, however, and this book was developed to conform with and support those efforts.

DPMA This text provides source material for all of the suggested topics in course CIS-1 of the Data Processing Management Association Education Foundation Model Curriculum for Undergraduate Computer Information Systems. The structure of this text follows the association's recommendation that the purpose of CIS-1 is to "place emphasis on computer requirements in organizations, history, hardware functions, programming, systems development, and computer operations."

ACM This text also recognizes the philosophy stated in the Association for Computing Machinery 1981 Information Systems Curriculum Report, and supports the opinion that "the demand for personnel having a combination of technical and organizational skills is relatively much greater than the demand for solely technical skills."

AACSB Additionally, this book follows the guidelines set out by the American Assembly of Collegiate Schools of Business, which suggest that students obtain a basic understanding of "management information systems including computer applications."

Both the authors and publisher of this text believe in the necessity for and importance of these standards, and continue to support and work with the many dedicated professionals involved in this important task.

Few introductory computer texts have successfully negotiated three editions. The rapid rate of change in information systems technology and methodology necessitates such drastic changes in coverage that most texts cannot withstand the adaptation required to keep them current and relevant.

In planning the third edition of *Business Computer Systems*, we wanted to maintain the fundamental philosophy and structure that users of the first two editions have found interesting and useful for their students. At the same time, we wanted to revise and add new material to make the book reflect information systems *today*. We wanted to help students become knowledgeable end-users — to give them a basic understanding of how computer systems are applied to meet business needs.

We quickly realized that the revision was a test of the very philosophy we have been espousing! Since the first edition we have been saying that if we organize our teaching around fundamental concepts, students will be able to adapt to changes in technology long after they have taken the course. If that's true, then the structure of this book, which is based on these concepts, should be flexible enough to accept the addition of new technology.

We believe that this edition bears out this philosophy. We have added new technology while retaining the book's conceptual design. The three conceptual frameworks that have consistently differentiated *Business Computer Systems* from other introductory computer texts, and have made each edition a success, are as follows:

1. The Five-Component Model
2. The Systems Development Process
3. Systems Concepts

TEACHING FUNDAMENTALS

We believe that students should have a broad background in the application of systems technology to the business environment. In particular, students graduating from this course should be able to answer the following questions based on our three conceptual frameworks:

1. The Five-Component Model: What is an information system?
2. The Systems Development Process: How are information systems developed?

3. Systems Concepts: What are the basic types of information systems?

We believe this text will successfully prepare the student to answer each of these questions. Let's now see how.

What Is an Information System?

An information system is more than just a computer with a program. As we explained in the first two editions of this book, an information system consists of five components: hardware, programs, data, procedures, and people. These five components interact to satisfy a set of user needs.

Many teachers have praised the effectiveness of this conceptual framework. They say it provides a structure for students to organize their learning. It enables them to tie together the many facts, concepts, and developments that are part of the dynamic field of business computer systems. Whenever students encounter a new piece of technology, they will know to ask: What hardware is required? What programs? How is the data organized? Which procedures will be required? Who will be needed? Such a discipline is simple and enduring. Students can benefit from it throughout their professional lives.

This text begins with three short cases. These cases illustrate the need for users to know about information systems. Two of the cases have successful outcomes because the key decision makers knew fundamental concepts. The third has an unhappy outcome because the key people lacked such knowledge.

The Five-Component Model was presented in one chapter in previous editions. In the third edition we have recognized the vital importance of *data* as a corporate asset. Thus, after introducing the Model we devote the major part of chapter 2 to one of the five components: data. In chapter 3 we focus on the four remaining components: hardware, software, procedures, and people. The concepts in both chapters are illustrated with an application familiar to all students: class enrollment.

How Are Information Systems Developed?

We view all students as future end-users. In many colleges, the introductory computer course is the only computer course that non-computer majors take; this may be their only opportunity to learn how computer systems should be developed. This knowledge is important not because these students will develop small microcomputer systems of their own, but rather because as end-users they will invariably participate in the development of computer systems, whether they realize this fact or not.

An introduction to systems development is critical for future end-users. Without an early exposure to this topic, majors are too likely to conclude that hardware or programming have more importance in systems development than they do. Students need to see the "systems" forest before they plunge into the "programming" or "application software" trees.

The single chapter on systems development in the second edition has been overhauled and now occupies two full chapters, chapters 5 and 6. Chapter 5 discusses the concepts, goals, steps, and tools used in systems development. Alternatives to traditional design techniques, such as prototypes and data flow diagrams, are presented here.

Chapter 6 illustrates systems development with a case study that does not presuppose that programs will be written in-house. Further, special considerations for microcomputer-based systems are included. The purpose of the case is to add interest and meaning to the systems development process.

Systems development concepts continue to be reinforced in chapters 7 and 8. Although these chapters specifically address sequential and direct access file processing, they do so in the context of systems development activity.

What Are the Basic Types of Information Systems?

Even in the age of the microcomputer it is important to teach students all the fundamental types of systems. The fact that the microcomputer has gained unprecedented popularity does not mean that systems that are prevalent on mini- and mainframe computers can or should be ignored. In fact, as microcomputer operating systems become more sophisticated, such knowledge will become valuable even to micro-computer users.

Thus, the fundamental types of systems are presented chapter by chapter in the following sequence:

- Chapter 7   Sequential File Processing
- Chapter 8   Direct Access File Processing
- Chapter 9   Database Processing
- Chapter 10 Teleprocessing & Distributed Processing Systems
- Chapter 11 Management Information & Decision-Support Systems

This organization is unique for an introductory computer text. Most introductory computer textbooks focus first on hardware, then on software, and so on. In this book you will not find a chapter on hardware, as such. Unlike most books, *Business Computer Systems* does not discuss each of the components in isolation. Instead, the material is covered by data organization. It is presented in the context of various types of systems.

The rationale for this approach is that each chapter presents a complete, integrated system. With this organization students learn, for example, not only what a disk drive is, but also how a direct access system can be utilized to satisfy information needs. We have used this organization because it has enabled thousands of students to relate technology to systems, and systems, in turn, to information needs in a better way.

THE THIRD EDITION: WHAT'S NEW?

Microcomputer Coverage

The single most significant change in this edition concerns the coverage of microcomputers. Since most students will encounter micros daily, we have integrated and expanded the coverage of micros and their hardware, software, acquisition, and uses. Our goal is to illustrate the impact of this tool called a microcomputer on business and the end-user.

In most cases we are not concerned with micros in isolation, but rather as components of information systems. Again, we focus on concepts and processes so that our discussion will continue to serve the student irrespective of what next year's microcomputer looks like.

In Module B we deal exclusively with micros. We present concepts pertaining to the three most popular types of microcomputer applications:

1. Word Processing
2. Electronic Spreadsheets
3. Database Management

Even though this module is concerned with micros, we have broadened the presentation by discussing these applications in a generic sense. We define the characteristics of each of these applications and describe features and functions that software should have. Through a wide range of applications, we also illustrate how these kinds of software can be used as personal productivity tools.

If you would like to use the conceptual material in this text as a "springboard" to hands-on instruction of specific packages, call Mitchell Publishing at (800) 435–2665. They have an array of tutorial lab manuals covering commercial packages, shareware, and educational software.

Management Information and Decision-Support Systems

The second most obvious change in this edition has been the addition of a chapter on MIS/DSS. As microcomputers proliferate, as end-user interfaces become easier to use and understand, as program generators and other productivity tools become more common, and as the general level of sophistication in the end-user community increases, more and more attention will be focused on the use of computers in the decision-making process. Therefore, students should be exposed to the management process and potential applications of computer technology in management.

However, this is easier said than done. Most students have trouble relating to basic business operations, let alone to the more sophisticated and airy dimensions of management tactics and strategy. Therefore, we have kept the discussion simple and down-to-earth. Concepts are illustrated in the context of a straightforward case that is introduced early in the text.

Expert Systems

Expert systems, or knowledge-based systems, are a branch of artificial intelligence that has come to have significance for business. The core of such a system is the ability to *infer*. This ability is new to business information systems, and so we believe that it is important to introduce it to students today. Thus, a discussion of expert/knowledge-based systems has become a special feature of the MIS/DSS chapter in the third edition.

Communications and Local-Area Networks

We have consolidated the chapters on teleprocessing and distributed data processing from the second edition. At the same time, we have illustrated the growing importance of local-area networks. Since many end-users procure and install LANs themselves, students need to be exposed to the fundamental concepts. Thus, we have added a major section to the teleprocessing chapter on this topic.

End-User Database Systems

It is becoming clear that databases can be designed to match the end-user's view of the business environment. Our new database chapter, chapter 9, reflects these changes in industry.

Systems Development

Kathleen Dolan was selected as a co-author of *Business Computer Systems* because of her expertise in the area of systems development. Kathy has experience as a systems analyst, teacher, and consultant in both education and industry. Users of the second edition will observe Kathy's contribution to the discussions of systems development in chapters 5 and 6.

The single chapter on systems development in the second edition has been overhauled and now occupies two full chapters. The first one, chapter 5, discusses the concepts, goals, steps, and tools used in systems development. Also featured here is coverage of end-user programming, prototyping, dataflow diagrams, data dictionaries, and structure charts. Then, in chapter 6 the systems development process is brought to life with a case study.

Modern Programming Modules

Users will also find that Kathy has completely reworked and modernized the programming modules, modules F, G, and H. The approach taken in these modules is unique. The emphasis is on problem-solving. The sample programs are broken down into several mini-programs, or modules. Each module is presented and explained as if it were a tiny program itself. Teaching this process illustrates that regardless of the size and complexity of a program, it can be broken down into small, easily understandable units.

BUILDING ON THE STRENGTH OF PAST EDITIONS

While adding new features and benefits to the third edition, we have maintained those aspects of the previous editions that users found most effective. Earlier, we discussed the primary features, namely the Five-Component Model, the Systems Development Process, and Systems Concepts. In addition, we have retained several other features.

Use of Vignettes

To some people technology is dry and boring. Nor does computer technology always relate to real-world situations. To add interest and facilitate the transfer of knowledge to business settings, this text contains many small cases and vignette applications. These stories illustrate the human aspects of developing and running business computer systems. They give students a chance to apply chapter material in solving actual business problems. In so doing, the stories illustrate how computers are used as tools and resources in today's competitive society.

Photo Essays

The third edition is enhanced by numerous photos, both in the body of the text and in these full-color photo essays:

1. Hardware: More and More for Less and Less

2. Microcomputers: How to Be a Smart Shopper
3. The Chip: The Heart of the Computer
4. Computers in Society: More Uses, More Users, and More Questions
5. Business Computer Graphics: Persuasive Power at Your Fingertips

These color inserts carefully combine text and photos to illustrate the uses of computers today and to stimulate students' interest and awareness.

Boxed Articles

Excerpts from business and computer magazine articles are organized into three categories—"Profiles," "Applications," and "Microcomputers"—and featured in each chapter. These boxes highlight contemporary, real-world applications of corresponding chapter topics. These supplemental readings add to the strong end-user orientation of the text. They help students understand how computer technology is used to solve problems, to increase productivity, and to gain a competitive edge.

Modular Approach

Introductory courses vary. Needs differ depending on the school, its location, the type of student, the teacher's approach, the surrounding business environment, and so forth. This text was organized in recognition of that fact; you will find eight independent modules in parts 4 and 5. These modules can be mixed and matched as you choose.

IN CONCLUSION

We believe that this text represents more than a third edition of a successful book. It represents the acceptance by thousands of teachers and students of the Five-Component Model as a valuable concept for understanding, and tool for teaching, the often difficult, complicated, dynamic material of an introductory computer course.

Our students benefit not from the bulk and detail of our knowledge but from grasping its essence. It is with lessons based upon simple and consistent concepts born of the breadth and depth of our own knowledge that our students are able to move forward to open new doors, explore new worlds, and surpass our own achievements.

SUPPORT PACKAGES

Business Computer Systems is supplemented by a complete range of ancillaries designed to help both the student and the instructor.

These ancillaries include the following:

1. Instructor's Guide
2. Student Study Guide/Casebook
3. Computerized Test Bank
4. Transparency Masters
5. Applications Software for the IBM PC for word processing (Word-Star 3.3), electronic spreadsheets (SuperCalc 3.0), and databases (dBase III Plus sampler)
6. Supplemental Microcomputer Lab Manual to support the step-by-step, hands-on instruction of WordStar 3.3, SuperCalc 3.0, and dBase III Plus sampler
7. Seventeen broadcast-quality Videotapes.

PRINCIPAL ACKNOWLEDGMENTS

In a project such as this there are always a few people whose contributions make all the difference. We extend a very special thank you to Leonard Schwab of the California State University at Hayward, and to Penny Fanzone of Essex Community College. Their extensive reviews were instrumental in the development of this edition of *Business Computer Systems*. We are also grateful to Randy Skelding of the Digital Equipment Corporation and Henry Gettenberg of Computerland for their technical support.

ACKNOWLEDGMENTS

Thanks to the following people who have provided helpful comments and other assistance in the preparation of this edition.

Gary R. Armstrong
Shippensburg University

Jack D. Becker
University of Missouri

Patricia Boggs
Wright State University

Elias R. Callahan, Jr.
Mississippi State University

Larry Clark
Cayuga Community College

Marilyn J. Correa
Polk Community College

Caroline Curtis
Lorain County Community
College

Joan Miley Danehy
State University New York,
Morrisville

Dennis Emmerich
Community College of Aurora

William C. Fink
Lewis & Clark Community
College

John H. Grose
Villanova University

Richard Hopeman
Villanova University

Bert Hurn
University of Missouri, Columbia

Peter L. Irwin
Richland College

Art Larson
University of Wisconsin,
Whitewater

Olof Lundberg
University of New Orleans

Charles H. Mawhinney
Indiana University of
Pennsylvania

Dick Meyer
Hartnell College

K. Mikan
University of Montevallo

John Palipchak
Pennsylvania State University

Earl J. Robinson
St. Joseph's University

S. G. Ryan
Baruch/CUNY

Tom Sarazen
Red Rocks Community College

G. E. Shaw
Macomb Community College

Erwin C. Vernon
Sinclair Community College

Tony Verstraete
Pennsylvania State University

Susan White
Catonsville Community College

Ken Wilson
Algonquin College

INTRODUCTION TO BUSINESS COMPUTER SYSTEMS

PART ONE

The four chapters in part 1 introduce you to business computer systems. Chapter 1 tells three stories about people and companies and their experiences in developing computer systems. Two of these situations turned out well, and the other one — well, you can read it.

Chapters 2 and 3 define business computer systems. You will learn about the five components of a business computer system, which will be illustrated by an example system that should be familiar to you — a system for monitoring class enrollment. These two chapters are very important; the concepts presented in them will be referred to throughout the text. Chapter 4 surveys the business applications of computers. It will help you relate computing to business areas that are of interest to you.

WHY STUDY BUSINESS COMPUTING?

CHAPTER 1

Ten years ago, computers were kept in the back rooms of major corporations. They did administrative data processing in a very controlled and restricted environment. Management's posture was that whatever happened behind the locked doors in the air-conditioned room was in the domain of computer specialists. Every now and then management had to throw a bag of money over the wall, but as long as that action kept the reports arriving more or less on time and more or less accurate, management had little to do with computing.

Today's situation differs in every way. Microcomputers pervade all levels of corporate life. Secretaries use word processors instead of typewriters, marketing analysts use electronic spreadsheets instead of wide sheets of accounting paper, executive assistants employ graphics packages instead of drawing boards to produce charts for the boardroom. Even the smallest organization can afford a computer, and many individuals have purchased their own computers to increase their professional productivity.

Computers have become the standard business equipment, and you will have to know about them to be competitive. Businesses value their corporate databases; a computerized list of registered customers is sometimes an organization's major asset. Using computers for strategic planning has become a way for one corporation to gain a competitive advantage over another.

Closer to home, computers enable people to do more things faster. This book was published more rapidly because it was written, edited, and typeset by computer. If you use a word processor, you can write a paper in half the time required by a student 10 years ago. You can make more changes, add more material, and reprint the changes more times than a student would have dreamed of in 1977. Because of the computer you can learn more, and learn faster, than your predecessors.

If you plan to be successful in business then you will have to learn how to use computers. If you do not know how to use them then you will not be able to keep pace with the competition. Computers can enable you to increase your personal productivity, increase the productivity of the business in which you work, and give you access to countless sources of valuable information.

There are few business applications that cannot benefit from computer use. Of course, not all computer applications are the same. They vary in terms of scope, objectives, size of computer required, number of people involved, amount of data used, and other factors. To illustrate the range of possibilities, three cases will be considered here. The first concerns a single individual, the second concerns a small department, and the third concerns a small company. Observe the way the nature of the computer system changes as the application involves more and more people.

These cases contain business and computer terms that you may not understand. Do not be alarmed by them. You do not need to understand

SENIOR PROGRAMMER ANALYST

Qualified candidate will be responsible for:

- Designing and coding complex programs and systems for clinical and research database applications.
- Assisting supervisor in the development of system design and specification.
- Maintaining, modifying and documenting all programs and systems.
- Providing ongoing support and training to the end-user for database applications.

Data Communications and Networking.

We are at the forefront of a myriad of technologies, offering professionals the opportunity to work with today's most sophisticated information Systems Group.

As data communications and networking leaders, we provide our customers with everything from public and private networks to new and emerging high technologies such as satellite networks. Our ability to deliver solutions is a direct result of dedicated professionals who strive to get closer to the mainstream of data communications and networking.

Strategic Marketing Associate

Working closely with the Manager of Strategic Marketing, you will research marketing data and financial information for new U.S. activities of our expanding, multi-national, high technology company. You will also establish and maintain a cross reference data bank.

FIELD TRAINING SPECIALIST

Microsoft, the leading manufacturer of computer software, is seeking a FIELD TRAINING SPECIALIST to instruct clients in the use of Microsoft products.

the details of these cases at this point. Try instead to get a feel for what can happen when people interact with computers.

MARY FORSYTHE

Mary Forsythe is a self-employed consultant who teaches seminars on effective communication to business and government personnel. She offers six courses on subjects such as basic communications skills, communication for managers, and coping with problematical employees.

Mary majored in dramatic arts in college and worked for the public relations department of a large auto manufacturer after graduation. She enjoyed the opportunities provided by a large organization, but ultimately she wanted more of a personal challenge, and so she started her own company.

Mary knew that most small businesses fail because of inadequate financing, so she tried to minimize her expenses. She rented a modest office and decided to do all of her own typing using a word processing program on a microcomputer. Mary had learned while working for the public relations department that she could compose, type, and print a letter faster herself using a microcomputer than she could by dictating the letter for preparation by a secretary.

Mary's interest in computers is limited to the results she can get from them. To her a computer is a tool for reducing her costs and thereby increasing her profit. She learned how to accomplish the several tasks she wanted from her word processor, and beyond that, she doesn't think much about computing. She is not interested in computer magazines, she could not care less about the latest whiz-bang gizmo, and she visits computer stores only when she needs more paper.

The Need for a Mailing List Application

About six months into her new business, Mary realized that she was busier than she wanted to be, and she wasn't making as much money as she thought she should. As she reflected on her business, she realized that she was making far too many after-dinner speeches (for free) and not giving enough professional seminars (for a fee). Part of Mary's problem was that she was an exciting and interesting speaker. This was also an asset, however, because many of the people who attended one of Mary's seminars wanted to attend another. In fact, she sometimes received letters from attendees asking about the availability of other seminars.

As she thought about these issues, Mary realized that she was underutilizing one of her assets — her contact list of prior seminar at-

PROFILE

"USE OF COMPUTER TECHNOLOGIES TO DEVELOP MORE SELECTIVE AND PROFITABLE MAILING PROGRAMS"

The Midwest's leading data processing service company, May & Speh, Inc., has formed a direct marketing information services company. It hopes to win business through its utilization of state-of-the-art computer technologies to develop more selective and profitable front-end mailing programs for clients.

The new firm intends to be a leader in sophisticated list preparation, and to develop strategies by using several unique services not available from traditional direct-marketing companies, claims Larry Speh, president of May & Speh Direct. He explains that the service will be marketed to its database clients, primarily to encourage greater use of target marketing. Hopefully, the service will result in fewer mailings yet more effective promotional pieces.

Clients buying this service, he says, could statistically analyze, score, and then rank their best customers and prospects before a mailing goes out. This could improve response rates and lower mailing costs, Speh points out. In addition, he notes, target marketing helps the clients determine profitability break-off spots in their mailing lists.

Among the other services offered by the company is a consultation/database management service, which works with a client's files and lists, building a database of marketing and financial information. This data is then used to maximize the effectiveness of mailings by automatically ranking customers and prospects for future profitability. The consulting service can also help reduce the inherent financial risk involved with direct mailings and provide analysis of previous mailings done by the client.

tendees. "Hmm," she thought. "I could obtain the membership lists of the organizations to which I've spoken, add member names and addresses to this list, and have a great resource for sending out seminar announcements. I could even customize the list — send announcements of management training seminars, for example, only to people who are managers."

The more Mary thought about this idea, the more she liked it. She also knew, however, that she did not know how to proceed. Her word processing program wouldn't support such a list, but surely something would? Mary knew that she needed some way to store names, addresses, and other business information in the computer, and some way to get the computer to print mailing lists based on selected criteria. And she was determined to find a way to do it. Some of Mary's problems are listed below:

- Identifying potential customers and collecting their names
- Targeting seminar advertising to potential customers
- Finding someone to develop her system
- Integrating her present word processing system with a customer mailing list

Developing the Application

As a struggling young entrepreneur, Mary did not have the financial resources to hire a consultant to solve her problem. What she lacked in money, however, she more than made up for in creativity. She called the president of the local chapter of the personal computer (PC) users group (usually, a group of more technically oriented microcomputer users who meet periodically to discuss trends, new products, new technology, and so forth) and made the following proposition: "I've heard that more technical computer people sometimes have trouble communicating. I'll give your group a one-day seminar on communications skills if you'll have one of your members develop a mailing list program for me."

The president of the group considered her proposal. He asked her a series of questions that enabled him to determine that what she wanted was feasible and probably wouldn't take more than a day of development time. He saw Mary's seminar as a potential fund raiser for the PC users group. "All right," he said, "we've got a deal."

As it turned out, the president himself had experience in developing applications like mailing lists, and within a week he arranged to meet Mary at her office. Together they identified a microcomputer database management system (DBMS) that would accommodate her mailing list and interface with the word processing program she already had. A DBMS, he explained, is a program that can store and report data for applications such as mailing lists. He even told her where she could go to obtain the best price.

The Results

Mary purchased the DBMS, and on the following Saturday the users group president developed a mailing list application for Mary's business. This application included forms (see figure 1–2) for entering and changing data and reports for printing the mailing labels (see figure 1–3). During the next week, Mary employed part-time typists to key in about a thousand names and other data that she had collected. Within two weeks she had her mailing list application up and running and was actually using it before she gave the seminar to the PC users group.

(To finish the story: Twenty-seven people attended her seminar, and the PC users group made $1134, much to the relief and pleasure of the president. The seminar was very well received, and Mary obtained two more seminar opportunities from people who attended.)

Mary's problem was a simple one. Her needs were straightforward and clear, her requirements were common, and there were many suitable products available. No one needed to develop any new programs to support her application. Additionally, Mary already knew how to use a microcomputer, and she was confident enough to try new applications. Further, Mary runs a one-person office, and she doesn't

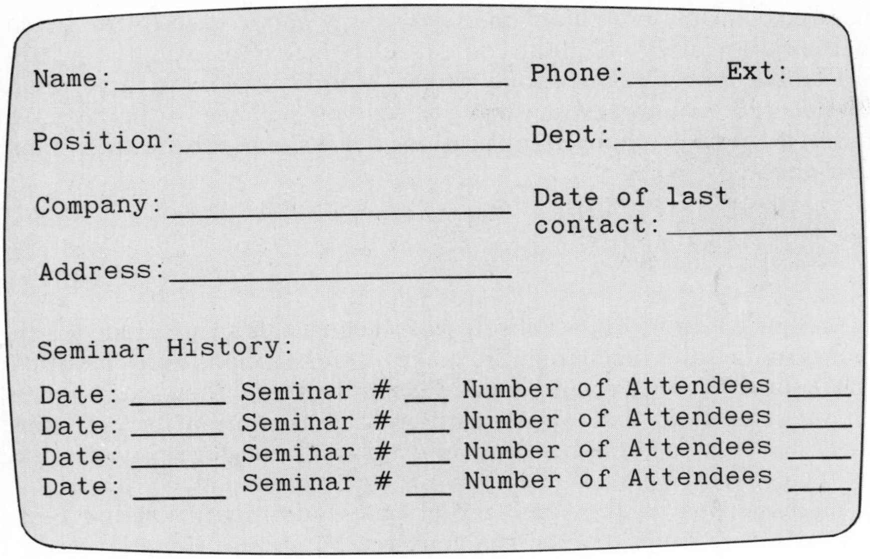

FIGURE 1–2
Data entry form designed for Mary Forsythe

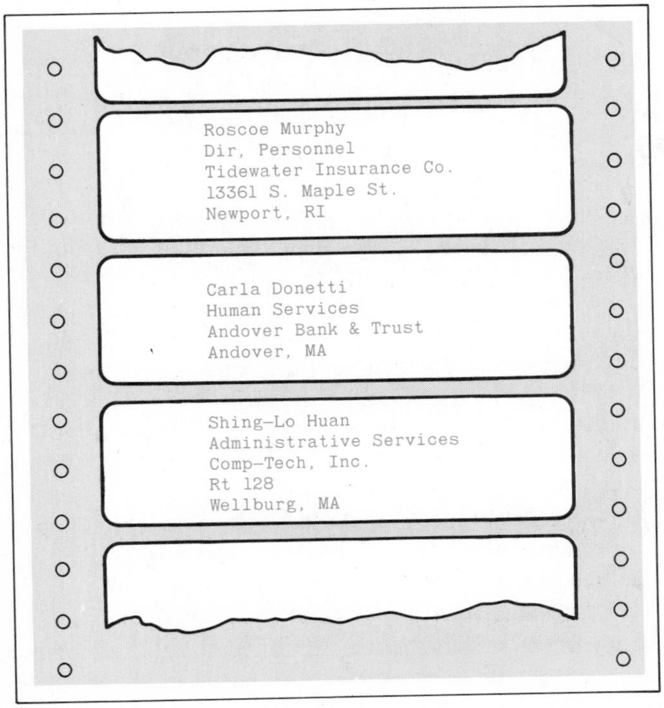

```
Name:_____   Phone:_____Ext:___

Position:_____   Dept:_____

Company:_____   Date of last
                          contact:_____

Address:_____


Seminar History:

Date:_____ Seminar #___ Number of Attendees ____
Date:_____ Seminar #___ Number of Attendees ____
Date:_____ Seminar #___ Number of Attendees ____
Date:_____ Seminar #___ Number of Attendees ____
```

FIGURE 1–3
Mailing labels produced by Mary Forsythe's system

```
Roscoe Murphy
Dir, Personnel
Tidewater Insurance Co.
13361 S. Maple St.
Newport, RI

Carla Donetti
Human Services
Andover Bank & Trust
Andover, MA

Shing-Lo Huan
Administrative Services
Comp-Tech, Inc.
Rt 128
Wellburg, MA
```

need to coordinate with anyone. She simply had to describe her needs to the expert, after which she could teach herself how to use the system.

If all computer applications were as simple as Mary's, there would be no need for courses like this one. As you will see in the next two cases, however, computer applications can become substantially more complicated.

BLAKE RECORDS AND TAPES

"I've had it!" said Ellen Gibson with disgust. "It's ridiculous for the clerks in the sales department to make all these graphs every month. It takes three people two and a half days to do it, and then management changes its mind and wants a different presentation for the board meeting. There's got to be a way to use a computer for this work" (see figure 1–4 and figure 1–5).

Ellen Gibson is the manager of sales administration for Blake Records and Tapes, a chain of four record stores. Her department

FIGURE 1–4

Clerks manually preparing graphs of sales

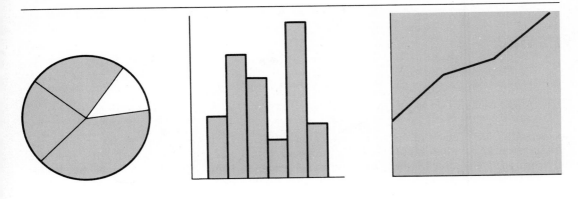

a. Example of a pie chart   b. Example of a bar graph   c. Example of an XY Plot

FIGURE 1–5
Sample graphs produced by Blake's
salesclerks

handles all the paperwork regarding sales, store inventories, and so forth. Ellen has a B.A. in education; after teaching elementary school for several years, she decided teaching wasn't what she really wanted to do. She returned to college and earned a degree in sales and marketing.

After graduation, Ellen joined Blake as a salesperson. She became an assistant store manager within a year, and six months later she was promoted to her present job. She works hard and has a good memory for sales facts. Her manner with people is friendly and easygoing. Ellen is known among sales personnel as the person to call for reliable sales data. Her subordinates think she is a fair and effective manager.

The Need for Computer Assistance

Ellen was upset about the time required to produce graphs of sales data. Blake's salesclerks had to perform the following tasks:

1. Copy weekly sales order data from computer report by hand
2. Sum data in different ways by hand (by date, record company, salesperson)
3. Make calculations on groups of data, generate sales predictions by hand
4. Portray results graphically using pie charts, bar groups, and XY plots (see figure 1–5)

Ellen had taken two computer classes in college — an introductory course and a course in systems development. She knew that a computer could save the clerks considerable work and frustration. She thought all the calculations and even the graphs could be prepared by computer, which would eliminate the greatest source of frustration for the clerks — redoing the calculations and graphs again and again while management decided what it wanted.

APPLICATION

"THE GRAPHIC REPRESENTATION MAKES INFORMATION EASILY DIGESTIBLE AND EASIER TO REMEMBER"

In today's information age, with time at a premium, graphic representation has been transformed from a nice field into a high-impact tool. It makes information easily digestible and hence easy to remember. If graphics are fun to look at, they are more likely to convince people.

At Empire Blue Cross/Blue Shield in New York City, Carolyn Sands turns out a wide variety of charts and graphs for special presentations every month. In the past she would make black-and-white mechanicals by hand, send them to the graphics department for the color additions

she required, and then have them photographed and processed into slides. Now Sands does all her designing at the computer. "It's an enormous time-saver and offers me much more flexibility in working with color," she says. A group of fifteen slides, for example, used to take her two or three days to develop. Using her computer she can now design the same material in about an hour.

Even if you've never used a computer before (or, conversely, even if you've never done anything artistic before), you'll find that a computer screen is a forgiving canvas that lends

itself to experimentation and the making of mistakes. "It's just like using a pencil and paper, but in this case the paper never gets dirty," says M. A. Hancook. As director of corporate communications at DPC & A, which designs economic evaluation software for the oil and gas industry, Hancook uses a computer to put together slide and transparency presentations. "The computer is so easy to manipulate that what used to take me 8 hours to accomplish now takes me just 15 minutes. It allows me to play 'what if' graphically."

Blake had a computer that was used for accounting and inventory applications. Ellen knew that it could be programmed to perform some of the salesclerks' calculations and to make the graphs. She discussed this use with the director of data processing (DP), Peter Wandolowski. He asked her to fill out a request form, which she had done once before over a year ago. She filled out another request, but she still received no response. Finally she complained loudly enough that Peter promised to send over a computer systems analyst when he could spare one from other work.

Analysis of the Problem

Two months later, the analyst appeared. His name was Fred Sanchez, and he was superb. He had 12 years of systems analysis experience, could communicate well, knew data processing inside and out, and had worked with the marketing department in a previous job. Unfortunately, he was available only part time.

In her computer courses Ellen had learned how important it is for computer people to understand requirements. Therefore, she asked Fred to present to her staff his understanding of their requirements when he was finished. She also wanted him to prepare a document summarizing the requirements.

Fred spent the next week with the sales administration staff. On Friday he presented his understanding of their requirements to Ellen and the clerks. They suggested only a few minor adjustments; they believed that Fred now understood their problems very well.

As Fred handed Ellen the requirements summary, he said, "Frankly, Ellen, I've got some bad news. If we try to develop these programs in-house, it will be at least a year before we get them done. We've got so much other work, and some of these programs will take some time to develop. We'll need a full-time analyst and a programmer."

He went on to explain that he had put the matter before Peter Wandolowski and had been told that no one was available. They would just have to make do with part-time help. Fred candidly told Ellen that this arrangement seemed unfair to all the people involved.

After Fred left, Ellen and her staff stared gloomily at one another. "Well, what will we do now?" Ellen asked.

"Maybe we should try the Yellow Pages," said one of the clerks sarcastically.

"Hey, that's not a bad idea!" said Ellen. "Maybe one of these new microcomputers I've been hearing about can do our job. Let's look into it!" Here are some of the problems encountered by Ellen:

- Sales summaries took too long to produce
- The data processing department was not responsive
- Sales staff had no background in programming or running a computer.

The Microcomputer System

Over the weekend, Ellen visited computer stores. She gathered information about programs called *electronic spreadsheets* (see module B) and about graphics packages. The graphics programs could produce outputs like those in figure 1–5. These systems supposedly would not require programming and could be used by inexperienced personnel with no computing background. "Do you suppose we could run a microcomputer ourselves?" she thought.

The next week was a busy one for the sales administration staff. In addition to their regular work, they investigated the possibility of buying a microcomputer. They called several stores and talked with the sales personnel. When they became confused, they called Fred. He came over one afternoon and they asked him questions until 8:00 that night. The following list summarizes the conclusions drawn from this conversation:

- An incredible variety of microcomputer hardware exists
- Select programs first, then appropriate hardware
- Off-the-shelf programs could perform 70 percent of processing
- Remaining 30 percent of programs would need to be written in-house
- Several suitable graphics programs exist

By the end of the week, Ellen had a good picture of the microcomputer alternative (figure 1–6). The advantages were that the computer could run on regular power, and it needed no air conditioning. Thus, the microcomputer could be located in the sales area and be controlled by the staff. Also, it was simple to operate, the electronic spreadsheet and graphics programs would do most of the required job, and the computer could be programmed by the staff in a language called BASIC.

The disadvantages of the system were that it would cost about $10,000 (although Ellen thought it would pay for itself in labor savings in less than 18 months), the microcomputer could not completely manage their job; some work would still have to be done manually. Also, the quality of the graphs would not be as high as those the clerks currently produced manually, though Ellen thought the graphs would be adequate. Finally, for the computer to perform calculations and create graphs, sales data would have to be entered into the computer, but there was far too much data for the clerks to type in. However, the data processing department already had the necessary data in its computer and, according to Fred, the microcomputer could get this data from the data processing department's computer via a communication line (like a telephone line). Fred said he doubted that Ellen would get much cooperation from the data processing staff, however.

Ellen thought seriously about this project. On Monday and Tuesday she prepared a proposal for management in which she discussed costs and benefits. She showed that, considering only labor savings, the project would easily justify its cost. Also, she discussed the data processing staff's busy schedule and explained how this project would relieve some of the burden on them.

Resistance from Data Processing

Ellen presented the proposal to her boss, the vice-president of sales, and Peter Wandolowski on Wednesday. Pete was vehemently opposed

FIGURE 1–6
Advantages and disadvantages of a microcomputer system

Advantages	Disadvantages
1. Can run on regular power and needs no special air-conditioning.	1. Costs $10,000.
2. Can reside in Sales Administration area and be controlled by the clerks.	2. Some manual work required.
3. Is simple to operate.	3. Graph quality not as high as manually prepared graphs.
4. Can be programmed in BASIC.	4. Needs cooperation of Data Processing for input data.

PROFILE

"A COMPUTER SYSTEM FOR AN EXPANDING SMALL BUSINESS"

Even fashion designers cannot escape the move into computerization. Dianne Benson of the Dianne B. Collection and owner of stores in New York City found herself taking the plunge when she opened her second store in 1981. Admitted Benson, "I had no education in computers and I thought, when they appeared on the scene and everyone was computerizing like mad, that this would be a process that would pass me by. Until I opened my second store."

Benson started with a Tandy Radio Shack computer, which she found inexpensive and easy to use. A consultant (the "computer doctor") customized the software so that it duplicated the manual systems Benson had developed.

With her Dianne Benson Men and Women store slated to open in April, she found that her computer system could not accommodate the sudden growth. But she resisted further changes for fear of becoming too technical. She continued to hire her staff for their fashion sense, not for their ability to use a computer. At a recent computer demonstration, however, she learned about features previously unknown to her and she was convinced enough to go ahead and plan upgrading. "It sounds like a dream to me," says Benson. "I can't wait till it happens."

to Ellen's buying a microcomputer. He expressed a dozen or so objections in a 30-minute, emotion-filled meeting.

To the vice-president of sales, some of the objections seemed rational. Pete believed that Ellen's staff was insufficient and unqualified to operate the system and that the system would require much more support than the microcomputer salespeople had said. Also, he was concerned about control of the data. How could the data processing department ensure that Ellen's data was current? Or that her staff would maintain adequate security and control? Or that they would take appropriate backup and recovery actions? He said that Ellen would eventually need professional data processing expertise and that the microcomputer would actually add to the data processing burden.

In addition to these concerns, Wandolowski appeared to be threatened. He saw this project as an infringement on his territory. If the sales department began managing computerized data resources, would accounting or purchasing or shipping be next? If microcomputers started popping up all over the company, would the data processing department be out in the cold? What would happen to his staff? Pete was adamantly opposed.

"Well, all right, Pete," responded the vice-president. "Since you're so opposed to this idea, let's put it before the vice-presidents' council. Maybe we can work out an official policy on microcomputer systems."

Later, Pete realized that he couldn't let the matter go before the vice-presidents. It was simply too risky; suppose their new policy

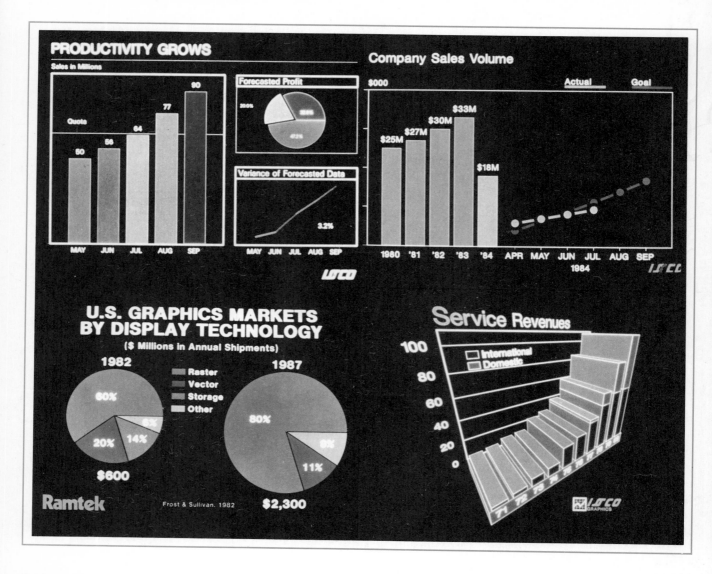

FIGURE 1–7
Computer-generated graphs

approved users' having their own computers? Would he have any control at all?

A Proposal for Ellen

By now, Pete had a keen appreciation for Ellen's business ability. He had to find a way to provide the service she wanted, or the long-range damage to the data processing department would be high.

The next day, Pete made another appointment with Ellen. He had done his homework. He explained to her the dangers and agonies of running a computer. What would she do when it didn't work? What if the vendor blamed her programming for the malfunction? Who would be responsible for the communication line that linked her computer with the main computer? What did she know about security, backup, recovery, and computer controls?

He asked how much she knew about selecting programs. Was she going to buy the source code? If not, what if the vendor went bankrupt? How could she tell whether the programs were any good? What if the programs contained errors? How much documentation would she receive? Would it be complete and accurate? What sort of maintenance agreement was she going to obtain for the hardware? If the hardware failed, how long would it take to get it fixed?

Once he discussed the potential problems, Pete reviewed Ellen's requirements. He had read Fred Sanchez's documentation and knew what needed to be done. He discussed the limitations of the programs that Ellen was planning to purchase and indicated a willingness to add custom programs to overcome those limitations. Finally, he presented a proposal: If Ellen would withdraw her request for a computer, he would make Fred Sanchez available full time, and data processing would acquire the programs and a microcomputer on Ellen's behalf; Pete wanted data processing to maintain control over microcomputer acquisitions.

Ellen considered the proposal. She wasn't overly concerned with the dangers of running a computer. Sure, they might make a few mistakes, but they would learn. On the other hand, did they want to learn? After all, their jobs were in sales, not data processing. She decided that if Pete would do as he promised, she would rather have data processing acquire the system than her staff.

"I'll tell you what, Pete," she responded, "I won't cancel my request for a system, but I will postpone it. If data processing can acquire the systems we need, on a timely basis, I won't raise the issue again. If you don't deliver, though, I will. And I'll have a document half-an-inch thick on how data processing failed."

"We'll deliver, Ellen. I assure you," said Pete, with a relieved sigh.

And they did. Whether from fear or respect for Ellen or a sincere desire to provide better service, Pete Wandolowski ensured that Ellen's department was satisfied. Within three weeks, the sales group had the basic capability it needed. The clerks were relieved of making most calculations. In two months they had an integrated system of purchased programs and programs developed in-house. The microcomputer resided in the sales administration area and was run by the clerks, all of whom had been trained by data processing personnel in the proper procedures for use, backup, and recovery.

Pete was satisfied as well. He had learned that, for some applications, microcomputers could actually save his staff work. Also, because of the success of the project, senior management established a policy that data processing would serve as consultants in the acquisition of all future microcomputer systems.

1.1   Mary Forsythe was not totally ignorant about computers. In fact, she knew quite a bit. List five or six things that Mary probably knew about computing that allowed her to solve her problem.

1.2   Mary is developing applications one at a time. She had a word processing application, and now she's adding a mailing list application. What are the risks of such a piecemeal strategy? What are the benefits?

1.3   Why do you think it took more than a year for the data processing department to respond to Ellen's request? What would you do if you were in Ellen's place?

1.4   Fred said it would take data processing over a year to develop the programs Ellen needed in-house; yet, as it turned out, only two months were required. Why?

1.5   Describe the two most important services that Fred provided to the sales administration department.

1.6   Ellen said she could save more than $10,000 in reduced labor expense if a computer could make sales calculations and draw the graphs. Does that seem reasonable to you?

1.7   List Pete's objections to the microcomputer. Which objections seem reasonable? Which objections seem motivated by his fear?

1.8   Summarize the risks in having the sales administration staff run their own computer.

1.9   Summarize the problems that the sales administration department might have in purchasing their own programs.

(continued)

A COMPARISON OF MARY'S AND ELLEN'S SITUATIONS

Mary's situation was considerably simpler than Ellen's. Because Mary was her own company she had none of the problems that Ellen had interfacing with other departments. Ellen needed data that was part of another system, used by another department, and administered by Pete's data processing department. Thus, Ellen's problem was more complicated to begin with, and became even more complicated when organizational politics entered the picture. However, despite the differences there were similarities.

Both Mary and Ellen eventually solved their problems. Each was able to identify a need, and although neither was a computer expert both realized that a computer solution was possible. Both were creative and took active roles in solving their problems. Both had some prior knowledge of computer applications. And although Mary was not herself aware of the range of software available to her, she was clever in finding someone who did know.

The next case is less happily resolved. Part of the reason for this is that the problem is more complex. Additionally, however, none of the key users of the system being developed had any knowledge of or experience working with computers.

TYCON CONSTRUCTION PRODUCTS

"Oh, no, not a traffic jam, too!" thought Chuck Swanson as he pulled to a stop behind a long line of cars on the freeway. It was a gray, rainy, early fall day, and Chuck had good reason to be upset. He was in the midst of problems at work, and he needed to be at his office early.

Chuck was 32 years old and the staff assistant to the director of marketing for TYCON Construction Products. His problems had begun nearly two years earlier. TYCON had been experiencing difficulties in processing orders. A boom in construction had caused manufacturers' deliveries to TYCON to be irregular, late, and sometimes even canceled. Thus, TYCON's inventory was erratic; customers and sales personnel couldn't depend on prompt deliveries. Furthermore, because some customers' payments were three, four, and five months overdue, the marketing department wanted to check customer credit before authorizing orders. Unfortunately, since TYCON had over 8000 customers, authorizations were extremely time consuming.

At this time, TYCON had a modest data processing department that was generally effective. The data processing manager, Tom Jackson, thought he could solve the order processing and credit authorization problems with a new, computerized order entry system.

A committee consisting of Chuck, Tom (as chairperson), an accountant, and a computer programmer was formed to study Tom's idea.

Chuck and the accountant told the computer people about the problem and their needs. The committee met five times over a period of three months and created a data processing proposal for management.

During these meetings, Chuck wished he had more knowledge about how to develop computer information systems. He was not sure that Tom understood his problem, and he couldn't see how the system was going to be developed if Tom didn't understand it. All in all, Chuck felt uncertain and vulnerable. Chuck had taken an introductory computer course in college, but all he had learned was facts about hardware and some programming in a language called BASIC. He wished he had learned more about systems and how they should be developed.

There was little he could do about it now. He helped the committee write the proposal as best he could. They recommended the formation of an order entry department with 12 clerks. Each clerk would have a video display terminal, or VDT, connected to the computer. (A terminal, which looks like a TV with a keyboard, is shown in figure 1–8.) The clerks would receive orders over the phone and use their VDTs to obtain inventory and credit information from the computer. If the materials were in stock and the customer's credit was good, the order would be approved.

To implement this system, TYCON needed to buy or lease a new computer and related equipment. Several programmers and computer operators also had to be hired. Tom Jackson said the system could be operational in 18 months.

This proposal was reviewed by Chuck's boss and eventually presented to Art Miyamoto, TYCON's president. (Figure 1–9 shows TYCON's organization chart.) Mr. Miyamoto liked the idea, but he thought the costs were too high. Because of recent sales successes, however, the company was in a strong cash position, and he approved the proposal but stipulated that the new system had to be operational in a year. Tom said that he could compress the schedule if he could hire one more programmer on a temporary basis. Mr. Miyamoto agreed, and the project was on.

The Project Starts

Once approval was granted, the committee stopped meeting, and Chuck didn't hear much from the data processing group. It was 10 months later when Mr. Miyamoto called a meeting with the original committee and Tom Jackson. He wanted to know the status of the project.

Tom presented a long list of problems (see figure 1–10). The new computer kept malfunctioning; two programmers had quit and had had to be replaced, and their programs had to be thrown out because nobody could understand them. Even worse, during testing the group had discovered that two programs didn't fit together, and one had to be

1.10 Do you think Ellen's decision to postpone her proposal was a good decision? What would you have done in her situation?

1.11 How did the sales administration department benefit from the cooperation of the data processing department?

1.12 How did the data processing department benefit from this situation?

FIGURE 1–8
Order entry clerks using video display terminals (VDTs)

rewritten. In addition, data processing hadn't known about a new product line, and another month or two would be required to incorporate it into the system. Further, order entry personnel still needed to be hired and trained, and procedures had to be developed. Altogether, Tom reported, it would be another six months before the system was ready for installation.

Mr. Miyamoto was furious. Why hadn't he been informed? Where did the $300,000 go that had already been spent? What were they going to do about the order processing problems for the next six months? Didn't Jackson know that they were losing business and creating ill will? Did

Jackson realize that TYCON existed to sell goods and make a profit and not to support every itinerant programmer and computer peddler?

After the meeting, Mr. Miyamoto stopped Chuck in the hall and told him to drop what he was doing. "Chuck," he said, "I have half a mind to cancel this project, but I don't want to lose the money we've invested. Spend some time with the data processing people and send me a memo about what you think we should do."

Chuck spent the next week with Tom Jackson and the data processing personnel. The data processing group seemed defensive, and they kept throwing terms at Chuck that he didn't understand. They claimed that many of the delays were beyond their control. The programmers also said that the requirements kept changing, and they had to redo their work. Chuck tried to find a document describing the requirements so he could see what they meant, but no such document had been prepared.

On the positive side, it was clear to Chuck that the data processing personnel were highly motivated. They had worked long hours and

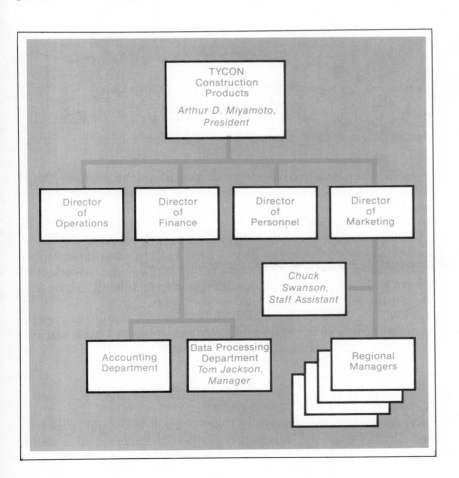

FIGURE 1–9
TYCON's organization chart

FIGURE 1–10
Tom Jackson reporting problems

were making an exhaustive effort to complete the system. Chuck decided to recommend continuing the project for six more months. His reasoning is shown in the memo in figure 1–11.

Mr. Miyamoto decided to go along with Chuck's recommendation. He asked Chuck, however, to help the project every way he could.

The next six months were as busy a time as Chuck could remember. He and Tom and most of the data processing staff regularly worked 10- to 12-hour days. Chuck was not qualified to help technically, so he tried to remove the administrative burden from Tom.

After five months of this hectic schedule, data processing was ready to implement the new order entry and inventory systems. Chuck and Tom checked with Mr. Miyamoto, and he told them to go ahead.

Problems Develop

At first, the new systems operated well; just a few small problems occurred. One time the computer displayed −5 cases of a siding product in inventory. Another time, several customers were accidentally dropped from the files. But, basically, the system operated well—especially considering the pressure under which it was developed.

At the end of the month, however, disaster struck. The existing computer billing system wouldn't work with the new order entry system. Something was wrong with the order data produced by the new system. The old billing system just wouldn't accept it. Figure 1–12 shows the relationship between the new order entry system and the old billing system.

Tom and the data processing staff worked through the weekend to determine what was wrong. They discovered a major design flaw in the order entry program. The person who had worked on it misunderstood how the billing system used order entry data. Much of the data needed

FIGURE 1–11

Chuck Swanson's memo

TYCON Construction Products

MEMO

July 17, 1987

TO: Mr. Arthur Miyamoto, President

FROM: Chuck Swanson

SUBJECT: Order Entry and Billing Systems

    I have reviewed progress on the order entry and billing systems as you requested. The following facts are pertinent:

    a. The project is definitely behind schedule. However, not all of the problems appear to have been Data Processing's fault. The computer vendor has caused several serious schedule slippages.

    b. Approximately $300,000 has already been spent or committed on this project. If we terminate it now, we will be able to recover only about $50,000 of this.

    c. Continuing this project for 6 more months will cost from $35,000 to $40,000.

    d. There is a significant chance that Data Processing will complete these systems within 6 months. The team members are highly motivated, and their enthusiasm is high.

    The cost of quitting now will be $250,000, plus we will still have order entry and inventory problems. The cost of continuing another 6 months will be $40,000, at most, and it is likely we will have a solution to our problems. In my opinion it is worth risking the $40,000 to continue the project.

by the billing system was in the wrong format, and some was simply unavailable.

Data processing worked furiously to correct the problem. By the end of the next week, it was apparent that another month would be needed to make the billing system operate. Tom reported to Mr. Miyamoto that TYCON would not be able to prepare bills for four or five more weeks.

Clenching his teeth, Mr. Miyamoto gave Tom a lesson in business. "Tom," he said icily, "if we don't send our customers their bills, they don't pay them. If our customers don't pay their bills, we don't receive any money. If we don't receive any money, we can't pay for our new computer and its staff, not to mention the other incidental expenses involved in running this company. It's called negative cash flow, and we can't have two months of it. Go back to the old system!"

"Mr. Miyamoto, we can't," responded Tom. "It will take us three months to reconvert to the old system. All the data has been changed because of the new prices you wanted. We don't have the new prices in the old files."

Within a week it was clear to Mr. Miyamoto that Tom was right. They were going to fall six to eight weeks behind in their billing. Mr. Miyamoto had to borrow money to cover the short-term loss of revenue. Ultimately, TYCON spent over $75,000 on interest payments because of the error.

By this point, Mr. Miyamoto had had enough. He hired a computer consulting firm to investigate the situation. A team of three people spent several days at TYCON talking with Chuck, Tom, the data processing staff, users, and customers.

Mr. Miyamoto Acts

Such was the situation that dreary fall day when the traffic finally started moving as Chuck drove to work. Chuck was analyzing inventory

FIGURE 1–12
Relationship between order entry and
billing systems

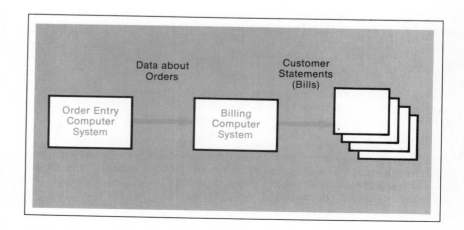

PROFILE

"THE SALES FORCE IS AN EXTENSION OF THE MARKETING RESEARCH DEPARTMENT"

Field sales personnel at Rothmans of Pall Mall Canada Ltd. have become market intelligence agents in a pilot program that equips them with hand-held terminals and enables their managers to view the resulting data in graphic form on videotex termi-nals. Using Telxon terminals, the salespeople record what they learn while making calls on retailers, such as shelf space allocated to Rothmans cigarettes and competitive brands and comparative prices, as well as answers to inquiries received from their managers. At the end of the day, they connect the terminals to tele-phones and send the information to a central computer. Simultaneously, they receive a new set of questions from their managers.

Primary benefits of the program, says project manager Tom Higgins, are "ease of recording information by the salesmen and greater flexibil-ity for managers who want, to find out and analyze certain types of infor-mation. Data for a research project can be turned up in a day or two."

The program "makes the sales force an extension of the marketing research department," says Paul Deninger, vice-president of market-ing at DISC. "When you have sales-people all around the country report-ing on competitors' daily activities, you give managers a powerful tool."

---

reports when Mr. Miyamoto's secretary called to ask Chuck to come to a meeting. Mr. Miyamoto, Chuck's boss, and the three consultants were present as Chuck sat down at the conference table.

"Chuck," Mr. Miyamoto began, "our consultants have analyzed our order entry project from the beginning, and they have given it some very low marks. They feel fundamental principles of systems design were ignored, and they question the professional competency of our data processing staff. Further, they believe we should have stopped the project as I wanted to five months ago.

"Consequently, I've decided to return to the old system, even though we will lose about $350,000 of our investment plus $75,000 in interest. Furthermore, I have this morning terminated Tom Jackson's employ-ment.

"Frankly, Chuck, I'm disappointed in your performance on this. I know you have limited knowledge of data processing, but it seems to me that you should have known that order entry and billing would be closely related. I think you should have seen this problem develop-ing when you wrote me your memo five months ago. Go back to your staff job and let's not have any more performances like this one."

Chuck felt terrible as he left the meeting. He felt sorry for Tom. He knew Tom had worked long hours to make the system successful. The experience hadn't been good for Chuck, either. Mr. Miyamoto was clearly displeased.

Later that night, Chuck tried to discover where he had gone wrong. He decided that the problem was that he just didn't know enough

QUESTIONS

1.13 Did Chuck have a chance? What could he have done differently before he wrote the memo to Mr. Miyamoto? What would you have done in his situation?

1.14 Do you think the memo in figure 1–11 makes sense? Do you agree with Chuck's reasoning?

1.15 What mistakes did Tom Jackson make? What could Chuck have done about them?

1.16 What mistakes did Mr. Miyamoto make? What could Chuck have done about them?

1.17 Do you suppose it is unusual for one data processing system to be dependent on another, as billing was dependent on order entry? What can companies do to eliminate problems like the ones TYCON had?

1.18 Do you think Chuck should have foreseen the billing problem? Would you have?

1.19 What can Chuck do now? What do you suppose his attitude is toward data processing? Can Chuck be effective on other computer projects?

1.20 Did Mr. Miyamoto really want to cancel the project as he says in the last meeting? Do you think he remembers how he truly felt?

1.21 Suppose Chuck had taken a business data processing course before the disaster. Describe three aspects of data processing he could have learned that would have helped him prevent the disaster.

about data processing. Some of the problems at TYCON Construction are listed below:

- System requirements not carefully defined
- Little user involvement in system development
- All programs developed internally
- No procedures for systems developers to follow
- Hardware and software were the only components that the data processing staff addressed, while hiring, training, and writing documentation were ignored until the last minute
- Chuck did not understand what was going on most of the time and he was easily baffled by the computer staff

Chuck's Mistakes

What should Chuck have known? If he had taken the course you are currently enrolled in, there is a very good chance that the project would have turned out differently and that TYCON would not have lost $350,000. First, Chuck would have known how a business computer system should be developed. He would have known some of the pitfalls to avoid. He would have insisted on a documented definition of requirements, which by itself could have prevented the billing problem.

Chuck would also have been aware of alternatives to Tom's plan and been certain that Tom at least considered them. He would have seen some of the mistakes that Tom made and had them corrected or recommended that the project be canceled in his memo. Finally, Chuck would have known what users are supposed to do for themselves, and what they can in all fairness expect from the data processing staff. He would have ensured that the users did their job and that data processing was providing appropriate support. He would also have known how important written documentation is during systems development, and he would have insisted on it.

Do not be alarmed if you cannot understand all of this discussion. You will learn about these concepts in this book. This is just a preview. What you should realize, however, is how important knowledge of computing is to every business professional.

A COMPARISON OF ELLEN'S AND CHUCK'S SITUATIONS

Do you think that Ellen is necessarily a better employee than Chuck? Did she work harder? No, actually Chuck worked *much* harder than Ellen. Chuck had three disadvantages. First, TYCON's problem was more complex than Blake's. The TYCON personnel had to develop their own programs (at least they thought they did), and they had to coordinate development among more people, as well as with the existing billing system. Second, the supporting data processing personnel at Blake were more competent than those at TYCON. Both Pete and Fred were able to provide the sales administration staff with the support they needed.

A third difference between Ellen and Chuck was that Ellen had some knowledge of computing. She had taken two classes in college, and she had some idea of how systems were supposed to be developed. She also knew many of the fundamental terms, so she was less likely to be intimidated by the data processing personnel and by outside experts. Her familiarity with the terminology allowed her to communicate with knowledgeable experts better than Chuck could. In addition, she wasn't afraid to ask questions, challenge people, and do work on her own. She had confidence in her ability and in the ability of her team. Thus, Ellen didn't work harder than Chuck — she simply worked more effectively.

THE MORALS OF THESE STORIES

Figure 1–13 summarizes the important characteristics of these three cases. The requirements for the computer system became progressively more complicated from the first to the third. This meant that the development process was longer and more complex. Additionally, the cases progressively required more and more in-house programming. Mary was able to implement her system with no programming at all; some programming was required at Blake; and at TYCON, the entire system was programmed in-house.

CASE	CHARACTERISTICS
Mary Forsythe Case	Simple, clear requirements
	Off-the-shelf programs
	Experienced, confident microcomputer user
	Creative solution to gain outside expertise
Blake Records Case	Clear statement of requirements
	Mixture of off-the-shelf and internally developed programs
	Ellen had knowledge of the systems development process
	Effective (if slow) data processing staff
TYCON Construction Case	Ambiguous statement of complicated requirements
	Internally developed programs
	Users were naive, inexperienced, and poorly educated
	Ineffective data processing staff

FIGURE 1–13
Characteristics of the three cases

Further, Mary and Ellen both had some computer experience. Mary was experienced in word processing on her computer. She had confidence in her ability to get what she wanted from the computer. Ellen had some knowledge of the systems development process. Poor Chuck, who needed it the most, had the least amount of knowledge. Chuck would have been far better off had he taken a college course like this one that discussed systems and their development. Finally, in the first two cases, the development of the systems was assisted by knowledgeable professionals; the staff at TYCON was simply over its head.

Given this summary, what are the morals to these stories? There are five (at least):

1. There is a difference between personal computer applications and computer systems that involve entire companies. Mary's problem was solved with a personal computer and some purchased software. She did not have to coordinate her needs with anyone else's. Ellen and Chuck each tackled problems that involved a number of other people and departments, so their systems were inevitably more complex than Mary's.

2. User involvement in the systems development process is critical to the success of the project. Both Mary and Ellen were users who were able to articulate their problems to the system developers. They both actively participated in the development process. However, users at TYCON were not involved in system development, except at the very beginning. Problems that should have been detected by users were not discovered until the system went into production. This was a disastrous mistake for TYCON. Furthermore, there is a vast difference between what a user (Mary or Ellen, for example) can contribute to the system development process and what a computer technician (the club president or Fred) can contribute. The perspectives of both users and technicians are required early on in order to lay the foundation for a successful project.

3. Computer information systems vary widely. Some systems serve only a single user or a single department. Other systems serve hundreds or even thousands of users and are more complex. Thus, if you've seen one information system you have *not* seen them all! Further, do not suppose that if you've learned how to run a spreadsheet on a microcomputer, you're ready to step into Tom Jackson's shoes.

4. It is considerably more difficult, expensive, and time consuming to develop programs in-house. It is so difficult, in fact, that, except in very unusual circumstances, it almost never should be done. Packaged, off-the-shelf programs are the key to success in the development of most computer information systems.

5. Knowledge of computer systems is very important for all business people — not just for computer majors. Further, knowledge of hard-

PROFILE

"IBM MARCHES STEADILY ONWARD IN THE VANGUARD"

Those surveyed were asked to rate the ten largest companies in their own industry according to eight key attributes. Ratings are on a scale of 0 (poor) to 10 (excellent).

In remaining the most admired company, IBM scored slightly lower than last year — 8.44 compared with 8.81 — but beat all comers on five of the attributes, one more than last year. IBM received the highest score awarded a company for any attribute, 9.4 for financial soundness. Though forced to kill the PCjr, a home computer that it had expected to be a huge success, IBM scored 9.19 for quality of management, the second highest score awarded for any attribute. IBM also ranked first for long-term investment value, use of corporate assets, and ability to attract, develop, and keep talented people. IBM's biggest decline in score was for innovativeness; it dropped from number 31 last year to number 78 this year.

KEY ATTRIBUTES OF REPUTATION

QUALITY OF MANAGEMENT	
Most admired	*Score*
IBM	9.19
J. P. Morgan	8.73
Boeing	8.46

LONG-TERM INVESTMENT VALUE	
Most admired	*Score*
IBM	8.74
Coca-Cola	8.04
Dow Jones	7.90

FINANCIAL SOUNDNESS	
Most admired	*Score*
IBM	9.40
Exxon	9.02
Dow Jones	8.90

USE OF CORPORATE ASSETS	
Most admired	*Score*
IBM	8.27
3M	7.94
Amoco	7.78

ABILITY TO ATTRACT, DEVELOP, AND KEEP TALENTED PEOPLE	
Most admired	*Score*
IBM	8.51
J. P. Morgan	8.21
Merck	8.14

ware, programming, and microcomputers is *not* enough. It is more important to understand the concept of information *systems:* how the hardware, programs, data, procedures, and people fit together. Additionally, you need at least a rudimentary knowledge of the process of building information systems.

A WORD OF ENCOURAGEMENT

Consider these three cases and realize that neither Mary nor Ellen nor Chuck wanted to work with data processing. However, in the course of their careers, they all needed knowledge about the use of computers in business. Any of these situations could occur in your career. As you progress through this course, think back to these people. Remember that the more you know about information systems, the more likely you are to be successful in your career.

If you are like many students, you may be uneasy about taking this course. You may be fearful that business information systems are something you won't be able to understand. That is unlikely. Most students, like Mary and Ellen, find that there is no magic to computing, and, contrary to popular belief, computing does not require a lot of math. If you'll invest the time, you'll probably find this course easier than you thought. The experience of hundreds of teachers has been that there are few college students who "just can't catch on." You will, however, need to invest your time.

▊ SUMMARY

There are important reasons for you to study business data processing even if you intend to work in some other area of business.

- Computers have changed business at all levels
- Computers are getting cheaper all the time, so they will see increased use in business and industry
- Computers can enable you to be more productive

In the future, many business people will be successful because of their ability to incorporate computer technology into their jobs.

WORD LIST

Database management system
  (DBMS)
Electronic spreadsheet
Video display terminal (VDT)

QUESTIONS TO CHALLENGE YOUR THINKING

To answer these questions, you will have to rely on your own intuition and experience. In later chapters, you may need to use additional references.

A. Speculate on how computers will affect your career. How will knowledge about computing help you?

B. Why are computers becoming so popular?

C. Neither Mary nor Ellen nor Chuck were data processing professionals, but their abilities to perform their jobs depended on their being able to work with data processing. Do you think this situation is rare? Is it becoming more common? Less common? Staying about the same?

D. Think of any two business people in any field — real estate, banking, manufacturing, insurance, sales, and distribution are all possibilities. Suppose both people are well qualified, but one has a knowledge of computers and what they can and cannot do. In what ways does the computer-literate person have an advantage over the other? How might their careers differ?

INTRODUCTION TO BUSINESS COMPUTER SYSTEMS: DATA

CHAPTER 2

The term *business computer system* will be used throughout this book. In this chapter you will learn what a business computer system is and what its components are. This chapter focuses on one of these components, data. This chapter will first introduce the concept of a computer system and then examine a computer system familiar to most students, one that monitors class enrollment to help with class scheduling. This example will illustrate a business computer system and show how its components interact. The definitions of these components will be used many times in the pages that follow. Be sure you understand them.

A *system* is a collection of components that interact to achieve some goal. A **computer system** is a collection of components, including a computer, that interact to achieve some goal. Note the word *including*. A computer system is not just a computer; it includes a computer as one of its components. **A business computer system** is a collection of components, including a computer, that interact to satisfy a business need. For example, some business computer systems produce payrolls, some compute taxes, some do accounting, and so forth.

Many business people are misinformed about the makeup of a business computer system. They think it is just a computer and that, if they buy one, their problems will be solved. Actually, the computer is only one of *five* components of a business computer system. Once the computer is obtained, many problems and considerable further expense remain.

THE COMPONENTS OF A BUSINESS COMPUTER SYSTEM

The five components of a business computer system are *hardware, programs, data, procedures,* and *personnel*. The presence of all components is required to satisfy a business need successfully; take any one of them away, and the need cannot be satisfied. Let's consider each of them in turn.

Hardware

The first component that we will consider is computer equipment, or **hardware**. Figure 2–1 shows a computer used by a bank. It is very large and is actually used to satisfy many different needs, not just one. There is a lot of computer equipment, so it may be helpful to divide it into categories. **Input equipment** is used to get data read into, *input* into, the computer. In Figure 2–1, line A points to a CRT, which generates information typed in through an input device such as a keyboard.

Processing equipment does the actual computing once the data has been input. Line B of figure 2–1 points to the **central processing unit**, or **CPU**. You can think of the CPU as the computer's brain.

Figure 2–2 shows a better picture of the CPU. Not very exciting, is it? Inside is a very complex electronic machine, but it's so small you can't

FIGURE 2–1
Two examples of a
computer

MICROCOMPUTERS

"A STRATEGIC TOOL THAT GIVES POWERFUL LEVERAGE IN MANIPULATING INFORMATION"

A new breed of user is emerging in the microcomputer world: the senior executive, who finds the microcomputer a strategic tool that gives powerful leverage in manipulating information. Not only are micros used on behalf of these executives, but more and more top managers are putting micros to work themselves.

The micro has gained widespread acceptance by decision makers in all the major business sectors: these include manufacturing, wholesale trade, retail, insurance, health and social sciences, transportation, government, construction, finance, utilities, and communications.

Micros are very conspicuous, used in 57% of companies overall and 73% of the large companies. Significantly, roughly one in three executives has a micro on his desk; 23% of executives have one at home as well.

An overwhelming 93% stated that their micro's performance is meeting or exceeding expectations.

Again, the major application (in 59% of the large companies surveyed) is decision support: providing an information and analysis infrastructure that supports much better informed decisions. This area covers budgeting, finances, what-if analyses of all types and general accounting (especially in smaller organizations).

see it. Visitors to computer centers are often disappointed with the appearance of the CPU; experienced guides usually spend most of the tour time on equipment such as tape drives. They are more exciting to watch but actually of much less importance.

Another category of computer hardware is **output equipment**. Data inside the computer is transferred to an output device so it can be accessed by the computer user. Line C of figure 2–1 points to a computer

FIGURE 2–2
The central processing unit (CPU)

FIGURE 2–3
User reading a computer printout

printer; this equipment produces wide printouts with holes in the sides, (an example is shown in figure 2–3.)

The fourth and final category of computer hardware is equipment used to store data. An example of this **storage equipment** is the tape drive indicated by line D in figure 2–1. Unfortunately, the CPU (the computer's brain) has a limited capacity to hold data. Consequently, storage equipment is needed to hold data that is not in use. This data is written onto tape and can be read back from tape when required.

To understand the need for storage, compare the CPU to your brain. You may have noticed that you have a limited capacity to hold data (say, for example, when you are taking a test). To help yourself, you put thoughts in a notebook. You read these thoughts into your mind when you need them. In this example, the paper serves as a storage device like the tape equipment in figure 2–1.

PROFILE

"ACCESSING WORDS AND NUMBERS BY COMPUTER IS BECOMING AN INCREASINGLY EFFICIENT WAY TO DO BUSINESS"

Electronic databases are libraries. You pay by the hour, generally, anywhere from $15 to $200 or more (often less at night) to obtain information from this library.

You once needed a master's degree in library science or equivalent skills to navigate through networks originally designed for and by techies. Now most networks are set up to be relatively easy to use. The most complicated, such as Lexis and Orbit, offer a day-long training session (for a fee). Others, such as Dow Jones News/

Retrieval, can be negotiated with only the help of the manual and a few hours of dedication. There is even one service, Easy Net, that scans other networks for you. If you find a listing you want to investigate, you pay $8 for up to 500 lines of full text. Otherwise, the trip around the databases is free.

Some electronic databases are for a particular industry, such as Lexis (for lawyers) or Inner-Line (for financial analysts). Others contain government-generated data, such as

the Bureau of Labor Statistics' Consumer Price Index.

Finally, information retrieved electronically can be used as raw data that you can manipulate with your own spreadsheet, word-processing or database programs, or with specialized software. Dow Jones, for example, offers several software packages for market analysis and portfolio management that allow you to manipulate data taken directly from databases on the Dow Jones News/ Retrieval network.

Programs

Figure 2–4 summarizes the five components of a business computer system and their subelements. We have just discussed hardware. The second component is **programs**. Most computers are general-purpose machines. They can add, subtract, and compare, but they are not designed to satisfy specific needs. A computer must have a program, or *sequence of instructions*, to satisfy a specific need. Thus, a computer with one set of programs might be used to design airplanes. The same computer with different programs could be used to do general ledger accounting or to process insurance claims.

Figure 2–5 shows a simple program that reads two numbers, labeled A and B, adds them, and prints the result. It also shows a portion of a more complex program used to enroll students in different classes.

Computer programs can be written in a variety of **computer programming languages**. Like human languages, these languages differ in vocabulary and structure. They all, however, have the same function: to instruct a general-purpose computer to satisfy a specific need. The first program in figure 2–5 is written in the **BASIC** language. The other one is written in a language called **COBOL.** Although there are several hundred computer languages, only about six or eight of them are commonly used. For one reason or another, the rest have not been accepted. Programming and languages are discussed in detail in part 4 of this book.

There is such a wide variety of programs that they are often divided into categories according to their function. Two categories that are used in business are **systems programs** and **application programs**. Systems programs control the computer. For example, they cause the computer to start and stop jobs, to copy data from one tape to another, and so on. Application programs are oriented toward a business need. They perform payroll, do accounting, and so on. The systems programs usually come with the computer, but application programs usually do not. Application programs usually must be developed or acquired separately.

Data

The third component of a business computer system is *data*. Before a need can be satisfied, all the pertinent facts must be gathered. This is a special problem for computer systems because all data must be put into some form the computer can understand before it can be read into the computer. Thus, data is entered by means of a keyboard of some type or else it is put into computer-readable form by some other means (figure 2–6).

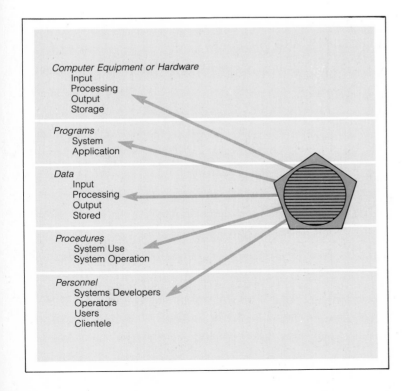

FIGURE 2–4
Components of a business computer system

FIGURE 2–5

Portions of computer programs written in BASIC and COBOL

```
10    INPUT A,B
20    LET C = A + B
30    PRINT C
40    END
```

```
IDENTIFICATION DIVISION.
    PROGRAM-ID.  CLASS01.
ENVIRONMENT DIVISION.
    INPUT-OUTPUT SECTION.
            .
            .
            .
            .
            .
            .
            .
DATA DIVISION.
    FILE SECTION.
FD  CLASS-MASTER
    LABEL RECORDS ARE STANDARD.
01  CLASS-MASTER-REC.
    05 CLASS-NUMBER                  PIC    9(4).
    05 CLASS-NAME                    PIC    X(10).
            .
            .
            .
            .
            .
            .
            .
PROCEDURE DIVISION.
    OPEN INPUT CLASS-MASTER.
    MOVE 0 TO EOF-FLAG.
            .
            .
            .
            .
            .
            .
```

APPLICATION

"THE SMART CARD IS BECOMING A FIXTURE IN EUROPE"

The smart card is fast becoming a fixture in Europe, for its adaptability as much as for its security features.

There are two ways of using cards at the point of sale. The first entails a handheld device called a certificator. This device is relatively inexpensive and hence appeals to merchants whose volume doesn't justify full-service point-of-sale terminals.

After the customer's card is inserted in the certificator, the customer punches in his or her personal identification number, or PIN. The microchip in the card verifies the PIN. If the PIN is valid, the certificator gives the merchant an authorization number, which is transferred to the sales draft to guarantee payment.

Merchants with large volumes of transactions use electronic payment terminals. These are cash registers that are linked into telecommunication networks and are capable of reading smart cards. Because the chip can verify the PIN, the need to secure the line is eliminated.

Even as this smart card program progresses, French banks are looking into a second strategy that would build on a concept originated by the French Postal, Telephone, and Telegraph Authority.

In 1985, the PTT began installing a system of pay phones that accept only preloaded smart cards. These cards are sold in two denominations. Once the value implanted in the chip is used up, the card can be discarded.

The French banks want to extend this concept to create an "electronic wallet." This would be a special-purpose smart card used for small purchases, such as movie tickets, that don't need on-line authorization.

Unlike the current PTT card, the supply of money in this proposed card could be replenished periodically. The technology is already available for this application.

The University of Paris, for example, now issues smart cards to its students. They use the cards to record current class schedules, classes taken, and grades received. In Nice, the smart card assures confidentiality when students dial in through Minitel for results of their baccalaureate examinations.

People in business computing distinguish between data and information. **Data** is defined as recorded facts or figures. **Information** is knowledge derived from data. Thus, data and information are not the same. A list of sales made during the past month by 15 sales agents is an example of data. A summation of the sales of each agent, together with the names of the top three, is an example of information.

Complete and correct data is essential for the successful operation of a business computer system. Computers are fast, but they have no intuition or judgment. They will work diligently with absolute gibberish and produce outputs of equal gibberish. "Garbage in, garbage out" is an old (30 years is old in this industry!) but appropriate saying in the computer business.

Computer data can be categorized in the same way that we categorized hardware (see figure 2–4). Thus, there is **input data** that is read into the computer for processing. There is **processing data** inside the CPU. There is **output data**, or results, that are usually in human-readable form. Finally, there is **stored data**. This data is written onto some storage device and saved for later processing.

FIGURE 2–6
Data-entry devices

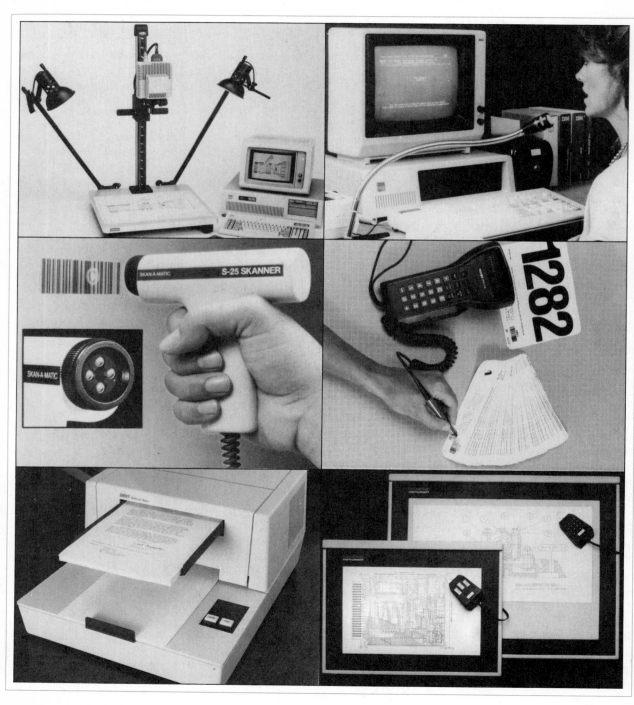

APPLICATION

"A HOME SHOPPING SOFTWARE PACKAGE HAS CHANGED THE WAY TO PURCHASE SUPERMARKET GOODS"

Fresh Systems, a Japanese corporation that franchises a home shopping software package to retailers, has changed the way many people in that country purchase supermarket goods. Instead of shopping the aisles, Japanese homemakers peruse catalogs; instead of conversing with checkers and bag boys, they beep their telephones at a computer.

At present, 90,000 Japanese homes are served by 10 retailers in the Fresh Systems network. Another retailer is scheduled to sign a franchisor agreement next month; its entry into the market will raise the number of households served by the system to 120,000. There are a total of 38 million households in Japan, with the population totaling 121 million.

Consumers order their groceries out of catalogs sent to the "members" in the retailer's franchise area. Retailers print both monthly and weekly black-and-white catalogs at their own expense, often inserting four-color flyers provided free by various manufacturers. (In the future, retailers are expected to start selling advertising to manufacturers to offset expenses.)

The prices for merchandise ordered from the catalogs are identical to the prices of the goods in the retailer's own store(s).

To order, the consumer simply calls into the computer of a local retailer, inputs a personal identification number, listens to a prerecorded tape that explains the ordering procedure, and then depresses the order number of the desired item(s) on the telephone keypad. There is no human contact, only the beeping of telephone push buttons.

The unmanned computer accepts orders 24 hours a day.

Data can be stored in a variety of ways. It can be recorded on magnetic tape (as on a tape recorder at home); it can be punched on cards; or it can be stored in other ways. The term **storage medium** refers to the type of storage used. Magnetic tape is a storage medium.

Procedures

The last two components of a business computer system go hand in hand. They are *procedures* and *trained personnel*. **Procedures** are instructions for people on the use and operation of the system. Procedures describe how people are to prepare input data and how the results are to be used. Procedures also explain what people are to do when errors are created and need to be corrected. Further, procedures explain how people are to operate the computer. They describe what programs to run, what data to use, and what to do with the outputs. Procedures must also describe what to do when the computer fails, or **crashes**.

Personnel

Trained people are the final component of a business computer system. People bring the other four components together and integrate the

PERSONNEL OVERALL SALARIES BY POSITION, 1985

Computer Operations

Manager, computer operations	$38,000
Supervisor, computer operations	27,800
Lead computer operator	21,000
Computer operator, Level A	18,400
Computer operator, Level B	16,100

Computer Operations Support Staff

Tape librarian	16,400
Data quality control clerk	16,300

Data Entry Operations

Supervisor, data entry	22,100
Lead data entry operator	16,800
Data entry operator, Level A	14,400
Data entry operator, Level B	13,100

Applications Programming

Manager, applications programming	41,700
Project leader (Lead programmer/analyst)	37,400
Systems analyst (Senior programmer/analyst)	32,600
Programmer/analyst	27,400
Programmer	22,800

Software Systems Programming

Manager, software systems programming	42,800
Senior software systems programmer	36,200
Software systems programmer	30,500

Database Management

Database administrator	37,400

Source: Administrative Management Society

computer system into the business environment. The major categories of personnel are *systems development personnel*, *operations personnel*, *users*, and *systems clientele*.

Systems development personnel design and produce business computer systems. **Operations personnel** run the computer. Salaries for various systems development and operations personnel can be seen in Figure 2–7.

Users are individuals who interact directly with the computer system. They provide input data and use computer-generated information to do their jobs. Examples are class scheduling clerks, order entry personnel, and airline reservation agents. Finally, the **clientele** of a computer system are people who receive the benefits of the system. Examples of clientele are students having their classes scheduled, customers ordering food or services, and passengers on an airline.

Once again, the five components of a business computer system are hardware, programs, data, procedures, and trained personnel. Without all five components, the business computer system will not operate.

APPLICATION

"CORPORATIONS ACHIEVING MAJOR FINANCIAL ADVANTAGE FROM STRATEGIC USES OF COMPUTERIZED DATA"

American Airlines gained major competitive advantage by using a detailed database of their customer travel information to restructure fares after deregulation. Both American Airlines and United Airlines gained market share by allowing travel agents to obtain information at terminals from their automated reservation systems.

Sears employs computerized information on its 40 million retail customers to reach targeted groups such as appliance buyers, gardeners, mothers-to-be, and to provide marketing for its insurance, brokerage, and real-estate subsidiaries.

Xerox cut manufacturing costs in its copier division by 18% in three years by strategic uses of information, which changed materials handling and inventory control practices. Xerox exchanges quality control information with suppliers to eliminate the expensive inspection of incoming parts. It gives suppliers its master manufacturing schedule so that they can ship parts at precisely the time Xerox needs them to keep inventories lean.

Equitable Life created a computer-assisted underwriting system for use at client sites, permitting annual renewal analysis for policies based on historical data. The system recommended changes in premium rates based on underwriting objectives and experience. Nearly 100 underwriters used the system daily. Its objective was to provide them with the decision-making skills of a top actuary.

The Santa Fe Railroad improved revenue ton miles/employee hour (a basic measure of railroad productivity) by 28% in four years thanks to a new relational database system with extensive user involvement.

How does this information relate to you? You already know more than Chuck Swanson did in the TYCON Construction case. If Tom Jackson presented his idea to you, you could ask, "Tom, where do you propose we get the data?" or "Tom, when are you going to define the procedures and train the users?" You could insist that these questions be answered adequately, or you could protect yourself by withdrawing from the project.

THE CLASS ENROLLMENT SYSTEM: THE PROBLEM

Let's now consider the components of a business computer system as they apply to a particular application. Specifically, let's consider a system that enrolls students in classes. As you read this application, think about the interaction of the five components: hardware, programs, data, procedures, and trained personnel. See if you agree that all five are necessary for the system to function.

The class enrollment problem is common to all colleges and universities. The various academic departments of the college or university decide to offer one or more sections of a large number of classes. The offerings are published in a class schedule. With the help of their

QUESTIONS

This section introduced many terms. The following questions will help you review them. You should also refer to the word list at the end of the chapter.

2.1 Define a business computer system.

2.2 What are the five components of a business computer system?

2.3 Describe one type of computer input equipment.

2.4 Describe one type of computer output equipment.

2.5 Describe one type of computer storage equipment.

2.6 What is a CPU?

(continued)

2.7 What is the purpose of a computer program?

2.8 Name and describe two types of computer programs.

2.9 Name four types of computer data.

2.10 Why is stored data necessary? Give two examples of storage media.

2.11 Explain the difference between data and information.

2.12 What is the difference between procedures and programs?

2.13 Explain three types of procedures needed for a business computer system.

2.14 Name four types of personnel who interface with a business computer system.

2.15 Explain the function of each category of people you named in the answer to question 2.14.

2.16 What is the difference between system users and system clientele?

advisers, students select courses from the schedule. They then fill out class request forms and submit the request forms to the administration.

As every student knows, conflicts occur. Some classes are requested by more students than can be accommodated. Other classes are selected by too few students to be taught economically. Consequently, the department administrators close some classes, add more sections of others, and drop sections of still others.

This leads to a chaotic process known as *add/drop*. Students who were unable to enroll in the classes they requested are given an opportunity to wait in long lines to enroll in other classes. Eventually this process concludes. The students finally get acceptable schedules or become so worn out by the system that they decide to take whatever courses they can get.

The basic functions of the class enrollment system are listed below:

1. Check student IDs against a list of valid students. Ensure that each student is enrolled in the university and is in good standing.
2. Check class requests for time conflicts. Eliminate conflicting requests when necessary.
3. Enroll students in requested classes as space is available.
4. Count the number of students enrolled in each class. Close classes when the maximum number have enrolled. Count number of attempts to enroll in class once it is closed.
5. Store student/class enrollment data for later use by add/drop, billing, grading, and other systems.
6. Print students' class schedules.
7. Print a summary report listing each class, the number of students enrolled, and the number of students attempting to enroll after the class is closed.

Student IDs are compared to a list of valid students to ensure that each requester is officially enrolled and in good standing. Then the requests of each student are examined to determine whether he or she tried to enroll in any classes that meet at the same time. If so, all but one of the conflicting requests are dropped.

Next, students are enrolled in classes as space is available. No classes are to have more than the maximum number of students specified by the department. If a class is closed, the system counts the number of requests for the class after it is closed. Data showing which students are enrolled in which classes is saved for processing by other computer systems. Finally, student schedules and a summary report are printed. The dataflow diagram in figure 2–8 should help you visualize the class enrollment system. We will study dataflow diagrams later on. For now you should know that each circle represents a process in the system, and that each arrow indicates data flowing from one process to another.

We will return to this system later in this chapter and again in chapter 3.

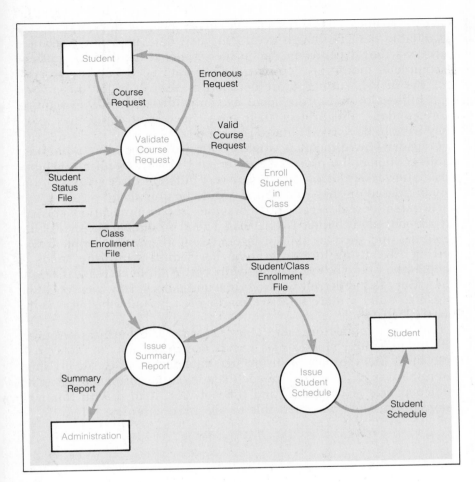

FIGURE 2–8
Dataflow diagram of the class enrollment system

▥ DATA

We begin our detailed discussion of the five components of a business computer system with a discussion of data. The other components are presented in chapter 3. At the end of this chapter we'll examine the data needed by the class enrollment system described in the preceeding section. First, though, we'll look at data from three different viewpoints: data as an organizational resource, data as it is processed by a business computer system, and computer representation of data.

Data as an Organizational Resource

Most of today's profitable companies share a common characteristic: Their decision makers have rapid access to accurate information that enables them to make effective business decisions quickly.

Good business decisions can be made only with timely access to reliable data (although access to good data does not guarantee success—that depends on the business skills of the decision maker). Incomplete, inaccurate, or inaccessible data spells disaster for all but the luckiest of corporate decision makers. It is for this reason that billions of dollars are spent by companies each year to acquire, store, update, and protect their data. Successful companies know they have to have good data to remain on top.

Consider how difficult it would be for a manufacturer to bid on a multi-million dollar project if the company's price, supplier, and labor cost data was outdated. Things were very different three years ago, and any bid based on those old figures would be unrealistic.

On a smaller scale recall Mary Forsythe, the communications specialist introduced in chapter 1. Mary had a good product in the form of her seminars and she was skillful in delivering them. Her problem was getting advertising literature about her seminars into the hands of people who would be most likely to hire her. Without access to the right data, Mary found herself wasting time and money. However, once she began to build a more selective mailing list her advertising became more effective.

Both the manufacturer and Mary use data as a business resource. The manufacturer studies past trends and projections to make realistic bids. Mary began by using her data for effective advertising; later she was able to analyze each seminar's performance based on audience, size of company, and time of year. Armed with this new information, Mary was then able to sell more seminars.

Data in a Business Computer System

Business people have long recognized data as an invaluable resource. In fact, data processing and information systems have been around much longer than computers. However, the sheer volume of facts that today's businesses must handle makes computerization a necessity. Computers are capable of dealing with large volumes of data in a short time and with a high degree of consistency. They are ideal machines for storing and processing data. Yet computers present challenges as well as advantages to business management. A manager must consider how a computer system handles each of the following functions:

- Data gathering
- Data verification
- Data access
- Data security

Data Gathering

Almost all the facts a business computer system must handle originate in the outside world, in the business environment. These facts must be collected through the process of **data gathering**. To gather pertinent facts, you must first identify the **data source**. For example, a customer, salesperson, or insurance agent might have data the system needs.

After determining the source of data, the data itself must be captured and entered into the business computer system. Someone must enter the data with an input device. Some input devices are operated by a company employee, for example an order-entry clerk might use a computer terminal. Other input devices are operated by system clients such as bank customers using automated teller machines. Input devices will be covered in chapter 3.

Data Verification

If data is to be relied upon, then it must be as accurate and error-free as possible. A well-designed business computer system will attempt to check for accuracy or reasonableness of input data values whenever possible. Unfortunately, no screening is 100 percent foolproof. In chapter 7 you will learn more about **data verification**.

Data Access

After data is gathered, entered, and verified, it must be stored within the computer system for future reference. The way in which data is stored in the computer will have an effect on how quickly and easily it can be retrieved and processed. The term **data access** refers to data storage, retrieval, and processing. Generally speaking, the quicker data can be accessed the more expensive is the development and maintenance of the business computer system. As you can see, there are always tradeoffs for the business person to consider.

You will learn in chapters 7, 8, and 9 how important it is for business people to carefully define their information needs before building a business computer system. For now you should know that business computer systems must often satisfy a variety of information needs. This is accomplished with effective data access — retrieving the correct facts and then summarizing, sorting, merging, reorganizing, and coordinating them to answer users' questions.

Data Security

Data, like any other valuable possession, must be protected. Specifically, through careful **data security** this important organizational resource must be protected from theft, unauthorized use, copying, sabotage, damage, and loss. Data in a computer system can be particularly vulnerable. Physically, magnetic storage media (disks, diskettes, tapes) are somewhat sensitive and fragile and can easily be damaged, which in effect destroys the stored data. Consequently, computer operators are trained in the art of handling expensive and valuable data storage devices and in making duplicate file copies, called **backups**.

Even more important than the care of the storage medium is preventing unauthorized access to data. Tapes and disks should be accessible only to authorized computer center or company personnel. Otherwise data can be copied, stolen, or altered. Often business computer systems allow many people to share the computer resources at the same time (via terminals, for example). This allows companies to centralize and share data among hundreds of people. Concurrently, the potential for unauthorized use increases dramatically, and data protection schemes must be complex to thwart would-be thieves and saboteurs.

Computer Representation of Data

You can see by now that data is a very important component of a business computer system. Long before there were computers people organized large amounts of data into manageable pieces. For example, thirty years ago all the data in an office was stored in file folders that were kept in rows and rows of cabinets. One set of cabinets might have held file folders for all of the company's customers, probably arranged alphabetically. Another set might have held file folders on all of the company's backorders, probably arranged by date.

Now that computer data banks are replacing file cabinets and folders, you should understand how data is organized into manageable pieces for the computer. In this section we will look at how data is actually stored inside the computer.

Bits

The basic building block for representing computer data is called a **bit**. The term *bit* is an abbreviation for **binary digit**. You know what a decimal digit is. It is one of the symbols 0, 1, 2, 3, 4, 5, 6, 7, 8, or 9. A binary digit is similar, but there are only two symbols: 0 and 1.

Bits are used as the basic building blocks for computer data because they are very easy to represent electronically. Bits can be represented by things that are either on or off. For example, we can say that a light represents a 1 when it is on and a 0 when it is off. Figure 2–9 shows a panel of light switches. If we define *up* as 1 and *down* as 0, then this panel represents the **bit pattern** 1101. Computers are not composed of panels of light switches, but they do have a variety of devices that are either on or off.

Bits are represented in various ways in different parts of a computer system. In the CPU, a bit is represented by the direction of flow of electricity or by the voltage at a particular location. On magnetic media such as tape, a bit is represented by the direction of magnetization; one direction represents a 0, and the opposite represents a 1. On a punched card, a bit is represented by the presence of a hole (1) or by the absence of a hole (0).

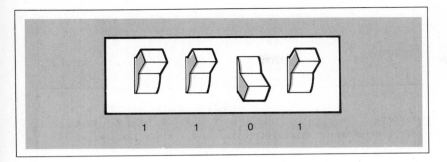

FIGURE 2–9
Panel of light switches representing bit
pattern 1101

Now, in the simplest terms, patterns of bits are used to represent
characters. A character is one of the letters A-Z; one of the digits 0-9;
or one of the special symbols, such as $, #, *. For example, the
pattern 000001 might represent an A; the pattern 000010, a B; and
so forth. The word *might* is used here because there is no single code.
The code used varies, depending on the type of computer system
and the type of equipment.

Punched-Card Data Representation

Although punched cards are infrequently used in the computer industry today, we will consider them here because they provide a good
vehicle for understanding data representation. The methodology for
representing data on tape and disk is similar to that described here.
The essential difference is that magnetization, rather than the presence or absence of holes, is used to represent the 1's and 0's.

Figure 2–10 shows a punched card. This particular type of card is
divided into 80 vertical columns and 12 horizontal rows. Each column
is used to represent one character. By convention, the top row is called
the 12-row, the next row is called the 11-row, and the next row is called
the 0-row. Then come the 1-row, the 2-row, and so on, to the last row,
which is the 9-row.

Each column represents a character. In figure 2–10, the character 0 (zero) is punched in column 36. By convention, this is done by
punching a hole in the 0-row and not punching any other holes in the
column. A 1 is signified by punching a hole in the 1-row only, a 2
by a punch in the 2-row only, and so forth. Letters and special characters are represented by two (or more) punches in a column. Thus,
the letter A is represented by punches in both the 12- and 1-rows. This
scheme is commonly called **Hollerith code**, after Herman Hollerith,
the inventor of punched-card data processing.

Now, if you think of a hole as a 1 and the absence of a hole as a 0, then
each one of these columns can be visualized as a bit pattern. Starting
from the top, the bit pattern for the character 0 (zero) is 001000000000,

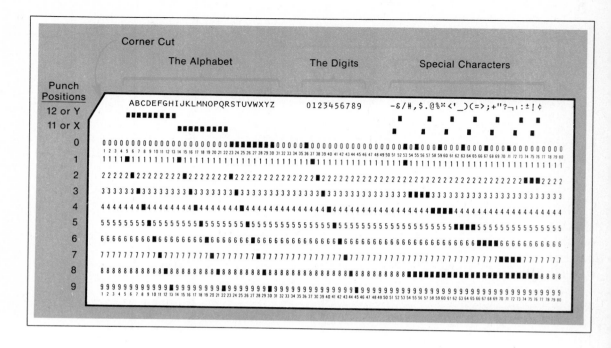

FIGURE 2–10
80-column punched card

because there is a 0 in the 12-row, a 0 in the 11-row, and a 1 in the 0-row, and 0's in all the other rows. The pattern for the character 1 is 000100000000, and that for an A is 100100000000.

Hollerith code is just one example of a way to represent characters. There are punched cards with 96 characters, and they use a different convention.

EBCDIC and ASCII Codes

One of the most common ways of representing data is the **Extended Binary Coded Decimal Interchange Code**, or **EBCDIC** (pronounced *ib–sa–dick*). EBCDIC is used to represent data on magnetic tape, on disk, and in main memory.

This code uses eight bits to represent characters. Figure 2–11 shows a portion of EBCDIC. There is no particular magic about the bit patterns. The fact that the pattern 1100 0001 represents an A and the pattern 1000 0001 represents an a has nothing to do with the name of the letters. The assignment of patterns to letters is arbitrary, and the designers of EBCDIC happened to choose these.

Notice that numbers are also represented in EBCDIC. When put in this coded form, numbers are considered to be textual in nature. When a number is represented in EBCDIC, no arithmetic can be done with it. The number only can be read, stored, or printed. The numbers in an address, such as 95th Street, would be put into this coded form.

Computers can store numbers in a form that permits arithmetic to be done as well. In fact, several such forms are available. Numbers can be stored as decimals, as binary integers (whole numbers), or as binary numbers with fractions. These formats are described in module C of part 4.

A second popular code for representing data in a computer system is the **American Standard Code for Information Interchange**, or **ASCII** (pronounced *ask-key*). Whereas EBCDIC uses eight bits, ASCII uses only seven. Figure 2–11 also shows a portion of the ASCII codes. ASCII is considered a standard in data communications, and is therefore used more frequently than EBCDIC in those applications. Some computers also use ASCII to represent data within the main computer memory.

Characters, Fields, Records, and Files

Before describing data further, we must define more terminology. As stated, a character is a single letter or digit. For example, a character might be a Q or a 6. Another term, **byte**, is often used synonymously with *character*. A byte is the collection of bits needed to represent a single character. Thus, in EBCDIC, a byte is a group of eight bits, while in ASCII a byte is a group of seven bits.

Although *character* and *byte* are synonymous, the terms are usually used in different contexts. *Character* is usually used when referring to

FIGURE 2–11

Portions of the EBCDIC and ASCII conventions

Character	EBCDIC Bit Pattern	ASCII Bit Pattern
$	0101 1011	010 0100
*	0101 1100	010 1010
)	0101 1101	010 1001
•		
•		
•		
a	1000 0001	110 0001
b	1000 0010	110 0010
c	1000 0011	110 0011
d	1000 0100	110 0100
•		
•		
•		
A	1100 0001	100 0001
B	1100 0010	100 0010
C	1100 0011	100 0011
D	1100 0100	100 0100

the logic or application of data. For example, a customer name could be 25 characters long. The term *byte* is usually used when referring to the physical size of hardware. For example, people might say that a main memory has 1 million bytes or that a disk file capacity is 10 million bytes.

A group of characters (or bytes) is called a **field**. Fields usually have logical meanings; they represent some item of data. Thus, the five or nine characters in a postal ZIP code are the ZIP code field; the nine characters in a social security number are the social security number field.

A collection of fields is called a **record**. A collection of fields about a student, for example, is called the *student record*. Figure 2–12 depicts a student status record. The numbers across the top of the record refer to character positions or columns. These numbers do not exist on the magnetic media; they are shown here just for reference. If this record were printed, the student number would appear in positions 1 through 9, the name would appear in positions 10 through 29, and so forth.

Note the use of abbreviations and special codes. Rather than write out lengthy grade levels like *sophomore*, abbreviations are used. Furthermore, the status code field contains numbers that are assigned mean- as shown in figure 2–12. These codes are set up as **conventions** when the system is designed. Thus, a 101 in the *code* field is understood to mean the student is an honor student who owes no tuition. When codes like these are used, they must be explained in procedures for users; otherwise, people will not know how to interpret results.

A collection of records is called a **file**. All the student status records together are referred to as the *student status file*. The class schedule file contains all of the class schedule records. Figure 2–13 summarizes

FIGURE 2–12

Fields in the student status record

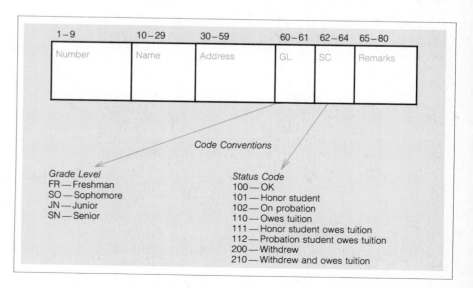

Code Conventions

Grade Level
FR — Freshman
SO — Sophomore
JN — Junior
SN — Senior

Status Code
100 — OK
101 — Honor student
102 — On probation
110 — Owes tuition
111 — Honor student owes tuition
112 — Probation student owes tuition
200 — Withdrew
210 — Withdrew and owes tuition

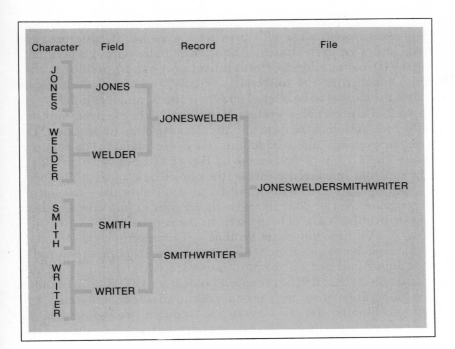

FIGURE 2–13
Relationship of characters, fields, records, and files

this terminology: *characters* are grouped into *fields*; fields are grouped into *records*; records are collected into a *file*.

THE CLASS ENROLLMENT SYSTEM: DATA

Figure 2–14 summarizes the data involved in class enrollment. The output data shows what the system is to produce; there are three types of output. *Student/class enrollment data* shows which students are enrolled in which classes. This data will be stored on tape to be used by other business computer systems that manage adds and drops, billing, grading, and so forth. The other two types of output are both printed reports. *Student schedules* will be given to students. The *summary report* will be used by administrators when they decide whether to add or drop class sections.

OUTPUT DATA	INPUT DATA
Student/Class Enrollment Data	Student Class Requests
Student Schedules	Student Status Data
Summary Report	Class Enrollment Data

FIGURE 2–14
Summary of data needed by the class enrollment system

There are also three types of input for the class enrollment system. *Student class request data* will provide the name, ID number, and desired classes for each student. The *student status data* is stored data listing the ID, name, address, status (honors, probation, and so on) of all students enrolled at the university. Finally, the *class schedule data* describes the classes to be offered and their times, and locations.

Figure 2–15 presents a **system flowchart**. This diagram summarizes the interaction of the data and the class enrollment program. The strange shapes are not accidental; they are standard computing symbols. The ☐ is a **document** or **report symbol**; in figure 2–15 it indicates that **mark-sense forms** (the ones that require a number-2 pencil; see figure 2–17) will be read and entered in the class enrollment program. Notice that the arrowhead goes in just one direction. This indicates that data is being sent to the program.

The ◯ is a **tape flowchart symbol** — it represents data stored on magnetic tape. We can see from the figure that three tapes are required — two for input and one for output. There are two more ☐ . These represent reports that will be prepared as documents. Figure 2–14 shows that two separate reports, the summary data and student schedules, will be printed. Finally, the ☐ , which is called a **processing symbol**, represents a program that will create the outputs from the inputs. In this case, the flowchart indicates that a program called *Class Enrollment* will perform this function.

There are six files in figure 2–15. Both the student status file and the initial class schedule file are on magnetic tape. For the time being, we will not be concerned with how the data got there. (This topic will be

FIGURE 2–15

Class enrollment system flowchart

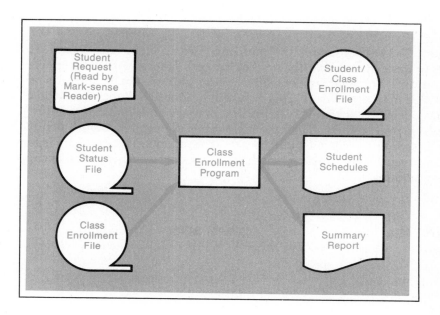

RECORD POSITION	FIELD CONTENTS
1-3	Class Number
4-30	Class Name
31	Section Number
32-35	Hours Meeting
36-40	Days Meeting (MTWRF)
41-43	Maximum Number of Students
44-46	Number of Students Enrolled
47-49	Number of Students Turned Away

FIGURE 2–16
Class schedule record format

discussed in chapter 7.) The format of the student status records was shown in figure 2–12.

The format of the class schedule records appears in figure 2–16. All the field contents are self-explanatory except perhaps *Days Meeting*. This field will have letters representing the days of the week that the class meets. A Monday-Wednesday-Friday class will have MWF. A Tuesday-Thursday class will have TR. Also, the number of students enrolled and the number turned away will initially be zero.

The remaining input file in figure 2–15 is the student request file. Students indicate their class requests by filling out mark-sense forms like the one in figure 2–17. These forms are read by a mark-sense reader. Data that is extracted from the forms is then stored in a student request file. The format of this file is shown in figure 2–18.

The computer display screen holds data for one student record. Once the operator sends this record to the computer, one of two actions will occur. Either the computer will begin processing the student request immediately (this will be discussed in chapter 8), or it will add the request to a file and .process the entire file later as a group, or *batch* (this will be discussed in chapter 7). For now, assume that the requests are collected and processed as a batch.

The remaining three files in figure 2–15 are output files. The student/class enrollment file lists classes and shows which students are in each class. We will not be concerned with its format here. The other two files are reports.

▥ SUMMARY

In this chapter you have begun to learn what business computer systems are all about. A business computer system is more than just a computer; it also includes programs, data, procedures, and trained people.

Data is one of the components of a computer, and it can be viewed in at least three ways.

QUESTIONS

2.17 Why is data considered an organizational resource?

2.18 What data might an automobile insurance company collect?

2.19 How does an automated teller machine (ATM) make sure that only the customer who owns a card is using it?

2.20 Name the four functions a business computer system must perform on data.

2.21 What is a bit? Why are bits used to represent computer data?

2.22 Describe the way characters are represented on punched cards.

2.23 What are EBCDIC and ASCII? What is their purpose?

2.24 Define the following terms: *character, byte, field, record, file*. How do these terms relate to one another?

2.25 Give an example of each of the terms in question 2.24.

2.26 What is a system flowchart?

2.27 Explain the meaning of ◯ , ▭ , and ▭ in a system flowchart.

2.28 Explain the conventions for status codes in the student status record (see figure 2–12).

FIGURE 2–17
Student class
request form

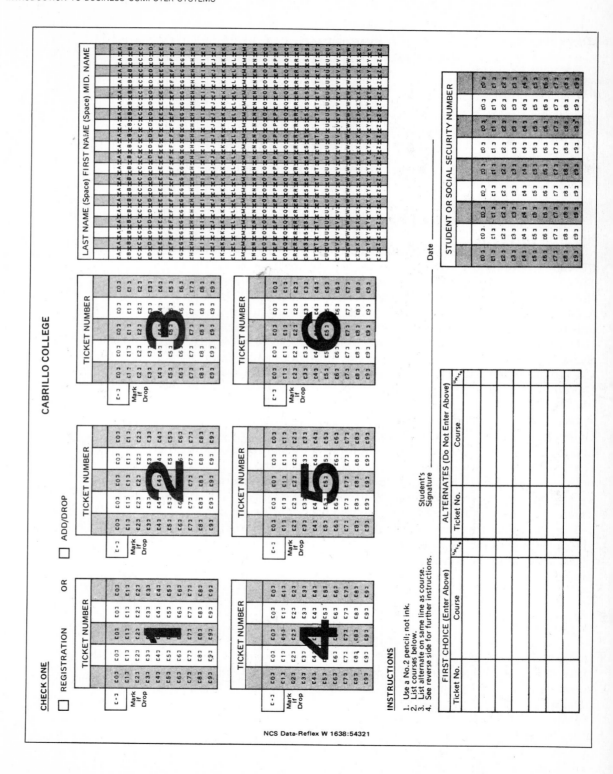

RECORD POSITION	FIELD CONTENTS
1-9	Student Number
10-29	Student Name
30	Number of Classes Requested (must be fewer than eight)
31–33	Class Number
34–60	Class Name
61	Section Number

Note: The last three fields repeat up to seven times.

FIGURE 2–18
Format of student request file

Data is an organizational resource. From data a business can derive the information it needs to make sound decisions. Therefore a business's data must be as accurate and current as possible. It must also be easily accessible.

From the computer system's point of view, data must be gathered, verified, stored and retrieved, and protected. How all this is done depends on the information needs of the business.

Data is stored inside the computer in arrangements of bits, each bit being like a switch that can be in either the "on" or "off" position. Several bits (usually six or eight) are called a byte and represent one character. One or more characters make up a field. One or more related fields are known collectively as a record, and many related records are stored together in a file.

In the next chapter you will look at the other four components of a business computer system.

WORD LIST

Many terms are introduced in this chapter. Terms that you should be sure you understand are listed here in the order in which they appear in the text.

Computer system
Business computer system
Computer hardware
Input equipment
Processing equipment
Output equipment
Storage equipment
Central processing unit (CPU)
Computer program
Computer programming language
BASIC
COBOL
Systems programs
Application programs
Data
Information
Input data
Processing data

Output data
Stored data
Storage medium
Procedures
Crashes
Systems development personnel
Operations personnel
System users
System clientele
System maintenance
Data gathering
Data source
Data verification
Data access
Data security
Backup copies
Bit
Binary digit
Bit pattern

Character
Hollerith code
Extended Binary Coded Decimal Interchange Code (EBCDIC)
American Standard Code for Information Interchange (ASCII)
Byte
Field
Record
Coding convention
File
System flowchart
Mark-sense form
Document or report flowchart symbol
Tape flowchart symbol
Processing flowchart symbol

QUESTIONS TO CHALLENGE YOUR THINKING

A. Suppose you are the computer center manager for a bank. What security measures would you use to protect your company's tape and disk libraries?

B. Daily sales data for a small shoe manufacturer is collected and stored on floppy diskettes. How would you ensure their security?

C. Suppose you are starting your own company. You plan to design self-contained mini-gardens for apartment and condominium dwellers. What data will you want access to? What are your sources? How will you gather this data?

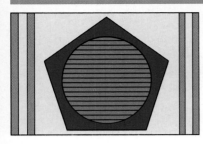

HARDWARE

More and More for Less and Less

End users input data from their desks.

▥ THE INPUT-PROCESS-OUTPUT/STORE CYCLE

The processing of data, or any computational activity, involves four fundamental functions. Information is **input** to the computer, it is **processed,** results are **output,** and data are **stored** in machine-readable form. Computer equipment can be classified according to these four primary functions.

Input equipment transforms information from a physical (often human-readable) form into data in a machine-readable form. **Processing equipment** transforms data into desired results. **Output equipment** transforms results from an electronic form into a physical or human-readable form. Finally, **storage equipment** saves data, in some machine-readable form, for subsequent processing. The difference between storage and input and output is functional rather than physical. Storage equipment also performs input and output functions, and often the same equipment is used for all three functions. However, the difference is that storage equipment does not translate between machine-readable and human-readable forms. Rather, it saves the data in magnetic, optical, or other machine-readable form.

As the following pages illustrate, there exists an incredible variety of equipment, most of which serves the same function. Why? Equipment — hardware and software — varies in performance (speed, capacity, and quality) and cost. Every year sees the rise of new technological innovations that improve performance or reduce costs, or both. When selecting computer equipment, the purchaser needs to know the system's immediate and future requirements in order to select sufficient (but not excessive) speed, capacity, and quality.

This modem is used to transmit data from the customer's computer via telephone to a typesetter.

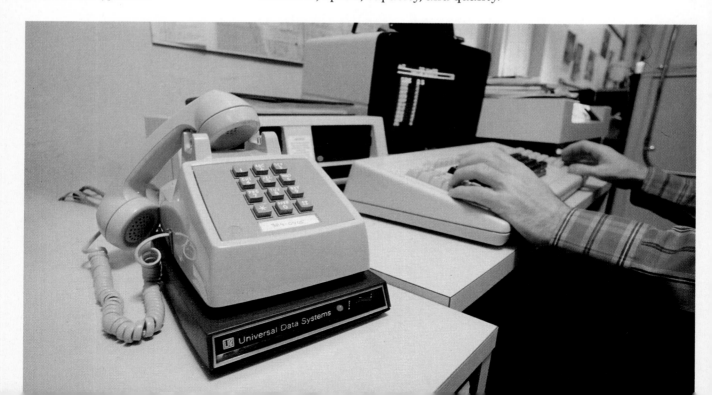

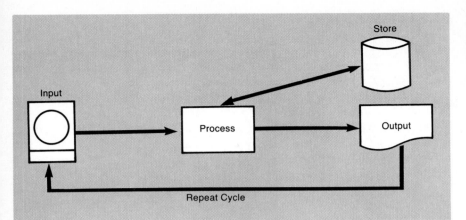

The input, process, output/store cycle.

Processing by a popular (Spectrum) minicomputer.

Output is viewed by a user as he enters data.

Keyboard data entry allows businesspeople to record information readily and quickly.

⊪ KEYBOARD INPUT

Keyboard input hardware requires a person to key in the data. Generally, the keyboard is similar to that of a typewriter. A video-display tube (VDT) is usually used for displaying data.

Keyboard hardware can be online or offline. If it is **online,** the keyboard is connected directly to a computer. Data flows from the keyboard device straight to the processing computer. If it is **offline,** the keyboard device ultimately produces a magnetic tape or disk. The tape or disk is later read by a tape or disk unit that is connected to the processing computer.

Most keyboard terminals contain a microprocessor. In less expensive terminals a simple microprocessor is used in order to reduce the cost of the terminal. However, a **smart** or **intelligent** terminal contains a powerful microprocessor that allows it to perform some of the functions of the processing computer. In addition to reducing the processing computer's workload, an intelligent terminal reduces the amount of communication required between the terminal and the processing computer.

Another type of keyboard operator is the **end-user** operator. An end user does not generally spend all the time keying data. Rather, keying data is only part of the end user's job. A bank teller using an online terminal is an example of an end-user operator. Although end users employ computer equipment in their jobs, they are generally not assigned to the data-processing department. Rather, end users work for another part of an organization. Bank tellers report to the head teller, not to the manager of data processing.

Today's banks utilize online data entry for accurate and current information.

End users input data from their desks.

Key-to-disk data entry.

Production data-entry personnel are employed by companies with continual data-entry needs.

Many organizations prefer end-user data entry. The end users feel that they have greater control when they do their own data entry. They must also live with their own mistakes, and, consequently, some companies find that the accuracy of data is higher when it is entered by end users.

Data entry via keyboards is very error prone. A production data-entry operator may key in hundreds of documents in a single day. Unfortunately, accurate computer processing requires accurate input data. Therefore, procedures to verify the accuracy of data input are crucial. For example, such procedures might involve manually counting the number of documents processed and comparing this count with a computer-calculated count, or adding, by hand, the amounts of all orders and comparing this sum to a computer-generated sum.

Data entry using a light pen.

The HP Touchscreen II personal
computer helps automate offices by
providing ready, quick, and accurate
access to data stored in minicomputers.

▦ NON-KEY INPUT

Keyboard input devices are slow for some applications. A variety of
other, special-purpose devices have therefore been developed.

Terminals have a **cursor** that show the user's position on the screen.
The cursor might be a blinking underscore, a highlighted square, or
some other, similar character. Moving the cursor around the screen
takes time. Most terminals have special keys for up/down, left/right
movement, but even with these keys cursor movement can be slow and
cumbersome. A **mouse** is a hand-held device for moving the cursor
quickly. The user moves the mouse around on a level surface, and the
cursor moves correspondingly. Moving the mouse left causes the cursor
to move left, moving it back (away from the user) causes the cursor to
move up the screen, and so forth.

A **light pen** is another device that reduces cursor movement and
keystrokes. A user with a light pen simply points the pen to the desired
spot on a screen and pushes a button. The terminal senses where the
light pen is located and responds accordingly. Light pens are often
used to select options from a menu on a screen. The user points the pen
to the menu item desired. With some terminals, the user can actually
use the light pen to draw on the screen.

UPC (Uniform Product Code) **bar codes** are used on grocery products. The bar pattern corresponds to an item number. The sensing
device sends the number to a computer for processing. UPC codes save
time not only for the clerk, but also for the people who would otherwise mark prices on the items. Furthermore, the grocery store can
change prices with minimal effort.

Digitizers sense marks on a document and convert those marks into digital data (whole numbers). For example, digitizers are used in the medical profession for storing X-ray pictures magnetically.

Paper strip scanners are used to input specially encoded files from paper. Some of these devices can also encode and write a file on paper. These devices are inexpensive and use technology similar to that used for UPC bar codes. A personal computer user can, for example, read in a properly encoded program published in a computer magazine, or transfer files between two computers by writing the encoded file to paper using one computer and reading it into another.

Optical character recognition devices are able to read a limited set of standard typefonts and translate the characters into machine-readable form. Some stores use them instead of UPC bar codes for reading prices on items being purchased—an advantage in that the customer and the machine see the same price. These devices are also used to input typewritten documents into a computer for updating, translating, or electronic mailing.

Computer designers and engineers have had only limited success with devices that recognize handwritten characters, because of the complexity of this problem. Usually, recognition is limited to a few characters such as digits. For example, a zip-code recognition device can save the postal service hours of labor.

Speech recognition devices translate spoken words into machine-readable form. A recognition device is **speaker independent** if it can understand words spoken by any speaker. A **speaker dependent** recognition device understands words spoken by one person only and must be trained by that person. Training involves having the intended user repeat several times each word in the device's vocabulary. The recognition device stores important characteristics of the speech sounds for later comparison.

Speaker-independent recognition devices can usually recognize only a few words (yes and no, and digits), as they must accommodate a variety of speaker's voices and accents. Speaker-dependent recognition devices are more widely used because they can recognize larger vocabularies (up to several hundred words) with greater reliability. The organization that coordinates organ-transplant donations in North America employs such a system.

Speech recognition devices are used by all manner of workers whose hands are not free to enter data, such as product inspectors, the handicapped, and researchers viewing objects under a microscope. Speech recognition devices are also employed for computer telephone polling, whose limited response requirements allow speaker-independent recognition devices to be used.

A scanner uses a low-grade laser to sense UPC barcodes in this grocery store.

The 'mouse' controls the movement of a cursor on the screen.

Processing inside a microcomputer occurs within one small hardware unit.

A microcomputer environment — this Macintosh computer sits on a desk top.

DEC's micro VAX provides minicomputer power in a small space.

▥ PROCESSING, HARDWARE, AND ENVIRONMENTS

Processing equipment includes the central processing unit (CPU) and main memory. There are three common types of CPUs: those used in microcomputers, minicomputers, and mainframes. The characteristics of the three types of processors are summarized in the chart at the end of this essay.

Main memory consists of thousands of on/off devices. Each on/off device represents one **binary digit** or **bit.** A **byte** is a group of bits that represents a single character, such as A or 7. Most computers have 8 bits per byte. In processing, the size of main memory is usually stated in bytes—for example, 256K bytes for a microcomputer. Although people often say that 256K equals 256,000, the letter K actually represents 1024. Thus, a 256-byte memory actually has 262,144 bytes. Common memory sizes are 256K, 512K, 1024K, and multiples of 1024K in the microcomputer area.

The distinction between the physical characteristics of microcomputers, minicomputers, and mainframes has almost disappeared due to advancing technology. Smaller minicomputers and microcomputers have become indistinguishable as have large minicomputers and mainframes. Networks of microcomputers with shared access to data storage and output services are beginning to take over minicomputer and mainframe applications.

The characteristics that define applications and environments also no longer fit neatly into the microcomputer, minicomputer, and mainframe categories, except in the general sense of small, medium, and large. The most important characteristics of a computer system are

A designer at a Sun Microsystem terminal.

whether it runs applications in an online, interactive mode or in batch mode, what sort of environment it resides in, and its processing power. The number of simultaneous users that an interactive system can accommodate is another important characteristic. This depends both on the processing power of the system as well as the software programs that run on it.

A user of an interactive system enters data and receives an immediate response from the system. A single-user system has one user and a multi-user system can have multiple users ranging from a handful to thousands. Clearly, the larger the number of simultaneous interactive users of a system, the more powerful the system must be. An airline reservation system that handles thousands of terminals requires the power of a mainframe computer. Business applications that require a few users, such as order entry, general ledger, inventory control, and the like typically use a minicomputer. Most single-user systems used

as personal assistants for word processing, electronic spreadsheets, personal databases, and educational programs are based on microcomputers.

An interactive computer system can be composed of a network of microcomputers that can share output and storage equipment. The cost of storage and output equipment, called **servers,** is amortized over all of the users of the system. A database server allows users on different microcomputers connected to the network access to the same data. A print server allows multiple users to share one, usually high-quality, printer. Unlike minicomputer and mainframe systems, the failure of one microprocessor affects only one user rather than the entire system. Also, the processing power of such a system can be incrementally increased by adding a single microcomputer. A popular use of a network of micros is in the area of computer-assisted design and manufacturing (CAD/CAM). The microcomputer network provides each user with the large amount of processing power required for interactive graphics while maintaining the minicomputer's advantages of centralized databases and shared output devices such as expensive, color printer-plotters.

Another type of interactive system is a specialized controller that receives information from and exerts control over other devices, such as temperature sensors and controllers, rather than users. These types of systems are based either on microcomputer, minicomputer, or mainframe applications, depending on the power and memory requirements of the task at hand. For example, both minicomputers and microcomputers are used to monitor and control power-plant operations, and both types are used to control circuit switching in the telephone system.

In batch mode, a large amount of information that has been entered offline is fed to a computer and processed without user interaction.

Most batch jobs are massive and require mainframe computers. Billing for credit cards and policy processing for insurance companies are business applications that run in batch mode on mainframe computers. Many science applications such as weather simulation and forecasting, or aircraft simulation, require large mainframes running in batch mode.

Microcomputers, usually desk-top computers, do not require a special environment and are typically run by their owner-user. Microcomputers used as specialized controllers and servers can be found in laboratories and equipment closets. Some minicomputers require a special air-conditioned environment, or contain sensitive data and are therefore kept in computer rooms, usually with controlled access. Other minicomputers are located in a user's work area, laboratories, and equipment closets, depending on their function. Most mainframes require very specialized environments with air-conditioning, raised floors, while some even require water supplies for water-cooled CPUs. Mainframes and related equipment are typically run by a highly trained operations staff in a formal and controlled operating environment. The workload of the computer is controlled by a preauthorized schedule.

The terminals for any computer system can be located near the computers, or thousands of miles away. External terminal users often access computers via dial-up phone lines. Because anyone can theoretically dial up the computer, prohibiting access to these machines by unauthorized users has become a major security problem. At the very least, access to these computers is usually controlled by passwords, which users must enter in order to use the machine. However, passwords are not that powerful a security measure. Where security is essential, either no external terminal access is provided, or special procedures are used to identify the caller. An example of this is a dial-up computer, which allows the caller to indicate who he or she is and where the call is coming from. The computer then hangs up, verifies the validity of the caller and the calling number, and calls the user back.

Processor and memory technology is constantly changing. Memory is becoming less expensive and smaller (1 megabyte is now available on a single chip). Processors, especially microprocessors, are becoming more powerful and less costly, and new concepts are developing every year. For example, an important new concept in processor design involves RISC (Reduced Instruction Set Computers) machines. The idea is that a processor will have fewer, or at least simpler, instructions, and therefore will execute them more quickly. The number of instructions needed to perform a given function, such as adding two numbers, may actually increase, but because the new instructions are so simple they can be executed more quickly than the few, complex instructions they are replacing. The commercial viability of this approach has not yet been determined, but most high-technology processor manufacturers have a RISC project in development and some have RISC-based products already on the market.

A CRAY II is an example of the ultimate mainframe environment.

An electronic publishing system can proceed from an idea to its representation in final copy in one sitting.

Line printers produce output at very high speeds.

▥ OUTPUT

Output equipment transforms results from electronic into physical form. One common output device is the CRT screen. CRTs are used both to display data being input and to display results.

Printers are a common output device. **Line printers** print a line at a time. **Serial printers** print only a single character at a time. **Full-character printers** print a complete letter the way a typewriter does. **Dot-matrix printers** print letters composed of small dots. Impact printers use hammers to transfer ink (either dots or characters) from a ribbon to the paper, as in a typewriter. Nonimpact printers use other, quieter techniques; **ink-jet printers** spray ink onto the paper, and **laser printers** fuse toner onto paper using a xerographic process like that of a copy machine.

How should a company choose among all of these alternatives? The answer again depends on the company's requirements. Speed and print quality are the most important characteristics, but cost and noise level should also be considered. For example, line printers are faster than serial printers, but the quality of print is not as good. Letter-quality output can be produced either by slow, full-character impact printers or by fast, dot-matrix laser or ink-jet printers. Impact dot-matrix printers are slower and produce less attractive output, but they are also less expensive. New technologies are constantly presenting new printer products with improved cost-performance characteristics.

Some companies store information on microfilm and microfiche rather than on paper, which is bulky and expensive. The procedure for transferring information from the computer to microfilm or microfiche requires a special-purpose microphotography device. The computer produces a magnetic tape containing the desired information. This tape is mounted onto the microphotography device which photographs the reports onto microfilm or microfiche. These devices are very expensive so many companies instead use a service bureau for microphotography. They send the magnetic tape to the service bureau and in turn receive the microfilm or microfiche back.

A more recent alternative to microfilm and microfiche for long-term storage is the **optical disk.** For example, banks use optical disks because they are highly reliable and the information can be retrieved by computer when needed. This is not true of microfilm and microfiche, which require humans to retrieve information. (This technology is also discussed in the section on storage.)

Voice output is emerging as a form of computer output. In its simplest form, a prerecorded message can be selected and played. Often the prerecorded message has been digitized (converted into digital signals) and compressed to simplify the storage and playback requirements. Examples are automobiles that instruct drivers to turn off their lights or inform them that their fuel level is low.

More sophisticated voice-output devices employ **text-to-speech** technology. This technology automatically translates text into spoken words. This procedure is more costly but it doesn't require that all phrases to be spoken be programmed in advance. This technology might be used by an executive to have a document "read" by a computer over the telephone.

Today's fastest printers use laser technology to print over a hundred pages a minute.

This Xerox plotter is the world's first narrow-format electrostatic color plotter.

The Hewlett-Packard Company's LaserJet 500 PLUS printer with its two, 250-sheet input bins, can print documents on more than one size and type of paper. More importantly, it's quiet!

Magnetic tapes provide an inexpensive and secure method of storing data in this tape library.

STORAGE

Some data must be stored because it is needed more than once. For example, for a payroll system employee name, address, pay rate, and other data are needed every pay period. Such data cannot be left in the computer's main memory for several reasons. First, main memory is very expensive and, for the largest computers, is limited to 32 million bytes (which may sound large, but even small companies need more than that). Furthermore, main memory is volatile. When the power is shut off, the contents of main memory are lost. Thus, computers need **secondary storage (memory)** that is less expensive and larger than main memory, as well as nonvolatile.

There are two fundamental types of secondary-storage equipment. Sequential devices allow only sequential access to the data. For example, to access the 50th record in a file or magnetic tape, the first 49 records must first be read. Furthermore, additions can only be made to the end of a sequential file, or wherever a large enough record was deleted.

Magnetic tape is the most common sequential-storage device. A variety of tape devices are available. The most common device uses tape that is similar to stereo tape but is ½-inch wide. Some microcomputer systems do use stereo tape, however. Tape is inexpensive; a 2400-foot reel of ½-inch tape can be purchased for $15. Because tape is cheap, it is often used for backup storage. Data that resides on other types of secondary storage is often off-loaded onto tape until it is needed.

The second type of secondary storage is direct-access storage, which is suitable for disks. Direct-access data can be accessed in any order on a disk. The 50th record can be obtained directly, without having to plough through the first 49 records.

There are several types of direct-access disk devices. All of them have a circular recording surface mounted on a spindle. The surfaces rotate under read/write heads. Data is recorded to or read from concentric circles called **tracks.** Hard or floppy magnetic disks are the most commonly used type of direct-access storage devices.

A most promising alternative to magnetic-disk storage is optical-disk storage. Optical disks are more permanent than magnetic disks and hold far greater amounts of data (up to a gigabyte per side). It isn't currently possible to erase optical disks. Once a track has been used it can't be reused (whereas magnetic disk space can be erased and reused repeatedly). However, the enormous amount of storage available on an optical disk makes it feasible to simply continue to write more and more on the same disk.

Compact disks are becoming popular for distributing information. In the future there will be cost-effective technology for writing information onto these disks as well.

The manufacturing of a disk surface takes place in a clean and controlled environment.

A 3½-inch floppy disk is inserted into a disk drive.

A COMPARISON BETWEEN MICRO, MINI, AND MAINFRAME COMPUTERS

	MICRO	MINI	MAIN
Main Memory (1000 bytes)	32–20000	2000–8000	8000–32000
Instruction Speed (millions per second)	.2–4	.5–5	5–100
Disk Storage (bytes)	.2–20 million	up to 1 billion	up to 20 billion
Cost	$500–$15,000	$50,000–$250,000	$500,000–$10 million +
Notes	Usually single-user	Single- or multi-user	Multi-user
	Often used in network with shared storage and output devices	Often sold by OEMs	Sold by vendor
			Extensive support
	Minimum vendor support		

QUESTIONS

1. Name and describe the four fundamental functions of processing data.
2. Describe the difference between online and offline data entry.
3. Describe the difference between production data entry and end-user data entry.
4. What steps can be taken to compensate for the error-prone nature of data entry?
5. Explain the use of **cursor**, **mouse**, and **light pen**.
6. Describe two keyboard data-entry devices.
7. Describe two non-key data-entry devices.
8. Distinguish between the hardware characteristics of microcomputers, minicomputers, and mainframes.
9. Distinguish between the processing environments of microcomputers, minicomputers, and mainframes.
10. Explain the difference between:
    a. Line and serial printers
    b. Full-character and dot-matrix printers
    c. Impact and nonimpact printers.
11. Describe the two fundamental types of storage hardware.
12. What is a mass-storage system?

INTRODUCTION TO BUSINESS COMPUTER SYSTEMS: HARDWARE, PROGRAMS, PROCEDURES, AND TRAINED PERSONNEL

CHAPTER 3

In addition to data, business computer systems also require hardware, programs, procedures, and trained personnel. Interestingly, programs are instructions that guide the hardware, while procedures are instructions that guide the people. In this chapter you will learn how the remaining four components combine with data to form entire business computer systems. When you complete this chapter you will have a solid foundation for the material in the rest of this book.

HARDWARE

It is convenient to classify hardware according to its function in relation to data. Thus, basic categories of hardware are input, storage, output, and processing hardware. In this section, we will discuss these categories and look at some important hardware devices. A more comprehensive catalog of hardware can be found in the hardware photo essay.

Input Hardware

Although there are literally dozens of kinds of input devices, only a few are commonly seen.

Terminals

Probably the most common input device in use today is the **terminal**. A computer terminal is actually made up of two devices used together and connected to the computer. One of these devices, the **keyboard**, is an input device. When a key is depressed a signal flows to the computer's central processing unit (the CPU will be discussed later) where it can be stored or processed. In many cases the program echoes the character back to the terminal and displays it on the second device, the **cathode ray tube** (**CRT**), which is an output device. Thus it appears that whatever is typed on the keyboard is also printed on the screen, although that is not always the case.

Terminals are also known as **video display terminals**, or **VDTs**. VDT is a more general term than CRT.

Key-to-Disk and Key-to-Tape Equipment

Other types of input hardware are **key-to-disk** and **key-to-tape**. These devices also use a VDT, but the VDT is not connected to the processing computer. Instead, data that is entered is copied onto magnetic media such as disks or tapes (these are discussed in the next section). The disk or tape can later be read into the processing computer (see figure 3–1).

FIGURE 3–1
Key-to-disk equipment

Special Input Devices

Additional input hardware include *mark-sense devices*; *optical character recognition (OCR) devices*, which read the characters produced by credit cards; *magnetic ink character recognition (MICR) devices*, which read the ink on checks; and *uniform price code (UPC) reading devices*, which are used to read prices in grocery and other stores. Other input devices include the light pen, the mouse, the joystick used in many videogames, specialized keypads, and the touchtone telephone. There are even some limited applications for voice input, although it is currently expensive and inflexible (the computer must learn the voice patterns of each user). Voice input is expected to become more common as time goes on. Many interesting input devices are illustrated in the hardware photo essay.

Punched Cards

For many years, the **punched card** was the workhorse for data entry. Cards were either punched by humans using card-punch machines or prepared by computer card punches (a computer output device). They were then sensed by card readers. Card input is slow and cumbersome; and, although punched cards are still occasionally seen today, they have by and large gone the way of real workhorses.

Storage Hardware

Two types of storage hardware are commonly used: magnetic tape and magnetic disks. They are called storage devices because they are used primarily to store computer data. Sometimes they are called input/output (I/O) devices because the computer first writes data on them (output), and later reads it back in (input).

Magnetic Tape

Magnetic tape devices read and write magnetic tape similar to the tape in your stereo (see figure 3–2). Instead of recording a continuous signal, however, they record digital data in the form of 1's and 0's. We will discuss magnetic tapes further in chapter 7.

Magnetic tape is relatively inexpensive, and it is easy to transport. For these reasons, many companies use tape to make backup and archival copies of their files and store them off site. Some microcomputer manufacturers offer a tape backup device for owners who have large-capacity hard disks (described in the next section).

For all its benefits, magnetic computer tape has the same disadvantages as the tape you use in your stereo. First, you can read the data only in sequence. If you want to read the 112th customer record on the tape, you must first read the 111 records that precede it. Second, if you want to add a new record or delete an old one, you must rewrite the entire tape. For these reasons, magnetic tape cannot be used for every application.

Magnetic Disks

A second type of storage hardware is the **magnetic disk**. Disks store data in concentric circles, called **tracks** (see figure 3–3). The 1's and 0's are recorded serially around the circle.

Three types of disks are common. **Floppy diskettes** (see figure 3–4) are used primarily in microcomputer systems. They are flexible (thus the name floppy) and are sealed in a protective envelope. A two-sided double-density diskette can hold about 350,000 bytes of data.

The second type of disk is the **conventional**, or **hard**, **disk** (see figure 3–5). Such disks are constructed of a stack of 5 to 20 hard recording surfaces mounted on a central spindle. The spindle revolves so that data can be read or written by the heads mounted on the ends of access arms. Some conventional disks can hold over 300 million bytes of data. A version of hard disk, called a **Winchester,** is available for microcomputers (see figure 3–6).

FIGURE 3–2
Magnetic tape

All of the disk devices are capable of direct access. This means that almost any data on the disk can be accessed without having to access all of the preceding data. Thus, record 112 can be accessed by reading the track on which record 112 resides. The first 111 records need not be accessed, as they must be with magnetic tape. With disks, it is unnecessary to read more than a single track of data to access a record. We will consider disk devices in greater detail in chapter 8.

Output Hardware

Although there are many types of output hardware, two devices are most common: terminals and printers.

Terminals

We have already discussed the terminal keyboard as an input device. We saw that a terminal's screen can be used as an output device as well. Responses to requests, messages, and reports can be displayed on the screen. Screens can also display intricate color graphics.

FIGURE 3–3
Disk surface

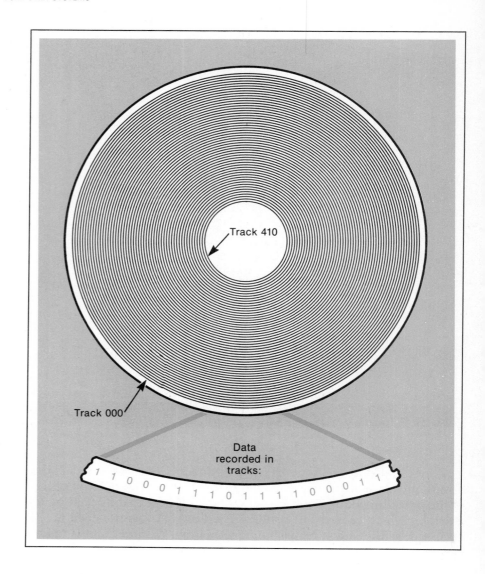

Printers

A second common type of output device is the printer. Although there are hundreds of different brands and models of printers, they can be classified in three ways, according to their mode of operation.

First, there are **serial printers** and **line printers**. Serial printers print one character at a time. They are similar to typewriters; in fact, the balls, or elements, that are used in IBM Selectric typewriters are used in some serial printers. Serial printers operate at speeds of 15 to 60 characters per second. Some serial printers can print in both directions so that time is not wasted on carriage returns.

Line printers print a full line at a time. Figure 3–9 shows a sketch of a line printer that uses a print drum with 136 print positions. At each position there is a band containing a complete set of characters. When a line is to be printed, the bands rotate to expose the correct character. The characters are then struck from behind by hammers, causing the line to be printed. A printer like this operates at 300 to 2000 lines per minute.

A second way in which printers are characterized is according to whether they are **impact** or **nonimpact** printers. With impact printers, the characters strike the paper through a ribbon. Both serial and line printers can be impact printers. Some nonimpact printers write on specially coated or sensitized paper. Other types of nonimpact printers spray ink on paper or use the same technique as photocopying machines. Figure 3–10 shows a laser printer that uses a xerographic process.

Impact printers can make several copies at a time, but they are noisy. Nonimpact printers are quiet, and some are much faster than impact printers. Speeds as high as 45,000 lines per minute are possible with ink-jet printers. Nonimpact printers cannot make more than one copy at a time, but their faster speed can compensate for this. It is likely that nonimpact printers will be used more and more in the future.

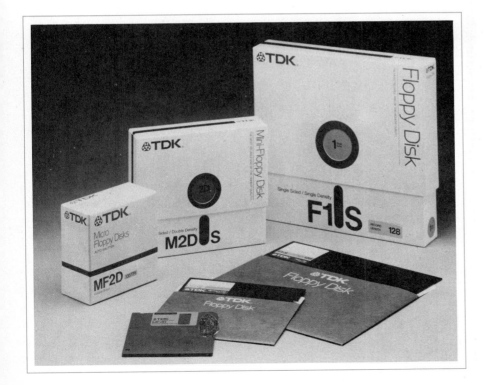

FIGURE 3–4
Floppy diskettes

FIGURE 3–5
Conventional or hard disks

A third categorization of printers is according to whether they are **full-character** or **dot-matrix** printers. Full-character printers print a whole character the way a typewriter does. Dot-matrix printers print an array of dots (see figure 3–11). Dot-matrix printers do not produce print of as high a quality as do full-character printers. However, they are cheaper and faster.

Figure 3–12 summarizes the categories of printers used in business computer systems.

Processing Hardware

The central processing unit (CPU) executes program instructions that cause data to be read, stored, written, or otherwise processed. CPUs

FIGURE 3–6
Winchester disk

have three functional parts: the **control unit**, the **arithmetic logic unit** (**ALU**), and **main memory**. The control unit interprets and executes instructions, moving data around in main memory and routing data between peripheral devices and main memory. (Peripheral devices are all of the input, storage, and output devices connected to the CPU.) The ALU performs arithmetic and comparisons when directed to do so by the control unit. It makes the results available to the control unit for further processing. Main memory holds program instructions and data during processing. Although CPUs are generally grouped into three classes—micros, minis, and mainframes—there is much overlap in terms of speed, capacity, and capability. For example, some of today's microcomputers are faster and more powerful than some mainframes of 10 years ago. It is becoming increasingly difficult to maintain the traditional distinction among CPUs. The following section offers some guidelines.

Microcomputers

Microcomputers are generally the cheapest and smallest computers (see figure 3–13). They are available from computer stores, business supply stores, and large department stores. Microcomputers initially

FIGURE 3–7
Characteristics of disks

DISK	CAPACITY (MAX)	SIZE	FIXED/REMOVABLE	USED ON
Floppy	360KB	3 ½ or 5 ¼ inches	Removable	Micros
Winchester	50MB	3 ½ or 5 ¼ inches	Fixed	Micros
Conventional	317.5MB	12 inches, up to 20 disks on one spindle	Fixed or removable	Minis and mainframes

PROFILE

"TECHNOLOGY DRIVEN WHEN MARKET DRIVEN IS THE MANAGEMENT RAGE"

For almost three years, nary a positive word was printed about Kenneth H. Olsen or the company he founded and leads: Digital Equipment Corporation. *Business Week* magazine, charmed by the apostles of personal computers and office automation, was a relentless critic of the minicomputer giant. A late 1984 cover story fingered DEC as a company that had fallen from "excellence." Olsen was chastised for a "seeming preoccupation" with past glories. DEC was condemned for its "bloated management" and for its failure to adjust to a personal-computer-based world.

Today, the prevailing winds have changed, and it is obvious to all that DEC is sailing ahead of the most powerful hard-blowing computer industry trends. With annual revenues approaching $7 billion, a strong financial position, a solid performance in the face of an industry-wide recession and market-taming products coming out almost monthly, DEC and Olsen's leadership are once again drawing praise.

It is amusing to see DEC and Olsen, in so many ways defiant of fashion, become fashionable once again. Olsen does not fit the modern image of the trim, endlessly exercising and self-improving executive. He is a heavy, slow-moving man, now 60 years old. He lives in a relatively modest and unpretentious home west of Boston. His company also seems oblivious to style. Corporate headquarters is still a grim and drafty old converted textile mill. The company exasperates Wall Street analysts with a no-layoff tradition that has whittled away at operating margins. Salesmen, remarkably, are not paid on commission. For a company its size, DEC has virtually no public recognition; this is at least partially the result of Olsen's disdain for television advertising. As if all of this heresy were not enough, DEC has been guilty of two more serious transgressions against the common wisdom. It has persisted in being "technology driven" at a time when "market driven" is the management rage. And the company has never been able to market a personal computer successfully. By sticking to his guns, by spurning the trends, by concentrating on the workhorse VAX architecture and the professional computer user, Kenneth H. Olsen has managed to silence his critics.

were bought by families for entertainment and education, by small business people, and by hobbyists. The accessibility of microcomputers and the development of inexpensive, high-quality software has resulted in an entire field of personal productivity aids, heavily used in business, industry, and government (see module B).

More and more business computer systems incorporate microcomputers: as personal productivity tools (for word processing and electronic spreadsheet calculations, for instance), as front-end processors to collect data and then process it and transmit it to a mainframe, as display terminals, or in various combinations.

A typical microcomputer includes two floppy-disk drives or one floppy- and one hard-disk drive giving it a storage capacity of from 5 to 20 million bytes; at least 256K of main memory, easily and inexpensively expanded to 2.5 million bytes or more; an instruction execution speed of 250,000 instructions per second; and graphics and commu-

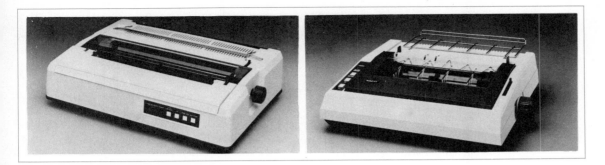

FIGURE 3–8
Daisy-wheel and dot-matrix printers

nications capabilities. The price of a microcomputer can be as low as $1,000. It can exceed $10,000, depending on the options you select.

CPUs are often classified according to the number of bits that make up a single instruction. Generally, the greater the number of bits in an instruction, the more powerful the CPU. Microcomputers generally have either 8- or 16-bit instructions, and there are some 32-bit micro-computers. Sixteen-bit micros are more powerful than 8-bit ones, and 32-bit computers are even more powerful.

(It is difficult to explain this concept further without discussing the details of CPU design. Consider an analogy using telephone numbers. A 7-digit number, xxx-xxxx, has the power to connect you to all the telephones within a given area code. A 10-digit number with an area code, (xxx) xxx-xxxx, can connect you to any telephone in North America. The larger number of digits gives you a greater range. In a somewhat similar way, the larger instruction size gives the computer more power per instruction.)

Microcomputers are most often single-user systems. Normally, only one person at a time can use a microcomputer. Thus, microcomputers

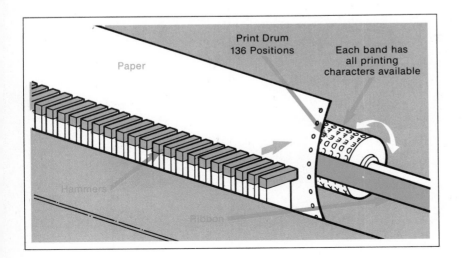

Paper

Print Drum
136 Positions

Each band has all printing characters available

Hammers

Ribbon

FIGURE 3–9
Print drum of a line printer

would be suitable for Mary Forsythe's word processing and mailing list applications and for the analysis application at Blake Records and Tapes, but they would be unsuitable for the order entry application at TYCON Construction.

Minicomputers

Minicomputers are the next group of computers in terms of size, speed, and expense (see figure 3–14). Minicomputers were first developed in the 1960s as small, special-purpose computers. However, as time went on, minicomputers became more and more powerful. In the late 1960s, general-purpose business minicomputers became available. Today, minicomputers have grown in capability so much that they overlap with the mainframe category of computers. The term *minicomputer* is prevalent, however, and you should know it.

Minicomputers are purchased from vendors rather than computer or department stores. They may be purchased directly from the manu-

FIGURE 3–10
Hewlett-Packard laser printer

FIGURE 3–11
Dot-matrix characters

```
2.00     4.00    50.00    210.00       0      25
0.20     0.40    50.00     55.00       0     175
1.50     4.00    62.00    375.00       0     300
2.00     6.00    66.00    298.00       0      75
0.63     1.25    49.00     51.03       0      40
1.50     3.00    50.00    604.50       0     200
0.63     1.25    49.00     44.10       0      40
0.30     0.70    57.00    243.00       0     300
1.88     3.75    49.00    535.80       0      20
```

facturer, or they may be purchased from **original equipment manufacturers (OEMs)**. An OEM is a company that buys hardware from the manufacturer; repackages it by adding special-purpose hardware, programs, or some other feature or service; and sells the new package. The term *OEM* is confusing. It implies that OEMs make hardware, but they do not; they repackage hardware.

Minicomputer vendors (manufacturers or OEMs) provide more comprehensive support than do microcomputer stores. Such vendors can make greater expertise available in the selection and acquisition of their products; they provide more comprehensive service; and they usually stay close to their customers.

A typical minicomputer has 2 to 8 million bytes of data in main memory and executes instructions at the rate of 1 to 4 million per second. The maximum amount of disk storage supported is about 1 billion bytes. Minicomputers have either 16- or 32-bit instructions. Some minicomputer manufacturers now produce a 64-bit supermini, making it yet more difficult to tell the minis from the mainframes. A typical minicomputer, including the CPU and an average amount of peripheral equipment, costs between $50,000 and $250,000.

FIGURE 3–12
Characterizations of printers

PRINTER	CHARACTERISTICS
Serial	Prints one character at a time.
Line	Prints a line at a time.
Impact	Can make multiple copies, but is noisy.
Nonimpact	Can make only a single copy, but is very fast and quiet.
Full Character	Prints characters like a typewriter, with possible high quality.
Dot Matrix	Prints characters using dots.

FIGURE 3–13
IBM, Apple, Tandy, and Fujitsu
microcomputers

PROFILE

"OPEN SYSTEMS MAKE ITS MACHINES ADAPTABLE TO THE INDUSTRY'S EVOLVING TECHNOLOGY"

The founders of Sun Microsystems Inc. are a study in contrasts and in the energy that drives a successful computer startup company. Andreas Bechtolsheim, a soft-spoken, German-born computer scientist who designed Sun's first workstation as an academic exercise, is prone to kicking off his Birkenstock sandals while pondering a microchip question. William N. Joy, Sun's software guru, is an irrepressible extrovert whose bushy hair and beard give him the look of an erudite mountain man. Then there is President Scott McNealy, the buttoned-down yuppie with degrees from Harvard and

Stanford, who yearns to play the world's top 100 golf courses.

The Mountain View (California) company has moved new technology to the workstation market, with an almost fanatical commitment to open systems that makes its machines adaptable to the industry's evolving technology. Apollo, the leader in the field, relies on proprietary designs, but Sun uses off-the-shelf parts and urges buyers to customize their product.

Sun's reliance on industry standards is a natural outgrowth of its humble origins. Bechtolsheim was pursuing a doctorate at Stanford

University when he set out to design a powerful computer using off-the-shelf components. But he needed money. In early 1982, before he could find a company that would pay to license the design, McNealy and Khosla, classmates at Stanford's business school, suggested starting Sun. They recruited Joy, the architect of an important version of the Unix operating system, which was then gathering momentum as an industry standard for engineering computers. Within a year the four had $4.6 million in venture capital and were shipping $1 million worth of computers a month.

Minicomputers are usually multiple-user systems. An average-sized minicomputer would be able to support 30 or 40 CRTs. Thus, a minicomputer would be suitable for TYCON's order entry system.

A minicomputer generally is located in a separate room, possibly with its own power supply and air conditioning. For security reasons, physical access to the room usually is controlled.

In the next few years, the minicomputer class of computers may well disappear. Large minis are becoming indistinguishable from mainframes, and small minis are becoming indistinguishable from micros. We may soon be left with just two categories: micros and mainframes.

Mainframes

The largest, fastest, and most expensive computers are called **mainframes** (see figure 3–15). These computers are nearly always purchased from manufacturers. Because of their size and sophistication, mainframe computers are sold with a great deal of support from the vendor. The vendor may well spend considerable time and money helping the customer select and install the hardware. Once the mainframe is installed, the vendor will be readily available to help resolve problems,

FIGURE 3-14

Digital Equipment Corporation VAX 780 minicomputer

QUESTIONS

3.1 Describe two types of input hardware.

3.2 Describe two types of storage hardware.

3.3 Describe two types of output hardware.

3.4 Explain the difference between serial and line printers.

3.5 Explain the difference between impact and nonimpact printers.

3.6 Explain the difference between dot-matrix and full-character printers.

(continued)

to service the mainframe and related equipment, and to make repairs when necessary. Maintenance is available on a 24-hour, quick-response basis.

A mainframe computer typically has 8 to 32 million bytes of main memory, and it executes instructions at the rate of 8 to 16 million per second. Disk (or similar) storage capacities may be as great as 10 to 20 billion characters. (Twenty billion is difficult to comprehend. Consider that a storage of 20 billion characters is large enough to hold 80 characters of data for every person living in the United States.) Mainframes typically have 32-bit instructions, although some very powerful mainframes have 64-bit instructions. Mainframes cost between $500,000 and $10 million or more.

Mainframes are multiple-user systems and can support 400 or 500 terminals while processing additional work. They require considerable power and air-conditioning facilities and so are always located in computer rooms. For security reasons, access to such rooms always should be controlled.

Characteristics of each of the three categories of CPU are summarized in figure 3–16.

THE CLASS ENROLLMENT SYSTEM: HARDWARE

The hardware requirements for the class enrollment system can be determined from the system flowchart shown in figure 2–15. The system requires at least one mark-sense form reader, a printer, and three tape drives. Only one printer is required because the reports can be produced one at a time.

Realistically, a single terminal would be unable to process the workload of a typical college. Instead, from 10 to perhaps 100 terminals would be needed. Therefore, a minicomputer or mainframe would most likely be necessary. Considering the amount of money that would be involved, CPU and other hardware selection for such a system would require careful analysis. We will consider such analyses further in chapter 5.

3.7 List three distinguishing characteristics of a microcomputer.

3.8 List three distinguishing characteristics of a minicomputer.

3.9 List three distinguishing characteristics of a mainframe computer.

Questions 3.10 through 3.12 pertain to the flowchart on page 79. Note: The ▢ symbol represents a terminal.

3.10 What computer hardware will be needed to run this program?

3.11 Is the customer order data input to the program or output from the program?

3.12 What data will be printed? What data will be stored?

FIGURE 3–15
CRAY-2 mainframe computer

▦ PROGRAMS

We will not discuss the details of programming and program languages in this section — that is done in part 4. However, you need to know more about programs than has been described so far. Consequently, in this section, we will discuss a logic pattern that occurs in many programs, and we will introduce two tools used by program designers.

Input/Process/Output Cycle

Think for a moment about how you would solve the class enrollment problem manually. You would probably schedule the classes for one student at a time. You would gather the data you need for the first student and the classes he or she requested. Then you would check for conflicts, closed classes, and so forth and produce a valid schedule. Finally, you would write the student's schedule. You would then proceed with the next student. When all of the student requests had been processed, you would be finished.

Think about this process for a moment. Can you see that it has three basic phases? There is a data-gathering phase, a processing phase, and a result-writing phase. These three phases are common to many business problems. In fact, this pattern occurs so frequently that systems developers have given it a special name. It is called the **input/process/output cycle**.

In one way or another, every computer program conforms to this pattern. Data is read into the computer and processed, and results are written. The cycle is repeated until all the data is processed.

FIGURE 3-16

Comparison of micro, mini, and mainframe computers

	MICROCOMPUTER	MINICOMPUTER	MAINFRAME COMPUTER
Main Memory (1000 bytes)	32 – 1000	2000 – 8000	8000 – 32,000
Instruction Speed (millions per second)	0.25	1 – 4	8 – 16
Disk Storage (bytes)	5 – 20 million	up to 1 billion	up to 20 billion
Cost	$1000 – $10,000	$50,00 – $250,000	$500,000 – $10 million +
Notes	Usually single-user Minimum vendor support	Multi-user Often sold by OEMs	Multi-user Sold by vendor Extensive support

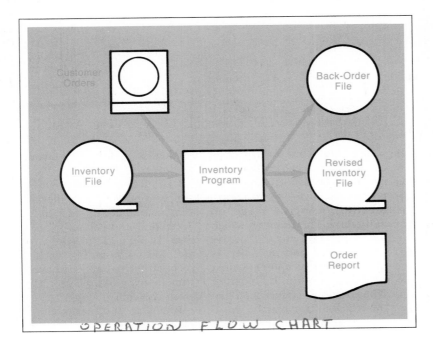

Flowchart for questions 3.10 through 3.12

OPERATION FLOW CHART

Top-Down Analysis

When preparing to write a program, many program designers begin by jotting down a list of program inputs and program outputs. They also identify all of the tasks the program will perform and determine the order in which they will be executed. In essence, a programmer who has to write a computer program is confronting a task not very different from any other problem-solving project.

The basic principle behind problem solving is this: Rather than attempting to solve a large, complex problem all at once, first break down the large problem into several small ones. Then solve each of the smaller problems. Finally, join together the solutions for the little problems and you form the solution to the big problem. This approach works well for writing a term paper, building a house, or developing a computer program. It is sometimes called **top-down analysis** because you begin at the top, the big problem, and work your way down to the small, manageable ones.

Program designers use **structure charts** like the one in figure 3–17 to show the small parts, or **modules**, that make up the whole program. The structure chart in figure 3–17 is for the class enrollment program. In the chart you can see that there are eight modules. The one on top, ENROLL STUDENTS, is able to call each of the other modules into action. A programmer would write program instructions to perform each function in the lower-level modules, then would write the code for ENROLL STUDENTS to execute each of the modules in the proper order. When this was done, the program would be complete.

APPLICATION

"VOICE RESPONSE EQUIPMENT IS BEGINNING TO TRANSFORM THE WAY BUSINESSES CONDUCT DAILY AFFAIRS"

The notion of a computer that responds to orders that are spoken rather than typed on a keyboard has long bedeviled inventors and inspired the plots of science-fiction movies. The 1980s however, have seen considerable progress in the field of speech recognition, and several machines are now on the market that respond to limited voice commands. The next few years are expected to make this mode of interaction between people and machine faster, easier, and more natural.

Sophisticated voice-response equipment that hooks up to existing computers, already being marketed by some 20 companies, is beginning to transform the way businesses ranging from the medical to the military conduct their daily affairs. And many suspect that the emergence of computers that can listen as well as speak will also mean new and diverse job opportunities.

One reason for these rosy projections is the breakthrough in tech-

nology in recent years. In the basic technology for speech-comprehension systems, the sound wave of a spoken word is converted into a number, usually binary, or made up of ones and zeros. This number, which contains within it codes that record its frequency and intensity, is then matched in the computer against words already stored in its memory bank. The computer screen then displays the written version of the word, or the computer responds with a piece of information, depending on the situation.

But until very recently most of these systems had limited vocabularies, were responsive only to a limited number of voices, required the speaker to pause between words, or had combinations of these faults. Now these faults are being overcome; the Kurzweil VoiceWriter, for example, which will be available in the middle of this year, has a vocabulary of nearly 10,000 words. The vocabularies of most systems now on the

market do not exceed several hundred words.

One sticky problem still to be solved concerns homonyms, different words that sound alike, such as "there," "they're," and "their"; "to," "too," and "two"; and "mettle" and "metal." Most computers with speech-recognition capability have a hard time figuring out the user's intended word choice.

But the International Business Machines Corporation has developed a system that through the use of statistics and information theory can place a word in its context, thereby choosing the correct word and discarding its troublesome homonym. Although IBM has yet to put a speech-recognition product on the market, or even to announce plans to do so, the company has spent a dozen years and millions of dollars on research and development. According to competitors and industry analysts, IBM is leading the race in speech-recognition technology.

Deciding on the proper order in which to execute instructions in a program is sometimes difficult, although it sounds simple. In the next section we will examine two tools that program designers use to help them do this.

Developing Program Algorithms

An **algorithm** is a set of specific actions to take to solve a problem in a finite number of steps. Computer professionals have developed many tools for this purpose, but two of the most popular ones are *pseudocode* and *program flowcharts*.

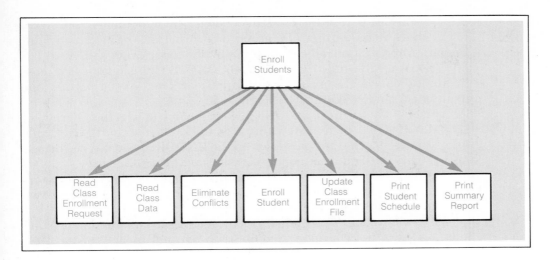

Pseudocode and Flowcharts

Pseudocode (*pseudo* means false; thus, false code) is an informal English equivalent of program logic. To write it, the programmer or analyst just explains in words what the program is to do. For an example, refer to figure 3–18, which shows pseudocode for one module in the class enrollment program. Pseudocode for the other seven modules has been omitted for the sake of brevity.

FIGURE 3–17
Structure chart for the class enrollment program

FIGURE 3–18
Pseudocode for part of the class enrollment program

```
BEGIN ENROLL STUDENTS

DOUNTIL THERE ARE NO MORE CLASS ENROLLMENT REQUESTS
     CALL READ CLASS ENROLLMENT REQUEST
     CALL READ CLASS DATA
     IF STUDENT STATUS CODE IS 200 OR 210
     THEN ADD 1 TO COUNT OF BAD REQUESTS
          ISSUE ERROR MESSAGE
     ELSE ADD 1 TO COUNT OF GOOD REQUESTS
          CALL ELIMINATE CONFLICTS
          CALL ENROLL STUDENT
          CALL UPDATE CLASS/ENROLLMENT FILE
          CALL PRINT STUDENT SCHEDULE
     ENDIF
ENDDO

CALL PRINT SUMMARY REPORT

END ENROLL STUDENTS
```

There is one paragraph of pseudocode for each module on the structure chart. A paragraph is a group of instructions treated as a unit. A paragraph's name indicates what function it performs.

The paragraph called ENROLL STUDENTS is the longest and most complex one in the program. Let's look at some of the pseudocode statements in ENROLL STUDENTS.

The first statement says DOUNTIL . . . , which means that a group of instructions is to be repeated until a condition is met. In this example, the statements that follow, down to the ENDDO, are to be performed repeatedly until all the student requests have been processed.

A group of statements that are performed repeatedly is called a **loop**, because the logic repeats, or loops back. In figure 3–18, the first two statements in the loop cause data to be read.

Next, the student's status is verified. Note the **IF statement**. Checking conditions is very common in computer programs; in fact, this capability gives programs much of their power. In figure 3–18 the IF statement is used to check student status in accordance with the conventions shown in figure 2–12.

As a result of this test, either an error message is issued or the student schedule is printed. (How would you like the schedule in figure 3–19?) After all requests have been processed, the summary report is written.

Do not be misled by the simplicity of these statements. Remember that figure 3–17 is *pseudo* code, not actual code. When the actual program is written in a programming language, many more details and more precise instructions must be specified. Pseudocode is a program designer's shorthand for organizing and developing program logic.

Flowcharts are a second way of organizing and presenting program logic. We have already seen one type of flowchart, called a *system flowchart* in figure 2–15. This flowchart showed how programs and files are related. Another type of flowchart is called a **program**, or **detailed, flowchart**. These flowcharts depict program logic. Figure 3–20 presents a program flowchart for part of the class enrollment program.

FIGURE 3–19
Sample student class schedule report

```
NAME:     SALLY J. PARKS

STUDENT NUMBER:  500004128                    GRADE LEVEL:  SOPHOMORE


CLASS                    HOUR        DAYS

ACCOUNTING               8           MTWF
COMPOSITION II           4           MWF
HUMAN SEXUALITY          CLASS FULL
STATISTICS               2-4         TR
AMERICAN HISTORY II  UNABLE TO SCHEDULE DUE TO CONFLICTS
```

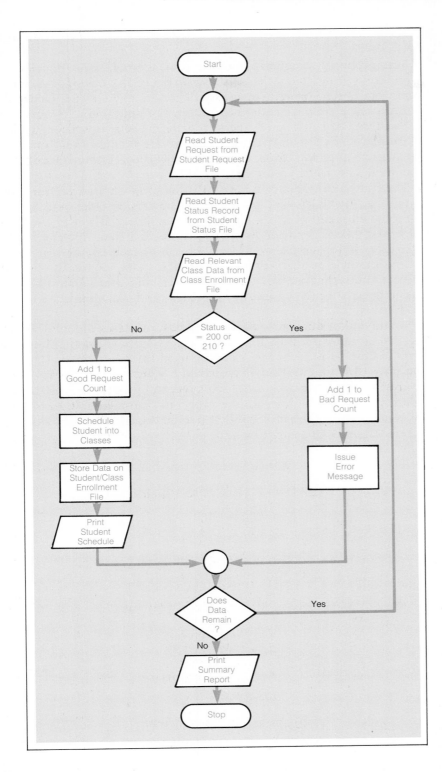

FIGURE 3–20
Flowchart for part of the class
enrollment program

This flowchart portrays the same logic shown in the pseudocode in figure 3–18.

You probably recognize most of the symbols from figure 2–15. However, two new symbols are shown in figure 3–20. The parallelogram represents a **read or write operation**. The data to be read or written and the file name are put inside the symbol. The diamond ◇ represents a **decision**. The condition that controls the decision is written inside the diamond, and the two paths coming out are labeled "yes" or "no" to answer the question. Thus, if the student status is either 200 or 210, the schedule will not be produced.

The computer industry is currently debating whether pseudocode or program flowcharts are better. Flowcharts are older and have an established position in the industry. Pseudocode is newer, but many experts think it is easier to produce and read than flowcharts. They also say that pseudocode is easier to keep current because it can be maintained on word processing systems (see module B of part 4). Others think that neither should be used and that some other technique is best. Both are used in industry, and you should be familiar with them.

We have described pseudocode and flowcharts as though their only use is to develop program logic, but in fact they have another important application. Both techniques can be used to document the logic of a program. Documentation is important when programs need to be changed, or when errors are discovered and programs must be fixed. Often the person who wrote the program is unavailable to make the change or fix the error. Even if that person is available, good documentation will make it easier to modify the program.

QUESTIONS

3.13 Explain the input/process/output cycle.

3.14 What does a structure chart illustrate?

3.15 Do all structure charts have the same number of modules?

3.16 Why are pseudocode and flowcharts necessary? Do professional programmers ever use them?

3.17 Explain the meaning of the pseudocode to the right of this question.

3.18 Convert the pseudocode in question 3.17 to a flowchart.

3.19 Explain the meaning of the flowchart on page 85.

3.20 Convert the flowchart in question 3.19 to pseudocode.

```
BEGIN AVERAGE-PARAGRAPH
    SET SUM TO 0
    SET COUNT TO 0
    DOUNTIL NO GRADES REMAIN
        READ NEXT SCORE
        ADD SCORE TO SUM
        ADD 1 TO COUNT
    END-DO
    SET AVG TO SUM DIVIDED BY COUNT
    PRINT AVG
END AVERAGE-PARAGRAPH
```

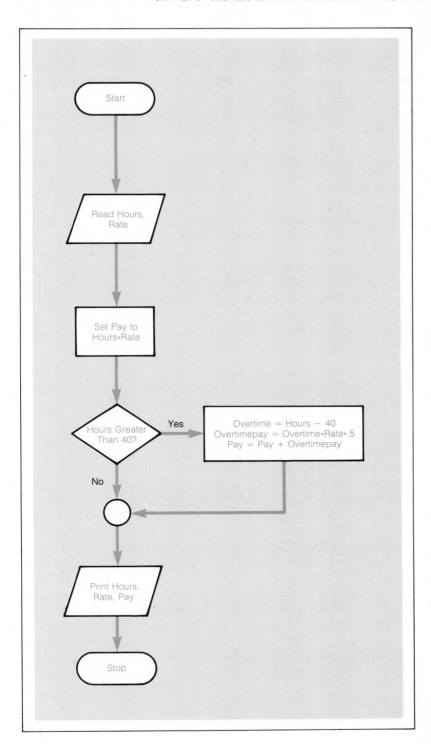

Flowchart for questions
3.19 and 3.20

▦ PROCEDURES

Superficially, it might appear that hardware, programs, and data are the major components of a computer system. In fact, many systems have been designed on the basis of this misconception. Unfortunately, as many businesses have painfully (and expensively) learned, two additional components are required. In this section we will discuss one of them, **system procedures**.

George Shelton tried to enroll in classes at a college that used a class enrollment system similar to the one discussed in the previous chapter. When George examined his class schedule, he found that the college thought he owed money. George went to the scheduling office to protest, but the people there sent him to the finance office. The finance office agreed with George; he owed no money. They didn't know what to do, however, so they sent him to the computer center. The computer center sent him back to the scheduling office. In desperation, George went to his adviser, who was sympathetic but didn't know what to do either. George went back to his room at the dorm, put his head in his hands, and wondered if college was for him after all.

The Need for Procedures

Why is George Shelton having this problem? Obviously an error has been made, but why can't it be corrected? Is the hardware incapable of correcting it? No. Can programs be written to correct it? Certainly.

George has a problem because of a lack of procedures. No one knows what to do.

In the early days of data processing, procedures were an afterthought, something users and the data processing staff worked out during systems implementation. Today, that is changed. Competent data processing personnel design procedures as part of the system. Procedures may be narratives, outlines, pseudocode, or flowcharts. (Yes, flowcharts are useful for more than just program algorithms.) Procedures often include lists, tables, and graphs. In fact, almost any format that clearly tells the reader how to do something is an appropriate procedure.

Procedures are needed by systems users, operators, and developers (see figure 3–21). Users need to know how to enter data and how to interpret results. They must understand any special responsibilities they have. For example, in the class enrollment system, the users (the scheduling clerks) are responsible for correcting or returning incorrect class requests. Procedures need to be written to tell them how to do this. Additionally, users need to know how to correct any errors that occur.

Procedures for operators explain how to run the system. Operators need to know who is authorized to make entries, what entries to expect,

USED BY	PROCEDURE
Users	How to prepare inputs
	How to interpret outputs
	User duties and responsibilities
	How to correct errors
Operators	Who is authorized to provide inputs
	What format inputs should have
	When to run jobs
	What to do with outputs
	How to run jobs — tapes to use,
	forms to mount, etc.
Developers	How to determine requirements
	Standards for systems design
	How to write and test programs
	How to implement new systems

FIGURE 3–21

Examples of procedures for users, operators, and developers

how often to run jobs, where output goes, and so forth. Operators also need to know the mechanics of running jobs, such as which tapes are to be read, what sort of paper is to be put into the computer printer, and how many tapes are to be written.

The first two types of procedures describe how to use the system and how to operate it. Users need one set of procedures while operators need another. In some cases, such as single-user personal computer systems, the distinction between user and operator is blurred; one person plays both roles. However, the need remains for both user procedures and operating procedures.

Finally, systems developers need procedures that specify a standard way of building business computer systems. These procedures explain how to determine requirements, how to develop systems designs, how to write and test programs, and how to implement new systems. We will study these activities in greater detail in part 2. The lack of systems development procedures was a major factor in the difficulties that TYCON Construction Products encountered.

Procedures are ineffective if they are lost or forgotten, and consequently they must be documented. **Documentation** is written procedures that should be evaluated by concerned personnel and approved by management. Documentation is extremely important, not only as a way to preserve procedures, but also as a way of ensuring that procedures are complete and comprehensible. Most computer systems have three volumes of documentation for each system: one for users, one for developers, and one for operators.

Procedure documentation serves several important functions. First, personnel training can be more efficient and effective if new people read documentation before, during, and after training sessions. Second, written documentation helps to standardize processing and thus improve the quality of service. Without documentation, someone like George may happen to find a knowledgeable clerk and receive good service. Another person may find a substitute clerk and receive poor service, which can lead to ill will among the system's clientele. Finally, documentation serves as a system memory. If the system is seldom used, people will forget the procedures. Documentation can also be used to recover from personnel loss if critical personnel quit or become otherwise unavailable.

THE CLASS ENROLLMENT SYSTEM: USER PROCEDURES

Figure 3–22 presents the table of contents for the user's volume of procedure documentation for the class enrollment system. The first section summarizes the system. The next three sections are concerned with input, processing, and output. The input section describes required input data and presents data formats and input procedures. Note the portion on how to verify data completeness and format.

The processing procedures for this system are minimal because the system is run entirely by computer operators. With some systems, however, the users have more responsibility, and the procedures would be documented in this section. Section IV, *"Output Procedures,"* summarizes the output generated by the system. It also defines the meaning of each output data item. Definitions are essential when output data items have several possible interpretations.

Section V, *"Error Correction Procedures,"* is crucial. This section explains what users should do when errors are discovered in computer input or on reports. This documentation either was unused or did not exist at the college where George Shelton attempted to enroll. Finally, there is a section listing names and phone numbers of critical personnel to be called in emergencies. This list can be invaluable when a problem occurs at a critical time (such as during class registration).

TRAINED PERSONNEL

The last of the five components of a business computer system is *trained personnel*. As mentioned previously, there are four types of people involved: systems development personnel (systems analysts, programmers, and programmer/analysts), operations personnel, system users, and system clientele.

Systems analysts are people who know both business and computing. When a system is being developed, systems analysts interview future users and determine what the requirements for the new system will be. They also design the computer systems to satisfy these requirements.

In the case of the class enrollment system, the systems analysts interviewed department heads, faculty members, scheduling person-

FIGURE 3–22
Example of user's procedure
documentation.

```
              CLASS–ENROLLMENT SYSTEM
           User's Procedure Documentation

                 Table of Contents


   I. System Overview
      A. System Functions
      B. System Flowchart
      C. Summary of User's Procedures

  II. Input Procedures
      A. Summary of Input Data Needed
      B. Student Class Request Data
      C. Student Status Data
      D. Class Enrollment Data
      E. Data Verification Procedures

 III. Processing Procedures
      A. Summary of Operation
      B. User Responsibilities

  IV. Output Procedures
      A. Summary of Output
      B. Student Schedules
      C. Summary Report
      D. Student/Class Enrollment File

   V. Error Correction Procedures
      A. Bad Input Data
      B. Incorrect Results
      C. Explanation of Error Messages

  VI. Critical Personnel
      (List of people and phone numbers for use in
      emergencies)
```

nel, college administrators, students, and computer center operators.
From these interviews, they determined the requirements, or the needs
to be satisfied, by the class enrollment system. Next, the systems
analysts developed a design by creating specifications for each of the
five components. The program component was then given to a programmer to build and test. Finally, the systems analysts developed a plan to
implement the system, and then they supervised this process.

Good systems analysts possess a rare combination of skills. They must be good at communicating with people; they must understand at least one business specialty; and they must know computing technology. Currently, systems analysts are in very short supply. If you would like to develop the needed skills, systems analysis would be an excellent career choice.

Programmers are computer specialists who write programs. These people need not be as good as systems analysts in dealing with people, nor do they need to know business as well. However, they must know more about computer technology. Specifically, they must know one programming language very well; most programmers know two or three languages. Programmers also understand the technical details of computing better than systems analysts do. Sometimes systems analysis and programming are combined into one job, called *programmer/analyst*. This job requires *all* of the skills just mentioned. A good programmer/analyst is a rare and valuable commodity.

Once a system is designed, developed, and implemented, development personnel should no longer be involved in it. Responsibility for using systems should lie only with users and operations personnel. Most systems that last more than a few months, however, must at some point be changed. When this time comes, the systems development personnel are called in to design and implement necessary changes in the system. Such modification is called *system maintenance*. These changes are not just changes in programs; they can be changes in hardware, data, procedures, or personnel as well.

To do their job properly, systems development personnel need to know the latest in computer technology. Training is thus a recurring need (see figure 3–23). One month out of every year is not an unusual amount of training time.

Operations personnel run the computer. They need to know how to start the computer, how to stop it, and how to run programs. They also need to know how to operate equipment like tape drives, card readers, and printers. When the computer fails, the operations personnel need to know what to do to minimize the damage, and they need to know how to restart the computer.

In a well-run data processing center, the majority of the processing is done according to a schedule. In addition, everything the operators need to know about running a system is documented. Therefore, neither systems development personnel nor users need be in the computer room. To enforce this measure, access to the computer room is often controlled by locks; only operations personnel are allowed in.

Operations personnel need to know how to run computer systems. They do not need in-depth knowledge of computing technology, nor even of how the computer works. Consequently, operations personnel usually have less technical knowledge than systems development personnel. A typical operator has three to six months of formal training followed by about the same amount of on-the-job training.

PERSONNEL	TRAINING REQUIREMENTS
Systems developers	Communication skills
	Business fundamentals and principles
	Programming languages
	Computer hardware
	Computer technology
	Project management
Operations personnel	How to operate computers
	How to handle failures
	How to run business computer systems
	Requirements for preventive maintenance
	Operations staff supervision
Users	How to prepare inputs
	How to interpret outputs
	Duties and responsibilities
	Forthcoming changes to systems

FIGURE 3–23
Examples of training needs of systems personnel

The third category of personnel are *system users*. These people generally have no formal training in computing (that's why you'll have an advantage). They do, however, have expertise in their business specialty. Users are often trained by the systems development personnel, although a large and growing business involved in computer-user training has been created in the last few years, particularly in the area of personal computer applications. **Initial training** introduces users to the system and its basic capabilities and teaches them how to accomplish their jobs. **Recurring training** is given periodically to remind users of how they should (or can) be using the system and to inform them of any new features that have been developed. If safety or public health is involved, users can also be given proficiency examinations during the recurring training sessions.

The last group of personnel is the *system clientele*. These are the people for whom the system is designed. You are a member of the clientele of a class enrollment system, of a grade-posting system, and of many other systems as well.

The clientele of a system are usually not available or even willing to be formally trained. Thus, systems are designed so that the knowledge needed by the clientele is negligible. The input and output forms for the class enrollment system, for example, are simple and self-explanatory. The same is true for billing, grade-posting, and other systems.

When the system is complex, the clientele are often guided by the system users. A good example occurs when you make an airline reservation. The reservation clerk obtains needed data by asking a sequence of questions and then enters this data. These questions, by the way, are often **prompted**, or requested, by the computer.

The first three lines of figure 3–24 show an example of prompting. The computer typed ORIGIN: and the clerk filled in *New York*. Next, the computer typed DESTINATION: and the clerk filled in *Los Angeles*. The

FIGURE 3-24
Example of computer prompting

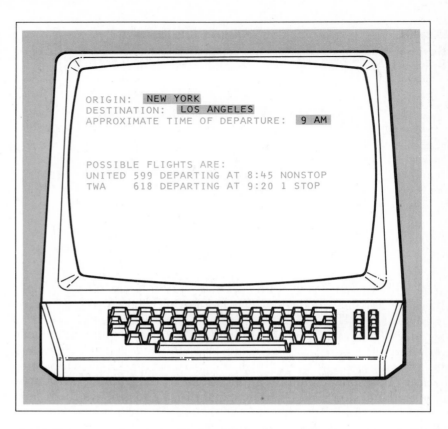

```
ORIGIN:  NEW YORK
DESTINATION:  LOS ANGELES
APPROXIMATE TIME OF DEPARTURE:  9 AM



POSSIBLE FLIGHTS ARE:
UNITED 599 DEPARTING AT 8:45 NONSTOP
TWA    618 DEPARTING AT 9:20 1 STOP
```

QUESTIONS

3.21 What are the three categories of system procedures? Explain the need satisfied by each type.

3.22 What does the term *documentation* mean? Why is documentation important?

3.23 What is likely to happen when no procedures are defined?

3.24 Describe the job requirements of a systems analyst.

3.25 Describe what a programmer does.

3.26 Compare and contrast systems analysts' jobs with programmers' jobs.

3.27 Explain what training is required for each of the following:
a. Systems analysts
b. Programmers
c. Operators
d. System users
e. System clientele

third line was done similarly. Then the computer responded with possible flights.

The need for trained personnel is so obvious that it is often overlooked. When users are not given formal training, system implementation is delayed until operators and users learn by experience, a slow and costly process. Furthermore, when personnel are not properly trained, they often use the system ineffectively or inefficiently. They may take one or two hours to accomplish a task that would take a few minutes if done properly. Untrained users are not able to service the clientele, either. This situation occurred in George Shelton's case.

Trained personnel are an important part of a business computer system. Users have a right to be trained by the development personnel. As a future business person, you should insist on proper training. You should plan time and expense for training purposes.

SUMMARY

If you have learned the material in this chapter, you understand more about data processing than most business people. If you know that a computer system consists of hardware, programs, data, procedures,

PROFILE

"EDGAR WILL REVOLUTIONIZE BOTH THE DISSEMINATION AND CREATION OF CORPORATE INFORMATION"

"Edgar" is the Electronic Data, Gathering, Analysis and Retrieval System at the Securities and Exchange Commission. Edgar's one-year trial has been so successful that it's slated to be expanded to accommodate electronic filings by the SEC's total population of 10,000 corporations by 1989.

With Edgar, access to information affecting securities markets will be almost instantaneous. Within an hour of receiving a public offering, for instance, Edgar will beam it to the SEC and state security administra-

tions. Simultaneously, the feed will be transmitted over one or two of the nation's telecommunications networks such as GTE Telenet.

That will enable anyone within reach of a personal computer and a modem, whether at home or in the office, to tap SEC regulatory news as soon as it breaks, much as they now can with on-line data services like Compuserve or The Source, says Kenneth Fogash, executive deputy director at the SEC.

One could, for example, compare

performance ratios among semiconductor companies. Sound easy? Not so, because many companies use different nomenclature and accounting methods to prepare balance sheets.

Edgar takes on this challenge by exploiting expert system technology — a branch of artificial intelligence that puts the knowledge of experts in computer software for use by nonexperts. Two elements make expert systems work: a knowledge base and an experience program that consults the knowledge base.

and trained personnel, then you will never be duped into thinking that if you buy a computer your problems will be over.

Hardware can be classified into the categories of input, output, storage, and processing.

Programs are instructions that a computer follows. Many program designers use top-down analysis, structure charts, pseudocode, and flowcharts to help them design programs.

Procedures are needed by users, operators, and developers of business computer systems. The nature of the documentation varies depending on the audience, but in every case procedures are step-by-step instructions for people to follow, just as programs are step-by-step instructions for a computer to follow.

Trained personnel are a key to a system's effectiveness. They include system developers, operators, users, and clientele. Each group looks at the system from a different perspective than the others.

Which of these components is the most important? We might as well ask which is the most important link in a chain. Without hardware, there is no computer system. Without programs, the computer won't solve a specific problem, for it is a general-purpose machine. Without correct data, the system can't accurately or meaningfully solve the problem. Finally, without procedures or trained personnel, the system can't be used. Each of these five components is required. Without any one, there is no *system*. There are only four expensive components waiting to be integrated.

WORD LIST

Many terms are introduced in this chapter. Terms that you should be sure you understand are listed here in the order in which they appear in the text.

Terminal keyboard
Cathode-ray tube (CRT)
Video display terminal (VDT)
Key-to-disk
Key-to-tape
Punched cards
Magnetic tape
Magnetic disk
Track
Floppy diskette
Conventional or hard disk
Serial printer
Line printer
Impact printer
Nonimpact printer
Full-character printer
Dot-matrix printer

Control unit
Arithmetic and logic unit (ALU)
Main memory
Microcomputer
Minicomputer
Original Equipment
   Manufacturer (OEM)
Mainframe computer
Input/process/output cycle
Top-down analysis
Structure chart
Module
Algorithm
Pseudocode
Paragraphs in pseudocode
Loop
IF statement in pseudocode

Program, or detailed, flowchart
Read or write operation
   flowchart symbol
Decision flowchart symbol
System procedures
Documentation
Systems analyst
Programmer
Programmer/analyst
Operations personnel
System user
System clientele
Initial training
Recurring training
Computer prompting

QUESTIONS TO CHALLENGE YOUR THINKING

A. Suppose a computer salesperson tells you the total cost of a computer system is $65,000 for the computer plus $410 per month for maintenance. How do you respond? What other costs might there be?

B. Computer hardware is available in a tremendous variety of speeds and capacities. In general, how can a business decide which computer to acquire?

C. Develop a system flowchart for an hourly payroll computer system. Assume that hours worked are recorded on time sheets and that there is an employee master file that contains pay rates, year-to-date totals, and so on.

D. Suppose you manage the clerks in a payroll office.

  1. Develop an outline of documentation for hourly payroll computer system procedures.

  2. Describe how the payroll clerks should be trained.

E. Describe what you believe is the appropriate amount of education for systems analysts, programmers, and operators.

F. What do you think will happen if a system is designed with

  1. The wrong hardware?

  2. Program errors?

  3. Improperly designed data?

  4. No procedures?

  5. Poor personnel training?

SURVEY OF BUSINESS COMPUTER SYSTEMS APPLICATIONS

CHAPTER 4

This chapter surveys the application of computing systems in business. As you read, you should gain a general sense of how businesses use computers and begin to relate computing to the areas of business you find interesting. You will also see that computing is important in every business field.

NEED FOR BUSINESS COMPUTER SYSTEMS

To appreciate the need for business information, imagine yourself as the president of a thriving business. You sit in the corner office, and as a manager you *plan*, *organize*, and *control* your business's activities. To do this, you need *information*. You need information about the company's performance, about competitors' performances, about new products, about costs, about inventories, about economic changes, about social changes, and on and on.

Why do you need this information? Your job is to make decisions and to get work underway on projects that you approve. To make good decisions and to plan successful projects, you need reliable and accurate information.

As president, when you need information, you ask for it. You access one or more of your company's *information systems*. Every company has information systems, whether they know it or not. The secretary outside your door who has last year's profit-and-loss statement is part of an information system, as are the contents of your file drawers, the annual report, and hundreds of other information sources.

An information system does not necessarily include a computer. An information system can be composed entirely of data, procedures, and personnel. Computer hardware and programs need not be involved. Information systems have existed for centuries — long before the computer was invented.

The focus of this book, however, is on business *computer* systems, a subset of business information systems. As you proceed through this book, you will study many different kinds of business computer systems and much computer technology. Do not lose sight of the forest for the trees. Remember that you are studying an information system, and the ultimate goal of the technology discussed is to provide better information to employees.

The proportion of computer-based information systems to manual information systems varies from company to company. Some companies do not have computers at all. Some companies have a few personal computers. Some companies buy computer service from other companies. Some companies have small computers that have just one purpose, such as inventory accounting or billing. At the other extreme, some companies have joined their business computer systems with their typing, copying, and communications systems, so that their entire

APPLICATION

"TEN WAYS TO GET AHEAD WITH INFORMATION TECHNOLOGY."

TELEMARKETING

Testing cold leads by telephone first — using computer runs to ferret out the best prospects — helps slash sales-force expenses and boost productivity.

CUSTOMER SERVICE

By letting customers tap into your database to track their orders and shipments, you build loyalty and smooth relations.

TRAINING

Training or retraining workers lets them learn at their own speed — and lets you cut training costs.

SALES

Giving salespeople portable computers so they can get messages faster and enter orders directly adds up to quicker deliveries, better cash flow, and less paperwork.

BETTER FINANCIAL MANAGEMENT

By setting up computer links between the treasurer's office and your banks you can obtain financial information faster.

PRODUCT DEVELOPMENT

By providing a toll-free number for consumer questions and complaints, you get ideas for product improvements and new products. In-house electronic publishing can help turn out product manuals faster.

LOCKING IN CUSTOMER

By creating exclusive computer communications with customers for order entry and exchange of product and service data, you can help thwart competitors.

MARKET INTELLIGENCE

By assembling and manipulating data on demographics and competitors, you can spot untapped niches, develop new products, and avoid inventory crunches.

NEW BUSINESS

Information technologies can now make whole new operations possible. Federal Express, for one, could not work without computer-equipped trucks and facilities.

SELLING EXTRA PROCESSING POWER

You can use off-peak processing power to develop completely new services for outsiders. That way, you can transfer some of the high costs of building your information network.

collection of information systems is computer based. There are millions (yes, millions) of companies in between these extremes (see figure 4–1).

FUNDAMENTAL TYPES OF BUSINESS COMPUTER SYSTEM SERVICES

Businesses use computers in a variety of ways, in part because the needs of employees differ. You, the president, have different needs than I, the warehouse manager. You manage the company, and I manage inventory. You don't care how many model 07Q56T portable stereo players there are in stock, and I don't care about the profitability of the

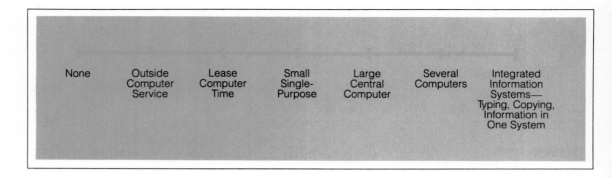

FIGURE 4–1
Range of computer use in business
information systems

Saskatoon store. (Unless of course the profitability of the Saskatoon store depends on my getting 600 model 07Q56T stereos there by tomorrow.) Our requirements for a business computer system are therefore different. I need the computer to keep track of events that affect inventory: How many items were received, how many were shipped to customers, how many are on backorder, and so forth. You need the computer to tell you more general information about the status of the business: Is the Saskatoon store doing better or worse than projected? What impact would closing the Saskatoon store have on the company's finances? Would increasing advertising increase business? What financial impact would laying off some workers have?

In general, *the higher the level of employee, the more likely the employee is to need information in summary form.* At each level of management, summaries, averages, and so forth are passed up to the next level. At the top, the information consists of summaries of summaries. We will discuss the information needs of management later in this chapter and in detail in chapter 11.

User needs can be categorized. Some users need the computer to be a record keeper. Some users need the computer to help them assess the company's actual performance as compared to its expected performance. Still other users need the computer to work out mathematical models of the business so they can change variables and observe the impact on the computer model. Three categories of computer system services have been developed to address those needs. They are called *transaction processing systems*, *management information systems*, and *decision-support systems*.

Why is this knowledge important to you? Because one day you will be a user of business computer systems. You should know what types of computer services are likely to serve you. You should know what to legitimately expect from a computer system. And you should know that some systems cost more and take longer to develop than others. You should also know what types of systems must be very carefully controlled, and which types are not vulnerable to criminal activity. In short, the more you know about business computer systems, the better prepared you will be to take your place in business.

Transaction Processing Systems

A **transaction processing system (TPS)** is a business computer system that processes data about the *operation* of a business or other enterprise. A *transaction* is the record of an event to which the company's system must respond; for example, data about an order that has just been shipped is a transaction. The company uses the transaction to update its business records and to produce appropriate documents. A shipment transaction usually increases a customer's balance due and decreases inventory. If the quantity in stock of that particular inventory item has fallen below the established reorder point, then the same transaction might also cause a purchase order to be issued and a corresponding entry to be made in the accounts payable records. A system that uses transactions to update company records is called a *transaction processing system*. Examples of transaction processing systems are order entry systems, airline reservation systems, and payroll systems.

To understand transaction processing, consider the rationale for business records. Why are such records necessary? Companies keep business records because

- They are required to by law.
- Records allow management to see the status of the business at a glance.
- Management uses the company's history (as recorded in the company's data) to make decisions and plans for the future.

If there were no records, how, for example, would a business respond when the IRS tax examiner came to evaluate the value of inventory? Without business records, the business would have to take the tax examiner out into the warehouse and say, "Here it is. Value it yourself."

The tax examiner would likely be dissatisfied with this answer. He or she wants the company to determine the dollar value of inventory. Furthermore, the examiner most likely does not want the value of the inventory today. The examiner wants to know the value two years ago, when the tax statement was filed.

Consider this situation and think again about the purpose of business records. Fundamentally, such records are needed to represent aspects of a business at some point in time. In a sense, the records that a company keeps about itself comprise a *model* of the company. Just as a photograph of a person represents the person, corporate data represents an actual company. The data is an extraction from reality.

Viewed in this light, transaction processing systems perform the function of keeping the **corporate data model** current and maintaining historical records of the business. When an event occurs to or in the

FIGURE 4-2
Transaction processing system

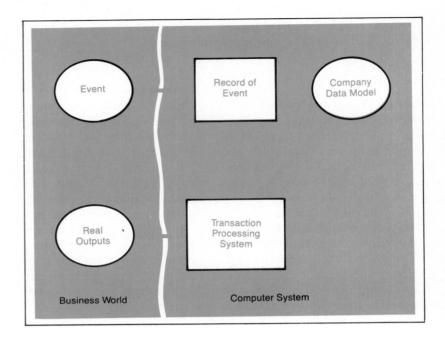

company, the stored data model does not *automatically* change itself. A transaction processing system receives a record of the event and makes appropriate changes in the data model.

A transaction processing system may also produce **real outputs**. Real outputs are documents issued to system clientele. Sometimes they are statements, such as purchase orders or invoices, and sometimes they are negotiable instruments, such as checks. The term *real* is used to emphasize the fact that the output is sent to the business world and is not simply a change to the data model. Figure 4-2 depicts a typical transaction processing system.

A transaction processing system may have hundreds of users, such as the clerks that use an airline reservation system and the tellers that use a bank system. A transaction processing system usually accepts a high volume of input and produces much output. Performance and reliability are critical. If a transaction processing system is slow or fails, the impact on the organization using it can be severe. Accuracy, precision, and reliability are critical in a transaction processing system. The key characteristics of a transaction processing system are the following:

• Concerned with day-to-day operations.
• Keeps data model current.
• Uses input transactions to change company's data model.
• Produces real output.
• Reliable and accurate.
• Keeps historical company data.
• Performs predictable, repetitive functions.

The other two types of computer services — management information systems and decision-support systems — provide help to users who must *plan* and *control* a company. Transaction processing systems serve users who are concerned with the *operation* of an organization. A transaction processing application would be concerned with keeping a record of the number of widgets in inventory at any given time. An MIS application would be concerned with whether or not the widget inventory is over or under the planned level. A DSS application would be concerned with the possible financial impact of changing the number of widgets carried in inventory.

Management Information Systems

A **management information system (MIS)** is a business system that provides past, present, and projected information about a company and its environment. An MIS does not necessarily require a computer, but today most do employ computers ranging from large mainframes to desktop microcomputers (see "Accessing MIS/DSS" later in this chapter). As is implied by the name, a management information system serves the needs of management.

Management's primary role in a company is planning. To plan properly, a manager must set realistic goals and state them in numbers so progress toward them can be measured. Here are some examples of quantified goals:

- Clerical staff will be reduced by 15 percent by the end of the year.
- Manufacturing will produce 200,000 of these items at a unit cost not to exceed $6.85.
- Sales personnel travel expenses will not exceed $50,000 in any quarter.

When programmed to, computers can compare budgeted and actual figures, looking for discrepancies and alerting management to potential problems. A management information system has access to data about plans and actual performance, and so it can provide managers with the information they need to make their business run more efficiently.

Because most MISs take their input from transaction processing systems, they are often not developed until the other systems are already in place. An MIS usually produces a variety of reports for management to study. Remember that the purpose of an MIS is to provide information for the benefit of human decision makers, not necessarily to act on it. For an illustration of this distinction, consider an MIS that tracks labor costs and discovers that actual costs exceed projected costs by 20 percent. The MIS notes this on a report — the MIS does *not* issue termination notices to 20 percent of the company's employees. If that decision is made, it is made by human managers, not by a computer system. (It could be programmed that way, but few companies would assign a computer system that kind of power — there

APPLICATION

"INFORMATION IS A VALUABLE ASSET THAT NEEDS TO BE MANAGED."

As computer-service divisions have moved from the back offices to a central role in the planning and managing of companies, employees with computer skills and an understanding of internal data management have become a valuable commodity.

The field of management information systems, popularly known as MIS, is today one of the fastest-growing fields of all. The Federal Bureau of Labor Statistics reports that the number of systems analysts, a mid-level MIS position, increased from 205,000 in 1980 to 359,000 in 1985 and is expected to grow to 520,000 in the next decade. Additionally, many businesses have made MIS directors into vice-presidents, which in many cases has tripled the number of employees reporting to them. "There is a big demand for individuals trained in MIS," said Jack Ahlin, director of management department information systems and administration for the International Business Machines Corporation (IBM).

MIS professionals are concerned with developing systems that will translate raw data into information that managers need to operate. "MIS professionals understand the link between information systems and strategy," said Patrick Marfisi, an electronics industry consultant at the Los Angeles office of McKinsey & Company.

MIS directors, sometimes called MIS executives, oversee all information systems and data-processing efforts, and as senior management they are responsible for determining how information systems can build a more profitable and efficient company. In many cases the MIS director reports directly to the chief executive officer of the company and is responsible for large budgets.

are often many more factors to consider in employee relations than just the numbers.)

MISs provide information to management so it can make decisions that will make the company run more efficiently. Here are some examples of reports and what management might do after studying them:

• Inventory status	Reduce inventory
• Manufacturing rejects	Improve quality control
• Sales performance	Redistribute sales regions
• Backorder summary	Increase inventory
• Summary of returned catalogs	Clean up mailing list

Some reports are produced on a regular, recurring schedule. For example, the inventory status report and sales performance report mentioned above might be issued every week. On the other hand, some MIS reports are produced on an exception basis. They are generated when an unusual situation occurs and management needs to be alerted. For example, the manufacturing rejects report mentioned in the list above might be issued only when the number of rejects exceeds some threshold figure. This is called an **exception report**. Although we do not know when an exception report will be issued, the events that cause it to be issued and the report itself are preplanned. This is an important characteristic distinguishing a management information system from a decision-support system, which we will examine in the next section.

Management information systems do not have the same needs for performance and reliability that transaction processing systems do. As long as a manager receives a report when it is expected, he or she does not care whether it took 30 seconds or 30 minutes to produce. Similarly, as long as the report arrives on time and is accurate, the manager does not care that the computer failed three times while preparing it. (This is true with one exception: The manager cares how much the report costs. Poor performance and reliability are inefficient and expensive.)

Management decisions that affect the entire company are often based almost exclusively on reports from an MIS. Therefore, the information must truly reflect the status of the company. However, remember that managers require more summarized data than do lower level workers. Therefore, the figures reported on an MIS report are often "round numbers" because managers need the big picture. The degree of precision of an MIS report only must be sufficient to prevent bad decisions from being made. By contrast, a transaction processing system must account for every penny in the company's coffers and every widget in stock.

Management information systems do not usually produce real outputs — their reports are used internally, and they have little direct effect on anyone outside the company. MISs deal with a much lower volume of input and output than transaction processing systems do. And whereas transaction processing systems are highly vulnerable to criminal activity, MISs are far less vulnerable. Consequently, the controls for an MIS are much less stringent than those for a transaction processing system. The key characteristics of an MIS are the following:

- Concerned with management and control of the organization.
- Gets input from data stored by TPS.
- Compares actual performance to plan.
- Produces regular, predictable reports.
- Output is used internally.
- Data is of an aggregate or summary nature — not necessarily precise.

Decision-Support Systems

Decision-support systems (DSS) are business computer systems that facilitate decision making by providing tools for **ad hoc data manipulation and reporting**. Decision-support systems may run on mainframes or on personal computers. Accessing a DSS is addressed in the final section of this chapter.

In this book, we will consider DSSs a specialized subset of management information systems (see chapter 11). Non-DSS MIS applications produce regular and recurring reports and other outputs, whereas DSS outputs are *irregularly produced and may or may not recur*. DSS applications are often used to solve one-of-a-kind problems or to assist special-purpose focus groups.

A DSS provides programs to retrieve, process, and report data in many different ways. Suppose, for example, that a large manufacturer is considering merging the sales forces of two regions. If this is to be done, management must develop new sales territories that provide for a fair allocation of customers to salespeople.

To develop this allocation, management will need reports about sales over a several-year period, broken down by salesperson and customer. Then management will want to try various alternatives and see how past sales would have been distributed for each of these alternatives. To evaluate these various plans, management will require that information be retrieved and processed in many different ways. Flexibility will be essential. Also, management will want to make this evaluation rapidly, perhaps within a week or so. When the evaluation is finished, there will be no recurring need for the reports generated.

Thus, the keystones of a DSS are *flexibility* and *speed*. Until recently, these attributes have been very difficult for computer systems to provide. Historically, systems development has been inflexible and slow. However, the new technology of relational database management (discussed in chapter 9) and high-level, nonprocedural languages (discussed in chapter 11) have made flexible, quick decision-support systems possible.

DSS applications do not consist of a single all-purpose program. Rather, DSS applications are supported by a number of different programs, which often include spreadsheet (see module B), database (see chapter 9), graphics, and other software. The key characteristics of a DSS are the following:

- Concerned with planning the future of the organization.
- Allows ad hoc queries.
- Reports not predictable, not recurring.
- Answers "what if" questions.
- Flexible.
- Provides fast performance.
- Low-volume output.
- Most input data imported from TPS.

SYSTEM SERVICES IN FUNCTIONAL BUSINESS AREAS

How are the three types of computer services applied to various business functions? In this section we will explore the use of business

QUESTIONS

4.1 What is an information system? Which companies have information systems? Does an information system require a computer?

4.2 Characterize the difference between the information needs of a company president and those of a warehouse manager.

4.3 List the three types of business computer system services defined in this section.

4.4 Explain the statement that data is a model of a company.

4.5 What is a transaction processing system? Describe two important characteristics of a transaction processing system.

4.6 What is a management information system? Describe two important characteristics of an MIS.

4.7 What is a decision-support system? Describe two important characteristics of a DSS.

4.8 How does an MIS differ from a DSS?

APPLICATION

"EXPENSIVE EXECUTIVE TOYS OR PRODUCTIVITY TOOLS?"

By the year 2000 the so-called executive workstation — more accurately known as the IVDT (integrated voice/data terminal) — will be on everyone's desk, replacing the telephone, the personal computer, the terminal, the modem, electronic mail software, and convenience devices like the calculator, desk and appointment calendars, the Rolodex, even telephone message and memo pads. Extra-fancy models may allow simultaneous communications in voice, text, graphics, image, and video. They might even take dictation.

A survey by Venture Development Corp. (Natick, MA) asked executives to indicate their interest in various IVDT features on a scale of one to seven. Most applications were given very positive ratings (over 2.5), and only one — the calendar — rated under 3.5. The following is a list of the features in order of interest.

1. internal database access
2. ability to run personal computer programs
3. telephone directory
4. single-key access to functions
5. ability to use phone and send data simultaneously
6. screen dialing

7. speed dialing
8. private database
9. electronic mail
10. external database access
11. voice annotation
12. memo writing
13. telephone call log
14. graphics generation
15. calculator
16. voice mail
17. calendar

---

computer systems in several business areas. Because there are literally hundreds of business applications for computer systems, we will focus on only four of the better known ones. Figure 4–3 shows one possible organization for a manufacturing company. (All manufacturing companies are not organized this way — this is simply an illustration.) Notice that the four major functional areas in the company are accounting, finance, manufacturing, and sales.

Accounting is concerned with recording events that change the financial status of the organization. Finance focuses on obtaining money for the company and evaluating how it is spent. Manufacturing designs new products, purchases raw materials, and fabricates the company's products. Sales gets the company's products into the marketplace.

Within each functional area are many users: some who perform daily operational tasks, and some who manage and plan. Computer systems have to serve all of their needs. Figure 4–4 shows the relationship of computer services to business functions. In this section you will begin to see how computers are used in business and what type of computer services — TPS, MIS, DSS, or combinations of these — serve users within each area.

FIGURE 4–3
Organization chart for a manufacturing company

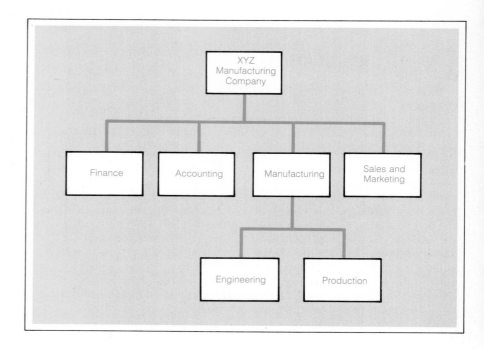

Accounting Applications

Of the primary functional business areas, accounting has been the most successful at using computers, and computer-based **accounting systems** have had great acceptance. Two major reasons account for this success. First, the nature of accounting makes computerization easy to implement. Accounting functions usually involve a high volume of data that must be processed and stored quickly. Accounting functions call for a high degree of accuracy. Processing requirements are not particularly complex (although computers can certainly handle complex calculations). Also, accounting functions are performed on a regular basis. Computers are masters at all of these things, so using computers in the accounting area of a business makes a lot of sense.

Second, there are historical reasons for the widespread use of computers in accounting. Repetitive tasks like posting transactions to accounts are time consuming and labor intensive. How many payroll clerks do you suppose would be needed to prepare the payroll for one of the major airlines? (And payroll is only one of many accounting functions.) Punched cards and punched-card readers were developed around the turn of the century to do simple calculations and were being used widely in business by the 1940s. The same companies that marketed punched-card devices began to develop and market computers for office use. Their first customers were, of course, the companies who were already using punched-card devices to do some simple accounting. Naturally, accounting functions were among the first to be computerized.

Now let us consider business computer systems that support the accounting functions of a business. Recall from chapter 2 the five components of a business computer system. To maintain accurate data, an accounting system needs (1) computer hardware of sufficient capacity, capability, and speed; (2) programs that correctly instruct the computer to modify data and produce reports; (3) accurate data to start with and accurate data about transactions (events of accounting significance); (4) procedures to enable people to operate the system and alter the data; and (5) trained personnel.

Characteristics of Accounting Systems

Several unique properties of accounting pose special requirements for accounting systems' programs and procedures. First, a high degree of control must be imposed on an accounting system. This is because accounting systems are used to maintain data about an organization's financial resources. That makes them targets for criminal activity. Theft can be concealed by altering the accounting records so that legitimate transactions appear to have occurred.

Second, accounting systems usually deal with large volumes of data. The input data must be converted to computer-readable format, which often involves manually keying the data, a very error-prone activity. Although computers can be programmed to detect many errors (see chapter 7), catching every one is almost impossible. Consider what

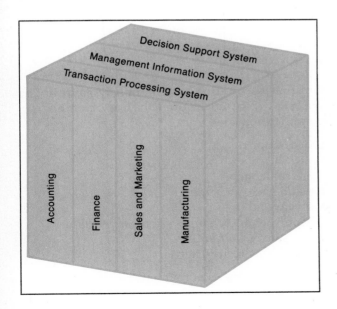

FIGURE 4–4
Relationship between computer system services and business functions

might happen if a vendor were paid $1000 instead of $100, simply because a clerk pushed the zero key too many times.

Do you see the dilemma facing anyone who wishes to develop a computerized accounting system? Errors can be very costly, so they must be avoided. At the same time, much accounting data must be entered using error-prone methods. The consequence of this dilemma is that much of the processing in an accounting system is done to identify and correct errors. Considerable processing is also done to provide **checks and balances** between the users and the data processing department and thereby reduce the likelihood of unauthorized activity.

Finally, accounting systems must produce an **audit trail**. An audit trail allows internal or external auditors to relate the summarized data in the accounting records to actual transactions. During an audit, auditors often want to trace a transaction (for example, a customer order) from its beginnng to its final resting place. If the order is processed by a computer, then auditors might want to examine the computer records. Clearly, it is of utmost importance that an auditor have a solid foundation in business computer systems.

Accounting systems usually include several subsystems. The accounts receivable system determines what money is owed to a company and collects it. The accounts payable system records purchases made on account by a company and pays for them. The payroll system tracks the services provided to the company by employees; pays employees wages; and keeps track of benefits, work hours, wages, and deductions. The inventory accounting system determines the number and cost of items a company has in stock. In every instance, events occur in the business world that must be recorded in the company's accounting records. By the end of this discussion you should see that accounting functions are supported primarily by transaction processing systems.

Payroll Computer Systems

Now, let's examine a familiar accounting system, **hourly payroll**. The requirements of this system are listed below. Observe that this is a transaction processing application.

1. Compute pay, taxes, deductions
2. Print paychecks
3. Produce entries for general ledger
4. Account for sick leave and vacation time
5. Print W-2 tax forms at year end
6. Accommodate new employees and changes to employee data
7. Account for ex-employees until year end
8. Minimize risk of error or unauthorized activity

The first two requirements are self-explanatory. The third requirement refers to the **general ledger**, or company accounts. The system needs to generate entries for accounting. These entries will reduce cash by the amount of the payroll, accrue taxes and FICA payments, and make other necessary bookkeeping adjustments.

Accounting for sick leave and vacation time requires the system to add time each pay period and deduct it as leave or vacation is taken. Reports must also be printed for the personnel department to use when authorizing vacations and sick-leave payments.

The requirement to print W-2 tax forms at the end of the year means that the system must keep track of total pay to date, total taxes to date, total FICA payments, and the total of any other taxable income. This data must be kept even for employees who leave the organization.

The next two requirements refer to changes that will be made to the employee master file. (The *master file* will be defined in chapter 7. For now, think of it as a file of permanent records.) As employees are hired, data for them must be added to the master file. Also, since pay rates are in the master file, changes must be made when employees receive pay increases. When an employee leaves the company, his or her record must be marked so that no new checks will be issued. The record cannot be deleted, however, until the W-2 form is printed at the end of the year. Finally, all of these requirements must be met in a way that minimizes the risk of errors and unauthorized activity.

Figure 4–5 shows a flowchart for the payroll system. It is broken into three **phases** to provide checks and balances between the payroll department and the data processing department. During phase 1, the changes to the master file are keyed (to tape in this case) and then edited by a computer program. **Editing** means the program will check the input to be sure it has the correct format, is plausible, and so forth. Note that no changes are actually made to the master file during phase 1. (The new symbol ▽ represents a **manual operation**.)

The report produced is called an **edit report**. The users must check this report, and if they are satisfied with the changes, processing to change the master file will be executed. At that time, a second report, called the master file **change report**, which shows changes actually made, will be produced.

The edit report, shown in figure 4–6, is reviewed by the payroll department. If it is correct, data processing is instructed to proceed with phase 2. If it is not, corrections are made, and phase 1 is repeated. This sequence allows payroll personnel to ensure that only correct and authorized changes are made.

In figure 4–6, the first two master file changes appear to be correct. However, the edit program detected an error in the third entry. This company has a convention that all employee numbers start with a 1. This number does not, so it is flagged as an error. The new employee data for Joy Johnson must be verified by payroll. The pay change for employee 17281 also appears to contain an error; the pay change probably should be 9.87, not 98.70. The program has not detected an

FIGURE 4–5
System flowchart for hourly payroll
system

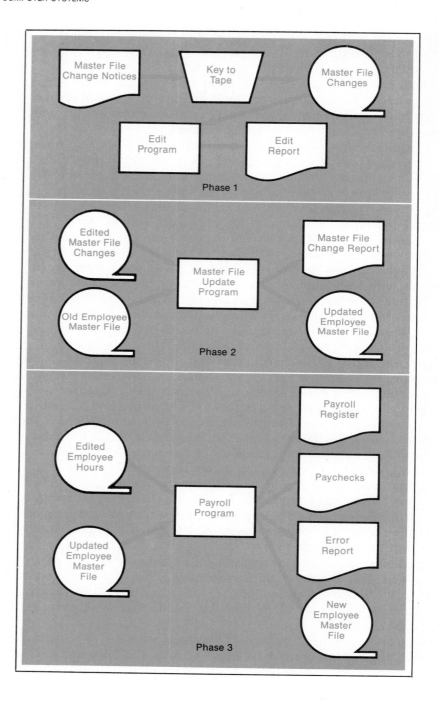

```
EMPLOYEE
NUMBER          EMPLOYEE NAME              TYPE OF CHANGE

12481           FRED PARKS                 PAY CHANGE TO 8.73
14618           SALLY BATTS                PAY CHANGE TO 7.50
*** ERROR IN NEXT CHANGE—INCORRECT EMPLOYEE NUMBER ***
02800           JOY JOHNSON                NEW EMPLOYEE
                ADDRESS                    1418 S. TAMARACK
                                           ALEXANDRIA, VA 01042
                DATE OF BIRTH              DECEMBER 11, 1944
                TITLE                      PRODUCTION ASSISTANT
                PAY RATE                   7.52
                DEPENDENTS                 3
                SOCIAL SECURITY NUMBER     522-00-1841
17281           ELMER NILSON               PAY CHANGE TO 98.70
16415           DOROTHY SUHM               PAY CHANGE TO 21.50
```

error, so the responsibility lies with the payroll department to accept or reject this change.

These discrepancies point out the need for good procedures and trained personnel. Without them, an error may go undetected. Perhaps, too, you can see why *all* business people need some knowledge about computers.

During phase 2, the edited changes are actually applied to the employee master file. When the master file change report is produced, the payroll department can check the edit report against it to ensure accuracy. If the phase 2 change report is correct, payroll authorizes data processing to perform phase 3. Otherwise, corrections are made, and phases 1 and 2 are repeated.

In phase 3, a file of employee hours is entered into the payroll program along with the updated employee master file. The hourly data has gone through an edit similar to that shown in phase 1. For the sake of brevity, it is not shown here. The program computes pay, taxes, and deductions; accounts for time off; and produces a new employee master file containing the new year-to-date totals. It also produces three reports. The *payroll register* contains the entries to be made to the general ledger and a list of every check written. Payroll uses this list to verify the amounts before signing the paychecks. The second report consists of the *paychecks* (see figure 4–7). The last report details any errors that have been detected—for example, a report of hourly work by a nonexistent or terminated employee.

This discussion demonstrates a typical accounting system. Can you see the need for user involvement to provide checks and balances over data processing? Note that the master files keep data about payments

FIGURE 4–6
Payroll master file edit report

FIGURE 4-7
Printed payroll check

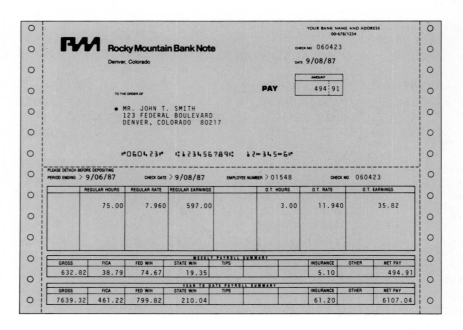

that can be used for audit and tax purposes. The payroll registers are another permanent record.

Other Accounting Computer Systems

The following is a list of common accounting systems. These will be briefly summarized here, and several of them will be discussed further in subsequent chapters.

- Payroll
- Billing
- Accounts receivable
- Accounts payable
- General ledger
- Inventory accounting

Billing systems generate bills or statements to customers. Figure 4-8 shows a typical billing statement. **Accounts receivable systems** keep track of debts owed to the company. Reports generated by this system are used for collection purposes, for checking credit on new orders, and for monitoring potential bad debts. Figure 4-9 shows a sample accounts receivable report.

Accounts payable systems produce checks to pay company bills. Since accounts payable systems generate checks, they usually have the same controls and phased processing as the payroll systems. A common accounts payable problem concerns discounts. Suppliers often offer price reductions if payment is made within a certain time period. The

```
                    CONSOLIDATED INDUSTRIES

                  STATEMENT OF ACCOUNT WITH

TAYLOR CONSTRUCTION PRODUCTS                    DECEMBER 1, 1986

   INVOICE          SHIPMENT DATE      DESCRIPTION          COST

   11046            10/20/86           ALUMINUM SIDING      $1148.12
   11982            11/04/86           FASTENERS               37.15
   12257            11/20/86           ROOFING MATERIALS     3894.84


   TOTAL DUE                                               $5080.11
```

FIGURE 4–8
Billing statement

company may or may not want to take the discount, depending on its available cash, the amounts of the debt and the discount, and other factors. Some accounts payable systems use these factors to determine the best time to pay debts.

General ledger systems maintain company accounts. They perform bookkeeping for the company. Balance sheets and income statements are usually produced, as well as other reports (see figure 4–10).

Inventory accounting systems maintain records of additions to and depletions of stock of finished or unfinished goods. Computer systems often are advantageous for inventory accounting, because some accounting techniques (last in, first out, or LIFO, for example) have sizable tax advantages but are complex. Without a computer, many companies cannot cope with the computational requirements of the more sophisticated techniques.

FIGURE 4–9
Accounts receivable report

```
                    CONSOLIDATED INDUSTRIES

                  AGED ACCOUNTS RECEIVABLE          DECEMBER 1, 1986

                                       BALANCE      BALANCE
                                       OVER 30      OVER 60       TOTAL
  CUSTOMER    CUSTOMER       CURRENT    DAYS LATE    DAYS LATE     BALANCE
  NUMBER      NAME           BALANCE

  37842       TAYLOR CONST.  $5080.11   $  0.00     $   0.00      $5080.11
  39148       ABC SUPPLIES       0.00    438.10        300.14       738.24
  40418       SHAKEWELL INC.   127.13    541.27       1384.17      2052.57
  41183       ZAVASKY INC.    2312.47      0.00          0.00      2312.47
  44817       ABLE ENTERPRISE 1497.12    348.97          0.00      1846.09
```

FIGURE 4–10
Balance statement

```
                        FRONTIER IRONWORKS

                     BALANCE STATEMENT          DECEMBER 31, 1986
                    (THOUSANDS OF DOLLARS)

          ASSETS                              LIABILITIES

CASH                    $  127     ACCOUNTS PAYABLE          $  197
ACCOUNTS RECEIVABLE        583     ACCRUED EXPENSES
INVENTORY                 317        EMPLOYEE BENEFITS          349
PREPAID EXPENSES            53        OTHER                     23
MACHINERY               1,483     PREFERRED STOCK             987
FURNITURE AND FIXTURES    275     COMMON STOCK              2,384
LAND AND BUILDINGS      1,788     RETAINED EARNINGS           686

TOTAL ASSETS           $4,626     TOTAL LIABILITIES        $4,626
```

QUESTIONS

4.9 What is the purpose of an accounting business computer system?

4.10 Why is much of the processing in an accounting system oriented toward error detection and correction?

4.11 Explain the purpose of the edit and change reports. Why are both reports needed?

4.12 Briefly describe three accounting business computer systems other than payroll.

As stated previously, almost all accounting applications are handled by transaction processing systems. There are some MIS/DSS applications having to do with *projections and estimating*, however. These applications are used to develop budgets and establish plans. Further, in construction and other industries that use bid systems, accounting systems are used to estimate project costs. In summary, the key characteristics of an accounting system are the following:

- Operational in nature.
- Records daily operations of organization.
- High volume of data.
- Data needs to be processed quickly.
- Needs high degree of accuracy.
- Processing not complex.
- Data needs to be accessed on regular, recurring basis.
- Supports many users.
- Vulnerable to criminal activity.
- Has impact on system clientele (customers).

Financial Applications

The finance function of an organization involves obtaining money for the company and planning and evaluating the ways in which the money is spent.

Just as accounting systems have certain characteristics that make them candidates for computerization, so do **financial systems**. First, financial calculations tend to be complex. In a finance course you might

APPLICATION

"RETAIL CHAINS MAKE STRATEGIC USE OF COMPUTERS."

Before Saks Fifth Avenue replaced its old-fashioned cash registers, it often took weeks for the venerable department store chain to accurately know what was selling and what to reorder.

Its technologically advanced competitors, on the other hand, were collecting precise sales data instantaneously, reordering best sellers within a day. The message was clear. "If I know during the day what's selling and you know a week later, I've got a big advantage over you," says Al McCready, a consultant with Arthur Young & Co., New York.

Without state-of-the-art systems, Norwalk, Connecticut-based Caldor could only collect daily sales data on 30% of its stores' 80,000 products. "We could track sales by class," explains James Guinon, chairman and chief executive officer of the discount unit of Associated Dry Goods Corp. "But the class will only tell you a cookie jar. It won't tell you it's a cookie jar with a red handle."

The lack of such data can mean shortages of what sells best. Caldor, for instance, stocks about 15 different barbecue grills ranging from Japanese hibachis to multiburner gas models, and "you've got to be very specific about which barbecues you've been selling, because during a sale you'll discover you don't have the one the customer wants," Mr. Guinon says.

The computer systems also help control big inventory costs by accurately forecasting each store's merchandise needs. "Fifteen years ago we were paying 6% interest to carry our inventory. Now we're paying 11% to 12% and think we're getting a break," says Mr. Schwartz of Caldor. "Every item I carry in stock for an extra month costs me twice what it used to."

In addition, such systems help retailers adjust quickly when a product is selling poorly, says Gordon Edelstone, a vice-president of Dylex's Tip Top division. "We can identify an item that looks like a dog and mark it down immediately and sell it even before [competitors] recognize the product isn't selling well."

Computers also help chains compete by reducing labor costs. Caldor, which plans to invest $15 million in computer hardware and software this year, expects savings equal to the salaries of five full-time employees for each store. "We promote 10,000 to 14,000 items in a weekly flier," explains Mr. Guinon. "In the past you had to mark down all these items manually, take off the old sales tickets and put the new ones on. The human effort was massive, and the

errors were massive."

During a sale under the new system, price tags are replaced by a single sign placed on a display designating the discount (for instance "Take 25% off the ticketed price") and the price is filed in the computerized checkout terminal.

Electronic mail is another benefit. Bentonville, Arkansas-based Wal-Mart Stores Inc. can send messages to 700 stores in less than one workday. Dylex's stores "used to take instructions for markdowns seven to ten days later than now," before the company's new point-of-sale terminals were installed recently, Mr. Schwartz says. Caldor expects electronic mail to save $2 million a year. "About 80% to 90% of the mail to keep the company going disappears," Mr. Guinon says.

Retailers say electronic ordering from suppliers is the next step in the technology of merchandising. It would save time and eliminate many retailers' out-of-stock troubles. A few big chains already are doing some electronic ordering.

study calculations for determining the rate of return on an investment, figuring interest rates, and computing present value. When you do you will see why these tasks are more easily done by computers than by people.

Another reason for using computer systems in finance is that the alternatives to be evaluated often involve complex interactions among variables that can be processed better by computers than by humans. For example, suppose a financial analyst estimates earnings of $10,000 on a $100,000 machine. The analyst might want to know what the impact will be on the earning potential of the machine if sales go up, say, by 20 percent. If sales go up by 20 percent, the machine will be used more. If the machine is used more, maintenance will increase, expenses will go up, and the amount of time the machine is available for use will decrease. If the availability of the machine decreases, a backlog will develop, orders may be lost, and so forth. Many of these interactions can be processed by financial computer systems more easily and accurately than by manual calculations.

Finally, financial planning involves answering many "what if" questions. Recalculating is frequently necessary to test the effects of changes in certain variables. For example, the financial analyst in the previous example might want to know the effect on the machine investment if sales decrease by 5 percent, increase by 10 percent, or increase by 15 percent. These kinds of questions can be answered easily by properly designed computer systems. The analyst may need to change only one or two input values and submit a new request to the computer to obtain the required answer. Calculating a solution to the new problem by hand might take nearly as long as determining the original solution.

Characteristics of Financial Systems

Financial systems have a totally different character from accounting systems. This is because most financial systems are used in *planning*, while most accounting systems are used to record data about the daily *operation* of a business. Consequently, most financial functions are serviced by decision-support systems, while most accounting functions are serviced by transaction processing systems.

Much of the data used in a financial system is based on summaries of accounting data. Other data is entered by financial analysts who change values of variables to observe the effects of the changes. Unlike accounting systems, financial systems require the entry of very little new data. As a result, lengthy procedures for detecting and correcting errors are not often found in financial systems.

What little output is produced is used internally in the organization—by planning committees, managers, boards of directors, and others who must steer the organization into the future. Financial systems themselves are not very vulnerable to criminal activity, but the information contained in output reports could be very interesting to competitors. Thus, one big difference between accounting systems and financial systems is this: Accounting systems themselves are vulnerable to criminal activity, and therefore they must be secured. Financial systems themselves do not require tight security, but the reports they produce must be protected from theft.

Compared to accounting systems, financial systems have relatively few users. Financial analysts are not as numerous as order entry clerks, stock pickers, accountants, sales people, and others involved in the daily operation of a business. Financial system users often are highly skilled, well-educated people. They require less training than many of the users of an accounting system. Also, finance departments tend to have lower turnover rates than accounting departments, so the need for recurring training is less. Procedures are often simple and informal.

As was mentioned earlier, calculations tend to be complex. This is no problem for a computer, of course. And recomputing a result based on new variables can be quickly and easily done by a computer. Transaction processing systems, on the other hand, usually involve very simple calculations (often addition and subtraction), but these calculations are repeated perhaps thousands of times, once for each new transaction entered.

Finally, financial data is often less precise than accounting data. Growth rates, interest rates, market shares, and so forth, usually are estimates. Absolute precision is rarely necessary in a financial system.

Examples of Financial Computer Systems

The following is a list of common financial systems:

* Capital expenditure analysis
* Financial planning
* Cash planning
* Merger analysis
* Credit analysis
* Electronic spreadsheets

Capital expenditure analysis is done to determine whether large and complex investments are worthwhile. Examples are analyzing costs and benefits for building a new manufacturing plant, introducing a new line of products, or adding a new division to a corporation.

Financial planning is another type of financial system. The purpose of financial planning is to project revenues and expenses over several years of operation. Another important financial system is **cash planning**. Usually, in business, money must be spent on a project for some time before money is made. This practice can lead to a cash shortage: The long-run financial picture is good, but bills can't be paid in the short run. Cash planning systems identify these situations before they occur and allow management to find supplementary sources of cash to cover the period when cash is short.

Some financial systems perform **merger analysis**. Here, data about two or more companies is entered into a financial analysis program, and a balance sheet and income statement are prepared assuming that

QUESTIONS

4.13 What are the responsibilities of people who specialize in finance?

4.14 What are three reasons financial personnel use business computer systems?

4.15 Compare and contrast a financial computer system with an accounting system.

4.16 Explain what each of the following financial systems does:

    a. Capital expenditure analysis
    b. Financial planning
    c. Cash planning
    d. Merger analysis
    e. Credit analysis

the companies have merged. This procedure allows management to learn the results of various merger strategies before a merger occurs.

A final type of financial system performs **credit analysis**. Banks, insurance companies, and other lenders use such systems to evaluate financial statements and determine the credit worthiness of potential borrowers. Similar systems are used by companies that buy stock or otherwise invest in other companies.

In recent years, financial personnel have begun to make extensive use of personal computers. Quite often, financial systems involve only a single user who employs the computer to make a series of slightly different financial analyses. Personal computers are ideal for this application, and electronic spreadsheet programs have become part of the standard tool kit for financial analysts. This topic will be presented in the final section of this chapter, "Accessing MIS/DSS," and in module B in part 4.

As you can tell from this survey, most financial applications are concerned with planning and thus are DSS applications. A few are TPS applications, but these are rare. One example occurs in very large corporations, where the treasury department moves large amounts of money from one account to another to obtain the very best return on the company's cash. In most cases, however, the finance department turns to the accounting department for the processing and recording of transactions. In summary, the key characteristics of a financial system are the following:

- Planning in nature.
- Calculations very complex.
- Calculations need to be repeated with new values in variables.
- Asks "what if" questions.
- Low volume of input and output.
- Precision not critical.
- Needs to produce timely answers.
- Output reports vulnerable to theft.
- Very few users.
- Little impact on clientele (customers).

Sales and Marketing Applications

Sales and *marketing* are two closely related fields that involve the selling of goods and services. People who work in these departments have widely varying responsibilities, including planning, management, and day-to-day operations. All three computer system services — TPS, MIS, and DSS — often will be needed within the sales and marketing division of a company. Let's start by looking at the characteristics of sales and marketing that cause them to benefit from computerization. To do this, we will discuss sales and marketing separately.

Characteristics of Sales Systems

Selling a company's product is an important function that requires skill and persistence. From the point of view of a company's business systems, however, a **sales system** requires simple and straightforward recordkeeping. Sales people present products to customers, answer questions, and handle paperwork such as contracts and order entry documents. After submitting an order on behalf of a client, sales personnel follow up to ensure delivery. When necessary, they investigate customer complaints and make adjustments. All of these activities require careful recordkeeping, which is easily accomplished by a computer system. Some of the facts that must be recorded are customer name, billing address, shipping address, item ordered, quantity ordered, date item is needed by, cost of item, terms, and method of shipment.

A busy company handles thousands of orders each day. Maintaining sales records (and interfacing sales with accounts receivable, inventory control, accounts payable and payroll) is a relatively easy task for a computer. The historical sales data captured by a sales system is important input to another group of people, those in marketing.

Characteristics of Marketing Systems

The primary functions of **marketing** are developing, pricing, and promoting a company's products. To guarantee a successful marketing campaign, a manager must know the product's future sales. Then, based on this knowledge, the manager can plan personnel; training; sales incentives; capital expenditures; and purchasing, production, and distribution needs. (Notice that the marketing function is one of *planning*, while the sales function involves day-to-day *operations*. MISs, and DSSs, support planning activities, while TPSs support operational activities.

Unfortunately, no marketing manager, market analyst, or computer system yet developed is clairvoyant, so there is no way for a manager to know for certain what future sales will be. However, it is possible to *forecast* sales reasonably well by studying a product's sales history (found in the sales records) and merging in other factors that effect sales. Let's consider a very primitive method for **sales forecasting**.

Suppose we can predict a product's sales for next month from its sales last month:

$$\text{Last month's sales} = \text{Next month's sales}$$

That would imply, incorrectly, that any product on the market always performed consistently. One factor we must include is that months have different numbers of business days. Thus, if last month had 22 days and next month has only 21 days, then our formula will be

$$\text{Last month's sales} \times 0.95454 = \text{Next month's sales}$$

Almost any clerk can perform this calculation. But it is more likely that a market analyst would base sales projections on a product's last 24 months' performance. Of course, each month has to be adjusted for the number of business days and other factors we will not even consider. This makes the formula more complex, although it can still be managed by a clerk with a calculator:

$$\frac{\text{Adjusted month 1 sales} + \text{Adjusted month 2 sales} + \ldots + \text{Adjusted month 24 sales}}{24} = \begin{array}{l}\text{Fore-}\\\text{casted}\\\text{monthly}\\\text{sales}\end{array}$$

Perhaps you can begin to see why computers are so useful in marketing. The calculation described here is far simpler than ones really used in business. But imagine having to perform even that simple calculation for 6,000 products at the end of every month. Clearly, computer power is called for.

Other factors besides sales history that effect sales are not obvious to anyone but market analysts. More variables market analysts might consider include the effects of past advertising campaigns on a product, competitors' reactions to a product, unemployment figures, discretionary household income, number of new housing starts, cost of energy, demographics of key marketplaces, and climatic conditions. There are literally hundreds more. This kind of data is not readily available through the sales history records. Therefore, market analysts must find the data, generate algorithms that use the data, and enter the data and the algorithms into the computer system. They must also adjust their algorithms as they collect more actual information about a product's performance. And they must realize that they are trying to predict the future, something that is impossible to do.

In summary, the sales function of a company handles day-to-day operations. It processes a high volume of input and produces a high volume of output, much of it real. Precision, accuracy, and performance are critical. Calculations are relatively simple, but the volume of processing is high. Much control must be exercised over the sales function because it is vulnerable to criminal activity.

By contrast, the marketing function of a company processes relatively little input and produces very little output. The output it does produce is used internally. Although the volume of input and output is low, the complexity of processing is extremely high. The same complex algorithms are often executed for hundreds or thousands of products many times each year. The marketing function of a company is to predict the future accurately enough to enable management to set reasonable goals and plan resources and expenditures. Thus, precision and performance are rarely critical in marketing systems. Also, marketing is not particularly vulnerable to theft or criminal activity, so controls can be more informal than those imposed on a sales system.

Many and varied computer systems support the sales and marketing functions of an organization. Transaction processing systems handle the recordkeeping for day-to-day operations in sales. Management information systems provide sales managers with feedback on product performance and sales personnel performance. Decision-support systems help sales managers predict the impact of realigned sales territories, incentive plans, and price structures; and they help marketing specialists forecast sales and plan for the production of new products. Let us now look at some computer systems that might be found in sales and marketing.

Examples of Sales and Marketing Computer Systems

The following is a list of common sales and marketing computer systems:

- Operational systems
    - Order entry
    - Mail order processing
    - Customer credit authorization
    - Order status
    - Advertising products

- Planning and management systems
    - Customer profiles
    - Product penetration
    - Sales agent effectiveness and commission calculation
    - Market analysis

The most common transaction processing systems involve **order entry**. These systems receive order requests, check inventory levels, prepare invoices, and so forth. Another common TPS does **mail-order processing**. Orders are received by mail and processed, and customer statements are prepared. Requests for backorders can also be printed. Forms used by a popular mountaineering and camping company are shown in figure 4–11.

Computer systems are also used to check **order status**. Some systems are designed to allow order entry clerks access to computer files using display terminals. Thus, an order can be monitored from order entry through production, packaging, and shipping, and the customer can be informed of its progress. This capability is especially desirable for companies that manufacture goods to order that take a long time to produce.

FIGURE 4–11

Forms used by REI Co-op

PLEASE USE REVERSE SIDE FOR SKI PACKAGES

Recreational
Equipment, Inc.
P.O. Box C-88125
Seattle, WA. 98188

FOR FAST TOLL FREE SERVICE PHONE:
Wash. Residents 1-800-562-4894
Alaska & Hawaii 800-426-4770
All other states 1-800-426-4840
Greater Seattle 575-4480
For Best Service Phone Between 7:00 am & 3:30 pm Seattle Time
TOLL FREE LINES NOT AVAILABLE FROM CANADA
Canadian Customers Please Call . . . . (206) 575-4480

MEMBER'S PERMANENT
MAILING ADDRESS   CO-OP NO. _____

SHIPPING ADDRESS, IF DIFFERENT
FROM PERMANENT MAILING ADDRESS

NAME _____   NAME _____

ADDRESS _____   ADDRESS _____

CITY _____ STATE_____ ZIP_____   CITY _____ STATE_____ ZIP_____

PHONE _____ AREA CODE_____   PHONE _____ AREA CODE_____

Is this an address change? ☐ Yes ☐ No

QTY ⑤	CATALOG NO.	CATALOG NO. 2nd Color Choice	SIZE	DESCRIPTION	PRICE	TOTAL

Shop R.E.I. by Mail or Telephone

Convenient. Order at your convenience. We are as near as your phone. No running from store to store.

Fast Service. Orders received by 3:00 pm are shipped the next work day.

Our Pledge of Quality. If any item you purchase from us proves to be unsatisfactory, please return it for a replacement or a full refund.

Send Your Friend a Catalog

Help your friend become a Co-op Member
We will send a current catalog

NAME _____

ADDRESS _____

CITY _____ STATE_____

FORM #186 REV. 10-78

SHIP MY ORDER:
⑨ ☐ SURFACE ⑩ ☐ AIR

**SHIPPING, HANDLING & INS.
U.S. ONLY**

Subtotal & Value	Surface	Air
0- 5.00	.35	.60
5.01- 10.00	.60	1.25
10.01- 25.00	1.00	1.75
25.01- 50.00	1.60	2.75
50.01-100.00	2.70	4.50
Over 100.00	3.20	5.50
Ski Sets @	4.00	10.00

Add $4.00 Per Package surface
or $10.00 Per Package air
for each ski package on
the reverse side.

Credit Card Number

Customer Sig. _____

Total—Ski Packages from other side	
Sub-total ㉕	
Current Sales Tax WA. & CA. only	
Shipping Charge	
Membership Fee ⑪	
Previous Due ⑫	
Total	

Method of Payment

☐ Check (U.S. Funds) ①
☐ Dividend ③
☐ COD ㉖
☐ Mastercharge ④
☐ Visa ④
☐ American Exp. ④

Expiration date _____

Thank you for your order!

a. Order entry form

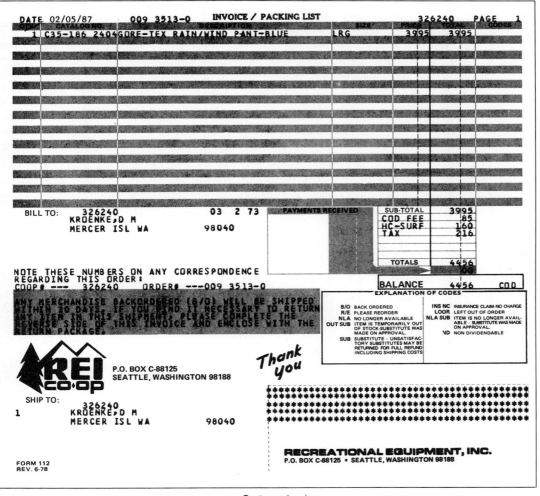

```
REI CASCADE PARKA-MNS-BLUE
LRG                    0150

M222002404   D03   $164.95
```

```
HEEL LOCATER
PAIR                   9313

M406600007   D08   >>$9.95
```

```
KASTINGER HIGH TOUR DOUBLE
BOOT  11               9319

M354402158   D08   $140.00
```

```
WONDER HEADLIGHT
4.5 VOLT               9345

M236000006   D02   >>$8.95
```

b. Picking Slip

INVOICE / PACKING LIST

DATE 02/05/87   009 3513-0   326240   PAGE   1

QTY	CATALOG NO.	DESCRIPTION	SIZE	PRICE	TOTAL	CODES
1	C35-186 2404	GORE-TEX RAIN/WIND PANT-BLUE	LRG	3995	3995	

BILL TO: 326240   03 2 73
           KROENKE,D M
           MERCER ISL WA   98040

PAYMENTS RECEIVED

SUB-TOTAL	3995
COD FEE	85
HC-SURF	160
TAX	216
TOTALS	4456

NOTE THESE NUMBERS ON ANY CORRESPONDENCE
REGARDING THIS ORDER:
COOP# --- 326240   ORDER# ---009 3513-0

| BALANCE | 4456 | COD |

EXPLANATION OF CODES

B/O BACK ORDERED
R/E PLEASE REORDER
NLA NO LONGER AVAILABLE
OUT SUB ITEM IS TEMPORARILY OUT
         OF STOCK-SUBSTITUTE WAS
         MADE ON APPROVAL.
SUB SUBSTITUTE - UNSATISFAC-
     TORY SUBSTITUTES MAY BE
     RETURNED FOR FULL REFUND
     INCLUDING SHIPPING COSTS

INS NC INSURANCE CLAIM-NO CHARGE
LOOR LEFT OUT OF ORDER
NLA SUB ITEM IS NO LONGER AVAIL-
         ABLE - SUBSTITUTE WAS MADE
         ON APPROVAL.
ND NON DIVIDENDABLE

REI CO-OP
P.O. BOX C-88125
SEATTLE, WASHINGTON 98188

SHIP TO: 326240
1   KROENKE,D M
           MERCER ISL WA   98040

Thank you

RECREATIONAL EQUIPMENT, INC.
P.O. BOX C-88125 • SEATTLE, WASHINGTON 98188

FORM 112
REV. 6-78

c. Customer invoice

A final type of sales and marketing system provides assistance to **advertising**. Mailing labels, form letters, and customized advertisements may be produced. Many companies have large files of customers' or potential buyers' names and addresses. Mailing labels can be produced easily from these files. Mailing lists on magnetic tape can also be purchased. Form letters and other types of personalized advertising commonly are produced as well.

Sales people use **customer profile reports** (figure 4–12) when making sales calls. Such reports are easily produced if order records are already stored on a computer-sensible medium. **Product-penetration reports** show the sales of various products in different geographic markets. Using such a report, a marketing manager might decide to increase advertising or to assign additional personnel to underdeveloped markets.

A **sales agent effectiveness report** (figure 4–13) shows the sales of products by sales agent. These reports help salespeople analyze their effectiveness in selling different products. Such reports also show commissions and bonuses earned. Sometimes these reports compare current sales effectiveness to prior years' performances.

FIGURE 4–12
Customer profile report

```
                            CUSTOMER PROFILES

                            SOUTHWEST REGION

                       PERIOD ENDING MARCH 1987

          CUSTOMER                     PRODUCT                 PURCHASES
   NAME               NUMBER    NAME              NUMBER    UNITS     AMOUNT

   ACE BILLIARD       10043     DISPLAY CASE      P1040       4      $1287.50
                                EXECUTIVE DESK    Q3877       1      $1150.99

   AJ ARCHITECT       70089     DRAWING TABLES    J8897      12      $4588.85
                                72-INCH TABLES    J9789       4      $1768.04
                                SECRETARY DESK    Q0446       4      $1238.79
                                EXECUTIVE DESK    Q3877       3      $3452.97

   DR. PAUL A AZURE   33879     EXECUTIVE DESK    Q3877       1      $1150.99
                                        •
                                        •
                                        •
```

```
                    SALES AGENT EFFECTIVENESS REPORT

                        FALL QUARTER, 1986

SALES AGENT              PRODUCT                       SALES
NAME              NAME           NUMBER      UNITS      AMOUNT

MARY PITTS        ZANSEN BOOTS    14327        319     $47,340
                  JET IV SKIS     36575        412      38,415
                  LAMBRETH POLES  55478        127       1,270


LENNY PORTZ       ZANSEN BOOTS    14327        450      66,780
                  NORDIC BOOTS    13788        139      27,845
                  JET IV SKIS     36575          7         653
                  K-3 SKIS        37782        539      73,422
                                    .
                                    .
                                    .
```

Market analysis systems are used to estimate the total sizes of markets; a company's share of each of them; and the distribution of markets across geographic areas, age groups, and demographic groups. For example, market analysis personnel may compare company sales over a period of time against the sales of its major competitors. This comparison may reveal that, although company sales are increasing, they are not increasing as fast as those of competitors. When management realizes that the company's share of the market is shrinking, it can decide how to respond.

As you saw earlier, this type of analysis often involves sophisticated algorithms and lengthy calculations. Computer systems ease the job of the market analyst and allow many more estimates to be prepared. Computer-generated estimates also are apt to be more accurate than manually prepared ones.

In summary, sales and marketing functions are supported by TPS, MIS, and DSS computer systems. *TPS* systems directly support company sales. They are similar to accounting systems. *MIS* and *DSS* systems are used for evaluating past performance and making plans. These systems are similar to those used in finance. The key characteristics of a sales system are the following:

- Both operational and managerial in nature.
- Produces regular, recurring output.

FIGURE 4-13
Sales agent effectiveness report

QUESTIONS

4.17 Explain the responsibilities of people who work in sales and marketing.

4.18 Explain the difference between sales systems and market analysis systems. Give an example of each.

4.19 Explain why sales operations systems are similar to accounting systems.

4.20 Explain why market analysis systems are similar to financial systems.

4.21 Why are computers used to perform market analysis? Can market analysis be done as effectively without computers?

4.22 Describe the purposes of two reports produced by a sales operation system.

4.23 Describe the purposes of two reports produced by a market analysis system.

- High volume of input and output.
- High impact on system clients (customers).
- Processing is simple.
- Needs to be precise.
- Needs fast response time.
- Vulnerable to criminal activity.

The key characteristics of a marketing system are the following:

- Planning in nature.
- Imports much input data from sales system.
- Produces little output.
- Complex calculations required.
- Calculations need to be repeated with new values in variables.
- Performs both regular, recurring functions and one-time functions.
- Precision not critical.
- Not very vulnerable to criminal activity.
- Few users.

Manufacturing Applications

A company's **manufacturing** department is responsible for transforming raw materials into finished products. Some of the activities in manufacturing involve day-to-day manufacturing operations. These include inventory control, tracing a product through the fabrication process, cost accounting, process control, and robotics. Other activities, such as designing new products, purchasing raw materials, and scheduling machines and facilities, primarily involve planning. Manufacturing can be a complex task requiring at least four distinct activities.

Manufacturing Functions

The first activity is **engineering**. The design of new parts or new machines is an engineering responsibility, as is the incorporation of new materials or new technology into existing products. Engineers are involved primarily in planning functions. They ask many "what if" questions during the design process.

Second is **procurement**. Manufacturing personnel must order sufficient raw materials to produce the desired quantity of finished goods. This task may seem simple, but consider the great variety and vast number of components needed to produce a television set, an automobile, or an airplane. Often the lead time for ordering raw materials is six months or more. Manufacturing must determine its needs at least that far in advance so that the raw materials will be available when needed. Once needs have been established, computers can be assigned the task of patrolling inventory records looking for items that must be reordered

PROFILE

"SOVIET INDUSTRY IS IN BIG TROUBLE WITH COMPUTERS."

Computers present several challenges to Soviet leadership. Presumably it worries about the military implications of the U. S. S. R.'s inferiority in computer hardware. Gorbachev must also be concerned about the computer's threat to the official Communist monopoly on ideas: a few Apple II computers hooked up to printers could make instant bestsellers out of dissident literates. So just about all computers in the Soviet Union are closely guarded in state-run institutions. Americans worry about hackers electronically breaking into institutions and gaining access to various business and military secrets. In the Soviet Union, things are reversed: the state's problem is to prevent any computers from breaking out of the institutions.

The U. S. S. R. has trouble producing modern computers: its leading entries are copies of mainframes that IBM stopped making six to ten years ago. And even these copies are inferior to those produced in East Germany. The best computer a Soviet manager could ordinarily hope to get his hands on would be an East German ES-1055 model, roughly similar to a third-generation IBM System 370.

Most managers who do have information systems run them with their own teams of specialists operating out of in-house computer centers. One alternative is to turn to a local service center — an institution somewhat similar to the time-sharing centers that flourished in the U. S. some 15 years ago. The service centers are strenuously encouraged by the state,

and the Soviet Communist party is a prominent customer. Some party officials originally viewed them as the ideal way for enterprises to use computers and also as a convenient way to ensure that information systems would be standardized throughout the Soviet Union. But years of squabbling over which ministry would control the service centers undermined this goal. The squabbling left the enterprises free to set up their own arrangements and left the state looking glumly at thousands of different and incompatible information systems.

and issuing purchase orders and providing data about these transactions to the accounts payable system.

The third manufacturing activity is **scheduling**. Manufacturing personnel want to schedule the use of their facilities so as to maximize productivity. For example, if a company has only two lathes, production should be scheduled to balance the use of these machines. Extra costs and delays will occur if the machines are overloaded at some times and idle at others. The production sequence needs to be arranged to allow uniform use of equipment.

Another scheduling consideration is **machine setup time**. Suppose it takes 10 minutes to set up a saw to cut table legs and 15 minutes to set up the saw to cut table tops. If five tables are to be produced, it makes sense to cut all the legs and then all the tops. Otherwise, if the saw cuts first the legs for one table, then the top, then the legs for the next table, then the top, and so forth, much time will be wasted changing the saw setup. Many firms have increased production 20 or 30 percent simply by scheduling machines and people more effectively.

Scheduling is clearly a planning function. It may involve very complex algorithms and many variables. Also, scheduling must be done quickly, which makes it a perfect task for a computer. A sudden failure on one production line means that another will have to be rescheduled to take up the extra work. Time is money in manufacturing, so the more efficiently scheduling can be done, the less money will be wasted.

The fourth and perhaps most familiar manufacturing activity is **fabrication**. Fabrication means making components and assembling them into finished products. Record keeping for this task includes capturing figures regarding production labor, labor to make tools and machines, and labor for inspections and other **quality assurance** procedures. In addition to labor records, manufacturing companies also need to trace the progress of each product through the fabrication process. A transaction processing computer system can easily record events that occur on the production line regarding labor and the status of each item.

As you can see, computer systems are used to support all four of these manufacturing activities. Some of these systems, particularly those supporting scheduling and engineering, are fundamentally **MIS** or **DSS** applications. Other systems, particularly those involved with events on the production line, are fundamentally **TPS** applications. For example, a production control system records the event of a product leaving one stage of manufacturing and entering another.

A special type of computer system that directly supports engineering and fabrication is called a **CAD/CAM** (for computer-assisted design/computer-assisted manufacturing) system. The design part of a CAD/CAM system allows engineers to modify designs over and over and to observe the effects of those modifications on a final product. This is similar to a decision-support system in that the engineers are essentially asking "what if" questions. The manufacturing part of a CAD/CAM system is used for process control and to direct robots. The system constantly gets feedback from the environment (such as how close a robot arm is to a sheet of metal) and sends messages to the robot as a result (such as to decelerate). This is more like a transaction processing system because there is much input, and events are anticipated and planned for.

Examples of Manufacturing Computer Systems

The following lists those computer systems commonly used in manufacturing:

- Materials management
    Materials requirements planning
    Inventory control
    Materials tracking

- Facility scheduling
  Machine balancing
  Production scheduling
  Operations research

- Process control
  Manufacturing machines
  Environment control
  Security systems
  Robots

- Engineering
  CAD/CAM
  Stress analysis
  Spatial conflict detection
  Electronic circuit evaluation
  Aerodynamics

Systems in the first category, **materials management**, support the planning of raw materials purchasing and the control of raw materials and finished goods inventories. They also enable tracking of materials through the production process. Figure 4–14 shows a **bill of materials** for a simple backpack. If a company wanted to make 1000 of these, manufacturing personnel would need to compute the amount of raw materials needed. If, in addition, the company wanted to make tents, sleeping bags, and other products, the total materials required would need to be computed. **Materials requirements planning (MRP)** systems eliminate the manual effort required to make these computations.

FIGURE 4–14
Bill of materials example

```
             BILL OF MATERIALS FOR

               HIKER BACKPACK

            PRODUCT NUMBER 14356

  MATERIAL            QUANTITY      DIMENSIONS (INCHES)

  CLOTH TOP              1          20x12
  CLOTH SIDES            4          8x22
  LEATHER BOTTOM         1          8x14
  VELCRO HOOK TAPE       1          6x1/2
  LEATHER TIEDOWN        3          3x2
  WEB STRAPS             2          2x35
  PADDED BELT            1          3x40
  THREAD                 1          400(FEET)
```

Inventory control systems maintain the right quantity of parts in inventory. Inventory personnel must maintain a delicate balance. They do not want to run out of parts, but on the other hand, they do not want to have too many parts. Excess parts must be paid for, and the cost of carrying inventory can be very high. Consequently, computer systems are used to keep track of the quantity of parts in inventory, the rate at which inventory is used, and the time required to receive a delivery once an order is made. These factors, together with the costs of the parts, are used to calculate the optimum reorder point and quantity for each part.

Tracking materials and finished goods is also accomplished using computer systems. Companies do not want to lose finished goods through accident or pilferage, nor do they want to lose material in the production line. Keeping track of materials can be a major task for a large manufacturer. Computer systems are used to process the large volume of data needed to do this.

Facility scheduling systems are another category of computer applications in manufacturing. Systems are used to help balance the use of machines and to minimize the amount of time wasted by machine setup or schedule conflicts. Since a typical manufacturer may have 50 machines and 500 products, production scheduling is not a trivial problem. A business specialty known as **operations research** uses mathematics to solve these problems. Computer systems are heavily used for the extensive calculations this research requires.

The next category of applications, **process control**, uses computer technology to control and operate machines. In addition to controlling manufacturing machines, these computers control air conditioning and heating, security systems, typewriters and copying equipment, and even timing equipment at sport events.

Perhaps the most exciting application of computer technology in manufacturing is robotics. A **robot** is a programmable manipulator designed to move materials, parts, tools, or specialized devices through a series of programmed activities [9]. (See figure 4–15 and also the computers and society photo essay.) Robots are especially useful for performing boring and repetitive tasks and for work in uncomfortable or dangerous environments.

The social implications of robotics are enormous. Robots could drastically reduce the need for manual labor in manufacturing companies in the next decade. They will certainly cause major changes in the skill levels of workers. A new, technical job will likely evolve that will require a person who has knowledge of computing, machinery, and manufacturing technology. Present-day blue-collar workers will need considerable retraining to be able to fill these new jobs.

The final category of manufacturing computer systems involves engineering and CAD/CAM. Systems are used to facilitate design in a variety of ways. Designs can be displayed on display screens, and

FIGURE 4–15
Robot

engineers can use the computer to make modifications. Once a design is approved, computer-assisted design systems translate design drawings into instructions for manufacturing machinery and robots.

Computer systems are also used for **stress analysis** of load-bearing structures and to check for **spatial conflicts** in drawings of large buildings. Other applications are the evaluation of electronic circuits and the investigation of the aerodynamic properties of cars, boats, airplanes, and rockets. In summary, the key characteristics of a manufacturing system are the following:

Engineering Functions
• Planning in nature.
• Low volume input and output.
• Ask many "what if" questions.
• Impact internal.
• Little room for criminal activity.
• Require high degree of precision.

Production Functions
• Operational and managerial in nature.
• High volume of input and output.
• Processing is simple, repetitive.
• Many users.
• Highly vulnerable to criminal activity.
• Require great deal of precision.
• Low impact on clientele (customers).

QUESTIONS

4.24 Describe four activities involved in manufacturing.

4.25 Define *process control system*.

4.26 Give an example of a process control system.

4.27 Briefly explain how computers are used to support manufacturing.

▒ ACCESSING MIS/DSS

Throughout this chapter we have discussed how managers, analysts, and engineers can use the information provided them by management information systems and decision-support systems. In this section we will explore some ways of accessing those sources of information.

Information Centers

The **information center** evolved after computer accounting systems had been established and managers realized that the computer records held a wealth of information they could use to be more productive and to make the company more profitable. However, at the same time this need was recognized, few managers knew enough about computers and computer systems to use them effectively. In fact, there are still thousands of top executives and middle managers who know far less about computer systems than you do (although they probably know much more about their business specialties.) The concept of an information center was developed to assist such people.

The function of an information center is similar to that of a library, except that instead of providing information services about books, it provides information services about information.

Companies have implemented information centers in a variety of ways. In some organizations, the information center contains one or more large mainframe computers that store summaries of data from the corporate operations (transaction processing) data. In these companies, users with DSS needs come to the information center for assistance much as a person seeks the assistance of a good research librarian. Personnel at the information center are in charge of obtaining needed data from the operations systems and making this data available to interested users. The information center also provides advice and assistance regarding the use of center facilities.

Although this type of information center was gaining popularity five years ago, personal computers have displaced it in many companies. Most DSS users want the independence and flexibility of having their own microcomputers.

This situation has led to information centers that operate as company-specific microcomputer/software/corporate-data service departments. This group provides advice and assistance regarding the use of microcomputers to meet DSS application needs. In such groups, information center personnel meet with DSS users and recommend hardware and programs. They also educate and train users in the use of hardware and programs and show them how to transfer corporate data to personal computers.

A new job, that of **information analyst**, is evolving in conjunction with the development of information centers. Information analysts have expertise regarding the information center's data and other resources, and they help users employ these facilities to obtain the information they need. This new job is something like that of a librarian. The information center librarian helps users but does not do their work. Users must obtain their own data and do their own research; the librarians are present to explain and to teach.

Executive Workstations

As executives and managers began to feel more comfortable with computer technology, and as more user-friendly systems were developed, the newest device to be found in an executive's office became the computer **terminal**. The terminal communicates with the company's mainframe computer(s) and allows an executive or manager access to up-to-the-minute data about the company (so long as transaction processing systems are updating the company's records as the events occur.)

In addition to simple access to corporate databases, the **executive workstation** also provides such services as **electronic mail** (messages can be sent from one terminal to another in an instant), calendar monitoring, and clerical support. Depending on the software that the user has available, a workstation can help a manager project sales, study past performance, examine the impact a new branch will have on the company, and perform many other analyses and tasks.

An executive workstation is a very sophisticated application of electronic and computer technology. Perhaps because of their sophistication and cost, they are not yet as popular as the more common personal computer.

Personal Computers

Personal computers, also known as microcomputers, are stand-alone computers, but if they are equipped with communications hardware and software, they can become computer terminals that access a company's mainframe. Ordinarily, a personal computer supports only one user. The goal of most managers and executives who use personal computers at work is to increase their personal productivity.

Because personal computer systems serve only one person, they are simpler than other types of business computer systems. An individual user can use a personal computer without worrying about coordinating with others. For example, an individual user can stop in the middle of a task and resume it later without hindering another user's processing. Further, a single user has only himself or herself to blame for mistakes that occur.

Personal computers can be used for many applications, and they are discussed in module B of part 4. In this section we will consider only how personal computers can assist managers and executives who need MIS or DSS support. Therefore, we will focus on electronic spreadsheets and personal databases.

Electronic spreadsheet applications support the analysis of numerical data. Spreadsheet programs are used to prepare time-oriented financial documents such as budgets and forecasts. For example, consider figure 4–16, which shows a spreadsheet application of a student budget based on the following assumptions:

a. Income is $400 per month.
b. Food is 35 percent of income.
c. Entertainment is 12.5 percent of income.
d. Savings is income minus housing and food expenses.
e. All accumulated savings are spent in December.

One of the main advantages of spreadsheets is that they are formula driven. Assumptions *b* through *d* in the preceding list can be expressed as formulas based on assumption a, the fixed amount of income. To prepare another budget, the user need only enter a different income

FIGURE 4–16
(a) Electronic spreadsheet output;
(b) Electronic spreadsheet after changing income

	INCOME	HOUSING	FOOD	ENTERTAINMENT	SAVINGS
SEPT	400.00	160.00	140.00	50.00	50.00
OCT	400.00	160.00	140.00	50.00	100.00
NOV	400.00	160.00	140.00	50.00	150.00
DEC	400.00	160.00	140.00	50.00	0.00
JAN	400.00	160.00	140.00	50.00	50.00
FEB	400.00	160.00	140.00	50.00	100.00
MAR	400.00	160.00	140.00	50.00	150.00

a. Student budget assuming $400 income per month

	INCOME	HOUSING	FOOD	ENTERTAINMENT	SAVINGS
SEPT	600.00	160.00	210.00	75.00	155.00
OCT	600.00	160.00	210.00	75.00	310.00
NOV	600.00	160.00	210.00	75.00	465.00
DEC	600.00	160.00	210.00	75.00	0.00
JAN	600.00	160.00	210.00	75.00	155.00
FEB	600.00	160.00	210.00	75.00	310.00
MAR	600.00	160.00	210.00	75.00	465.00

b. Student budget assuming $600 income per month

amount, and the spreadsheet program will make all of the calculations necessary using the formulas for assumptions *b* through *d*.

For example, suppose the student wants to know how the budget would differ if income were $600 instead of $400. To answer this question, the student need only enter the new amount, and the spreadsheet program produces the results shown in figure 4–16b.

Spreadsheet applications require the purchase of a spreadsheet program. Typical programs are Lotus 1-2-3, Multiplan, Supercalc, and PC-Calc.

Spreadsheets are used for management information and decision-support applications. They are useful for comparing actual figures to budgeted ones, and they can easily be manipulated to show the effects of changes in variables. Probably one of the most useful tools for today's executive or manager is the electronic spreadsheet.

Another application for a personal computer is the **personal database**. Like spreadsheets, databases can be used for both individual and business-wide applications. The key distinction is the number of users. A personal database application has one user; business applications have more than one.

This distinction may seem trivial, but it has important implications. As will be discussed in chapter 9, shared data is hard to manage. When there are multiple users, special procedures need to be developed to prevent one user from making unacceptable changes to shared data. Such problems do not occur with personal database applications.

The purpose of a database application (personal or business-wide) is to keep track of things. People develop personal database applications because they want to keep track of something in their personal or professional sphere. For example, a secretary might use a database application to keep track of correspondence; or a salesperson might use a database application to keep track of customers: when they were last visited, what their buying preferences are, and so forth.

Database applications require a program called a **database management system (DBMS)**. Common personal computer DBMS programs are R:base System V, dBASE III + , and pfs:file. These programs provide facilities to develop processing menus, data entry forms, and reports. Many DBMSs include easy-to-use languages that allow people, with a little training, to extract and manipulate data easily. These are called *user-friendly* database management systems and are perfect for business people who are not computer experts and do not want to become computer experts.

Depending on the complexity of the application and the particular DBMS product in use, it may be necessary to write programs to support the personal database application. If so, most users hire programmers to develop the application on their behalf, although more sophisticated users sometimes develop programs themselves. We will consider this topic further in chapter 11 and module B.

QUESTIONS

4.28 Name three ways to access a management information system or a decision-support system.

4.29 Why are electronic spreadsheets used by so many managers?

4.30 Describe a business problem that cannot be solved by an electronic spreadsheet program.

4.31 Why are personal computers more widely used by managers and executives than executive workstations?

4.32 What is the function of an information center?

4.33 Describe three applications for a *personal* database in the sales division of a company.

Data can be entered into a personal database by the user (such as the salesperson who is tracking his or her own sales calls), or it can be **downloaded** (copied) from the corporate database. Do you see the implications for this in terms of MIS and DSS? Managers and executives can download the information they need from the company's central files and then manipulate it with programs and spreadsheet facilities to make plans, develop budgets, produce sales forecasts, identify slips in the progress of a project, and so forth. More and more information is becoming more readily available to the users who need it most.

Many methods are available to today's managers and executives for accessing the information needed to make sound business plans and decisions. They include the information center, the executive workstation, and the personal computer. More methods undoubtedly are being developed that will make information access even easier.

▓ SUMMARY

Computer systems can provide different services for different users within a company. The most fundamental type of computer service is provided by a *transaction processing system (TPS)*. Transaction processing systems support the day-to-day operations of a company. They typically handle much input and produce much output. Most of the output from a TPS is issued to system clients, such as customers and vendors. Thus, these systems must be timely, efficient, accurate, and precise. A company usually exercises a great deal of control over a TPS.

Another type of computer service is called a *management information system (MIS)*. As its name states, an MIS provides information to managers, which they can use to make business decisions. Reports are anticipated and planned for and are almost always used internally. MISs do not usually process much input, though they often extract data stored by a TPS. MISs enable managers to set goals and then measure progress toward these goals. Project control is an important aspect of management.

A third type of computer service is provided by a *decision-support system (DSS)*. A DSS is actually a collection of programs that allow managers to build models of a company and measure the impact of changing one or more variables on a model. A DSS is similar to an MIS; the major distinction is that DSSs allow ad hoc, or unanticipated, inquiries, while MISs are programmed to produce certain reports according to a certain schedule. Like MISs, DSSs are used internally and do not require stringent controls. Much of a DSS's data is extracted from one or several TPSs.

Within the business world are thousands of systems that help users in one way or another. In accounting, transaction processing systems represent the bulk of computer services. Accounting systems are concerned with day-to-day operations of the company. In contrast, financial systems rely heavily on MIS and DSS — they process transactions only very rarely. Financial systems exist for planning, not day-to-day operations. Sales functions in a company are operational in nature and consequently are supported by TPSs. Sales management, that is, measuring the performance of products and sales representatives against goals, requires MIS support. Marketing, on the other hand, is concerned with planning. DSSs help market analysts do their jobs better and more quickly. Finally, manufacturing functions are widely supported by a broad mix of computer systems because the functions of manufacturing are so diverse. Thus, you will find TPS, MIS, and DSS systems in use in the manufacturing division of a company.

As you can see, almost every area of business has the potential to benefit from some level of computerization. That is why getting a solid foundation in business computer systems is so important for you — you are bound to encounter them, regardless of what business specialty you choose.

Accessing management information systems and decision-support systems has become easier as more user-friendly interfaces have been developed. *Information centers* help executives or managers get information, without having to search for it themselves. *Executive workstations* allow managers personally to access company data as well as a communications network. They are more powerful, more sophisticated, and more expensive than the ubiquitous *personal computer*. A personal computer is very versatile — it can be used as a terminal to access a corporate database and services on the mainframe computer, and it can also be used as a stand-alone device. When used by itself, a personal computer can be a wonderful productivity aid to managers, salespeople, secretaries, and others. Software such as electronic spreadsheets and personal database management systems provide computer power to anyone who wants to learn how to use them.

WORD LIST

Information systems
Transaction processing systems (TPS)
Corporate data model
Real output
Management information systems (MIS)
Exception report
Decision-support systems (DSS)
Ad hoc data manipulation and reporting
Accounting system
Checks and balances
Audit trail
Hourly payroll system
General ledger
Phased processing
Editing
Manual operations flowchart symbol
Edit report
Change report
Billing system
Accounts receivable system
Accounts payable system

General ledger system
Inventory accounting system
Financial system
Capital expenditure analysis
Financial planning
Cash planning
Merger analysis
Credit analysis
Sales
Marketing
Sales forecasting
Order entry system
Mail-order processing system
Order status system
Advertising system
Customer profile report
Product-penetration report
Sales agent effectiveness report
Market analysis
Manufacturing
Engineering
Procurement
Scheduling
Machine setup time
Fabrication

Quality assurance
CAD/CAM system
Materials management
Bill of materials
Materials requirements planning (MRP)
Inventory control system
Facility scheduling
Operations research
Process control system
Robot
Stress analysis system
Spatial conflict analysis system
Information center
Information analyst
Terminal
Executive workstation
Electronic mail
Personal computer
Electronic spreadsheet
Personal database
Database management system (DBMS)
Download

QUESTIONS TO CHALLENGE YOUR THINKING

A. If you are interested in management:

1. What is PERT? How does it work, and are computers necessary for PERT applications? What is CPM? GERT?

2. Suppose you managed the production of a newspaper. How might you use the computer to reduce your operating costs? to provide better reader services?

3. Interview one of your management professors. Find out other ways the computer is used to assist manufacturing personnel.

4. What role does a top-level manager have in the development of business computer systems? What is a steering committee, and how can it be used to control computer projects?

B. If you are interested in accounting:

1. What are the potential dangers of using computers for accounting purposes? What steps can be taken to reduce these dangers?

2. Interview one of your accounting professors and ask how computers have changed accounting. How do CPAs treat computer sys-

tems during an audit? Find out what SAS-3 is and why it is important to both data processing and accounting.

C. If you are interested in finance:

1. Find out if your computer has a package of financial programs. If so, determine the interest rate on a loan with a principal of $73,000 to be paid off in 72 payments of $1450 per month.

2. Ask one of your finance professors about financial planning and how it has changed since the advent of the computer.

D. If you are interested in sales and marketing:

1. How are computers used to support marketing directly? Find out about a system that produces mailing labels. How can such a system detect whether or not a duplicate label is on the mailing list (a common and important problem with these systems).

2. How are computers used to perform market forecasts? Has the ability of marketing people to make these forecasts changed since the advent of the computer?

E. If you are interested in manufacturing:

1. What is MRP? Do MRP systems always use the computer? Why or why not? What do you suppose is the major computer problem in using an MRP system?

2. Bill of materials processors are very common manufacturing systems. What, specifically, do they do? Could this activity be done without a computer?

3. Investigate the application of robots in manufacturing. How many robots exist? Which industries are using them? What types of work are they performing? Who are the major vendors? What posture have unions taken toward robots?

FUNDAMENTAL BUSINESS COMPUTER SYSTEMS

PART TWO

Part 2 of this text discusses fundamental business computer systems. First, the book discusses how they are developed, and then it describes the characteristics of fundamental system types. Chapter 5 outlines a general process for developing systems and introduces some useful development tools. That process is then illustrated in chapter 6 with a case adapted from the experience of an actual business.

The systems development process as described here works equally well whether micros, minis, or mainframes are ultimately selected. In fact, more and more microcomputers are being incorporated into larger business systems.

The remaining chapters in this part discuss two system types. Chapter 7 discusses sequential file processing systems, and chapter 8 discusses direct access file processing systems. Looking ahead, chapter 9 in part 3 discusses business database systems. All business computer systems are based on one of these system types.

Observe that the fundamental system types are characterized by the way in which they organize and process data. When we discuss the five components of a system, data is the middle component. On one side of data is hardware executing programs; on the other side of data are people following procedures. Since data is the interface between machines and people, it makes sense that we use data organization to characterize systems.

THE SYSTEMS DEVELOPMENT PROCESS

CHAPTER 5

In this chapter, we discuss the ways in which business computer systems are developed. This information will be important to your career whether or not you become a computer professional. For example, if you become a business manager, you will need to know this process to ensure that your employees develop systems correctly. If you become a business user, say, a supervisor of payroll, you will need this information to protect yourself. You will need to know what is happening, what your role should be, what you can fairly expect from the experts, and so forth. Finally, if you make the computer profession your career, you will need to know how to proceed when developing a system. This chapter will be your introduction. To become a qualified systems developer, however, you will need several courses in systems development and computer technology as well as a year or more of experience.

People develop computer systems to help them solve problems. Consequently, systems development is simply one special application of basic problem-solving techniques. The steps we take to solve problems are well known:

1. Define the problem.
2. Identify alternative solutions and select one.
3. Develop the selected solution.
4. Implement the solution.

Computer system developers follow the same four steps. In this chapter we will see how this model is applied to computer systems development. In the next chapter we will follow a particular company's experiences in applying these principles to a system development project.

PROJECT MANAGEMENT

The development of a business computer system is usually an expensive undertaking requiring the coordination and cooperation of many individuals. Therefore, system development projects, like any business projects, must be *managed*. Management consists of two complementary activities, planning and control, and assumes the existence of defined goals and objectives. *Planning* means scheduling what is to be done by whom, to what level of acceptability, and when. *Control* means maintaining a record of what people have actually accomplished, comparing actual performance to planned performance, and taking corrective action when necessary. An introduction to the fundamentals of **project management** will help you to understand business computer systems development.

Overview

Management of computer system development is essentially the same as management of any project. The entire project is subdivided into phases and, usually, each phase into tasks. The four problem-solving steps referred to earlier become the four stages of a systems development project. They are the

1. Requirements stage
2. Evaluation stage
3. Design stage
4. Implementation stage

Each stage is designed to produce a **deliverable**.

A deliverable is a clearly identified product whose acceptance marks the end of a project phase. Suppose you were building a bridge. Before drawing detailed blueprints of the bridge you would first have to build a scale model. The model is a deliverable. Once the scale model is accepted by a review board you can move from the general design phase to the detailed design phase. Acceptance of the deliverable thus marks the end of one phase and the beginning of the next one.

In business computer systems development, most deliverables are documents. They might be reports, drawings, programs, or something else. To be acceptable, deliverables must be readable (written in English, drawn neatly and legibly, following any appropriate rules), and someone besides the author must be able to judge their accuracy and acceptability.

When a project is initiated, skillful managers not only specify the work that is to be done; they also establish acceptance criteria for each deliverable. Then, as each document is delivered, it can be compared with the acceptance criteria for control purposes. If management does not specify acceptance criteria, it will not know if each phase was conducted properly and correctly.

Having broken the project into phases and having identified the end products of each phase, a project manager can develop a preliminary budget and schedule, based on knowledge of the general scope of the system and the availability of resources such as analysts, users, and software. To visualize a schedule better, a manager can draw a chart like the one in figure 5–1. Throughout the entire project the manager **reviews** the project team's progress and compares it to the schedule. Depending on how finely the project has been subdivided, these reviews can take place as often as once a week.

If reviews happen frequently enough, a project manager can spot problems and address them before it is too late. For example, a manager might add more people to the team, insist on more cooperation from the user, or purchase a software package to help the development

146

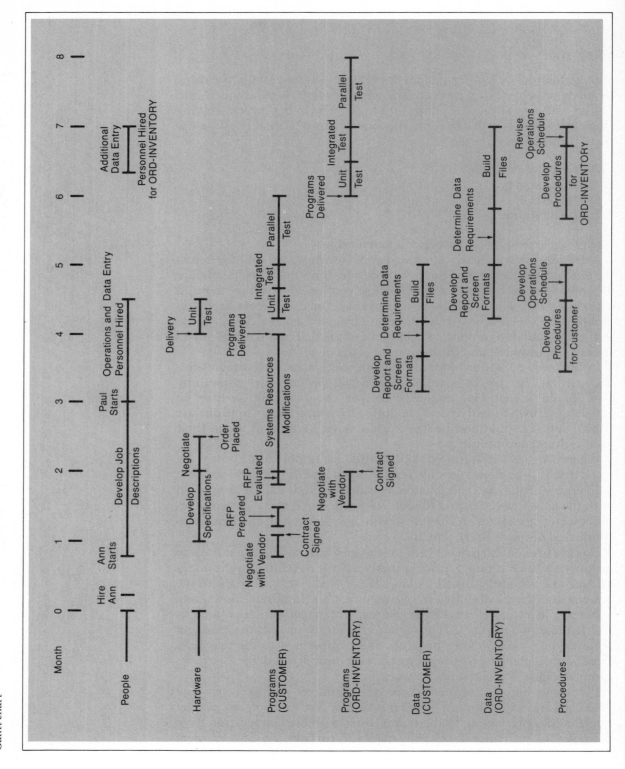

FIGURE 5-1
Gantt chart

team. Alternately, a manager might identify an insoluble problem and be forced to adjust the schedule.

One thing business computer systems developers have discovered over the years is that pictures do speak louder than words. The once-popular 300-page narrative system specification has yielded to the more readable and less ambiguous pictorial system specification. Graphics are used very heavily during systems development because they are more easily interpreted by all the people involved in the project — users, systems analysts, computer operators, managers, database administrators, and so forth. Later in this chapter we will explore some of the graphic tools currently used in systems development.

Project management, then, means breaking the project into steps, identifying what is to be accomplished during each step, defining the deliverables from each step, scheduling time and personnel for each step, and then tracking actual progress against scheduled progress and making necessary adjustments to keep the project moving. Let's now look at the systems development process and the deliverables for each of the steps we identify.

THE SYSTEMS DEVELOPMENT PROCESS

A business computer system is a group of five components that interact to satisfy a business need. To develop a system, you must select, install, and establish the interaction among these five components. You will need to select and install hardware (unless a suitable computer is already available). You will need to obtain programs. You will need to design data and build the initial files. You will need to design procedures for people to follow, and you will need to train the people who will be involved. Building such a system can be a complex job. The process described in this section breaks this complex job down into simpler pieces.

The following is a list of the four stages of the **systems development process**:

- Determine requirements
- Evaluate alternatives
- Design
- Implement

This sequence of stages has evolved over time. It has been forged out of the mistakes and disasters of many systems development projects. Today, most business computer professionals agree that these activities, in the order listed, are the best way to ensure that an effective system is developed. (Professionals may disagree on the names of the stages and on the packaging of activities into each of the steps, but there is a general agreement on the basic behaviors listed above.)

Requirements Stage

The first step in a systems development project is to determine what the system is supposed to do—the **requirements**. As shown below several actions must be taken to make this determination:

- Form project team
- Define problem
- Determine specific requirements
- Assess feasibility (can be done after problem definition as well)
- Obtain management approval

The first is to form a project team.

Form Project Team

The project **team** should include both users and computer professionals. The users are primarily responsible for developing requirements and ensuring that the system meets the intended need. The computer professionals build the components of the business computer system to satisfy those user requirements. Sometimes, the best results are achieved if the project team is led by a user, rather than by someone from the data processing department.

The skills needed by members of the project team will change over time (see figure 5–2). In the early stages, users have a major role. The need for technical personnel such as programmers is limited in these stages. During design and implementation, however, this situation reverses. Technical personnel have major responsibilities, and users have less to do, at least until the final stages of implementation. Thus, personnel may be assigned to the project intermittently. Generally, however, the project manager should remain constant throughout the project.

FIGURE 5–2
Project team composition in each stage

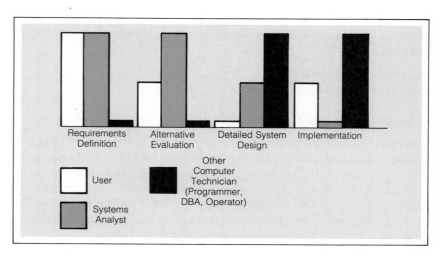

APPLICATION

"A PROPERLY PLANNED INTERVIEW CAN BE AN ANALYST'S BEST TOOL."

While the methods of obtaining useful information from the user vary greatly, the personal interview will bring the best results and best understanding, if conducted properly. The properly planned interview can be the analyst's best business tool in the tool kit.

An important key to excellent interviewing skills is the ability of the analyst to prepare to deal with the different personalities and attitudes of the people being interviewed. If the analyst can modify personal style to complement the personality of the interviewee, then a channel of communication will be established that will allow ideas to be effectively communicated and the needed information to be obtained.

Studies indicate that verbal messages convey 7%, intonations convey 38%, and body language conveys 55% of the total message. Body language is the key factor, and the alert and well-informed analyst and interviewer should take advantage of this fact during the interview.

Listening has specific goals as they relate to the interviewee as an employee:

1. To raise the level of employee motivation.
2. To increase the readiness of subordinates to accept change.
3. To improve the quality of all managerial decisions.
4. To develop teamwork and morale.

Active listening is characterized by a nonjudgmental attempt on one person's part to allow the other person to explore a problem. Use of body language that encourages openness and acceptance should motivate the employee to participate in the interview more fully, and this should be the interviewer's goal in obtaining information. As with other attitudes, openness encourages similar feelings in others.

Determine General Requirements

The first task of the project team is to **determine the general requirements** of the system. This is the step at which the problem to be solved is defined.

A problem is a perceived difference between *what is* and *what ought to be*. Therefore, to define the problem, the team must clearly define the present situation and then describe the desired situation. A problem is a *perceived* difference. In some lucky situations, the team will discover that the problem is only a perception, that the problem does not truly exist. In this case, the team will have saved considerable time and expense by focusing early on problem definition. More than one company has developed an elegant solution to a nonexistent problem or even to the wrong problem. As carpenters say, measure twice and cut once.

Meeting the needs of users is the constant problem that system developers must address, so the deliverable is a list of user requirements. In all but the most unusual cases, the new computer system will replace a system that is already in operation (it may be a manual system, a computerized one, or a combination). Therefore, the project team may need to have a thorough understanding of the company's present operations. Learning this is time consuming and expensive, so most project teams approach the problem in at least three steps: they determine the *general* requirements of the system, they estimate whether or not a computer solution is *feasible*, and if it is they identify more *specific* requirements.

Knowing what is happening today in a company is an important first step in systems development. Determining what should be happening comes as a result of studying what is happening and by skillfully interviewing key users. This is a lengthy process, but a very necessary one. Studies have shown that if the project team does not develop a clear picture of their goals and objectives, the group is almost certainly doomed to failure.

After general requirements are established, the project team must consider whether, in the group's opinion, developing a computer system to meet the requirements is possible. This is called *assessing the feasibility of the project*.

Assess Feasibility

At some point (or perhaps at several points) during systems development, the feasibility of the project is evaluated. This **feasibility evaluation** usually occurs after general system requirements are defined, after specific requirements are defined, or at both times.

The purpose of the feasibility study is to determine as early as possible whether the project is *not* worth continuing. The project's team objective is to abandon an infeasible project before serious costs have been incurred. In fact, throughout the entire project the team's primary goal is to maximize the probability of success and to minimize the cost of failure.

The team considers three dimensions when evaluating feasibility. The first dimension is **technical feasibility**. For this portion of the evaluation, someone with computer expertise determines whether or not the problem to be solved is amenable to a computer solution. Has such a problem ever been solved by computer? Or, if not, is it likely that this problem can be solved by computer? For example, producing customer invoices can feasibly be done by computer. Deciding whether or not to change personnel policies cannot.

Once the technical feasibility is verified, then **cost feasibility** is examined by developing rough cost estimates. The approximate size and capacity of the computer required are determined. This information can be used to get a rough estimate of the cost of the computer itself. However, other costs are also involved. Programs must be purchased or developed, data must be converted, procedures must be developed, and personnel must be trained. These are all initial costs. Added to these are the operational costs incurred as the system is used. Power, maintenance, and salaries of operations personnel are examples of these operational costs.

Again, rough cost estimates are used. The purpose of the cost feasibility step is to determine whether the cost of a computer system solution is in the right range. For example, if the cost of the system is $100,000, and the estimated worth of the solution is $10,000, then a computer solution to the problem is cost infeasible.

The third dimension of feasibility evaluation is **schedule feasibility**. If the computer system requires a year to develop, and if a solution must be found in six months, then the proposed system is infeasible. For example, if a system is needed to compute taxes that are due on April 15, and if the system cannot be completed until July 4, then the proposed system is schedule infeasible. Another solution must be found.

Again, a feasibility evaluation can be done at any point in the systems development process. In the first stage, it is most frequently done after the general requirements have been defined and again after specific requirements have been determined. The deliverable from this task is a written summary of the feasibility study.

Determine Specific Requirements

The next task within the requirements stage is to **determine the specific requirements** of the new system. Whereas the problem definitions in the prior step are broad in scope, the requirement definitions in this step are narrow and focused. At this point, *specific* needs of the users are determined and documented. An example of a specific requirement is the following: The VDT screen for order entry must show customer number, name, address, and credit limit.

It is vital that future system users be involved in determining specific requirements. Studies have shown that the number one cause of failure in a business computer system is a lack of user involvement during requirements definition. If users are not involved, the requirements are often not realistic. In addition, if users are not involved, they have no psychological stake in the new system. In fact, they may be motivated to cause the system to fail. But if users have participated in the development of requirements, they feel a part of the process and are as eager as anyone to see the system succeed.

Studies of unsuccessful systems development projects have shown that a major reason for failure is that data processing personnel have developed business computer systems for users without really understanding the users' needs. There are two complementary reasons for this. First, data processing personnel are usually computer people first and business people second, if at all. Even with a strong background in some business applications, most systems analysts lack enough knowledge of detailed requirements to develop a system adequately without cooperation from the user. Second, users, who understand their problems better than anyone else, often have a difficult time understanding computer folks and articulating to them their needs. Users often do not know what to expect from the data processing people nor their own responsibilities during system development (you will have an advantage here). Only disaster can result when users cannot or do not state their needs clearly enough to direct the computer people. The problem, of course, is communication.

Fortunately, tools have been developed that allow each side to communicate with and clearly understand the other. These tools — the dataflow diagram and supporting documents — are presented in a later section, and their use is illustrated in the case study in chapter 6. Systems analysts and users employ these tools *jointly* to define system requirements. During the early stages of systems development users must commit almost as much time and effort to the project as analysts. After this, user participation drops off, and users can return to their other work. But without user involvement, the systems development project is almost certainly doomed.

System requirements focus on three topics:

1. Business functions
2. Data
3. System characteristics:
   Data currency
   Access speed
   File activity
   System flexibility
   User friendliness

The user can identify **business functions** by completing the sentence "I want the system to. . . ." For example "I want the system to determine the optimum date on which to pay an invoice," or "I want the system to issue refunds to customers within 30 days of a return."

Having identified the functions, the team can then determine what **data** must be captured and stored within the system. For example, to issue a customer refund, a system needs the customer's name and address, the amount of the refund, and the date the item was returned.

Finally, the user must establish requirements for some key **system characteristics**. You will see in chapters 7, 8, and 9 how these requirements influence the processing style adopted, whether sequential, direct access, or database. The key characteristics are **data currency**, **access speed**, **file activity**, **system flexibility**, and **user friendliness**.

Data currency refers to how up-to-date the stored data must be. No one but the user, who knows how the business operates, can determine this requirement. At one university it may be adequate to post tuition payments to student accounts monthly, while another university might require weekly or even daily updates. One manufacturer might need inventory balances updated as soon as material is received at the warehouse, while another manufacturer might be satisfied with recording receipts every other day.

The *speed* with which the user needs to access records is another key system requirement, one that will have a major impact on the alternative system designs that will be considered during the next stage. In the banking business, customers expect to go to any branch of their bank and ask for their current balances. Consequently, the data for all accounts for each customer must be instantly accessible. Similarly, airline reservation systems must show at any moment how many (and which) seats are available for a particular flight. Other systems do not require instant access to data. For example, a university might print transcripts within five days of a student's request. This clearly does not require instant access to a particular student's grade record.

File activity refers to the proportion of stored records that are read or updated during a work period (perhaps one day or one shift). The user must study the business's history to determine this requirement. In a payroll system, for example, the entire personnel file is used when the company issues payroll checks. But in one business day at a mail-order company perhaps only 5000 customers out of a customer base of 2 million place orders. The payroll system uses 100 percent of its records, while the order entry application uses only one-quarter of one percent of its records. This characteristic will have a major impact on the type and organization of data storage chosen, which will have a ripple effect on the other components of the system.

Flexibility refers to the nature of problems the system is likely to be called on to solve. Some problems are predictable by their nature. Payroll is issued weekly, transcripts are mailed two weeks after the semester closes, customers make bank deposits and withdrawals every day, and so forth. These are fairly standard accounting applications and are not expected to change very much. However, some computer systems are developed to answer ad hoc questions — to solve problems no analyst or user anticipated during development. In chapter 4 we distinguished between transaction processing systems, management information systems, and decision-support systems. The user, with the help of a systems analyst, must decide which general category the new system falls into. You will see in chapters 7, 8, and 9 how important this distinction is, and the impact it has on designing the final system.

Finally, the project team must get a handle on how *user friendly* the new system must be. This depends largely on who the hands-on operators will be. If the system will be run primarily by professional computer operators, then system documentation, screen displays, messages, and so forth can be more technical. But if some or many users, or even system clients, interface directly with the system (through terminals, automatic teller machines, telephones, and so on), then much care must be taken to ensure that the system can easily be used by everyone involved.

The user requirements — functions, data, and key system characteristics — are documented in a journal or other written record. This journal must specifically state what the new system is to do. It becomes a storehouse of the team's knowledge about the new system. Further, documenting the requirements forces the team members to understand them. Because the requirements specification document states clearly and unambiguously the system goals, it becomes the yardstick to measure the project team's success in meeting those goals. At the end of the project the team can answer the question: Does the system accomplish what it is supposed to?

The deliverable from this task, then, is a written requirements specification. It identifies the business functions this system will carry out, the data needed for those functions, and requirements for the five key system characteristics. At this point you are not concerned with how the system will operate, only what it must do to help the user. Decisions regarding computers, data formats, screen designs, and so forth are addressed in later stages.

Obtain Management Approval

Once the problem has been defined, the specific requirements have been determined, and the technical, cost, and schedule feasibility have been evaluated, the problem statement, requirements specification, and feasibility report are presented to management. If management believes that the problem has been well defined, that the requirements are complete, and that the project is feasible, then a go-ahead decision is issued. Otherwise, management may direct that a part of the work be redone or may cancel the project.

Such **management approval** is mandatory. Management must have an opportunity to influence the flow and direction of the systems development project. As you will see, management approval is required at the end of all four stages of systems development. A written statement of management approval is issued at this point.

Evaluation Stage

After the requirements have been determined, alternative general system designs are developed and **evaluated**:

- Identify alternatives
    (hardware, programs, data, procedures, people)
- Evaluate alternatives
    Cost/benefit
    Subjective evaluation
- Obtain management approval

Each alternative design specifies hardware, programs, data, procedures, and personnel required to solve the business problem.

Identify Alternatives

The objective when specifying alternatives is to find three or four feasible alternatives that will fulfill the user's requirements. To do this, each of the five components of a business computer system is considered in light of the requirements. Then an alternative is created by specifying the hardware, programs, data, procedures, and personnel needed to meet the requirements.

Sometimes, one of the business system components is the same for all alternatives. For example, if a company already has a computer, then the hardware may be the same for each alternative. In some cases, the data needed may be the same, or the procedures to be used may be equivalent. When this correspondence occurs, the component that stays the same does not form part of the alternative.

Developing an alternative is an iterative process. The five components are interdependent. A decision on one may change the others. This may necessitate going back and reassessing other components. For example, one type of computer hardware might seem feasible until the personnel component is discussed and the team discovers that a systems engineering specialist would be required to put the computer together and keep it running. Such an alternative would probably be eliminated.

One of the most influential components in system development is the program component. Decisions here have a major impact on all other components. There are three common ways of acquiring programs: buying general application programs off the shelf from a vendor, buying off-the-shelf programs and altering them to meet specific needs, and writing programs from scratch. No one approach is best in all situations — the best approach varies with the system requirements. The most important factors to consider are delivery time, uniqueness of system requirements, and development cost. Let's consider these factors with respect to each method of obtaining programs.

There are literally thousands of **off-the-shelf programs** available for thousands of general business applications. Off-the-shelf programs are written to meet the needs of many users — if these packages are too specific, then not enough copies will be sold. For example, one payroll package might work equally well for a manufacturer, a dentist, and a restaurant owner. Consequently, for any common business problem off-the-shelf software may already exist. *Purchasing* software rather than *developing* it from scratch has many advantages.

Off-the-shelf programs are available almost as quickly as you can pay for them, so development time is nil. Most program bugs are already worked out, and they are (or should be) fully documented and ready to install and use. In the long run, buying off-the-shelf programs is the fastest, cheapest, and easiest way to acquire programs.

On the other hand, the available software may not precisely meet the user requirements that were identified in the previous stage. This gives rise to two additional possibilities: (1) modify the user requirements to match the available software to gain the advantages of buying versus building or (2) alter off-the-shelf software to gain at least some of the advantages.

Altering off-the-shelf software is more expensive than simply buying and using whatever is available, because you must add the extra expense of designing, building, testing, and documenting the changes. Sometimes the original developer can be persuaded (for a price, of course) to make the needed changes. This will protect the warranty of the software. Another approach is to hire someone to make the changes or to make them yourself (very risky for any one other than a professional programmer). Regardless of who does it, altering purchased software costs time and money.

The advantage, of course, is that in addition to the general needs addressed by the software package, the user's specific needs are also met. However, if the user's needs are truly unique, you may be forced into the last alternative, *writing programs from scratch.*

Custom-tailored programs are programs specifically designed and coded to meet the system's requirements. You may elect to hire a software firm to do this, free-lance consultants, or full-time computer programmers. Most business professionals do not have the time, interest, or skills to undertake such a project themselves. This is by far the most expensive and time-consuming approach of the three.

However, developing your own custom software will ensure a perfect fit between the system and the users' needs. The other two approaches sometimes only approximate them, though they cost less and are installed sooner. Figure 5–3 compares the three ways of acquiring programs.

During the alternative evaluation stage, the approach taken for programming will greatly influence the other components. All trade-offs must be considered. The deliverable from this task is several alternative general system designs, as well as a summary comparing the alternatives.

FIGURE 5–3
Ways to acquire programs

	OFF-THE-SHELF SOFTWARE	ALTERED SOFTWARE	CUSTOM-BUILT SOFTWARE
DEVELOPMENT TIME	Fastest	Depends on extent of alterations	Slowest
PERFECT FIT TO UNIQUE REQUIREMENTS	Probably not	Possibly	Almost guaranteed
COST	Cheapest	In the middle	Most expensive

APPLICATION

"PROTOTYPING HAS MANY ADVANTAGES OVER TRADITIONAL METHODS."

Most systems developers currently use an approach that was described some 20 years ago to develop today's computer information systems. This development approach, which is usually termed the Traditional Life-Cycle approach, uses a linear path of analysis, design, development, and implementation phases.

However, the traditional approach to systems development has recently come under question as information systems grow in complexity and systems development times extend into years. Prototyping has been suggested as an alternative.

Prototyping could be the answer because it responds to the contemporary problems. Although common in the engineering disciplines, prototyping of information systems is relatively uncommon. In fact, the term information systems prototype has no unique definition. The dictionary provides several definitions for the word "prototype," but the one most appropriate to information systems is one "that serves as a model for one of a later period."

An information system's prototype is an early version of a system that contains the most important features of the later production system. The prototype is a model — much like the model used to test a new automobile before it is put into production, or a building before the concrete is poured. With an information system's prototype, the intended users get an early picture of the final production system. This picture allows the users to evaluate the design before the production system is built and implemented.

The traditional development approach differs from the prototyping approach in one key aspect: The traditional approach assumes that user requirements can be precisely specified before system construction is attempted. Prototyping, on the other hand, incorporates a learning process into system design. It assumes that precise user requirements are *not* always definable before system construction. While experimenting with a prototype system, users identify, evaluate, and refine production systems requirements.

ADVANTAGES

Prototyping has many advantages over the traditional approach. Some of these advantages are that prototyping:

1. Gets the user more actively involved in system design and development.

2. Provides the user with a tangible means of comprehending and evaluating the proposed system.

3. Achieves more meaningful user feedback in terms of their needs and requirements.

4. Develops better relationships between systems people and user groups.

5. Results in fewer post-implementation change requests with lower maintenance costs.

Although prototyping has some problems, it is a vital tool in the development of today's complex information systems.

Evaluate Alternatives

Once the alternatives have been identified, the next step is to evaluate them and select one. Then the best alternative is compared to the value of the problem solution, and a decision on whether or not to continue is made. If the decision is to proceed, the design stage will begin.

Basically, alternatives should be evaluated by comparing the dollar values of benefits to costs. One way to do this is to form ratios of benefits to costs. The alternative with the highest ratio is selected. You will learn more about the process of **cost/benefit analysis** if you take a course in systems development or business finance.

In some cases, a formal evaluation of costs and benefits is not performed. Instead, the project team, together with management, meets to assess the alternatives. A decision regarding alternatives is then made on a more subjective basis.

The deliverable from this task is a general system design that the project team recommends as the best solution to the problem.

Obtain Management Approval

At the conclusion of this stage, the selected alternative is presented to management. Management may have concerns that were not addressed by the project team. If so, these issues may need to be studied. Otherwise, management will budget the necessary funds and approve the start of the next stage. Thus, the deliverable from the second stage of systems development is an approved general system design, a budget, and usually, a schedule for the next stage.

Design Stage

The third stage of the systems development process is designing the system in detail. As shown in figure 5–4, by *system* design we mean that each of the five components of a business computer system is designed. Insofar as hardware is concerned, the term *design* is used loosely. Very rarely is computer equipment built; usually it is purchased or leased. Here, **design** means determining the detailed specifications of the equipment needed and then ordering it from a vendor.

If programs are going to be purchased off the shelf and used as is, negotiations with a vendor might begin now. If they are going to be purchased and altered, then detailed specifications for the alterations are now developed. Finally, if programs are going to be custom built, they must be carefully specified and designed. This is often the most time-consuming part of program development. If the

FIGURE 5–4

Tasks and deliverables for detailed system design

HARDWARE	PROGRAMS	DATA	PROCEDURES	PEOPLE
Specifications	Detailed specifications for custom-built programs or program alterations (may include prototypes)	Specific file, screen, and report formats	User procedures for normal processing and failure recovery	Job descriptions
				Organizational structure
			Operations procedures for normal processing and failure recovery	Training needs
	Purchase orders for off-the-shelf programs			

design is done properly, the actual coding or programming may be done quite rapidly.

Prototyping is an approach to designing custom-built programs. A prototype is a model of the real system programs, offering the user just the skeletal features that are of interest: screen displays, error messages, dummy reports, prompts at the terminal, and so forth. The user can actually use the prototype as if it were the real thing to get a feel for the system interfaces. The development team can get important feedback from the user early enough to make design changes when they are easy and inexpensive to make. A prototype can be quickly changed until the user is satisfied. And the user can see how the system will work — before approving the design. Once approval is granted, the actual system can be built based on the prototype.

The other three components of the system must also be designed. Decisions are made about data formats, including input forms, storage file structures, and layouts of outputs such as reports. Decisions about data are influenced greatly by the key system characteristics the user specified early on: data currency, access speed, file activity, flexibility, and user friendliness. Procedures that describe how users will employ the system, as well as how the operations personnel will run the system, must be designed. Finally, job descriptions are prepared, the organizational arrangement of users and operations personnel is designed, and training programs are developed. The deliverables produced for each component during the design stage are summarized in figure 5–4.

Obtain Management Approval

The design stage is also approved by management. At this phase, however, management may not have the expertise to assess the work that has been done. Therefore, independent experts may be hired to assist in the **design review**. Even without such expertise, it is important for management to review the design and stay involved in the project. Quite often, good managers will detect a fly in the ointment, even if they do not understand the technical details. In addition, if the detailed system design necessitates organizational changes (which is often the case), then management's approval will be required.

If work is proceeding satisfactorily, approval will be granted for implementation. Because of the highly technical nature of many of the documents produced during design, many people might be called upon to approve the deliverables. Users approve screen and report designs, for example, but the data processing manager would approve program design. The company's training director might be called on to approve training objectives and vendors. All approvals must be in writing. Ultimately, company management must make the overall decision to implement the system, often based on the recommendations of the individuals who approved portions of the design.

Implementation Stage

The last step in systems development is **implementation**. As shown below, this step has three primary tasks: construction, testing, and installation. At the beginning of this final stage a firm and detailed implementation schedule is developed by the project manager.

- Construct
    - Install hardware
    - Install (or write) programs
    - Build files
    - Document procedures
    - Hire and train personnel
- Test
    - Test each component individually
    - Test system
- Install
    - Plunge
    - Parallel
    - Pilot
    - Phased
- Obtain management approval (of completion)

Construction

At this point, hardware and programs that have been ordered are installed and tested for correct operation — the system is **constructed**. (Actually, this step varies according to the project. We have assumed that hardware and programs are ordered during design. If the lead time is short, however, orders may not be placed until implementation.)

If programs are being written instead of purchased, they are coded and tested at this step. Test data files are built. The conversion of the actual data to computer format is begun. Procedures are documented and tested by operations personnel and by users. Needed personnel are hired, and necessary organizational changes are made. Training materials are prepared, and initial training is completed.

Testing

Testing usually has two different phases. First, as the hardware and programs become available, they are tested as separate **components**. Hardware is tested using test plans and procedures provided by the vendor. Programs are tested according to vendor procedures or by the programming staff. Once these components have been tested, then a **system test** of all five components is made. During this test, the critical users and operations personnel follow defined procedures. An evaluation is made to determine whether or not the system is ready for installation. If so, installation proceeds. Otherwise, the system is corrected and retested.

The system testing process varies widely, depending on the complexity of the system, the number of personnel involved, and the degree to which the programs have already been used. A program that has just been constructed obviously will require more testing than a program that is currently used at 200 sites.

Installation

Proper **installation** of a business computer system is vital. If installation is done poorly, users will develop doubts and hostilities toward the system, even if it is an excellent one.

There are two groups of installation strategies. The project team selects one option from each group. The choice of options in the first group determines whether the old system will be retained or abandoned altogether while the new one is being tried; the choice of options in the second group determines how much of the new system is installed at once. Let's consider the first decision: plunge versus parallel installation.

The first installation strategy is to **plunge**. The new system is started, and any existing manual systems are stopped. This strategy can be *very dangerous*. If the new system has some errors or other difficulties, there is no backup. This strategy is used rarely, if ever. However, if the cost of running parallel far exceeds the risk of failure taking the plunge, plunging might be considered.

A second strategy is to run the new system in **parallel** with the old system. If any problems develop, there is a backup. This approach is expensive because two systems must be supported for some period of time. Still, many companies view this expense as a form of insurance.

Thus, the project team decides whether to install the new system and run it parallel to the old one (expensive but safe) or to take the plunge (cheaper but risky). The team must also decide how much of the system to install at once. Here three options exist: (1) install the entire system, (2) install the system in phases, or (3) install the system in pilot locations. Installing the system all at once means that the complete system is made available to all of the users right away.

When a **pilot** strategy is followed, the new system is implemented for a small part of the clientele. For example, a company might install a system for part of their customer base, say, the customers in the state of Minnesota. Once the system is working correctly, it can be used for all customers. The pilot strategy limits the damages in case the new system works incorrectly.

QUESTIONS

5.1 Name the four stages of systems development.

5.2 Describe tasks to be accomplished during the requirements stage.

5.3 List the deliverables produced by the requirements stage.

5.4 Describe tasks to be accomplished during the evaluation stage.

5.5 List the deliverables produced by the evaluation stage.

5.6 Describe tasks to be accomplished during the systems design stage.

5.7 List the deliverables produced by the systems design stage.

5.8 Describe tasks to be accomplished during the systems implementation stage.

5.9 List the deliverables produced by the systems implementation stage.

Finally, **phased** installation means implementing the system in parts. For example, for an integrated order entry/inventory system, a company could install just the inventory part of the system and verify it before implementing the order entry portion. Any of these strategies — installing the system all at once, piloting it at select locations, or implementing it in phases — can be coupled with either the parallel or the plunge approach. The costs and benefits of each installation strategy must be considered, along with the nature of the system being installed.

Not surprisingly, the deliverable from this stage of systems development is a fully operational business computer system.

Figure 5–5 summarizes the steps of systems development as they relate to the five components.

▥ SYSTEMS DEVELOPMENT TOOLS

During the first two stages of systems development, requirements definition and alternatives evaluation, a number of graphic **systems**

FIGURE 5–5
Summary of systems development stages for the five components

FOUR DEVELOPMENT STAGES	FIVE COMPONENTS OF A BUSINESS COMPUTER SYSTEM				
	HARDWARE	PROGRAMS	DATA	PROCEDURES	PERSONNEL
REQUIREMENTS STAGE	Determine cost/technical/schedule feasibility. Form project team and steering committee (if necessary). Determine user requirements. These requirements then determine requirements for the five components.				
EVALUATION STAGE	Determine vendors of needed equipment.	Off-the-shelf, altered, or custom-built software	File organization and processing styles	Ways to meet users needs — depends on other components	Organizational structure (users, operations, systems development)
	Determine costs and dollar value of tangible benefits. Identify intangible benefits. Compare costs and benefits; select best alternative if cost-justified.				
DETAILED DESIGN STAGE	Determine specifications. Initiate procurement.	Specifications for custom-built software or software alterations; purchase off-the-shelf programs.	File contents Data formats Relationship to programs	Design users and operators procedures.	Develop or procure training programs.
IMPLEMENTATION STAGE	Install and test.	Write programs, document, and test.	Create and test production files.	Document and test.	Conduct training. Test with rehearsals.
	Choose parallel or plunge; choose all at once, pilot, or phased.				

APPLICATION

YOURDON, INC.

Founded in 1974, Yourdon, Inc., has attained a position of leadership in the software engineering field through training, consulting, software, and publishing activities. Training courses are taught throughout the world, and the skills learned in Yourdon classes have contributed to the successful systems development effort of more than 100,000 professionals in thousands of organizations. Yourdon, Inc., pioneered the systems development tools known as the Structured Techniques, which are now widely used as an **EDP** development standard.

The curriculum in the Structured Techniques covers the complete systems development life cycle and continues to provide the information processing community with current courseware.

The Yourdon Consulting division is a staff of senior-level consultants dedicated to providing solutions to the many information processing challenges. They offer technical consulting services that combine experience in Yourdon Techniques with expertise in the areas of quality assurance, strategic planning, systems development, project management, and information modeling.

The Software Engineering Workbench is a family of software products assisting software engineers in every aspect of systems development. The Analyst Toolkit automates the process of structured analysis.

development tools are frequently used. One popular tool is the *dataflow diagram*, and its supporting documents, the *data dictionary* and *process specifications*. These are useful during the first two stages because they can be easily developed, reviewed, and interpreted by users and systems analysts alike. Thus, they are a good communication device. They are also clearly definable deliverables, and versions of them can mark the end of some systems development stages.

You learned in the previous section that two related problems in systems development are the inability of systems analysts to read the users' minds and the difficulty users have articulating their business needs to computer personnel (fortunately, you will not have this problem). Using the tools we are about to discuss will not guarantee success, but it will surely improve the team's chances for success.

Of course all the tools in the world are useless if either side is uncooperative. Systems analysts must make a real effort to understand the user's business, to help identify the user's problems, and then to design a system that addresses the user's needs. Users also must make a sizable time commitment during the early stages of development. Time spent defining requirements for a new system means time lost performing the user's normal business activities. Time, in the business world, is money. Such a costly commitment can be made more palatable and more productive by using tools developed especially for the task of requirements definition. Speeding up the process allows the user to return to business more quickly.

FIGURE 5–6
Dataflow diagram

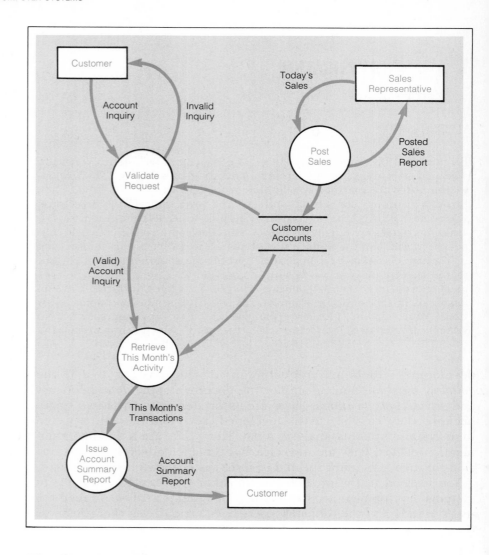

The Dataflow Diagram

The **dataflow diagram**, or **DFD** (figure 5–6), illustrates a business system. One of its many strengths is that it allows us to study the functions in a business without worrying about which tasks are done by people and which are handled by computer. To a dataflow diagram, a task is a task.

The graphics used in a DFD are limited to these: a circle ○ represents a **process**, or function; an arrow → is called a **dataflow**, and it represents input to a process or output from a process; parallel lines ═ represent a **file** or other data storage; a rectangle ☐ represents a **terminator**, either the source of raw input to the system or the receiver of system output. Let's take a look at each of these.

The Process

A process is a task, usually a business-related one. The name of the process appears in the circle. The name of a process is best stated as a short (two- or three-word) sentence, such as "Issue customer statement" or "Calculate regular loan payment."

The Dataflow

The dataflow is a named arrow going into a process (input) or coming out of one (output). The direction of the arrow indicates whether the dataflow is input or output. A dataflow helps us visualize data produced by one business function that is used as input for some other business function. A network of processes and dataflows helps us identify relationships between various parts of a business system.

The File

A file is defined as any place we store data so we can retrieve it later. By this definition, businesses use lots of files: rolodexes, file cabinets full of manila folders, schedules written on chalkboards, and lists, to name a few. Computerized disk and tape files are other examples.

On a DFD the name of a file should indicate the data that is stored there, rather than the physical characteristics. For example, "the second file cabinet from the wall next to Mary's desk" is not as appropriate as "the employee personnel file," though both may refer to the same file.

A dataflow going into a file indicates that the file is updated by the process; a dataflow coming out means that the file is read by the process, but not changed by it in any way (see figure 5-7).

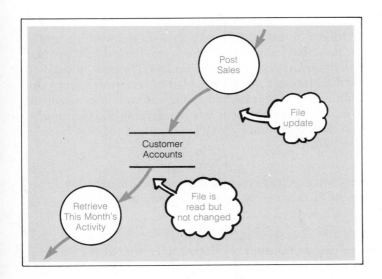

FIGURE 5-7
File updates and reads on a dataflow diagram

The Terminator

On some dataflow diagrams we show the source of a system's input and the destination of its final output. A terminator can be a person, another company, a department within the same company, a government agency, another system — almost anyone or anything with whom the system interfaces. The name of a terminator is written inside the rectangle.

Armed with this brief description of dataflow diagrams, turn back to figure 2–15, the description of the class enrollment system. Can you interpret it? Systems analysts use DFDs frequently because with them an analyst can quickly illustrate his or her understanding of a user's business system, and the user can quickly review this understanding. If there are errors on a DFD, they can be easily seen. Consequently, when the analyst is wrong, he or she is very visibly wrong. It is important that errors be detected and addressed very early in systems development.

If the analyst does understand the user's business, the new business computer system is more likely to meet the user's real business needs. Users are expected to review analysts' DFDs (a large time commitment), but many users draw their own documents to be incorporated with the rest of the system documentation. If you take a course in systems development, you will probably learn how to draw and use DFDs. That will be just one more advantage you have over other business people.

A dataflow diagram illustrates two important aspects of a system: the functions of a system and their data interfaces. There are two other documents used to support the dataflow diagram; namely, the data dictionary and process specifications.

Data Dictionary

A **data dictionary** might be better named a glossary of system terms. The function of our data dictionary is to define clearly all dataflows and files on the dataflow diagram in terms of their parts. The parts are called *fields*. This standardization enables users, systems analysts, programmers, managers, database administrators, and anyone else involved with the system to use the same term when referring to documents, records, and files. A data dictionary entry for the class request form in figure 2–17 appears below:

class request form = type of request + student name + student number + at least 1 course choice

course choice = course number + units + alternate course number + alternate course units

Process Specifications

Naming a function does not mean you know how to perform it. A **process specification** defines how to perform a process identified on a dataflow diagram. A given process might eventually be computerized, or it might be carried out by people, but that has no bearing on the process specification. For example, the algorithm used to amortize a loan is the same for a clerk and a computer. A process specification for the Post Sales process seen in figure 5–6 appears in figure 5–8.

```
POST SALES

For each of today's sales
   1. Get the customer's balance from the customer
      accounts file
   2. If today's sale is a purchase:
         a. Add total sale to customer's balance
         b. Write purchase line on Posted Sales Report
         c. Add total sale to grand total of purchases
      Otherwise (today's sale is a return):
         a. Subtract total sale from customer's balance
         b. Write return line on Posted Sales Report
         c. Add total sale to grand total of returns
   ENDIF

Write both grand totals on the Posted Sales Report

END POST SALES
```

FIGURE 5–8
Process specification for Post Sales

In summary, a dataflow diagram identifies business functions and their interfaces, the data dictionary defines the data, and process specifications describe how to perform each function. They are produced as deliverables during the requirements definition stage (at that point they show business functions and business data required by the new system) and are modified during the evaluation stage (at that point they incorporate features and data needed not only by the business, but also by the computer and programs). The DFDs, data dictionary, and process specifications for the alternative system that is selected are then used as input for the next step, detailed system design.

▓ SUMMARY

Systems development has four fundamental stages. Each stage can be broken down further into several steps, shown on the next page.

QUESTIONS

5.10 What is a dataflow diagram?

5.11 Why are dataflow diagrams preferable to narrative descriptions of a business computer system?

5.12 What does a circle on a DFD represent?

5.13 What does an arrow on a DFD represent?

5.14 What does a pair of parallel lines on a DFD represent?

5.15 What does a rectangle on a DFD represent?

5.16 What two documents support a dataflow diagram?

5.17 What is the purpose of each of the documents named in the answer to question 5.16?

- Determination of requirements
    - Form project team
    - Define problem
    - Study feasibility
- Evaluation of alternatives
    - Cost/benefit analysis of several system designs
- Detailed system design
    - Draft specifications for hardware and purchased programs
    - Design files, databases, reports, screen displays
    - Write detailed program specifications
    - Design user and operator procedures
    - Hire new people
- Implementation
    - Install equipment
    - Install purchased programs; code and test in-house programs
    - Convert or build data files
    - Document procedures
    - Train users and operators

There are also some tools that can be helpful during systems development. They are:

- Dataflow diagram, which shows functions and their data interfaces
- Data dictionary, which names and defines the composition of dataflows and files
- Process specifications, which describe how to perform each function

WORD LIST

Project management	File activity	System test
Deliverable	System flexibility	Installation
Review	User friendliness	Plunge installation
Systems development process	Management approval	Parallel installation
Requirements stage	Evaluation stage	Pilot installation
Project team	Off-the-shelf programs	Phased installation
General requirements definition	Altered programs	System development tools
Feasibility evaluation	Custom-tailored programs	Dataflow diagram (DFD)
Technical feasibility	Cost/benefit analysis	Process symbol
Cost feasibility	Design stage	Dataflow symbol
Schedule feasibility	Prototype	File symbol
Specific requirements definition	Design review	Terminator symbol
Business function	Implementation stage	Data dictionary
Data currency	Construction	Process specification
Access speed	Components test	

QUESTIONS TO CHALLENGE YOUR THINKING

A. Locate a company that has recently developed a system using off-the-shelf programs. Interview the systems development personnel, the operations personnel, and the users. Did the company follow a process similar to the one described in this chapter? If not, how did the process differ? Has the system been successful? What would any of the personnel involved do differently if they were to develop the system again?

B. Locate a company that has recently developed a system using altered programs. Conduct an interview as described in question A.

C. Locate a company that has recently developed a system using custom programs. Conduct an interview as described in question A.

A CASE APPLICATION

CHAPTER 6

Chapter 5 described the systems development process in abstract terms. To help you relate this process to reality, this chapter will describe the experience of one company that implemented a new system.

▥ ELLIOT BAY ELECTRONICS

We begin our case study with a look at the company and its problems. Then we will see how the company decided to form a committee to consider developing a computer system of its own to help solve some of these problems.

The Company

Elliot Bay Electronics is a wholesale distributor of electronic components. Most of its 6,500 customers are retail stores. It lists 4,500 items in its catalog and stores its inventory in three large warehouses.

EB Electronics bills its customers at the end of each month. Customers have an incentive to pay their bills within 30 days, because each customer is offered a special discount. The discount varies from one customer to another, and it is based on each customer's total purchases during the previous four quarters. As a result, more active customers are eligible for a higher discount than are less active ones.

When EB instituted the individual discount policy, the company saw an increase in sales, a dramatic decrease in the number of delinquent accounts, and an improvement in cash flow. The discount policy has become a permanent feature of EB's way of conducting business.

In 1985, Elliot Bay experienced severe growing pains. The company bought out another electronics distributor, and suddenly its customer base doubled. Shortly thereafter, EB added several new product lines, and the number of customer accounts exploded to 6,500. By the middle of the year, EB Electronics was filling over 65,000 orders per year. Sales were 3.5 million — up nearly 300 percent from 1.2 million in just three years. The sales department was thrilled.

However, neither accounting nor shipping were able to keep up with the increase in business. All orders were processed manually. The backlog of orders was growing. It sometimes took weeks to open a new customer account and a month or more to post a sale. The accounting department had already hired four more clerks to help with the

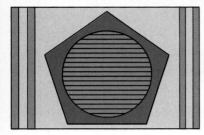

MICROCOMPUTERS

How To Become a Smart Shopper

Word-processing requirements in law offices typically originate with dictation. Documents often call for the inclusion of standard legal elements.

Which microcomputer should I buy? What do I need to buy to go with it? How do I choose software? What kind of printer do I need?

People buy microcomputers for many reasons. Some want to manage personal business accounts, some want to keep up with stock prices, some want to manage small business records, and on and on. For most, a microcomputer is a major purchase. Although computer hardware is continually decreasing in price, and may indeed be the least expensive component, other costs such as software, training, other computer devices, and supplies are financial considerations. And, as if it were not difficult enough just to decide when to buy a microcomputer, there are dozens of options available for most components.

So how do you decide what to buy?

There is a process for developing a system, regardless of the application. The process has four basic steps:

1. Define your requirements
2. Identify and evaluate your alternatives
3. Select the alternative that is best for you
4. Install, use, and evaluate the system.

To demonstrate this systematic process, consider a hypothetical case involving the initial purchase of a microcomputer system.

Searching for suitable microcomputer hardware and word-processing legal software requires first selecting several sample documents produced regularly by the law firm.

Typing legal transcripts and inserts is both tedious and error prone. Making an insert into a legal document means that the whole document has to be retyped from scratch.

As a basis for selecting a microcomputer, a series of requirements is established and listed. This list, in effect, becomes a shopping and selection guide.

STEP ONE: DEFINE YOUR REQUIREMENTS

A computer dealer should be able to understand and recommend workable solutions for business problems.

Chris Peterson is a legal assistant in a small law firm. She learned to use word processing, spreadsheet, and database microcomputer software at school. However, she now works in an office that prepares all documents manually with an electric typewriter.

In addition, Chris handles some of the firm's legal research. In visiting local libraries, she has learned about legal database systems that hold promise for her firm. She understands that, if she had a microcomputer workstation, she could use these same resources.

Lynn Allen, the attorney for whom Chris works, is aware that it is taking a considerable amount of overtime for the young and growing firm to keep up with the work volume. Lynn and Chris decided to attend a seminar on the use of microcomputers in a legal practice sponsored by the local bar association. They also shared articles about microcomputer applications from professional journals and business publications. After visiting several other law firms that were successfully using microcomputers, Lynn and Chris decided that their own office could benefit from a microcomputer system.

Chris and Lynn gave a lot of thought to their requirements for a microcomputer system. They listed the requirements needed for the present and foreseeable future:

Evaluate the computer store while waiting for help from a salesperson. The initial approach and questions by the salesperson can be important indicators of the quality of a store's service and expertise.

A. A WORD-PROCESSING REQUIREMENT

1. The system must be able to process and store documents up to 100 pages in length
2. Since legal documents often use standard forms and text passages, the system must be able to move sections of text from one file to another
3. The system should allow the user to create subject listings of contents for each document, and have the ability to search for specific listings throughout all documents.

B. A SPREADSHEET REQUIREMENT

1. There must be an ability to create numerical documents and to move them into the word-processing documents.

C. A MAILING-LIST REQUIREMENT

1. To meet the need for legal notifications, the system must have the capability for building and maintaining mailing lists, and for using those lists to generate multiple copies of letters and briefs to different people.

D. A HARDWARE REQUIREMENT

1. Because of the firm's extensive legal text library, the system should have a lot of memory
2. The system should be able to utilize online legal databases.

E. A PRINTING REQUIREMENT

1. The printer should produce attractive, readable, high-quality legal documents
2. The printer must be able to "feed" stationery, and to address envelopes.

F. A "BACK-UP" REQUIREMENT

1. The system should allow for the easy creation and storage of all documents produced on it.

G. A BUDGET REQUIREMENT

1. The total purchase price should be in the range of $7000 to $9000.

Software selection is the key element in the purchase of a microcomputer. The software will determine the features and capabilities required of the microcomputer itself.

In addition to listing their requirements, Lynn and Chris selected several sample documents of the type produced regularly by the firm. Chris agreed to visit several microcomputer stores to evaluate the software and hardware that would best meet their requirements. She also was to prepare sample documents and print them out on the system of her choice.

▥ STEP TWO: IDENTIFY AND EVALUATE ALTERNATIVES

Prepared with the requirements checklist, Chris faced the first challenge: Where to buy? After visiting four stores she realized that there are major variations in the types of hardware, software, service, and sales support available from store to store.

Chris decided to go back and ask several of the law firms visited earlier how they'd selected a store. After getting quite a few tips, she came up with a list of guidelines for narrowing down her options.

Choosing a Microcomputer Store

Here are some tips for choosing a store:

- Look for stores that attract business people; avoid stores that look as though they are havens for hobbyists or technical experts.
- Look for stores that carry a limited number of hardware brands. If a store carries a large number, be suspicious about their ability to install and service what they sell.
- Look for stores that are authorized to do warranty work. If you buy from an unauthorized dealer, you may not be eligible for equipment warranty coverage.
- Evaluate the sales staff carefully. Beware of salespeople who attempt to sell you equipment before asking about your specific needs. Also avoid those who make heavy use of computer jargon. A qualified salesperson will take the time to find the software and hardware that will best meet your needs.
- Find out the kinds of training available to you from the store. Also find out what kinds of support will be available for any software packages you purchase. Be sure that the store will meet your own needs.
- Ask the store for names of other customers for whom they have installed hardware and software.
- Ask for a formal proposal. Review it carefully to make sure that it covers all of your requirements and is within the established price range.

In shopping for a microcomputer, you should resist the temptation of rushing headlong into keyboarding and instead establish some realistic requirements first, such as your precise needs and some specifications for the computer.

▥ STEP 3: SELECT THE ALTERNATIVE THAT IS BEST FOR YOU

Chris visited a total of six computer stores, then chose the one she felt would give her the best help and support. She recalled how the salesperson at the one store listened to her requirements, and then asked her numerous questions about the business. How many briefs do you handle each week? How long are they? How many clients does each attorney have at a time? Which word processors did you work with in school? After about 45 minutes, the salesperson suggested that Chris prepare documents on two word-processing packages and one spreadsheet package available in the store.

All packages were useable on several brands of computer. Chris asked to try out the packages on a couple of them. The salesperson

Selecting a microcomputer should begin with a serious, detailed review of the work to be done and the conditions under which the system will be used.

An initial understanding of the work to be done will dictate the selection of application software packages to be reviewed and tested.

loaded the software, showed Chris how to run it, then left her to work on the sample documents. Chris experimented with the packages on both machines. She liked all of the packages, but one of the computers felt more comfortable. Chris picked up the literature on the hardware and the software, and went back to the office to share her findings with Lynn and the other attorneys. Chris learned that microcomputer software can fall into several categories.

Choosing Microcomputer Software

Here are some tips on choosing microcomputer software:

- Word-processing software should be considered by any user with a need to prepare typewritten materials. The ability to easily edit documents can result in significant productivity gains. Also consider the need to send multiple copies of the identical letter to different people — a mailing list capability.
- Spreadsheets should be selected by people who work with columns and rows of numbers. The spreadsheet should easily recalculate all affected totals when a single number is changed. Determine if you need to reproduce or compare numerical totals graphically.

- Database programs allow you to store, sort, and retrieve large amounts of data from many sources.
- Integrated software usually takes word-processing, spreadsheet, and database functions, and permits interchange between the different functions. Additional features of graphics and other communication between user and computer are common.
- Utility software takes care of the miscellaneous tasks that you may need. Included are easy recovery of files, productivity packages, and fancy printing.
- CAD (Computer-Aided Design) is the computer replacement for the draftsperson's table. Mechanical and architectural drawings can be created easily with this type of software.
- Communications software allows one microcomputer to share information with another. Communications may be through a local area network or over phone lines to any other computer.
- Graphics software continues to be an exciting part of computing. Graphics software exists that creates maps or builds business graphics. Desktop publishing combines the features of word processing with the graphics capabilities available to produce camera-ready page images.

To get you started reviewing application software packages, the salesperson will typically demonstrate the equipment and the features of the software.

The following week, Chris returned to the computer store. She selected the word-processing and spreadsheet packages. Then she told the salesperson she was now ready to talk about hardware. Reviewing Chris' requirements, the salesperson suggested several options. All of them, he said, would meet those requirements.

Several of the systems requirements were dictated by the software Chris had chosen. For instance, the word processor required 256K of memory and a 20 megabyte hard disk for data storage. Still other requirements were dictated by taste, such as Chris' preference for the amber monitor over the green one.

The salesperson encouraged Chris to pay special attention to the printers. There were so many to choose from, each one offering a unique combination of features and benefits.

Printers

Here are ways to tell the differences between one printer and another:

- The technology used to print characters:
  dot-matrix printers print dots in a pattern that looks like a letter
  impact printers strike a print element such as a Selectric ball against

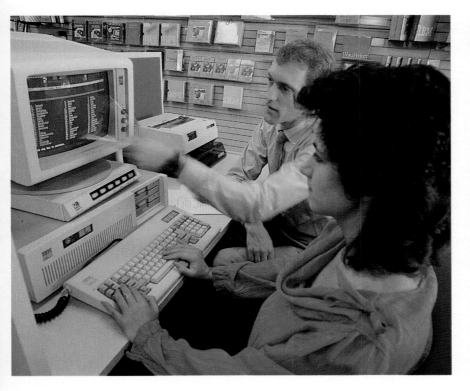

Hands-on practice is an important part of the process of evaluating your potential microcomputer system.

As part of the hands-on practice session, Lynn captures portions of test documents brought along for this purpose.

an inked ribbon and transfer the character to the paper laser printers use a photographic process somewhat similar to that used in photocopiers.

- The quality of output:
  letter quality
  near letter quality
  draft quality.
- The width of paper the printer will accept:
  eight-inch width for standard correspondence
  up to fourteen inches wide for financial reports.
- The method of "feeding" the paper: some printers have sprockets that feed paper continuously.
- The speed of the printer — which is stated in characters per second.
- The ability to print envelopes.

The salesperson made his recommendations to Chris, also listing a few alternatives. Interestingly, the total price was below $7000, which more than met the budget requirements. He specifically suggested the following:

- A word-processing program that included a calculating function for relatively simple arithmetic calculations, as well as mailing and indexing functions

Detailed attention to the features and capabilities of printers is an important part of system configuration.

As part of the system selection process, the system's requirements in the form of supplies — including diskettes, ribbons, and paper — are studied.

- A spreadsheet program that would let data be transferred to the word-processing program
- A microcomputer with 512K of memory, to allow for processing of the longer documents
- A 20-megabyte hard disk for the storage of many lengthy documents
- A letter-quality dot-matrix printer
- A communications program with a built-in modem for online research
- A service contract
- Software upgrades (new releases) for six months
- A supply of diskettes for backups for the disk.

   Chris and Lynn reviewed the proposal, and concluded that it met the requirements list initially developed for the system.
   Chris returned to the store, finalized the purchase, and began to prepare a place in the office for the system. New furniture was ordered, and new procedures for training and computer useage were developed. Procedures for taking good care of the new system were also discussed and developed.

Back at the office, preliminary decisions about system configuration and components are reviewed in detail. A final visit to and another demonstration at the computer store are also planned.

Microcomputer Care

Here are some tips for taking good care of a computer system:

- A computer system should be exposed to no more of a harsh environment than you are. The temperature should be between 64 and 80 degrees, and covers should be used to keep dust from the machine.
- Diskette heads should be cleaned regularly with proper equipment.
- Practice good habits of handling diskettes. Never touch the exposed part of the magnetic medium, as your fingers can leave traces of oil that cause data loss. Insert the diskette carefully into the computer — never force it. Never bend the diskette. Avoid magnetic fields such as those found around monitors or radios. Always replace the diskette in a protective jacket.
- Consider a protection device to give you uninterrupted power. A loss or a surge of power could damage your computer and cause a loss of data.
- Clean your computer case with mild soap and water. Clean the screen with a glass-cleaning substance.

An important step that precedes equipment installation is attendance at a class held in the computer store. Instruction should cover the specific hardware and software to be used.

▥ STEP FOUR: INSTALL THE SYSTEM

As soon as the equipment arrived, a store representative came to the office to assemble and test the system, go over the documentation manuals with Chris, and answer any questions. He also spent time going over the store's liberal service policy with her again, which impressed her a lot.

Six months later, Chris realized that the microcomputer system was loaded with work — unable to take on growing volumes. To increase capacity, it was obvious that the existing system would have to be expanded either through a new work station or through additions to the existing equipment. By this time, everyone in the office knew what to do: The staff met to discuss and specify the new requirements.

Thus, the cycle repeats itself. The systems development process reviewed in this insert is usable whenever information processing needs arise. For your further use, the process is described in greater depth in another chapter.

The microcomputer system is ready for installation.

A microcomputer can be put to productive use in a short time.

Your Insurance: Good Service

Computer service may be provided by several sources. A dealer may have someone on staff capable of running simple diagnostic routines and replacing malfunctioning parts. This person should also be able to deal with problems such as memory failures, diskette drive replacement, and power supply replacement.

How do you evaluate your dealer's service personnel? Ask about their previous training. Manufacturers often certify technicians for training on their product. Make sure your dealer has a spare parts kit on hand. At a minimum, your dealer should always have a stock of replacement parts.

The service you get often depends on whether you have a service contract. A service contract is a type of insurance policy on your computer equipment. Some contracts cover all parts and labor in the event of a failure. Others provide "loaner equipment." Still others provide on-site service or 24-hour phone service.

A second method of service is provided by large, nationwide service organizations. These organizations are usually based in major cities. Because they are typically large they are equipped with many repair people. Still, make sure that they are familiar with your particular equipment before signing an agreement.

A third and final source of equipment and repairs is the manufacturer itself. This source is rarely appropriate for complete systems, and tends to be more expensive.

QUESTIONS

1. What are the four steps in the system development process?
2. Does the list of requirements developed by Chris and Lynn seem adequate? What can you add to the list?
3. What measures can be used in evaluating microcomputer stores?
4. Can you think of other ways in which Chris could have researched the use of microcomputers in legal offices?
5. Was it important that Chris take sample documents along to the microcomputer store? How should Chris react if the store refuses to let her prepare the documents on demonstration hardware and software?
6. Why is it important to select proper software programs before hardware is investigated?
7. Develop your own list of procedures for staff training and daily use of the microcomputer system to be installed in the legal offices.

individual discount program, but the department manager felt that things had gotten out of control.

At the end of each quarter, every customer's discount rate had to be recalculated and written in his or her records. What had taken four or five days when the customer base was only 1,200 was now taking three weeks. Often during those three weeks, an outdated discount rate was being applied to sales. Customers complained that the discount rate should have been higher, and sales people complained that it should have been lower. The problem was that every customer's record had not yet been updated.

To place an order, the purchasing agent for a retail store sent a purchase order form like the one shown in figure 6–1. Each purchase order was differ-

FIGURE 6–1
Purchase order form from a customer of Elliot Bay Electronics

HORIZON ORDER FORM
TV and Electronics
P.O. Box A-8000 • Phoenix, AZ 85029 • Phone 1-800-362-4894

CITY _____ STATE _____ ZIP _____
(Is this an address change? ☐ Yes ☐ No)

QTY.	CATALOG NO.	SIZE	DESCRIPTION	PRICE

Shop by Mail or Telephone

Convenient. Order at your convenience. We are as near as your phone. No running from store to store.

Fast Service. Orders received by 3:00 pm are shipped the next work day.

Our Pledge of Quality. If any item you purchase from us proves to be unsatisfactory, please return it for a replacement or a full refund.

Sub-total _____
Tax _____
Shipping _____
Total _____

☐ Check Enclosed   ☐ COD   ☐ Mastercharge   ☐ Visa

_____   _____   _____
Credit Card Number   Expiration Date   Customer Signature

FORM 101 REV. 10-80

ent, but every one included the company's name, the billing address, ship-to-address, account number, and a list of the items the customer wanted to buy.

Most customers calculated the total amount of their purchase less the discount. When a purchase order arrived at EB Electronics, all calculations had to be double-checked. Order entry clerks had to look up the customer's credit limit and discount rate and the price of each item. Then the clerk computed the total cost of the order. Sometimes the customer's billing address changed, so the clerks updated this data on the customer's record while they were processing the order. If the order was correct, or at least nearly correct, it went to the warehouse, where the goods were picked from inventory. All the items in stock were shipped to the customer. Items that were out of stock were backordered by EB, and the customer's order went into the backorder file. When the backordered goods arrived, they were shipped to the customer (see figure 6–2). A list of items that had been shipped went back to accounting so the purchase could be posted to the customer's account.

As you might imagine, all sorts of errors and problems developed. Customers often made mistakes when ordering. Sometimes the customer account number was in error; sometimes the item numbers were wrong. Very often customers made errors in arith-

metic when they calculated their totals or used an incorrect discount rate. Some customers prepaid their orders, and the checks they sent were made out for the wrong amount. If the check amount was too high, the customer received a credit; if it was too low, the customer was billed for the difference.

EB's backorder file had grown so much that buyers did not know what quantities to order. They often ordered 100 units of an item only to discover that 150 units were already backordered and orders were still coming in. To prevent this situation from occurring, some buyers ordered very large quantities. Then warehouse space became a problem. The cost of carrying the large inventory reduced company profits. This gravely concerned EB's management.

To be fair, this manual system was designed when Elliot Bay had fewer than 1,500 customers and did about $500,000 in annual sales with 6000 products. It worked fine then, but it was no longer suitable. However, management had to spend so much time coping with the day-to-day problems that no time was taken to devise a new and better system.

In addition to these problems, EB was having trouble with its mailing list. EB had hired a company that provided computer services (called a **computer service bureau**) to produce the mailing labels for the quarterly catalog and monthly sales flyer. Once

FIGURE 6–2
Processing of an order at EB Electronics

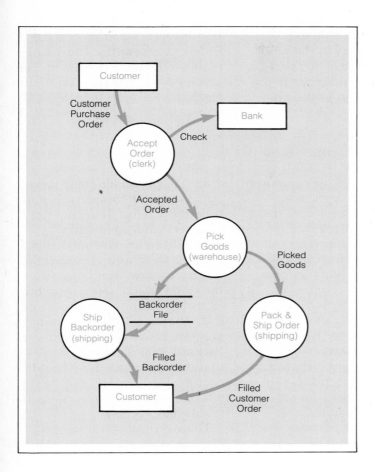

a week, EB sent data about new customers and address changes for existing customers to the computer service bureau. This data was supposed to be incorporated into the mailing list.

In 1985, 32 percent of EB's quarterly catalogs were returned. Nearly one-third of the addresses were incorrect. Elliot Bay was spending a small fortune on full-color catalogs that never got to their proper destinations. EB had repeatedly discussed this problem with the service bureau in previous years. The bureau was either unwilling or unable to improve the accuracy of the output.

In early 1986, EB's board of directors decided to investigate the possibility of the company's acquiring its own computer. The board members hoped to use the computer to relieve the accounting clerks of some of their problems posting sales and calculating individual discounts.

They hoped to be able to improve the accuracy of the mailing list. They also hoped that the computer could be used to find better ways of controlling inventory and processing orders. A committee consisting of an accountant, a buyer, and an inventory supervisor was formed.

The Computer Committee

The first meeting of the computer committee occurred in early April, 1986. Within a few minutes, the members realized that none of them knew anything about computers, nor did they know anyone at Elliot Bay who did. Consequently, the committee decided that the first order of business was to hire someone with computer expertise. They placed the ad shown in figure 6–3 in two local newspapers. One of the committee members said, "Let's place it under *P* for *programmer*," so they did.

They had four applicants. The first two were unsuitable. One wanted part-time work, and the other was inexperienced. The third had been a programmer for several years. He talked very impressively about the job he had done building an "online bill of materials processor" for a large manufacturing company. Unfortunately, none of the committee members knew what that was. (You will, before you finish this course.) They weren't especially impressed, however, because they didn't want to do any manufacturing. This programmer told them that he had experienced great success with a Hewlett-Packard 3000® computer and that that was what they should acquire. With the HP 3000, he would be able to develop the programs they needed.

The fourth person, John Abrams, did not actually apply for the job. He was an independent, freelance consultant. He wanted to sell them his services to develop the data processing department and systems. John had an impressive record of

FIGURE 6–3
Ad for a programmer placed by EB Electronics

WANTED

A programmer to select a computer and write programs for a mail order retail company. Salary negotiable depending on experience. Send resume to P.O. Box Z, care of this newspaper. An equal opportunity employer.

accomplishments in a variety of businesses, but the committee wasn't looking for a consultant. They nearly decided not to invite him for an interview. However, since they had had only three other respondents, they decided to invite him.

The interview with John Abrams went as follows:

Committee Chairperson: "John, we're not actually looking for a consultant. As I said on the phone, we've talked with a good many applicants. We think we've found two or three possibilities. However, since you're so interested, we decided to spend an hour with you. What can you do for us?"

(John didn't believe a word of this. He could tell from their ad that they didn't know much about business computer systems. He also knew that programmers were in short supply. He doubted that they had had six applicants, if that many. He judged these opening comments to be the bravado of someone who didn't know what he was doing but was coping as best he could.)

John: "Look, let me come right to the point. It's obvious that you have a good business. The outlook for your company is very bright. You committee members are probably very good at your business specialties. But it's equally obvious that you don't know very much about data processing."

"You ran an ad for a programmer to select a computer and develop programs for your business. First of all, programmers don't usually select computers. Someone called a data processing manager does that, with the assistance of people called systems analysts. So what you really want is a data processing manager and possibly other data processing personnel.

"Second, you say you want to develop programs. What you really want to do is develop something called a business computer system. Programs are only one of five components of such a system. The other components are hardware, data, procedures, and trained people. Are you going to have a programmer develop those?

"Finally, how do you know you want a computer? Have you done a feasibility study to see if a computer can solve your problems? Do you know how much a computer costs? Do you know how big a computer you want? Do you know how long it will take you to develop the business computer system?"

Chairperson: "Well, John, it's true we aren't experts at data processing. You may have a valid point or two. We were thinking that a Hewlett-Packard 3000 computer might be what we need."

John: "The HP 3000 is a good machine. However, there is a great deal of computer hardware to choose from. It's difficult to make a good choice until you know specifically what you want the computer to do. There might

PROFILE

ARE STRUCTURED METHODS FOR SYSTEMS ANALYSIS AND DESIGN BEING USED?

The roots of the structured methodologies can be traced to the 1960s when tools were needed to design increasingly complex systems. Systems developed in the 1960s were often late, over budget, expensive in resources used, and poorly suited to users' requirements. Unsuccessful projects were usually impossible to salvage. Each new system was designed from scratch, without the benefits of prior efforts. Early efforts to solve these problems led to the introduction of structured design methodologies in the 1970s. Structured analysis tools and techniques were then introduced to develop better requirements for good design.

The goal of the structured methods was to provide an orderly and manageable process for developing systems that met user requirements. By enabling designers to manage complexity and by introducing the concepts of decomposition, modularity, and structured program logic, the structured tools made it easier to modify systems in repsonse to changing user requirements.

Two general types of structured methodologies led to designs based on data flows and data structures respectively. The data flow techniques, developed by Yourdon and DeMarco, describe processes and information flows which, in turn, are used to develop a hierarchical design. The data structure techniques, developed by Warnier-Orr and Jackson, are based on the idea that a model of data structure is essential for good system design. The Warnier-Orr

methodology starts with the analysis of hierarchical data structure and then determines a program structure that parallels the data structure.

Structured design, a technique developed by Yourdon and Constantine, provides a methodology for transforming data flow diagrams into program structures. Major emphasis is given to the design of modular system structures, with each module carrying out a single, well-defined function. While the emphasis on modularization is valuable for breaking down a system into subsystems and establishing interfaces, structured design provides little help with detailed design specifications.

In practice, systems designers have used specific tools from the structured methodologies during various phases of the systems development life cycle. The designer must choose which tools are best suited to a particular design environment and modify them as needed to meet the needs of a specific project.

A study of systems development practices in 1984 examined the characteristics of 73 projects, as well as practices for determining requirements. The projects they studied averaged 10.5 months in duration, cost an average of $103,000, and required fewer than 1,000 staff days. Fifty-four percent of these systems were new projects, and 33 percent entailed the re-design of existing systems. The majority were written in COBOL.

Of the sixty-three systems development methodologies in use reported

by project leaders, 26 were purchased from consulting firms or software vendors and 37 were developed in-house. Most of the projects were initiated by formal request (58.3 percent) or by feasibility study report (15.3 percent). During the initial analysis effort, the primary technique used was both individual and group interviewing (48 percent), but one-fourth of the respondents began their analysis by developing a paper model or a prototype (26 percent). In about three-fourths of the projects, requirements analysis had to be repeated because additional requirements were discovered or users changed their minds.

Another study of the effectiveness of methodologies and tools used in software-development projects at Bell Laboratories found that the software projects being worked on were real-time applications (43.8 percent) and business applications (23.5 percent). The results of the study showed that the major obstacles to software development were inadequate and changing user requirements, and that tools and methodologies being used in software development were perceived as being effective. Structured methodologies (Yourdon, Jackson, top down, pseudocode) used primarily in the design phase were considered effective, but many respondents had reservations as to their degree of effectiveness. Unnamed, unspecified, "up to the individual" methodologies were considered losers and actual impediments to effective design.

A study in 1985 found that although

most of the respondents acknowledged the benefits of using structured tools in requirements analysis and design, these tools were not being widely used in actual systems development projects, largely because of their lack of acceptance by data processing professionals, and the fact that they were perceived as time-consuming to use.

Most of the projects described by respondents were initiated by formal systems request. The most frequently used methods in requirements analysis were interviewing, traditional systems flowcharts, and data dictionary. In detailed design, the most frequently used tools were pseudocode and traditional program flowcharts.

be better computers for you.

"Finding programs may well turn out to be more important than finding the hardware. Do you know if there are suitable programs that you can buy off the shelf? Can you tailor existing programs to your needs? Or do you have to develop your own programs from scratch?"

This conversation continued for an hour or so. Finally, John brought it to a close with this statement:

John: "Let me summarize my position. I'll help you decide if a computer system is for you. If it is, I'll lead you through the process of acquiring the staff and equipment. I'll help you develop the business computer system you need. It will likely take a year or more to get this done. My bill for this service will depend on the amount of time it takes me. The more you do, the less my services will cost. Based on my past experience, I'd say it will probably cost between $10,000 and $25,000.

"If we come to an agreement, I will agree to structure it so that you can terminate my services during the management review at the end of any stage of work in case you're dissatisfied. Before we sign anything, why don't I give you a two-day course on how to develop a business computer system? I'll charge you $1000, which is less than my usual fee, for two days of instruction. You can listen to me and hear my philosophy before you make any larger commitment."

After John left, the committee discussed his proposal for some time. They liked what he said. He seemed to know what he was doing, but $20,000 seemed a lot to pay for nothing more than advice. Finally, they decided to hire John to teach the two-day course. They would think about what to do after that.

"Well," said the accountant with a chuckle, "we could always run an ad under *D* for *Data Processing Manager*, or maybe under *M* for *Manager, Data Processing*."

SYSTEMS DEVELOPMENT AT EB ELECTRONICS

The next week, John Abrams presented the two-day seminar at EB. In addition to the computer committee, all the vice-presidents and department managers were invited.

The course had two parts. In the first part, the components of a business computer system were summarized. This discussion was very similar to the material presented in chapters 2 and 3 of this book. In the second part of the course, the process of developing a business computer system was considered. This part of the course was similar to chapter 5.

At the conclusion of the course, John suggested that, if EB did proceed with a systems development project, a steering committee should be formed. This committee would be composed of senior-level managers who would set the general strategy for computer systems development and use and who would approve work at the end of each stage of the systems project. John suggested that EB form this committee if the results of the feasibility study were positive.

At the end of the two-day course, the project committee felt that they had a much better idea of what developing computer systems involved. Because of their new knowledge, however, they also felt more vulnerable.

The committee considered their options. They were convinced that they needed some outside expertise to help them. They didn't know whether to hire a data processing manager, hire John as a consultant, or hire another consultant. They wanted to hire a data processing manager, but they didn't know what kind of person to look for. If they hired the wrong person, discovering this and then correcting their error might take a long time. Considerable money might be wasted.

They finally decided to hire John, but they hedged. They hired him just to help them with the first step, determining requirements. After that, they would decide whether or not to hire him for more assistance. John agreed to these terms, and the next week the requirements stage began.

The EB Requirements Stage

The first task was to form a project team. John suggested that the team be composed of the computer committee (accountant, buyer, and inventory supervisor) and himself. The board of directors approved this suggestion, and the three people were released from their normal duties to participate in the computer project.

Neither John nor the EB personnel knew whether off-the-shelf programs were available to solve EB's problems. They decided to examine requirements down to a level of detail that would enable them to determine whether suitable off-the-shelf programs were available. If they were not available, then portions of the requirements study would need to be repeated to gain additional details.

For five days, John and the computer committee visited EB personnel in the departments that seemed to be having the greatest problems. The committee wanted to gain an understanding of these problems and define them. They also wanted to gain a general sense of where computer systems might be useful. Using the facts they learned during the interviews and their own understanding of pieces of EB's business system, the team constructed a preliminary data-flow diagram (see figure 6–4). They also drafted a skeletal set of process specifications:

1. Maintain customer file
   Adds new customers to file
   Changes customer's name, address, phone number

2. Write mailing labels
   Marketing has not yet decided what it wants. This process might print adhesive labels to stick to catalogs. It might write a diskette or tape file of labels that a catalog printing company will use to print labels onto catalog covers before binding.

3. Compute discount
   Calculates discount for each customer, records discount amount on each customer's record, issues discount notice to customer

4. Post customer purchase
   Rejects indecipherable purchase orders
   Prices order

Sends order to customer service if no customer account is found
Reduces inventory record by quantity purchased
Posts backorders to backorders file; increases backordered amount on inventory record
Posts amount and date of purchase to customer's record
Issues picking slip to warehouse

5. Maintain inventory file
   Adds new item to inventory
   Deletes obsolete inventory items
   Changes inventory item details such as vendor, price, buyer

6. Issue inventory list
   Produces inventory report

7. Receive goods
   Posts to inventory file goods received from vendors

8. Issue backorder report
   Produces report of backordered items for buyers

9. Issue backordered item
   Produces picking slip for backorder that can now be filled

10. Accept returns
    Backs purchase of returned item(s) out of customer record
    Increases quantity on hand on inventory record
    Issues credit to customer

11. Issue invoice
    Issues invoice to every customer

FIGURE 6–4
Preliminary dataflow diagram for EB
Electronics

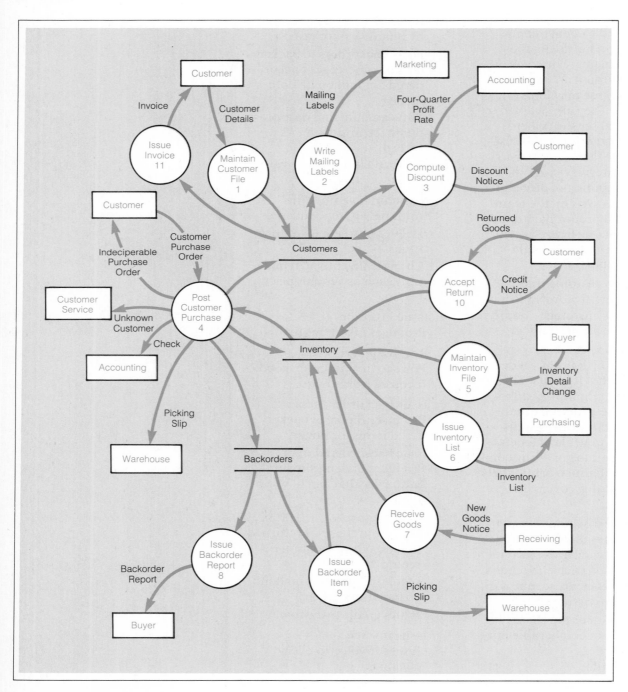

In addition, they began drafting a data dictionary:

backorder = customer account number + item number + customer name + customer address + quantity backordered + date backordered

customer = customer number + name + address + telephone number + date of last order + current discount + four quarterly purchase totals

inventory item = item number + description + size + buyer + vendor + vendor price + quantity on hand + customer price + warehouse bin location + number on backorder

picking line = quantity + item number + description + size + bin location + backordered indicator

picking slip = shipping label + order number + date + picking lines

They knew that their system would need lots of data, and building the data dictionary early in the project gave them a feeling for the size of the task ahead. As you study the three documents, try to get a general understanding of EB's business.

At the end of the preliminary study all of the team members felt more attuned to the company's problems rather than only the ones affecting themselves. Having a "big picture" made the team more eager to develop a computer system that would benefit everyone. They added to their preliminary dataflow diagram, data dictionary, and process specifications a narrative summarizing EB's problems as they saw them. Their report had seven points:

First, there was a need to keep an accurate file of customer names, addresses, and four-quarter purchases. This file was needed for monthly billing, for the catalog and other mailings, and for discount computation. This file needed to be updated accurately whenever a customer moved or a new customer ordered. The committee learned that the service bureau had not been able to keep an accurate file because their own staff made too many keying errors when entering changes.

Accurate customer numbers were crucial. If a customer misstated his or her number on an order, or if it was incorrectly keyed, sales would be posted to the wrong customer. A more accurate way to enter customers' numbers had to be found.

Second, all of the problems regarding quarterly purchase totals and discount computation related to inaccuracies in the customer file. If this file were accurate, computing discounts at the end of each quarter would be simple.

Third, purchasing and inventory personnel needed a list of items in inventory. This list should show item name, item number, name of the buyer responsible for purchasing the item, name of the vendor who supplied the item, and other data. Such a list was necessary because EB was adding about 100 items and deleting about 10 items a month. Several typewritten lists of items existed. Unfortunately, they often disagreed with one another. Consequently, orders were being taken for items no longer carried in stock, and the purchasing department was buying items no longer listed in the catalog.

Fourth, the most time-consuming part of processing an order was verifying prices and checking the computation of the amount due. Orders could be processed much faster if a computer system computed the amount due. Order processing personnel wanted to give the computer the customer number, the item number, and the quantity for each item on the order, and then have the computer calculate the amount due.

Fifth, the manual records of the items in inventory were a mess. At the last physical check of inventory, nearly 70 percent of the counts were in error. Shipments had arrived but had never been entered in the inventory records. Goods had been shipped and billed but were never taken out of the records. A computer system to keep track of inventory would be very helpful. John remarked, however, that a computer system would be useless unless the inventory management procedures in the warehouse were improved.

Sixth, orders were currently being filled in a chaotic manner.

A picker took the customer's copy of the order and walked through the warehouses filling a basket with the items ordered. Whenever the picker couldn't find an item, it was marked for backorder. Sometimes this was an error. The goods were actually in the inventory, but the picker didn't know where to find them. In this case, the item was backordered even though it was available.

Much of this chaos could be eliminated if a computer system processed the orders and generated picking slips. The system could keep an inventory file and determine whether or not each item was available. If an item was available, the computer could print its bin location on the picking slip. If an item was not available, it would be marked "backordered" on the picking slip. The picker then would not waste time looking for it. The computer could also generate backorder recommendations for buyers and reduce the number of unnecessary backorders.

Seventh, the computer could probably be used for other business functions, such as payroll, accounts payable, and general ledger accounting. However, there were currently no major problems in those areas. Such applications could easily be deferred until the immediate problems were solved.

Feasibility Study

After the problems were defined and documented, the computer committee and John considered the feasibility of developing business computer systems to solve any or all of these problems. John stated that, from a technical standpoint, all of the problems could be solved by computer. He knew of several companies that were using computer systems to perform similar functions. Consequently, the technical feasibility was considered certain.

From cost and schedule standpoints, however, feasibility was not so easy to determine. The costs and dates for developing systems depended on how many of the problems were to be solved. After considerable discussion, the committee decided to rank the requirements. They tentatively broke development into three phases, as shown in figure 6 – 5.

During phase 1, the customer master file and discount systems would be developed. During phase 2, the inventory and pricing systems would be developed. The purposes of the inventory system would be to keep a master list of the items in inventory

and to maintain a count of the items in stock, on backorder, and so forth. The pricing system, given the item numbers and quantities, would then calculate the total amount due for each order. Phase 1 had to be completed prior to phase 2 because the pricing system needed accurate customer numbers and discounts for preparing invoices.

A prepicking order processing system would be developed during phase 3. The system would accept the customer number, the item number, and the quantity of each item ordered. From these inputs, it would produce a picking slip, show items on backorder, and generate order recommendations for buyers. Phase 3 could be completed only after phases 1 and 2 were finished.

The cost and schedule of the phases depended very much on whether suitable programs could be found off the shelf, whether programs would need to be altered, or whether programs would be custom developed. John suggested that the team be

PHASE	SYSTEMS TO BE DEVELOPED

1	Customer Master File System including:
	    Master file maintenance
	    Purchase updates
	    Discounts
	    Mailing labels

2	Inventory Master File System Inventory Accounting System Order Pricing System

3	Prepicking Order Processing System including:
	    Picking slip generation
	    Backorder management
	    Order recommendations

FIGURE 6 – 5
Three phases for EB's systems development

PHASE	INITIAL EXPENSE	ANNUAL OPERATING EXPENSE
1	$100,000	$200,000
2	$275,000	$400,000
3	$600,000	$650,000

Assumptions:
1. Computer hardware is leased.
2. Growth in customers and sales is 10 percent per year.

conservative when planning. "Let's assume," he said, "that all programs must be custom developed. If the project is feasible for this worst case, it will be feasible if we find programs to use or adapt."

Figure 6–6 shows cost estimates developed by the project team, assuming custom programming. The initial expense category includes the costs of hardware installation, program development, data conversion, procedure development, and training. It does not include the cost of hardware. Since the team assumed that the hardware would be leased, the cost of leasing was included as an operating expense.

Operating expenses shown in the figure include the costs of the leased hardware, program and data maintenance, operating personnel salaries, training, and an allocation for overhead (a share of the expenses for lights, heating, buildings, taxes, and so forth). John explained that, if EB decided to buy computer hardware, the initial expenses would increase, but the operating expenses would decrease.

As the team examined the costs, it became apparent that phase 1 by itself would not be cost justified. The cost was too great for the service; finding another service bureau would be a better solution. However, it appeared that both phases 2 and 3 would be cost justified if they were implemented in addition to phase 1.

Considering schedule, John said that EB could not realistically hope to accomplish all three phases in the immediate future. Far too many tasks needed to be accomplished. Data processing personnel needed to be hired, the equipment needed to be selected and installed, and the other components of the systems needed to be developed. John predicted a disaster if all of the problems were addressed at the onset.

After two days of thinking and discussing, the committee estimated that phase 1 would take about one year, phase 2 would take about 14 months, and phase 3 would take about two years. This estimate of phase 3 assumed that inventory personnel would make changes to their procedures on schedule. Thus, if EB started the project in May 1986, the earliest that all three phases could be finished would be July 1990 (see figure 6–7).

Management Approval

To summarize, the computer committee found that all three phases were feasible from a *technical* standpoint. However, phase 1 by itself could not be cost justified. Phase 1 followed by phase 2, or phase 1 followed by phases 2 and 3, could be cost justified. Finally, the phases were *schedule* feasible if EB could wait one year for phase 1, slightly over two years for phase 2, and about four years for phase 3.

The findings, phases, and results of the feasibility study were documented in a 15-page report. The report was sent to the board of directors, the president, and the vice-presidents. The board requested a meeting of top management and the project team. Basically, the board was pleased with the quality of the analysis and the work that had been done. They were disappointed that four years would be required for the company to have complete capability, but they observed that they had no choice. As one director said, "We have to proceed; let's just hope that not all of the programs must be developed from scratch."

Some managers tried to get the computer committee to reduce the estimates of time required for custom programming. However, John had forewarned the committee about such attempts, and they adamantly refused to give in. As John had said, "Nine women can't make a baby in one month, no matter how badly someone wants them to."

In the report to management, the computer committee had recommended formation of a steering committee. The board of directors thought this was an excellent idea. They suggested that the president and all the vice-presidents be involved initially. They also recommended that John Abrams be retained for the next phase of work and that the project team continue with its present members. With this preliminary work accomplished, the president instructed the team to proceed with development for phases 1 and 2. Phase 3 would be deferred until these phases were completed. The project team was instructed to report to the steering committee at the conclusion of the evaluation stage.

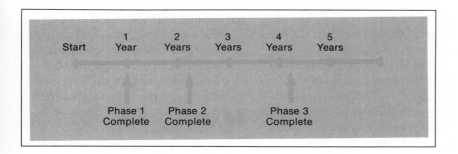

FIGURE 6–7
Timing of EB's systems development phases

PROFILE

INTECH

InTech is a pioneer in the development and introduction of integrated software for the professional systems analyst. The company is committed to providing automated design tools that utilize innovative technology, and to supporting its customers who use a variety of structured analysis and design techniques.

Intech was formed by systems development professionals to provide new and more highly integrated tools to assist in the design, documentation, and generation of information systems.

Excelerator, InTech's first product, has been received enthusiastically by systems analysts, data-processing managers, and computer educators. The installed base of users has grown rapidly since the shipment of release 1.0 in August 1984, and InTech, headquartered in Cambridge, Massachusetts, has grown to support its customers at numerous corporations, universities, and government agencies.

Detailed Requirements

According to figure 5–3, after the problem is defined, the next task is to determine specific requirements. If custom programs must be developed, the requirements statements need to be very detailed. In spite of their earlier assumption, however, the team hoped that suitable off-the-shelf or altered programs could be found. The team did not want to perform a detailed requirements study unless it had to. Consequently, at this point the team changed course to assume that off-the-shelf or altered programs could be found.

Specifically, the team decided to determine the functions and features that EB would need for both customer and inventory systems. They would not attempt to determine details such as screen formats, report layouts, and the like. John reminded the team, however, that if suitable programs could not be found off the shelf, then this work would need to be done later.

A list of the functions and features required for the customer master file and discount systems is shown on page 189. These statements describe the general nature of the work to be done, but they do not provide the details that would be necessary to make alterations or develop custom programs.

The general requirements are that the customer master file must be maintained, allowing for additions, deletions, and changes to certain fields. Adequate editing and controls must also be provided to ensure that all transactions are posted to the correct accounts.

Here is a list of specific requirements:

1. Add new customers daily; allow for corrections

2. Modify name, billing address, phone number; allow for corrections

3. Post amount of order to customer's quarterly purchases

4. Back out amount of return from customer's quarterly purchases

5. Compute customer's discount; record discount on customer's record; issue discount notice; issue summary report

John derived from the original dataflow diagram (figure 6–4) a smaller one, this time encompassing only the part of the business pertaining to the customer master file and dividends (figure 6–8). The team had carefully

FIGURE 6–8
Reduced DFD of customer and discount systems

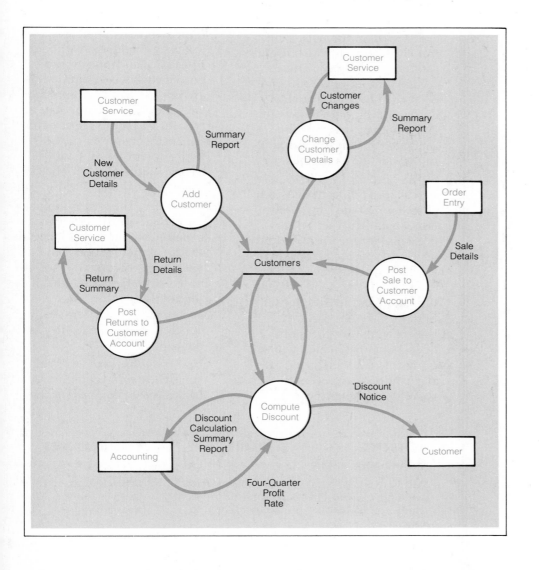

defined the scope of its study; John now led the team through an investigation of user requirements as they pertained to the customer master file (figure 6–9). The customer master file currently contains records for about 6,500 customers, and it is growing at the rate of about 1,000 customers per year. Each customer is assigned a unique customer account number. Here are the team's findings:

1. *Currency of the data*. The customer master file must be current within one day. This means that new customer records must be added at least daily, and changes to existing customer records must be made daily. Purchases and returns must be posted at least daily.

2. *Access speed*. Because customer updates do not have to be done instantly, there is no pressing need to ensure rapid access to specific records, at least not during phase 1. The customer service department indicates that its staff will better serve the customer if they can answer questions over the phone, which will require faster access speed in the future. Also, access to specific customer records

seems likely to be a requirement of phase 2, order pricing. Looking ahead, although access speed to the customer master file is not yet a requirement, it should be anticipated for future phases.

3. *File activity*. In one business day less than 2 percent of the records in the customer file are referenced (for purchases, returns, record changes, and the addition of new accounts). Approximately 20 new customers are added, and about 1300 sales and returns are posted each week. Catalogs are published each quarter, and sales flyers go out once a month, and these require that the entire customer file be read to print mailing labels. On the whole, though, the file is not very active.

4. *Flexibility*. The customer master file will be used for simple accounting functions. None of the team members nor the users they interviewed anticipate using the data in this file for anything other than accounting. Thus, the team concluded that flexibility is not a priority.

5. *User friendliness*. At this early stage the degree of user-friendliness required for this

FIGURE 6–9
Other characteristics of the EB customer master file system

CAPACITY	CURRENCY	ACCESS SPEED	FLEXIBILITY	USER-FRIENDLINESS
6,500 records; add 1,000 per year	Within one day	Must have quick access to specific customer record (phase 2 requirement)	Will remain stable; used only for accounting applications	Depends on whether batch or online applications are selected

system cannot be determined. It depends on who will actually be interfacing with the system. If order entry clerks will be entering data online, then user friendliness will be extremely important. On the other hand, if professional data entry operators enter data via key-to-disk equipment, then there will be fewer noncomputer users to whom the system must be friendly. The team will defer establishing a requirement on this subject until alternative systems are addressed during stage 2.

John and the project team repeated the preceding steps — drawing a small dataflow diagram for the scope of one phase and then identifying special system characteristics — for each of the remaining phases.

When the system requirements were developed and documented, the team met with EB management and key users. Management wanted the users to attend this meeting to reduce the likelihood that a key function or feature would be omitted. The general conclusion of the meeting was that the requirements were fundamentally complete and that the team should proceed to identify and evaluate alternatives. Management understood that requirements would have to be determined in greater detail if programs needed to be altered or custom developed.

QUESTIONS

6.1 Summarize why Elliot Bay Electronics decided that the company needed a business computer system.

6.2 What should EB's ad have said for the company to find the help it actually needed?

6.3 What is the role of the steering committee?

6.4 Why did the team assume that custom programs would be needed when preparing the cost and schedule estimates?

6.5 When the project team determined the detailed requirements, they assumed that off-the-shelf programs could be found, yet when they were preparing cost and schedule estimates, they assumed that custom programs would be needed. Why did they make this switch?

The EB Evaluation Stage

Reminding the team of the five components in a business computer system, John recommended that they begin their investigation with programs. Hardware is easier to find, he pointed out, but what good would it do to have the hardware selected, if the necessary programs would not run on that equipment? Therefore, the team began to look for programs for both customer and inventory systems.

Programs

The project team members began by calling companies that had similar needs. They called other distributors, as well as wholesalers with similar inventories. In addition, John brought in several catalogs of programs for the team to study. See reference [32].

One of the team members talked with EB's president, who suggested that they call several companies belonging to their trade organization. These companies provided other leads. Finally, John contacted two hardware vendors and asked their sales representatives for assistance. The hardware salespeople were willing to cooperate because they knew that there would eventually be a hardware sale.

The team found that there were several programs available for keeping customer data. John reminded them that merely performing the functions listed earlier was not enough. Any programming package they considered must also adhere to the system constraints listed in figure 6–9.

Using that list as a guideline, the team promptly rejected 80 percent of the packages. Some could not accommodate enough data; some allowed only batch updates to sequential files (you'll learn about this in chapter 7); some were far more sophisticated (and expensive) than EB needed.

One element was the same for all of the packages, though. None of them could calculate individual customer discounts at the end of each quarter. Consequently, the team predicted that EB would purchase a package with a pretty close fit and then have it altered to meet the company's special needs.

Having studied all of the candidate programs carefully, the project team concluded that only one program package would allow for the growth in the number of customers that EB expected. That program was called CUSTOMER.

The team was relieved to find many more choices available for inventory processing. Two of them would provide all the capability that EB currently needed and, with some alteration, might even be able to support the phase 3 requirements. These two programs were called ORD-INVENTORY and STOCK-PILE.

Hardware

The CUSTOMER program would run only on hardware supplied by vendor X. This vendor had a large number of computer systems, which were arranged in families. For example, one **family of computers** was the System 25, with models I, II, and III. John explained that converting from one computer to another in the same family usually is not difficult. Since EB planned to expand its data processing activity during phase 3 and beyond, John recommended that they pick a computer that met their current needs and that was at the low end of a family. Then, as their needs expanded, they could switch to the model II or III. If they picked the top model of a less powerful family, they would have to switch to another family or even to another vendor's computer as their needs expanded. This approach would likely be time consuming and expensive.

The ORD-INVENTORY program would run on hardware available from either vendor X or vendor Y. Vendor Y had only one family of computers, but it appeared that EB's needs could be met by one of the computers at the low end of the family. Thus, computer equipment from either vendor X or Y seemed feasible.

The alternative inventory program, STOCKPILE, would operate only on hardware from vendor Y. No version of STOCKPILE existed for vendor X hardware. The vendor said that a version could be developed for vendor X computers, but this would require an additional cost. John recommended that the team not consider this possibility as a realistic alternative. "Let's not be their guinea pig," he said. Figure 6–10 summarizes the program and hardware alternatives.

Data and Procedures

As the project team discussed the data and procedures for the new systems, they discovered that data and procedures were nearly the same for all of the hardware and program alternatives. Data requirements did not change from one computer to another. Consequently, they decided not to include data and procedures as part of the alternatives to be presented to management. They would be designed and developed later.

Personnel

The last of the five components of a business computer system is trained people. The team decided that three groups of personnel would be necessary: systems development personnel, operations personnel, and data entry personnel.

Two alternatives were possible for the systems development personnel. Either they could be permanent, or the systems development expertise could be obtained by using temporary or contract

SYSTEM	PROGRAM	HARDWARE
Customer	CUSTOMER plus alteration	Vendor X
Inventory	ORD-INVENTORY	Vendor X or Y
Inventory	STOCKPILE	Vendor Y

FIGURE 6–10
EB's alternative programs and hardware

personnel. EB could hire temporary help directly, or it could contract for development with an independent company (sometimes called a **software house**).

In addition to systems developers, data entry personnel needed to be hired, and both they and the users needed to be trained. (Data entry personnel would do the bulk data entry; users would do some, less voluminous data entry and would also process orders and make queries of the data.) The team thought that

four data entry employees would be required for both systems. Eight to 10 users in customer service, order processing, the warehouse, and shipping would need to be trained.

Finally, operators would be required to run the new computer. The team decided that, initially, EB would need only eight hours per day of operation. John recommended that two operators be hired. A third, backup operator could be obtained by training one of the data entry clerks to run the computer.

FIGURE 6–11
Two alternative organizations proposed for EB

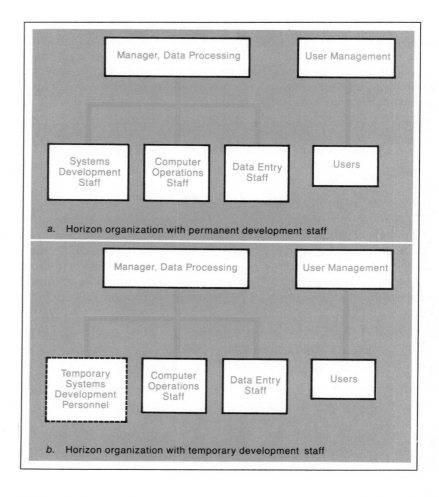

a. Horizon organization with permanent development staff

b. Horizon organization with temporary development staff

	PROGRAMS	HARDWARE	ORGANIZATION
1	CUSTOMER (with alteration) ORD-INVENTORY	Vendor X	*a* or *b*
2	Custom Customer ORD-INVENTORY	Vendor Y	*a* or *b*
3	Custom Customer STOCKPILE	Vendor Y	*a* or *b*
4	Custom Customer Custom Inventory	Vendor X or Y	*a* only

FIGURE 6−12
EB alternatives

EB's Organizational Alternatives

The team proposed two alternative organizations, as shown in figure 6 – 11. In the organizational structure shown in figure 6 – 11a, the data processing manager supervises three groups: systems development, computer operations, and data entry. The systems development staff would be permanent EB employees. In the second alternative (figure 6 – 11b), only the operations and data entry groups have permanent employees. The second organizational alternative assumes that systems development personnel are hired on a temporary or contract basis.

The Complete Alternatives

Considering these facts together with the organizational charts shown in figure 6 – 11, the project team developed four basic alternatives, listed in figure 6 – 12.

Alternative 1 assumes that EB buys CUSTOMER and ORD-INVENTORY program products. CUSTOMER would need to be altered to include the capability to produce discount rates. Hardware would be purchased from vendor X, and either of the organizations shown in figure 6 – 11 could be used.

Alternative 2 assumes that ORD-INVENTORY is purchased and that hardware from vendor Y is acquired. Since CUSTOMER does not operate on vendor Y hardware, EB would need to develop its own programs for customer processing. Alternative 3 is the same as alternative 2, except STOCKPILE is purchased instead of ORD-INVENTORY. Both of these alternatives could use either of the organizational structures in figure 6 – 11.

Alternative 4 assumes that EB custom develops programs for both the customer and inventory applications. Hardware could be acquired from either vendor, but only the organizational structure in figure 6–11a would be feasible. The team believed that, with so much custom programming, permanent staff would be necessary.

This discussion of alternatives has abbreviated some actions that would need to be taken. Realistically, more details would be addressed. Figure 6–13 lists some of the other factors that the EB project team considered.

Evaluation of Alternatives

The EB project team decided to perform an informal cost/benefit analysis. They decided to develop estimates of costs for each of the alternatives and then to compare those costs to benefits. The accounting department had already developed estimates of the amount of money being wasted because of ineffective inventory control (duplicate items, sales lost due to out-of-stock conditions, wasted labor hours, and so forth). These estimates could be used as a rough guide for the value of the new system. In addi-

FIGURE 6–13
Considerations when developing systems alternatives

SYSTEM COMPONENT	ISSUES CONSIDERED
Hardware	Type of CPU Amount of main memory Type and amount of tape, direct access, and other storage equipment Type and number of terminals Type and number of data entry devices
Programs	Number and type needed Off-the-shelf, alteration, or custom Language choice Expandability
Data	Number of files and rough format Type of data organization Data input media Report formats

Procedures	Users
	    Input activities
	    Use of outputs
	    Data editing and control responsibilities
	
	Operations
	    How to use equipment
	    How to operate systems
	    Backup and recovery
	    Control responsibilities

FIGURE 6–14
Summary of costs for EB alternatives

ALTERNATIVE	DEVELOPMENT COSTS		ANNUAL OPERATIONAL COSTS
1	ORD-INVENTORY	$ 30,000	
	CUSTOMER	30,000	
	Alterations	10,000	
	Computer X	120,000	
	Total	$190,000	$490,000
2	ORD-INVENTORY	$ 30,000	
	Custom Customer	50,000	
	Computer Y	100,000	
	Total	$180,000	$490,000
3	STOCKPILE	$ 25,000	
	Custom Customer	50,000	
	Computer Y	100,000	
	Total	$175,000	$490,000
4	Custom Inventory	$ 80,000	
	Custom Customer	50,000	
	Computer Y	100,000	
	Total	$230,000	$490,000

tion to these tangible benefits, there would be intangible benefits, such as better customer service, more satisfied customers, and better information for management decisions. The team decided not to attempt to place dollar values on these benefits, but just to list them.

Thus, the team decided to present to management the cost estimates of the alternatives, the accounting department's assessment of the value of improving inventory control, and a summary of intangible benefits. Management could use this data for a subjective decision, or they could request further evaluation using present value and other financial management techniques, as described in reference [31].

The results of the cost study are presented in figure 6–14. The annual operational costs are the same for all four alternatives. The development cost of alternative 3, $175,000, is the lowest and that of alternative 4, $230,000, is the highest. Observe that the CUSTOMER program with alterations would cost $40,000, whereas, according to the team estimate, only $50,000 would be needed for custom development.

The accounting department had estimated that over $600,000 could be saved in one year alone from better inventory management. This figure did not include the benefit of more accurate customer data, but clearly some benefit would accrue. Thus, any of the alternatives would appear to be a desirable investment.

QUESTIONS

6.6 Why did the team begin with programs when investigating alternatives?

6.7 What is a family of computers? How is the selection of a computer influenced by computer families?

6.8 Why didn't John want to hire the STOCKPILE vendor to convert STOCKPILE for use on hardware from vendor X? Would such a decision ever make sense?

6.9 Describe the two different organizational possibilities for Elliot Bay Electronics.

6.10 Comment on the recommendation of alternative 1. Do you agree? Under what circumstances would one of the other alternatives make sense?

Management Review

The team documented its findings and presented the results to management. Management was pleased with both the quality and the direction of the work. During the meeting, costs were discussed, but management also wanted to know about risks and schedules. The team stated that alternative 1 definitely would have the lowest risk because it involved the least amount of new development. The schedule for alternative 1 would be shortest; roughly eight months would be needed to develop the customer and inventory systems. Alternatives 2 and 3 would both take about a year each, and alternative 4 would require slightly more than two years.

One manager wondered why these estimates varied so much from the initial estimates (see figure 6–6). The team explained that the initial estimates had been made conservatively, assuming that programs would have to be custom developed.

With off-the-shelf and altered programs, however, the team believed the new estimates to be realistic.

Management had no trouble deciding how to proceed. Given the lower risk and quicker schedule, alternative 1 was chosen, even though it was more expensive than alternatives 2 and 3. As one manager remarked, the $15,000 difference between alternatives 1 and 3 was insignificant in light of the savings achieved by having the system in place four months earlier.

Considering organizational alternatives, Elliot Bay's management wanted to proceed slowly. Their attitude was, "Let's find a qualified manager of data processing and hire the needed operations and data entry personnel, but wait to acquire permanent systems development personnel. We may need to do this later, but let's try development with a software house first."

The EB Design Stage

During the design stage, specifications for each of the five system components are developed. For components that must be purchased, the procurement process is started. Starting the purchasing process during design is especially important for

components such as hardware that require a long lead time.

We will consider design for each of the five components of the EB customer and inventory systems. First, however, the team had more requirements work to do.

APPLICATION

"YOU CAN CUT DEVELOPMENT TIME BY UP TO 70%."

What's the best way to design and write complete and correct software? The various answers to that question have been debated since the computer's inception. A new approach that combines the advantages of two popular strategies — prototyping and structured methodology — may offer the best answer yet. The debate over software development methods continues because while methods have come and gone the problem remains. Systems still have bugs, often exceed the time and money budgeted for them, and many times deliver less than expected.

Prototyping combines design and development into an ongoing, interactive process of building prototypes, testing them, writing modifications, and retesting the system until the system is complete. The principal advantage of prototyping is the involvement of the user in system design and analysis. Prototyping moves directly from the outlining of systems requirements to coding, bypassing the traditional pause to translate requirements into specifications. Users work as insiders to ensure the system's accuracy. Users can "kick the tires" rather than study diagrams and specifications. Another key benefit of prototyping is flexibility. If, for instance, one segment of a system requires a data conversion effort that won't be complete for months, that section won't hold up a separate module that's needed right away. You can start seeing benefits from a system right away. Prototyping also focuses efforts on the most immediately important elements of the system, rather than spreading resources over the entire project. A carefully planned prototype has development milestones built in to affirm realistic projections for delivery dates, and budget concerns, and to mark modules or programs for future development. Prototyping is an extremely valuable method when additional funding is anticipated.

Structured methods provide a rigid framework of outline, design, and development steps, that, in theory, eliminate or vastly reduce the chance for error, omission, and budget-busting delays. In structured methodology, management can decide (based on the information systems proposal done in the second stage) whether to proceed with the project, or to seek other ways of accomplishing the same tasks.

Another valuable advantage of structured methodology is the structured walkthrough in the third and fourth stages. The structured walkthrough is a dress rehearsal by the design and programming team for the system users and management. After presentation of design, programming, or testing work, the session is opened up for questions. Relevant modules or programs can then be incorporated into the system.

More Requirements Work: Altering the CUSTOMER Package

The CUSTOMER package of programs that EB was going to purchase met all their requirements except one: It would not compute individual discounts. Consequently, programs to provide this service needed to be written. Before that could be done, however, requirements for discount computation had to be determined.

The project team visited both the customer service and the accounting departments to obtain requirements for discount computation. They identified the outputs that were needed, the inputs that had to be provided to produce those outputs, and the special controls required because discounts would affect the profitability of each sale. The team also visited the vendor of CUSTOMER to ensure that the necessary alterations could feasibly be done.

John drafted specifications for the alterations. The dataflow diagram (figure 6–15) indicated that discounts would not be recorded on any customer's record until an audit report (Discount Calculation Summary Report) had been sent to the accounting department. The process

specifications below summarized what each program was to accomplish:

1. Calculate discount
   For each customer:
      Compute discount (discount = total of last four quarter's purchases × four-quarter profit adjustment × 0.036)
      Record customer and discount in Discounts file
      Write discount line on report
   End
   Issue Discount Calculation Summary Report

FIGURE 6–15

Dataflow diagram for alterations to CUSTOMER

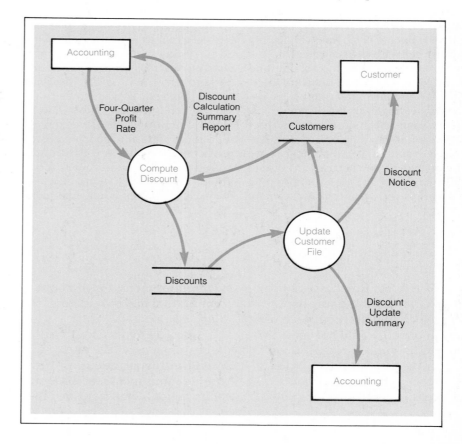

2. Update customer file
   For each discount:
     Retrieve matching customer record
     Update customer record with discount
     Age four quarterly purchase totals
     Format notice details
     Issue notice
     Issue line on discount update summary
     End
     Issue Discount Update Summary Report

John also designed all of the reports the programs would produce, although they are not illustrated here. He produced some mock reports with dummy data and asked the users for feedback. Then he changed the report formats until they met the users' needs.

EB would later supply these documents — the dataflow diagram, process specifications, and report formats — to the software house that would make the alterations. By doing this, the company could be sure that the alterations were what they had really wanted and asked for.

Once the requirements were identified and approved by the users, the team proceeded with the design stage.

People

The project team decided to focus initially on finding critical personnel. They knew this might take some time, and they wanted to start personnel searches before proceeding with other design tasks. The EB project plan is summarized in figure 6 – 16.

As it turned out, finding the data processing manager was easier than the team had expected. EB interviewed five different people for the job and eventually selected one of their own employees, Anne Franklin. Anne had worked both as a computer operator and as a data entry clerk in a previous job. She had come to Elliot Bay Electronics as a supervisor in the customer service department. Consequently, she had the right background, she was known to be a reliable and efficient worker, and she was immediately available.

Anne was able to switch from her job in customer service to the project team within two weeks. After that, she was gradually given more responsibility and, within several more weeks, she became leader of the project team. John worked with Anne to develop job descriptions for the computer operations and data entry personnel. Once these job descriptions were finished, a personnel firm was engaged to locate potential employees. The lead operator and the supervisor of data entry needed to be hired first. Other personnel could be hired later, as the project entered

202

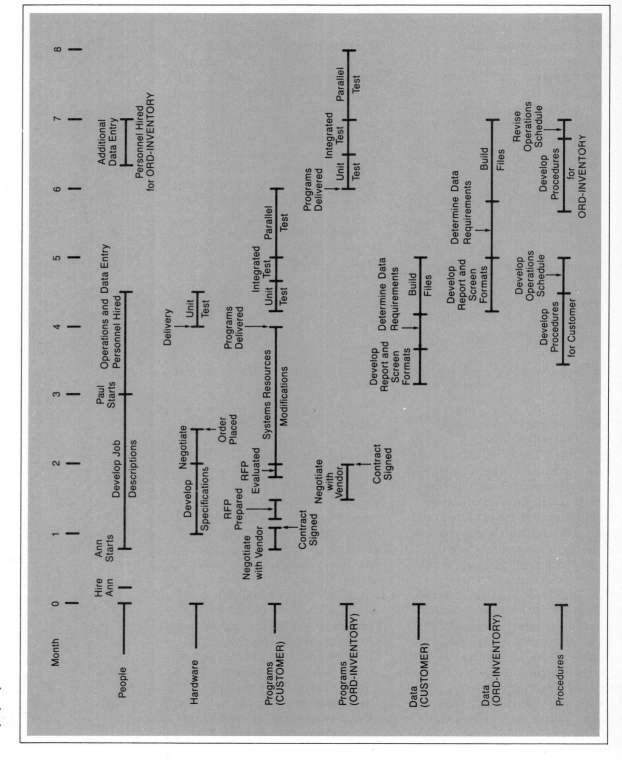

FIGURE 6-16
EB project plan

the implementation phase.

Within a few weeks, Paul Brooks was hired as lead operator. He was scheduled to begin work for EB four weeks before the equipment was to arrive. This schedule gave him time to become familiar with EB's needs and to obtain vendor training. Anne worked with Paul to hire the second operator.

Next, Anne hired the supervisor of data entry. Other data entry personnel were hired by Anne, working with the new supervisor.

Hardware

To order hardware, the project team needed to develop specifications, negotiate with vendors, and sign an order. Using current and expected workloads, the project team consulted with the vendors of the CUSTOMER and ORD-INVENTORY programs to determine specifications. The specifications included the model of the CPU, the amount of main memory, the amount of disk storage, the number of terminals, and other similar characteristics.

Given the specifications, EB began negotiations. The company hired an attorney who specialized in computer law to complete negotiations and write adjustments to the contract proposed by the computer vendor. Hardware was placed on order for delivery in six weeks.

Programs

The team needed to negotiate with vendors and order both the CUSTOMER and the ORD-INVENTORY packages of programs. They also needed to find a software house to make the alterations to CUSTOMER programs necessary to calculate discounts.

Anne, John, and the attorney met with both vendors, negotiated acceptable terms, and signed contracts. The vendors provided documentation and scheduled training for EB personnel. Not only were the operators and data entry personnel trained, but the users in the customer service, order processing, warehouse, and shipping departments were trained as well.

The vendor of CUSTOMER did not want to make the alterations necessary to calculate discounts but did recommend two companies that were qualified to perform such work. John and Anne prepared a **request for proposal** (or **RFP**), which is a written statement of the work to be performed, and a request for cost and schedule commitments. They sent the RFP to both companies and then met with representatives in person. Responses to the RFP were received in 10 days, and John and Anne selected one of the vendors, Systems Resources, to make the modifications. According to the terms of the contract, EB's CUSTOMER programs and specifications for the alterations were to be delivered to Systems Resources. Systems Resources would then make the alterations necessary to calculate discounts and deliver the complete package within six weeks. (Without telling Systems Resources, John and Anne allowed eight weeks in developing the schedule in figure 6–16.)

Data

EB Electronics had three major design tasks to complete for the data component. First, they needed to determine the specific formats they wanted for screens and reports. When EB personnel were trained in the use of CUSTOMER and ORD-INVENTORY products, they were taught how to tailor screen and report formats. For example, the ORD-INVENTORY product had three different screen formats from which to choose. The EB users needed to decide which format they wanted. Later, during implementation, the project team would provide parameters (inputs) to ORD-INVENTORY to cause those formats to be generated.

The second data design task was to determine the data needed to establish initial files. For example, for the customer system, EB would need to build a starting customer file. It would include customer name, address, and other fields of data. At this point, the team needed to determine exactly what those other fields would be. The team made this determination by reviewing the requirements statements, especially the data dictionary, discussing needs further with users, and reviewing the documentation of the CUSTOMER and the ORD-INVENTORY products.

The team also needed to learn where the initial data was located in the company and to design a procedure for obtaining that data. Once the programs had been installed, the data would be keyed and the initial file constructed.

The third design task concerned recurring data. What data would be gathered during business operations? To a large extent, the design of the CUSTOMER and ORD-INVENTORY programs would determine what data would be needed. The project team needed to understand these requirements and ensure that necessary data would be available. In several cases, the project team found that new forms needed to be designed. For example, the form that EB was using for order returns did not specify all the data that needed to be entered in the new system.

Procedures

The final design task was to develop procedures for computer operations, data entry personnel, and users. Procedures were needed for both normal and failure-recovery operations.

Both the CUSTOMER and ORD-INVENTORY packages included operations and user documentation. The project team reviewed this documentation and modified it where necessary to conform with EB's standard operational practices. Also, several of the order processing users complained that the documentation was unclear, so the project team wrote supplements that were easier to understand.

According to the contract with Systems Resources (the software house making the modifications to CUSTOMER), user and operations documentation for the changes and additions to the CUSTOMER product were to be delivered. John and Anne provided Systems Resources with an outline of the documentation they thought would be appropriate.

Anne and Paul worked together to develop the initial computer operations schedule. This schedule documented when programs were to be started, when reports were to be produced, where the reports were to be sent, when to perform file backup, and so forth. Anne stipulated that inputs and requests for computer runs were to be received by data entry personnel, processed by the computer operators, and returned to the data entry personnel. This scheme provided control over the activities of the operations department (see module D).

Once procedures had been designed and documented, the team moved on to implementation.

The EB Implementation Stage

Recall from figure 5 – 9 that implementation includes three phases: construction, testing, and installation. EB was actually developing two systems: customer and inventory. Therefore, the company had to perform construction, testing, and installation tasks for each system. The scheduling of these tasks for the two separate systems is shown in figure 6 – 16. Refer to this diagram as you read the next sections.

Construction

During construction, the hardware was installed. (The installation of hardware is not the same as the installation of the *system*.

All five components must be installed and tested before the system can be installed.) Programs were delivered, and the vendor assisted Anne and Paul in placing them on the computer hardware. At this point, optional program features were selected, and the formats of screens and reports were specified.

Once the programs were available, the initial data files could be built. Data entry and user personnel followed the procedures developed during design to build the files. Edit reports were closely examined to ensure that only correct data was stored. John continually reminded the team that the first uses of the systems had to be successful to obtain the users' confidence. Failures would occur if bad data was stored in the initial files: garbage in, garbage out.

As these construction activities were taking place, users and operations and data entry personnel were trained. Some of the training was provided by the vendors, and other training was done by Anne or Paul.

Testing

Each of the five components was tested individually, and then an integrated dress rehearsal was conducted. Hardware was tested by the vendor as soon as it was installed. Paul and the other operator then conducted their own tests to ensure that the hardware was operating. They found a problem in the way that one of the disk units had been connected to main memory. The vendor was easily able to correct the error.

Programs were tested using test data supplied by the vendors. (Systems Resources supplied data for their modifications.) Then John and Anne ran their own tests to verify program operation. They found that two reports were not formatted correctly. The formats were easily corrected with changes to program inputs. One of the control reports produced by the Systems Resources program also had an error in it. Anne called it to Systems Resources' attention, and the report was fixed within a week.

Data was tested by examining printouts of the initial files. This was a time-consuming task. Incorrect data that had been identified during construction was examined again to ensure that it had been properly changed.

Anne and Paul discussed procedures with the users and operations and data entry personnel, and they answered questions. By this time, the team thought the personnel were well prepared.

After each of the components had been tested separately, an integrated test was conducted using sample data. Operations personnel started jobs in accordance with the schedule, the users and data entry personnel entered data, sample reports were produced, and so forth. Several problems were identified that resulted in adjustments in the procedures.

Installation

The project team had decided to use a parallel installation strategy. The new systems would be run while the old systems continued operation. As shown in figure 6 – 16, the team planned to implement the customer system first and the inventory system two months later.

The customer system was installed, and use began. At the end of each week, the reports of the new system were compared to reports from the accounting department and the service bureau. Nearly all of the differences between them were the result of errors that the accounting clerks or service bureau had made. At the end of the month, the discount system was run just as it would be run at the end of the quarter. (It was not the end of a quarter, but John and Anne wanted to see if the discounts could be computed correctly before paying the Systems Resources bill.) No significant errors were found.

At the end of the month, the team recommended to management that the clerks in the accounting department no longer post sales to customer accounts or calculate discounts. The team also recommended that the service bureau activity be stopped. With that decision, the customer system was then up and running.

Next, the team turned its attention to the inventory system. (Actually, the installation and unit testing of ORD-INVENTORY had been accomplished while the parallel test of CUSTOMER was in progress. See figure 6 – 16.) ORD-INVENTORY installation was more difficult because more people were involved. Order processing, warehouse, and shipping personnel all had a role. As with the customer system, a parallel strategy was used. Orders were processed by the old manual system as well as by the new computer-based system. This duplication caused considerable extra work for the employees, and there was considerable grumbling. Management held firm to the plan for a parallel installation, however, and an entire month's orders were processed both ways.

One problem with the interface between the inventory and the customer systems occurred, but by and large the implementation went smoothly. Several users were dissatisfied with their report formats (they hadn't bothered to review and approve the prototypes). "I didn't understand what this would really look like," was one of the comments. Basically, however, both sys-

QUESTIONS

6.11 Why did the project team return to requirements work after the evaluation stage? What requirements work did the team do?

6.12 Using figure 6 – 16 as a guide, explain the actions taken by the project team to design and implement the customer and inventory systems.

6.13 In figure 6 – 16, what would have happened if the hardware had arrived late? What would have happened if Systems Resources had delivered the altered programs late? What would have happened if the customer system had been a failure?

6.14 Describe what you think are the major reasons that the EB systems development was successful.

tems were operational, and the projects were complete eight months after management had approved the alternatives. Since this was right on schedule, management was exceedingly pleased.

▦ SUMMARY

Elliot Bay Electronics enjoyed a good system development experience, due largely to the knowledge and expertise of John Abrams. The company could have made many costly errors along the way, but in hiring John they gained a wealth of system development knowledge.

When you find yourself in a business considering a first-time computer system or adding on to the one in place, review what happened at EB. Recall the amount of time and effort users were expected to put forth. Remember that neither Rome nor a working business computer system was built in a day. Systems development takes time and effort. Follow the four steps for each of the five system components. Using these as guidelines, you will be sure to do a thorough job.

WORD LIST

Computer service bureau
Family of computers
Software house
Request for proposal (RFP)

QUESTIONS TO CHALLENGE YOUR THINKING

A. Suppose a friend who owns a small record shop asks you for advice about what type of computer to buy for her business. How do you respond? Make a list of all the questions she should ask a computer consultant who offers to develop such a system. Make a list of all the deliverables she should insist upon from the consultant.

B. A very large manufacturing firm in the Midwest recently cancelled the installation of a manufacturing/inventory control/accounting/marketing system because the project had gone over budget by $1.6 million and was already 24 months late. The company had spent over $4 million on system development already. Why do you suppose the company would decide to do such a thing? How far over budget and behind schedule should a project be allowed to get before drastic action is taken by a company?

C. A common problem in business is the conflict between marketing and engineering: Marketing sells to a customer something that does not exist and then expects engineering to build it in time for delivery. Engineering, on the other hand, often wants to continue testing and improving a product until it approaches perfection, frustrating the salespeople who want to get it into the marketplace. Suppose you worked for a software company that builds general-purpose software for business applications. What problems do you anticipate between marketing and development (the equivalent of engineering)? If marketing does sell a software package that does not (yet) exist, how can the development team deliver it in the shortest amount of time? Is perfection a realistic goal? Can some resources be adjusted to speed things up? Does adding more people to the development team speed up development?

SEQUENTIAL FILE PROCESSING SYSTEMS

CHAPTER 7

Concepts mentioned in chapters 4 and 5 will be developed in the next three chapters. In chapter 4 you learned that business computer systems fall into three categories: transaction processing, MIS and DSS systems. Each category serves a certain group of users or solves a different type of problem.

In chapter 5 you learned that during system development, the user is responsible for identifying certain key system characteristics, such as whether instant access to data is needed and whether the system will answer predictable business questions or ad hoc inquiries. You read that these factors are used during the second stage of system development to determine alternative system designs. That decision is made in part by selecting one of several ways to organize and access data: *sequential file processing*, *direct access file processing*, or *database processing*. This chapter discusses sequential file processing, chapter 8 discusses direct access file processing, and chapter 9 discusses database processing.

The fundamental difference between file processing systems and database management systems is that file processing systems are patterned after manual record-keeping systems, while database management systems are not.

In a manual record-keeping system, a file folder is the basic storage unit. A file folder usually contains all of the details about a particular person, object, or event. For example, each student enrolled in a university or every customer with an account at a department store might have one file folder. When specific details are needed about the object of a file — say, a customer — someone pulls the entire file folder and extracts the relevant data. Additions to, deletions from, and changes to the contents of the folder might be made. Then the entire folder is returned to its place in the file cabinet.

File processing systems — sequential and direct access — are patterned after the manual record-keeping system just described. Though the terminology might be different, the fundamental concepts are the same. The basic storage unit is called a **record**, and it contains many **fields**, each field representing one detail about an object. When all or part of a record is needed for processing, the file processing system retrieves the entire record. Additions, changes, and deletions can be made, and then the record is returned to a storage device.

A computer programmer who writes a program that needs access to only part of a record must nevertheless know many details, including the physical organization of the file itself and the description and location of every field in every record (even though only some of the data is needed.) In addition, the programmer is responsible for retrieving the correct records from a file, not an inconsequential task. (You will learn how to do this in this chapter and in chapter 8.)

Database management systems are based on an entirely different principle. Whereas a file processing system uses a record as its unit of storage, a **DBMS** can retrieve fields. Therefore, a program that needs access to only certain fields simply requests those fields — the **DBMS** retrieves them and makes them available to the program for processing. Additions, changes, and deletions can be made, and then the **DBMS** returns the data to a storage device.

The result of this is that a computer programmer needs to know very little about the physical aspects of files and records. Those details are stored and maintained by the DBMS. In addition, a DBMS handles all aspects of locating and retrieving data, so programmers are relieved of those burdens as well. From a programmer's standpoint, a DBMS is easier to use than a file processing system.

As you study chapters 7, 8, and 9 you will see that each approach to file processing satisfies different system requirements. While no approach is inherently better than the others, each one's characteristics make it more effective than the others in some instances. In general, sequential file processing satisfies most transaction processing applications in which instant access to particular records is *not* required, a large percentage of the stored records are referenced each time the system is run, and ad hoc inquiries are not involved.

Direct access file processing is the preferred approach in transaction processing systems that require instant access to specific data and that reference only a small percentage of the records each time the system is run. Figure 7 – 1 compares sequential with direct access file systems.

Database management systems (DBMSs) are very sophisticated systems, based largely on direct access file processing. MIS and DSS systems, which usually require quick access to data stored in not one but many related files, and which are expected to field what-if questions, can be supported only with database processing. DBMSs are available for handling everything from large corporate databases to personal computer applications.

Any of these three alternatives could be used by Elliot Bay Electronics (chapter 6), and we will refer to that company for examples. In this chapter you will learn the characteristics of a sequential file system. Then you will learn how each of the five components of a business computer system is affected by a decision to use sequential files.

WHAT ARE SEQUENTIAL FILE SYSTEMS?

Sequential file systems are business computer systems that have a special property: the records in files are processed in sequence. Think of your stereo tape player. You listen to songs in sequence. When you have a tape with a song that you like in the middle, you must either listen to the preceding songs or fast-forward through them. Sequential file systems are similar. To find a record in the middle of the file, all the records preceding it must be read first.

FIGURE 7–1
Comparison of file processing systems

	SEQUENTIAL	DIRECT
TYPES OF ACCESS	Batch	Batch or online
DATA ORGANIZATION	Sequentially by key value	Sequentially and by index
FLEXIBILITY IN HANDLING INQUIRIES	Low	Very high
AVAILABILITY OF UP-TO-DATE DATA	No	Yes
SPEED OF RETRIEVAL	Slow	Very fast
ACTIVITY	High	Low
VOLATILITY	Low	High
EXAMPLES	Payroll processing	Airline reservations
	Billing operations	Banking transactions

Figure 7–2 shows a system flowchart for the EB customer master file system. This is a sequential file system. Data about customer changes, such as new customers or address changes for existing customers, is keyed onto magnetic tape using a key-to-tape device. The resulting file is called the change transaction file. This file and the old customer master file are read, and a new customer master file is created. Now consider a problem: Suppose there are 100 changes to be made to a file that has 100,000 customers in it. How are the correct master file records to be found? If the first transaction says to change the address of customer number 10, how is customer 10's master file record to be found?

Think about your tape player. Suppose you have a tape of nursery rhymes, and you want to play "Lucy Locket." If you don't know where "Lucy Locket" is located on the tape, you will have to search the tape from the beginning until you find it. You might do this by using fast forward to advance the tape 10 feet and then listening. If you do not hear "Lucy Locket," you would advance the tape another 10 feet, listen again, and so forth. If there are 50 nursery rhymes on the tape, you can expect, on the average, to search over 25 nursery rhymes to find the one you want.

Now suppose you want to listen to three nursery rhymes: "Ding, Dong, Bell," "Lucy Locket," and "Rub-a-dub-dub, Three Men in a Tub," in that order. If you don't know where these are located, you will have to search the tape three times. You may have to search over 75 (3×25) nursery rhymes before you find all three.

You can improve this process if you put the nursery rhymes on the tape in some order, say, alphabetical order. Then, assuming you want to listen to the three rhymes in alphabetical order, you can search first for "Ding, Dong, Bell" and play it. Then you can search for "Lucy Locket" and play it. Then you can find and play "Rub-a-dub-dub." At worst, you will only have to search through the tape once.

You can also catch mistakes more easily. Suppose you are searching for "Ding, Dong, Bell," but you find "Deedle, Deedle, Dumpling" followed by "Jack Sprat." What does this mean? It means "Ding, Dong, Bell" is not on the tape. If it were, it would be between "Deedle, Deedle, Dumpling" and "Jack Sprat." Thus, by having the rhymes in order, you eliminate having to search the whole tape to find that "Ding, Dong, Bell" isn't there.

Now consider Elliot Bay's customer master file of 6,500 records. If the customers' records are in no particular order in the file, then, on the average, we will have to search 3,250 records to find the ones we want. Therefore, to find master file records for 10 customers, 32,500 (10 × 3,250) records will have to be searched.

On the other hand, if the customer master file is sorted by number, and if we also sort the required changes by number, then we can find

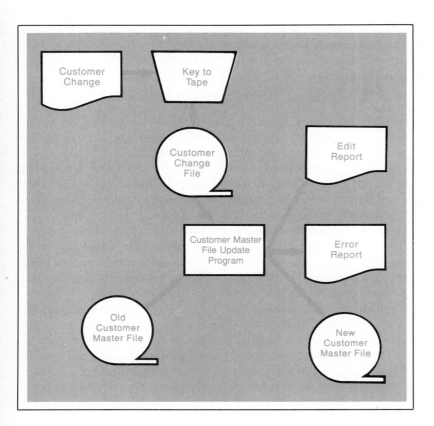

FIGURE 7–2
Elliot Bay's customer master file maintenance system

all the records in one pass through the file. Invalid numbers can also be identified quickly.

The essence of sequential file processing is that the records are sorted into some order. They are processed one after another in that order. *A sequential file system is a business computer system in which the files are sorted and processed in some predefined order.* This sorting saves considerable searching, and processing can be extremely fast.

Data for Sequential File Systems

Sequential file systems data has several identifying characteristics. First, there are two types of files. **Master files** keep data about continuing relationships. Examples are master files of employees, of customers, and of suppliers. Master files are usually relatively stable. In Elliot Bay's case, a few (as a percentage) new customers may be added, and some customers may be deleted, but by and large, the same customers are processed month after month.

Transaction files contain records about events. When these records are processed, changes are made to master files, or other outputs are produced. Transaction file inputs are erratic. For example, changes to the customer master file for one month will likely be completely different from changes for the next month. In figure 7–2 the customer change file is an example of a transaction file.

A second characteristic of a sequential file system is that a master file is completely rewritten whenever any records in the file are changed. This is because the records must be kept in some order. If a new record is to be **inserted**, the file must be rewritten to make room for the record. (Similarly, to add a new nursery rhyme, the stereo tape needs to be rewritten.) If a record is to be **deleted**, the master file has to be rewritten to eliminate the unneeded record.

If a record is to be **modified**, the file has to be rewritten because the modified record may be larger or smaller than the existing one. Even if the record length does not change, the file is rewritten because of the difficulty of inserting the modified record in just the right place.

Have you ever tried to record a song in the middle of a group of songs? It is easy to accidentally delete the end of the prior song or the beginning of the next song. It also is easy to create a tape with a blank spot. These problems exist on magnetic tape, too, which is one reason that records on sequential files are not modified in place.

A third characteristic of a sequential file system is that transactions are usually processed in batches. The master file will be completely rewritten whether 1 percent or 100 percent of the records in the file are changed. Therefore, the more changes that can be made in one run, the better. Figure 7–3 shows a graph of the average time (per updated record) required to update a file plotted against the size of the transaction file. The bigger the batch, the shorter the average time to

PROFILE

"A SEQUENTIAL FILE SYSTEM THAT WOULD BE USER FRIENDLY"

Sequential file processing is widely used for many business applications. It is especially efficient when most or all of a file must be accessed at once. Notice how many of the reports described here require entire files of data rather than a few specific records.

When Alan Freifeld went shopping for a point-of-sale (POS) system last year, he knew exactly what he was looking for—"a system that would be user friendly, easy to [operate] and fairly easy to implement ... something that we could control, that had a future to it and that we wouldn't outgrow," explains the MIS director for Secaucus, New Jersey-based National Brands Outlet.

Armed with those requirements, Freifeld shopped the POS market and ultimately purchased a system that, he feels, not only meets his needs for today, but also for the years ahead.

A store manager or supervisor can request up to six different reports by inserting a security key into a specific terminal and then entering a code. Those reports include:

1. A list of readings by terminal that includes sales, returns, discounts, return discounts, number of gift certificates issued, net merchandise sales, and net tax amount.
2. Credit card transactions by terminal including the total number and dollar value of sales and returns made by credit cards.
3. Sales totals by employee. The report lists the total number and dollar value of sales and returns performed by each sales clerk so that commission checks can be issued by the home office.
4. Department totals. This report gives a list of the net sales and returns by each of the chain's 35 departments. It is further broken down into two main categories appearing at the bottom of the report: clothing and haberdashery. In each of these groups, the manager sees a complete breakdown by sales, returns, and discounts.
5. A reading by clothing and haberdashery categories. This type of report eliminates the break-out by department and just summarizes the results.
6. A summary identical to that of the fifth report for all terminals combined. Unlike the previous reports, this one can only be generated by the master terminal.

process a transaction. Since transactions are processed in batches, sequential file processing is sometimes called **batch processing**.

Magnetic Tape Data Representation

Recall from chapter 2 that the basic building block for representing computer data is called a **bit**. A bit is a *binary digit*. Bits are grouped together to form **bytes**, or characters. Characters are represented in columns across magnetic tape.

Figure 7–4 shows a section of **magnetic tape**. Bits are represented on magnetic tape by magnetized spots. If the spot is magnetized in one direction, it is considered to be a 0. If it is magnetized in another direction, it is considered to be a 1.

If you turn a section of tape on its side, its format is like a punched card. However, instead of having a fixed number of characters (the

FIGURE 7–3
Average time to update a sequential file

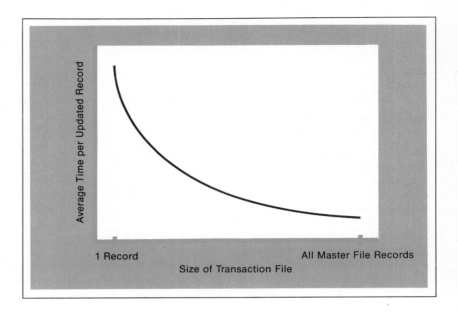

card in chapter 2 had 80), it can have as many characters as the tape is long. The section of tape shown in figure 7–4 has 8 characters. Instead of having 12 rows as the punched card did, the tape has 9. These are called **tracks**. Each character is represented by a column across the nine tracks.

For nine-track tapes, characters are represented using **EBCDIC** (Extended Binary Coded Decimal Interchange Code). With this code, eight bits are needed to represent each character (see figure 2–14). For example, the character "A" is represented as 1100 0001, the character "B" as 1100 0010, the number 1 as 1111 0001, and the number 2 as 1111 0010.

Characters are stored on tape by writing their codes in the lower eight tracks. Thus, to store the character 1, a 1 is written in the bottom track, 0's are written in the next three tracks, and 1's are written in the four tracks after that (see figure 7–4). To store the character "A", a 1 is written in the bottom track, 0's are written in the next five tracks, and 1's are written in the next two tracks.

If you're following this discussion, you have a burning question. What about the ninth track? Why have a nine-track tape to hold an eight-bit code?

The ninth track is called the **parity track**. It is used to help detect errors. Before the tape is written, a convention is established that the tape will be written in either **even** or **odd parity**. If even parity is used, each column of the tape is to have an even number of 1's. If odd parity is used, each column is to have an odd number of 1's. The parity track is used to make each column obey the convention.

Suppose the convention is even parity. To represent the character 1 in EBCDIC, a 1 is written in the first track, then three 0's, and then four 1's. A total of five 1's are in the column. However, since each column is supposed to have an even number of 1's, a 1 will also be written in the parity track. After this is done, the column has six 1's, making it even, as it is supposed to be.

To represent the character 3, 1's are written in the bottom two tracks, then two 0's, and then four 1's. A total of six 1's are in the column. Since this column has an even number of 1's, a 0 is written in the parity track. Examine figure 7–4, and you will see how the parity track is used to give every column an even number of 1's.

How does this process help check for errors? Given an even-parity convention, if the tape unit misreads one of the tracks (reads a 0 as a 1, or a 1 as a 0), it will sense an odd number of 1's. Since the convention is even, the unit has made an error and will reread the character or stop. Furthermore, if the tape has been damaged by mishandling, the tape unit will detect **parity errors**.

If you work around business computer systems, you will undoubtedly hear someone say, "That tape is full of parity errors." This statement simply means that either the tape is damaged, or the equipment is malfunctioning.

The code in figure 7–4 is not the only way data is represented by computers. There is another popular code that uses just six bits. Tape units that commonly process this code have only seven tracks.

QUESTIONS

7.1 Define *sequential processing*.

7.2 Why are records sorted in sequential files?

7.3 Explain the difference between master files and transaction files.

7.4 Why are transaction records usually batched in sequential file processing?

7.5 Why do master files need to be completely rewritten when they are changed?

7.6 What is a bit? Why are bits used to represent computer data?

7.7 Describe the way characters are represented on magnetic tape.

7.8 Define *parity* and explain how it is used for error checking.

▥ ELLIOT BAY'S CUSTOMER MASTER FILE SYSTEM

Figure 7–5 shows a version of EB's customer master file system. The change transaction file is keyed using a **key-to-tape device,** and the old and new customer master files are stored on tape. A printer is used to output the reports. Transactions are keyed directly to tape, but they

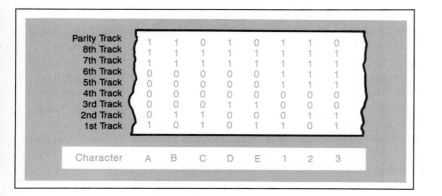

FIGURE 7–4
Character representation on nine-track magnetic tape

FIGURE 7–5
Tape-oriented customer master file
system

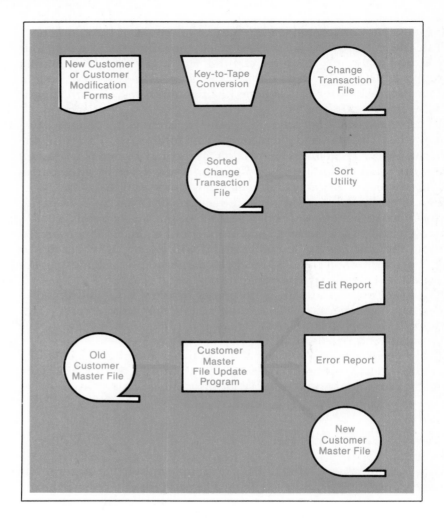

are keyed in no particular order. Consequently, they must be sorted according to customer number. After they are sorted, the order of the transaction records will match the order of the master file records.

For the system depicted in figure 7–5, EB clerks initiate a change to the customer master file by filling out a change request form. This form goes to data entry, where it is keyed on magnetic tape. A machine and operator performing key-to-tape data entry is shown in figure 7–6. The tape that is generated can be a cassette tape like those used for home stereos, or it can be a reel of 1/2-inch tape commonly used for computers.

The record format for the change transaction file is shown in figure 7–7. The data entry personnel fill in this data on the terminal screens, and a tape is created that has one record for each change.

FIGURE 7–6
Operator using key-to-tape equipment

The record code field tells the update program what function to perform. A 1 in this field means to add a new customer, a 2 means to delete a customer, a 3 means to change customer data, and a 4 means to print the customer's record. This last action is taken to determine what data is on the customer's master record.

The contents of the other fields in the change record vary, depending on the value in the record code field. For codes 2 and 4, only the customer number need be specified. For code 1, all the data must be specified. For code 3, only the customer number and the data to be changed must be specified. Figure 7–8 shows some examples of change records.

COLUMN	CONTENTS
1	Record code
5–10	Customer number
11–30	Customer name
31–70	Customer address
71–80	Customer phone

FIGURE 7–7
Change transaction file record format

```
1   201143FRED J. PARKS          316 E. TAMARACK, LOS ANGELES      CA94123 2135551201
1   201144MARY ABERNATHY         934 S. LARCH, ALEXANDRIA         VA02034 2033812347
2   101234
1   201145PETE WANDOLOWSKI       1123 17TH STREET, APT 6, MIAMI   FL11234 6053457769
3   001214 MARY HOPKINS
2   000109
4   000044
4   109877
3   154347REX BAKER
```

FIGURE 7–8
Change transaction data

HARDWARE FOR SEQUENTIAL SYSTEMS

Two types of media are commonly used for the storage of sequential data: magnetic tape and magnetic disk. Magnetic disks are used for sequential file processing on mainframes, minis, and micros. Magnetic disks are capable of sequential as well as other types of processing. We will consider disk media in chapter 8. Magnetic tape is used primarily with larger systems, such as mainframes. Magnetic tape will be discussed in this chapter, but note that sequential file processing is exactly the same when magnetic disks are used.

Characteristics of Magnetic Tape Files

For the EB Electronics application, both old and new customer master files are stored on tape. Figure 7–9 shows a typical magnetic tape format. The tape has a **header** section that contains the tape serial number, identity of the owner (such as the payroll department), and so forth. Then for each file on the tape, there is a file header that names the file and gives its date of creation and other identifying data. (More

FIGURE 7–9
Magnetic tape format

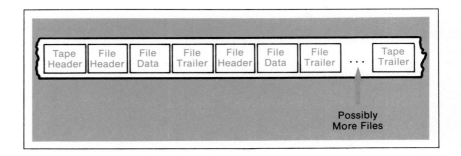

than one file can be on a tape, although in EB's application there would be just one.)

The records in the file are stored after the file header. Following all the records, a file trailer repeats the file header data. It indicates the end of the file. If the tape contains another file, this grouping of file header/data/file trailer is repeated for as many files as are on the tape. Finally, the tape has a **trailer** that repeats the tape header data and signifies the end of recorded data on the tape. The headers and trailers are sometimes referred to as **labels**. A tape with headers and trailers is called a *labeled tape*.

This description generally applies to all labeled tapes. Slight variations exist among manufacturers, but the format is essentially the same. Equipment can be forced to write tapes without labels, but this is bad practice. Without labels, the computer cannot verify that the correct tape has been mounted. If the wrong tape is mounted, valuable data may be lost. When tapes are labeled, the computer system will ensure that a tape that is mounted is the one that is called for.

Figure 7–10 shows a reel of tape with a **write-protect ring**. This ring must be in place before the tape can be written. Because the operator must insert the ring, this action is protection against someone's inadvertently writing on a tape that was supposed to be read. The equipment simply won't write unless the ring is in place.

Figure 7–11 shows a simple schematic of a tape read/write unit. As the tape passes under the read/write heads, the magnetic spots are either sensed (read) or created (written). Typically, a tape unit will read or write one record and then stop, read or write another record and then stop, and so forth. Consequently, the tape moves forward in

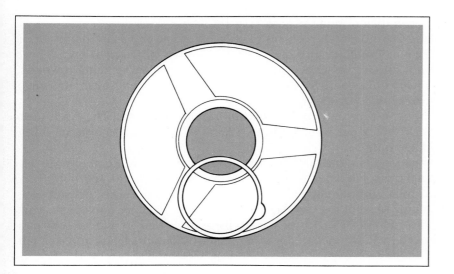

FIGURE 7–10
Tape volume with write-protect ring

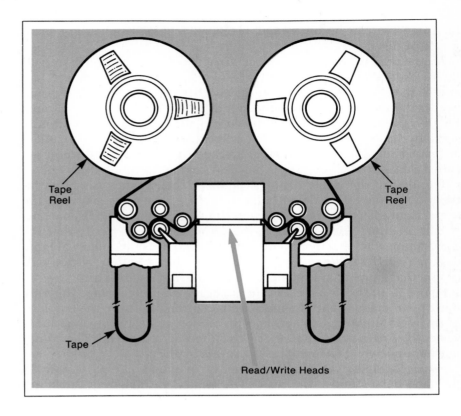

jerks: a quick move followed by a stop, a quick move followed by a stop. To give the equipment time to stop, there is a gap between the records on the tape, called the **interrecord** (or **interblock**) **gap**. This gap may be ½ inch or more in size.

You may have seen pictures of magnetic tape drives in movies or on television. Typically, the tape reels are shown whirling at great speed and not moving in jerks at all. That's because they're being rewound. Hollywood likes action, and a tape drive actually reading or writing is apparently not dramatic enough.

Magnetic tape can be recorded in various **densities**. These are measured in **bytes per inch**, or **bpi**. Typical values are 800 bpi, 1600 bpi, and 6250 bpi.

Consider EB's master file. According to figure 7–12, there are 120 characters per master record. If a tape is recorded at 1600 bpi, then 0.075 inch will be required to hold one customer record. Do you see a problem? Most of the tape will be used for interrecord gaps. If the gaps are 0.5 inch, 0.075 inch of data will be followed by 0.5 inch of gap, followed by 0.075 inch of data followed by 0.5 inch of gap, and so forth. (See figure 7–13.)

POSITION	CONTENTS
1–6	Customer number
7–26	Customer name
27–66	Billing address
67–76	Customer phone
77–82	1 quarter purchases (xxxx.xx)
83–88	2 quarter purchases (xxxx.xx)
89–94	3 quarter purchases (xxxx.xx)
95–100	4 quarter purchases (xxxx.xx)
101–102	Discount
103–109	Credit limit (xxxxx.xx)
110–115	Date account opened
116–120	Salesperson this account

FIGURE 7–12
Customer master file record format

Record Blocking

To prevent this situation, records can be **blocked**. This means a group of records can be written or read together as a unit, or **block**. Figure 7–14 depicts a tape with a **blocking factor** of eight records per block. In this case, a block will take 0.6 inch (8 × 0.075) of tape and be followed by 0.5 inch of gap.

How much tape will be required to hold EB's customer master file? There are 6,500 records. If they are blocked at 8 records per block, then 813 blocks will be needed. Each block and its adjacent interblock gap require 1.1 inches. Consequently, 895 inches, or 75 feet, of tape are required. Reels of magnetic tape are available in lengths of 800, 1200, and 2400 feet, so the master file will fit on one 800-foot reel. There will be plenty of tape left over for headers and trailers. How much tape would be required if the blocking factor were 4? If it were 15?

You might be wondering why there are any gaps at all. Why not compress the data into one long record? The reason is that a block must be read into main memory in its entirety. A portion of main memory, called a **buffer**, must be set aside to receive the record as it

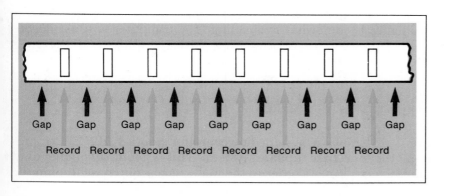

FIGURE 7–13
Elliot Bay's customer master file record format on tape

FIGURE 7–14
Schematic of tape with blocking factor of 8

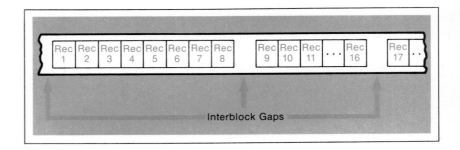

Interblock Gaps

QUESTIONS

7.9 Why does figure 7–5 call for change transactions to be sorted?

7.10 What is the purpose of the record code field in figure 7–7?

7.11 What are the two types of media most frequently used for the storage of sequentially organized data?

7.12 What is a labeled tape? Should most companies use labeled or un-labeled tapes?

7.13 Explain what file headers and trailers are.

7.14 Sketch the layout of a labeled tape that has three files.

7.15 What does *bpi* stand for? What are typical bpi values for magnetic tapes?

7.16 What is the purpose of the write-protect ring?

7.17 What is the purpose of the inter-record gap? What is its disadvantage?

7.18 What is record blocking? Why is blocking done?

7.19 How much tape would be required to hold the EB Electronics customer master file if the blocking factor were 4? If it were 15?

7.20 How long would it take to read the EB customer master file if the blocking factor were 4? If it were 15?

7.21 How long will it take to read 250,000 200-byte records recorded at 1600 bpi?

7.22 How long will it take to write 250,000 200-byte records recorded at 6250 bpi?

comes in from the tape. If EB's master file were one long record, then 6,500 × 120 bytes, or 780,000 bytes, of main storage would have to be set aside for the buffer. Although many computers have that much memory there are better uses for it. Consequently, records are usually blocked into units of more manageable size, such as 1000 or 2000 bytes.

Magnetic Tape Speeds

How long will reading or writing EB's customer master file require? The time to process a tape has two components: the time required actually to move the data, and the time required to start and stop the tape between blocks. The time required to move the data depends on the speed of the tape and the recording density. A typical speed (called the tape **transport speed**) is 200 inches per second. Thus, at 1600 bpi, a total of 320,000 bytes can be transferred per second. The EB master file has 780,000 characters, so 2.5 seconds (780,000 divided by 320,000) will be needed to read or write the tape.

In addition, time is required to start and stop the tape between blocks. A typical time interval to stop and start a tape is 0.003 second. Assuming EB has 6,500 customer records blocked 8 per block, then 813 blocks will be needed. At 0.003 second for stop and start, a total of 2.5 seconds will be needed. Thus, the total time to read or write the entire EB master file is five seconds.

This figure is somewhat misleading. The computer will not devote all of its time to reading or writing this tape; other activities will interfere. Still, about five seconds is a realistic estimate.

▥ PROGRAMS FOR SEQUENTIAL FILE PROCESSING

Figure 7–15 shows a system flowchart for another EB Electronics system, the purchase update system. This system adds the total amount of a customer's order to the four-quarter purchase total in the master record. This is a typical sequential file system.

A Sequential File Record-Matching Algorithm

In figure 7–15, the transaction records are sorted into the same order as the master file records. Then they are read by an update program. The update program matches a transaction record with the corresponding master file record, makes adjustments to the master data (here, by adding the order amount to the quarterly total), and writes the new master record.

Records will be matched by customer number. The master file will be kept in order of customer number, and the transaction file will be sorted by customer number. Fields that are used the way customer number is used in this example are called **control fields** or, sometimes, **keys**.

FIGURE 7–15
EB purchase update system

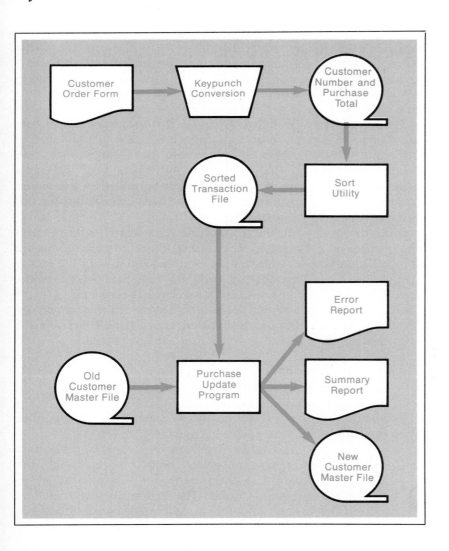

TRANSACTION FILE		MASTER FILE	
CUSTOMER NUMBER	**AMOUNT OF SALE**	**CUSTOMER NUMBER**	**OTHER MASTER DATA**
100010	007.95	100010	
100020	124.85	100020	
100040	382.17	100030	•
100045	081.29	100040	•
100050	176.76	100050	•
EOF		100060	
		100070	
		EOF	

FIGURE 7–16

Data for purchase update program

Some master records may have no matching transactions, which means that some customers made no purchases. In this case, the program will copy the master record from the old master file to the new one without making any changes. On the other hand, if a transaction record cannot be matched to a master record, an error condition exists, which must be noted on an error report.

Figure 7–16 lists data that could be entered into a system like the purchase update system in figure 7–15. Each transaction record contains a customer number and the amount of a recent sale. Each master record has a customer number and other data that is not shown. If we examine this data, we see that customer 100010 is on both the transaction file and the master file. The 7.95 will be added to his or her master record. Then the program reads the next transaction record and compares key field values again.

This time the number on the transaction record (100020) is greater than the number on the master record (100010), so the updated master record is written to the new master file, and the next master file record is read. The numbers match this time, so 124.85 is added to the customer's balance, and the transaction record is replaced with the next one on the file. Once again, the number on the transaction record is greater than the number on the master record (100040 > 100020), so the updated master record is written to the new file, and the next master record is read.

This time a customer has made no purchases. Customer 100030's record is written, unchanged, to the new master file. Notice that the key field on the transaction record is higher then the key field on the master record both when all update transactions have been applied and when there are no transactions for a master record.

After copying 100030's data, the program must read another master record to see if it matches transaction 100040. Sure enough, this record matches the current transaction record. Consequently, 382.17 is added to 100040's quarterly total. The program now reads the next transaction, writes the updated master record to the new file, replaces the master record, and compares key fields again. This time the key field on the transaction record (100045) is less than the key field on the master record (100050). When the key on the transaction record is less than the key on the master record, the program has detected an unmatched transaction. This is an error because purchases can be made only by customers who EB has on file. 100045 is not in the master file. If it were, it would have come before 100050, because the records are in numerical order. In this case, the program prints the unmatched transaction, 100045, on the error file. Then it reads the next transaction record. It is 100050, which matches 100050 on the master file. The 176.76 is added to the master record.

When the program tries to read the next record from the transaction file, it finds EOF. **EOF** stands for **end of file**. Here, it simply means that there are no more file records to be read. All systems have ways of notifying a program that the records in a file have all been read. However, the way this is done depends on the type of computer and the language of the program. Your instructor can show you how your computer notifies programs that EOF has been reached.

When the program encounters EOF on the transaction file, it copies all the remaining records from the old master to the new master. If it did not do this, then all the remaining records in the master file would be lost. In this case, customer records 100060 and 100070 are copied unchanged to the new master file.

It could happen that the master file runs out of data before the transaction file does. If it did, then all remaining records in the transaction file would be erroneous. They would have no matching records on the master file. In this case, they would be copied on the error report.

Program Logic for Record Matching

Figure 7–17 shows a **structure chart** for the purchase update program. A structure chart is a tool for designing programs. Each box on a structure chart represents a **program function**, or **module**. (You will learn more about structure charts in module F in part 5 or if you take a course in a programming language such as Pascal or COBOL.) According to figure 7–17 this program contains six modules. The one called Update Master File with Purchases calls the other five modules in the correct order. Each of the subordinate modules does what its name states.

Figure 7–18 shows **pseudocode** for the controlling module, Update Master File with Purchases, and figure 7–19 shows pseudocode for two of the subordinate modules. Remember that pseudocode is a tool that enables a program designer to develop program logic without becoming bogged down in the details of any particular programming lan-

FIGURE 7–17
Structure chart for purchase update
program

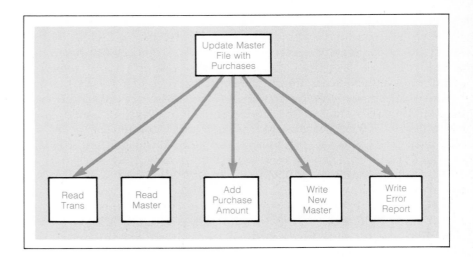

guage. (A flowchart for the controlling module can be seen in figure 7–20). The controlling module begins by setting two variables, EOF-MASTER and EOF-TRANS to zero. The two variables need explanation. EOF-MASTER is used to tell the program when EOF is detected on the master file. Initially, EOF-MASTER is set to 0, meaning EOF has not been reached. When the read module detects the end of the master file, it will set EOF-MASTER to 1. The same is done for EOF-TRANS. Variables used in this way are sometimes called **EOF flags**; if the flag is up (1), the file end has been reached.

After the flags are set, the first record is read from each file (CALL READ-MASTER, CALL READ-TRANS). Figure 7–19 shows the pseudocode for each of these modules. (Pseudocode for the other three modules has been omitted for the sake of brevity.) Notice that each of the read modules simply reads the next record from the file and checks to see if EOF has been reached. If EOF has been reached it sets the flag to 1.

The next section of pseudocode in figure 7–18 is the heart of sequential record-matching logic. This section includes everything from DOWHILE to ENDDO. DOWHILE EOF-TRANS = 0 AND EOF-MASTER = 0 mean the instructions that follow (up to ENDDO) will be repeated until one of the files is exhausted. When that happens, program control will skip to the instructions following ENDDO. One of three cases will be true for each pair of records.

CASE 1 occurs when the key fields of the master and transaction records match. The program will apply the customer's purchase to the master file record and then will get another transaction record to replace the one it just applied (there could be more than one purchase for a given customer).

CASE 2 occurs when a matching customer record is not found for a transaction record (the key field of the master record is greater than the key field of the transaction record). The transaction is an error and must be printed on the error report. Then the program replaces that transaction with another one.

CASE 3 occurs when there are no more transactions for a master file record. Either all the transactions for that customer have been applied, or there simply are no purchases for that customer at this time. In either case, the master file record is written to the new master file. The program then replaces the master file record it just finished processing with a new one by calling the module that reads the master file.

Notice that in each case one new record is read to replace the one just processed. Then, with a different pair of records, control returns to the beginning of the **loop**, where the program checks for the end of file. (A loop is a group of instructions that are repeated.) If neither file has run out, the program selects one of the three cases and acts on it.

FIGURE 7–18
Pseudocode for Update Master File with Purchases module

```
BEGIN UPDATE MASTER FILE WITH PURCHASES
   SET EOF-TRANS TO 0, EOF-MASTER TO 0
   CALL READ-TRANS
   CALL READ-MASTER
   DOWHILE EOF-TRANS = 0 AND EOF-MASTER = 0
      CASE 1: CUSTOMER-NUMBER (MASTER) = CUSTOMER-NUMBER (TRANS)
              CALL ADD-PURCHASE-AMOUNT
              CALL READ-TRANS
      CASE 2: CUSTOMER-NUMBER (MASTER) > CUSTOMER-NUMBER (TRANS)
              CALL WRITE-ERROR-REPORT
              CALL READ-TRANS
      CASE 3: CUSTOMER-NUMBER (MASTER) < CUSTOMER-NUMBER (TRANS)
              CALL WRITE-NEW-MASTER
              CALL READ-MASTER
   ENDDO
   DOWHILE EOF-TRANS = 0
      CALL WRITE-ERROR-REPORT
      CALL READ-TRANS
   ENDDO
   DOWHILE EOF-MASTER = 0
      CALL WRITE-NEW-MASTER
      CALL READ-MASTER
   ENDDO
END UPDATE MASTER FILE WITH PURCHASES
```

Eventually one of the files is completely processed, and EOF is detected. Then control passes to the next section.

Each of the next two sections of pseudocode in figure 7–18 flushes the remaining records out of one of the files. The first one (DOWHILE EOF-TRANS = 0) writes all the remaining transactions to the error report. This module is used when the program detects the end of the master file before the end of the transaction file. If there are no more master file records, any remaining transactions must be errors.

The second section (DOWHILE EOF-MASTER = 0) copies all remaining master file records to the new master file. This is used when the program detects the end of the transaction file first. If there are no more transactions, then none of the remaining master records can be updated. Only one of these loops will be executed each time the program is run, but we never know which one it will be.

The need to match transaction and master records is universal to sequential processing. Consequently, this algorithm, with a few modifications, could be used for a large class of sequential processing programs. For example, consider the master file maintenance problem summarized in figure 7–5. Additions, deletions, and modifications are to be made to the customer master file. With slight modifications, the algorithm shown in figure 7–18 could be used to solve this problem. The major difference is the action to be taken once two matching records are found.

Sorting

So far in this chapter, we have skipped lightly over **sorting**. However, sorting is an important activity. The sort depicted in figure 7–15 would actually be done by a computer program, most likely by a **system utility** — that is, a program provided by the computer vendor to

FIGURE 7–19
Pseudocode for read modules

```
BEGIN READ-TRANS
   READ TRANS RECORD
   IF END OF FILE
      SET EOF-TRANS TO 1
   ENDIF
END READ-TRANS

BEGIN READ-MASTER
   READ MASTER RECORD
   IF END OF FILE
      SET EOF-MASTER TO 1
   ENDIF
END READ-MASTER
```

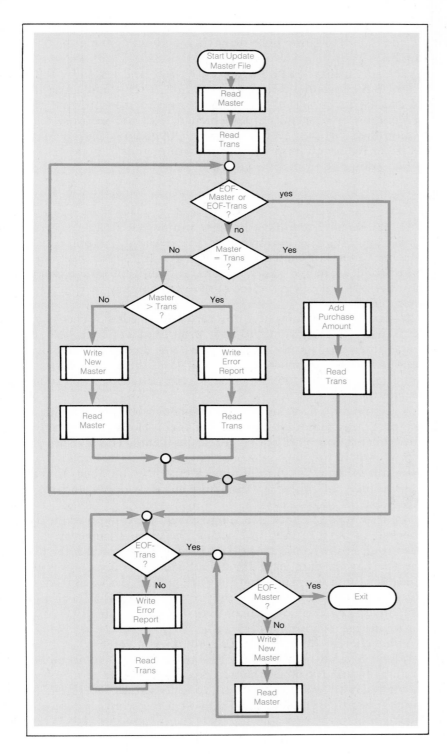

FIGURE 7–20
Flowchart for Update Master File with Purchases module

perform a common activity. Examples of other utilities are programs to copy data, to dump files (print their contents), to merge files, and so forth.

The **sort utility** would have been written and tested by the vendor. Elliot Bay personnel would simply run it. They would enter the name of the file to be sorted, the fields to use in the sort, and the order (ascending or descending) in which to sort the records. The utility would then sort the records and put them on an output file. If the data to be sorted is too large to fit into main memory at one time, tape or other storage equipment would be required.

Data Validation

Thus far we have assumed that programs always receive correct data. Unfortunately, that is unrealistic. *Experienced programmers plan on incorrect data.* For example, we know that Elliot Bay's service bureau had produced many errors because it could not enter the customer number correctly. The service bureau's keypunch operators made too many errors.

A good business computer program always **edits** or checks the input data. If the data is known to have been produced by keyed entries or some other error-prone method, checking should be extensive. If the input comes from a master file on, say, tape, then less checking need be done, assuming that the data was heavily edited as it was added to the master file.

A seemingly infinite number of errors can be made in data. Clearly, the program cannot check for all of them. However, certain types of checking are commonly done. A **reasonableness check** verifies that the input data items have reasonable values. For example, the update program in figure 7–15 might check customer numbers to make sure they include only numeric characters, have six digits, and are positive numbers.

Another type of check is a **range check**. Here, input data items are checked to be sure they fall within the correct range of values. EB Electronics may have a rule that no order can exceed $2000. If so, then the purchase update program should edit the transaction record purchase amounts to ensure that they are greater than 0 and less than or equal to 2,000.00. A program that reads ages might check to be sure that all ages entered are greater than 0 but less than, say, 100 (depending on the users' optimism).

Value checks can be made if the number of values that a data item can have is small. For example, the value for sex should be M or F or perhaps blank. No other characters are acceptable. If a company has 10 plants numbered 1 through 10, the only values acceptable for plant number are the numbers 1 through 10. The records in figure 7–7 had a code field in the first column. Its value is supposed to be 1, 2, 3, or 4. A value check could and should be made on this field.

Value checks can be made on a portion of a field as well. For example, a company may establish the convention that all part numbers are to start with 1. If so, programs can edit part numbers for a 1 in the first position.

Check digits also facilitate program editing. Here, a digit is added to a field to verify the accuracy of the rest of the field. For example, consider EB's customer numbers. They have six digits. Suppose we add together the digits in each of the numbers. For instance, for the number 100040, the sum is 5; for the number 123456, the sum is 21. To create a check digit, we take the number in the ones column of the sum and append it to the customer number. This forms a seven-digit number. Thus, 100040 becomes 1000405 and 123456 becomes 1234561.

Now suppose a data entry operator is to enter customer 1000405, but miskeys the customer number as 1000505. The program will sum the first six digits of the number and get 6. Since the 6 does not agree with the last digit (the check digit), an error will be detected. If 1234561 is miskeyed as 2234561, the check digit of 1 will not agree with the computed digit of 2 (the sum of 2, 2, 3, 4, 5, and 6 is 22).

This is an example of a type of **self-checking number**. Note that this scheme will not catch all errors. If 1234561 is miskeyed as 2134561, the check digit will not catch the error. The sum of the first six digits is still 21, even though the first two digits have been transposed. Another type of check is required to detect this error.

What kind of a check can be used for the value of the purchase amount of the transaction file of the purchase update program? Range and reasonableness checks can be made, but they are not conclusive. If 555.00 were keyed for 055.00, neither of these checks would detect the error. Unfortunately, the program by itself cannot improve the checking of these amounts. Instead, this checking must be supplemented by manual checks performed by users and operations personnel. We will discuss this type of checking in the next section.

▦ PROCEDURES FOR SEQUENTIAL FILE PROCESSING

We discussed the general nature of systems procedures in chapters 2 and 3. We will not repeat that discussion here. However, sequential file systems do impose some special requirements on systems procedures. Those special needs will be discussed in this section.

Correct data is important in all business computer processing, but this is especially true in sequential systems. Because transactions are processed in batches, an erroneous update can easily slip through. It is very hard for humans to ensure the accuracy of every item in a 1500-item list, for example. Furthermore, once an erroneous update is made to a record in a sequential system master file, it is particularly difficult to fix. The entire file must be rewritten to change just one record.

QUESTIONS

7.23 What is a control field? How is it used for sequential file processing?

7.24 Describe the condition that occurs when:

   a. There is a record in Elliot Bay's customer master file that does not match a record on the transaction file.

   b. There is a record in Elliot Bay's transaction file that does not match a record on the customer master file.

7.25 Why does the matching algorithm include a routine to copy the remaining customer records to the new customer master file?

7.26 What is EOF? What role does EOF detection play in the matching algorithm?

7.27 Explain what the DOWHILE statement means.

7.28 Explain what the CASE statement means.

7.29 What is a sort utility? Is this utility a machine or a program?

7.30 Define the following edits and give one example of each:
   a. Reasonableness
   b. Range
   c. Value
   d. Value (portion of a field)
   e. Check digit

7.31 Why are edits not conclusive?

7.32 Modify the pseudocode shown in this chapter to perform master file maintenance (add new customers, delete customers, change customer details). Assume that the master records have the structure illustrated in figure 7–12 and the transaction records have the structure illustrated in figure 7–7.

Two types of procedures are employed to reduce the likelihood of errors. First, updates to master files are often made in two phases. During the first phase, a dry run (dress rehearsal) is made; all of the processing is done, but the master file is not updated. A report of changes to be made is generated, and this report is examined by users. Any erroneous changes are corrected and resubmitted or removed for other corrective action. This type of processing was described previously in the discussion of accounting in chapter 4.

Figure 7–21 shows a two-phased approach for Elliot Bay's purchase update system. The edit program checks the transaction customer master number and purchase amount fields. Both reasonableness and range checks can be made on these fields. Also, a form of value check can be made on the customer number. To do this, the program checks the customer number value by searching the master file for a matching number. If one is found, the number is assumed to be correct.

If the master file is large, this procedure for verifying customer number may be too expensive. In EB's case, reading the 6,500-record customer master file takes very little machine time. But a master file of 200,000 records would require more time than is judged practical. If so, then the transaction data will be edited, but the check on the customer number will not be made until the actual update is done.

Unfortunately, even the check against the master file is inconclusive. If a valid customer number is found on the master file, it is not a guarantee that *the* correct number was entered. It only guarantees that *a* valid number was read. A check digit can be used as well, although, as explained in the last section, this technique is also inconclusive. In truth, no check is conclusive. A variety of checks are made in the hope that any errors will be caught by at least one of them.

The edit report is sent to users by the data processing department and checked. Errors are sent to data entry for correction or are corrected in other ways. Then the edit run is repeated. After errors are fixed the second phase is run. The master file now is updated.

Another procedure often used with batch systems is making manual calculations and comparing them to the computer program's results. For example, the number of transaction records can be counted by the users before they submit them to data processing. Later, when the edit report is available, the users compare this **transaction count** to a count made by the transaction processing program. In this way, users can detect when transactions are duplicated or lost. It is crucial for users to check this number on both the edit and the final update reports.

Batch Totals

An extension of these transaction counts is known as a **batch total**. Here, the users manually compute the total amount of all purchases in

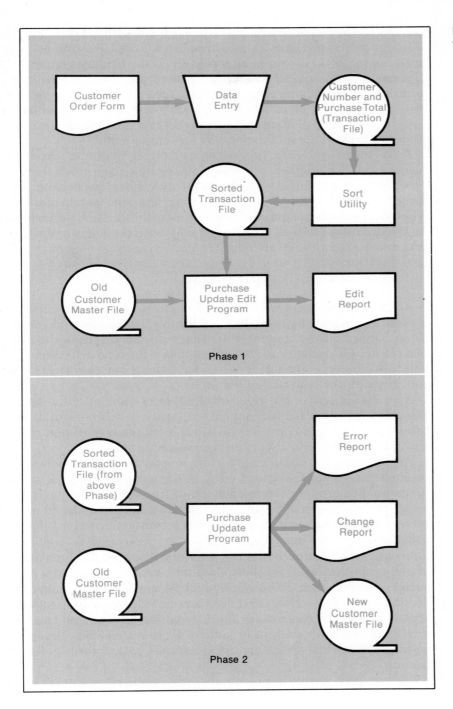

FIGURE 7–21
Two-phased purchase update system

the batch. They then submit the orders to data entry. Later, when the edit report comes back, users compare the total determined by the program to the total computed manually. If the two disagree, then the difference can be traced to its cause. There may have been a manual addition error, a keying error, a missing record, or even an error in the program. If the batch is very large, it may be divided into subbatches to ease the burden of identifying errors. In this case, the program must be coded to print the subbatch totals for comparison.

Thus, users and data processing personnel maintain checks and balances on one another. Simple counts or totals are produced by the two groups using different methods. If they agree, processing is continued. If not, the error is found and corrected. This system works only when both groups are aware of their responsibilities and perform their tasks correctly. Perhaps you can see why both the users and the data processing staff are considered parts of the system.

Backup and Recovery Procedures

In addition to procedures for use, error detection, and error correction, a well-designed system also has procedures for **backup and recovery**. What happens if the computer malfunctions or crashes in the middle of a master file update run? What happens if the tape drive breaks and ruins the master file tape? What happens if an operator spills a soft drink on the transaction file tape?

Here we see one of the great advantages of sequential file systems. Whenever a master file is changed, a completely new copy of the file is produced. If the old copy is kept, along with the transaction records, then the new copy can always be reproduced.

For example, the master file for the first week in January is used to produce the one for the second week. In turn, the second week's master file is used to produce the one for the third week, and so forth. If, for some reason, the master file for the third week is lost, it can be recreated from the second week's file. The transaction records for week 3 are just processed again.

A sequential system that is run weekly will generate 52 master files in one year. How many of these should be kept? Although the answer varies from application to application, a general rule is that three generations of master files and their associated transactions should be kept. Thus, when the master file for the fourth week of January is produced, the first week's file and transactions can be released (see figure 7–22). This procedure is sometimes called **three-generation backup**.

Backup and recovery procedures are very important. There are countless horror stories of companies that have been "dead in the water" because a critical system could not be recovered. Luckily, backup and recovery is easily done for sequential systems. For other

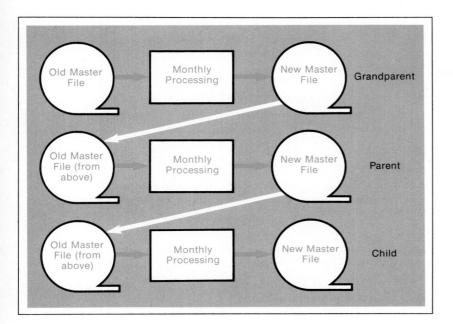

FIGURE 7–22
Child-parent-grandparent processing

types of systems, it becomes much more difficult and expensive. (We will see this situation in chapter 8.) It becomes no less important, however.

To review, procedures for sequential file systems have three unique characteristics. First, a two-phased approach is often employed: An edit run is made and then an actual update. Second, control mechanisms, like transaction counts and batch totals, are often employed by users and data processing personnel as checks and balances. Finally, backup and recovery is accomplished by keeping at least three generations of master files and associated transactions.

PERSONNEL FOR SEQUENTIAL FILE PROCESSING

Users and operations personnel are the two groups involved with the use of a sequential file system.

Users

Users have two major responsibilities for which they need to be trained. First, users need to know what the control procedures are and what they are supposed to do. If transaction counts are to be made or batch totals produced, the users need to know what to do, how to do it, and what to do with the results. The design of effective control

PROFILE

"A SERVICE TO PROVIDE BUSINESSES WITH TIMELY, ACCURATE, AND INEXPENSIVE PAYROLL PROCESSING."

Automatic Data Processing, Inc. (ADP) was founded in 1949 as a service to provide businesses with timely, accurate, and inexpensive payroll processing.

During the past 35 years, the company's services have grown from the processing of simple payrolls to include the most complex business and financial applications and information requirements.

Today the company uses more computers and data communications systems than any independent computing service company in the world to serve more than 125,000 clients in North America, Western Europe, Brazil, and Hong Kong. In brief ADP:

1. Serves more than 125,000 companies, from very small firms to most Fortune 500 listed firms.

2. Processes more than 250 million paychecks a year for over 7 million workers in the United States, Canada, Europe, and Brazil.

3. Provides customer services for over 1,500 banks.

4. Operates one of the largest shared Automatic Teller Machine (ATM) networks in the United States, handling 2 million banking transactions monthly.

5. Manages computerized accounting, inventory, and management services for over 5,000 auto, truck, farm, and construction equipment dealers.

6. Prepares over 3 million automotive collision repair estimates annually for insurance companies — including eight of the ten largest auto insurers in the United States.

7. Operates 50 data processing centers worldwide.

procedures is worthless if the procedures are not performed. Sometimes users take their control responsibilities lightly. They incorrectly assume that computer systems are infallible. Sometimes users simply do not understand how the system works.

Second, users need to know how to correct bad data. If an error is discovered during an edit run, it is easily corrected. If, however, an error gets through the edit and is applied to a master file, it may not be so easy to correct.

For example, suppose the price of an item in inventory is incorrectly stated in a master file. If orders for the item are processed with the incorrect price, it may be very difficult to correct the erroneous orders. Furthermore, once the correction is made, strange results can occur. A customer can order the part under one price and return it under another. If the first price is less than the second one, the customer may make a profit. Consequently, error correction procedures need to be designed carefully, and users need to be trained in how to use them.

Operators

Operations personnel need to be trained in three major areas when executing sequential systems. First, they need to know about the two-phased activity; they must not initiate master file updates until the transaction data has been inspected and approved by users. Second, operations personnel need to know the backup and recovery procedures. They must be able to perform them without assistance from users or the data processing staff. A call at 3:00 A.M. to find out what to do because the system crashed should be a rare event.

Finally, operations personnel must follow defined procedures for handling sequential files — especially master files. In addition to obtaining user approval before updating master files, the operations personnel must release old versions of master files at the appropriate time. This requirement may sound simple, but when a tape library has thousands of tapes and when many sequential systems are in use, it is easy to mount the wrong tape. File-handling procedures need to be carefully designed and well documented. Operations personnel need to be trained to use them.

In many organizations, a **data control clerk** has a role in controlling sequential processing. This clerk, whose office normally is just outside the computer room, receives job requests for processing and job outputs, such as reports, after processing. The task of the data control clerk is to ensure that inputs are complete before processing. The clerk also ensures that jobs are processed when (and only when) they are supposed to be processed, and that all outputs are produced and delivered to the appropriate users. The data control clerk is thus a liaison between users and the operations staff.

▥ SUMMARY

This chapter surveyed the first of the three basic types of organizing and processing data: sequential file organization. We began by discussing the general nature of sequential systems. These systems usually have two types of files: master and transaction. We found that, when master files are changed, a new copy of the file is created. Changes are not made in place in a sequential master file. Sequential systems are designed to process transactions in batches. Although transactions could be processed one at a time or a few at a time, such processing would be expensive because all of the master file must be copied.

We discussed the data and hardware used for sequential processing. Data is represented by bit codes. One common bit code is EBCDIC. Data is recorded in tracks, or columns, across the tape.

In addition to data and hardware, we discussed sequential-file-oriented programs. A common problem is matching transaction records with master file records. Pseudocode of a record-matching algorithm was illustrated. The importance of program editing was emphasized, and several types of edit checks were described.

Finally, procedures and personnel requirements for sequential systems were discussed. The need for control procedures providing checks and balances between users and data processing was described.

QUESTIONS

7.33 Why are errors easy to make with sequential file processing systems? Why are they hard to fix?

7.34 Explain the two-phased change process described for EB's purchase update system.

7.35 What is a batch total and how is it used?

7.36 Describe backup and recovery procedures for sequential file systems.

7.37 Explain the three-generation backup procedure.

7.38 Describe two user responsibilities for sequential systems.

7.39 Describe three operations personnel responsibilities for sequential systems.

Backup and recovery procedures for sequential file systems were defined. Again, it was stressed, the best-designed procedures are worthless if they are not followed. Consequently, training for both users and operations personnel is crucial.

Sequential file systems are very common. They have advantages over other kinds of systems. They are relatively simple, they are fast, and they can be easily backed up and recovered. Unfortunately, they suffer one severe limitation: Direct access to a record is impossible. To read record 1000, the first 999 records must be read or at least passed over. In the next chapter, we will describe a type of file processing that does not have this disadvantage.

WORD LIST

Record	Tape header	Pseudocode
Field	Tape trailer	EOF flag
Sequential file processing	Tape labels	Loop
Master file	Write-protect ring	Sorting
Transaction file	Interrecord gap	System utility
Insert operation	Interblock gap	Sort utility
Delete operation	Recording density	Edit
Modify operation	Bytes per inch (bpi)	Reasonableness check
Batch processing	Record blocking	Range check
Bit	Block	Value check
Byte	Blocking factor	Check digits
Magnetic tape	Buffer	Self-checking number
Tracks	Transport speed	Transaction count
EBCDIC	Control field	Batch total
Parity track	Key	Backup and recovery
Even parity	End of file (EOF)	Three-generation backup
Odd parity	Structure chart	Data control clerk
Parity errors	Program function	
Key-to-tape equipment	Module	

QUESTIONS TO CHALLENGE YOUR THINKING

A. A county government maintains records about the ownership of parcels of land. The legal description of the property, the name and address of the owner, and the date and price of purchase are recorded. The county wants to design a sequential file system to maintain this data.

1. How should this file be sorted?

2. If the length of the record is 150 bytes, how long would reading or writing 45,000 of these records require if the records are stored in a magnetic tape file?

3. Draw a system flowchart of a tape-oriented system to maintain this file.

4. Write pseudocode to insert, delete, and change the owner in these records.

B. A music production company keeps records about concerts it produces. The company keeps a record of the name of the group, the date, the place, and the gross revenue for each concert. It wants to keep this data in a computer file and periodically compute the average revenue for each group as well as the average revenue at each place. Assume that the company handles 50 groups and produces concerts in 200 places. The total number of concerts given so far is 3500; 500 concerts a year are produced.

1. Design a system to keep needed records.

2. Draw a system flowchart of your recommendation in question B1.

3. Develop pseudocode for a program to add concerts to this file.

4. Develop pseudocode for a program to compute the averages.

C. Describe in detail a good application of a sequential file system.

D. Describe an ineffective application of sequential file processing.

DIRECT ACCESS FILE PROCESSING SYSTEMS

CHAPTER 8

There are two fundamental ways of organizing and processing data. One of them, sequential file processing, was presented in chapter 7. In this chapter, we will discuss the second type, **direct access** file processing. Looking ahead, we will discuss in chapter 9 an advanced data processing technique — database processing — that is based on direct access file processing. Keep in mind that none of these techniques is uniformly superior to the others. Each has its own advantages and disadvantages. The choice among these three approaches depends on the system requirements.

THE NATURE OF DIRECT ACCESS PROCESSING

The distinguishing characteristic of a direct access system is that records can be accessed (read or written) from a file in any order. In contrast to sequential processing, there is no need to read all preceding records to get to a particular record. Further, there is no need to rewrite all of the file when a record is changed, inserted, or deleted.

We compared sequential systems to a stereo tape recorder. In a loose way, we can compare a direct access system to a stereo record player. You can play the third song on a record without having to play the first or second. However, direct access computer systems can record data, whereas your record player cannot record music. Before considering how these systems operate, let's examine the need for such a capability.

The Need for Direct Access Processing

Suppose you want to withdraw money from your bank account using a cash machine on a local street corner. You insert your card and then key in the amount of money you want to withdraw. If the bank keeps the balance of your account in a sequential file, you will have to wait while the file is searched to find your account. If there are a large number of depositors at your bank, this search may take five minutes or more. You will become impatient as will those waiting in line for you to finish. Perhaps you will find another bank. The bank needs to be able to access your account balance directly – without sequentially searching through the depositors' records until yours is found.

Suppose you decide to buy a new stereo. You want to pay for it using your Mastercard, Visa, or other bank card. A stereo is an expensive purchase, so the salesperson must call for a credit authorization before he or she can accept your credit card. If the bank card processing center keeps all of its credit information on a sequential file, you and the salesperson will have to wait for the credit file to be searched. All of the records preceding yours in the file must be read. The search could take several minutes or more. To provide better service, the bank card processing center needs direct access to accounts.

Suppose you call a parts distributor for an auto part or similar product. You want to know whether the part you need is in stock before you drive across town. If the distributor keeps the inventory records on a sequential file, and if there are many records in this file, you may have to wait some time for the inventory file to be sequentially searched. Again, the distributor needs direct access to the inventory file records.

In general, a direct access capability is called for when the batching and sorting of transaction records is infeasible. The bank cannot ask you to find 50 other people who want to withdraw money and then require all of you to line up in ascending order according to your account numbers to obtain money (see figure 8–1). The bank must be able to take the transactions (withdrawal requests) one at a time and in random order.

FIGURE 8–1
Here's what could happen without direct access capability

PROFILE

"TRW'S PRODUCT IS INFORMATION."

Direct access is crucial to the efficient updating of credit data. Consider the impact of sequential file processing on TRW.

TRW Information Services division's data center in Anaheim, CA, can be compared to a plant that manufactures information. TRW's product is information; it collects and markets consumer and business credit data. The division's data center stores information on more than 120 million consumers and 8 million businesses and sends 350,000 credit reports a day via high-speed communications lines to up to 25,000 subscribers with terminals at 40,000 locations.

"The manufacturing plant that produces our credit reports is our data center and its computers," says Al Duey, the division's director of computing services. "Reliability is critical to our business. If computers shut down, it's like closing the doors to a store."

TRW delivers reports containing credit information within ten sec-

onds of a request by a subscriber. "Subscribers to our system don't stay online, roaming through our database asking questions or doing searches," explains Delia Fernandez, director of public affairs for the informations services division. "They ask for one particular report, on either a business or consumer." Typically, TRW subscribers receive reports on teleprinters. Subscribers with CPU-to-CPU connections get electronic responses that can be stored in the customer's computer.

TRW also receives credit information from subscribers. Because the majority of TRW subscribers have computerized accounting departments, subscribers typically provide updated information on magnetic tape. More than 2,000 magnetic tapes arrive each month from consumer credit customers and more than 1,000 magnetic tapes and diskettes containing business credit data arrive from businesses.

Information is placed into TRW's online database only after complet-

ing a long journey. TRW continuously revises its online database — at a rate of more than 250 million updates a month. When tapes containing updates arrive at the center, they are first read by IBM tape drives. The data is then moved to a disk that analyzes the information, corrects any errors, and formats data before sending it to an IBM 3851 mass storage system. The mass storage system acts as an intermediate storage device, where data resides before it is sent to the online database. The information that subscribers access is stored on IBM and Control Data disk drives.

"TRW has one quarter trillion bytes' worth of data in mass storage," explains Ken Romans, technical services manager. "We also have about that much storage available on disk drives. The difference is that the disk drives fill almost the entire computer room, but the mass storage system is a blue box that fills only one corner of the room."

Because a direct access system can process transactions in any order, it can always substitute for a sequential system. If transactions happen to arrive in batches in presorted order, it won't matter to the direct access system. The system will process them as if they were random. You may wonder, then, why businesses use sequential systems at all. Why not use direct access systems for all applications? The answer is cost. Direct access systems cost more to design, to implement, and to operate than sequential systems do. Therefore, they are used only when the benefit is worth the cost.

Possible Direct Access Systems at Elliot Bay Electronics

When John Abrams discussed direct access systems at Elliot Bay, he described two possible applications. Figure 8–2 shows a system flowchart for a direct access customer master file system. Requests for changes to the customer master file are submitted to the data entry clerks at terminals. These clerks enter the changes in the master file program via terminals. Each change is made immediately to the customer master file. Note the symbol ▭ .This symbol refers to **direct access media**, which we shall discuss in the next section. Direct access devices serve the same storage function as tape drives, but they have direct access capability.

The advantage of this system over a sequential system is that the clerks have immediate access to customer records. If they need to know what the contents of a record are, they can bring the record up on the screen and examine it. Also, changes can be made immediately. The clerks do not need to wait for data entry operators to prepare input files.

Does EB Electronics need a direct access capability for this application? That is a good question, one that will be hard for EB to answer. As John explained in his presentation, either a sequential or a direct access system is feasible. The direct access system will allow immediate access to the customer data, but it will also cost more to develop and operate. EB will have to decide whether the benefits are worth the costs.

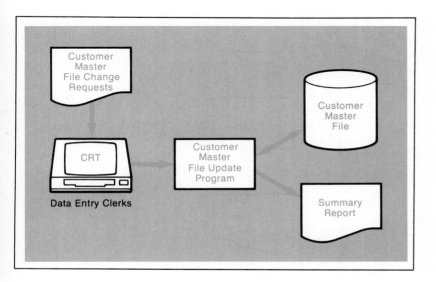

FIGURE 8–2
Direct access customer master file maintenance

Order Pricing Application

The second example John described concerned the order pricing system illustrated in figure 8–3. In this example, items are picked and packed and then moved to a shipping area. Here, a clerk extracts a copy of the picking slip from each order and sends it to data entry. There the data entry personnel prepare a tape file of input data for the order pricing program.

For each order, the order pricing program obtains the price of each item, multiplies the price by the quantity of the item shipped (a process called **price extension**), and computes the total cost of the order. The outputs are priced invoices that are shipped with the orders and a magnetic tape file of customer numbers and order amounts. This file is input to the accounts receivable business computer system (not shown).

For each order to be priced separately, the prices must be on a direct access file. If they were not, then the entire price file would have to be sequentially searched for each item. Extensive searching would be required just to find the prices of a few items on each order. Such searching would be a very time-consuming process. Instead, the program shown in figure 8–3 reads the item number for each item on the order and uses this number to obtain the price of the item directly from the product price file. Then the price extension is done, and the process continues.

FIGURE 8–3
Order pricing system

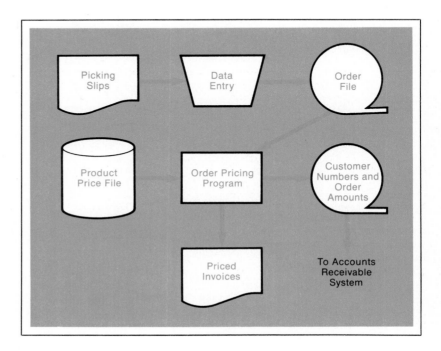

PROFILE

"THE SYSTEM HANDLED 45% OF ALL AIRLINE RESERVATIONS MADE IN THE U.S."

Robert Crandall—chairman, president, and chief executive officer of American Airlines and its parent company, AMR Corp.—guided the development of SABRE (the Semi-Automated Business and Research Environment), a classic in the strategic use of information systems.

SABRE is a worldwide travel information system based in Tulsa, Oklahoma, and a famous example of direct access file processing. According to American's count, the system handled 45% of all airline reservations made in the U.S. last year as well as 20% of all reservations for car rentals and 10% for hotel rooms. AMR employs 2,400 data processing employees. Its DP shop runs two IBM 9083s, two IBM 9090s (specially configured versions of the IBM 3083 and 3090) and an Amdahl Corporation 470V/8.

Crandall says it was his "great good fortune" to be exposed to the business possibilities of DP early in his career as manager of computer programming at Hallmark Cards, Inc. and head of data processing at Trans World Airlines.

He sees more possibilities right now, which is why he recently rehired Max Hopper, the man who developed SABRE and built a reputation for innovation at American. Hopper had left the airline for a short stint at Bank of America, but reclaimed a post at American—senior vice president of information systems—seven months ago.

The following is an interview Crandall gave to Computerworld Features Director George Harrar:

"Will you use SABRE to take you into different markets, such as insurance or retailing?"

"That's conceivable, although our highest priority is the application of the technologies we're good at to the business we know best. Whether there are applications to which we can bring those skills outside the airline business, I'm not sure. Our initial readings of the marketplace are that we're likely to have a pretty full plate in the aviation business for some time to come."

What is Max Hopper's mandate?

"What we've said to Max is that we want to be a more important participant in the data processing and communications marketplace, with a primary focus in commercial aviation and a secondary focus in any other industry where we have proprietary capabilities that will allow us to earn higher than average rates of return. And we've said we've got the dollars to fund those efforts."

"Do you have any problem internally at American convincing others who aren't as sold as you are on the value of information systems?"

"The people in top management are familiar with the technologies and are committed to the notion that we cannot remain the traditional airline. They are aware that sensible and aggressive use of these techniques is a good way to go.

"If we don't reduce our labor cost, we're not going to be in business. The only way to reduce the percentage of the revenue dollar devoted to labor is somehow to do the job in a way that is less labor intensive. The only answer I know is the application of technology. We are driven here both by conviction and necessity.

"Max and his guys spend a lot of time figuring how we can most efficiently staff the airplanes, where we can most efficiently put crew bases—a variety of things that have allowed us to make consistent progress towards wasting less manpower."

"At what stage is the worldwide communications network you are building?"

"We have established locations for 14 nodal sites, something like a Bell central office. We have four or five of those currently installed; the others are going forward in various states of construction. It will have a tremendous amount of growth capability."

Facts and Figures: American Airlines' Sabre System
Miles of data circuits: 700,000
Peak message capacity: 1,200/sec
Fares in data base: 13.5 million
Rates of fare change: 35,000/day
Number of terminal devices: 75,000

Online and Offline Systems

A system in which a user can communicate directly with the computer's CPU is called an **online system**. An example of an online system is the master file maintenance system illustrated in figure 8–2. Data entry clerks can communicate directly with the CPU via terminals. (We will discuss online systems in chapter 10.)

In contrast, the user of an **offline system** has no direct communication with the computer's CPU. An example of an offline system is the order pricing system illustrated in figure 8–3. Data entry clerks using the order pricing system have no direct link to the CPU. They prepare inputs offline with key-to-tape equipment. In short, the terms "online" and "offline" refer to the user's relationship to the computer — a direct link is online while no direct link is offline.

Direct access file processing is used with both online and offline systems. Direct access file processing systems allow rapid access to specific data, a feature that is desirable in most online systems. In fact, most online systems use direct access file processing (or database processing, which is based on direct access), because it is much faster than sequential file processing. However, not all direct access systems are online. Many offline systems, such as the order pricing system shown in figure 8–3, use direct access too. Do not make the mistake of assuming that direct access systems are *always* online systems.

We will now consider each of the five components of a direct access business computer system. Hardware and data will be considered first, followed by programs, procedures, and personnel.

▥ DATA AND HARDWARE FOR DIRECT ACCESS PROCESSING

The most common type of direct access device is a **disk storage unit** (figure 8–4). It has two basic components. A **disk pack** is a collection of disks with **recording surfaces**. It looks much like a stack of phonograph records mounted on a spindle (see figure 8–5). The disk pack is mounted on the disk storage unit. It revolves at high speeds. (Speeds of 50 to 75 revolutions per *second* are typical.)

The surfaces of the disks are coated with an easily magnetized substance. Data is recorded on each disk in concentric circles, as shown in figure 8–6. These circles are called **tracks**. Our comparison with a phonograph record is not perfect; the tracks on a disk surface are not continuous like the groove in a phonograph record is.

Figure 8–7 presents a schematic of a disk storage unit and its associated read/write heads. These heads are used to read data from or write data to the tracks. In most disk units, the heads are attached to access arms that move together to position the heads at any track on the surfaces of the disks. Suppose a disk pack has 10 recording

QUESTIONS

8.1 How does direct access processing differ from sequential file processing?

8.2 Is a bank card processing company for Mastercard or Visa apt to keep credit information on a direct access file or a sequential file? Why?

8.3 Since a direct access system can always substitute for a sequential system, why have sequential systems at all?

8.4 Why is the EB customer master file system shown in figure 8–2 called an *online system*?

8.5 Are all direct access systems online systems?

FIGURE 8–4
Disk storage unit

FIGURE 8–5
Disk pack

FIGURE 8–6
Disk surface

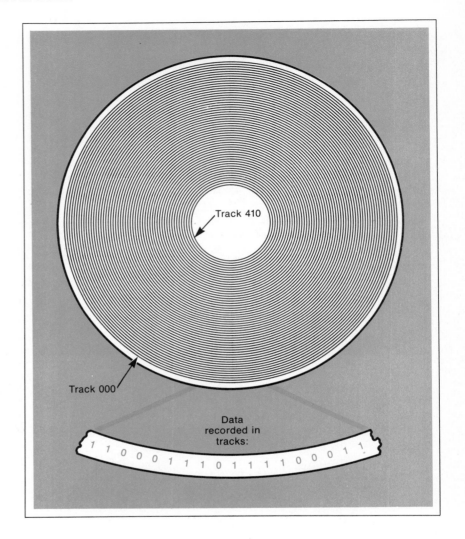

surfaces. When the access arms are fixed in a position, 10 tracks can be read—one on each surface. When the arms are moved to another position, another 10 tracks can be read. The collection of tracks that can be read when the access arms are stationed in a position is called a **cylinder**.

A relatively long period of time is needed to move access arms on a disk drive, so hardware engineers designed a way to reduce the time spent in mechanically positioning the read/write heads. Rather than recording (or reading) an entire disk surface at a time (that is, fill up the outside track, move in one track and fill up that one, move in one more, and so forth), they designed their equipment to fill the track accessed by the first read/write head, and when that one is full to keep the access arms in the same position, switch off the first read/write head and switch on the one below it (electronic switching is much faster than mechanical movement). When that track is full, its read/write head is turned off and the next one down is turned on, allowing the track below it to be accessed. This continues until all of the tracks that can be reached with the access arm in that location are full. Only then does the equipment actually move to a new position, giving access to the next cylinder of recording space. Recording one cylinder at a time is therefore much faster than recording one surface at a time.

Not all disk storage units have **movable read/write heads**. Some units have fixed heads. **Fixed-head** units have one read/write head per cylinder. Consequently, they are more expensive than movable-head units. They may be faster, however, because no time is spent moving the read/write heads to the correct cylinder.

Some disk storage units permit the disk pack to be removed. Thus, packs containing different files can be mounted in the same unit. For other systems, the disk pack must be fixed. Figure 8–8 shows one type of removable disk pack called a **Winchester disk** or **data module**. The

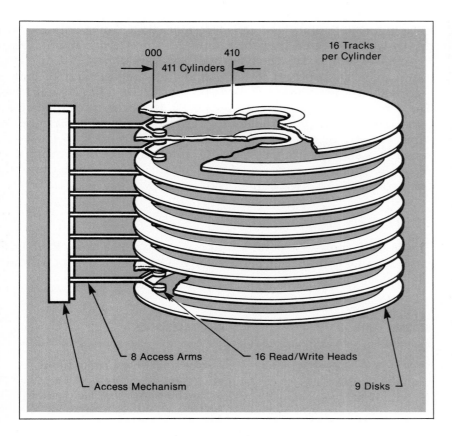

FIGURE 8–7

Schematic of disk storage unit and its read/write heads

FIGURE 8–8
Data module

disk pack and the access arm and heads are encased in a plastic housing, and the entire package is removed. Data modules are more expensive than disk packs like the one shown in figure 8–5, but they have higher reliability and can store more data. Some data modules are so well protected that they require no preventive maintenance. Figure 8–9 summarizes the types of disk storage units.

You may be surprised to learn that the same amount of data is recorded on a small inner track as is recorded on a large outer track. The data is just recorded more densely on the inner track than on the outer one, thus keeping the data transfer rate constant. Because the same amount of time is required for an inner track to make one revolution as for an outer track, the same amount of data must be recorded. Otherwise data would have to be transferred faster from the large tracks than from the small ones.

Data Layout on Disks

Figure 8–10 shows a general layout of data on a disk track. Each track has a starting point that is permanently marked on the track, followed

FIGURE 8–9

Summary of disk characteristics

TYPES OF DISK STORAGE UNITS	CHARACTERISTICS
Fixed or movable heads	Fixed heads have one head per track.
Fixed or removable packs	Fixed packs stay in the unit. Removable packs can be interchanged. (Packs with disk and access arms removed are called *data modules*.)

by a track header, and then blocks of data. The track header contains the name of the track and other system data. As with tape, the application data is recorded in blocks that are collections of one or more logical records. (A block can include several EB Electronics customer master file records, for example.) However, with disks, each block is preceded by a block header that identifies the block, gives its length, and may indicate the contents of the block. Each computer system has its own layout peculiarities, but the general structure is similar to that shown in figure 8–10.

The capacity of a disk pack depends on the type of unit and its manufacturer. Capacities vary from several million characters to 350 million or more. For example, the Hewlett-Packard (HP) 7935H disk storage unit has 1321 cylinders per pack; each cylinder has 13 tracks; and each track can contain up to 23,000 characters, or bytes. The total

FIGURE 8–10
Layout of data on a disk track

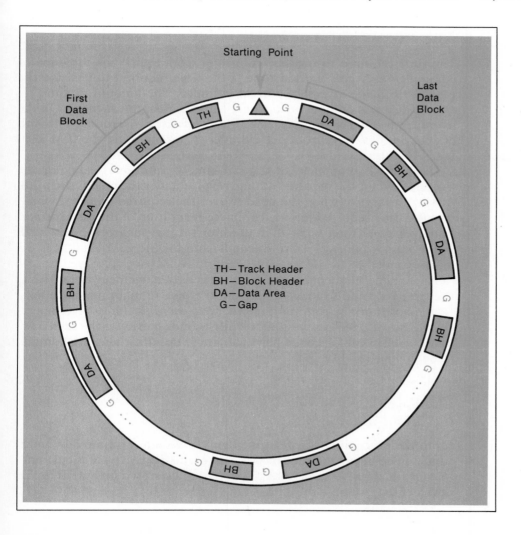

capacity is just over 404 million bytes. The IBM 3380 disk storage unit has 885 cylinders per pack, each cylinder has 15 tracks, and each track can contain up to 47,000 bytes. The total capacity for the IBM 3380 is 630.2 million bytes.

Not all of the stated capacity of a disk pack can be used for application data. Some of the space will be used for system data, like addresses, block lengths, and so forth. Some will be used for interblock gaps. Depending on block sizes and other factors, somewhere between 75 and 95 percent of the available space can be used for application data.

Recall from chapter 6 that the Elliot Bay customer master file has 6,500 records, each 120 bytes long. This is a total of 780,000 bytes. The file would easily fit on either of the two devices just discussed. It would fit on many other devices from other manufacturers as well.

Data Transfer Time on Disks

The time required to transfer data to or from a disk has three major components. **Access motion time** is the time required to position the read/write heads over the correct cylinder. The amount of time required depends on how far the access mechanism must move. On the average, the HP 7935H takes 24 milliseconds (a millisecond is 1/1000th of a second) to move from one cylinder to another, and the IBM 3380 takes 16 milliseconds.

The second component of transfer time is **rotational delay**, or the time needed for the required data to revolve under the read/write head. At best, it is zero (when the head is over the required data); at worst, it is the time required for one complete revolution of the disk surface. The average of the two is often used for timing purposes. For the HP 7935H, this time is 11.1 milliseconds, and for the IBM 3380, it is 8.3 milliseconds.

The final component of transfer time is **data movement time**. This is the time required to move data from the disk to main memory (for a read operation) or from main memory to the disk (for a write operation). The HP 7935H takes 0.001 milliseconds per byte; the IBM 3380 takes 0.00033 milliseconds per byte. These specifications are summarized in figure 8–11.

Processing Times for EB Electronics' Customer Master File

From the preceding transfer-time figures, we can estimate how much time will be needed to read or write all of the EB Electronics customer master file data. Assume that the data will be stored on an HP 7935H device. First, suppose the data is read sequentially.

DEVICE TYPE	AVERAGE ACCESS MOTION TIME	ROTATIONAL DELAY TIME	DATA MOVEMENT TIME
HP 7935H	24 ms	11.1 ms	0.00100 ms per byte
IBM 3380	16 ms	8.3 ms	0.00033 ms per byte

Note: ms = milliseconds

FIGURE 8–11
Typical time requirements for disk units

Reading the File Sequentially

EB has 6,500 120-byte records in the master file. Let's assume eight records are blocked together. Therefore, there are 813 blocks of data. With the HP 7935H, we can assume that 23 of these blocks will fit on each track. Consequently, 813 divided by 23, or 36, tracks will be required. Since there are 13 tracks per cylinder on the HP 7935H, a total of 3 cylinders will be required to hold the data.

Now, consider each of the components of transfer time. For access motion time, an average of 24 milliseconds will be required to find each cylinder. Therefore, 3×0.024, or 0.072, seconds will be required for access motion. For rotational delay, an average of 11.1 milliseconds will be required to find each block, so 813×0.0111, or 9, seconds will be required. Finally, a total of 780,000 bytes of data must be transferred. Thus, $780,000 \times 0.001$ milliseconds, or .78, seconds will be required to transfer the data. Thus, the total time to read or write the EB customer master file is 9.85 seconds.

The time required to read or write the data for the IBM 3380 is not vastly different and will be left as an exercise.

Randomly Reading the File

How much time will be needed to read one of these records randomly? Unless we are lucky, we will have to move the access arm to a new cylinder to find the block. On the average, this movement will take 24 milliseconds for the HP 7935H. The unit will also have to wait for the record to come under the read/write head. On the average, this will take 11.1 milliseconds. Thus, 35.1 milliseconds will be required to find the record.

Once found, the entire block (not just the record wanted) must be read, because the unit is designed to read only whole blocks (not parts of them). There are 960 bytes per block, so, at 0.001 milliseconds per byte, a total of 0.96 milliseconds will be required to read the block. In total, then, 36.06 milliseconds will be required to read the record. Since there are 6,500 records in the file, a total of about 234.4 seconds, or about 3.9 minutes, will be required to read the file in random order.

Compare this to the answer we obtained for reading the file sequentially. To read a record randomly, 36.06 milliseconds are needed. To read the same record in sequential order, only about 2.6 milliseconds are required.

Why is there such a big difference in the times required to read the file? There are two reasons. First, for direct access processing, the access arms must move back and forth across the disk pack. Second, for sequential processing, when a block is read, all eight records in the block are processed. For direct access processing, when a block is read, although only one of the records in the block is needed, all eight records in the block must be read. Therefore, each block is read eight times instead of just once. This fact accounts for the balance of the extra time.

Other Direct Access Hardware

In addition to conventional disk storage units, two other types of direct access media are in common use. One is called a **floppy disk** or, sometimes, just a *floppy*. This medium is similar to a **conventional** or **hard-disk** storage unit, but it is comprised of only one disk (like a

FIGURE 8–12
Floppy disks

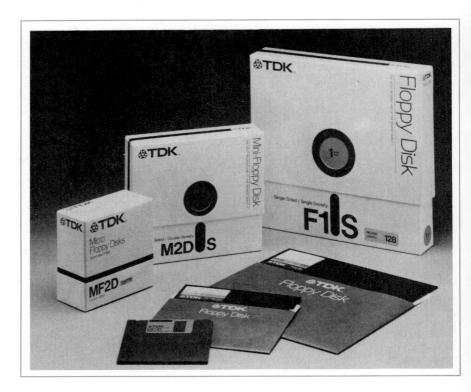

FIGURE 8–13
IBM 3850 mass storage subsystem

phonograph record) instead of a stack of disks. Further, this disk is flexible; hence, the term *floppy*.

The arrangement of data on a floppy is very similar to that on the disks previously described. One difference is that floppies, because of their design, can hold less data. A floppy disk might have two recording surfaces, with 70 tracks per surface and 7680 bytes per track. The total capacity for such a disk is just over 1 million bytes (compared to over 400 million bytes on some hard disks). Also, the time for access motion, rotational delay, and data transfer are considerably longer for floppies. Figure 8–12 shows several floppy disks.

Another type of direct access device is actually a hybrid or combination of tape and disk technology. Figure 8–13 shows a **mass storage device**. Data is stored on small rolls of magnetic tape and then moved, or *staged*, to direct access devices as needed. After the data is processed, it is moved from disk back to the small rolls of tape. The capacity of this unit and of similar units manufactured by other companies is typically in the range of 400 billion bytes. Thus, mass storage devices provide very large-capacity direct access capability.

The cost per byte of stored data is less for a mass storage unit than for the several pure direct access devices required to yield the same

QUESTIONS

8.6 Define the terms *disk storage unit*, *disk pack*, *disk*, *track*, and *cylinder*.

8.7 The XYZ 2000 disk pack has 10 surfaces, 200 tracks per surface, and 10,000 bytes per track. What is the total capacity of the XYZ disk pack?

8.8 What is the difference between a record and a block?

8.9 What is access motion time? Rotational delay? Data movement time?

8.10 Average access motion time for the XYZ 2000 is 50 milliseconds to move from one cylinder to the next. What is the access time required to read a file of five cylinders sequentially?

8.11 Rotational delay for the XYZ 2000 is 10 milliseconds. What will be the total rotational delay time for reading 500 records?

8.12 The XYZ 2000 transfers data at the rate of 0.001 millisecond per byte. How much time will be required to read 500 records if they are 200 bytes long?

8.13 What is the total time required for the XYZ 2000 to read sequentially a file of 500 records, 200 bytes long, that occupies five cylinders? (The records are not blocked.)

8.14 Why does it take so much longer to process a file randomly than it does to process a file sequentially?

8.15 What is a floppy?

capacity. The disadvantage is that the data must be staged from tape to disk and back. This staging, however, is automatic; it requires no human intervention. These units, by the way, are fascinating to watch. If you have the opportunity to see one, don't pass it up.

▓ DIRECT ACCESS DATA ORGANIZATION

Records must be uniquely identifiable, a fact you learned when studying sequential file processing systems in the previous chapter. Each record contains a field whose value is different from that of every other record in the file — an account number or a part number, for example. In a sequential file, records are arranged according to the value in the key field, that is, relative to each other. This correspondence between the value of the key field and the relative position of a record in the file makes it easier to locate a record than if all the records were jumbled up randomly.

Direct access file processing systems also require records to have unique key fields, but the physical arrangement of records within the file is different from that of sequential files.

A record stored on disk is located at a specific physical address: It is a certain distance from the center of the disk (cylinder number), on a certain recording surface (track number), and a certain distance from a reference point on that track (record number). Thus, if you know the cylinder, track, and record number of a particular record, accessing it can be almost instantaneous. (Sequential files are not organized this way.)

The fundamental problem for direct access processing is to convert a key field value to the physical address of the record on a direct access device. There are two primary techniques or file organizations for doing this. One is called **random**, or **direct**, **file organization**, and the other is called **indexed sequential file organization**.

Unfortunately, the terminology as used in industry is confusing in this area. To review, the two types of file processing are sequential and direct access. Under the category of direct access file processing are two file organizations: random, or direct, and indexed sequential. Thus, the term *direct* is used in two ways: as the name of a type of file processing and as the name of a type of direct access file organization. To make matters worse, the term *random* is used in the same two ways.

In this book, we will use the term *direct* to refer only to a type of file *processing* (in contrast to sequential file processing) and the term *random* to refer only to a type of file *organization* (in contrast to indexed sequential file organization). This is awkward, but it can't be helped. Industry uses the terms this way, and you should be aware of its terminology.

Random File Organization

The first way of converting a record key field value to a physical disk address is called **random file organization**. This method treats the characters in the key field as a numeric value (remember that even letters are stored internally as a binary number code). The technique is to perform a calculation called a **hashing algorithm** on the key field value that results in a physical disk address. Thus, the value of a key is arithmetically manipulated to determine a record's location in a file.

For example, suppose Elliot Bay has an inventory file of less than 1000 items. One way of determining record locations would be to take the last three digits of the part number as the address of the record. Thus, part number 12345 would be assigned record location 345 on the file, part number 14592 would be at location 592, and so on.

As you can see, a problem occurs if two different parts have the same last three digits. Both part 12345 and part 32345 are assigned location 345. One way to solve this problem is to put one of these records in location 345 and to put the other in the next available location. Thus, the calculated address is the place to start looking for the record. This addressing scheme is summarized in figure 8–14. Other ways are used but are not important for your understanding of business computer systems (at least in this course).

When this file is first created, the direct access device is formatted with 1000 empty records. These records can be thought of as empty buckets or placeholders. Then the file is loaded with the inventory data by assigning the records to file locations according to their last three digits.

Can you see the problem that could occur if the file were completely full? Suppose that when the 1000th record is loaded, the only remaining empty record is record 999. Further, suppose that the part number of the last item is 12000. Its assigned location is zero, but the next available location is 999! For this reason, randomly organized files should be only 60 to 70 percent full. Even so, similar problems can occur.

Now, how does the system find a record? Given part number 12345, it will first find the record at location 345. If record 12345 is in location 345, the system will stop because the desired record has been found. If not, it will read the next record and so on until record 12345 is found. To modify a record, the system will first read the record into main memory as just described, then modify the record contents, and then write it back out to the location in which it was found. To delete a record, the system will first find it and then replace it with an empty record, or indicate that the record is deleted by putting a special mark on it (a question mark in the first position, for example).

This discussion has assumed that the records are unblocked. If there are several inventory records per physical block, then the algorithm

FIGURE 8–14
Allocating records to random file using last three digits

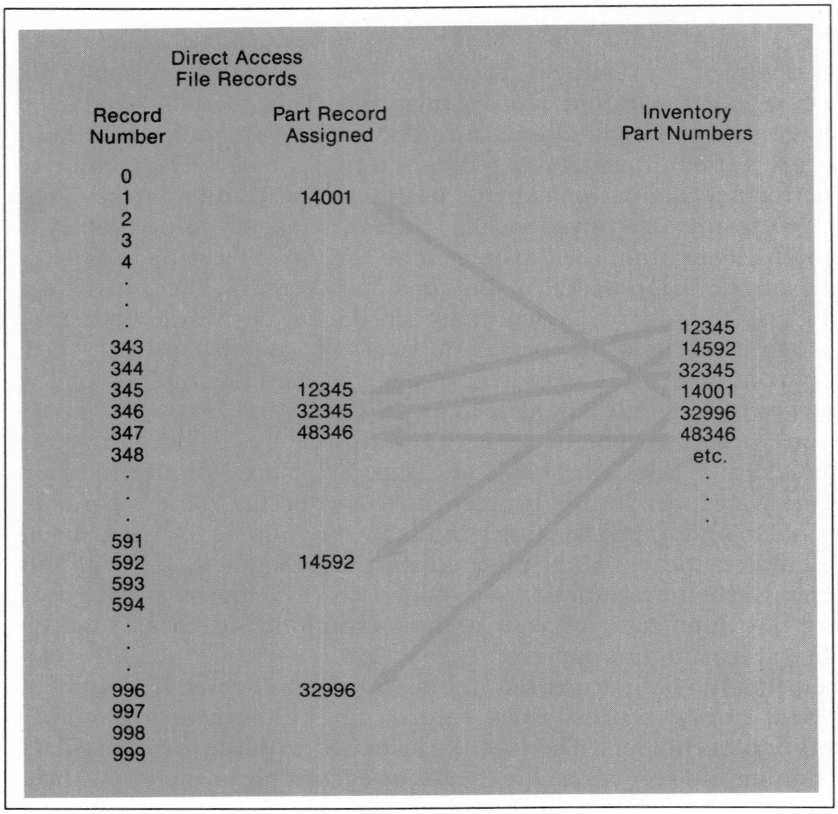

for computing addresses must be a little more sophisticated. Otherwise, the process is nearly the same.

Random file organization is the fastest direct access file organization. Unfortunately, it suffers from several disadvantages. First, the records are allocated to the file in a seemingly haphazard fashion. If the records are read in the order in which they are stored on the direct access device, they are not in any logical sequence. That would make it difficult for Elliot Bay to issue a list of inventory items in part number sequence without some further processing. Second, it is hard to expand a randomly organized file. If Elliot Bay wants to have 10,000 items in inventory, the file and some of the programs must be altered. Finally, as mentioned, randomly organized files should never be full. Consequently, 20 or 30 percent of the file space is wasted. However, in spite of this, when an application calls for very fast retrieval, random organization can be effective.

Indexed Sequential File Organization

The second file organization that allows you to determine a record's disk address based on the value of its key field is called **indexed**

sequential organization. Indexed sequential organization stores almost all of the records in a file in key sequence (like sequential file processing). However, indexed sequential files also include lists of keys and pointers, called indexes, that enable the system to quickly determine the track and cylinder on which a record is stored.

Indexes work much the same way as the index to an encyclopedia. One index tells you in which volume you will find a topic you are interested in. Then an index in that volume tells you on what page you will find the topic. Finally, when you locate the page, you scan it to locate the topic. (In contrast, sequential processing would have you scan each page of each volume, starting at "aardvark," until you eventually hit the topic you were looking for.)

With indexed sequential file processing one index points to the cylinder on which a desired record will be found. Then an index on that cylinder points to the correct track. Once there, the system scans the records on the track sequentially until the correct one is located (thus the name "indexed sequential"). Indexed sequential organization is very versatile in that it can accommodate both sequential processing and direct processing.

Since records are to be kept in key sequence, inserts pose a problem. Rather than rewrite the entire file as is done with sequential processing, indexed sequential organization puts the new records in their correct places on a track and moves the last record on the track to a special place called an **overflow area**. Thus, in figure 8–15, when record 12 was inserted, record 20 was moved to the overflow area; when record 14 was inserted, record 15 was also moved into the overflow area.

When the file in figure 8–15b is processed sequentially, the system will read records 5, 10, 12, and 14 from track 1. It will then find records 15 and 20 in the overflow area. Then it will process the records on track 2. Thus, all of the records will be retrieved in the correct order.

Indexed sequential organization is an excellent compromise between straight sequential and pure random file organizations. It is most useful in applications that call for both sequential and direct processing. A good example is credit card authorizations. At the end of the month, the credit file is processed sequentially to produce the customer bills. However, throughout the month, it is processed directly for credit authorizations.

Unfortunately, like all compromises, indexed sequential organization has disadvantages. Sequential processing is slower for an indexed sequential file than for a sequential file. Direct processing is slower for an indexed sequential file than for a random file. Also, the overflow areas take up extra file space. Finally, after many inserts, record retrieval becomes slow. Figure 8–16 summarizes advantages and disadvantages of sequential, random, and indexed sequential file organizations.

QUESTIONS

8.16 What is a key?

8.17 What are the two possible meanings for the term *direct processing*?

8.18 What are the two possible meanings for the term *random processing*?

8.19 Which of the two meanings of *direct processing* will we use in this book? Which will we use for *random processing*?

8.20 In the random file organization shown in figure 8–14, to what location will part number 45897 be assigned? Where will part number 22345 be assigned? Where will part number 22345 actually be stored?

8.21 Why should a randomly organized file never be completely full?

8.22 Name three disadvantages of random file organization.

8.23 Does an indexed sequential file allow direct access or sequential processing?

8.24 How are inserts made to an indexed sequential file?

8.25 Describe a good application for random file organization.

8.26 Describe a good application for indexed sequential file organization.

FIGURE 8−15

Inserts in an indexed sequential file.
a. Before inserts. *b.* After inserting
records 12, 14, 47, 48, 49

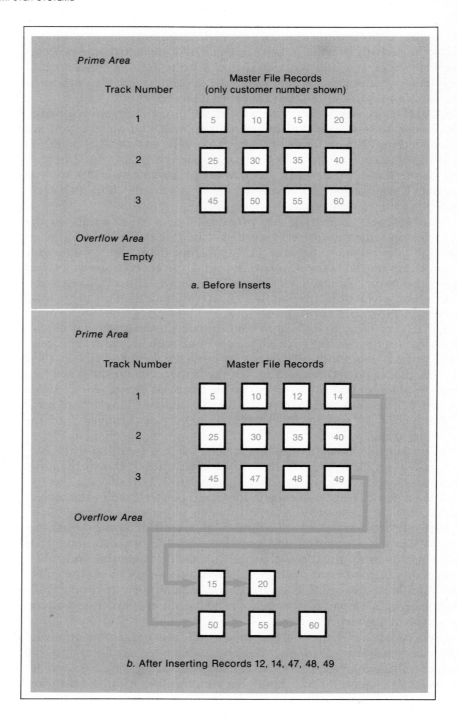

PROFILE

"TWA USES A COMPUTER TO TRACK TRAINING."

Direct access to specific records can be easily handled by a computer system. In the system described here, users at online terminals around the world instantly access data on any of more than 5,500 individuals—with just a few keystrokes.

While maintenance and engineering computer systems are becoming standard throughout the airline industry, TWA is taking computerization one step further. It uses a proprietary computer program to track the training of the more than 5,500 mechanics who work on its aircraft.

Dubbed the "Maintenance Training Record System," the program was developed in less than a year by the manager of the maintenance

data processing and two data processing staffers. TWA, the nation's 11th largest transportation company, has run the system on a DEC VAX 11/750 minicomputer since January 1983. Users in the field have access to the system via a network of remote terminals.

The system provides a complete training history for each of the airlines' mechanics as well as mechanics from other airlines who also service TWA aircraft. TWA flies into 62 airports in the United States and has its own mechanics stationed at 22 of them. Mechanics for other airlines provide service at airports little serviced by TWA. For instance, United Airlines mechanics work on TWA

planes in Salt Lake City when necessary. TWA also has its own mechanics stationed at 11 of the 17 foreign airports it serves, relying on foreign airlines' staffers at the remaining six sites.

TWA annually spends an estimated $5,000 to train each of its mechanics. Upon completing a course, the instructor updates the file of each mechanic trained, including mechanics from other airlines who are trained in TWA's procedures for its own airliners. "It gives you ready access to all the relevant skills information on the individual," says TWA's staff vice president of maintenance support, Joseph Nemecek.

PROGRAMS FOR DIRECT ACCESS PROCESSING

Programs that use direct access file processing are easier for a computer programmer to write than programs that use sequential file processing. One reason for this is that in a direct access file processing system the burden of locating a specific record is handled by a special program called the **operating system** (see module E). The programmer

FIGURE 8–16
Comparison of file organizations

FILE ORGANIZATION	ADVANTAGES/DISADVANTAGES
Sequential (tape or disk)	Simple to use Fast and efficient for large batches Cannot update in middle of file
Indexed sequential (disk)	Can update in middle of file Both sequential and direct processing are possible Processing may be slow
Random (disk)	Can update in middle of file Processing is very fast Has wasted file space

simply identifies the key and the system software actually finds and retrieves the matching record.

In contrast, a programmer who writes a program that uses sequential files must write the complex program logic to ensure that the correct records are retrieved at the right time. In actuality, though, direct file processing is much more complex than sequential file processing. It only seems easier because the operating system does much of the difficult work. Now let's see how Elliot Bay handled their direct file processing system.

▥ ELLIOT BAY'S CUSTOMER MASTER FILE UPDATE

To view a direct access application program more closely, we will consider the EB Electronics customer master file update program shown in figure 8–2. Again, a clerk at a terminal enters requests to the update program. The program then accesses the direct access customer master file. For this example, we will assume that this file has indexed sequential organization and that the key is the customer number.

Four basic actions can be taken in maintaining a master file. Records can be inserted, deleted, modified, and read. Corresponding to each of these actions is a command that the application programmer may use. Thus, when he or she codes the INSERT command, the operating system will cause a new record to be added to the file. Now, since this is a direct access application, the operating system needs to know what to call the new record — that is, what the key of the new record will be. Usually this key value is specified in a command such as INSERT 123456 INTO CUSTOMER MASTER FILE. This command means insert a new record whose key is 123456 into the customer master file. The data for the new record will also be supplied by the application program, but the way that this is done depends on the language used. (Ask your instructor to explain how it is done in the language you use.)

Examples of other indexed sequential commands are DELETE 123456 FROM CUSTOMER MASTER FILE, REPLACE 123456 IN CUSTOMER MASTER FILE, and READ 123456 FROM CUSTOMER MASTER FILE.

Recall that the commands for processing a sequential file named only an operation (such as READ) and the name of a file. The identity or key of the record was not needed. The next record in sequential order was assumed to be the one to be processed.

A Direct Access Program for EB's Customer Master File

Figure 8–17 shows a structure chart for EB's customer master file maintenance program. Pseudocode for the controlling module appears

FIGURE 8–17
Structure chart for customer master file
update program

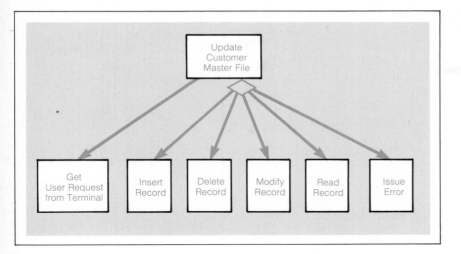

in figure 8–18. This pseudocode references three files. MASTER FILE
is the indexed sequential file having the customer data. SUMMARY
REPORT is a printed report of the actions taken by the clerk at the
terminal. This report documents changes that have been made for
later reference if errors are discovered. The third file is called TERMI-
NAL; it corresponds to the terminal employed by the user.

At first, considering a user at a terminal as a file may seem odd.
However, because the user supplies data to the program, and because
the program outputs data to the user, the terminal is like a storage file.
Therefore, terminals are often processed as files in application programs.

The structure chart in figure 8–17 indicates that the customer
master file update program is comprised of seven modules. In addition
to pseudocode for the controlling module, Update Customer Master
File, pseudocode for two subordinate modules, Insert Record, and
Delete Record, can be found in figure 8–19. Pseudocode for the other
modules has been omitted for the sake of brevity.

Examine the logic for the main module, Update Customer Master
File. The program begins by opening the files. (This means that the
operating system will take whatever action is necessary to prepare to
use the files.) Then it calls a subroutine that asks the user to enter a
request code. A request code of 0 means stop, I means insert, D means
delete, M means modify, and R means read. The program will reject
anything else the user enters and will ask the user again to enter a
request code.

Once the program gets a user request code it begins a loop that will
be repeated until the user enters a zero. The controlling module simply
examines the request code and calls the appropriate subroutine to
handle it. Notice on the structure chart that there is one subroutine for

```
BEGIN UPDATE CUSTOMER MASTER FILE
  OPEN MASTER FILE, SUMMARY REPORT, TERMINAL
  CALL GET-USER-REQUEST-FROM-TERMINAL
  DOUNTIL USER REQUEST = 0
    CASE USER REQUEST
      CASE 1: USER REQUEST = "I"
              CALL INSERT-RECORD
      CASE 2: USER REQUEST = "D"
              CALL DELETE-RECORD
      CASE 3: USER REQUEST = "M"
              CALL MODIFY-RECORD
      CASE 4: USER REQUEST = "R"
              CALL READ-RECORD
      CASE 5: USER REQUEST NOT = "I" AND "D" AND "M" AND "R"
              CALL ISSUE-ERROR
    END CASE
    CALL GET-USER-REQUEST-FROM-TERMINAL
  ENDDO
  CLOSE FILES
END UPDATE CUSTOMER MASTER FILE
```

FIGURE 8–18
Pseudocode for customer master file
update module

each request code and one to handle errors. Each time the user enters a request code, one and only one of these five subroutines will be invoked. The diamond symbol ◊ on the structure chart highlights this aspect of the program.

After one function has been performed (or an error message issued), the program asks the user for another request code and then waits for the user to respond. When the user responds with a zero, program control passes to the instructions following the loop. In this program the next instruction closes the files, and the program terminates.

Now examine the logic for two of the subordinate modules in figure 8–19. In both cases the program gets a key field (and maybe other data as well) from the user at the terminal and then checks to see if that customer is in the master file. If the customer is in the file and the user is trying to add a new customer with the same number, the program rejects that request. Conversely, the user can delete only those customers who are in the master file. An error occurs if the user tries to delete someone who does not have a record on file. The other two subroutines, MODIFY-RECORD and READ-RECORD, are similar.

Characteristics of Direct Access Programs

If you compare the pseudocode shown in figure 8–18 to the pseudocode for making updates to the sequential file shown in figure 7–18, you will find that the direct access pseudocode is simpler. It is simpler because there is no need to match records against one another, as there is in sequential processing. In actuality, direct access processing is much more complex than sequential processing. Most of the extra work, however, is taken care of by the operating system so the application programmer does not see it.

Because the customer master file is an indexed sequential file, it could also be processed sequentially. Therefore, the pseudocode in figure 7–18 could be used to update the customer master file with sales data. In fact, EB's customer system could very well use indexed sequential processing. EB could construct the customer master file as an indexed sequential file and use direct processing to update the customer records with sales data. EB could use direct access processing to maintain current customer data and add new customers. The company could also use sequential processing to generate customer invoices at month end and to update everyone's discount at the end of each quarter.

Random organization of direct access files places more burden on the application programmer than indexed sequential organization

FIGURE 8–19
Pseudocode for insert and delete modules

```
BEGIN INSERT-RECORD
  GET CUSTOMER DATA FROM TERMINAL
  READ CUSTOMER FILE
  IF CUSTOMER IS ON FILE
  THEN ISSUE ERROR MESSAGE
    DISPLAY "CUSTOMER CANNOT BE ADDED—ALREADY ON FILE" ON TERMINAL
  ELSE FORMAT NEW CUSTOMER RECORD
    WRITE NEW RECORD ON FILE
    ISSUE LINE ON SUMMARY REPORT
    DISPLAY "NEW CUSTOMER ADDED TO FILE" ON TERMINAL
  ENDIF
END INSERT-RECORD

BEGIN DELETE-RECORD
  GET CUSTOMER NUMBER FROM TERMINAL
  READ CUSTOMER FILE
  IF CUSTOMER IS ON FILE
  THEN DELETE RECORD
    ISSUE LINE ON SUMMARY REPORT
    DISPLAY "CUSTOMER DELETED FROM FILE" ON TERMINAL
  ELSE ISSUE ERROR MESSAGE
    DISPLAY "CUSTOMER CANNOT BE DELETED—NOT ON FILE" ON TERMINAL
  ENDIF
END DELETE-RECORD
```

QUESTIONS

8.27 When performing direct access I/O, the application program must specify an extra parameter. What is it?

8.28 Why consider a user at a terminal as a file?

8.29 Although direct access processing is complex, it is easy for an applications programmer to code. What programs handle the complex aspects?

8.30 Write the pseudocode for the Modify Record and Read Record modules in figure 8–17.

does. To understand it fully requires more detail than is probably necessary for your business career. Consequently, we will not view pseudocode for a randomly organized file. See [27] and [56] for discussions if you are interested. For now, it will be sufficient to remember that random organization exists and that it is one of two major types of direct access file organization.

Direct access file organizations are not standardized across makes and models of computers. The syntax of commands, as well as the details of the file organizations, vary from one computer to another. The commands described in this section are generalized. They do not correspond to any particular manufacturer's language. Furthermore, some operating systems provide a wider variety of direct access organizations. These organizations are variations and extensions of the two basic types described here. If you understand these two organizations and their capabilities and limitations, you should be able to understand other variations that you encounter.

PROCEDURES FOR DIRECT ACCESS PROCESSING

"Let's suppose," said John Abrams, "that EB Electronics has the customer master file in an indexed sequential file and that clerks make changes to this file directly using a customer update program. Could a clerk accidentally delete the wrong customer? Would this be hard to do? Also, could a clerk change his or her own sales amounts and thereby get an extra-large discount the next quarter?"

These questions started a loud and active conversation during which the project team discovered an important fact: *Although direct access systems have many advantages and are easy to use, they are also very hard to control*. Errors are easily made, and data is vulnerable to unauthorized activity. As the discussion progressed, John explained how systems procedures can be used to control direct access systems. He described two categories of procedures: those used for normal operations and those used when a system failure occurs. We will consider the procedures for normal operation first.

User Procedures for Normal Operation

Users need to know how to perform each operation on the file. Therefore there should be a written procedure that describes the steps a clerk takes to add, or insert, a new customer. Procedures for deletion, for modification, and for reading should also be written.

The insert procedure is summarized in figure 8–20. When the clerk receives a customer order, he or she first determines if the customer has ordered before. If so, then no insert is needed. If not, the clerk

```
CHECK FOR PREVIOUS ORDER
IF NO PREVIOUS ORDER
   THEN CHECK DATA FOR COMPLETENESS
      IF INCOMPLETE
         THEN CONTACT CUSTOMER FOR MORE DATA
      END-IF
      CHECK FILE ON BAD RISKS
      IF NOT ON BAD-RISK FILE
         THEN ADD CUSTOMER TO CUSTOMER FILE
         ELSE SEND ORDER TO CUSTOMER CREDIT FOR PROCESSING
      END-IF
END-IF
```

FIGURE 8-20
User procedure for adding customer to customer file

verifies that the customer's name, address, and phone number are complete. If more data is needed, the clerk contacts the customer to obtain the necessary items. Then, a search is made of the bad-risk file to determine the customer's credit worthiness. If no entry is found in the bad-risk file, the customer record is added using the update program. If an entry is found, the order is sent to customer credit for processing there. Customer numbers are assigned by the update program and are printed and returned to the customer when the order is processed.

Why is this procedure necessary? Without it, as John explained, clerks may enter new customers with incomplete data, or they may not know what to do if some data is missing, or they may add customers who have caused problems in the past. Each clerk may take a different action, and the results will be unpredictable. Worst of all, some requests with insufficient data may neither be inserted nor returned to the customer. Thus, the situation may occur in which someone submits an order to EB and then never hears from the company. Finally, without procedures, there will be no means for reporting errors and for correcting them when they occur.

The Need for Procedures

Think for a moment about the "computer errors" publicized in the news. Frequently, these are not *computer* errors at all, but errors in procedures or errors in following procedures. Suppose that EB Electronics implemented this system with poorly defined procedures and, as a result, two customers' records were intermixed; say, one customer was assigned another customer's address. If that happened, one person could receive another person's order, and someone else could receive a bill for goods that he or she never received. These errors might incorrectly be blamed on the computer.

The problems that can be caused by incorrect modifications and deletions are even worse. If a clerk modifies the wrong customer record, say, when changing a customer name, then two errors are generated: The desired name change is not made, and another customer's name becomes incorrect. If the wrong record is deleted, a customer will inexplicably disappear from the file, while a customer that was to have been deleted is retained.

Because of these potential difficulties, modification and deletion procedures usually call for some type of verification before the action is taken. For example, the clerk may first read a customer record and verify that the name on the file is the name that is on the change request form. If not, the change is not made.

The verification step can be coded in the program. Thus, when the clerk types in the number of a customer to be deleted, the program will display a message like "THIS IS THE RECORD OF JOHN PARKS IN OMAHA, NEB. IS THIS THE RECORD YOU WISH TO DELETE?" If the clerk then types YES, the deletion is made. Otherwise, the deletion is not made, and the clerk must find the correct number or return the deletion request to obtain the correct data.

Error-Correction Procedures

If procedures are well designed and documented and if clerks are trained in their use, many errors will be detected before the customer master file is incorrectly modified. In spite of this, however, some erroneous changes will be made. When errors occur, procedures are needed to correct the errors.

For example, suppose a customer writes to Elliot Bay complaining that his address has not been changed, even though he requested a change several weeks previously. To determine the source of the error, a supervisor or other employee could check past records. He or she could examine past change request forms to find out whether EB had received the request. If it had been received, the supervisor could find out whether it had been processed, and if so, when and by whom it was processed. Then the supervisor could examine the summary report for that date to determine what happened. If a change was made in the wrong record, the supervisor could initiate action to correct both of the records involved.

Observe that the supervisor cannot just correct the record for the customer who complained because the other customer's record would remain in error. Also, note the need for data about past processing. Both the old change request forms and the summary report are required to find the error. Error-correction procedures need to be carefully designed ahead of time so that necessary data and training can be developed.

Control Procedures

A third type of procedure concerns controls. Data entry clerks could willfully make erroneous changes for their own gain or for the gain of their associates. The only certain control is to maintain accurate records of the transactions processed and to compare them with the source documents. Generating such log files is especially critical in an online direct access file processing system, because without a record of the transactions that are entered there can be no control over the system. Contrast this with sequential file processing systems and batch direct access file processing systems, which use transaction files as input. In those cases, all transactions are automatically "logged."

When transactions are logged a supervisor is able to compare the activities recorded on the summary report with the customer change request forms. Every change made to the master file should correspond to an authorized change request form. If changes are made to the master file that do not have matching change request forms, the supervisor should investigate them to be certain that they are authorized. This investigation can be a long and exhausting process if there are many changes. In some cases, it suffices to check summary data. Thus, the summary report may print the total number of insertions, the total number of deletion documents, and so forth. If the counts do not agree, then a more detailed investigation can be conducted.

In summary, the normal-use procedures for the users of a direct access system have three primary purposes. First, they must specify how the users are to employ the system to obtain correct results. This procedure includes actions to be performed when special situations occur. Second, the procedures must detail what actions are to be taken to correct errors when they are discovered. The procedures should include steps for ensuring that all the data needed to correct an error is saved for a reasonable period of time. Finally, procedures must be designed to provide checks and balances against unauthorized and possibly criminal activity. Procedures are especially important for direct access systems because users have a much greater impact and work more independently than with other types of systems. Users need procedures that explain:

1. How to use the system to accomplish their job.
2. How to correct errors.
3. How to ensure that only authorized activity occurs.

Operators' Procedures for Normal Operation

The computer system operators also need to follow system procedures. The operations staff needs to know how to start programs, what files to mount in the direct access equipment, and how to stop programs. Additionally, security procedures need to be defined so that computer operators know who has authorized access to the programs and data, and when.

Unlike tape files, direct access files are not always dismounted. If data resides on a disk pack that is not removable, or if a removable pack is left in place for some reason, then the data can be readily accessed. Whereas an operator is required to mount a tape volume, no action at all is required to access an available direct access file.

This fact is both an advantage and a disadvantage. Not mounting files is less work for the operations staff, but on the other hand, it results in less control. The operators do not necessarily know what users and programs are accessing the data.

Several controls can be developed to counteract this disadvantage. First, users can be assigned **account numbers** and **passwords**. These are special numbers or code words. If the user cannot provide the correct number or code word, then the computer will not allow access to certain programs. Users in the shipping department, for example, can be restricted from the programs in the customer service department if they do not know the customer service account numbers and passwords. Further, files themselves can have passwords. A user may have to specify one password to use a program and another password to access a critical file. Passwords also can be restricted as to specific functions. One password may permit read-only access. Another may allow both reading and inserting. A third may allow reading, inserting, deleting, and modifying.

The operations staff may be involved in setting up passwords. If so, they need procedures. Further, they need to know the importance of passwords and of not circumventing them for the users' convenience.

Another procedural responsibility of operations is to run computer jobs only in accordance with established schedules. These schedules are set up to ensure that all the computer workload can be accomplished in a timely manner; they also serve as a control measure. Because the user of a direct access system can have nearly unlimited ability to modify the contents of a file, such systems are often restricted for use only during normal business hours. The hope is that the activity will be adequately supervised during this time.

Thus, procedures need to be defined that describe what programs are to be run at what times. The operations staff also needs to have a procedure for making exceptions to the schedule. This procedure may merely be the name of someone to call to authorize changes in the schedule.

A final procedure for the operation of a direct access system is periodically to obtain **backup copies** of the direct access files. This need can be met by copying or dumping the direct access data to a tape file. New generations of master files are not created as a by-product of processing, as they are in sequential systems. Updates are made in place. When they are made, the old data is lost. If the file is damaged in some way, the data can be restored only from a backup copy.

APPLICATION

"HOW CAN THEY BACK UP FILES THAT ARE CONTINUOUSLY BEING UPDATED?"

Data processing managers are discovering a storage problem that seems to be ticking toward disaster. Their users are coming to depend on interactive mainframe applications as much as 24 hours a day and those applications are causing disk files to grow exponentially. Meanwhile, batch jobs must also be run. The problem is finding enough free system time between on-line and batch processing to complete the tasks of backing up critical disk files to tape.

It is not unusual to find hundreds of gigabytes of disk storage attached to large-scale mainframes, but the more those data files are needed for production jobs the less time there is to copy them. The backup window that has traditionally existed between the daily interactive and nightly batch processing cycles is closing inexorably, and that is creating severe operational problems for large users. Running backup jobs during either production period causes inefficient system usage or, worse, risks degraded performance.

With total disk capacity projected to continue to grow at 50% each year, fueled primarily by less costly and denser DASDs, it doesn't seem as if the problem will get much better anytime soon. "The (backup) window is too narrow as it is," observes Nick Allen, program director of the Gartner Group, a market research firm in Stamford, Conn. "And it's only going to get worse with more data that needs to be backed up."

"Banks are the best example. With their 24-hour operations, how can they back up files that are continuously being updated?" asks Jane Morse, a senior staff member within the Information Systems Group at the consulting firm of Arthur D. Little of Cambridge, Mass. For data constantly being updated, total read-write capability would be needed, but that is a development that industry gurus say is still over the horizon. "Perhaps a box that attaches between the computer and a DASD would do the trick," theorizes DPCE's Skaw. "It would send the data that needs to be backed up directly to tape while the computer continues processing."

Even if a company is able to keep pace with its backup storage chores, it has to be able to quickly find the required tapes to return its data center to full operation. The number one priority, in the event of an emergency, is tape accessibility, whether files are stored off-site at a third party's facility or at a company-owned site.

Firms large enough to have their own warehouse to accommodate the ever-growing number of backup tapes still make multiple copies of each file, storing one version in a nearby or out-of-town company-owned facility, another with a third party.

"Survivability of the data is the key," says Travelers' Horansky. Toward that end, Travelers, like a number of large companies, has set up a systems assurance group to monitor in-house tape library services, off-site vaulting, and other related disaster recovery services. "There are about 20 people involved. Some are more involved in planning, while others are involved with implementation," Horansky notes.

Unfortunately, according to Arthur D. Little's Morse, many companies are not paying as much attention to the backup and recovery issue as they should. "As companies become more dependent on their computers, they have to know where their backup is in the event the data is lost — and data is lost," she emphasizes.

"It should be similar to that famous question asked before some television stations' late news: 'Do you know where your children are?' ", Morse says, adding, "Do you know where your backup is?"

Backup Procedures

Procedures need to be defined that tell the operations personnel when and how to back up the direct access files. Procedures should also be defined for the operations supervisors to check periodically on backup activity to ensure that it is being properly performed. This step is crucial. Many companies have learned through great agony and expense how important appropriate backup is for direct access systems. Operators need procedures that explain:

1. How to start and stop programs.
2. Which files to mount on devices.
3. How to assign account numbers and passwords.
4. How to maintain integrity of the security program.
5. How to run jobs in accordance with the established schedule.
6. How to handle exceptions.
7. How to back up direct access files.

User Procedures During Systems Failure/Recovery

When a failure occurs in a direct access system, both the users and computer operators need procedures describing what actions they should take. Users need to know what to do while the computer is out of operation. Later, they need to know what to do when the computer first becomes operational again. If the system is online and the users rely on it for the performance of their jobs, they need to know what to do while the system is down. For example, if bank tellers use an online direct access system to post deposits and withdrawals to banking accounts, the tellers need to know what to do when the system fails. Do they continue to accept deposits? If so, what data do they gather for entry in the system when it is again running? Can the tellers allow withdrawals? If so, how do they verify account balances?

The problem for Elliot Bay is not as severe as it might be for a bank. If the customer master file update program won't work, the data entry clerks can simply wait until the system is operational: They have no customers waiting in line. If EB uses direct access processing to price orders, failure might be more disruptive. The shipping area may fill up with orders that have been filled but not priced. The picking of new orders may have to be deferred until the shipping area is cleared. In this case, procedures have to be developed describing what to do until the system is again functioning.

Once the system is repaired, users need procedures describing their recovery activity. Usually, some work must be redone. The amount of rework depends on the severity of the error, the adequacy of the backup and recovery techniques, and luck. Users need procedures for determining how much work must be redone. For example, the users of EB's customer update program could check to see if the last five changes they made to the file were recovered. If not, then the users might go back 25 changes to see if they were recovered. Continuing in this way, the users could discover how much work needed to be redone. Sometimes the operations personnel can help; they may know that the files were recovered accurately as of 8:00 in the morning and that all subsequent changes must be redone.

Operators' Procedures During Systems Failure/Recovery

For computer operators, recovery of a direct access system is a three-step process. First, the operators must have a procedure for determining the general source of the problem. It might be a direct access device malfunction, a CPU or memory failure, a program error, or some other problem. Operations personnel need to know which of these sources of error is at fault so that they can notify the appropriate personnel.

This notification is the second step of recovery. Since operations personnel generally are not trained or experienced in fixing problems, they call in appropriate experts to make repairs. Consequently, they need a list of names and phone numbers for repair purposes, as well as special instructions for the large variety of errors that can occur.

Once the repairs are in progress, operations personnel can begin preparing for the final step of recovery: recovering files and restarting programs. Whenever an unscheduled stop of a direct access computer system occurs, there is always a chance that some data is lost. If the computer fails in the middle of an update, for example, part of the record may be changed and part may not be changed.

To recover from this failure, restoring the file to its condition before the failure and restarting the programs where they were when they were interrupted is necessary. This is easy to say but difficult to do. The file can be restored from its most recent backup copy, but then all of the changes since the backup was made must be reapplied. The computer can take this action if all of the changes have been recorded. Otherwise, the users will have to reenter all of the transactions since the backup copy was made.

Since these backup and recovery activities are so complex, operations personnel need detailed procedures to follow. Procedures for recovery from system failure are summarized in figure 8–21.

To review, direct access systems can be much easier to use than sequential systems. However, this ease of use means that errors can be

PERSONNEL	PROCEDURES
Users	What to do while the computer system is inoperative What to do when the computer system first becomes operational
Operators	How to detect the general cause of the failure Whom to contact to have the problem fixed How to restore files and restart programs

FIGURE 8–21

Procedures for recovery from system failure

made more easily and that unauthorized activity is harder to control or prevent. Further, direct access systems are considerably more difficult to back up and recover than sequential systems. This difference is caused by the fact that updates are made in place and no backup files are generated as a by-product of processing, as they are with sequential systems.

These disadvantages can be counteracted only by people following well-designed and well-documented procedures. It is impossible to counter these disadvantages with more hardware, a faster CPU, or other types of equipment. Thus, the careful design of procedures for both users and operations personnel is crucial to the successful implementation and use of direct access systems.

PERSONNEL FOR DIRECT ACCESS PROCESSING

The final component of a direct access business computer system is trained personnel. Again, there are two groups to be trained: users and operations personnel. Both groups need training in using the equipment and following established procedures.

User Training

Users need to be trained in how to prepare inputs and how to use outputs. If the direct access system is offline, then this training is similar to that for users of sequential systems. If the system is online, then users need to be trained in the use of terminals or other devices.

Generally, users will be more comfortable if they are given some minimal introduction to computer processing during this training. Also, they need to be assured that they cannot ruin millions of dollars of computing equipment from their terminals. (They may, however, be able to ruin data files, so they should be trained in how *not* to do that.) After these preliminaries, users should be shown how to use the terminals.

When they have learned how to use the equipment, users need to be trained in the use of procedures. They should be given the documentation that they will have on the job and shown how to accomplish their job using the computer system and the documentation. Even the best procedures are worthless if users do not understand or believe in them. Therefore, users should be given procedure rationale. Some activities may seem silly or inconsequential when considered just from the user's viewpoint. When this is the case, the users will often stop following the established procedures. To prevent this situation from occurring, users should be given insight into the reasons for all procedures.

Operator Training

Training for operations personnel is similar to that for users. Operators need to be taught how to use the direct access equipment and how to perform any special maintenance or testing activity. They should be shown how to handle removable disk packs and the like so as to minimize the chance of equipment damage. Finally, operations personnel need training in the established procedures. As indicated previously, backup and recovery is especially important for direct access processing, and operations personnel should be trained and rehearsed in the backup and recovery procedures. Periodic inspections should be made to ensure that the procedures are known, remembered, and followed.

▥ SUMMARY

This chapter has presented an introduction to direct access file processing systems. We began with a discussion of the need for direct access processing. In those situations in which sorting and batching are not feasible, direct access capability is required. We then discussed the characteristics of each of the five components of a direct access business computer system. Direct access hardware includes hard disks, floppy disks, and mass storage equipment. Direct access data can be organized in either of two basic forms. Indexed sequential file organization permits both direct access and sequential processing. Random organization can be very fast, but it permits only direct access processing.

We described the pseudocode for a direct access program to maintain the Elliot Bay customer master file. The program itself is actually simpler than a sequential program because many functions are taken care of by the operating system. We then described procedures for direct access processing. The importance of these procedures cannot be overemphasized. Direct access systems are easy to use; this ease of use means errors can easily be made. The only effective controls over these errors are well-designed and well-implemented procedures. Finally, we briefly looked at the training requirements for direct access system users and operations personnel.

Chapter 9 in part 3 describes an advanced way of organizing and processing data that is based on direct access processing: database systems. When you finish that chapter, you will understand all three ways of organizing and storing data: sequential file processing, direct access file processing, and database processing. All business computer systems are built around one of these.

QUESTIONS

8.31 What are the two categories of procedures needed for direct access systems?

8.32 Describe three types of procedures for users of a direct access system?

8.33 What procedures do operators of an online system need?

8.34 What user procedures are needed when a direct access system fails?

8.35 What operations procedures are needed when a direct access system fails?

8.36 Describe training needed by users of direct access systems.

8.37 Describe training needed by operators of direct access systems.

WORD LIST

Direct access
Direct access device flowchart
   symbol
Price extension
Online system
Offline system
Disk storage unit
Disk pack
Disk recording surface
Track
Cylinder

Movable read/write head disk
   storage device
Fixed-head disk storage device
Winchester disk
Data module
Access motion time
Rotational delay
Data movement time
Floppy disk
Conventional disk
Hard disk

Mass storage device
Key
Random file organization
Direct file organization
Indexed sequential file
   organization
Hashing algorithm
Overflow area
Account numbers
Passwords
File backup copies

QUESTIONS TO CHALLENGE YOUR THINKING

A. Estimate the amount of time required for an IBM 3380 to read the Elliot Bay Electronics customer master file both sequentially and randomly. Use the same file data as used for the HP 7935H estimates. The IBM 3380 performance characteristics are summarized in figure 8 – 11.

B. Although random and indexed sequential file organizations are standard, many computer systems have special varieties of them. Find out what variations your computer has and compare them to random and indexed sequential as described in this chapter.

C. Find out whether your college or university has business computer systems using direct access technology. If so, investigate the five components of the direct access system. In particular, determine whether or not you believe the procedures in use are sufficient. Are they well documented?

SYSTEMS IN THE MIS ENVIRONMENT

PART THREE

Parts 1 and 2 of this text presented fundamental information about business computer systems and basic file-processing technology. Part 3 examines the more advanced systems that have been developed in the past several years. In the MIS environment the computer is called upon to be many things to many people, specifically to managers at different levels who perform different business functions. Consequently, computer systems have been developed to address a wide spectrum of business needs, far beyond those that you learned about in part 2.

In chapter 9 you will learn about database processing, and why it is so much more powerful and flexible than file processing. In chapter 10 you will learn about teleprocessing and distributed processing, techniques that allow system components, such as people and data, to be hundreds of miles apart and yet work together. Finally, in chapter 11 you will study management information systems and decision support systems from the manager's perspective.

All three chapters in this part deal with sophisticated systems that evolved because the simpler centralized file-processing systems were inflexible and restrictive. All three chapters deal with topics that are very important to any business person: In every case, the computer is used as a tool to increase a company's productivity, either by giving people faster access to better data, by locating parts of the system in different geographical areas where those parts will be most effectively used, or by helping managers to plan and control their businesses.

DATABASE PROCESSING

CHAPTER 9

File processing systems satisfy many business needs, particularly in those situations where there are few users, where stored data can be easily partitioned, and where files do not need to be integrated. Most simple, straightforward systems can be easily supported by simple, straightforward file processing.

In other situations, though, file processing systems are not adequate to meets an organization's information needs. Some transaction processing systems and almost all MIS and DSS systems involve multiple users, multiple data files, and multiple views of stored data. On top of that, users of MIS and DSS systems need quick answers to unanticipated questions. File processing systems are simply not designed to handle such needs.

Database management systems (DBMS) are programs that take a more sophisticated approach to data storage and retrieval. Database management systems pick up where file processing systems leave off. In fact, database management systems actually use direct access to store and retrieve data, but the organization and format of database data are very unlike those of direct access files. DBMS takes advantage of the speed and versatility of direct access storage, but in a different way than file processing.

One of the great advantages of a DBMS is that the system itself locates and retrieves the data a user wants (figure 9–1). Even computer programmers do not need to know the location and format of data records — they can simply ask for data within a computer program and the DBMS retrieves it for them. This is very different from file processing. Finding data in files is like finding a book in the library. You can locate a specific book by searching the shelves (sequential file processing) or by looking up the book's location in the card catalog (direct access file processing). Either way, you eventually must go to the shelves and get the book yourself.

Using a DBMS is more like asking a research librarian to find the book you want. You identify the book by its title, author, and copyright date. The librarian returns in a few minutes with the book you asked for. How the librarian found the book is not your concern. Did the librarian look up the book's location in a card catalog? Are the books arranged by author, by title, by subject, by copyright date, by size, or by cover color? You don't need to know. That is information the librarian cares about, but not you. You can also ask the research librarian to find all of the books by a certain author. Or you can request all of the articles published in the past five years on a certain topic. The librarian is able to retrieve all of this information for you. The advantage of this approach over the do-it-yourself method is obvious. But the disadvantage is also obvious: You have to pay the librarian.

A DBMS is the research librarian for an information store. A user is able to ask for information about a certain topic (for example, data

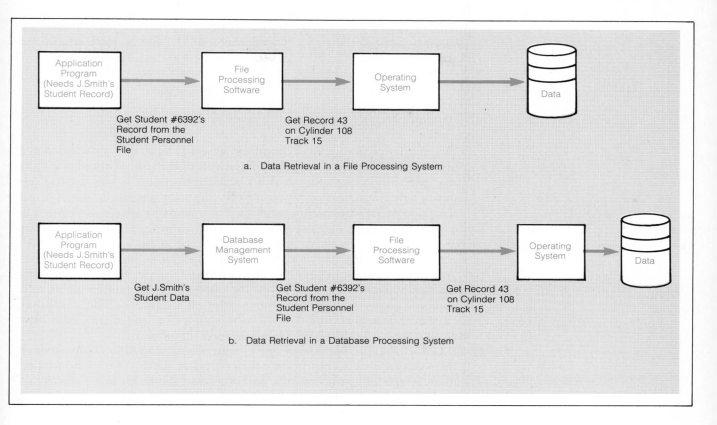

a. Data Retrieval in a File Processing System

b. Data Retrieval in a Database Processing System

about a student or about a professor's teaching load for this semester), and the DBMS retrieves the data from the database. DBMSs provide tremendous flexibility and power, far beyond that which is available from file processing systems.

In this chapter you will learn why database management systems were developed to replace file processing systems. Then you will learn the principles on which database processing is based. Finally, you will learn how the selection of a database management system affects each of the five components of a business computer system.

As you learn about database processing you might wonder why *all* computer systems do not store their data in a database. One reason, already mentioned, is that database management systems can be expensive. Another reason is that many companies already have working file processing systems in place and are reluctant to convert them to database processing. A third reason for why all systems do not use database processing is that database systems are considerably more complex to develop and to maintain. The decision to implement a DBMS is made by comparing the costs and benefits of a DBMS to the costs and benefits of a file processing system. File processing will be

FIGURE 9–1

Comparison of data retrieval in file processing and database processing systems better in some cases and database processing will be better in others. The one that satisfies the users' needs at the lowest cost should be selected.

THE NEED FOR DATABASE PROCESSING

The challenge facing any computer system is to enable a user to enter and retrieve data in a way that is natural to the user. This means that the user should be able to think about an object in the user's own terms, and not in terms imposed by a computer system. To understand this, you must first understand what is meant by *object*. An **object** is something a user is interested in and can name. Some objects that might be found in a university are students, professors, and transcripts.

A user who needs transcripts should be able to ask for transcripts and get them. Similarly, a user who adds a grade to a student's transcript should be able to do that just as if the transcript were a piece of paper with spaces for grades to be added. The computer system should accommodate the user's view of a transcript, regardless of how the actual bits and bytes are stored in a disk file.

Unfortunately, users often have been required to alter their views of the real world to accommodate the computer. Thus, a user who wished to enter student grades at the end of a term might be asked to submit to the data processing department a form (see figure 9–2) on which is written a student's ID followed by repeating pairs of course numbers and grades received. This data would subsequently be entered into the computer system to update the student's records. But the form that the user is expected to use may not even vaguely resemble a transcript. It might resemble a transaction record that is meaningful to the computer, but is not particularly meaningful to the user who must complete it.

One major problem of information systems development is that computer engineers have expected the user community to alter its point of view to match that of the computer. Now software engineers are finally realizing that it is possible and preferable to design systems that allow users to retain their own, noncomputerized, world views. Computer software can be built to translate the user's view into the computer's view and vice versa. Some database management systems more closely approach this objective than others, and none has yet reached it. Still, the result of this discovery is that systems are being developed that are much easier for users to use than older systems.

Database management systems are far superior to file processing systems in representing three aspects of real-world objects: representing variable-length objects, representing multiple data views, and representing relationships among objects.

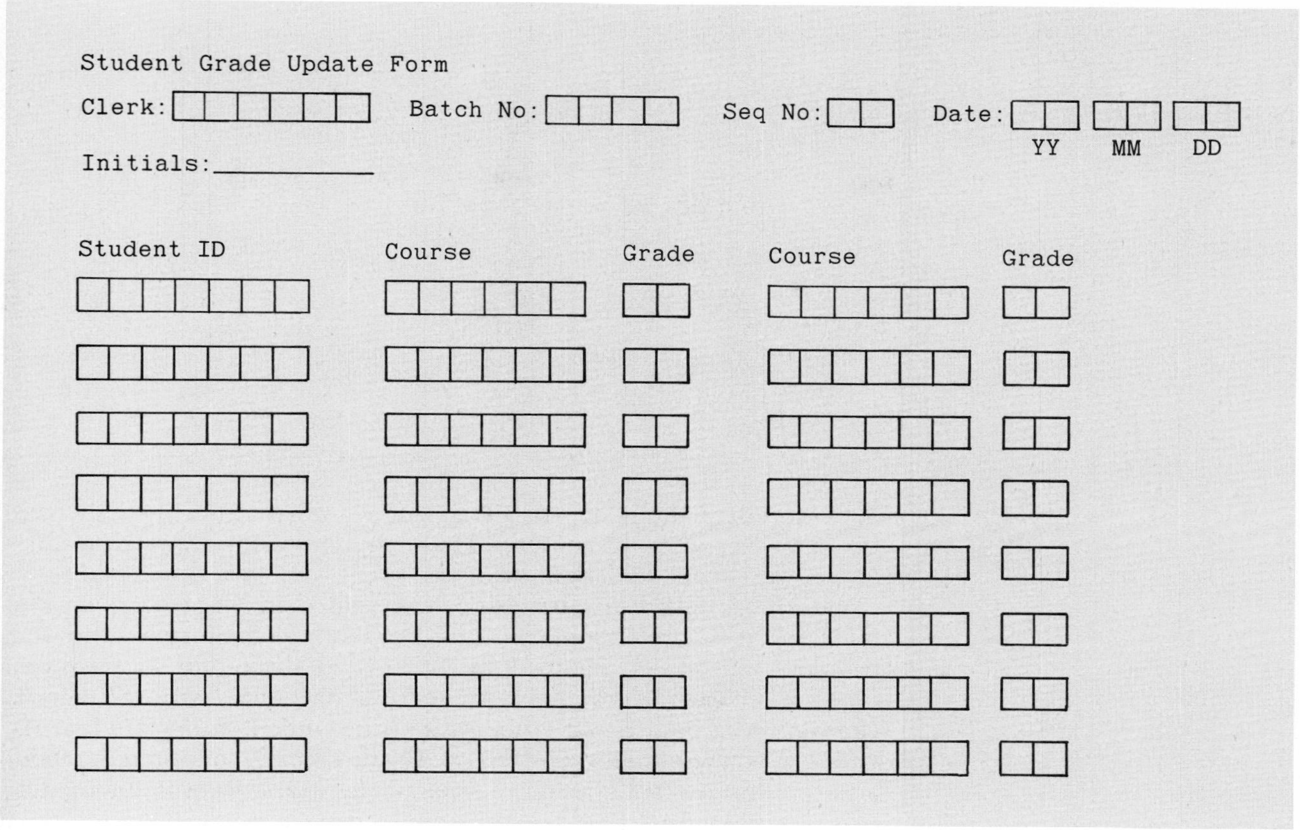

```
Student Grade Update Form

Clerk: [ ][ ][ ][ ][ ]    Batch No: [ ][ ][ ][ ]    Seq No: [ ][ ]    Date: [ ][ ] [ ][ ] [ ][ ]
                                                                              YY    MM    DD
Initials: _____


Student ID              Course          Grade     Course          Grade

[ ][ ][ ][ ][ ][ ][ ]   [ ][ ][ ][ ][ ][ ]   [ ][ ]    [ ][ ][ ][ ][ ][ ]   [ ][ ]

[ ][ ][ ][ ][ ][ ][ ]   [ ][ ][ ][ ][ ][ ]   [ ][ ]    [ ][ ][ ][ ][ ][ ]   [ ][ ]

[ ][ ][ ][ ][ ][ ][ ]   [ ][ ][ ][ ][ ][ ]   [ ][ ]    [ ][ ][ ][ ][ ][ ]   [ ][ ]

[ ][ ][ ][ ][ ][ ][ ]   [ ][ ][ ][ ][ ][ ]   [ ][ ]    [ ][ ][ ][ ][ ][ ]   [ ][ ]

[ ][ ][ ][ ][ ][ ][ ]   [ ][ ][ ][ ][ ][ ]   [ ][ ]    [ ][ ][ ][ ][ ][ ]   [ ][ ]

[ ][ ][ ][ ][ ][ ][ ]   [ ][ ][ ][ ][ ][ ]   [ ][ ]    [ ][ ][ ][ ][ ][ ]   [ ][ ]

[ ][ ][ ][ ][ ][ ][ ]   [ ][ ][ ][ ][ ][ ]   [ ][ ]    [ ][ ][ ][ ][ ][ ]   [ ][ ]

[ ][ ][ ][ ][ ][ ][ ]   [ ][ ][ ][ ][ ][ ]   [ ][ ]    [ ][ ][ ][ ][ ][ ]   [ ][ ]
```

Representing Variable-Length Objects

FIGURE 9–2
Data entry form for entering students grades

Few things are more baffling to a computer user than such questions as "How long is a transcript?" The user wants to answer, "It depends on how many courses a student has completed." Data processing personnel, though, need to define fields and records of a certain length for the computer. When technology was not advanced enough to allow the computer to take the user's perspective, users had to shift their perspective from the real world, in which transcripts do indeed vary in length, to that of the computer, in which all transcripts are the same length (though some contain more blank spaces than others, another concept that baffles most people who are not computer engineers). The user's frustration is revealed in the complaint, "If the computer is so smart, why can't it look at things from *my* point of view?" Let's take a closer look at a transcript.

A transcript, like the one in figure 9–3, is an object you might find in a university. It can be named, described and recognized by, say, the registrar. The transcript in figure 9–3 indicates that John Smith, a freshman, has completed four courses. As he completes more courses the length of his transcript will grow (not the paper itself, but the

FIGURE 9-3

A transcript: an example object

```
            University City College
                 Transcript
                  12/31/86
     John Smith       Accounting        1298-4791
                       1990
                  Credit
        Class        Hours        Date        Grade
     Eng 101          3.0         F86           A
     Hist 105         3.0         F86           B
     Math 151         3.0         F86           A
     Bus 100          3.0         F86           B
```

information printed on it). Furthermore, other students will have taken fewer or more courses. Thus, the length of transcripts does indeed vary from student to student.

Variable-length objects can be represented in file processing systems, but it is cumbersome to do so. Database technology handles this problem very easily. Figure 9–4 shows a database that contains two types of records: one for Student and one for Grade. Student records contain basic data about students such as student name, student ID, address, phone number, and major. Grade records contain data about a particular student's grade in a particular class. Data items include class name, student ID, date, and grade received.

Suppose the registrar needs to print John Smith's transcript. The DBMS responds by first locating John Smith's student record, and then finding all the Grade records that match John's student ID

FIGURE 9-4

University database containing student and transcript objects

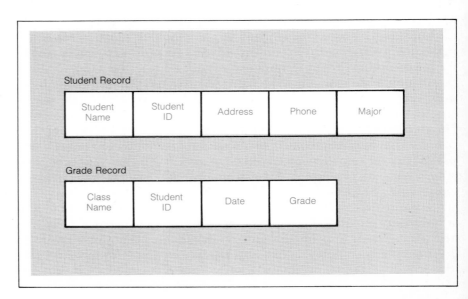

number. In this way (and unbeknownst to the registrar) the DBMS constructs from the stored data a transcript, a variable-length object. Notice that from the registrar's perspective the computer appears to keep a file of transcripts ready to be printed. Yet there is no such thing as a transcript record — a transcript is derived from other records when it is needed. Also, as a student earns more grades, more grade records with that student's ID number simply are added to the database.

Multiple Views of Data

Figure 9–5 shows several objects that might be important in a university. Most of the objects are tangible: They are either people (such as students) or reports (such as class rosters). Other objects, such as teaching load, are less tangible, but no less real.

If university personnel were asked to supply a list of facts that needed to be kept for each of the objects in figure 9–5 they might look like the ones below:

- Student   = name + student ID + address + telephone number + major + advisor + one grade for each completed course
- Professor   = name + department + degree
- Class   = class name + room + date + teacher + time
- Class roster = class name + teacher + one grade for each student who completed the class
- Advisee   = student assigned to a professor for academic guidance
- Teaching load = courses a professor is teaching this semester
- Transcript   = student name + one grade for every completed course

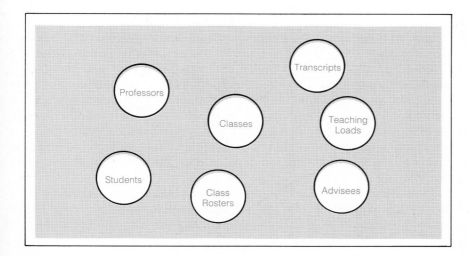

FIGURE 9–5
Objects in a university

Given each user's view of various objects, it is the database designer's responsibility to distill the minimum amount of data that will need to be stored to accommodate all those views. Take, for example, the object called *student*. Sometimes a student is important just as a student. Sometimes a student is the owner of a transcript. At other times, a student is merely one of many advisees assigned to a professor. A student can be viewed in many different ways, depending on the situation.

Multiple views of data cannot be represented in file processing systems without generating large amounts of redundant data. For example, a file processing system might contain a file called *Transcripts*, which contains student names, IDs, and grades organized by student. Another file called *Class Roster* might contain student names, IDs, and grades organized by course. As you can see, much of the data is duplicated. What is wrong with this arrangement? Actually, several problems arise when data is stored in this fashion.

First, there is much **redundancy** in the data. A student's name, home address, campus address, major and year of graduation might be stored in several files. Updating such data can be troublesome. Suppose a student moves from one dormitory to another—all of the files containing address information must be updated. Trying to do this is time consuming and error prone, and when it is not done correctly this can be frustrating for the user and for the student.

Database management systems eliminate much data redundancy. They are built upon the principle of integrated, centralized files. To the extent possible, each fact about an object is stored in only one place. The end result is that changes to data can be made quickly and completely.

Another problem with storing separate redundant files in a file processing system is that the **data is not integrated**. Therefore, answering ad hoc inquiries can be very difficult or impossible. For example, suppose someone files a complaint against the university for bias in grading, claiming that professors in each department give higher grades to their own majors than they do to students from other majors. To investigate this claim, the university needs a report showing the average grade given to majors and nonmajors by all the faculty members in the university. To prepare this report, data in a faculty file and data in a transcript file have to be combined in some way. As no program to do this would already exist (this is an unanticipated need), a programmer will have to develop a program to extract data from the files and produce the report. The trouble is that this combination is likely to require more time to develop than the university has prior to the hearing.

Unlike file processing systems, DBMSs address this problem very well. Even without the help of a computer programmer, a user in the university would probably be able to produce the grading report in very little time. In fact, one of the major factors pushing database development has been the user's need to quickly retrieve data about many different objects at once. File processing systems have proven woefully inadequate in answering unanticipated questions. Database management systems, however, excel at it. (Is it any wonder that decision-support systems are built on databases rather than on file processing?)

Now look at the diagram in figure 9–6. A DBMS would store records only for Professors, Students, Classes, and Grades. From these records it can derive all the data needed to represent professors, students, advisees, classes, teaching loads, transcripts, and class rosters. Notice that there is no actual stored record for transcript, advisee, class roster, or teaching load. But all of the elements needed to construct those objects are available from the four record types in the database. Consequently, each user's view of the objects important to him or her can be supported by the DBMS. Also notice that some of the objects share common data. For example, student, transcript, class roster, and advisee all include student name. These objects are said to *overlap*.

Representing Relationships Among Objects

Things in the real world are often associated with one another, and the association itself is important to track. In the university example an association exists between a student and a professor that makes a student an advisee (or the professor an advisor, depending on your perspective). This association is intangible, but it certainly is important, especially when the time arrives to plan next semester's course of studies. In database terminology an association between two objects is called a **relationship**.

Database management systems are designed to easily and flexibly represent relationships among objects. File processing systems are not. File processing systems are usually forced to introduce redundant data to accommodate relationships among records in several files. For example, a file processing system might contain one Student file, and

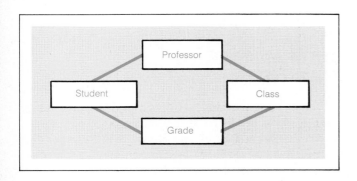

FIGURE 9–6
Database records in a university

each student record might contain the name, office location, office phone number, and office hours of the student's advisor. Likewise, in the file called Professors each faculty record might include a list of student advisee names along with each advisee's campus address, year of graduation, and last contact date. All of the problems associated with redundant data previously described are present in this situation.

Database management systems, on the other hand, do not duplicate data. Instead, they incorporate into the database a link between a student's record and the appropriate faculty advisor's record (we'll see how this might be done later in this chapter). The relationship that exists between a student and a professor is represented more easily in a DBMS than in a file processing system. If an advisee is reassigned to another faculty member, the links are easily and quickly adjusted. If a professor's office hours change, only his or her record needs to be modified, because all of that professor's advisee records simply point to the professor's record — they do not actually contain the advisor's office hour data (contrast this with the file processing system previously described).

Relationships between things in the real world change rapidly and unexpectedly. File processing systems cannot be updated fast enough to keep pace with changes in the real world. Consequently, users of file processing systems often are frustrated. Although database management systems usually cannot respond instantly to relationship changes in the real world, they do respond significantly faster than file processing systems.

Look at the diagram in figure 9–7. This diagram indicates the data records that would be stored in the university database. Lines between one record type and another indicate relationships between records that the database would have to maintain to represent all of the objects described here. In fact it is accurate to say that an object (such as transcript) is derived from data (such as student name and grade received) and relationships (the link between a particular student and a particular grade). Similarly, an advisee list is derived from professor and student data and the relationship between a particular student and a particular professor. Figure 9–8 shows what database records representing some of the objects might look like.

⫿ FUNDAMENTALS OF DATABASE MANAGEMENT SYSTEMS

In this next section you will learn the basic principles upon which database management systems are built. Such background is unnecessary for someone who only *uses* a DBMS, but if you ever help develop a DBMS in your business career, or if you are considering a career in information systems, you will find this information useful.

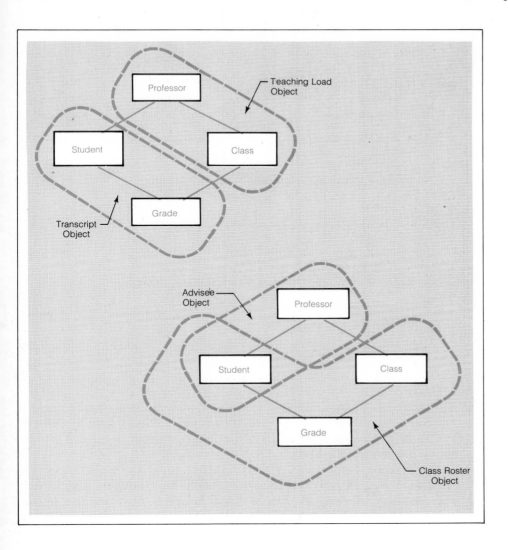

Professor

Teaching Load Object

Student

Class

Grade

Transcript Object

Advisee Object

Professor

Student

Class

Grade

Class Roster Object

A **database** is a self-describing collection of integrated records. **Self-describing** means that the format of the database is recorded within the database itself. Contrast this with file processing systems in which the format of a file is defined in every program that references it. This means that when a file's format changes, every program that references it must be modified to reflect the change. To appreciate how inefficient this is, you should realize that some companies maintain thousands of application programs referencing hundreds of files. One format change can mean updating hundreds of programs, a time-consuming and error-prone activity.

Databases, however, are self-describing: The format of the database is stored on disk with the data, not in the application programs that

FIGURE 9–7
Database records and objects that can be derived from them

FIGURE 9 – 8
Database records needed to represent student, transcript, professor, and advisee objects in a university database

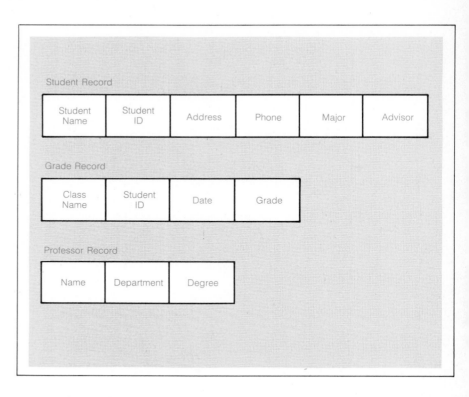

use the data. Thus, if changes need to be made, they are made once, to the **database directory**. (The directory is also called a **data dictionary**, not to be confused with the data dictionary system development tool described in chapter 4.)

The database directory describes the contents of the database, including such facts as record formats, field locations and lengths, and the location of various lists of links between records. The phrase **integrated records** means that relationships among records, like the student/grade relationship inherent in transcripts, are represented. In the example in figure 9 – 4 the Student ID field served as a link between student and grade records. As you will see in the section on database data, there are many ways of representing record relationships.

Database Applications

An **application** consists of one or more programs that use a database to meet the requirements of users. Usually, these requirements involve the need to keep track of something — dollars, people, projects, equipment, inventory, or something else. An application is the interface between a user and a database. In a sense, an application sits on top of the database and serves as a window into the data, as shown in figure 9 – 9.

Database applications have four major components: reports, forms, transactions, and menus. First, to keep track of something, people want **reports**. To produce accurate reports, the application must have accurate, up-to-date data. This implies that there be a way of adding new data and updating data that resides in the database. For this purpose, the application needs display **forms** for data entry and editing.

If an application is simple and straightforward, the forms can be used to process all of the changes to the database. For example, Mary Forsythe's customer database in chapter 1 could readily be kept current with a simple input/edit form for her customer data. If the application is more complicated, however, the user will need to be guided through the change process. When an object consists of portions of several records, the changes that can and should be made will not be obvious to most users. For example, consider the database in figure 9–8. What changes should be made to the university database when a professor

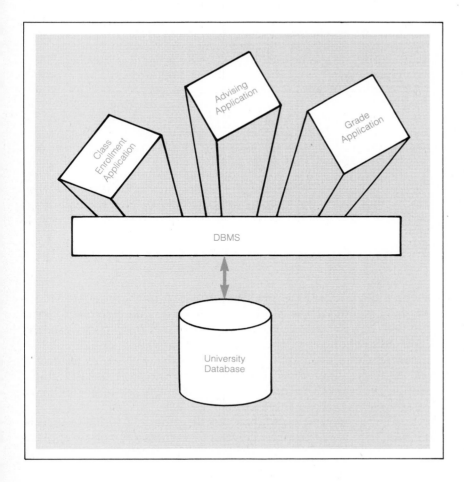

FIGURE 9–9
Applications as a window to the database

APPLICATION

"IDENTIFY ALL INFORMATION REQUIREMENTS OF A USER."

DATABASE DESIGN AND MODELING

Under traditional system development efforts, files were constructed to furnish programs of unique sets of data, arranged and sequenced in the manner easiest for each program to use. This gave rise to the creation and maintenance of a large number of files: extract files, re-sorted files and the like.

Often, several files contained duplicate data and caused problems for users and programmers because of the need to maintain the same information in more than one place. Because DBMS technology eliminates the need to establish redundant data files and promotes the organization of data for use by multiple applications, system designers and theorists developed the concept of database design.

Database design is the technique of developing logical and physical arrangements of data that can be accessed through a DBMS. It is essentially a three-step process; gather data requirements, develop logical data relationships, and implement the physical representation of data.

In gathering data, a designer must identify all information requirements of a user community. Past, present and future uses of data must be considered in establishing a data base that will serve a universe of potential applications.

The key is in identifying the entities that are significant to an organization, such as clients, vendors, or automobiles, and identifying the attributes that relate to those entities: client name, vendor ID or automobile color.

The designer then must determine which attributes, often more than one, identify an entity. Social Security number, for instance, identifies an individual, but so does address, home telephone number and blood type.

Next, the designer must organize the logical relationships between entities, a step known as "data modeling." The designer must consider whether and how entities are related: Can a client own more than one automobile? Can more than one vendor serve the same client?

The designer also must consider whether a relationship has any value to the user community. Clearly, an auto insurer must know whether a single policy-holder possesses more than one automobile, while the Division of Motor Vehicles might concern itself only with each individual owner-automobile relationship.

The last step in database design is to physically develop the databases that optimally organize the data and their logical relationships.

leaves the university? If the professor's record in the professor file is simply deleted, all of the students who have that professor as an advisor will be left unattached. This will generate a data integrity problem. Other changes will need to be made as well.

To prevent these problems, programs can be written to guide the user through the change process. Such programs are usually called **transaction programs**, or simply *transactions*; they are essential for all but the simplest database applications.

The last component of a database application is a series of **menus**. Menus guide the user through the various components of an application. For example, a menu may display a list of options such as Add,

Change, or Delete Student Data. The user will make a selection from the menu, and the appropriate transaction programs will be initiated.

Types of Databases

There are four fundamental kinds of databases, as shown in Figure 9–10. The simplest databases support a single application and are used by a single person. Mary Forsythe's customer database in chapter 1 is an example of a **single-application, single-user database**. Databases of this type are usually processed on microcomputers, although they could be processed on other computers as well.

The second type of database is **multiple application, single user.** An example of this type is shown in figure 9–11. This database is used by a teacher to keep track of courses taught, students advised or taught, and grades given. This database supports three applications. One application, Preparation, is concerned with courses and reference materials used in them. The second application, Student, is used to maintain data about students whom the teacher has advised or taught. The third application, Grading, is used to record class grades. Databases like this are also commonly stored on microcomputers.

A third type of database supports a **single application but multiple users**. Databases of this type are common in packaged software for mini and mainframe computers. For example, a publisher of accounting software has embedded a DBMS into its general ledger package, as shown in figure 9–12. The DBMS creates a database that is used only for general ledger accounting. It supports multiple users in an online, transaction processing mode. Sometimes companies develop single-application databases in house for their own processing. This is usually done either to save development time or because there is little overlap from the single application to other applications.

The final type of database is one that supports **multiple applications and multiple users**. These databases are the most sophisticated and complex of the four types. They occur primarily on mainframes, although some are processed by minicomputers and, rarely, on local

FIGURE 9–10
Four types of databases

	SINGLE USER	MULTIPLE USER
SINGLE APPLICATION	Typically on microcomputers	Minis, mainframes Often with packaged software
MULTIPLE APPLICATION	Typically on microcomputers	Mainframes, minis Usually developed in house Complex

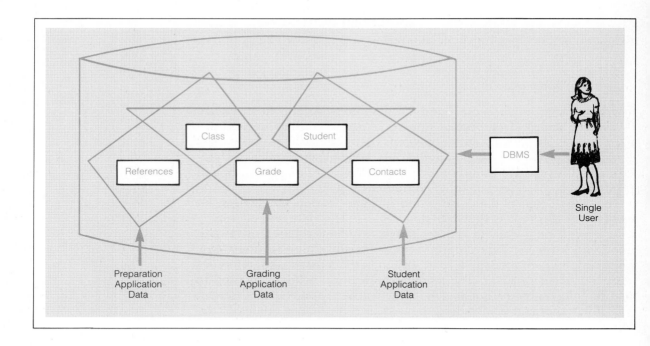

FIGURE 9–11
Single-user, multiple-application
database

QUESTIONS

9.1 Give an example of an object that fits naturally into a single record of a file processing system. Give an example of an object that does not.

9.2 Give two examples of record relationships that might occur for a database that supports the campus bookstore.

9.3 Suppose a bookstore maintains a database that contains records about books, publishers, and classes. Describe two views of Book data.

9.4 Explain the statement that the DBMS acts like a data librarian.

9.5 Using your answer to question 9.2, show database records that represent the two relationships.

(continued)

area networks of microcomputers (see chapter 10). Such databases are generally developed in house for one-of-a-kind problems.

Major corporations have multiapplication, multiuser databases for integrated processing of corporate data. For example, a large company may have an order entry system that is integrated with inventory, shipping, and purchasing. When items are ordered, picking slips are generated for the warehouse, shipping documents are prepared, and when appropriate, orders for replenishment of inventory are prepared. Such large and complicated databases are difficult to set up and require significant administrative support.

Fundamental Types of Record Relationships

To understand how database processing works, you need to understand two concepts. First, three fundamental types of record relationships can be used to model objects and relationships. Second, database structure can be expressed in a number of different ways, called data models.

A database is a self-describing collection of integrated records; in other words, a database is a self-describing collection of files and *relationships among records* in those files.

The phrase *relationships among records* is critical. If a database were only a group of files, then those files would not be integrated. The student records in a student file, for example, would have no correspondence with professor records. In a database, a facility must be provided to relate records to one another.

What are record relationships? Database experts have determined three basic ways in which records can be related.

Hierarchical Record Relationships

The first relationship type is **hierarchical**, or **tree**. A tree is a collection of records in which all of the relationships between record types are one-to-many. Figure 9–13(*a*) shows an example of a tree relating department records to employee records. Each department has many employees. However, each employee works in only one department. This **one-to-many relationship** is symbolized by the single/double-arrow notation in figure 9–13(*b*).

Figure 9–14 shows a tree of records for a checking application. Three record types are involved. The first is the customer record, the second is a checking record, and the third is a transaction record (canceled checks). Again, notice the one-to-many relationships. Each customer can have many checking accounts, but an account corresponds to only one customer (joint accounts are considered to be one customer with

9.6 Suppose a book purchase consists of data about the student purchasing the books and data about each book purchased. Sketch records that could be stored in a database to represent the object called "Book Purchase."

9.7 A class roster is a list of final grades given in a course. Describe how the records in figure 9–8 would be processed to produce a class roster.

9.8 Define these terms:
  a. Database
  b. Directory
  c. Integrated records
  d. Application

9.9 Name and describe the four components of a database application.

(*continued*)

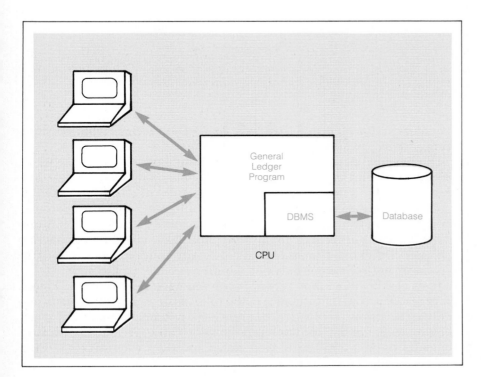

FIGURE 9–12
Single-application, multiple-user database

FIGURE 9–13
Example of a tree relating departments to employees

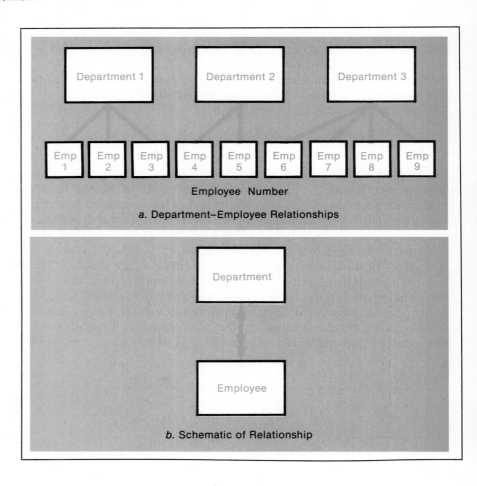

a. Department–Employee Relationships

b. Schematic of Relationship

9.10 Explain the differences between single- and multiple-application databases. Give an example of each.

9.11 Explain the differences between single- and multiple-user databases. Give an example of each.

two names). Each account can have many transactions (checks), but a transaction corresponds to only one account.

These record structures are similar to family trees. In fact, the terms **parent** and **child** are sometimes used to define one record's relationship to another one. In figure 9–13, department records are parents, and the employee records are children. In figure 9–14, the customer records are parents, and the checking account records are children. Checking account records are also parents (to the checking transaction records). Checking transaction records are children only. In a tree structure, each child has only one parent.

Trees can involve many record types and have several levels. Figure 9–15 shows a tree that illustrates the relationships among records in a multiapplication, multiuser database at a bank. There are seven record types, six one-to-many relationships, and three levels. Most of the early database products were based on tree structures for storing and retrieving data (this topic will be covered in a later section).

Network Record Relationships

The other two kinds of record relationships are *simple* and *complex networks*. These allow a record to have more than one parent. Figure 9–16 shows a **simple network**. Here, an order record has two parents: a customer record and a salesperson record. Notice that in a simple network there are multiple parents, and the parents are *different* types of records. Put another way, in a simple network all relationships are one to many, even though some records may have more than one parent.

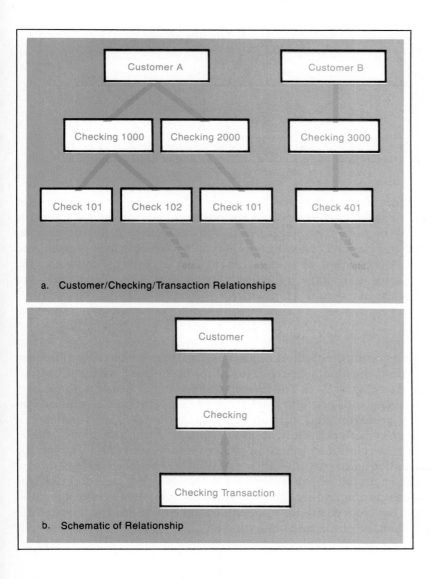

a.   **Customer/Checking/Transaction Relationships**

b.   **Schematic of Relationship**

FIGURE 9–14
Example of a tree relating customers and accounts

FIGURE 9–15
Schematic of bank relationships

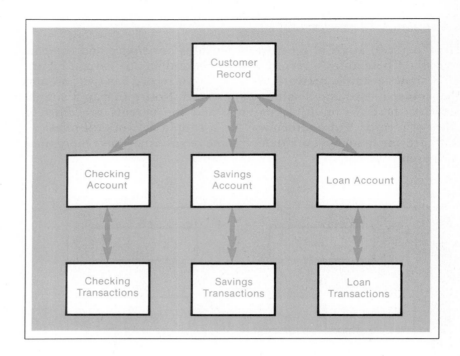

The third record relationship is called a **complex network**. In a complex network a record can have multiple parents, and the parents can be of the *same* type. Figure 9–17 shows a complex network among student and class records. One student is enrolled in many classes, and a class is composed of many students. In a complex network, the relationships are many to many. The terms *parent* and *child* are meaningless in a complex network.

Application of Record Relationships

The three types of record relationships are important because they are used to describe objects and relationships in the user's world. Consider objects from figure 9–5. The records are Professor, Student, Class, and Grade. Using those database records we can represent a relationship between professor and student to form the object called *advisee*, a relationship between student and grade to form the object called *transcript*, a relationship among student, grade, and class to form the object called *class roster*, and a relationship between professor and class to form the object called *teaching load*. We can describe the relationships among these records more completely with the terminology just developed. Figure 9–18 shows the relationships among professor, student, grade, and class records.

Sketches like figure 9–18 are used to develop database designs. If you are the user of a new database application, you may be asked to review sketches like this. Knowledge of record relationships will enable you to communicate better with data processing personnel.

Data Models

Objects are found in the real world. Records are bits of information stored in a computer system. Database developers have had to invent ways of organizing, storing, and retrieving records in order to represent real-world objects. As a result, several data models have evolved upon which database products have been based.

A **data model** describes the physical structure and the processing of a database. Most experts would agree that the three most important data models are the *hierarchical data model*, the *network data model*, and the *relational data model*. Of the three, the relational data model is the most recent development, and also the most important one for users to understand.

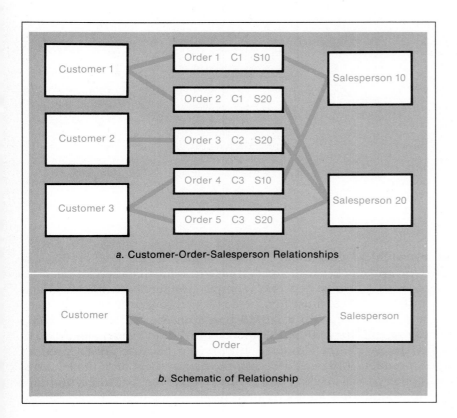

FIGURE 9–16
Illustration of a simple network

a. Customer-Order-Salesperson Relationships

b. Schematic of Relationship

FIGURE 9–17
Illustration of a complex network

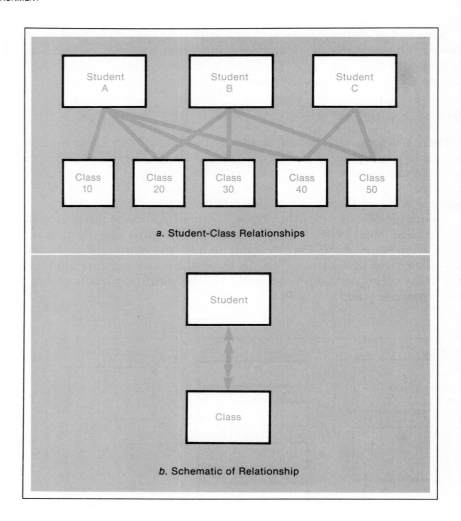

a. Student-Class Relationships

b. Schematic of Relationship

Hierarchical Data Model

The **hierarchical data model** was developed in the late 1960s. It is called *hierarchical* because it uses trees to model all data relationships. Databases that involve networks (nontree structures), such as the database in figure 9–18, must first be converted to tree form before they can be represented with a DBMS based on the hierarchical model. Because of this limitation, the hierarchical data model should have died a timely death. However, it survived because IBM's premier DBMS product, IMS, was based on the hierarchical data model. IMS, which otherwise is an exceedingly fine product for multiuser, multiapplication databases, kept this data model — including its shortcomings — alive beyond its time.

Hierarchical databases present several problems. First, the model upon which such products are based restricts each child record to only one parent. Next, all of the objects that any users will ever want to derive from the database must be defined when the database is created. Thereafter, specific records must be accessed by following the paths established during the database's creation. Finally, lower-level records can be accessed only by starting at a parent record and working down from there. Consequently, using a hierarchical database is somewhat difficult.

Remember that the hierarchical data model was one of the earliest data models. In spite of shortcomings, products based on this model were still more powerful than file processing systems. Some problems were solved with the development of another data model, the network data model.

Network Data Model

The **network data model**, an improvement over the hierarchical model, achieved prominence in the early 1970s, primarily because of the work of CODASYL (the group that developed the language COBOL in the 1950s). In the early days of database processing, CODASYL formed a group called the database task group (DBTG) to study database processing and to develop a standard that was to serve the same role as the COBOL standard. This group developed a data model that could represent both hierarchies and simple networks directly; hence, it became known as the network data model.

The major difference between a DBMS product based on the network data model and one based on the hierarchical data model is that

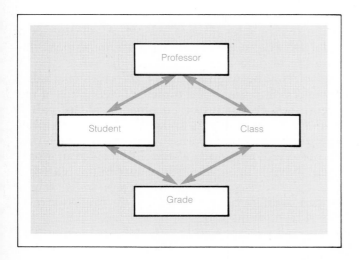

FIGURE 9–18

Simple network record relationship in a university database

a network database allows a child record to have multiple parents, whereas a hierarchical database does not. Thus, network databases are easier to use than hierarchical ones. The simple network illustrated in figure 9–18 is easily implemented in a network database.

Other problems with hierarchical databases were carried into network databases: All relationships had to be specified during the database's creation, and lower-level records could be accessed only through their parents.

The **CODASYL DBTG data model** has been the basis for many DBMS products such as IDMS, a product licensed by Cullinet Software, and has been the foundation of many successful database applications. In 1975 the DBTG model was unsuccessfully nominated as a national standard. It probably would have been successful except for the promise offered by a third data model, the relational data model.

Relational Data Model

Whereas the hierarchical and network data models arose from the ranks of information systems practitioners, the **relational data model** arose from the theory of relational mathematics. The relational model represents data in a form that is more convenient and natural to the user. Initially, the problem with this model was that DBMS products based on it had unacceptably slow performance. This problem has been addressed by many vendors, and today many relational DBMS products with more than acceptable performance exist.

The relational model is useful not only as the basis for a DBMS product, but also as a design tool. System developers can translate requirements into relational database designs. These designs can be reviewed by users for completeness and accuracy and then transformed into whatever model — relational, network, or hierarchical — is employed by the DBMS product to be used.

In concept, the relational model is very simple. A **relation** is a two-dimensional table. (Don't confuse *relation* with *relationship*. A relation is analogous to a file of data about objects of the same type. A relationship is an association between records.) The rows of a table represent particular objects and are called **tuples**. The columns of the relation, or table, represent properties of an object and are called **attributes**. Figure 9–19 shows student data and grade data represented in tables. A row of the student relation represents a student, and a row of the grade relation represents the grade a student received in a particular class. Relations have a fixed number of attributes; variable attribute structures like the advisee object in which a professor might be assigned many students cannot be represented in the professor relation. Another table must be built instead.

The terminology surrounding the relational model is confusing. The formal terminology is *relation*, *attribute*, *tuple*. To avoid complexity,

FIGURE 9–19
Student and grade relations in a
relational database

Student-Name	Student-ID	Phone	Major
John Parks	1234	555-1212	Accounting
Mary Franklin	4890	523-0010	Finance
Fred Bentz	5314	428-9000	Accounting
Sally Hernandez	6741	555-8700	Info Systems

Student Relation

Class-Name	Student-ID	Class-Grade
ACCT 101	1234	B
ACCT 200	6741	A
ACCT 400	6741	A
IS 200	1234	B
ACCT 101	4890	C
ACCT 400	5314	C
IS 400	5314	B
FIN 280	1234	B
FIN 480	5314	A

Grade Relation

some vendors of DBMS products use the terms **table**, **column**, **row**; and others use the terms **file**, **field**, **record**. We will use the formal terms when discussing the relational data model.

The essence of the relational model is that, as far as the user is concerned, record relationships are *stored in the data*. In Figure 9–19, a grade tuple is related to a particular student tuple because there is a match in the Student-ID data item of the two tuples, and for no other reason. Furthermore, with the relational model, tuples are processed in relation to one another using matches of data values. Thus, in **SQL** (one popular relational language), to print the name and grade of all students, you would enter:

```
SELECT    STUDENT–NAME, CLASS–GRADE
FROM      STUDENT, GRADE
WHERE     STUDENT–ID.STUDENT = STUDENT–ID.GRADE
```

QUESTIONS

9.12 What is another way of saying a database is a collection of integrated files?

9.13 Describe a hierarchical record relationship. Give an example.

9.14 In the example you gave in question 9.13, which records are parents and which are children?

9.15 Describe a simple network relationship. Give an example.

9.16 Describe a complex network relationship. Give an example.

9.17 What is a data model? Name three important data models.

9.18 Explain how the hierarchical and network data models differ.

9.19 Explain how the relational data model can be used as a design tool.

9.20 Define the terms *relation*, *attribute*, and *tuple*.

9.21 Explain how relationships are stored in data. Use the example of the relationship between author and book records.

9.22 Describe three criteria used to judge whether a DBMS is a true implementation of the relational model.

Observe that Student-name arises from the Student relation in figure 9–19, and Class-grade arises from the Grade relation. The SQL statement has caused data from two relations to be combined on the basis of matching Student-ID values.

There is considerable debate among experts as to what constitutes a true implementation of the relational model. For the purposes of this text, three criteria are used: (1) multiple relations can be stored in a single database, (2) relationships are stored in the data (or at least appear to be to the user), and (3) the DBMS provides a language by which any data can be accessed by attribute and relation name. This last point means that not only can data be retrieved or changed by attribute and relation name, but also that any data item can be used to qualify a query. Unlike other database models, a data item used to qualify a query need not have been defined as a **key field**. (Remember that a key field uniquely identifies a record. Some records are identifiable with multiple keys—a student record might have two keys: student ID and student name.) For example, consider the following SQL statement:

```
SELECT    STUDENT—NAME, CLASS—GRADE
FROM      STUDENT, GRADE
WHERE     STUDENT—NAME.STUDENT = STUDENT—NAME.GRADE
          AND MAJOR = ACCOUNTING
```

In this query, the attribute Major, a nonkey field, is used to qualify tuples. With the relational model, every attribute can be used as a key. This opens the door to ad hoc queries against the database, something that hierarchical and network databases cannot do adequately.

The relational model is a vast improvement over other database models. Any piece of data can be accessed almost directly, without tracing through parent-child paths, and relationships can be developed on the spot—they do not have to be anticipated when the database is created. This makes databases much more flexible and accessible to users.

Let us summarize the previous two sections. Objects in the real world need to be represented in a database. Database designers accomplish this by establishing records and somehow linking them together to represent relationships among them. Record relationships fall into three categories: hierarchies, simple networks, and complex networks. Several standard formats for storing and retrieving database records, called *data models*, have been developed. Each model improved upon the previous ones in terms of flexibility or capability. The most promising one so far is the relational data model.

All data models provide access to integrated data, and so they more closely parallel the real world than file processing systems do. However, nothing is free in this world. In the next section you will learn about how each component of a business computer system is affected by your choice of DBMS and what prices must be paid for flexible access to stored data.

THE FIVE COMPONENTS OF A DBMS

Database management systems offer flexible and fast access to integrated data. The most significant difference between DBMSs and file processing systems is in the data component. Of course, all components — hardware, programs, data, procedures, and personnel — are affected by a DBMS. But the data component is by far the most significantly altered by database technology.

Database Data

A concept essential to understanding the data component of a database system is that systems data, sometimes called **overhead data**, is created to allow processing by keys and record relationships. Because of this overhead data, the size of a database may be 200 or 300 percent greater than that of the original application data. The exact amount depends on how many keys and record relationships are represented as well as the particular DBMS product in use.

Regardless of the data model, the methods used by a DBMS to store and retrieve data will be very complex and entirely transparent to the user.

We will look at two examples that are typical of the structures used: indexes and linked lists.

Indexes

Consider first the need to retrieve data by more than one key (recall that a key is a data item used for direct access to stored records.) Suppose that we have a group of customer records in a direct access file and that the key for this file is the customer number. A hashing algorithm is applied to the customer number to determine a record's relative position in the file (see chapter 8).

Now suppose that, in addition to accessing the records by account number, the users want to access them by ZIP code. One way to do this is to read the entire file, looking for all the records with the desired ZIP code. However, this search is time consuming if the file contains many records and wasteful if few of these records have the desired ZIP code.

To make this process more efficient, some database systems build a file of overhead data called an **index** (or, sometimes, an **inverted file** or **inverted list**). This index is similar to an index for a book. It shows which records have which ZIP code values. Figure 9–20 pictures such an inverted file.

FIGURE 9–20
Example of an inverted file

ZIP CODE VALUE	CUSTOMER RECORDS HAVING CORRESPONDING VALUE
01418	5, 7, 8
22042	1, 2, 4, 11
55520	9, 10
98040	3, 6

If a user or application program wants to know all of the customers with ZIP code 22042, the DBMS will search for 22042 in the index. It will find 22042 as the second entry. Then the DBMS will use the indicated record numbers to find the customer records desired. Thus, record locations 1, 2, 4, and 11 contain customer records with ZIP code 22042.

Whenever customer records are added, changed, or deleted, the DBMS modifies the index. If there are several indexes (there will be one for each key in use), modifications of them will become burdensome. That is a price of additional access capability.

Linked Lists

Record relationships can also be represented by linked lists. Suppose that we want to represent the one-to-many relationship between departments and employees. Assume that both types of records are loaded on a direct access file, as illustrated in figure 9–21. Locations 1, 3, and 5 hold department records. The other locations hold employee records.

To represent the relationships, we will add a **link field** to each record. This field has a record location, or address, of another record. In a department record, this link field points to the first employee record for that department. In an employee record, the link field points to the next employee in the same department. The last employee record in a department has a zero in the link field.

Examining figure 9–21, we see that department 100's link field points to record position 2, or employee 20's data. Thus we know that employee 20 is in department 100. Employee 20's link field points to record position 7, which contains employee 80. Finally, employee 80's link field points to position 10, which contains employee 15's data. The link field for employee 15 is 0, indicating that there are no more employees in the department. Thus, employees 20, 80, and 15 work in department 100.

If you follow the links in the other records, you will discover that employees 25 and 70 work in department 200 and that employees 30 and 40 work in department 300.

Data structures like this one are called **linked lists**, because link fields are used to maintain relationships as lists of data items. Linked lists can also be used to represent multiple keys.

Database Hardware

Database applications seldom require special hardware. They may, however, require *more* hardware. On microcomputers, most database applications require at least a hard disk, and 512K bytes of memory are required for most microcomputer DBMS products.

On mini and mainframe computers, more direct access file space is usually needed because of the database overhead data. Furthermore, database processing places a greater burden on the CPU because of the processing required. Thus, a larger, more powerful CPU may be needed.

In some specialized applications, companies have found it advantageous to use **database machines**. Such machines are special-purpose computers whose sole function is to manage the database. The database machine is connected to a second CPU that does applications processing. The database machine stores and retrieves data on behalf of the application processing computer. To date, database machines have had limited acceptance.

Database Processing Programs

Figure 9–22 shows the relationships of programs involved in the processing of a multiuser, multiapplication database. Messages arrive at the CPU and are accepted by the operating system. This system is a program that manages the computer's resources and controls the flow of processing. The operating system sends messages to the appropriate application program. For example, at a bank a deposit transaction

FIGURE 9–21
Linked lists used to represent record relationships

RECORD NUMBER	LINK	RECORD TYPE	CONTENTS
1	2	D	Department 100 data
2	7	E	Employee 20 data
3	4	D	Department 200 data
4	8	E	Employee 25 data
5	9	D	Department 300 data
6	0	E	Employee 40 data
7	10	E	Employee 80 data
8	0	E	Employee 70 data
9	6	E	Employee 30 data
10	0	E	Employee 15 data

FIGURE 9—22

Program relationships in the database
environment

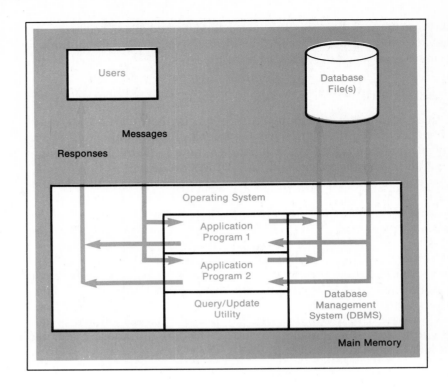

(message) would be delivered to the deposit processing application
program. To process the transaction, this program may need to
retrieve data from the database or store data within the database.
When these functions are needed, the application program calls on the
database management system for service. The DBMS obtains or stores
the data as instructed. When the application program has completed
the transaction, it sends a response, via the operating system, back to
the user. (See chapter 10 for information about the receipt and delivery of messages.)

The processing for single-user and single-application databases is
similar, but simpler than that shown in Figure 9—22. In a single-user
database, multiple messages would not go to the operating system. In
a single-application database, only one application program would be
involved.

Functions of a Database Management System

The primary functions of the DBMS are listed below:

1. Store, retrieve, and update data
2. Provide a data dictionary
3. Recover from failure

4. Provide security facilities
5. Provide utility facilities
6. Control concurrent processing

First, the DBMS must store, retrieve, and update data. The DBMS must allow users to directly access records using one or more keys. In fact, as mentioned, relational DBMS products must allow direct access by every field (attribute) of the file (table). Second, the DBMS should provide a *data dictionary*, or user-accessible catalog of data descriptions. The user should be able to access the dictionary to determine the contents of the database.

The third major function of a DBMS is to recover from failure. Computers fail; processing can stop unexpectedly; disk heads crash and ruin data. When events such as these occur, the DBMS must have facilities to support recovery. For example, restoring the database from a previous backup and reapplying any changes made must be possible.

Another function of the DBMS is to provide security facilities. The database is a valued resource. With powerful query languages, data can be readily accessed, both by authorized and unauthorized users. Therefore, the DBMS must provide passwords and other protective measures. Observe that the DBMS cannot provide security. The DBMS can provide only facilities for people to use so that *they* can provide security.

The fifth function of the DBMS as listed above is to provide utility services. The structure of the database may change. When such a change occurs, the database may need to be unloaded, altered, and reloaded. If so, programs to perform these services are needed. Rather than force each organization using a DBMS to write its own programs, the vendors of the DBMS provide generalized utilities that perform these services. Other utilities clean up files by consolidating unused space; improve the efficiency of the overhead data, and back up the database.

Finally, in a multiuser environment the DBMS must provide facilities to control concurrent processing. A database is a shared resource. Many different application programs and many different users can access it concurrently. When two users try to modify the same record at the same time, errors can be generated.

To prevent these problems from occurring, DBMS products must supply special commands to lock records that might be modified or deleted. When the application program issues one of these commands, the DBMS will not allow other users to access the record until the first user is finished. Chapter 10 discusses the concurrent update problem in greater detail.

There are other, more sophisticated functions of a DBMS, but they are beyond the scope of this text. See [48] and [56] for more information.

APPLICATION

"WHAT DATABASE TECHNOLOGY WILL OFFER DURING THE NEXT FIVE TO TEN YEARS."

The technology behind database management systems is continually evolving. A picture of it is based primarily on three factors: the demands and inertia of the marketplace, the current research and development, and the history of the last 15 years.

DATABASE ARCHITECTURES

Textbooks on data management usually list three major architectures or models for database management systems: hierarchical, network, and relational. The utility of this taxonomy will rapidly diminish in the next few years as systems evolve toward the three-schema architecture. The three-schema architecture makes fundamental distinctions between the internal (physical) schema, the external (user-viewer) schema, and the conceptual (enterprise-wide) schema.

We might expect the current relational craze to give way to more robust systems that employ all ANSI three-schema architectures to deliver a high level of data independence.

DISTRIBUTED DATABASES

The amount of discussion and number of technical papers concerning distributed databases is out of proportion to what has been accomplished in this area during the past ten years and to what the real requirements are. The performance, recovery, reliability, and procedural coordination problems of distributed databases is limited, so for most users

any capability would have to be cheap, transparent, and foolproof, and development of such a general product is still far in the future.

DATABASE MACHINES

Database machines are beginning to make an impact in the marketplace, but very slowly — much more slowly in fact than many people had forecast. The Britton-Lee machine has proved somewhat popular in the large minicomputer arena and a new offering for mainframes is too new to have established any trend. Teradata on the other hand has gone straight for the large-scale IBM markets with an SQL-compatible language; results to date have been somewhat disappointing.

Database machines will continue to make inroads, especially into dedicated, large-database application environments. These applications naturally demand the kind of performance that specialized hardware can offer, and a large, single-application workload can be used to justify capital expense and a dedicated hardware solution, which managers in more general environments tend to eschew (particularly from third parties).

DATA DICTIONARIES

The data dictionary is the sleeper in the what the future holds for databases. Sure, data dictionaries have been around for some time, and most

installations still haven't figured out how to use them in an efficient and effective manner. But they are the key to integration in the database environment and we haven't even scratched the surface yet in learning what can be with them.

The data dictionary will become the database for a wider circle of information systems activities. In particular, it will contain information about activities that occur earlier in a system life-cycle, such as planning and functional requirements analysis and design. This information will then be used to automatically generate prototype and production applications. Project management, scheduling, test control, documentation, and other ancillary functions associated with system development can be assisted through use of the data dictionary.

INTEGRATION

The level of integration among the components of a vendor's data management offerings is one of the main considerations used in evaluating modern products. Every vendor is working to tighten the level of integration among the main elements of its product line; typically these include the DBMS itself, the data dictionary, the query language, the report generator, and the applications generator. In several cases, what appears to be integrated is really interfaced. For example, an intermediate file must be output from the dictionary and then input to the database definition generator; the database cannot be generated directly from the dictionary.

END-USER FEATURES

Now that most database packages have their own application generator capabilities, the next big push in product development will be aimed at end-user features. Improvements in end-user inquiry and update capabilities can be expected, including a foray into expert systems and artificial intelligence. Natural language inquiry systems will become much more popular during the next two years as new techniques move from the laboratory to the marketplace.

Categories of DBMS Products

DBMS products fall into three major categories, as summarized below:

1. Mainframe DBMS Products
   Designed for large multiuser, multiapplication databases
   Manage databases of from 50 million to 1 billion bytes
   Cost $100,000 to $200,000
   Examples: ADABAS, IDMS, IMS
2. Minicomputer DBMS Products
   Designed for multiuser, multiapplication databases; frequently used for multiuser, single-application databases
   Manage databases of from 10 million to 400 million bytes
   Cost about $10,000
3. Examples: TOTAL, IMAGE, ORACLE
   Microcomputer DBMS Products
   Designed for single-user, and single- or multiapplication databases; multiuser possible with local area networks
   Manage databases of from 50,000 to 15 million bytes
   Cost $500 to $700
   Examples: dBASE III Plus, Rbase System V, Knowledgeman

Products for mainframe computers are intended to support large multi-user, multi-application databases. Such databases range in size from 50 million bytes up to 1 billion bytes. Products in this category typically cost in the $100,000 to $200,000 range. Examples of products in this category are IMS, IDMS, and ADABAS.

Minicomputer DBMS products are scaled down versions of mainframe products. They are generally accessed by multiple users, but quite often they support single-application databases. Such databases vary in size from 10 million bytes up to 400 million bytes. Minicomputer DBMS products cost around $10,000. Examples are TOTAL, IMAGE, and ORACLE.

DBMS products for microcomputers generally support single-user and both single- and multiple-application databases. These products are designed to be easy to use because both the users and the developers in this market are relatively inexperienced. Some microcom-

QUESTIONS

9.23 Suppose a company has a database that includes a file of sales data. One of the fields of records in this file is month of sale. How many entries will an inverted file in this field contain?

9.24 Sketch an example for the situation described in question 9.23. Use the format shown in figure 9–20.

9.25 Consider the example shown in figure 9–21. Suppose a department that has employees 72, 82, and 92 is added. Also suppose that employee 20 is moved to the new department. Sketch the appearance of the file after these changes are made. Use the format in figure 9–21.

9.26 Do database systems require any special hardware? Do they require any additional hardware?

9.27 Explain the roles performed by the operating system, the application program, and the DBMS during the processing of a multiuser, multiapplication database.

9.28 How would your explanation in question 9.27 change for the processing of a single-user database? for a single-application database?

9.29 Describe the six major functions of a DBMS.

9.30 Explain the difference between an application program and a query/update utility.

9.31 Describe the major differences among DBMS products for micro, mini, and mainframe computers.

9.32 Why do application programs contain special commands to process a database?

9.33 What does a data dictionary contain? How is it used?

(continued)

puter DBMS products support a limited amount of multiuser processing on local area networks (see chapter 10). Databases in this category range in size from 50,000 to 15 million bytes. Microcomputer DBMS products typically cost $500 to $700. Example products are dBASE III Plus, Rbase System V, and Knowledgeman.

Using the DBMS

Users can interface with the DBMS in one of two ways. First, they can use application programs that call the DBMS for service. In the system shown in figure 9–22, for instance, the user would send a message or transaction to the applicable application program. In the course of processing the transaction, the program would call the DBMS.

The second mode of access to a database is through a **query/update utility**. This utility is a program or a portion of the DBMS that provides generalized access to the database. Query/update programs are not application programs in that they do not solve problems such as order entry or inventory. Instead, they are used to access records and perhaps to modify them. The user names a file and gives the key or keys for the records desired. The query/update program responds with qualifying records. Commands are available to insert and delete records as well. The SQL examples in the previous section are typical query commands.

For the system shown in figure 9–22, a query/update command would be entered like any other command. The operating system would route it to the query/update utility instead of to an application program.

Database-Oriented Application Programs

Application programs are different in a database processing environment than in a file processing environment. The ability to process records by many keys and by record relationships is a characteristic unique to database processing. Common programming languages do not have commands or statements for such processing. For example, the BASIC language has INPUT and PRINT statements, and the COBOL language has READ and WRITE statements, but these are inadequate to initiate the powerful actions a DBMS can perform.

In response to this problem, some DBMS vendors have defined **special commands** for the application programmer to use. These commands augment the standard language statements. Because these statements are not part of the standard language, the language translators (or compilers) cannot process them. Therefore, the application program with special database commands is first translated by a program, called a **precompiler**, supplied by the DBMS vendor.

DBMS products for microcomputers provide both query/update utilities and program access, although none (as yet) support precompilation as described here. They also provide a third method of access: their own languages. In the early days of microcomputing, languages such as BASIC did not support DBMS calls. Rather than wait for this capability to be added, the early DBMS developers designed their own languages. In many cases, the languages were not especially good, but they met the early need. Once program libraries were developed with these languages, they became established. From a purist standpoint, this development is regrettable, since established languages such as COBOL, PASCAL, and C were perfectly acceptable, given a precompiler interface.

Procedures for Database Processing

The procedures necessary for database-oriented business computer systems are extensions of those required for more basic types of processing. Like other systems, database systems must have user procedures explaining how to use the system under normal and abnormal operating conditions. Procedures must also be developed that utilize the DBMS security features to ensure that only authorized personnel can perform authorized activity.

Since database applications are often online, the procedures for control, error correction, and recovery described for direct access processing in chapter 8 pertain to database processing as well. To implement these procedures, programmers need to be taught how to use DBMS facilities. Controls need to be developed to ensure that programmers follow these procedures. Additionally, users need to be instructed to follow procedures, and periodically, managers should verify that procedures are being followed.

Regarding backup and recovery, users must have procedures describing what they should do when the system is unavailable due to failure. They should know how best to carry on their responsibilities, what data to keep, and what to do first when the system becomes operational.

In addition to these procedures for programmers and users, procedures must be developed and documented for operations personnel. These procedures should explain how to run the system, how to perform backup and recovery operations, and how to control the system to ensure that only authorized activity occurs.

Procedures for Sharing the Database

For multiuser database applications, special procedures must be developed because the database is a shared resource. Without careful management, users can interfere with one another. For example, consider the database depicted in figure 9–14.

Suppose that a customer who has a checking account and a bank loan decides to move to another city. In the process of moving, the

9.34 Identify a way that microcomputer DBMS products allow databases to be accessed other than through a query/update utility or a standard programming language.

customer closes his or her checking account. If the clerk in the checking department deletes both the customer's checking account and the customer's record, then information about the customer's loan may be lost. This is because, when the customer record is deleted, the loan record will not have a parent. Depending on the DBMS in use, records without parents may be deleted automatically.

A simple solution to this problem is to have the checking department clerk examine the database to determine whether the customer has accounts in other departments. However, the clerk may be processing a subset of the database that does not include the loan or savings records. If so, he or she will be unable to determine whether the customer has other accounts.

This example illustrates the problems that can occur in database processing. These problems occur not only because the data is shared, but also because the data is integrated — there is only one customer record for all checking, savings, and loan processing.

Processing Rights and Responsibilities

To prevent users from interfering with one another, the company must determine the **processing rights and responsibilities** for all users. For each record (or even each field), the company must decide which users can read, insert, modify, or delete data. Furthermore, each of these users must have a procedure to follow when performing the activity.

Figure 9–23 shows the processing rights negotiated at the bank. All departments can access customer records, but only the new accounts department is allowed to add, modify, or delete such records. (Further, when deleting records, they must follow the procedure shown in figure 9–24.)

Authorities for the other record types are shown in the remainder of figure 9–23. Note that the checking and savings departments are allowed to read each other's records. They can thus check to make sure

FIGURE 9–23
Department processing rights for the bank database

COMMAND	CUSTOMER RECORDS	CHECKING AND TRANSACTION RECORDS	SAVINGS AND TRANSACTION RECORDS	LOAN AND TRANSACTION RECORDS
Read	New Accounts Checking Savings Loan	Checking Savings	Savings Checking	Loan
Insert	New Accounts	Checking	Savings	Loan
Modify	New Accounts	Checking	Savings	Loan
Delete	New Accounts	Checking	Savings	Loan

```
SEND REQUEST FOR CUSTOMER DELETION TO CHECKING, SAVINGS, AND
    LOAN DEPARTMENTS
IF ALL THREE DEPARTMENTS APPROVE DELETION REQUEST
    THEN IF CUSTOMER HAD NO SAVINGS OR LOAN ACCOUNTS
            THEN DELETE CUSTOMER RECORD
            ELSE CHANGE CUSTOMER STATUS TO INACTIVE
                CHANGE ADDRESS IF APPROPRIATE
        END-IF
    ELSE DEFER OR DESTROY DELETION REQUEST IN ACCORDANCE WITH
        DEPARTMENT INSTRUCTIONS
END-IF
AT YEAR END, SEND TAX FORMS FOR SAVINGS AND LOAN ACCOUNTS
    DELETE ALL INACTIVE CUSTOMERS
```

that transfers from savings to checking (or checking to savings) are successfully made.

FIGURE 9–24
Bank procedure for deleting customer records

Figure 9–24 shows the procedure that new accounts personnel must follow when a customer record is to be deleted. First, the checking, savings, and loan departments must all certify that the customer's accounts are successfully closed. If all three concur, and if the customer had no savings or loan accounts, the record is deleted.

If the customer had savings or loan accounts, the record is marked inactive. It will not be deleted until the close of the calendar year, because year-end statements must be sent to the savings and loan customers for tax purposes. If the customer's record were deleted, the bank would have no address to send the statements to.

This discussion has illustrated the decisions the bank must make about processing rights to ensure that users' activities do not interfere with one another. A similar community-oriented view must be taken when considering changes to the database structure.

For example, suppose that the checking department wants to add a code letter to the customer number in the customer record. Making such a change will affect the savings and loan departments. Most likely they will have to change their application programs as well as their forms and documents. Clearly, the code letter change cannot be made without agreement from these departments.

Suppose that these other departments oppose the change. Negotiations will then have to be conducted to determine the best solution for all concerned. If the code letter change is so important that it justifies the additional expense and effort to the savings and loan departments, then it will be done. Otherwise, another way must be found to satisfy the needs of the checking department.

The point of this example is that changes to the database can be made only after the needs of all users have been considered. To consider them

PROFILE

"DATABASE PROFESSIONALS HAVE SUDDENLY BEEN ELEVATED TO A UNIQUE LEVEL OF POWER, RESPECT AND VISIBILITY."

Because of the strategic value placed on corporate information resources, database professionals have suddenly been elevated to a unique level of power, respect, and visibility. "The database administrator must administer all the technical aspects of the corporate data resource under one umbrella," explains Arvid Shah, senior staff consultant, Performance Development Corp., Princeton, NJ.

"Very few people start out in DBA at the entry level," says Brian Krueger, DP placement manager, Robert Half of Wisconsin, Inc., Milwaukee, WI. "Normally, you must work up to the position through an applications path consisting of database programming and systems analysis." This evolutionary process can take anywhere from four to eight years. However, a "fast-tracker" may become a DBA within two or three years.

According to Ken Brathwaite (Software Design Associates, Inc., Union, NJ), DBAs should be responsible for:

1. Improving the effectiveness and efficiency of DBMS use, and its overall performance.
2. Offering assistance to end users experiencing DBMS problems.
3. Ensuring that adequate validation procedures are used for all transactions.
4. Providing ongoing staff training and keeping up-to-date on database technology.
5. Developing long-range plans to meet current and future DBMS requirements.

Database administration represents the fastest growth area in the DP profession, and the trend toward relational DBMS and database machines adds luster. Control over data storage may ultimately determine the future success of DP.

effectively, procedures for change must be developed. The procedures describe how changes can be suggested, how the input of all using departments is received, and how the change decisions will be made. Such procedures bring order to the change process and ensure that all proposals receive fair and adequate consideration. They also ensure that all departments have a chance to express opinions.

Database Personnel

Database environments have users, operations personnel, and systems development people just as all other business computer sytems do. In addition, however, there is a need for someone to manage and protect the database resource. For a small database on a microcomputer, this administrative function is a part-time job. For a large multiuser, multiapplication database, this function may be assigned to a group of people.

Databases are shared, and, since the beginning of the human race, whenever people have to share something, conflict develops. In a broad sense, the job of the **database administrator (DBA)** is to anticipate conflict, provide an environment for the peaceful resolution of conflict, and protect the database so that it can be used effectively. The DBA has three separate functions, as summarized below:

1. Manage data activity
   a. Processing rights
      (1) Provide focal point for negotiating
      (2) Document
      (3) Enforce
   b. Concurrent update and backup and recovery problems
      (1) Define problems
      (2) Develop solutions and standards
      (3) Ensure that adequate training is done
      (4) Evaluate problems
2. Manage database structure
   a. Manage schema and subschema designs
   b. Determine data standards
   c. Document database structure
   d. Manage changes to structure
3. Evaluate DBMS performance
   a. Resolve performance problems
   b. Determine need for new features

Managing Data Activity

First, the DBA manages data activity. Note the wording here. The **DBA** does not perform data activity (inserting accounts, canceling checks, and so on); users do that. The **DBA** *manages* this activity.

As discussed in the last section, the processing rights of all users must be carefully determined. The DBA is the focal point for negotiating these rights. The DBA meets with the users to determine who wants to do what to which data. The DBA is (or should be) an unbiased arbitrator for resolving any conflicts. As time goes by, the business will change and user needs will change. The DBA serves as a focal point for changing the user processing rights as necessary.

Once processing rights have been determined, they need to be documented. The DBA is responsible for developing this documentation. The DBA is also responsible for enforcing processing rights. If a department or individual violates the agreed-on policy, complaints are given to the DBA. The offender is informed of the need to follow the policy. More stringent measures are taken if necessary.

Since the DBA is charged with the responsibility for protecting the database, the problems of concurrent update and of backup and recovery are important to him or her. First, the DBA must determine what the potential problems are and how serious they can be. These problems vary from one DBMS to another, as well as from one

QUESTIONS

9.35 What procedures do users need for operation of a database system? What do they need for backup and recovery?

9.36 What procedures do operators need for operation of a database system? What do they need for backup and recovery?

9.37 Explain why the activities of one user must be coordinated with the activities of another.

9.38 What does the phrase *processing rights and responsibilities* mean?

9.39 What procedures are needed to ensure orderly change to the database structure of a multiuser database?

9.40 What does *DBA* mean?

9.41 In a broad sense, what is the job of the DBA?

9.42 What are the three major functions performed by the DBA?

9.43 Does the DBA perform data activity? If not, who does?

9.44 What role does the DBA have in defining processing rights and responsibilities?

9.45 What is the DBA's responsibility with regard to concurrent update and backup and recovery problems?

9.46 What does the DBA do with regard to developing database structure?

9.47 What is the major management problem of the DBA?

9.48 What qualities and characteristics should the DBA have?

application to another. Once the problems are known, the DBA meets with users, operations personnel, and the systems development staff to develop solutions.

As mentioned previously, part of the concurrent update solution may be to develop standard ways of processing the database. Application programs may need to lock records before they are updated, for example. In addition, standard procedures must be developed for backing up the database. Procedures for recovery are also important.

The DBA is also responsible for ensuring that the means used to solve concurrent update and backup and recovery problems are documented. All involved personnel from the user and operations departments must be trained. Although the DBA may not do all of this documenting and training, he or she must make sure that it gets done.

Finally, the DBA is charged with the responsibility for investigating problems that occur and for finding solutions to prevent their recurrence. The DBA may meet with involved personnel to change standards, procedures, processing rights, or other activity.

Managing Database Structure

In addition to managing data activity, the DBA must also manage the database structure. If the DBA has been appointed at design time, he or she leads the tasks of defining the database structure. Multiapplication databases must allow users or application programs to accomplish their assigned tasks and must support the negotiated processing rights.

Defining the database structure is the same as developing data standards for the company. Users must agree on how many characters will be in the customer account number, for example, or which fields will be in the customer record. Further, the relationships that can exist among records must be standardized. Again, whenever more than one person develops a standard, conflict will develop. The DBA is responsible for resolving this conflict.

Once the database structure and related standards have been determined, the DBA ensures that the decisions are documented. The DBA must also ensure that the database is developed in accordance with these decisions.

Business is a dynamic activity. No structure, however well developed, will last without change. Users will want to add new capabilities or to change existing procedures. The operations staff will want to add new equipment or to change computers. The systems development staff will find a better way to do things.

The DBA is charged with the responsibility of managing change to the database structure. As discussed in the section "Procedures for Database Processing," such changes must be made carefully. If not, a change made for the benefit of one user will cause problems for others.

To manage change, the DBA must receive requests for changes and periodically present these requests to a group representing all user, computer operations, and systems development groups. Potential changes should be discussed with the representatives of each group. In a subsequent meeting, the changes should be discussed again and potential problems identified. If no conflicts exist, or if ways of eliminating the conflicts can be found, the changes can be made. This change process is managed by the DBA.

Evaluating DBMS Performance

A third area of DBA responsibility concerns **DBMS** performance. Because the DBA is the focal point for conflict resolution, when users complain that the system performs too slowly or that it costs too much to run certain jobs, the DBA will be involved. He or she will serve as an interface between the users and the operations and systems development staffs.

Sometimes the performance problem can be resolved by **tuning**, which means changing DBMS parameters set at installation time. The amount of main memory allocated to the DBMS is an example of such a parameter. Other performance problems can be fixed by cleaning up the database using utility programs supplied by the vendor. In some cases, a high-performance feature of the database can be acquired. At worst, a more powerful CPU can be obtained.

Vendors of DBMS products periodically announce new features at extra cost. When such announcements are made, the DBA must determine whether the new features are needed. The DBA considers each feature in light of user requirements. Again, the DBA will meet with users, operations personnel, and systems development personnel to make this determination.

SUMMARY

Database processing is a technique for organizing and manipulating data files in an integrated manner. Database management systems were developed because file processing systems have trouble adequately representing objects in the real world. Three specific areas in which file processing systems have proven inadequate are in representing variable-length objects, multiple views of data, and relationships. DBMSs can represent these things and can therefore more readily support the user's view of stored data.

Databases are built upon records that can be linked, or related, to each other in many combinations. This permits the construction of many different objects. Record relationships are of three fundamental types: hierarchies, simple networks, and complex networks.

Knowledge of record relationships is not as important to users as it is to database designers and other computer personnel who work with a database.

There are three basic database designs, or data models, upon which many database products have been built. They are the hierarchical data model, the network data model, and the relational data model. The relational data model offers the most flexibility of the three and is useful not only as a data model but also as a database design tool. In the relational data model all data is stored in two-dimensional tables, and relationships among records are built into the tables with linking fields. This is easy for users and data processors to understand.

Selecting a DBMS over a file processing system affects each of the five business computer system components, most significantly the data component. To respond quickly to user requests, a DBMS must store much overhead data in addition to application data. Very complex programming also is required to maintain both application data and the lists, tables, and so forth that are overhead.

A DBMS has six major functions: storing, retrieving, and updating data; providing a user-accessible directory; controlling concurrent processing; recovering from failure; providing security facilities; and providing utility services. DBMSs are accessible through query/utility programs and also through application programs.

Procedures must be developed to resolve conflicts that are bound to arise because a database is a shared resource. The database administrator is responsible for resolving conflicts, as well as ensuring the successful operation of the database. The job of the DBA is to anticipate conflict, provide an environment for the peaceful resolution of conflicts, and protect the database so it can be effectively used.

WORD LIST

Database management
Database management system
    (DBMS)
Object
Variable-length objects
Multiple data views
Redundant data
Data integration problems
Record relationships
Database
Self-describing
Directory
Data dictionary
Integrated records
Application
Reports
Forms
Transaction programs
Menus
Single-application, single-user
    database
Multiple-application, single-user
    database

Single-application,
    multiple-user database
Multiple-application,
    multiple-user database
Hierarchical, or tree,
    relationship
One-to-many relationship
Parent
Child
Simple network
Complex network
Many-to-many relationship
Data model
Hierarchical data model
Network data model
CODASYL DBTG data model
Relational data model
Relation
Attribute
Tuple
Table

Column
Row
File
Field
Record
SQL
Key field
Overhead data
Index
Inverted file
Inverted list
Link field
Linked list
Database machine
Query/update utility
Special DBMS commands
DBMS precompiler
Processing rights and
    responsibilities
Database administrator (DBA)
Tuning

QUESTIONS TO CHALLENGE YOUR THINKING

A. Suppose that you work for Elliot Bay Electronics (see chapter 6). The director of data processing asks you whether EB needs a database capability. How do you respond? What would be the advantages to EB? The disadvantages? How should EB determine whether or not a database is appropriate?

B. Show how indexes could be used to represent all three types of record relationships.

C. Show how linked lists could be used to represent nonunique keys.

D. Extend the structure in figure 9–21 to represent simple networks. Extend it to represent complex networks.

E. Locate a nearby organization that is using a DBMS product. Interview a responsible person to find out the name of the DBMS, its cost, and

how satisfied the organization is with it. How long did the conversion to the database take? Did any special problems occur that other organizations should avoid? Has the support from the vendor been adequate?

F. Locate an organization that is using a multiuser database. Determine whether any special procedures have been instituted since the database was installed. How does the organization handle concurrent update problems? Have processing rights and responsibilities been negotiated and documented? Have there been conflicts among users? Has the company appointed a DBA? If so, what are the DBA's responsibilities? What organizational or management problems have developed since the database was implemented?

TELEPROCESSING AND DISTRIBUTED PROCESSING SYSTEMS

CHAPTER 10

Until the mid 1960s, most data processing was done on centralized, batch-oriented computers. However, for many business applications bringing the data to the computer center for processing was undesirable or infeasible. The movement and delivery of the data on punched cards, magnetic tape, printed reports, and so on took too long and was too expensive.

Businesspeople began to wonder whether telephones or other communications facilities could be used to transfer data. Today, a wide range of capabilities for such data transfer has been developed.

THE NATURE OF TELEPROCESSING SYSTEMS

Simply stated, **teleprocessing** is data processing at a distance. The term is derived from a combination of the terms *telecommunications* and *data processing*. You know by now what data processing is, so only the term *telecommunications* needs to be defined.

Telecommunications is communicating at a distance, usually using some form of electromagnetic signal similar to that used for radio and television. The subject of telecommunications is a broad one that includes the transmission of voice, messages such as telegrams, facsimiles (pictures), and data. The latter form of telecommunications, called *data telecommunications* or *data communications*, is concerned with moving data from point to point, from terminal to computer, and even from computer to computer.

Now we can be more specific. A business teleprocessing system is a business computer system in which one or more of the five components are physically (geographically) distributed and the components are connected into a system using telecommunications facilities. All forms of telecommunications can be used. Data communication is used to transfer data from one site to another, voice communication is used to integrate distributed personnel, and message communication is used to implement distributed procedures.

Three Examples of Teleprocessing Systems

The system used at Elliot Bay Electronics represents the simplest form of teleprocessing system. Data entry clerks use terminals to process the direct access files for the customer master file and inventory systems (see figure 10–1). This system is considered a teleprocessing system because the clerks and the terminals are physically removed from the computer.

This system is a simple one. Most clerks are in the same building as the computer, and the others are not more than 100 meters (about 300 feet) away from it. As is frequently the case, all of the hardware is supplied and maintained by the same vendor, a situation that elimi-

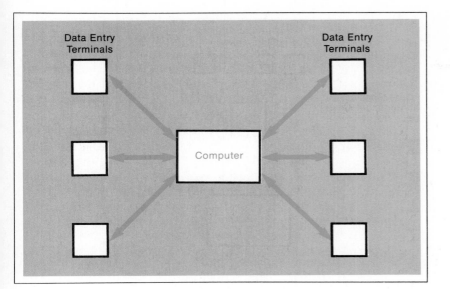

FIGURE 10–1
Teleprocessing system used by Elliot Bay
Electronics

nates compatibility problems. Both the CPU and the operating system are designed to support just this type of teleprocessing. Only a modest amount of work is required to install the hardware. (The other four components may require extensive work, however.) Consequently, Elliot Bay does not need a staff specialist for communications processing.

Figure 10–2 shows the teleprocessing equipment configuration for a medium-sized bank that has three branches and operates a bank card authorization center. In addition to the terminals, there are cash machines and a **remote job entry (RJE) station**. The RJE station has a card reader, a printer, and a terminal for the operator to use. This equipment is used to submit batch jobs from the remote card processing center.

The bank's teleprocessing system is considerably more complicated than Elliot Bay's. The communication lines are much longer and involve the telephone company and other organizations. The hardware is supplied by several vendors. Getting it all to work together is not easy. Maintenance and troubleshooting can be complicated when one vendor blames any problems on other vendors. Further, the operating system was designed to be general purpose. Someone must tailor it to the bank's environment. The bank needs at least one communications and operating system specialist on staff to install and maintain the hardware and programs.

The bank has less control over the terminal environment than does EB. The equipment may be misused, abused, or even fraudulently used. Since the applications are financial in nature, efforts must be

FIGURE 10–2
Teleprocessing equipment configuration
for medium-sized bank

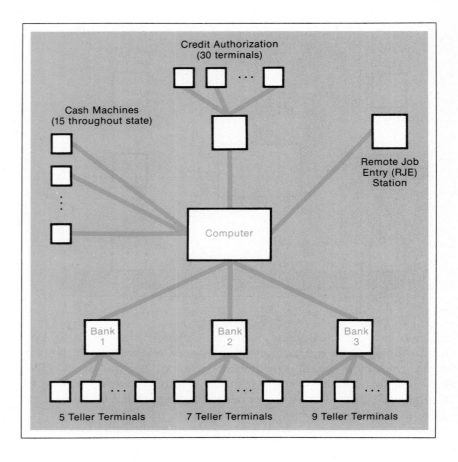

made to provide security. Finally, **response time** (the time it takes the computer to respond to a request or statement) is important to the bank. If response is too slow, customers will be kept waiting in line, and customer service will suffer. This differs from the Elliot Bay case, in which clerks, not customers, must wait.

The third teleprocessing configuration, that for Worldwide Shipping Company, is depicted in figure 10–3. Clearly this third configuration is the most complex of the three examples. Here, computer users in Alaska, Hawaii, and Europe communicate with the company's headquarters in New York. Not only are multiple vendors involved, but multiple communications media are used as well. Phone, microwave, satellite, and other types of communications equipment are used. All of the equipment must work together in spite of different speeds, conventions, and vendors.

Additional problems occur because of the international link. Europe, Canada, and the United States have different laws and customs. Furthermore, the equipment is designed to operate to different standards. Because this system is a large and complex configuration,

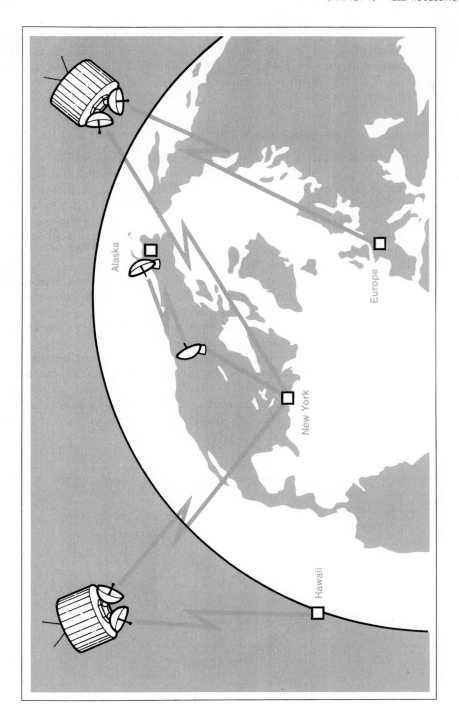

FIGURE 10–3
Teleprocessing configuration for
Worldwide Shipping Company

multiple CPUs are involved. Some computers will be used to handle communications resources and traffic but not to process data. This company may use several hundred terminals. To build this system and maintain all the equipment requires a large staff of communications specialists.

Rationale for Teleprocessing Systems

Businesses develop teleprocessing systems for two major reasons. First, because a business is geographically distributed and its data originates, is processed, and is used at different places. In the example of the bank, customers transact business at a local bank, but the data is processed at a central facility. Output such as the bank's financial statements then go to the bank's headquarters at still another location.

The second reason that teleprocessing systems are developed is economy. A central facility is established so that every bank does not need separate data processing facilities. The banks are connected to the central facility via telecommunication links. This system allows the business to gain **economies of scale**, or cost reductions, by having one large computer instead of several smaller ones.

Unfortunately, these economies of scale do not extend indefinitely; as more systems are added to the central computer through teleprocessing, the facility becomes hard to manage and expensive to operate. Figure 10–4 shows the average cost of data processing as it relates to the size of the computing facility. At first, the average cost decreases as

FIGURE 10–4

Average cost of data processing versus size

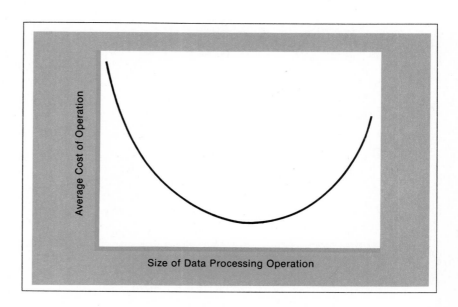

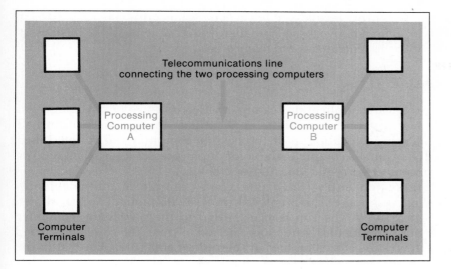

FIGURE 10–5
Example of distributed processing using two computers

the size increases, but at some point the computer becomes hard to manage and the average costs go up.

When a single, central computer becomes too large to manage effectively, another will be acquired and some applications transferred to it. At this point, the company will have two (or more) teleprocessing systems (see figure 10–5). Usually, these systems need to communicate to share data or facilities. Consequently, they are connected using telecommunications. The result is one large teleprocessing **network**, with applications processing occurring at two separate sites. This setup is called **distributed processing**, because the processing of application data is distributed on two or more computers in the teleprocessing network.

To review, there are three major configurations of data processing systems. In the first, called **centralized processing**, processing is centralized on a single computer. Applications are batch oriented; inputs arrive at, and outputs depart from, the computer center on physical media like cards or printed reports.

In the second major configuration, called **teleprocessing**, the components of the business computer system are geographically separated but united into a system by telecommunications equipment. Processing of the data is still done on a single computer, however. Finally, in the third configuration, called **distributed processing**, the system components are geographically separated, and applications processing is done on more than one computer.

In the early days of teleprocessing, data processing services evolved from centralized to teleprocessing to distributed configurations. Ten years ago, some businesses skipped the centralized stage and installed teleprocessing systems to begin with. Elliot Bay Electronics is a case in point. Recently, businesses have been connecting microcomputers with local area networks to form distributed systems; these businesses skip both the centralized and teleprocessing stages.

Teleprocessing Applications

Teleprocessing applications can be divided into two broad categories: offline and online. For **offline** applications, the data is transmitted from a remote location to the processing computer and stored. When a batch of data is complete, the computer processes it and then returns the output to the remote location as a batch.

Remote job entry (RJE) is a good example of offline teleprocessing. A computer run is entered via RJE equipment like that shown in figure 10–6. The run is transmitted to the processing computer and stored on its files. After some period of time, the run is processed and the results stored on files at the central computer. Later still, the outputs are sent to the RJE station for printing.

Batched data transmission is another example of offline processing. Here, groups of data are sent to the central computer in batches. For example, a day's worth of sales data may be sent. The batch of data is then processed by one or more application programs at the central computer. The results are then returned to the remote terminal and printed as a batch.

FIGURE 10–6
Remote job entry (RJE) station

APPLICATION	TELEPROCESSING SYSTEM
Offline	Remote job entry
	Data transmission
Online	Query and response
	Transaction processing
	Online program development

FIGURE 10−7
Types of teleprocessing systems

For **online** teleprocessing applications, the remote terminal is connected directly to the processing computer. Data is not sent in batches. Rather, a single record or message is sent; it is acted on by the processing computer, and the results are returned. Then another message is sent, and so forth.

Query and response systems are online applications. Here the user sends a request for such information as "How many seats are available on Flight 102?" The processing computer determines the answer and returns it to the terminal. Such questions are acted on one at a time, not in batches.

Transaction processing is another online application. The user sends a transaction such as "Add $1000 to account number 123123," and the processing computer takes the indicated action. A message is then returned indicating whether the operation was successfully executed or not.

Online program development is a third example of online applications. Users write programs at terminals by sending one line of code at a time to the processing computer. The computer then either translates the code and stores it, if it is correct, or stores the code for later translation. Either way, the user sends one line at a time. Unlike RJE, the program is not sent as a batch. Figure 10−7 summarizes these classifications of teleprocessing applications.

COMPONENTS OF TELEPROCESSING SYSTEMS

In this section we will describe three of the five components of a teleprocessing system: hardware, programs, and data. Procedures and personnel, while important, are not markedly different from procedures and personnel described in previous chapters and will not be discussed here.

Teleprocessing Hardware

A variety of specialized equipment and techniques are required to support a teleprocessing system. In fact, there is so much to this subject that it easily fills a two-semester course. In this section, the

QUESTIONS

10.1 From what two terms is the word *teleprocessing* derived?

10.2 What is telecommunications?

10.3 Define a business teleprocessing system.

10.4 Why is a medium-sized bank's teleprocessing system more complicated than Elliot Bay's?

10.5 What are the two major reasons for developing a teleprocessing system?

10.6 What does the phrase "economies of scale" mean?

10.7 How does centralized processing differ from teleprocessing?

10.8 How does teleprocessing differ from distributed processing?

10.9 Describe an offline teleprocessing application.

10.10 Describe an online teleprocessing application.

terms you are most likely to encounter in your business career will be defined.

Transmission Media

Many types of media can be used to transmit signals. The simplest and easiest is a pair of wires that connect the terminal to the computer. The most sophisticated is a satellite. In between these extremes are telephone lines, radio, cable television lines, optical cables, and so forth. These media are classified according to their *speed, mode,* and *type.*

The **speed** of a communication line is measured in **bits per second (bps).** Transmission media fall into three groups, based on speed. The slowest group is called **narrowband** and permits communication at the rate of 45 to 150 bps. A simple pair of wires will allow narrowband communication. The second group is called **voice grade** and permits maximum transmission rates of 1800 to 9600 bps. These lines are called voice grade because their speeds are typical of those that can be obtained over a voice-oriented telephone line.

Regular telephone lines like those in your apartment or home can be used for data transmission. However, such lines allow a maximum of only 2400 bps processing. To obtain higher speeds, a line must be leased from the telephone company and given special conditioning. Only then is the maximum speed of 9600 bps possible.

The third category of communication lines is called **wideband**; these lines permit very high-speed communication at the rate of 500,000 bps or more. Optical cables and electromagnetic communication via satellite are good examples of wideband service. Figure 10–8 summarizes these three categories.

Communication line speeds are sometimes given in another unit, called **baud**. This term refers to the number of times per second that a line signal can change its status. It is not the same as bps; speed in terms of baud is less than speed in terms of bps. For data processing purposes, the term *bits per second* is always more informative than baud, and you should use it.

In addition to speed, communication lines are classified according to **mode.** Two modes are possible: *analog* and *digital.* **Analog lines** carry signals that are continuous waves. The sounds of a siren and of a

FIGURE 10–8
Speed of communication lines

LINE SPEED	TRANSMISSION RATE
Narrowband (telegraph)	45 to 150 bps
Voice grade (telephone)	1800 to 9600 bps
Wideband (microwave or satellite)	500,000 bps or more

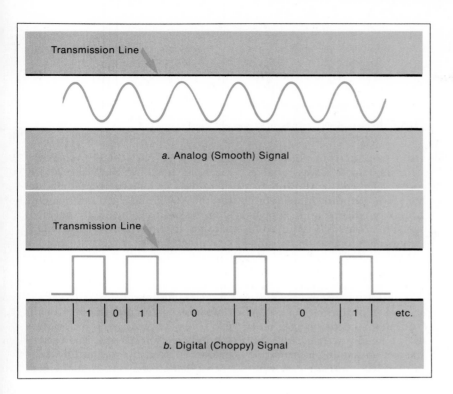

FIGURE 10–9
Modes of communication lines

smooth melody can be thought of as analog signals. Voice telephone lines are analog lines (see figure 10–9a).

Digital lines carry signals that have sharp peaks and valleys. The sounds of a barking dog and of a dripping faucet are similar to digital signals. The graph in figure 10–9b illustrates a digital signal.

When a terminal sends a message to the central computer, it does so by sending a series of bits. Thus, it might send the sequence 1, 1, 0, 1, 0, 1. As you might guess, such a message is more easily carried by a digital line than by an analog one. The peaks of the digital line can be used to represent 1's, and the valleys can represent 0's (see figure 10–9b).

Sending a series of bits on an analog line is not as simple. Somehow the continuous signal must be transformed to carry the bits. This transformation is called **modulation** and **demodulation**.

Figure 10–10 shows a common type of modulation called **frequency modulation**. This type works by causing the signal to oscillate faster to represent a 1 and to oscillate slower for a 0. **Amplitude modulation** works by making the signal larger (louder) for a 1 and smaller (softer) for a 0.

To transmit digital signals over an analog line requires a special device called a **modem**, or *modulator-dem*odulator. As shown in figure

APPLICATION

"DIGITAL SIGNALS USED BY COMPUTERS AND PRINTERS ARE SENT LONG DISTANCES."

The first thing most people want to know about a modem is its baud rate, or speed. Actually, the term "baud" is a misleading one, since it doesn't necessarily reflect the true throughput of a modem.

A better way to view modem speed is by bits per second (bps), a measurement of the quantity of information sent in a given length of time. Since typical modem use results in 10 bits being sent and received for each character, you can consider the number of characters sent to be one-tenth the number of bits per second (e.g., a 1200-bps modem sends and receives at the rate of 120 characters per second).

The process of transferring in-

formation to and from your computer via modem involves what is commonly referred to as protocol. Whether you are sending information (uploading) or receiving it (downloading), some control is required to assure that the information is transferred properly. The simplest of these controls is known as handshaking, the way that each machine tells the other when it is and is not ready to accept more information. For example, if your machine is storing what it receives, it needs to tell the other machine to stop sending information and wait while it stores to disk what has already been received.

The most common handshaking protocol in telecommunications is

start/stop or XON/XOFF. When the receiving machine can't accept any more data, it sends a special character, the XOFF, and the other machine stops sending until it receives another special character, the XON, signaling that it is ready to receive again.

Most communications packages now provide one or more common error-checking protocols, such as the Christensen (Xmodem) or Kermit protocols, as well as a proprietary error correction scheme. The various protocols are not compatible with each other, so be sure that the software you choose supports a protocol that is also available to the machine with which you'll be communicating.

10–11a, when the terminal sends a message to the central computer, it sends its digital message to the modem. The modem encodes the message into an analog signal and sends it over the analog communication line. At the other end, another modem receives the analog signal and converts it to digital (binary) form.

The third classification of communication lines is by **type**. A communication line can be *simplex*, *half-duplex*, or *full-duplex*. A **sim-**

FIGURE 10–10
Analog signals representing 1, 1, 0, 1, 0, 1 using frequency modulation

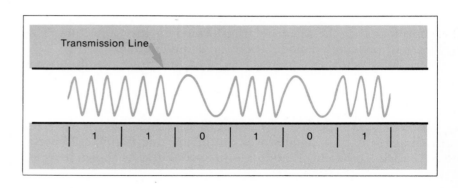

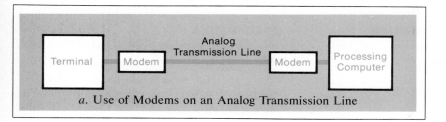

a. Use of Modems on an Analog Transmission Line

FIGURE 10–11
Use of modems

b. Modem

plex line is designed for one-way transmission; that is, a signal can go from the terminal to the central computer, but not back. Simplex lines are cheap, but they are not very useful for business teleprocessing.

Half-duplex lines can carry a signal in either direction, but only one way at a time. Thus, the terminal can send a message to the computer, but the computer must wait until the terminal is finished before it sends a message back. Half-duplex lines are like a road that is wide enough for only one car.

Full-duplex lines can carry messages in both directions simultaneously. Thus, while the terminal is sending a message to the computer, the computer can be sending a message to the terminal. A good application for a full-duplex line is an RJE station. While the terminal

FIGURE 10–12
Summary of characteristics of transmission lines

LINE CLASSIFICATION	CHARACTERISTICS
Speed	Narrowband (45 to 150 bps maximum)
	Voice grade (1800 to 9600 bps maximum)
	Wideband (500,000-plus bps maximum)
Mode	Analog (modems required)
	Digital
Type	Simplex (one-way transmission)
	Half-duplex (one way at a time)
	Full-duplex (both ways simultaneously)

is sending the computer a job, the computer can be sending the terminal the results from a previous job for printing.

The characteristics of communication lines are summarized in figure 10–12.

Line Management

A common problem in telecommunications processing is that the terminals are not active enough to keep the lines busy. In this situation, several terminals can be connected to the same line, as shown in figure 10–13. This is called a **multidrop** configuration, because the terminals are "dropped off" the line.

When several terminals share the same line, a potential problem is created. If two or more of them use the line simultaneously, their messages will become garbled. To prevent this problem from occurring, two line management methods are used.

In the **polling** method, the central computer asks each terminal if it has a message to send. If so, the terminal is directed to send it. The central computer then asks the next terminal, and so forth, in round-robin fashion. In figure 10–13, the terminals are polled in the order 5, 4, 3, 6, 2, 1, 5, 4, 3, 6, 2, 1, and so forth.

Polling works well, but it can waste CPU time. If none of the terminals has a message to send, the CPU is asking a lot of questions for nothing. A second technique, called **contention**, overcomes this disadvantage.

When a line is managed by contention, each terminal listens to the line before sending a message. If the line is busy, it waits a period of time and listens again. Eventually, when the line is not busy, the terminal sends its message. When two terminals start to send messages at the same time, they notice the contention and stop. They then wait different lengths of time and try to send their messages again.

Contention is similar to a human discussion without a leader. It works well as long as no one speaks too frequently and as long as no one speaks very long at a time. Using this comparison, if a terminal sends messages too frequently, or if it sends a single message that is too long, then other terminals will incur long delays in sending messages. Additionally, to work well, the line must have considerable excess capacity. Otherwise, terminals will get too many busy signals.

Like so many data processing alternatives, neither polling nor contention is better in every situation. Polling allows the line to be busier but requires CPU time; contention requires idle time on the line but does not involve the CPU. It becomes a question of which is cheaper — CPU time or line capacity.

Polling and contention are also used in the coordination of processing of local area networks as you will see in the discussion of local area networks later in this chapter.

Multiplexors and Concentrators

Typically, a communication link operates at much faster speeds than a terminal operator. A medium-speed line transmits data at the rate of 9600 bps, whereas a human reads at about 50 bps and types at about 15 bps. Further, there are human delays for thinking time. To reduce this imbalance, two types of communications equipment are used: multiplexors and concentrators.

A **multiplexor** receives several slow-speed transmission lines and combines them into one high-speed line. One method, shown in figure 10–14, is called **time-division multiplexing**. Here, five 300-bps lines are combined into one 1500-bps line. Each slow line is allocated one out of every five character positions on the fast line. If it has nothing to send, a blank character (shown as b in the illustration) is sent in its position.

Note that, on the receiving end, the signal must be demultiplexed into its components; in this case, there would be five outputs. Demultiplexing is similar to a line at the post office. People (messages) enter in

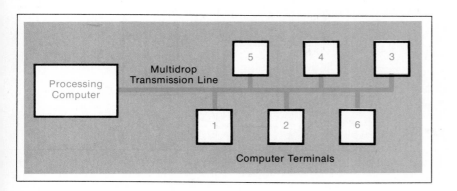

FIGURE 10–14
Operation of multiplexor

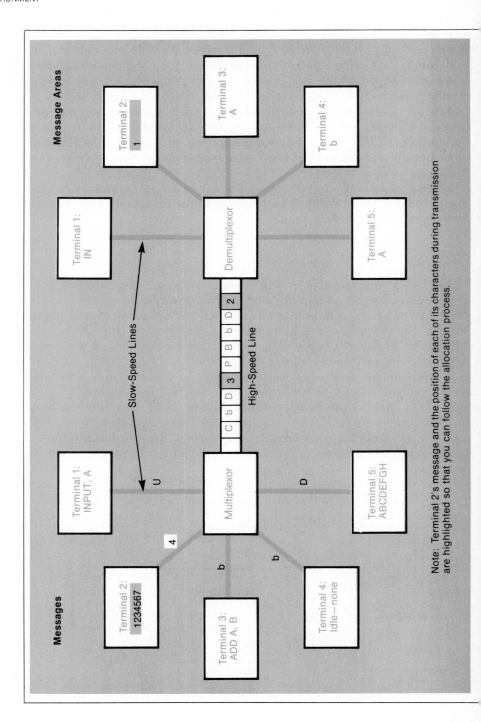

one line and are distributed to windows (terminals). Unlike the post office, however, a message must go to a specific terminal.

A **concentrator** is an intelligent multiplexor. It combines several slow-speed lines into a single fast line, but it does this more efficiently and performs other services as well. Concentrators allocate time on the fast line in accordance with need. For example, instead of allocating every fifth character to a terminal, it allocates many characters to busy terminals and no characters at all to idle ones. Blanks are not sent.

Additionally, concentrators can compress data by removing repeated characters and by more sophisticated techniques. The compressed data is sent over the transmission line and then decompressed into its original format. Concentrators provide error detection and correction capabilities not found in multiplexors.

Also, some terminal equipment operates on a different character code than others. (Remember EBCDIC and ASCII in chapter 2?) One terminal may represent characters with a seven-bit code, while another uses nine bits. A concentrator can convert all of these codes to a single convention.

Finally, concentrators can help the central computer to manage communications equipment. For example, a multidrop line might be connected to a concentrator. If so, the concentrator can poll the terminals and send their messages down the fast line to the central computer. This relieves the CPU of the responsibility of polling and also reduces traffic on the fast line. Figure 10–15 shows such an application.

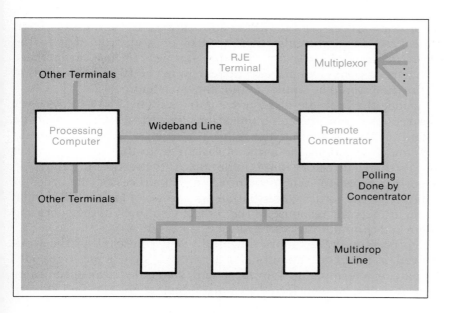

FIGURE 10–15
Example of remote concentrator application

QUESTIONS

10.11 All communications media can be classified according to speed, _____ , and _____ .

10.12 Narrowband communications lines transmit at the rate of _____ to _____ .

10.13 What are two other speeds of communication lines (besides narrowband)?

10.14 What are the two communication line modes?

10.15 Which mode is closer to the format of computer data?

10.16 What is the function of a modem?

10.17 Name the three communication line types.

10.18 Explain the difference between polling and contention.

10.19 Explain the difference between a multiplexor and a concentrator.

10.20 List five functions that can be performed by a concentrator.

10.21 How is polling different from multiplexing?

Do not confuse polling and contention with multiplexing and concentration. The objective of polling and contention is to allow multiple terminals to share the same line but with no change in line speed. The message leaves the terminal and is received at the central computer at the same speed. On the other hand, multiplexing and concentration allow the line to be shared by combining several slow-speed lines into one fast line.

Programs for Teleprocessing Systems

Three types of programs are used in the teleprocessing environment: the *operating system, communications control programs*, and *application programs*. The **operating system** controls the processing computer's resources (not including communications equipment), the **communications control program** coordinates message processing, and the **application programs** process the users' requests. See module E for more about operating systems.

The Communications Control Program

Communications control programs (CCP) control and coordinate the transfer of messages between terminals and application programs. Figure 10–16 shows a schematic of the contents of main memory of the processing computer. The operating system is shown at the top of the memory. As messages are delivered to the processing computer, they are received by the operating system and delivered to the CCP.

The CCP determines whether the message is to be acted upon immediately (an online application), or whether it is to be stored on a file for later processing (an offline application). If the message is an online type, the communications control program routes it to the correct application program. If databases were in use, a database management system would also appear in figure 10–16. Its position and function would be similar to that shown in figure 9–22.

Consider the example of an order entry system. The CCP receives order requests from the communications hardware via the operating system. It determines that the request is to be acted upon immediately, and it identifies the name of the program that processes such requests from a directory that it maintains. It then sends the request to the correct program. When the program has processed the order, it sends a response (order confirmation, for example) to the CCP, which, in turn, directs the response to the correct terminal via the operating system and communications hardware.

Teleprocessing systems are amazing when you think of the work involved. In the case of a national order entry system, a message could originate on a terminal in Tampa, be sent 3000 miles to a concentrator in Los Angeles, be transferred to a processing computer, and eventu-

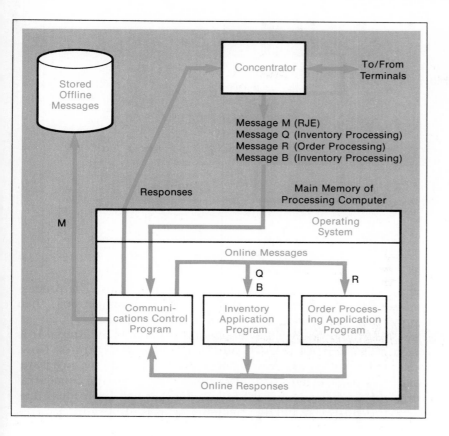

FIGURE 10–16
Programs involved in communications
processing

ally find its way into the correct program residing in a main memory of 16 million bytes. It is then processed, and a return message retraces all of these steps. The entire operation must take no more than a few seconds.

Protocols

For a message to be routed through this maze of equipment, it must be packaged. When you want to send a package through the mail, you wrap it and put *to* and *from* addresses on the outside. A similar technique is used to package messages. As shown in figure 10–17a, header and trailer data are added to a message for routing and error control purposes. The header shows where the message is to be delivered and where it is from. The trailer contains parity bits for error checking. In fact, in some systems, the trailer has enough data so that any errors can be detected and corrected without retransmission.

There is a difference between the way post office packages and teleprocessing messages are wrapped, however. In teleprocessing

FIGURE 10–17
Message-packaging techniques

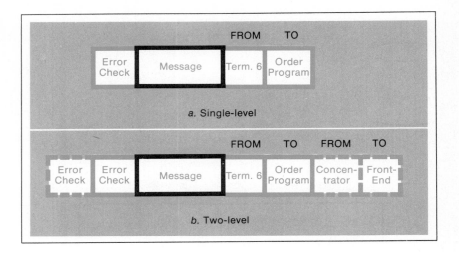

applications, a message may be wrapped several times. The process can be compared to putting a package inside a bigger box, then rewrapping and readdressing it, and so on, several times.

Consider an order entry transaction that originates in Tampa. It is wrapped as shown in figure 10–17a and sent to the concentrator. Now, the message is marked for delivery to the order processing program. The concentrator does not know just where that is. So, the concentrator wraps the message again, specifying another concentrator in Los Angeles as the *to* address and the concentrator as the *from* address. This procedure is shown in figure 10–17b.

When the message is received at the concentrator in Los Angeles, the outer layer of packaging is removed. Another one may be added. This time, the *to* address is the processing computer, and the *from* address is the Los Angeles concentrator.

The number of layers of packaging depends on the complexity of the communications facilities. In one important international standard, the International Standards Organization Open Systems Architecture [66], up to seven levels of packaging have been defined.

The term **protocol** is used in the communications business to refer to the way that a message between two communicating programs is packaged and handled. Because the equipment used by a communications system is likely supplied by several vendors, it is important that national and international standards on protocol be used. If two computers, say, concentrators in two different locations, conform to the same standard, they can interface successfully with each other. However, if they use different protocols, then they cannot be used together. Consequently, an important consideration in the design of a communications facility is ensuring that all components operate on the same protocol.

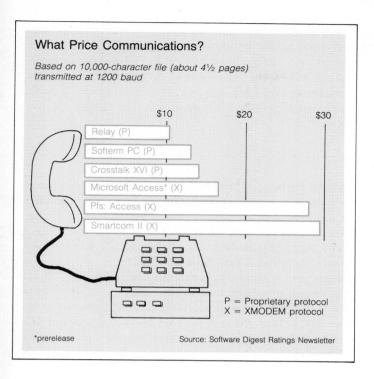

What Price Communications?

*Based on 10,000-character file (about 4½ pages)
transmitted at 1200 baud*

Relay (P)
Softerm PC (P)
Crosstalk XVI (P)
Microsoft Access* (X)
Pfs: Access (X)
Smartcom II (X)

$10 $20 $30

P = Proprietary protocol
X = XMODEM protocol

*prerelease   Source: Software Digest Ratings Newsletter

If you ever buy communications equipment, you may hear the terms **asynchronous** and **synchronous protocols**. Asynchronous protocols send packages containing only one character. Synchronous protocols send packages containing many characters. Asynchronous protocols result in slower processing, but because only a single character is sent, coordination is simple. Synchronous protocols are faster, but coordination is more difficult.

Teleprocessing Application Programs

Two **application programs** are shown in figure 10–16. One performs inventory processing. The other is used to process customer orders. In reality, there might be many more application programs. Messages are delivered to these programs and processed. When results are available, they are sent back to the communications control program and routed to the terminal that is waiting for a reply.

In figure 10–16, four messages are being transferred to the processing computer by the concentrator. The first will be sent to the inventory application program, the next will be sent to the order processing program, the third will be sent to the inventory application program, and the fourth will be stored in the file for later processing.

Note an important detail. Although there may be many order entry clerks, there is only one order processing program. As transactions arrive for order processing, they will have to wait in line just as people do at the grocery store. When the order processing program is finished with an order, it will take the next one in line and so forth. If orders arrive faster than the order processing program can handle them, a wait will develop.

Coordinating Concurrent Updates

Because the processing computer has only one CPU, it cannot process two orders that are truly simultaneous. Instead, it will do some processing on one, then some processing on another, and so forth, until both are completed. However, the computer works so fast that it appears to the users that their orders are processed simultaneously. This type of processing is called **concurrent processing**.

Examine the concurrent processing summarized in figure 10–18. Here, the order processing program read an inventory record for clerk A and then read the same record for clerk B. Next, clerk A took the last item from inventory and updated the inventory record. Subsequently, clerk B took what he or she thought was the last item from inventory and updated the record. At this point, the inventory showed 0 items for that part, but the last part had been issued twice.

This is called the **concurrent update problem**. It can occur in any system in which more than one user is allowed to update the same file. To get around the problem, programs have to be written to place **record locks** before updates are made. The record is locked by giving exclusive control of it to one user. Other users cannot obtain the record until the first person is through with it.

FIGURE 10–18

Example of concurrent update problem (sequence numbers show the order of computer processing between the two clerks)

CLERK A'S ACTIVITY	CLERK B'S ACTIVITY
1. Read inventory record for item X.	
	2. Read inventory record for item X.
3. Take last item X from inventory.	
	4. Take last item X from inventory. (Clerk B's copy of the record does not show that clerk A just took the last one.)
5. Set item count to 0.	
	6. Set item count to 0.
7. Replace item X inventory record.	
	8. Replace item X inventory record.

Teleprocessing Data

In the teleprocessing environment, data is subject to three special considerations. First, data must be available through direct access processing; sequential file processing takes far too long.

The second consideration for teleprocessing data concerns its vulnerability. Efforts must be made to preserve the accuracy (or **integrity**) of the data. Because the data is **online**, and because there can be multiple users of the same data, the files can easily be changed incorrectly. Furthermore, because the files are shared, when problems develop, determining who or what is responsible is difficult.

Consider a nation-wide order entry system. Suppose that an order entry clerk confuses two part numbers. He uses the part number for bolts whenever he means to order diesel engines, and he uses the part number for diesel engines whenever he orders bolts. Chances are that, after two or three days, the order entry files will be a mess. There will appear to be a great backlog of diesel engines. Furthermore, other order entry clerks will be misinformed. If one of them tries to enter an order for a diesel engine, he or she will be told that there is a great backlog. The company may lose an important order.

As another example, suppose the company has two order files: one for customer orders and one for in-plant orders for items used in production. If the order entry clerk accesses the wrong file (which is possible, because both files are online), havoc will result on the production line. This, by the way, will all be blamed on the computer, even though the order entry clerk is at fault.

Because data is online, and because data integrity can be a problem, adequate **security** must be provided for the files. At a minimum, all online files should be protected by **account numbers** and **passwords.** Only users with certain account numbers should be able to access the file. Additionally, these users must be assigned passwords that restrict the actions they can take. For example, read-only passwords might be used.

The account number restriction will prohibit users in purchasing, say, from accessing order entry files. The passwords will keep order entry clerks from making unauthorized changes to order entry files. These features are needed not just to keep computer criminals out. They are needed to bring control and order to everyday business activity.

In addition to these precautions, some businesses use **encryption** to protect their data. Encryption is the coding of data so that it is unintelligible. Substituting one character for another is a simple encryption scheme. More sophisticated techniques are needed for highly sensitive applications.

Data can be encrypted when it is sent over communication lines and when it is stored in the files. Encryption is *not* effective unless the

QUESTIONS

10.22 What types of programs are used in the teleprocessing environment?

10.23 What are the functions of the communications control programs?

10.24 Illustrate the packaging of a message with a three-level protocol.

10.25 What is a *protocol*?

10.26 Explain the difference between asynchronous and synchronous protocols.

10.27 If there are 10 order entry clerks, all performing the same function, must there be 10 order entry programs? Why or why not?

10.28 Describe the concurrent update problem. How can it be prevented?

10.29 Describe methods used to preserve data integrity and provide security.

programs that do the encrypting and that use the data are protected from would-be infiltrators as well.

To review, there are three special considerations for data in the teleprocessing environment. The data must be online, and consequently, data integrity must be carefully managed. Finally, because online data is vulnerable, security is vital.

DISTRIBUTED PROCESSING SYSTEMS

In this section, we will discuss **distributed data processing systems**. The term *distributed* is used because applications are processed on computers that are distributed throughout a company. Distributed processing systems are business computer systems in which multiple computers are used to run application programs.

Two Examples of Distributed Processing Systems

Distributed data processing is not the same as teleprocessing. Figure 10–19 shows a teleprocessing system. In this figure, users and terminals are distributed. There may also be multiple computers; for example, special computers may be used to control the flow of data from the teller terminals to the main processing computer. However, only a single computer will process application programs. Applications processing is *not* distributed.

ERD Pharmaceutical

Figure 10–20 shows a distributed processing network used by a pharmaceutical company. This system has three computers: the central applications processing computer, a computer for managing communications, and a computer for processing marketing applications. This system is different from a teleprocessing system because there are two computers doing *applications* processing: A microcomputer does marketing analysis, and a mainframe does other applications processing.

Therefore, the distinguishing characteristic of a distributed system is not that users or terminals are distributed. It is not that there is more than one computer in use. The distinguishing characteristic of distributed processing is that more than one computer processes *application* programs.

Distributed processing allows applications processing to be done in the best place for the application — not in the place where a large, centralized computer happens to be. This arrangement has two advantages. First, it can be cheaper. When applications processing is moved toward the user, there is less traffic on the communication lines. There is no need for the data to be sent to a centralized location for process-

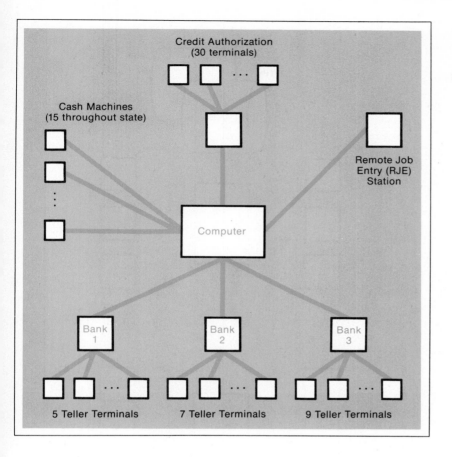

FIGURE 10–19
Teleprocessing equipment configuration for medium-sized bank

ing and for the results then to be returned. Thus, communications costs go down.

Second, distributed processing gives users greater control over the data and its processing. Often users operate distributed computers. They can determine the data to be processed, the order of processing, and the quality of service. Also, users in one department are not inconvenienced by users in another department if each group of users has its own computer.

If you view data processing as a method of producing information from raw data, then data processing is a type of manufacturing. In these terms, distributed data processing is similar to distributed manufacturing. The computer (plant) is moved close to the location where the product is needed.

An **applications node** is a computer in a distributed network that does applications processing. Each applications node has a computer, programs, data, procedures, and users. Thus, each node has all of the components of a business computer system. However, within this

FIGURE 10–20
ERD distributed processing system

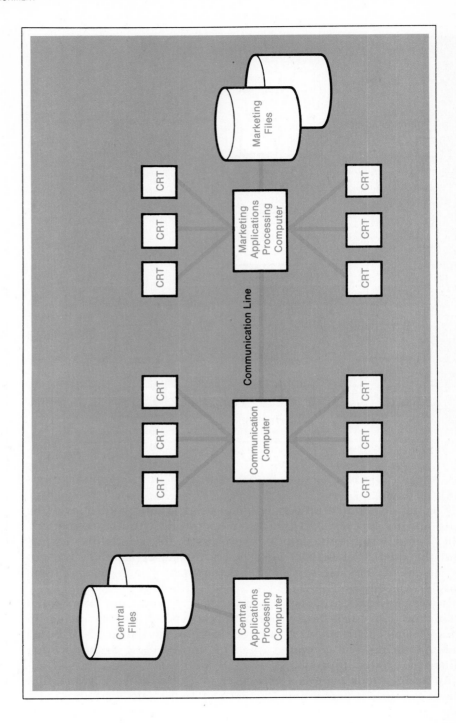

definition is a wide range of capability because there can be variation in how much these components are distributed.

Examine the pharmaceutical company's distributed network in figure 10–20. Once a day, all of the sales data is sent from the central applications computer (a mainframe) to the marketing department's computer (a micro) over the communication line. This data is saved in a local file. The marketing analysis department later scans this data and copies parts of it to several other files. These files are then used by analysis programs to produce marketing reports. Marketing analysts also examine the data in these files using a query utility.

This is a simple distributed system. There is only one distributed computer, and it processes only marketing-related data. The flow of data is one way; the marketing department does not send any data back to the mainframe. Thus, marketing analysis does not change any files used by any other department. If a mistake is made, only the marketing department will suffer the consequences.

In this system, the mainframe is a **master** and the microcomputer is a **slave**. The mainframe decides when to send the data, and it decides what data to send. There is no interaction between the two computers to determine what to do. Further, the mainframe never receives data from the micro. No interactions are initiated by the micro. Finally, since the mainframe keeps a copy of everything it sends to the microcomputer, the mainframe is not dependent on the micro for any data.

FRAMCO Distributing

Figure 10–21 shows a distributed data processing system that is more complex than the pharmaceutical company's. FRAMCO Distributing has seven locations throughout the United States and Canada that operate as autonomous profit centers. Each location is considered to be an independent company. Each location manager shares in the profits made by his or her company.

Each location has its own computer and does its own data processing. However, for reasons of compatibility and maintenance, the programs are the same, and the files have a common format. The programs are used for order processing, inventory, and accounting. There are customer, price, inventory, order, and general ledger data files.

Additionally, FRAMCO headquarters has a computer of its own. It receives data from the other seven computers and produces consolidated financial statements. It also extracts marketing and other data that is used by centralized purchasing and planning departments. Consequently, each location's computer must be able to communicate with the headquarters computer. Furthermore, the applications nodes must be able to communicate with each other.

FIGURE 10–21
Computer network for FRAMCO
Distributing

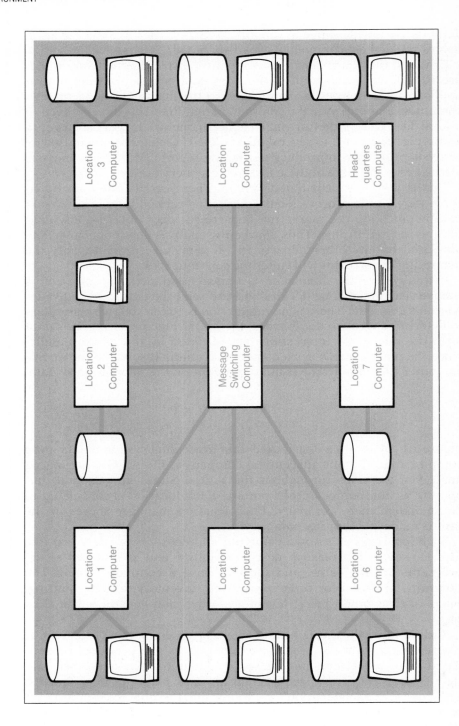

According to FRAMCO policy, if one location is out of a part, it must try to locate the part at another location. Before the distributed system was developed, order clerks did this verbally over the telephone. This procedure was too slow to be effective. Consequently, FRAMCO built the distributed system so that all seven location computers could communicate with one another. Now, when the local inventory does not have a part in stock, the local computer determines if another FRAMCO location has it. If so, the part is ordered from the other location. This processing is done by the computers. The order entry clerks need not telephone or initiate any other direct, human intervention.

Considerations for Distributed Computers

The distributed network shown in figure 10–21 is considerably more complex than the one in figure 10–20. First, there are eight computers instead of just two. FRAMCO must operate all of these, ensure that they are properly maintained, and have them repaired when necessary. Also, programs must be maintained for each computer. Because all of the computers are the same, this task is not as difficult as it could be. However, maintaining seven uniform copies of a program is difficult. Whenever changes are made to one program, great care must be exercised to ensure that the same changes are made to all copies of it. If not, over a period of time the programs will diverge. Processing will not be identical at each location.

Another complexity of the FRAMCO system is that there is no clear master/slave relationship. The eight computers operate as **colleagues**. As with humans, equality requires more frequent and more sophisticated communication. The computers can request services from one another, but they must be prepared for rejection. Another computer may be too busy, or it may be inoperative. Furthermore, while a computer is requesting a service from one computer, it may be receiving a request from a different computer. All of these actions must be coordinated, and the processing must be done systematically, without error.

Finally, unlike the ERD system, FRAMCO's computers are very **data dependent** — they rely on one another for data. No computer in the network possesses all of the FRAMCO data. Backup and recovery must be carefully performed at each node so that no data is lost. This demands both close coordination of activity and careful data management.

Characteristics of Distributed Systems

As with teleprocessing systems, the components of a business computer system in a distributed environment are physically distributed.

In the FRAMCO example, the consolidated financial statements are produced by hardware and programs at headquarters. The personnel, including users, of this system are also at headquarters. However, the data and the procedures for obtaining the data are distributed throughout the company.

In contrast to a teleprocessing system, however, a distributed system has at least one complete business computer system resident at each applications node. The node has processing hardware, programs, data, procedures, and users for at least one system. This fact is one way to discriminate between teleprocessing and distributed systems.

Evolution of Distributed Systems

As you can imagine, distributed systems are complex to develop. In fact, almost no company starts out to build a distributed computer system. Instead, a company usually moves to a distributed system in one of two ways. The first way is that a company with a very large central computer may decide to **offload** some of its processing to a distributed computer. This usually happens when the central computer processing load is so big that it is hard to manage. There may be so many systems to run that the operations staff has trouble scheduling them. The quality of service may be poor because it becomes impersonal. Also, cost considerations may indicate that expanding the existing computer is more expensive than acquiring an additional, smaller one. (Refer to figure 10–4.)

Another common reason for offloading a central computer is that the systems development staff is far behind in development efforts. In some companies, it takes 18 months or more before work starts on a new project. In these companies, the users sometimes become so frustrated that they acquire systems with off-the-shelf programs to install and run themselves. (Recall Blake Records and Tapes in chapter 1.) The systems development staff may be happy to be relieved of another request. This situation can lead to problems, however, if the system is not properly integrated into the rest of the company's data processing operations.

A second way a company can move to a distributed system is to *build up to it*. Here, the company may have one applications processing computer that is too small for the current workload. Instead of upgrading the computer, however, the company decides to buy more small computers. This strategy is common with microcomputers. A department may have several applications running on autonomous computers and want to connect them so that they can share data. In this case, companies usually install and operate local area networks as described in the next section.

Often a company builds up to distributed processing if local control of information resources is important. In FRAMCO's case, for example, each location is considered to be an independent company. FRAMCO therefore decided to let each location have its own data processing center under its own operational control. It would have been feasible for FRAMCO to develop a centralized teleprocessing system, but the company decided not to do this for organizational and political reasons.

U.S. Navy Rear Admiral Grace Hopper, one of the pioneers of the data processing profession, has presented an interesting analogy about distributed systems. She says we should think about the pioneers as they struggled across the Great Plains. When they wanted to move a rock, they would hitch an ox to the rock. If the rock was so big that the ox couldn't move it, they didn't attempt to grow a bigger ox; instead, they used two oxen for the job.

A company with a distributed system uses the same technique. Instead of trying to build a bigger computer, it uses two or more computers to accomplish its work.

Advantages of Distributed Systems

Distributed processing systems have several advantages. First, they can be less expensive than a large centralized system. It is often cheaper to use minicomputers and microcomputers to perform a task than to use a larger mainframe. If the data processing organization operates on the right-hand portion of the graph in figure 10–4, it will be cheaper to obtain additional, smaller computers. Distributed systems can also reduce data communications costs because data is processed close to the source rather than being sent away for processing.

Second, distributed systems give the users greater control over the processing of their data. Often users operate the computer themselves. They can determine the quality and the scheduling of the services they receive. Additionally, distributed systems can be useful in companies in which the systems development staff is behind in their development schedules. Off-the-shelf programs may be available that will successfully accomplish the users' tasks.

Finally, distributed systems can be tailored to the company's organizational structure. For example, FRAMCO has seven autonomous locations that are connected on a more or less equal basis. This decentralized configuration matches the company's philosophy of decentralization. Other companies have computer configurations that complement their hierarchical organization. At ERD, for example, the central mainframe is a master of the marketing department's micro. Each of these systems meets the needs of the organizational structure of the company that owns it.

The advantages of distributed processing systems are summarized in figure 10–22.

FIGURE 10–22
Summary of distributed processing systems

ADVANTAGES	DISADVANTAGES
Can be less expensive	More complex to build
Greater control to users	Close coordination required for data compatibility
Quicker development if off-the-shelf programs can be used	Greater need for standards and documentation
Tailored to organizational structure	Problems of multivendors

QUESTIONS

10.30 Why may distributed processing be cheaper than teleprocessing? Refer to figure 10–4 for your answer.

10.31 How does distributed processing give the user greater control?

10.32 What is an applications node?

10.33 Give two reasons that the pharmaceutical company's distributed system is simpler than FRAMCO's system.

10.34 Why may a company decide to offload its centralized or teleprocessing computer system?

10.35 Why may a company decide to install new computers even though its existing computer could be expanded to meet its needs?

10.36 List the advantages and disadvantages of distributed systems.

10.37 Explain the statement, "A distributed system can be tailored to a company's organizational structure."

Disadvantages of Distributed Systems

Distributed processing systems also have several disadvantages. First, they are complex to set up. Communications facilities must be obtained. The computers must be connected to one another. Furthermore, the programs must be made to interact with one another. Close coordination is required throughout the distributed system to ensure that all data is compatible. Confusion will result if, for example, one division of a company reports sales data from the previous month, and another reports sales data from the current month.

Additionally, distributed systems are often run without the guidance of data processing professionals. This policy is risky unless the personnel are well trained and have complete, well-written documentation of all necessary procedures.

Finally, distributed systems often use a mixture of equipment. The computers may be supplied by a variety of vendors; the communication lines, by other vendors; and the programs, by still other vendors. In this environment, compatibility can be a problem. Making the equipment operate together may be difficult. Also, recovery may be difficult if one vendor inaccurately claims that a problem is due to another vendor's equipment. Figure 10–22 also summarizes the disadvantages of distributed processing.

LOCAL AREA NETWORKS

A **local area network (LAN)** is a system of from two to a dozen or so computers connected via a short-range, high-speed data path. *Short range* means the microcomputers reside within a few thousand feet of each other. *High speed* means data transfer as fast as 50 million bits per second, or about 6 million characters per second. Each computer on the LAN is referred to as a **node**. Although, strictly speaking, a node can be any type of computer, most nodes on LANs in use today are microcomputers.

LANs are primarily used for communicating within a work unit. For example, a LAN might be used to support employees in an accounts

APPLICATION

"INNOVATIONS IN LANS AND MICRO NETWORKS ARE EMERGING."

Low-cost local area networks (LANs) can be implemented by MIS managers to link self-contained working groups of two to ten PCs, with a relatively small investment of $50 to $500 per node. Such LANs offer most of the benefits of larger networks, providing a centralized database that is easy to access and maintain. Safeguards are available to prevent unauthorized access to private information. Spreadsheet, word processing and database management software can also be supported.

Typically, working groups in large organizations will use personal computers such as the IBM PC family and nonprogrammable terminals linked to mainframes or minicomputers such as IBM 3278s or 5251s. It also is becoming common for working groups to use a dedicated minicomputer, such as an IBM System/36, in conjunction with PCs. In this instance, the minicomputer is a "departmental computer" that can perform functions not handled effectively by PCs.

Technical considerations. In a micro network, three kinds of PCs may be designated: a "user" PC that uses shared resources, a "server" PC that provides resources for sharing, and a "master" PC that acts as both "user" and "server" simultaneously. All PCs linked in a network can be used as normal standalone workstations and still perform network functions.

There also are high-performance dedicated servers that can support large numbers of users. However, they require unique hardware and software that pushes up the cost per node, often without a corresponding increase in flexibility or processing power. A more cost-effective approach is to rely on the departmental computer for large-volume centralized storage, use high-speed printers and gateways to mainframes, and IBM PC ATs as master PCs for increased performance. A micro network employing the master PC concept can provide a high degree of information and resource sharing.

Changing technologies and increasingly sophisticated requirements of PC users have put new demands on MIS managers. Their role has moved beyond the technical into corporate information and communications policy development. Innovations in LANs and micro networks are emerging just as MIS managers are beginning to chart new territories in PC technology and systems.

receivable department, a loan processing department, or a product marketing department. Except in very small companies, LANs are seldom used for company-wide applications.

Local area networks provide three types of service. First, LANs provide communications **message processing**, by which the users of computers in the LAN can transfer messages to one another. For example, in figure 10–23, users at any of the nodes can send messages to users at any other node. If the user at node 1 sends a message to node 4, the message will be routed through nodes 2 and 3.

The second service provided by a LAN is the **sharing of peripherals**. This is especially advantageous for situations in which members of a group need occasional access to expensive equipment such as a laser printer, a sophisticated plotter, or fast, large-capacity disks. In figure 10–23, any of the computers on the LAN can send documents to the laser printer connected to node 1.

FIGURE 10–23
Example of a local area network (LAN)

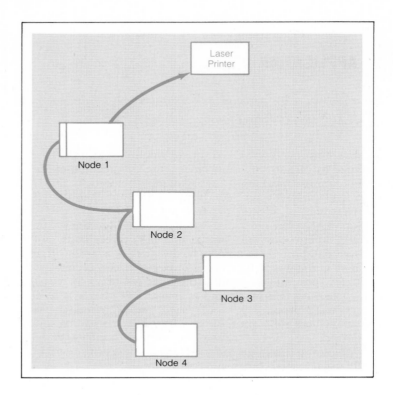

The third service is the **sharing of databases**. To provide this service, a database is stored on the disk of one of the nodes, and a DBMS, or portion thereof, is installed to process it at the request of other nodes. The computer that manages the database is sometimes called the **file server**. (Since this node is managing a database, not a file, this may be a poor term. Unfortunately, poor or not, it is the term commonly used.) In figure 10–24, a database and DBMS have been stored on node 3. When nodes 1, 2, or 4 need data, they send requests to this node for processing.

LAN Hardware Design

A variety of LAN hardware designs exist. These designs vary in their communications capacity, the configuration of computers, and the protocol or methodology used for managing communications traffic.

LAN Capacity: Baseband versus Broadband

Regarding capacity, the two major alternatives are **baseband** and **broadband**. Baseband systems have lower capacity than broadband systems, but they are simpler and cheaper. The capacity of typical baseband systems varies between 1 million and 10 million bits per second. Ethernet is an example of a commercial baseband system. The capacity of broadband systems reach as high as 50 million bits per second. Wangnet is an example of a commercial broadband system. Baseband systems are more common among networks of microcomputers, primarily because of their lower cost.

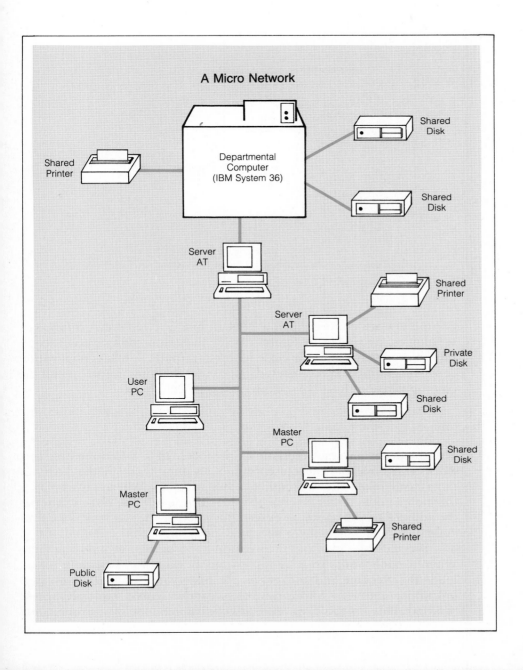

FIGURE 10–24
Local area network (LAN) with database
file server

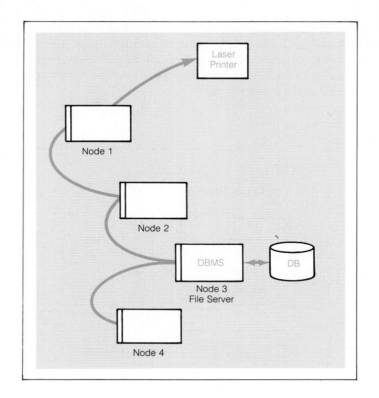

LAN Topology: Ring versus Bus

Computers are connected in a LAN in one of two configurations, or
topologies, as shown in figure 10–25. In a **ring configuration**, computers are connected to a closed-loop data path. A **bus configuration**
consists of computers connected in a string; the computers hang off the
communications line like socks hanging on a clothesline.

LAN Protocol: Token Passing versus CSMA

The third design characteristic is protocol. In a **token-passing network**, transmission packets continuously flow through the LAN. In
most cases, token passing requires a ring topology. When a token passes
through a node, it can be empty or full. If it is full, the node examines
the address on the packet to determine whether the message is for that
node. If it is, the message is accepted, and the token is emptied. If it is
not, the message is allowed to continue is journey around the ring.
When a node wants to send a message, it waits for an empty token,
loads the message and address on the token, and sends it on its way.
Another common LAN protocol is **carrier-sensed multiple access
(CSMA)**. This protocol, which is used with bus topology, implements

the contention line management technique discussed previously. When a node wishes to transmit a message, it waits for a pause in the traffic on the line and then sends the message. With this protocol, two nodes can attempt to broadcast a message at the same time. When this event, which is called a **collision**, occurs, the nodes wait an interval of time and then rebroadcast. Obviously, the nodes must wait for different intervals of time; otherwise, collisions would occur indefinitely. The protocol is sometimes referred to as CSMA/CD, where *CD* stands for collision detection.

Hardware Components

LAN hardware consists of three major components: the line, network intelligence electronics, and possibly, special-purpose computers. For the line, some networks use **coaxial cable** similar to that used for cable television. Others use **twisted-pair** wire similar to that used for telephones.

Intelligence electronics is provided by a **network adapter card**, which each node is required to have. This card, which plugs into one of the expansion slots, contains the circuitry for managing the line and sending and receiving messages.

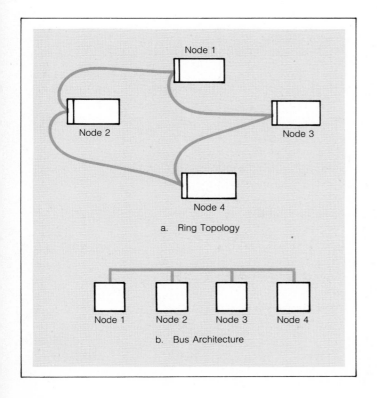

FIGURE 10–25
LAN topologies

APPLICATION

"IN SEARCH OF DATACOMM EXPERTISE."

Infosystems' third annual Datacomm Usage Survey found that a lack of trained staff, varied equipment choices, and the "vendor gap" pose management problems as firms grow into data communications.

Although only 13 percent of all companies responding to the survey have separate datacomm managers, that number rises to 24 percent among companies with 1000 or more employees. In the heavily communications-dependent banking and transportation industries, about 30 percent of those surveyed have datacomm managers.

In companies with datacomm managers, more than half report to an MIS executive, according to the study. In companies with more than 500 employees and no separate datacomm expert, the MIS manager assumes direct datacomm control 40 percent of the time. In businesses with 500 or fewer employees, however, datacomm responsibility is handled by the DP manager in about 45 percent of the firms surveyed.

Regardless of how responsibilities are delegated, datacomm expertise is at a premium. Lack of trained staff and/or technical knowledge were among the most oft-cited problems of those surveyed. Summarizes one respondent, "This is a new area for us, and we are having to learn the hard way how to do things."

Compatibility is another issue that continues to raise the hackles of many users. Cutting to the heart of the problem, one individual points to the "vendor gap between what is technically feasible and what it really takes to get things working reliably."

PRODUCTS AND SERVICES

	Presently Use	Plan to Add In Next 12 Months		Presently Use	Plan to Add In Next 12 Months
Terminals	92%	30%	PBXs: Voice	45%	7%
Modems	92%	30%	Carriers (common value-added packet switching)	45%	14%
Printers	92%	26%	Converters (protocol interface, etc.)	43%	21%
Microcomputers	82%	27%	Diagnostic and test equipment	31%	16%
Communications software	72%	23%	Local area networks	30%	35%
Micro-to-mainframe links	56%	43%	Network management systems	22%	21%
Private line	52%	16%	PBXs: Voice and data	15%	19%
Communications processors	49%	16%	PBXs: Data	13%	10%
Multiplexors	49%	20%	Database	100%	100%

Local systems remain the highest priority, with 43 percent planning on expanding either "moderately" or "substantially," according to the study. This is down from the 53 percent that planned similar expansion last year. One third of those surveyed expect growth in long distance systems, but that number is down 20 percent from a year ago. Metropolitan area systems are expected to suffer the greatest growth stagnation, as only 19 percent of respondents plan to expand in this area, compared to 52 percent in 1985.

The survey also indicates a reduction in the planned purchase of individual products and services. Of the 17 products and services listed, only two show signs of measurably higher growth than last year — local area networks (LANs) and network management systems. Thirty-five percent of survey respondents plan to add LANs in the next 12 months and 21 percent expect to implement network management systems, both up four percent from last year.

Three products that appear to be approaching a saturation point are terminals, modems, and printers. More than 90 percent of respondents presently use such equipment. As a result, estimates of purchasing for this year, while still strong, are showing signs of leveling off. Microcomputers, in use at 80 percent of the companies surveyed, would appear to be following a similar pattern. Future purchases of these products are likely to depend increasingly on the vendors' ability to provide added value or specific niche functionality.

Some LAN vendors provide special-purpose CPUs for use as file servers. These CPUs are designed to provide especially fast service for the LAN. Alternatively, vendors also allow standard-issue microcomputers to be used as file servers. Special-purpose CPUs sometimes include tape or other hardware for backing up file contents. Typical LAN configurations are shown in figure 10–26.

LAN Programs

Figure 10–27 illustrates the relationships of software in the main memory of a LAN node. The application calls on the DBMS, which in turn calls on the operating system for processing all I/O requests, including opening and closing files and reading and writing data. When the operating system receives a request, it determines if the request can be processed on the local node. If so, the request is sent to the local I/O processing subsystem. If not, the request is sent to the network I/O processing subsystem, which accesses the network via the network adaptor card.

SUMMARY

This chapter introduced the major concepts of business teleprocessing systems. The terms *teleprocessing* and *telecommunications* were defined, and three examples were presented. A business develops teleprocessing systems because the business enterprise is geographically distributed, as well as for economic reasons. Because of economies of scale, it can be cheaper to have one central computer with communications capability than to have many disconnected, distributed computers.

QUESTIONS

10.38 What are three types of service provided by LANs?

10.39 What is the main difference between baseband and broadband systems?

10.40 What are two types of LAN configurations?

10.41 Describe two LAN protocols.

FIGURE 10–26

Possible configurations in a local area network. Notice that the computers are physically connected with one another via cables.

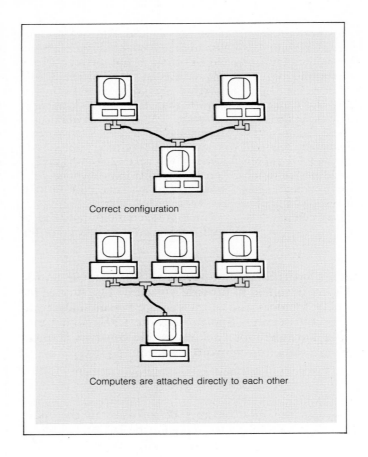

Correct configuration

Computers are attached directly to each other

Three stages in the growth of computer capability were identified: *centralized processing*, in which all computing is done in batch mode on a single computer; *teleprocessing*, in which all computing is done on a single computer, but the users are connected via telecommunications equipment; and *distributed processing*, in which computing is done on distributed computers.

In a distributed data processing system, application programs are run on more than one computer. These computers are connected to one another via communications lines. Distributed systems are like teleprocessing systems in that the terminals and users are distributed and more than one computer can be used. However, distributed systems differ from teleprocessing systems in that application programs are run on more than one computer. In a teleprocessing system, the application programs are run on a central computer.

A wide variety of distributed data processing configurations exist. Computers can be connected in master/slave relationships, or they can be connected as partners or colleagues. The nodes of the distributed networks can be microprocessors or large mainframes. Distributed computers can be totally interconnected, or there can be few connections. Distributed computers can be autonomous and independent, or they can be interconnected and very interdependent.

Distributed processing has several advantages. It may be cheaper than teleprocessing because communications costs are less. Distributed systems also allow users to have more control because the computer is located close to the need for the data processing services. Further, a distributed system can result in reduced development time if off-the-shelf programs can be found that meet user requirements and can be integrated into the distributed system. Finally, distributed networks, because of their flexibility, can be tailored to the organizational structure of the company.

Distributed processing also has several important disadvantages. First, such systems are difficult to build, and close coordination is required to maintain data compatibility. Second, there is a greater need for standards and documentation. Finally, distributed systems usually involve multiple vendors, and this requirement can lead to maintenance problems.

A local area network is a type of distributed processing system in which from two to a dozen computers are connected via a short-range, high-speed data path. LANs are used primarily within a work unit to provide message processing, sharing of peripherals, and sharing of databases. LANs vary in their communications capacity, the configuration of computers, and the protocols used.

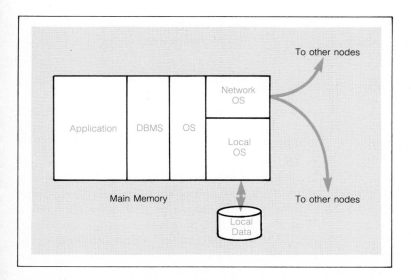

FIGURE 10–27
Relationship of programs on a LAN node

WORD LIST

(In order of appearance in text)

Teleprocessing	Amplitude modulation	Passwords
Telecommunications	Modem	Encryption
Data communications	Communication line type	Distributed data processing
Remote job entry (RJE) station	Simplex line	system
Response time	Half-duplex line	Applications node
Economies of scale	Full-duplex line	Master/slave relationship
Distributed processing	Multidrop line	Colleague relationship
Centralized processing	Polling	Data dependency
Offline processing	Contention	Offload processing
Batched data transmission	Multiplexor	Local area network (LAN)
Online processing	Time-division multiplexing	Node
Query and response systems	Concentrator	Message processing
Transaction processing	Operating system	Sharing peripherals
Online program development	Communication control program	Sharing databases
Communication line speed	(CCP)	File server
Bits per second (bps)	Protocol	Baseband
Narrowband	Asynchronous protocol	Broadband
Voice grade	Synchronous protocol	Ring configuration
Wideband	Application program	Bus configuration
Baud	Concurrent processing	Token-passing protocol
Communication line mode	Concurrent update problem	Carrier-sensed multiple access
Analog line	Record locks	(CSMA) protocol
Digital line	Online data	Collision
Modulation	Data integrity	Coaxial cable
Demodulation	Data security	Twisted-pair wire
Frequency modulation	Account numbers	Network adapter card

QUESTIONS TO CHALLENGE YOUR THINKING

A. Suppose you worked for Elliot Bay Electronics (chapter 6). Would you recommend a teleprocessing system or a distributed processing system at EB? What about a LAN? How would you determine if any of them is appropriate at EB?

B. Find an organization that has a teleprocessing system. Interview the director of data processing or other responsible individual to find out how they do backup and recovery. What backup files are kept? How often are they obtained? How are transactions saved? How is recovery performed? What procedures are there for users and operations personnel? Are there any special programming restrictions?

C. In the past few years several notorious crimes have been committed using teleprocessing systems. Pick any one of them and find what you believe was the cause or causes of the crime. Was the problem hardware, programs, data, procedures, or personnel? What can be done to prevent the recurrence of the crime in the future?

D. Suppose that Elliot Bay Electronics decided to open retail stores and to add several warehouse shipping points. Would distributed data processing be appropriate? If so, should data processing costs or other considerations play a role in determining the locations of new installations? Assume that EB opened stores in Los Angeles, Anchorage, Denver, Atlanta, and Boston. Assume also that warehouse/shipping points were located in Los Angeles, St. Louis, and Richmond. Describe one feasible distributed processing configuration. Show where applications nodes and equipment like concentrators, message switchers, RJE stations, and terminals could be located. Describe communication lines connecting the hardware.

E. For some organizations teleprocessing is more appropriate than distributed processing. For other organizations, just the opposite is true. Characterize the organizations for which teleprocessing is more appropriate and those for which distributed processing is more appropriate. How are they structured? What management philosophies are prevalent? How is senior management rewarded? What services do their customers expect? What products do they buy and which do they sell? Describe other characteristics you think are important.

F. Local area networks (LANs) are becoming very important to many businesspeople, especially young, non-data processing managers. Determine why this is so by researching articles on LANs in both computing and business periodicals.

MANAGEMENT INFORMATION AND DECISION-SUPPORT SYSTEMS

CHAPTER 11

Chapter 4 presented a brief overview of management information systems and decision-support systems. In this chapter we discuss MIS and DSS and their roles in supporting business managers and decision makers more thoroughly.

You will recall from chapter 4 that there are two broad categories of business computer systems: transaction processing systems (TPSs), which maintain data about a company's daily operations; and management information systems (MISs), which assist managers in the areas of planning and control. A special subset of MIS is called decision support systems (DDSs). DSSs allow managers to make ad hoc queries about the system. This distinguishes DSS from other MISs, which answer anticipated questions, usually through regular, recurring reports or exception reports.

In this chapter we will first review the history of MIS. Then we will discuss management's information needs by defining management and describing how information requirements vary. A common cycle for business activity also will be illustrated. Next, we will consider MIS, first summarizing TPS applications and then summarizing MIS services and applications. Finally, DSS will be defined. We will describe DSS components, summarize several DSS applications, and indicate likely future directions for DSS.

▦ ORIGINS OF MANAGEMENT INFORMATION SYSTEMS

Data processing originated in the mid 1950s when large companies began to automate the processing of accounting records. Through the late 1950s and early 1960s, information processing capabilities expanded, and the records of more and more business activities were processed by computer systems. Until the mid 1960s, information systems were designed simply to keep track of day-to-day operations. These early computer systems produced fixed, standard reports that displayed facts about a company such as labor costs, inventory levels and account balances.

These early information systems satisfied some important needs but they did not provide all the information that managers wanted. A major problem was that early systems were isolated from one another. For example, a system that processed production records was entirely separate from one that processed labor expenses. The production manager, who viewed the department as a single entity might want to know how much labor was required for particular production jobs. Answering this question meant that the production data and labor data had to be integrated. Early computer systems were file processing systems, and integrating data in separate files is difficult to do. Another problem was that managers did not want the same level of detail as operations personnel did. Some means of giving each level of employee the appropriate level of detail had to be devised.

APPLICATION

"COMPUTER ANXIETY IN MANAGEMENT: THE PROBLEM IS NEITHER EXTENSIVE NOR SEVERE."

Computer anxiety has been suggested as a possible explanation for the tendency of some managers to sidestep direct involvement with computers, by delegating computing tasks to technically literate subordinates or avoiding computing altogether. This has led to the prediction of a crisis in the white-collar work force: that computer-anxious managers will derail the white-collar productivity movement because they are afraid to use microcomputers and other new computer technologies. We see no such crisis. Our results suggest that the issue of computer anxiety among managers is overblown. Although computer anxiety is indeed a very real phenomenon, it may not be nearly as widespread as once thought.

Yet there is still disagreement about the actual extent of the computer anxiety problem among managers. Some studies report a high incidence of computer anxiety accompanied by extreme physical, phobic symptoms such as stomach cramps and cold sweats. An Exxon Office Systems study yielded quite different results when it found that most of the 5000 managers surveyed significantly overestimated the degree of fear and other negative attitudes of company personnel regarding computers, and consistently underestimated the level of computer literacy of the overall white-collar work force.

Here are some common beliefs about computer anxiety:

- Older managers will exhibit higher levels of computer anxiety.
- Managers with high math anxiety will also exhibit high computer anxiety, as these may be very similar psychological phenomena.
- Analytical cognitive-style managers will be less computer anxious than heuristic types.
- Managers with more computer knowledge will have less computer anxiety.
- Managers who are negative about the overall impact of computers on society will have high levels of computer anxiety.
- Women will have higher levels of computer anxiety.
- External locus-of-control managers will exhibit higher levels of computer anxiety than internals.
- Managers with high levels of trait anxiety will exhibit higher levels of computer anxiety.
- Managers with greater computer experience will suffer less computer anxiety.
- Managers with negative overall attitudes about microcomputers and their usefulness in the workplace will have higher levels of computer anxiety.

It appears that computer anxiety has three kinds of roots: psychological, educational, and operational. The *psychological* roots are tied to profound personal traits that manifest themselves as technological alienation, and it is unlikely that these trait-based origins of computer anxiety can be quickly treated. The correlation between computer anxiety and math anxiety found in this study points to the existence of these psychological roots. *Educational* roots refer to anxieties caused by lack of education and knowledge about the capabilities and particularly about the limitations of computers. Terms such as "artificial intelligence" and "expert systems" elicit some managers' fears that their jobs are threatened by computers, as were the jobs of clerks and manufacturing workers in the last era of computerization. That managers with higher levels of computer anxiety were negative about the overall impact of computers on society is evidence of the educational roots of the problem. Education about the limitations of computers may be successful in alleviating this component of computer anxiety. Finally, the *operational* roots stem from simple concerns about where the power switch is, how to insert diskettes, etc. Increased computer experience for managers — a hands-on microcomputer training course, for example — would be a quick and inexpensive way to treat this source of computer anxiety. The strong inverse correlation found between computer anxiety and computer experience confirms this contention.

Systems that were developed to meet the newly recognized needs of management were called *management information systems*. It was a good name. It implied that management, too, could benefit from computers. It also was broad enough that every manager could come to expect that his or her pet project would be included.

Unfortunately, early MIS development projects were disastrous. Computer professionals had underestimated the difficulty they would have developing systems to meet managerial needs. Although aggregating data into monthly or other totals was not too difficult, integrating data turned out to be quite difficult. Remember, these were all file processing systems.

Furthermore, managers were hard to please. Their requirements were vague, their needs changed from month to month, and systems couldn't be adapted fast enough. Further, no one was sure that all of the information provided to management actually improved decisions. Many cost overruns and missed schedules occurred as these systems were developed.

These early disasters were not entirely fruitless, however. A new technology for integrating data arose out of the ashes of MIS disappointments. This new technology was called **database processing** (chapter 9) because it concerned the organizing and processing of *bases* of integrated data (as opposed to *files* of isolated data).

With database processing, many of the earlier promises of MIS became technically feasible. By the mid 1970s, MIS had transcended its negative reputation, and it again became respectable. Unfortunately, with such a checkered career, the term *MIS* has been applied broadly and inconsistently. In fact, quite a few speeches and papers have been devoted to the question: "What is MIS?"

Given all this confusion, you may wonder, "Why bother?" The answer is that the term *MIS* does refer to a valid service, and this service is quite important. As more data is generated, as technology changes, as decision-making processes become better understood, as managers become more able to articulate their needs, systems will be devised to provide better information to managers. The potential benefit of this better information is enormous. Whereas making an accurate statement about how many widgets are in inventory may earn (or save) a few thousand dollars, improving the quality of long-range strategic planning by the chief executive may earn (or save) millions or billions of dollars. Thus, even though the water surrounding MIS is murky, the subject is well worth studying.

INFORMATION FOR MANAGEMENT

To understand MIS and DSS, you first need to understand management's information needs. What do managers do, and why do they need information to accomplish their objectives? Once we have answered these questions, we can discuss MIS and DSS.

What Is Management?

Management, according to the classic definition, is the planning, organizing, and controlling of business activities. Accordingly, managers define goals and objectives, organize resources to accomplish those goals, and adjust the allocation of resources to ensure that goals are attained.

Business managers each supervise one **business unit.** That unit might be a team of 3 or 4 people, it might be a department of 15 or 20 people, or it might be a division of hundreds or even thousands of people. Larger units are usually broken into subunits.

In figure 11–1, for example, the warehouse division of Elliot Bay Electronics (the unit) is composed of the receiving, order filling, and shipping departments (the subunits).

The manager of each unit (and subunit, sub-subunit, and so on), sometimes in conjunction with other personnel, defines goals and objectives for that unit. Each department in the warehouse division at EB is assigned certain responsibilities. The receiving department is responsible for stocking the warehouses with goods from vendors, the order filling department picks the stock to fill customers' orders, and the shipping department prepares orders for shipping and arranges delivery to customers.

Business units are allocated resources they use to achieve their goals. Resources might include people, raw materials, equipment, procedures, and money. For example, each department in figure 11–1 has a budget. Each manager is expected to assure that the unit meets its objectives within the allocated budget.

At Elliot Bay it is the warehouse manager's job to allocate resources and to **plan** their use in ways that will most efficiently meet the

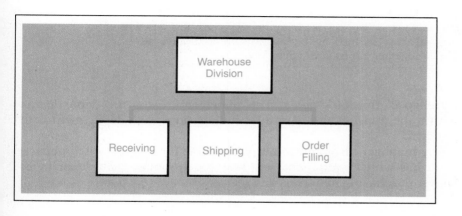

FIGURE 11–1
Division of a business unit

APPLICATION

"INFORMATION OFFICERS BRIDGE THE GAP BETWEEN THE TECHIES AND MANAGEMENT."

Wanted: chief information officer. Company seeks individual to bridge large gap between senior managers, who know little about computers, and data-processing personnel, who know less about business. Applicant must be able to translate the language and ways of the "techies" to the brass, and vice versa — so that high tech can be applied to better effect. Ample opportunity for rewards, headaches.

The want ad is apocryphal and the job doesn't always bear this title. But it's becoming an increasingly common one at all kinds of companies — and at a very senior level.

The reason: The leapfrogging advance of technology has, in many cases, surpassed companies' ability to apply it well. It also has given rise to alien cultures within companies — old-line managers, on the one hand, and new-breed data-processing wizards on the other. Never, it seems, shall the twain meet. Rarely, it's grumbled, are they pulling in the same direction.

One big problem: Data-processing managers, called management information system (MIS) officers, often treat technology as an end in itself, with little regard to its application. "They aren't sharp enough as business people," says Herbert Z. Halbrecht of Halbrecht Associates Inc., which recruits MIS officers. "They're like Moses bringing the Israelites almost to the promised land. They'll never be able to cross the river themselves."

That's where this new breed called the chief information officer comes in, straddling the spheres of general management and technology. The CIO ranks high in the corporate hierarchy, often reporting directly to the chief executive officer. He knows the company's business well, and knows just enough about technology to view it as a valuable tool, rather than an end in itself. Under various names, the chief information officer now exists at about a third of the nation's major companies, according to John Diebold & Associates, a New York-based technology consulting firm.

At BankAmerica Corp., for instance, Max D. Hopper is streamlining an array of inefficient systems, pieced together haphazardly over the years by corporate fiefdoms. At HNG/InterNorth Inc., J. Ronald Knorpp is trying to employ computers as a better competitive tool in the newly deregulated pipeline industry. At Northwestern National Life Insurance Co., David W. Haskin is working to get the sales and system people to know — and understand — one another.

Yet at a lot of companies, the idea of such an executive still meets resistance. Victor E. Millar, a managing partner at Arthur Andersen & Co. and a strong proponent of the chief information officer, says most companies rebuff him when he proposes it.

In some cases, he says, it's just never considered enough of a priority to get the chief executive to move on it. His own huge accounting firm, for instance, hasn't gotten around to getting a chief information officer, Millar says, even though "we desperately need one." There also can be resistance from senior managers, who fear the prospect of one person controlling the flow of data. In companies — as elsewhere, of course — information is power.

warehouse division's goals. The manager creates the departments within the division and identifies the functions each department is to perform.

The manager also determines who works for whom, which department has which equipment, and how much money each department has for purchasing materials and services.

Most importantly, the manager **controls** the activity in the warehouse division by checking to see if each department is meeting its goals according to plan. A skillful manager does this by constantly asking and getting answers to questions: Are orders being filled on schedule? Is the receiving department working more overtime than was budgeted? Does warehouse 2 have some extra stock carts that can be used in warehouse 3? Is trying to ship every order within 24 hours realistic? Depending on the answers to these and other questions, the manager may make changes within the division.

The best managers rely on experience, intuition, and accurate information. Computer systems cannot provide the first two items, but they are certainly able to provide managers with information. In the next section you will learn how different managers need different kinds of information from a computer system.

Management Information Needs

In the early days of MIS, systems developers painfully learned that management's needs for information are many and varied. As shown below in figure 11–2, these needs depend upon the manager's functional area, on the level of the manager's position, and on the amount of structure in the problem to be addressed. We will consider each of these in turn.

Information Needs Vary by Functional Area

Information needs vary by functional business area. To illustrate this, consider managers in various departments.

Sales managers need information of a short-term nature. For example, they might need to know:

- How the sales staff is performing compared to plan
- The sales summary by region and by product line
- The amount of sales needed next week to meet sales quotas

FIGURE 11–2
Variation of management information needs

INFORMATION NEEDS VARY BY FUNCTIONAL AREA	LEVEL OF MANAGER	DEGREE OF STRUCTURE
Sales	Strategic	Structured
Engineering	Tactical	Semistructured
Marketing	Operational	Unstructured
Manufacturing		
Finance		
Personnel, Administration, etc.		

Engineering managers, on the other hand, need information of a long-term nature. They might need to know:

- How technology is changing
- The products likely to be in demand next year
- What competitors have better designs
- The reason for why those designs are better

The marketing department, the liaison between sales and engineering, wants information about both the near and the long term. Marketing managers might need to know:

- Sales trends in the past six months
- The total sales for next year, based on the assumption that the present trends continue
- The size of the current market
- The size of the market next year
- The cost and return of expanding a production line

Manufacturing managers need information for planning and control. They might need to know:

- The quantity of each product that needs to be produced this month, next month, next quarter, and next year
- The efficiency of the production process
- Whether production has improved since last year
- How their plant compares with the industry average
- How the production cost of a product can be reduced

Financial managers need information about the history of their company, its current status, and its future direction. They need to know:

- Past sales
- Expenses
- Any change in their company's financial status since the previous statement
- Their company's current financial position, including cash, receivables, payables, and inventory levels
- Anticipated income from future sales
- Future expenses
- When and if there will be a cash surplus
- When and if their company will need cash

Personnel, administration, international, general management, and other departments will also have varying needs for information. These differences are important to understand because the design of an effective MIS requires that the developers have in-depth knowledge of the functional business areas involved.

APPLICATION

"DECISION SUPPORT SYSTEMS (DSS) FOR MARKETING MEAN DIFFERENT THINGS TO DIFFERENT PEOPLE."

Marketing research analysts want Decision Support Systems (DSS) that allow them to perform the sophisticated techniques they use in their work, for example regression analysis of variance. Product managers view DSS as providing the ability to access all of the various types of information they must monitor during promotions or advertising campaigns.

Perhaps the most used "buzzword" for DDS is "integration," and this is probably the most important feature of the many systems on the market. Integration means that various external data can be stored in a single database together with different types of internal data, for example orders processed, shipments, pricing, and allocations.

Data-processing experts view DSS as a comprehensive system that:

- includes an integrated, relational database of internal and external information
- has a state-of-the-art database management approach
- provides applications models (software that allows the user to per form specific calculations)
- contains report-generation capabilities (software that produces both standard and ad hoc reports)
- is based on a fourth-generation language (a user-friendly computer language that allows a non-computer person to interact with the system and/or to build models, reports)
- has a graphics feature (software that produces a variety of graphs)

Let us look at the information needs of the functional areas in Elliot Bay Electronics. Notice that the needs of the different departments tend to overlap.

The order entry department needs information about customers, such as their addresses, discount rates, and special shipping instructions. Accurate quantities and prices for the items in inventory and the current status of previous orders and backorders are also needed. The sales department wants to know such things as who are our best customers? Which are the most and least active items in stock? How do current sales figures compare to those for this time last year? Can we reduce the number of backorders? The buyers in the purchasing department need accurate information about inventory levels, shipments received from vendors, and which vendors offer the best prices and the most flexible delivery schedules. In addition, the buyers need to be aware of the levels of sales activity in the different product lines, and they need to know the marketing plan: Which items are going to be promoted, which items are going to be added to the product line, and which items are about to be discontinued. The warehouse managers want information about stock usage and inventory levels. Can we cut the amount of stock on hand and still fill our orders on time? If we add another product line, do we have enough warehouse space?

Information Needs Vary by Level of Manager

The type of information needed depends on the level of the manager as well as functional area. Managers and the problems they solve can be divided into three levels. The highest-level managers participate in **strategic planning** and problem solving. These managers define a company's corporate goals, examine the company's strengths and weaknesses, and determine corporate policies in keeping with the company's goals and objectives. Strategic planning focuses on the long-range status of the company.

The second level of manager is involved in **tactical problem solving** and decision making. These managers identify what has to be done to meet the corporate goals. For example, if a strategic goal is to increase market share by 5 percent, the tactical problem is figuring out how to do that. Managers at this level might propose:

- Increasing the size of the sales force
- Changing the composition of the sales force
- Increasing advertising
- Developing new promotional programs
- Designing new products

The information that tactical problem solvers need is different from that needed by strategic planners.

The third level involves **operational problem solving.** Managers at this level figure out **how** to accomplish tactical objectives. For example, if a tactical decision were made to increase the sales force, an operational manager would have to determine how to do it. The manager might propose adding sales personnel to all regions or only to specific geographic markets. The manager would decide whether to use a recruiting agency or hire new sales personnel directly.

Observe that as we change focus from strategic to tactical to operational issues, we reduce the time frame. Strategic issues are long-term, tactical issues are intermediate-term, operational issues are short-term issues. Consequently, each level of manager needs a different type of information. The ways in which information needs vary by level of manager are summarized in figure 11–3. The questions are ones that might be asked by the management at Elliot Bay.

As you can see, managers at all levels require information to solve their problems. The kind of information they need varies with the kinds of questions they need to answer. Figure 11–4a shows part of a report that might be used at the operational level: a detailed listing of each item in inventory, the quantity on hand, and its location in the warehouse. The reports in figure 11–4b contain information about the sources for each item in inventory and the amount of business done with each of the suppliers. Management would use this information when considering the tactical decision to add or change vendors. The strategic evaluation of company performance would include informa-

FIGURE 11–3
Levels of information needs

LEVEL OF INFORMATION NEED	TIME FRAME	EXAMPLE QUESTIONS
Strategic Issues	Long term	What is our corporate mission? Are we achieving our goals? Should we grow by acquiring a chain of retail stores?
Tactical Issues	Mid term	Should we add a telemarketing department? Should we add or change vendors? Should we establish regional warehouses?
Operational Issues	Short term	Do we have all the items in stock to fill the Olympic Stores order? Should we schedule overtime in the shipping department this weekend? Should Jones be promoted to manager of the receiving department?

tion from many sources, some of the reports needed at this level are shown in figure 11–4c.

Information Needs Vary by Degree of Structure

Perhaps the greatest difficulty in developing an effective **MIS** is that so many of the problems managers face are not cut and dried. They are often complex, multi-dimensional issues that defy simple solutions.

Problems actually fall on a continuum, as shown in figure 11–5. A highly structured problem is one that can be solved with a specific procedure or algorithm. Highly structured problems are readily solved with computer systems because goals are clearly defined, only certain alternatives are feasible, and the costs of each alternative are easy to determine.

Consider an example of a highly structured problem. Suppose we want to choose one of three vendors to supply red transistors at the minimum cost. Suppose the cost per transistor is equal to the unit price of the transistor plus the shipping cost. To choose the vendor, we simply add the two costs together for each vendor and pick the vendor having the lowest total cost.

FIGURE 11–4a
Report used at the operational level

PARTS LIST: STOCK STATUS AS OF 10/01/86					
PART #	DESCRIPTION	QTY. ON HAND	QTY. ON ORD.	WHSE.	AISLE/BIN
123	Green diode	500	50	1	3/4
236	Red transistor	1000	0	3	1/6
457	Blue resistor	250	100	2	2/18

FIGURE 11–4b
Reports used at the tactical level

VENDOR ANALYSIS: QTR. ENDING 9/30/86

VENDOR NAME	#	PART #	DESC.	QTY.	$
Ace Supply	226	123	Green diode	2000	500.50
		418	Blue transistor	500	150.85
		619	Red capacitor	800	237.62
				Total	888.97
A to Z Mfg.	637	236	Red transistor	1500	478.26
		712	Yellow diode	550	193.58
				Total	671.84

PARTS PURCHASED: MONTH ENDING 11/30/86

PART #	DESC.	VENDOR NAME	#	QTY.	$
123	Green diode	Ace Supply	226	1500	375.00
		A to Z Mfg.	637	200	40.00
		Comtronics	956	1000	220.00
				Total	635.00
187	Gray fuse	Fusecom	567	500	100.00
		Raytek Inc.	891	1200	228.00
				Total	328.00

This example is highly structured for several reasons. Notice that the goal is clear: We are only concerned with minimizing costs. The choices are clearly delineated: There are only three vendors to consider. Finally, measuring costs is easy: We simply ask the vendors.

Now consider a problem on the other end of the continuum. Suppose you are a senior executive at Elliot Bay. You have noticed that employee morale has been steadily declining, and turnover has been high. The executives are meeting in order to develop a statement of the "corporate culture" that EB will begin to develop. How does the group proceed?

This problem is highly unstructured. The goal is obscure. Is it to improve morale, reduce turnover, or something else? What is "corporate culture"? Each executive has his or her own definition. What is the purpose of publishing a statement? If the purpose of the meeting is to improve employee morale, will a statement do that? How are the rights of stockholders to be compared to the rights of employees? This problem leads to questions of ethics and values, subjective assessments of situations, and so forth. It is unlikely that a computer system will be able to solve this problem.

Between these two extremes are problems that are semistructured. For example, suppose Elliot Bay wants to know whether it should

SALES SUMMARY
FIRST QUARTER 1986

SALE PROJECTIONS
FIRST QUARTER 1987

SALES SUMMARY
FIRST QUARTER 1987

INVENTORY CLASS	REGION	SALES
Transistors	1	10,000
	2	8,000
	3	5,000
	Total	23,000
Microprocessors	1	20,000
	2	14,000
	3	16,000
	Total	50,000
Switches	1	10,000
	2	3,000
	3	7,000
	Total	20,000

FIGURE 11–4c
Reports used at the strategic level

institute a campaign to improve customer service. First, they need to know the customers' perceptions of the service they already receive. Do they want more variety in stock, faster delivery time, a toll-free number for inquiries and orders, a phone line for technical support, or more courteous service from company employees? Once these questions have been answered, alternatives can be suggested to improve each area. Each alternative will have a price, and some will cost more than the value of the estimated benefit. For example, the toll-free

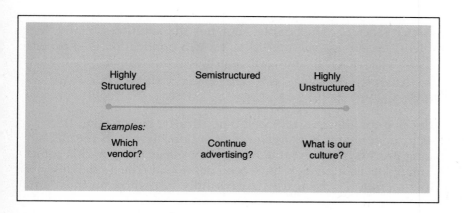

FIGURE 11–5
Problem structure continuum

number for ordering is relatively easy to implement, while the phone line for technical support implies the employment of at least one person who is expert in a variety of technical areas. The alternatives with the highest rate of return, those that promise the greatest increase in sales for the amount of money spent, will be selected.

Can a computer system assist managers in arriving at some decisions? Yes, of course. As you have learned throughout this text, computer systems can be used to solve algorithmic problems. Consequently, managers can enter figures into their computer and have it respond with reports that compare alternatives, costs, and potential benefits. It is unlikely, however, that a computer will suggest possible solutions, such as the toll-free line or a technical support service.

Once improvements in customer service are implemented they should reflect higher sales, more repeat customers, and fewer complaints. But suppose that doesn't happen. New decisions need to be made—more unstructured questions need to be answered. Will you discontinue the improvements to save money and alienate the customers you already have? Or are you committed to looking further and spending even more?

There are three distinguishing characteristics of unstructured problems:

- The solution objectives are ambiguous, numerous, and not operational
- The process required to achieve an acceptable solution cannot be specified in advance
- It is difficult to say either in advance or after the fact which user steps are directly relevant to the solution achieved.

In other words, unstructured problems are ones in which we find *a* solution (maybe not the best one, either) by muddling through, and, having muddled through have little idea of how we did it.

From this discussion it should be clear that some management problems are sufficiently structured so that they are amenable to MIS-based solutions. For others, an MIS application can provide useful assistance (comparing sales before and after the changes in customer service, for example), but not the solution. Finally, some problems are so unstructured that an MIS application is of no practical use. The trick is to know which problems are which.

The Business Activity Cycle

To develop an effective MIS and, specifically, an effective DSS, you need to understand how business uses information in the decision-making process. Considerable research has been done on this subject, and many decision models have been developed. The model described in this section has been used successfully in several business situations. Other models could be used as well.

Figure 11–6 shows a **business activity cycle** consisting of four major stages: **action, appraisal, specification,** and **decision.** This model is cyclical because it continuously repeats. A decison is made that leads to an action that leads to an appraisal, which starts the cycle again.

To clarify this model, consider its application to another Elliot Bay situation. Suppose the managers of the marketing and sales departments decide to implement a sales promotion: They *decide* to award an additional discount to dealers who increase their orders to a specified level. The promotion is started with an *action* — notifying dealers of the new policy. Once the action is underway, EB's managers *appraise* its success. If the promotion is achieving its goals, the managers turn their attention to other issues. If the promotion does not appear to have had an appreciable impact on sales, management will need to *specify* new alternatives and decide upon one.

According to the model in figure 11–6, the managers will appraise the situation and develop a problem definition. Recall from chapter 4 that a *problem* is a perceived difference between what should be and what is. In this case, the problem is that the promotion is not increasing sales. With this problem definition, the company will *specify* alternatives for correcting the situation. For this example, alternatives might be to cancel the promotion, increase advertising, develop more promotional material, and so forth. The alternatives are then consid-

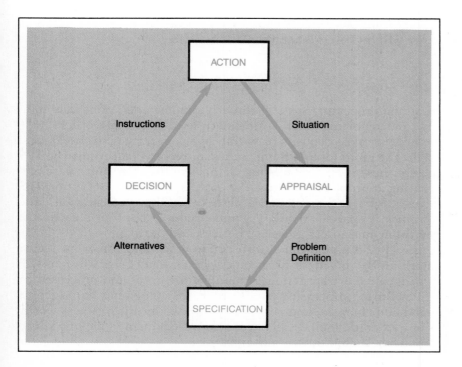

FIGURE 11–6
Business activity cycle

(continued)

QUESTIONS

11.1 What are the two broad categories of information systems? How do they differ?

11.2 Describe the relationship between MIS and DSS.

11.3 In what ways did computer professionals underestimate the difficulty of developing MIS?

11.4 Define *management*.

11.5 Describe ways in which managers plan.

11.6 Describe ways in which managers organize.

11.7 Describe ways in which managers control.

11.8 What three factors affect management information needs?

11.9 Give examples of ways in which management's information needs vary by functional business area.

11.10 Give examples of ways in which management's information needs vary by level of manager.

11.11 Give examples of ways in which management's information needs vary as problems vary from structured to unstructured.

11.12 List three characteristics of an unstructured problem.

11.13 Describe the business activity cycle.

ered by the decision maker, and a *decision* is made. This decision leads to *action*, which starts the cycle over again.

In reality, the order of activity may not follow this process, and specific problem statements, alternatives, and so forth may not be developed. There is evidence, however, that managerial decisions actually improve if all steps are followed. In spite of this fact, the business activity model is a good approximation of most business situations. In fact, the systems development process described in chapter 5 is a special case of this cycle.

Effective MIS and DSS applications were developed in order to provide useful information at all stages of this cycle. This will be discussed more thoroughly in the next sections.

MANAGEMENT INFORMATION SYSTEMS

In the chapter introduction, we divided information systems into two major groups: transaction processing systems and management information systems. We said that TPSs support day-to-day operations while MISs support management. However, it should be evident that management depends on operations. Therefore, any system that benefits operations also benefits management. Thus, it is more appropriate to say that **all** systems support management; transaction processing systems support **both** operations and management, whereas management information systems support **only** management. Since this is true, we will review TPS and then discuss MIS.

Review of Transaction Processing Systems

Transaction processing systems directly support operations (and indirectly, management). Such systems are used to process orders, take reservations, make deposits or withdrawals, generate paychecks, and so forth. The input for a TPS is a request or record of an event. The TPS processes these inputs by making changes in the company's data and generating appropriate outputs. For example, a hotel reservation TPS receives a request for lodging, accesses the hotel's reservation data, determines if space is available, and produces appropriate outputs (reservation guarantees, rejection notices, and the like).

Figure 11–7 is a diagram of transaction processing. An event occurs in the Elliot Bay business: a customer phones in an order for item 123. A record, called a **transaction,** is made of the event and processed by the TPS. During processing of the order, the company's data records are read and changed, and output is generated for the business world. This output could include an order acknowledgment, a picking slip, a shipping label, a backorder, and an invoice.

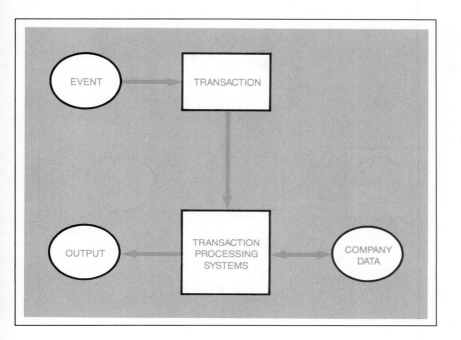

FIGURE 11–7
Diagram of a transaction processing system

In this diagram, the term *company data* is purposely left vague. This data can be a single file, several files, or one or more databases.

Characteristics of transaction processing systems are summarized below:

- Support company operations
- Create and maintain data model
- Utilize standardized processing
- High performance and reliability are essential
- Backup, recovery, and disaster planning are mandatory

As stated, a TPS supports operations and creates and maintains the organizational **data model.** A TPS also is a standardized system. For example, orders are processed today the same way they were processed yesterday, and the same way they will be processed tomorrow. Some change does occur with TPS applications; such change, however, is slow and evolutionary.

Transaction processing systems have two other important characteristics. First, since a TPS may have hundreds of users, performance and reliability are critical. If a TPS is slow or fails, the impact on the organization can be severe. Second, the data model must be kept accurate and intact. If the data model becomes inaccurate, transactions will be incorrectly processed. Widgets will be sold that do not exist, for example. This means that backup, recovery, disaster planning, and similar protective measures are essential.

11.14 In the sales promotion problem described in the preceding section,
a. Which functional areas are involved?
b. What level of management is involved?
c. Is this a structured or an unstructured problem?
d. What information is needed to solve the problem at each of the four stages of the business activity cycle?

11.15 In the customer service problem described in the previous section,
a. Which functional areas are involved?
b. What level of management is involved?
c. Is this a structured or an unstructured problem?
d. What information is needed to solve the problem at each of the four stages of the business activity cycle?

FIGURE 11–8
Diagram of management information
system at Elliot Bay

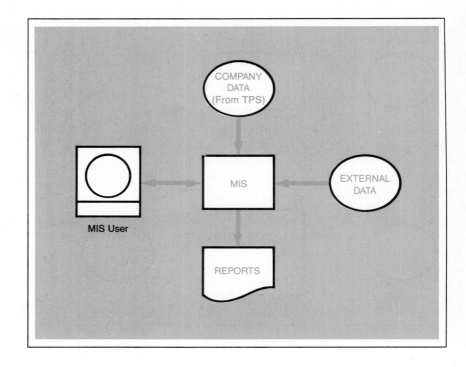

Characteristics of MIS

A management information system is a business system that provides past, present, and projected information about a company and its environment. By definition, an MIS does not require a computer, but in practice, most MISs do use computers.

A diagram of an Elliot Bay MIS is shown in figure 11–8. The MIS programs use the company data model generated by the TPS. This model is typically the most comprehensive and complete source of data about the company. Observe that the MIS does not change this data.

Management information systems may also use other sources of data, particularly data about the environment outside of the company itself (the external environment). Examples are general economic data, industry sales and forecasts, financial reports of similar or competitive companies, and so forth.

MIS services fall into three major categories: those that provide regular, recurring reports, those that produce exception reports, and those that answer ad hoc inquiries. In the first group are MIS services that produce **regular and recurring reports.** For example, Elliot Bay may have an MIS that produces weekly summaries of new orders. Management reviews these reports to determine the appropriateness of inventory levels. These reports can be compared to reports from previous periods to detect trends. They can also be used to rearrange the allocation of stock pickers, shipping employees, and other resources. Reports such as these would be produced on a regular schedule and would tend to be stable over time.

A second category of MIS services is **exception reporting.** Elliot Bay MIS programs in this category may look for unusual and exceptional conditions. For example, a program could be written to compare sales of products to the sales plan. When sales of a particular product line increase significantly faster than planned, the MIS produces an exception report for the purchasing department. This report alerts the buyers to the unusual demand and the need to increase orders to the vendors. Similarly, if sales are significantly below the planned level, other managerial decisions can be made.

The third category of MIS services is **decision support.** Typically, this service is used by management to improve the quality of a particular decision. For example, suppose Elliot Bay is considering adding a new product line. If this is to be done, management must develop new sales plans, new advertising, new catalog copy, and new vendor sources. Before making this decision, management needs to determine the impact of the decision on sales expenses, warehouse space, and other factors.

In a way, a DSS is a tool kit that managers can use to access company and other data, process this data, and present results. A DSS generally is directed at solving a specific, short-term problem: How shall we reorganize the sales department? Should we acquire company XYZ? Hence, the DSS tool kit must be flexible and easily tailored to widely differing problems. We will discuss DSS in greater detail later in this chapter. Characteristics of MIS applications are summarized below.

- Support company management
- Produce regular and recurring reports
- Generate reports of exceptional conditions
- Provide decision support tools

Consolidating Information

The amount of information any human being can assimilate is limited. Successful senior managers often have prodigious memories, but even so, their memories do have limits. Clearly, the manager of a $5 billion company cannot assimilate the myriad details necessary to run the production line. Information must be consolidated for managers; the higher the level of management, the greater the consolidation necessary.

The developers of MIS applications need to consolidate information as the MIS is designed. There are two primary techniques for consolidating information: **aggregation** and **generalization.** To aggregate data, we combine like data across categories. For example, we can aggregate daily sales data into weekly or monthly sales totals. We can group the purchases of items by vendor as shown in figure 11–4b, or we can group individual items into product classes and show their sales by region as shown in figure 11–4c. Observe that once we have made the combinations, we lose some information. We can no longer tell how many purchases we made from Ace Supply, or if the unit price varied from order to order. Likewise, in the Sales Summary, we can no longer identify the best-selling microprocessor or the largest customer within a region.

When we generalize, we combine unlike objects, but we ignore their differences. For example, we may divide sales personnel into two categories: *new* and *experienced*. We could say that salespeople will be allocated to the *new* cateogry if they have less than six months of sales experience. If they have more than six months experience, they will be allocated to the *experienced* group. Clearly, all salespeople who have more than six months experience are not equally experienced. Some may have seven months' experience and others may have 20 years of experience. Still, for the purpose of generalization, we ignore these differences.

In another example of generalization, we can combine the inventory records of parts from different product lines. For example, we might total the dollar value of all microcomputer parts. When making this total, we ignore the fact that the parts are totally different.

Although both aggregation and generalization are necessary and appropriate, they do have a cost. Whenever we aggregate or generalize, we lose information, usually details.

However, we must use aggregation and generalization to reduce the bulk of information that a manager must assimilate. MISs are supposed to answer managers' questions. Therefore, the goal of an MIS developer is to aggregate and generalize in such a way that the only unanswerable questions are those that the manager will not need to ask.

MIS and the Business Activity Cycle

Examine the business activity cycle shown in figure 11–6. Management information systems potentially have a role in each of the stages of this cycle. During the appraisal step, an MIS can be used to extract data from the corporate data files to better determine the current situation and help define the problem to be solved. During specification, the MIS can be used to help formulate alternatives. Infeasible alternatives can be identified and discarded early in the process. The MIS can also be used to store and retrieve alternatives.

Clearly, there are many uses for MIS at the decision step. Financial models can be constructed to evaluate the impact of different alternative selections, and statistical analyses can be performed to estimate

APPLICATION

"ORGANIZATIONS ARE ALREADY MAKING DSS A REALITY."

Every day, Steve Anderson sits at his terminal at the Atchison, Topeka & Santa Fe Railway Co. offices in Topeka, Kan. He types in his password and logs onto the railroad company's operations expeditor (OX) software system, developed inhouse. As Anderson plugs in a set of commands he is soon enmeshed in OX's railroad car tracking subsystem. Very quickly Anderson sees which freight cars are scheduled to be used that day at various locations across the country. He also sees which cars are lying idle and what empty cars are being hauled to other areas.

Typing in a few more commands, Anderson leans back and watches as the computer flashes the effects of moving some freight cars from Clovis, N.M. to Barstow, Calif. The screen indicates the cars would be better used in Topeka. The OX system has just answered Anderson's what-if question and, perhaps, saved thousands of dollars in the bargain.

At Genrad, Inc., a Waltham, Mass., electronics firm, Donald Sundue, corporate director of management information systems (MIS), looks at the massive monthly operations report sitting beside him. Instead of picking it up, he punches instructions into his terminal. Sundue's screen quickly displays a condensed electronic version of the report, presented by means of the Command Center, a decision support system (DSS) from Pilot Executive Software, Inc. of Boston, Mass. A few more keystrokes and Sundue has gleaned, consolidated and printed what he wanted from the

report without flipping through any pages.

Both the above sketches represent real uses of DSS. At the Atchison, Topeka & Santa Fe Railway, the company's OX system has been touted in some circles as the most extensive user-developed computer system in the U.S., if not the world. OX also represents what DSS is supposed to be all about: putting computing power in the hands of users.

The DSS concept got its start early with financial applications and has deviated little from this financial touchstone. Early mainframe-based DSS products such as Interactive Financial Planning System (IFPS) from Execucom Systems Corp., Austin, Texas; Focus from Information Builders, Inc., N.Y.; and System W from Comshare, Inc., Ann Arbor, Mich., were the inspiration for a number of large, financially driven DSS products that, until the arrival of the IBM Personal Computer, had a stranglehold on the DSS concept. Financial DSS programs are extremely data-driven and their supporters look askance at some of the more intuitive, abstract input to many decision-making programs now on the market for personal computers.

The IBM Personal Computer has had a twofold effect on DSS. First, it has done much to take DSS out of the old grasp of the DP department and into the lap of the user. Almost every DSS vendor now offers a micro version of its mainframe DSS product. Second, by downloading data from the mainframe onto a micro-

computer and merging the data with programs such as Lotus Development Corp.'s 1-2-3, the user can create more open-ended, personalized DSS applications than is possible when tied to a mainframe.

An example can be found at the F. W. Woolworth Co. in New York, where the retailer's MIS department is working with users in its information center to migrate mainframe IFPS applications to IBM PCs. Using Execucom's Dataspan conversion software, programs written in COBOL and other non-Execucom languages can be converted to IFPS format without the use of programmers. Barry Putt, F. W. Woolworth's manager of corporate business applications, said divisional managers are using IBM PCs to create personal financial modeling projects using using such cryptic tools as variance analysis, return on investment trees and profit center scenarios.

The future of DSS is tied to fourth-generation languages and the ability to make the communication between user and system as natural and easy as possible. David Tory, senior vice-president of planning at Computer Associates, Inc., the Jericho, N.Y. producers of CA-Financial Planner, a mainframe-based DSS, offered an explanation: "The whole orientation of DSS is toward languages users understand. DSS people are finally beginning to use the tools to make software a function of the computing environment, not the computer system itself."

or project future conditions. Finally, MIS report writing and graphics capabilities can be used to communicate the decision. We will see examples of each of these applications in the next section.

DECISION SUPPORT SYSTEMS

It would seem that just about any system that supports a decision could be called a DSS.

A decision support system (DSS) is an *interactive* computer system that *helps* decision makers use *data* and *models* to solve *unstructured* problems. The keywords are italicized. A DSS is interactive; thus, the user is part of the DSS. Additionally, a DSS helps managers decide; it does not make decisions. A DSS is an assistant in the same way that a research librarian is an assistant. Further, a DSS employs data and models of the enterprise and is helpful in solving unstructured problems.

Components of a DSS

A DSS is a business computer system, and as such, it has the five major components we have discussed before: hardware, programs, data, procedures, and people. The hardware that early DSS used was mainframe computers or minicomputers. Today, many DSS applications use or at least involve microcomputers.

A DSS is a problem-solving environment; it is a workbench for decision makers, and thus there is no single DSS program. Rather, a DSS includes several types of programs. First, the DSS needs a **database management system** (DBMS) to access the potentially large volumes of complex data (see chapter 9).

Second, the DSS includes programs that perform **statistical analyses,** such as regression analysis, analysis of variance, factor analysis, and so forth. It is not important that you understand statistics (for this course), only that you realize that statistics are important in business.

A third category of DSS programs is comprised of packages that facilitate **financial modeling.** An electronic spreadsheet (see module B) such as LOTUS *1-2-3* is one example. Other more sophisticated programs are available as well. Such programs could be used, for example, to estimate a change in a company's balance sheet if another company is purchased for certain cash payments over a ten-month period. Financial modeling programs can also be used in determining the impact of selling stock at various prices or of consolidating two company divisions, or in other similar situations.

Finally, a DSS includes general-purpose **query, report writing,** and **graphics** software. That software allows a user to easily extract data, and produce written documents and charts. To date, no single DSS program includes all components. Companies do not buy a DSS program. Rather, they buy at least one program of each of the types discussed here. DSS programs are summarized below:

- Database management
- Statistical analysis
- Financial modeling
- Query, report writing, and graphics

The primary source of data for a decision-support system is the data maintained by transaction processing systems. Quite often, DSS data is extracted from one or more corporate database. Data also may be purchased from outside sources or developed within the DSS itself. For example, the results of one DSS application can be saved and used as input to another.

Since DSSs address unstructured problems, no standardized procedure exists for using them. In the Elliot Bay order entry system, for example, the process of recording a customer order is standardized. But DSS procedures tend to be one of a kind. In fact, the decision maker or analyst may have to try several different techniques, learning as he or she goes. Further, the experience gained on one study may not be useful in other studies.

Suppose Elliot Bay considers opening another warehouse somewhere in the eastern part of the United States. The management wants answers such to questions as: How many customers do we have in each of the eastern states? How much business do we do with them? What is the market like? How many competitors do we have in the area? How much would another warehouse reduce delivery time and shipping costs for our customers. How would a new warehouse affect the shipping costs we pay our vendors? If we decide to open the warehouse, where should it be located? What will the management structure be? How will we coordinate activities between the new warehouse and our other sites? Will the new warehouse carry a complete line of stock? Will higher sales offset the additional administrative expense?

To answer these questions, the DSS will need company data about customers, orders, sales, inventory, vendors, and administration. In addition, data about market conditions and competitors will be necessary. Programs can analyze the various combinations of alternatives — locations, warehouse sizes, sales volumes, shipping costs, and so on — to estimate the costs and benefits of each. Elliot Bay management will evaluate the alternatives, make the decision, and then move on. The particular combination of data needed to solve this problem may never be needed again.

You will recall from chapter 4 that there are many ways to access a DSS. Some companies provide their executives with assistants called *information analysts*. Other companies have built and staffed *information centers*. Still other executives use their own terminals or PCs to directly access a DSS. In some cases users connect their microcomputers to the information center (or corporate) mainframe or mini and **download** data from the information center or corporate database.

Although a DSS is a kind of management information system, its characteristics are somewhat different from those systems that produce regular reports and exception reports. These characteristics are summarized below:

- Solve unstructured, one-of-a-kind problems
- Produce reports as needed; reports may be unique
- Manipulate data in a variety of ways
- Provide information quickly
- Use microcomputers and information centers

DSS Applications

Since 1980, a wide variety of DSS applications have emerged. The following three cases illustrate the use of DSS in business.

Tasty Baking Company

Tasty Baking company manufactures cupcakes, pies, and other desserts and snacks. Sales in 1980 were almost $180 million in 25 states across the United States. When Tasty needed to replace its mainframe computer, the company selected a system that could not only provide transaction processing, but would also facilitate flexible, ad hoc querying of the corporate database.

Tasty installed a Univac mainframe computer and purchased MAPPER, a database management system that provides generalized query and report writing capabilities to users. Once the system was installed, the data processing department taught a 10-hour class to a number of middle-level executives.

The manager of operations learned to use MAPPER to access sales and inventory data in the database. He used this information to balance inventories with sales demands at various distribution points. Since he learned to use the system himself, he did not need to wait for the data processing staff to generate new reports as his needs arose. The data processing department did provide a coordinator, however, to assist executives when they develop new applications.

Marine Terminals Corporation

Marine Terminals Corporation operates shipping and receiving facilities at major ocean ports in California and Alaska. In 1983, Marine Terminals used a decision-support system to analyze financial data and operating procedures when building a supply base terminal near Santa Barbara.

Marine Terminals wanted to know the financial effects of various methods of financing the terminal. Also, the terminal could be constructed in several configurations. Under one scenario, ships were loaded and unloaded only during regular working hours. Under a second scenario, ships were serviced on a 24-hour-a-day schedule. The first scenario required more berths, but labor costs were lower. The second scenario required fewer berths, but labor costs were higher.

To address these issues, the vice president of marketing purchased a microcomputer and a financial planning package. He analyzed a series of alternatives and calculated the financial results in terms of net present value of invested capital, income, taxes, operating costs, and similar measures. The results of these analyses were displayed in color on the microcomputer. Slide pictures were taken of the screen images and used to present the results to management and potential investors.

International Harvester

International Harvester is a billion-dollar manufacturer of heavy trucks, farm, and construction equipment. In 1980, they employed over 87,000 people worldwide. In 1982, International Harvester endured a six-month strike at the same time that sales were declining in their major markets. As a consequence, they needed to restructure their debt (they had to raise money to make payments to or pay off creditors).

For such a large corporation, debt restructuring is a complicated problem. How much money would the company need? The answer depended on what would happen to sales in the future and on decisions management would make regarding production and staffing levels. If the company raised too much money, then they would pay interest needlessly or sell stock that need not be sold. On the other hand, if they raised too little money, obtaining more money from banks in the future would be difficult; management can make only so many trips to the well.

Several years prior to this situation, International Harvester had formed a DSS group as part of the corporate planning office. The DSS group worked closely with the corporate treasury department to evaluate the debt restructuring problem. Together the groups created models that simulated the company's cash needs and estimated costs for various restructuring alternatives. The results of these studies were used to negotiate new loans with International Harvester's banks.

DSS in the Future

The decision support systems of today no doubt will be superseded by more robust, easier-to-use, and more effective systems in the future. Microcomputers are becoming more and more powerful, and no end to this trend is in sight. As microcomputer disk capacities increase, more data will be available for DSS analysis. Further, as microcomputer CPUs become faster, they will be able to run very sophisticated programs.

APPLICATION

"PROVIDE EXPERT ADVICE AND KNOWLEDGE SUPPORT TO COMPANY MANAGEMENT."

By 1990, knowledge-based advisory systems built and delivered on symbolic processing machines will be "the ground floor, even in general-purpose computing," predicts Symbolics, Inc. Chairman Russell Noftsker. "That's a trend that I'd say is unstoppable at this point.

"Commerical users of computers right now are primarily managing and digesting the records of business — processing those records. A lot of what goes on is aimed at enhancing management's understanding of the records and transactions of business," he adds.

As time goes on, more and more knowledge will be applied to that process via machine, he emphasizes.

According to Noftsker, the trend is toward a point at which the computer systems "can serve as information advisory systems, where they're actually drawing conclusions and telling you what's going on in your business as opposed to just running out reams of paper that you have to dig through and understand. I think that business wants to go in that direction."

DP PREPARATIONS

So how are DP shops bracing for the transformation?

"Just in the past nine months they are beginning to buy into it," Noftsker remarks.

He notes, "We've started seeing the MIS departments actually go looking for these kinds of capabilities and trying to figure out how they could take advantage of them."

Noftsker suggests that DP search out those areas in which to provide expert advice and knowledge support to their company management. "And then start implementing those support capabilities before your management comes in and says, 'Why don't you guys have this?' "

In addition to the hardware technology, other technologies are developing as well. Knowlege about human perception will be used to develop more effective user interfaces. Knowlege about human cognition will enable DSS architects to build systems that mirror human patterns of thinking. Knowledge about the decision-making process, both for individuals and for groups, can be coupled with computer communication technology to provide group-oriented DSSs.

Undoubtedly, too, **artificial intelligence** will be applied to decision-support systems. Some **natural language** products, such as INTELECT, CLOUT, and GURU (see figure 11–9), already are available. With these systems, the user can express queries in natural language (in English, for example). The systems do the best they can to understand and process the query. When these systems become confused, they ask for more information to clarify the question.

Natural language will be extended in the future. At some point, executives will be able to address their computers in the same manner as they address their assistants today. This communication will be spoken as well as conducted via a keyboard.

Eventually, natural language will be combined with DSS and expert systems (discussed in the next section). Subject-matter expertise will be programmed into DSSs, and managers will be able to consult with them. For example, a microcomputer could be programmed with DSS facilities and expert knowledge about taxes. This microcomputer could participate in the evaluation of financial alternatives that have tax consequences. With natural language, communication with this microcomputer could well be spoken.

KNOWLEDGE SYSTEMS

Knowledge systems are computer applications that store representations of human knowledge and process it to make conclusions. As shown in figure 11–10, knowledge systems can be used to interpret, predict, diagnose, design, plan, control, and so forth. Knowledge systems are sometimes referred to as **expert systems**; however, the term **knowledge systems** is preferred because it is less presumptuous.

```
SHOW ME THE SALESPEOPLE

Jones
Smith
Abernathy


SORT THEM BY NAME

Abernathy
Jones
Smith


SORT THEM BY NAME DESCENDING

Smith
Jones
Abernathy


JUST THE ONES WITH SALARY GREATER THAN 40,000
```

SALESPERSON	SALARY
Jones	42,986
Abernathy	67,348

```
HOW MUCH DID THEY SELL?
```

SALESPERSON	SALARY	AMOUNT
Jones	42,986	1,345,989
Abernathy	67,348	3,429,083

FIGURE 11–9
Examples of natural language query processed by CLOUT™. CLOUT is a registered trademark of the Microrim Corporation.

Most knowledge systems are not sufficiently robust to qualify as true experts.

Knowledge systems technology has been applied to a wide variety of problem domains. Below you will find several of the better-known knowledge systems:

- **MEDICINE**
  Mycin diagnoses and prescribes treatments for meningitis and bacteremia infections. The Stanford University Medical Experimental Computer Facility developed it in the mid-1970s.
- **TRAINING**
  Steamer teaches naval officers, through simulation, the techniques needed to run a steam propulsion plant similar to those used in many ships. The U. S. Navy Personal Research and Development Center developed it in cooperation with Bolt, Baranek and Newman, Inc.
- **COMPUTER SYSTEMS**
  Xcon configures VAX-11/780 computers on a daily basis for Digital Equipment Corp. DEC and Carnegie-Mellon University developed it and implemented it in June 1971.
- **CHEMISTRY**
  Dendral estimates the molecular structures of unknown compounds by analyzing mass spectrographic, nuclear magnetic resonance and other data. Stanford University developed the system.
- **ENGINEERING**
  Delta uses diagnostic strategies to identify and help maintenance workers correct malfunctions in diesel electric locomotives. The research and development center of General Electric Co. developed Delta.

FIGURE 11–10
Generic categories of knowledge engineering applications

CATEGORY	PROBLEM ADDRESSED
Interpretation	Inferring situation descriptions from electronically sensed data
Prediction	Inferring likely consequences of given situations
Diagnosis	Inferring system malfunctions from observations
Design	Configuring objects knowing their constraints and limitations
Planning	Designing actions
Monitoring	Comparing observations to plan
Debugging	Prescribing remedies for malfunctions
Repair	Executing a plan to administer a prescribed remedy
Instruction	Diagnosing
Control	Interpreting, predicting, repairing, and monitoring system behaviors

PROFILE

"SPERRY CORP. HAS INVESTED HEAVILY IN EXPERT SYSTEMS."

In September 1984, Sperry Corp. announced its initial plunge into artificial intelligence with the establishment of its Knowledge Systems Center in Bloomington, Minn. Now, less than two years later, in what may be remembered as one of the fastest ramp-ups in AI history, Sperry is in the midst of developing 30 expert systems, along with 20 additional AI projects.

One expert system that is near implementation is Sperry's Printed Circuit Card Fault Analysis package. As early as April, Sperry could install this system in three of its defense division factories (Clearwater, Fla.; Pueblo, Colo.; and St. Paul, Minn.), according to Lawrence Walker, director of Sperry's Knowledge Systems Center. This package would enable an engineer with two weeks of training to employ a Lisp workstation connected to a probe to diagnose problems in PC cards "that many $1.5 million testers couldn't," Walker says. Sperry estimates that the pack-

age will save the company as much as $10 million once it is up and running.

One of its best known expert systems, the Airline Revenue Optimization package, which Sperry built in conjunction with Northwest Airlines, is scheduled to go into production some time this year. The system is intended to aid Northwest and other airlines decide the best price to charge for each seat on each flight in order to maximize revenues. The system weighs such factors as date of departure, prices charged by competing airlines, number of passengers to date, etc.

To write these expert systems, Sperry engineers employ Texas Instrument Inc.'s Explorer workstations and Intellicorp's KEE (Knowledge Engineering Environment) software. Sperry repackages, resells and services TI's and Intellicorp's products for its own customers. It also conducts joint development, bids and training with these two partners,

Walker adds.

Any expert system that Sperry decides to sell in the commercial market will be called a "Power Pack." Walker defines Power Packs as database-like collections of generic knowledge and certain functions common to a specific industry. This type of package, which will operate on top of KEE, will prevent Sperry from having to fully customize each expert system for each customer. "Customers don't really want the final answer anyway," Walker claims. Primarily for security reasons, they usually prefer to finalize systems themselves, he says.

The first Power Pack that Sperry will offer will probably be Simkit, a general simulation package for factory operation, which was developed with Intellicorp, Walker says. The Airline Revenue Optimization package will be the next probable Power Pack, he predicts.

- **GEOLOGY**

   Dipmeter Advisor estimates the subsurface geological structure of an area by analyzing dipmeter logs and other pertinent geological data. Schlumberger-Doll Research developed the program.

This technology is just now emerging, and the full impact is not yet known. Some people believe that knowledge systems could have the same impact on such professions as accounting or law that automation had on the factory. Others believe that this claim is overstated and that the contribution of knowledge systems will be much more modest.

Inferencing

The concept of **inferencing** is key to understanding the value of knowledge systems. In this context, inferencing is the the process of combining two or more facts, implications, relationships, or other knowledge items to form a conclusion. For example, suppose we know that A implies B and that B implies C; given these statements, we can infer (or make an inference) that A implies C. Consider a more direct example. Suppose that the following rules pertain to the operations at EB Electronics:

a. Transitors are always shipped in the number 27 carton.
b. The total outside dimensions of the number 27 carton are less than 45 inches.
c. Packages with total outside dimensions of less than 45 inches are always shipped via air freight.

Given these implications, a knowledge system could infer that transistors are always shipped via air freight.

An operational knowledge system would have dozens or perhaps hundreds of such rules together with additional facts. The system would ask the user for information about the problem to be addressed and then apply the rules and other knowledge to make inferences about the problem. Mycin, perhaps the most famous knowledge system, has hundreds of rules, which are used to diagnose infectious diseases.

Knowledge Representation

In addition to the rules just described, knowledge systems contain **representations of other knowledge** in the problem domain. For example, a knowledge system at EB Electronics might include a list of products, a list of customers, and a list of employees. This data could be used in conjunction with rules to determine how to ship particular orders.

Although knowledge systems and database systems arose independently, recently the two have begun to merge. Databases can support knowledge systems by storing large volumes of facts. At the same time, inferencing techniques can improve DBMS processing. For example, the natural-language interface product, CLOUT, uses inferencing techniques to process queries stated in English.

Knowledge Systems Development

Knowledge systems can be developed in many ways. Early systems were developed in special-purpose programming languages such as PROLOG and LISP. These languages differ from procedural languages such as BASIC or COBOL in that they allow the expression of rules and

FIGURE 11–11a
Dialog with a knowledge system.
Sample PROLOG program.

```
person (X, gotbucks) :-
        club (X, Y),
        cost (Y, Z),
        Z > 200.

person (X, fewbucks) :-
        club (X, Y),
        cost (Y, Z),
        Z < 101.

club (john, ski).
club (mary, scuba).
club (fred, jogging).
club (rosemary, racketball).
club (roger, mountaineering).

cost (ski, 500).
cost (scuba, 650).
cost (jogging, 5).
cost (racketball, 100).
cost (mountaineering, 125).
```

a. Sample PROLOG program

facts in a direct manner. Figure 11–11a shows a sample PROLOG program containing knowledge about people and their activities. Figure 11–11b shows a sample execution of this program.

PROLOG, LISP, and other special-purpose languages require highly skilled programmers to develop the knowledge application. Further, a long period of time is required for such development. Greater productivity can be achieved if the application is developed in what is known as a **knowledge system shell**. These shells are essentially knowledge system development workbenches that allow less sophisticated users to develop their applications with greater productivity. Examples of such shells are the TI Personal Consultant, M.1, and KEE.

The Unrealized Potential of Knowledge Systems

There currently are very few operationally useful knowledge systems. Most systems that have been developed have been far more successful as research tools than as commercial products. Considerable work is underway throughout the computer and related industries to develop practical knowledge systems, and this work may pay dividends in the near future. *If* operationally useful knowledge-based

FIGURE 11–11b

Execution of program.

```
>club (Who, ski)?

Who = john
>
>
>club (rosemary, Which)?

Which = racketball
>
>

>person (Who, gotbucks)?

Who = john

Who = mary
>
>
>
>
>person (Who, fewbucks)?

Who = fred

Who = rosemary
>
>
>
>
>person (Who, nobucks)?
NO
>
```

b. Execution of program

MIS and DSS applications can be developed, their impact on business will truly be revolutionary.

Throughout the history of artificial intelligence, there have been many more promises than there have been results. Artificial intelligence is interesting to the public at large, and often the conservative statements of knowledgeable researchers have been exaggerated in the press. Natural-language translators were first promised in the mid 1950s; rudimentary translators are just now becoming available.

To summarize, you should be aware of the existence of knowledge systems, and you should understand that they can potentially have great impact on business — particularly on MIS and DSS applications. You should also realize, however, that operationally useful capabilities are currently rare and that it may be some years before truly practical applications are developed.

▓ SUMMARY

Two basic types of business computer systems are transaction processing systems (TPS) and management information systems (MIS). Transaction processing systems support both the operation and management of an organization; management information systems support the management of an organization. Decision-support systems (DSS) are a subset of management information systems.

MIS arose from the operational processing of the early 1960s. Early MIS applications were unsuccessful because the technology for integrating large volumes of data had not yet been developed. This shortcoming led to the development of database processing technology. This technology, in turn, enabled the development of effective MISs in the 1970s.

The function of management is to plan, organize, and control. Managers allocate resources to ensure goals are accomplished within budgets. Information needs for managers vary by functional area, by level of manager, and by the degree of structure in the underlying problem. Most business activity can be represented by a four-stage process: Action, appraisal, specification, and decision. Information needs vary with the stage of this process and MISs are able to support management at each stage.

Management depends on operations, so TPSs, which benefit operations, also benefit management. A transaction is a representation of a business event. Transactions are processed by accessing and updating a company's data and by generating outputs for the business world.

An MIS provides past, present, and projected information about a company and its environment. An MIS reads the organizational data generated by a TPS; it accesses external data as well. An MIS produces both regular and recurring reports and exception reports. Another category of MIS application is DSS.

Decision-support systems are interactive computer-based systems that help decision makers use data and models to solve unstructured problems. DSSs are business computer systems and have the five general components: hardware, programs, data, procedures, and people.

QUESTIONS

11.16 Explain why transaction processing systems benefit managers.

11.17 Describe four characteristics of transaction processing systems.

11.18 Describe four characteristics of management information systems.

11.19 Describe two ways that information can be consolidated.

11.20 What is the cost of information consolidation? How can the designer of an MIS minimize this cost?

11.21 Name and describe business information needs at each stage of the business activity cycle.

11.22 Define *decision-support system*.

11.23 Describe the components of a DSS.

11.24 Name four types of programs needed in a DSS.

11.25 Summarize one of the DSS case applications described in this chapter.

11.26 How do knowledge systems differ from other computer systems in their approach to problem solving?

11.27 Define the term "inferencing".

11.28 Why are there no commercially useful knowledge systems today?

Knowledge systems are only in their infancy now, but one day they will enable people to participate in a dialog with a computer system in order to solve unstructured problems. That dialog might even be done in English rather than a special computer language. Increasing capacities of microcomputers as well as new technology in human and artificial intelligence will one day give rise to knowledgeable and easy-to-use decision support systems.

WORD LIST

Management information
   system (MIS)
Decision support system (DSS)
Operations
Management
Transaction processing system
   (TPS)
Database processing
Outputs
Inputs
Planning
Organizing
Controlling
Strategic planning
Tactical problem solving

Operational problem solving
Business activity cycle
Action
Appraisal
Specification
Decision
Transaction
Company data
Regular and recurring reports
Exception reports
Aggregation
Generalization
Database management system
   (DBMS)
Financial modeling

Query
Report writing
Graphics
Information analyst
Information center
Information assistant
Download
Artificial intelligence
Natural language
Knowledge systems
Expert systems
Inferencing
Knowledge representations
Knowledge system shell

QUESTIONS TO CHALLENGE YOUR THINKING

A. Interview a business manager. Find out how he or she uses computer technology to facilitate his or her productivity. How have computer systems helped? How have they hurt?

B. Survey the microcomputer industry trade publications for articles about decision support. How do they agree with this chapter? How do they disagree? Do the packages that are offered as "decision support" software conform to the definition of DSS in this chapter? If not, explain why you think this discrepancy exists.

C. Survey computer publications for articles on knowledge systems and expert systems. What technological problems are yet to be overcome? Where is most of the research in this field taking place? What do you think will be the impact of knowledge systems on business?

SPECIAL COMPUTING TOPICS

PART FOUR

In this part we present five optional modules on topics that may be of interest to you. These modules are independent; they can be read in any order. However, you should complete chapters 1, 2, and 3 before studying these optional topics.

MODULE A
HISTORY OF DATA PROCESSING

MODULE B
PERSONAL COMPUTER APPLICATIONS

MODULE C
NUMERIC REPRESENTATION AND COMPUTER ARITHMETIC

MODULE D
COMPUTER CRIME, SECURITY, AND CONTROL

MODULE E
SYSTEM PROGRAMS, OPERATING SYSTEMS, AND PROGRAMMING LANGUAGES

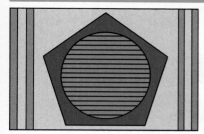

BUSINESS COMPUTER GRAPHICS

Persuasive Power at Your Fingertips

A picture is worth a thousand words, but why? Some experts believe that there are fundamental differences between the way the human brain processes words and the way it processes pictures. Words are processed one at a time. Visual images, on the other hand, seem to be processes in parallel. Many separate brain circuits processed different parts of the visual image simultaneously. Consequently, humans are able to assimilate more data graphically than they can reading words or tables of data.

"Not only can graphics applications save corporate time and money, but they are also another step toward converting data processing into a strategic and competitive weapon."

Alan Paller, AUI Data Graphics

▥ WHY GRAPHICS?

Every picture tells a story, but some pictures tell it better than others. Hence, the art of computer graphics — the professional polish of sharp, lively images that allow your audience to focus on the important aspects of your presentation.

Computer Graphics has quickly become one of the fastest growing fields in the computer applications industry. Why? Several reasons, among them lower hardware and software costs and advances in computer graphics technology.

Another significant reason for the growing demand for and popularity of graphics is that people today are more visually oriented than in the past. Not only are they attracted to colorful graphics; they expect them.

Graphics: Yet another computer application that can offer companies improved sales effectiveness and satisfied customers.

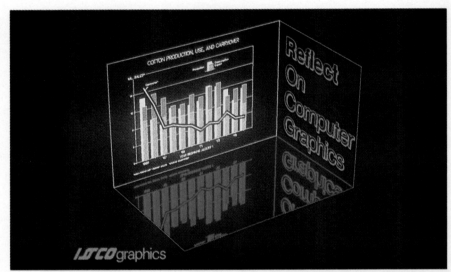

Business graphics would be worthless if they did not satisfy a need. Obviously they do.

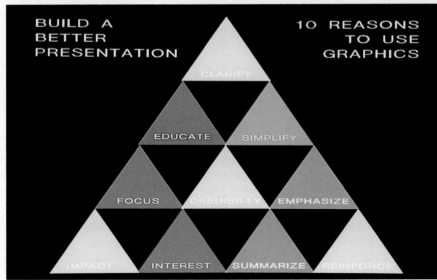

▥ GRAPHICS: A TREND

Research done by a magazine, Personal Computing, found that almost half of their subscribers already use a microcomputer for presentation graphics. Within the next year, an additional 36% plan to begin using microcomputer graphics.

The amount of dollars spent on computer graphics over the past few years reflects this trend.

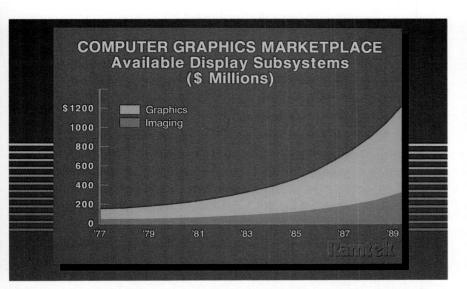

The business graphics marketplace is booming. Graphics hardware and software are becoming more and more sophisticated, providing more options as to how you display information.

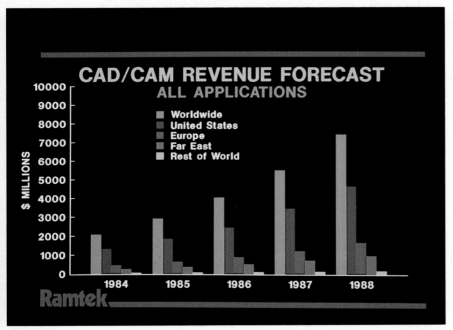

While computer-aided design/-computer-aided manufacturing (CAD/CAM) still represents the largest segment of the computer graphics industry, the emergence of business graphics has helped to move the technology into the commercial sphere.

▥ HARDWARE: WHAT'S REQUIRED FOR YOUR MICROCOMPUTER?

The capacity to generate and display graphics is a prerequisite for using presentation software.

Once you have a microcomputer, the minimum hardware includes:

- Monitor (color is best)
- Enough RAM for the program and any special data storage
- Input devices, such as the keyboard or joystick
- Printers, from dot matrix to color plotter
- On-line storage devices
- A graphics board or addition, depending on the microcomputer

Several sources of presentation hardware.

HARDWARE

Color Digital Imager Bell and Howell, 411 Amapola Ave., Torrance, CA 90501; (213) 320–5700

Datacom 35 Photographic Sciences Corp., PO Box 338, Webster, NY 14580; (716) 265–1600

HI PC Pens Plotters Houston Instrument, 8500 Cameron Road, Austin, TX 78753; (800) 531–5205

HP Graphics Plotters, LaserJet Hewlett-Packard Corp., 16399 W. Bernardo Drive, San Diego, CA 92127; (800) 367–4772

IBM Color Printer, Color Jetprinter IBM Corp., PO Box 1328, 1000 N.W. 51 St., Boca Raton, FL 33432; (800) 447–4700

Matrix PCR Matrix Instruments, Inc., 1 Ramland Road, Orangeburg, NY 10962; (914) 365–0190

Polaroid Palette Polaroid Corp., 575 Technology Square, Cambridge, MA 02139; (800) 225–1618

VideoShow General Parametrics Corp., 1250 Ninth St., Berkeley, CA 94710; (800) 556–1234

Videoscope, Multiscan projectors Sony Corp. of America, Sony Drive, Park Ridge, NJ 07656; (201) 930–6432

More and more for less and less. That trend applies to graphics software as well as graphics hardware.

▥ SOFTWARE: WHAT'S MOST IMPORTANT?

Once you've had experience developing and using business graphics, you'll become a more critical user. You'll become especially sensitive to the capabilities of graphics software to make your presentations more effective.

Several sources of presentation software.

SOFTWARE

Chart-Master, Sign-Master, Map-Master   Decision Resources, Inc., 25 Sylvan Road South, Westport, CT 06880; (203) 222-1974

ExecuVision, Concorde   Visual Communications Network, Inc., 238 Main St., Cambridge, MA 02142; (617) 497–4000

GEM Graph, WordChart   Digital Research, Inc., 60 Garden Court, PO Box DRI, Monterey, CA 93942; (800) 443–4200

Graphwriter, Freelance   Graphic Communications, Inc., 200 Fifth Ave., Waltham, MA 02254; (617) 890–8778

Harvard Presentation Graphics, PFS:Graph   Software Publishing Corp., 1901 Landings Drive, Mountain View, CA 94043; (415) 962–8910

Inset   American Programmers Guild, Ltd., 12 Mill Plain Road, Danbury, CT 06811; (203) 794–0396

Microsoft Chart   Microsoft Corp., 16011 N.E. 36th Way, Box 97017, Redmond WA 98073; (206) 882–8088

PC Storyboard   IBM Corp., PO Box 1328 1000, N.W. 51 St., Boca Raton, FL 33432; (800) 447–4700

Show Partner   Brightbill-Roberts & Co., 120 E. Washington St., Suite 421, Syracuse, NY 13202; (315) 474–3400

Quality and easy of use rank as the most important graphics software attributes, according to users.

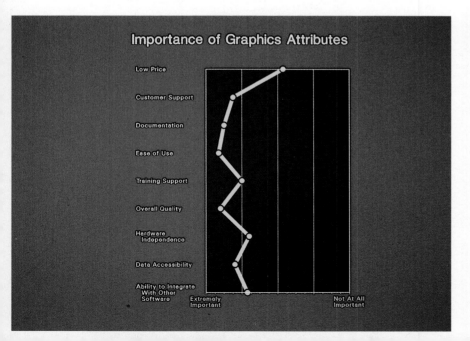

Importance of Graphics Attributes

Low Price
Customer Support
Documentation
Ease of Use
Training Support
Overall Quality
Hardware Independence
Data Accessibility
Ability to Integrate With Other Software

Extremely Important — Not At All Important

▦ RUNNING THE SOFTWARE: THE EASY PART

With the appropriate software and hardware, your microcomputer will let you prepare a professional-looking presentation — from start to finish — in one sitting.

No longer does this user have to create an image in his head.

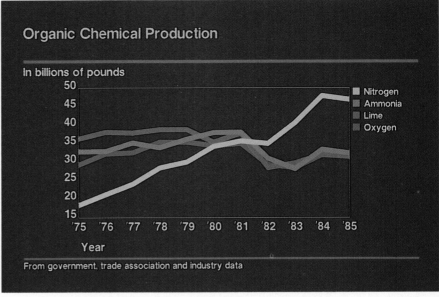

Adding color helps get the point across more effectively than black and white.

This experienced user of business computer graphics says that the process of developing graphics forces him to present his information more succinctly.

Artistic talent isn't a necessary prerequisite, either. Let's say you want to create a graph in Lotus 1-2-3. Basically, these are the steps you would follow:

1. Title your graph and the categories of your data or information
2. Enter your data or information
3. Select the kind of graph you want the program to create
4. Name the data range to be shown on the graph
5. Decide how to use the X and Y axes
6. Choose your colors (if you have a color monitor)....

And poof! The computer does the drawing for you. Often it's that simple.

This user doesn't have a printer. She prefers to photograph her graphics while they are displayed on the screen. She uses the resulting prints and slides in visual presentations.

Some spreadsheet programs, such as Lotus, include graphing programs. This integrated feature makes it easy for this user to take information or data directly from his electronic spreadsheet and put it into a graph.

Even though graphs do not supply all the details of the raw data, they make it easier for this user to recognize trends and conditions.

▓ APPLYING COLOR FOR IMPACT: HELPFUL HINTS

Andrew Corn, Admaster, Inc., a design and production agency, suggests the following elements of design in creating a presentation:

- Maintain good contrast such as dark text and brightly colored graphics set against a light background.
- Choose appropriate colors — yellow, blue, and green are usually good choices.
- Fill charts with bright, solid colors. They're pleasing to the eye and easy to distinguish.
- Spare the colors, don't spoil the picture. More than five colors in one graphic will overshadow the message.
- Accentuate with color — bright color to emphasize, darker or lighter colors to anchor the remaining pieces.
- Adapt color to your environment. Factors like lighting and audience size should influence your use of color.

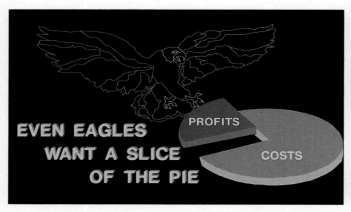

Company logos can be displayed on the screen to help viewers associate a company name with its products.

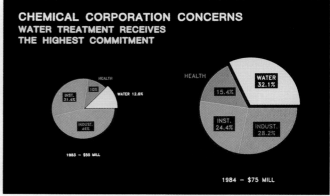

The pie chart is popular and widely used for simple business applications.

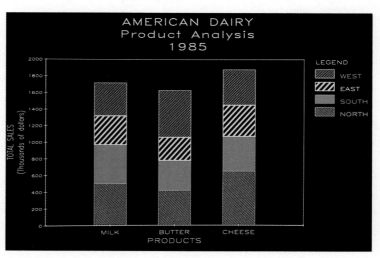

Bar charts are commonly used to illustrate business data.

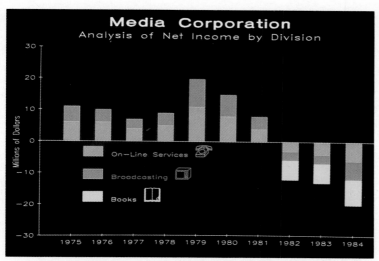

Bar charts may be stacked one on top of the other to summarize the income of several divisions.

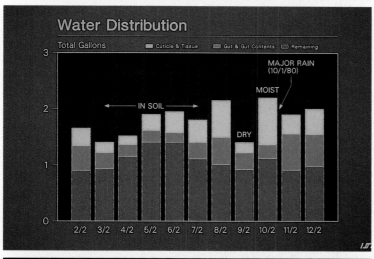

This bar chart illustrates the impact of contrast; that is, the use of light text and of brightly colored graphics set against a dark background.

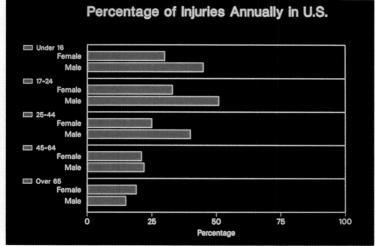

Bar charts can be drawn horizontally or vertically. The selection of this format is useful for a change of pace to get, or retain, the viewer's attention.

▥ KNOWING WHAT YOU WANT TO SAY: THE CHALLENGE

But slick isn't everything. Once you've learned how, putting your chosen medium to work for you is the easy part.

What makes some graphs effective, valuable, and memorable when so many are unnecessary or misleading? What is your challenge?

Line graphs are excellent for displaying financial and daily, weekly, monthly, quarterly, and yearly data. It is also possible to plot more than a single relationship on the same chart for purposes of comparison.

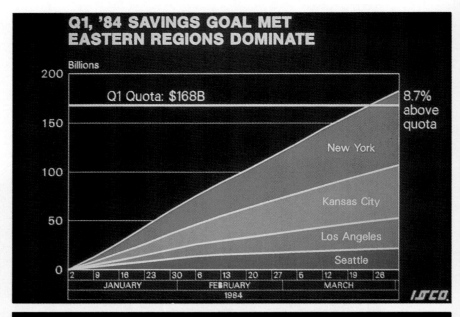

Three-dimensional graphics are far less common than bar graphs or pie charts. Most users aren't willing to spend more for the required hardware and software. But for some users the benefits outweigh the costs.

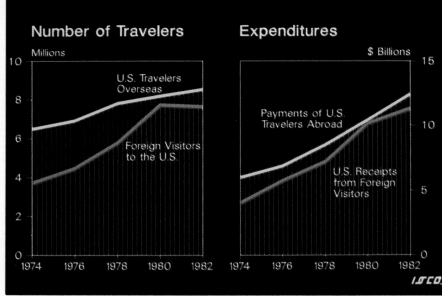

Filling in spaces with color can dramatize and add meaning to the presentation of data.

Above all, it's how well you know your audience and the information you want to communicate.

Computers can generate vast quantities of data, but more data is not necessarily better for your reader. Concepts can confuse and numbers can numb without the instant translation that pictures can relate.

Again, the art of computer graphics is to focus the viewer's attention, to communicate, to persuade.

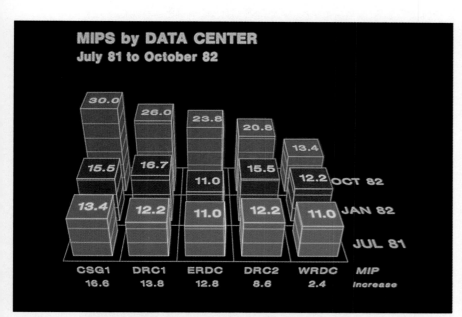

This three-dimensional graphic provides an interesting presentation of a bar chart.

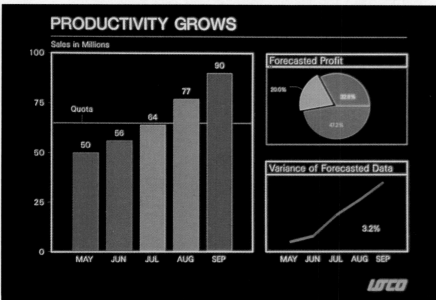

Pie, line, and bar charts may be designed to illustrate the same information. However, bar charts can incorporate the widest range of variables through the use of colors and different shadings.

Using different types of charts in one presentation gives the viewer several perspectives from which to analyze the data.

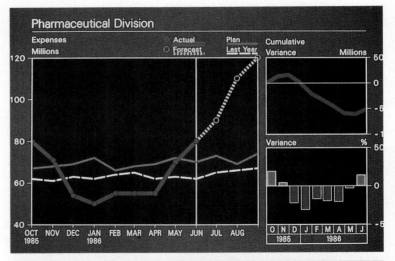

Bar and line charts can be combined to give both the big picture and the detailed picture simultaneously.

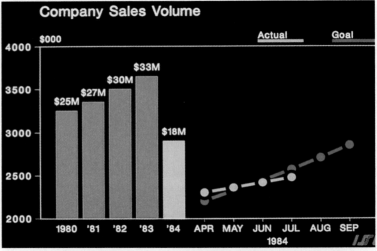

This combination of charts gives managers immediate access to key performance indicators, allowing them to reinforce outstanding performance quickly and to anticipate weak performance before it becomes critical.

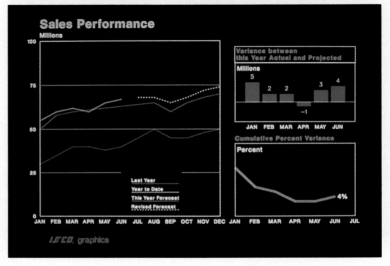

▦ HOW TO BE PERSUASIVE

Microcomputer graphics are a tool for the professional to use in accomplishing business objectives. Common objectives of business graphics are:

- To evaluate past relationships between variables
- To project expected relationships for decision-making
- To monitor ongoing business operations
- To find and demonstrate trends and deviations
- To communicate information to a targeted individual or group
- To sell your ideas — and yourself!

First, what point do you want to make? Answering this question will be your biggest challenge. To do so, you must first gain an understanding of the essential ingredients of a persuasive presentation: your audience and the information you want to communicate.

Once you've answered this question, then and only then are you ready to select the data and graph type that will best illustrate your point.

Graphics is likely to be the key communication aid of the next decade.

A recent study from the Wharton School of Business demonstrated that those who used graphics in their presentation enjoyed shorter meetings, and that they also achieved consensus quicker than those who did not use graphics.

Commercial art and photography shops offer you an alternative to enlarging an image yourself.

⦀ TYPICAL BUSINESS APPLICATIONS

The number of applications of computer systems continues to grow.

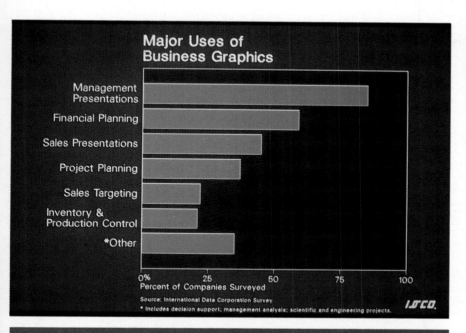

Uses of business computer graphics are not only increasing but spreading into all areas of business. Still, graphics are used primarily for management presentations and summaries.

3M is just one of the many companies that now prepares and delivers "on-call" graphics.

3M has an alternative for users who would rather not, or who can't afford to, purchase a computer system and develop their own graphics: graphics by phone—24 hours a day, seven days a week.

Here's how it works:

1. Choose a format from the more than 100 displayed in their format guide

2. Relay your choice to 3M with a keyboard of any microcomputer that has telephone communication capability

3. Within two days your 35mm slide, overhead transparency, or full color print will arrive.

▥ WHAT'S AHEAD?

In the midst of the changes, the measure of an effective business graphic remains constant. The important consideration is whether or not actions will result from the graphic, whether decisions will be made on the basis of it.

Computer graphics stands at a crossroads: It can either be supported as a personal tool for presentations or as a strategic resource for decision-making. Many successful organizations have discovered that their strongest approach combines and supports both these aspects of computer graphics.

QUESTIONS

1. What are two of the many reasons the use of computer graphics is increasing in the business world?

2. What are the minimum hardware requirements for a microcomputer graphics system?

3. Name three attributes of microcomputer graphics considered important by users.

4. Identify three guidelines to be considered in the use of color graphics.

5. Describe three business objectives that can profit from the use of business computer graphics.

6. What are three important considerations in creating presentation graphics?

7. What is the greatest challenge in creating effective computer graphics?

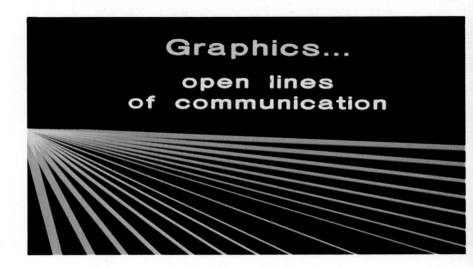

HISTORY OF DATA PROCESSING

MODULE A

The history of computing began thousands of years ago when people first started to count on their fingers. In fact, fingers and toes were probably (who knows for sure?) the earliest computational devices. As business and commerce developed, however, a need arose for a calculator with a capacity greater than 20.

The **abacus** shown in figure A–1 is an early form of such a calculator. Different versions of it were used for centuries by people of many nations and areas of the world. The abacus was used even before numbers were represented in writing. Other computational devices were constructed throughout the centuries. The numerical wheel calculator (figure A–2) was the predecessor of the adding machines and manual calculators that commonly were used before the electronic calculator. The slide rule (figure A–3) was another type of computational device.

CHARLES BABBAGE AND HIS MACHINES

As far as we know, **Charles Babbage** is the father of computing. This amazing man was far ahead of his time. He developed the essential ideas for a computer over 100 years before the first computer was constructed. He was so advanced that practically none of his contemporaries appreciated him. In addition to computing, Babbage made contributions to mathematics, optics, underwater navigation, railroads, industrial engineering, mechanics, and other fields.

Many of the mistakes that Babbage made continue to be made today, and so it is worth considering his life's activities in some detail.

FIGURE A–1
Abacus

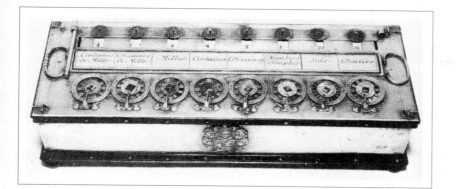

Babbage's Life

Babbage was born in England in 1792 (George Washington was still
alive). His father was a wealthy banker who left him a sizable fortune.
Babbage says he suffered from high fevers, and so he was sent to a
private tutor "with instructions to attend to my health; but, not to

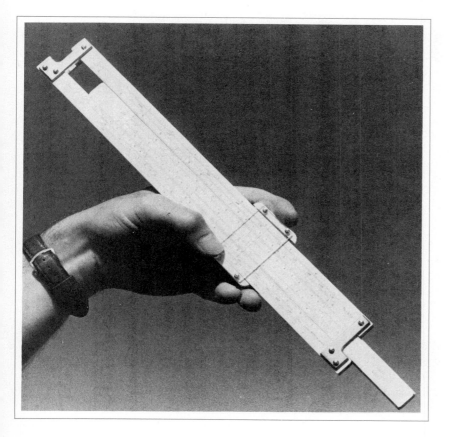

FIGURE A—3
Slide rule

press too much knowledge upon me: a mission which he faithfully accomplished" [88, p. 11]. Babbage relates, "My invariable question on receiving any new toy was, 'Mamma, what is inside of it?'" Apparently, if she couldn't answer, he tore it apart.

Sometime prior to 1822, Babbage and his friend John Herschel were checking data calculated for the Astronomical Society. In frustration, Babbage remarked to Herschel, "I wish to God these calculations had been executed by steam." (Steam engines were common.) In 1822, Babbage proposed the design of a **difference engine** composed of gears and wheels (see figure A–4). This engine would automatically compute functions of the form

$$y = a + ax + ax^2 + \ldots + ax^n$$

In 1823 the British government granted Babbage money to build the engine. The first government-sponsored computer project was on. Like

FIGURE A–4
Babbage's difference engine

most of those to follow, the project fell behind. By 1833 the government had invested 17,000 pounds ($85,000 at the 1823 rate of exchange), and only part of the difference engine was completed. Meanwhile, Babbage's active mind had been extending the possibilities of automated computing. By 1834 he had developed the idea of an **analytical engine**. The analytical engine would compute *any* mathematical function. It embodied most of the concepts that early computers did.

In 1834 Babbage asked the government whether it wanted him to finish the difference engine or start on the analytical engine. After eight years of frustrating correspondence, Prime Minister Robert Peel told Babbage that the government was going to abandon the project. This case may have established a record for governmental delay.

The analytical engine had a main memory that Babbage called the *store*. It was to have room for 1000 variables of 50 digits each. It had an arithmetic and logic unit that he called the *mill*. Programs for the mill were written on punched cards. The engine would drive a typesetter. It had logical capability and could ring a bell or take other action when a variable passed zero or exceeded the capacity of one of the words. All of these operations were to have been implemented mechanically.

People had a hard time understanding the concept. Mathematicians asked Babbage how the engine would use logarithms. He told them that it wouldn't need logarithms because it could compute any function. Some people didn't believe this claim, so he showed them how it could be programmed to ask an attendant to supply a logarithm from a library of cards. Furthermore, it would check for the correct logarithm. The procedure he described in 1864 is exactly the same as the procedure used today to check tape labels (see chapter 7).

Ironically, Babbage got more attention from outside England than from within. He had two automated devices in his home: a clockwork woman who danced and a part of the difference engine. He reported that his English friends would gather about the dancing lady, whereas an American and a Hollander studied the difference engine. In fact, a Swedish printer, George Scheutz, built the only complete version of the difference engine (except for one made recently by IBM). Babbage was delighted and helped Scheutz explain it.

We know about the analytical engine largely from a paper written by an Italian, L. F. Menabrea. This paper was written in French and translated into English by **Ada Augusta, the Countess of Lovelace**. There is interesting social commentary here.

Ada Augusta was the only legitimate daughter of the poet Lord Byron. She was an excellent mathematician and understood Babbage's concepts perhaps better than anyone. In 1842, when she translated Menabrea's paper of 20 pages, she added 50 pages of "notes." Babbage wanted to know why she didn't write a paper of her own. "I never thought of it," she replied. In fact, she didn't sign her translation or her notes, but used the initials *A. A. L.* instead. Apparently, ladies didn't do such things.

However, ladies could go to the race track. The Countess loved racing, and it may have been inevitable that she would use the difference engine to determine horse bets. Apparently, it didn't work too well. She lost the family jewels at the track. Her mother, Lady Byron, had to buy them back.

The Countess died of cancer at the age of 36, just 10 years after reading Menabrea's description. Her death was a big loss to Babbage and perhaps to the world. The programming language ADA is named after Ada Augusta Lovelace.

Babbage was a fascinating person. Charles Darwin reported lively dinner parties at Babbage's home. Another person complained of barely being able to escape from him at 2:00 in the morning. Babbage once said that he would be glad to give up the rest of his life if he could live for three days 500 hundred years in the future.

Lessons We Can Learn from Babbage

Many of the errors Babbage made have been repeated again and again in the computer industry. For one, Babbage began with vague requirements. "Let's compute numbers by steam" sounds all too much like "Let's use a computer to do billing." Much more precise statements of requirements are necessary.

Second, it appears that Babbage started implementing his plans before his design was complete. Much work had to be redone. His engineers and draftsmen often complained that they would finish a project only to be told the work was wrong or not needed because the design had been changed. The same complaint has been made by countless programmmers since then. Another mistake Babbage made was to add more and more capability to his engines before any of them was complete. As his work progressed, he saw new possibilities, and he tried to incorporate them into his existing projects. Many data processing systems have remained uncompleted for the very same reason.

Work on the difference engine was set back considerably by a crisis over the salary of Babbage's chief engineer, Joseph Clement. Clement quit, and Babbage had little documentation to recover the loss. Further, Clement had the rights to all the tools. Who knows how many systems projects have failed because indispensable programmers quit in the middle? Working documentation is crucial for successful system implementation.

Even Lady Lovelace's losses at the track have a lesson. Systems ought not to be used for purposes for which they weren't designed. The computer industry has experienced much inefficiency because systems are applied to problems for which they weren't designed.

There was no electronics industry to support Babbage's ideas. All of the concepts had to be implemented in mechanical components, and

BABBAGE'S MISTAKES

Vague problem definition and requirements
Implementation started before design was complete
Requirements added during implementation
Working documentation not complete
Dependency on one person
System used for unintended purposes
Grandiose plans that exceeded existing technology

FIGURE A–5
Mistakes Babbage made that are still made today

the tolerances were so fine that they could not be manufactured within the limitations of nineteenth-century technology. Furthermore, Babbage's plans were grandiose. Building a computer with a 1000 50-decimal-digit numbers was a large task. He might have been more successful if he had completed a smaller computer first and then built credibility with his government and solidified his funding before starting on a larger one. Many government-sponsored projects fail today because of a lack of technology to support grandiose plans. The lessons we can learn from Babbage are summarized in figure A–5.

We do not know what impact, if any, Babbage's work had on future development. One pioneer, Howard Aiken (discussed later in this chapter), reported that he worked for three years before discovering Babbage's contributions. We do not know about the others.

HERMAN HOLLERITH

In the late nineteenth century, the U.S. Census Bureau had a problem. The bureau was supposed to produce a census of the U.S. population every 10 years. However, the 1880 census took seven and a half years to finish. By the time the census data was processed, much of it was no longer useful. Furthermore, at the rate that the population was growing, the Census Bureau was afraid that the 1890 census would not be finished before the 1900 census was due to begin.

In 1879, the bureau hired **Herman Hollerith** to help them. He worked for the Census Bureau for five years and then started his own company. Hollerith designed and managed the construction of several punched-card processing machines (see figure A – 6).

In 1889, the bureau held a contest among Hollerith and two competitors to determine whose system was the fastest. Hollerith's system required only one-tenth of the time needed by his nearest competitor. Using this equipment, the first count of the 1890 census took only six weeks! However, the final, official count was not announced until December 1890.

Hollerith's equipment was an extension of the work of the Frenchman Joseph Marie Jacquard. Jacquard designed looms in which punched cards controlled the pattern on woven material. In Jacquard's looms,

FIGURE A – 6
Hollerith's punched-card machines

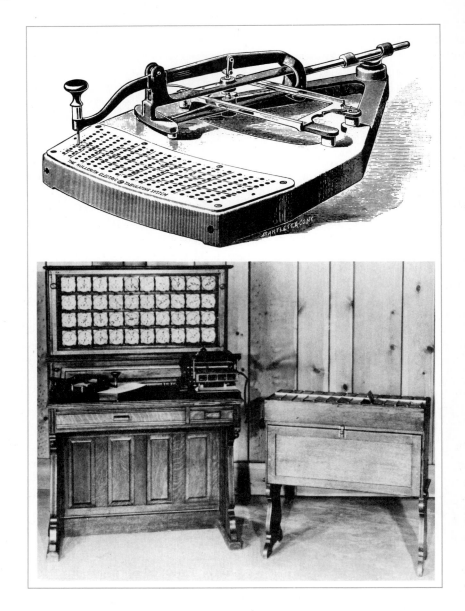

FIGURE A – 6
Hollerith's punched-card machines

needles fell through holes in the cards. The needles lifted threads so as to produce a pattern. This technique had been used in the weaving industry since 1804.

Hollerith extended this concept by using the cards to control electric circuits. Data was punched on three-by-five-inch cards and fed into a machine that moved the cards over a group of pins. If there was a hole in a card, the pin would fall through the hole and touch a pan of mercury. This contact closed a circuit and registered on a meter. Apparently, the machine worked so well that the humans became exhausted. There is a story that occasionally someone would pour all of the mercury into a nearby spittoon. The machine would stop, and everyone could rest.

Hollerith decided he had a marketable idea. He sold his equipment to railroads and other large companies that had computational problems. This step represented the start of the punched-card industry. Hollerith built up his business and then sold it to the company that later was to become IBM (International Business Machines). Hollerith didn't know it, but he was setting the pace for many entrepreneurs to come. Hundreds of computer people have done the same thing he did. They have taken a good idea, developed it, formed an attractive company, sold it, and enjoyed many trips to the bank. Perhaps you can do the same.

The punched-card industry was the beginning of automated data processing. The earliest business computer systems were developed around punched-card technology. Companies found that to use this new technology successfully, they needed to build systems composed of hardware, programs, data, procedures, and trained personnel.

Programs? Well, sort of. As the punched-card equipment became more sophisticated, it became possible to change the wiring of the equipment to make it do different things. People who changed the wiring were doing an elementary form of programming. Programming as we know it today did not exist until stored-program computers were developed in the middle of the twentieth century. However, the concepts used in business computer systems started evolving with the 1890 census. The idea of developing systematic procedures to direct machines to turn data into information was born in that year.

▥ EARLY COMPUTERS

In 1937, **Howard G. Aiken** proposed the use of electromechanical devices to perform calculations. He was a professor of applied mathematics at Harvard at the time, and the IBM Corporation gave him a grant to pursue his ideas. IBM was active in the punched-card industry.

In 1944, Aiken and IBM completed an electromechanical calculator called the **Mark I**. This computer had mechanical counters that were manipulated by electrical devices. The Mark I could perform basic arithmetic, and it could be changed to solve different problems (see figure A–7).

At about the same time, the U.S. government signed a contract with the University of Pennsylvania to develop a computer that would aid the military effort during World War II. As a result of this contract, **John W. Mauchly** and **J. Presper Eckert** developed the first all-electronic computer, called the Electronic Numerical Integrator and

FIGURE A–7
Mark I computer

Calculator, or **ENIAC**. Unlike the Mark I, ENIAC had no mechanical counters; everything was electronic.

Although Mauchly and Eckert are often given credit for developing the first electronic computer, this apparently is not completely true. Their work was based in part on work that had been done by **John V. Atanasoff**. Atanasoff was a professor at Iowa State University, and in 1939 he had developed many ideas for an all-electronic computer. In 1942, he and a graduate student, Clifford Berry, completed an electronic computer that could solve systems of linear equations.

ENIAC (the Mauchly/Eckert machine) was used to perform many different calculations. It had 19,000 vacuum tubes, 70,000 resistors, and 500,000 soldered joints (see figure A–8). The ENIAC could perform 5000 additions per second. It used 150,000 watt-hours of power a day—so much that, when it was turned on, the lights in one section of Philadelphia dimmed. Unfortunately, it was inflexible. Changing its program meant rewiring the machine and thus required considerable time and resources. Since it could be changed, it was programmable; however, it was not programmable in the sense that we understand the term today.

In the mid 1940s the mathematician **John von Neumann** joined the Mauchly/Eckert team. Von Neumann proposed a design for a computer that stored programs in its memory. He also developed other concepts that were to become the foundation for computer design for thirty years. Two computers evolved from this work: the **EDVAC** (Electrical Discrete Variable Automatic Computer) and the **EDSAC** (Electronic Delay Storage Automatic Calculator). Both machines stored programs. EDSAC was completed in England in 1949 and EDVAC in the United States in 1950.

At the time, the potential of these machines was not understood. Atanasoff couldn't get support from Iowa State. The administration thought that there would be a need for only three or four of these devices throughout the United States. Furthermore, in the late 1940s none of the ENIAC-EDVAC staff was promoted to full professor at the Moore School of Engineering. People didn't seem to feel the work was going to be very important.

Another social commentary: The first programmers for the Mark I and the ENIAC were women. U. S. Navy Rear Admiral **Grace Hopper** programmed the Mark I, and **Adele Goldstine** programmed the ENIAC. Both of these women were talented mathematicians. Their presence undoubtedly helped to establish women's strong position in the computer industry.

John Mauchly and Presper Eckert decided to follow in Hollerith's entrepreneurial footsteps, and in 1946 they formed the Eckert-Mauchly Corporation. This ripe young company was purchased by the Remington-Rand Corporation. Their first product was **UNIVAC I** (Universal Automatic Computer). It was the first computer built to sell. The Census Bureau took delivery of the first one in 1951, and it was used continuously until 1963. It now resides in the Smithsonian Institution (see figure A–9). Sperry Rand still manufactures a line of computers under the name *UNIVAC*, although these computers are a far cry from the UNIVAC I.

Meanwhile, other companies were not idle. IBM continued development on the Mark I computer and eventually developed the Mark II through Mark IV, as well as other early computers. Burroughs, Gen-

FIGURE A–8
The ENIAC, a first-generation computer

FIGURE A–9
UNIVAC I

eral Electric, Honeywell, and RCA also were busy with computer developments.

IBM took an early lead in the application of the new computer technology to business problems. The company developed a series of business-oriented computers and sold them to their punched-card customers. Because IBM had a virtual monopoly on punched cards (which they had been unsuccessfully sued for by the U.S. government in the 1930s), they were in a strong position to capitalize on the new technology.

Furthermore, IBM had an extremely effective marketing philosophy. They emphasized solving business problems. They developed products that were useful to businesses, and they showed business people how to use those products. IBM provided excellent customer service and good maintenance.

This philosophy paid off. Some other companies had better computers, but their computers weren't packaged to provide total solutions to business problems. IBM was the first company to understand that wise business people don't buy the best *computer*; they buy the best *solution* to their problem. Today, many vendors have adopted this philosophy. They sell solutions to business problems, not just computers. However, the fact that IBM understood this first has much to do with the company's strength in the computer market today.

The computers manufactured in the 1950s are often called **first-generation computers**. Their major components were **vacuum tubes**. Most of them used magnetic drums as their primary storage devices. Main memory as discussed in this book did not exist at that time.

Because of the number and size of the vacuum tubes, these computers were huge. Furthermore, they generated tremendous amounts of heat, were expensive to run, and experienced frequent failures. A large first-generation computer occupied a room the size of a football field. It contained row upon row of racks of tubes. A staff of a half-dozen people was required just to change the tubes that burned out.

COMPUTERS IN THE 1960s AND 1970s

In the late 1950s and early 1960s, vacuum tubes were replaced by **transistors**. This development led to **second-generation computers**. These computers were much smaller than vacuum-tube computers, and they were more powerful. A new type of main storage was developed. It was called **core memory** because it used magnetized, doughnut-shaped cores. The term *core* is still used today. Some people use core synonymously with *main memory*, but this usage is incorrect, because most main memories today do not contain magnetic core.

The first high-level programming languages were developed during this stage. First-generation computers were programmed in **machine code**, but second-generation computers were programmed in **assembly language** and English-like **high-level languages**, such as FORTRAN and ALGOL (see module E). Further, primitive operating systems were installed on second-generation machines. Operating system programs controlled the use of the computer's resources.

Most second-generation computers could run only one program at a time. Therefore, to speed things up, certain input and output operations were done **offline**. For example, punched cards were read and their contents copied to tape without the computer's involvement. Then the tape was read into the computer and processed, and the generated output was written to tape. The tape was then dismounted and printed on a separate machine. This process was followed because tape units could read and write much faster than card readers or printers could operate. Figure A–10 shows the IBM 7094, a typical second-generation computer.

Most of the business computer systems at this stage were designed for accounting. The computer was used to produce checks for payroll and accounts payable and to keep track of inventories. General ledger was also computerized. However, processing was done in batches. Inputs were gathered into groups and processed, and outputs were produced. Applications such as order entry that required interaction could not be handled.

In the 1960s, the **third-generation computers** became available. In these computers, **integrated circuits** were used instead of transistors. An integrated circuit is a complete electrical circuit on a small chip of

FIGURE A–10
A second-generation computer: the IBM 7094

silicon (see figure A–11). Because of these chips, third-generation computers are smaller and more powerful than second-generation computers. Figure A–12 compares the sizes of vacuum tubes, transistors, and integrated circuits.

Vast improvements were also made in programming for third-generation computers. Sophisticated operating systems were developed. These systems allowed many programs to be executed concurrently. Slow input and output operations such as card reading or printing could be performed in the background: One job would be in processing while another was being read and the output of a third was being printed. The computers ran programs and every now and then took a little time to handle slow I/O operations. This arrangement eliminated the need for the offline processing typical of second-generation computers. Figure A–13 shows a typical third-generation computer.

Third-generation computers also supported interactive, **online processing**. Users could interact with the computer to perform functions like entering orders or making airline reservations online. Although some online processing had been done by earlier, military systems, these applications were very specialized and not economical. The third generation of computers allowed online processing to be a standard operation.

Minicomputers appeared in the mid 1960s. Initially, minis were small, special-purpose machines designed for military and space applications. Gradually, however, the capability of these machines has increased to the point that the more powerful minicomputers and the less powerful mainframes have overlapped. Figure A–14 shows a

Digital Equipment VAX minicomputer, a very powerful machine that exceeds the capability of many so-called mainframes. Thus, it now is hard to distinguish between the two categories of computers. (See chapter 3 for more discussion of this topic.)

THE FOURTH GENERATION

The fourth generation of computers is characterized by **very large-scale integration (VLSI)**. With VLSI, thousands of transistors and other components can be placed on a single quarter-inch silicon chip. In fact, an entire CPU can reside on a single chip. The computer that may have occupied a football field in 1952 today is less than half the size of a penny.

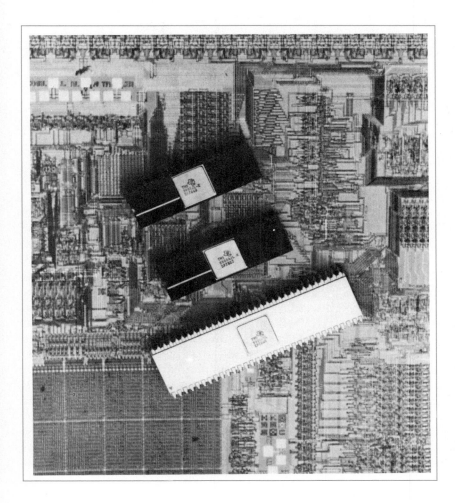

FIGURE A–11
Integrated circuit on a silicon chip

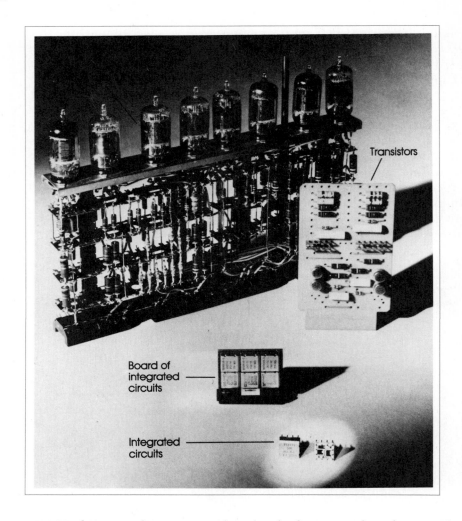

VLSI chips can be mass-produced, which means that they can be manufactured and sold in quantities of thousands. Because so many are sold, the costs of research, development, and tooling are spread over many items. Thus, VLSI chips are extremely cheap. A circuit that may have cost $50,000 10 years ago can now be purchased in quantity for $10 or less. Thus, VLSI technology has caused a tremendous decrease in the price: performance ratio of new computers.

A computer on a chip is called a **microprocessor**. When the chip is installed with electronics to perform input and output processing and other functions, it is called a **microcomputer**.

Microprocessors were not designed with forethought. They just happened. The companies that manufacture silicon chips found ways to put more and more circuitry on the chip. They were increasing the

FIGURE A–13
A third-generation computer:
the Honeywell 6000

circuitry to support other products. For example, the Intel 8008, a microprocessor, was originally intended to be the controller for a CRT terminal. For a variety of reasons, the chip was not used for this purpose.

Because Intel had developed the product, however, they put it in their catalog. To their surprise, apparently, it sold very well. The company saw the demand, put a design team together, and a year later introduced the Intel 8080 microprocessor, shown in figure A–15. This product has become one of the most popular microprocessors. Other manufacturers quickly followed suit. Today there are dozens of microprocessor products to choose from. While there was no such thing as a microprocessor in 1969, by 1975 750,000 microprocessors were in use and by 1984 that figure had exploded to 100,000,000.

All of this development means that computers have become cheaper and cheaper. Some experts believe that the cost of computer CPUs will soon be essentially zero. At least, the cost will be negligible compared to that of other components of a business computer system.

These inexpensive microprocessors may well lead to entirely new computer architectures. Since microprocessors are so cheap, it becomes feasible to develop and market **supercomputers**, or computers that are banks of many microprocessors. For example, a supercomputer could be a 100 × 100 array of microprocessors. It boggles the mind to consider the power of such a machine.

FIGURE A–14
The DEC VAX minicomputer

Computers in the 1980s

During the 1980s there have been some exciting developments both in the large mainframe environment and in the area of microcomputers. All of these developments have affected business in some way.

Off-the-Shelf Programs

The most significant cost of business computer systems is the cost of the development process itself. A lot of money and time must be invested to develop a new business computer system. One significant development in the 1980s is the acceptance of **off-the-shelf software**, even by large corporations. Recall from chapter 5 that three ways of acquiring programs are to write them yourself, to buy them off the shelf and use them as they are, and to buy packaged software and alter it to fit your needs. Until recently, many companies were distrustful of any software developed "NIH" ("not invented here"). As software development costs continue to rise, new development projects continue to be backlogged, and as high-quality software packages become available, more data processing managers are turning to off-the-shelf software to satisfy at least some user needs.

Prototyping

Another significant development in the area of system development is the concept of **prototyping**, discussed in chapter 5. Recall that a prototype is a skeletal system that users can work with very early during system development. This hands-on experience enables users to more accurately define their requirements and to reject unsatisfactory features of a system while it is easy and inexpensive for the developers to make changes.

Fourth-Generation Languages

A third improvement for developers of mainframe systems is **fourth-generation languages (4GLs)**. 4GLs are *non-procedural* languages (unlike COBOL, BASIC, Pascal, and hundreds of other languages). Some are easy enough for users to learn and use, though the more powerful 4GLs are too technical for use by an ordinary business person. In the hands of a skilled programmer, a 4GL can increase programming productivity by as much as 200 percent.

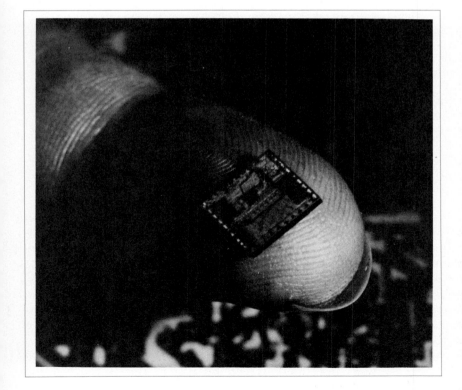

FIGURE A–15
The Intel 8080 microprocessor

APPLICATION

"THE ULTIMATE FACTORY TECHNOLOGY: COMPUTER-INTEGRATED MANUFACTURING."

The fully automated factory is finally emerging from the mists of theory and conjecture (see figure A−16). One of the toughest problems—getting disparate computers and machines to communicate with each other—is well on the way to being solved. That will make way for the ultimate factory technology: computer-integrated manufacturing. With CIM, the U. S. can "compete favorably with any offshore manufacturer," declares Patrick J. Zilvitis, president of Martin Marietta Data Systems.

The basic premise behind CIM is that by totally automating and linking all of the functions of the factory and the corporate headquarters, a manufacturer would be able to turn out essentially perfect, one-of-a-kind products—at the lowest possible cost and delivered almost overnight. With a computerized factory, greased liberally with expert systems and other forms of artificial intelligence, a company could:

1. Conceive new products on a computer-aided design (CAD) system that would allow designers to optimize their ideas.
2. Pass the CAD data electronically to a computer-aided engineering (CAE) system to verify that the design will do the job intended and can be made economically.
3. Extract from the CAE data the information needed to make the product. The information would be sent to a computer-aided manufacturing (CAM) system. The CAM system would send electronic instructions for making the product to computer-controlled machine tools, robotic assembly stations, and other automated equipment on the shop floor.
4. Coordinate with computerized management systems, such as manufacturing-resource planning, which keeps a running tab on the consumption of parts and materials, and manufacturing-process planning, which helps schedule production for op-

timum efficiency. In addition, the mainframe computer in the factory would continuously update the corporate data banks used by marketing, finance, purchasing, and other headquarters functions.

This facile factory will have a profound impact on how manufacturers do business. "No part of the entire company will be untouched by the change," says Thomas G. Gunn, director of the manufacturing consulting group at Arthur Young and former vice-president for CIM at Arthur D. Little Inc.

For starters, a CIM factory will be so flexible that it will be able to make the first copy of a product for little more than the cost of the thousandth. As a result, says Erich Bloch, who left International Business Machines Corp. in 1984 to become director of the National Science Foundation, "organizations optimized for economies of scale may become obsolete."

What impact will the use of fourth-generation languages have on software development? If the biggest deterrent to custom programming is the time and cost of developing programs (and maintaining them later), then will 4GLs eliminate that problem? Rather than settle for off-the-shelf programs that almost (but not quite) meet their needs, will users insist on custom programming? Will fourth-generation languages eventually be developed that *any* user, even an inexperienced one, can easily learn and implement? What impact will such a development have on the people currently in data processing? Of course, we do not have the answers to these questions. Only time will tell what systems development will be like in the 1990s. But the changes just described are probably indicative of what is to come.

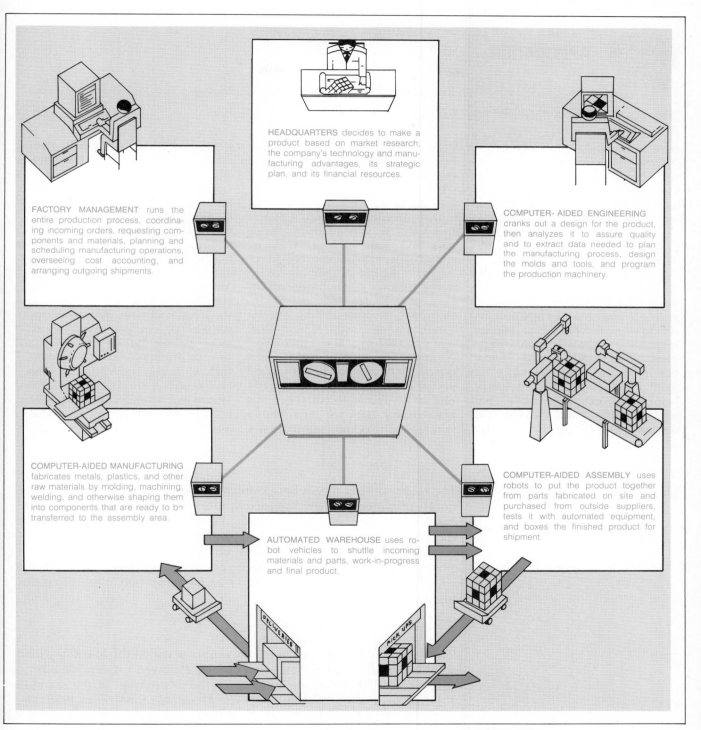

FIGURE A –16
The factory of the future

APPLICATION

"THE KEY TO SUCCESS IN THE MICROCOMPUTER SOFTWARE BUSINESS."

Innovative products are the key to success in the microcomputer software business, says Ed Esber, president and chief executive officer of Ashton-Tate. Like many large software houses, Ashton-Tate pursues innovation more through careful acquisition rather than internal product development.

Since it was founded in 1980, the Torrance, CA-based vendor has been mining the micro software landscape. It acquired its chief product, the dBase series of database management systems (DBMSs), from an independent developer who later joined the software house. Framework, Ashton-Tate's integrated database, word-processing, spreadsheet, and telecommunications package, was originally developed by Forefront

Corp. of Sunnyvale, CA. Last December, Ashton-Tate bought Multimate International Corp. of East Hartford, CT, and its line of word-processing software for $23 million.

With these three main product lines, plus a book-publishing business and some add-on products, Ashton-Tate has become the third-largest independent micro software house, behind Lotus Development Corp. (Cambridge, MA) and Microsoft Corp. (Redmond, WA). Ashton-Tate has grown from a $3.6 million outfit in 1982 to a $145 million corporation. For its most recent fiscal quarter, which ended in April, it reported a $5.1 million profit on $41 million in revenues. Although this performance lagged slightly behind that of the previous quarter, sales

were up 72 percent and profits more than doubled over the corresponding quarter a year ago.

Ashton-Tate's plans to branch into mini and mainframe software may hold ramifications for its micro software users. For example, Esber says he plans to start charging users a fee for "support, training, systems engineering help, and product updates." Although micro software vendors typically don't charge users extra for services, Esber notes that mainframe vendors do not give such services away. Ashton-Tate is also moving to cash in on several new markets, such as local-area networking. Last November, it announced dBase III Plus, which allows simultaneous file access by many multiple users over a LAN.

The Microcomputer Explosion

The most exciting recent developments have taken place in the area of microcomputers. When microcomputers first appeared during the early 1980s they were almost immediately snubbed as playthings for the computer hobbyist. But their sophistication, power, small size, portability, and software rapidly changed the minds of even the cynics. The 1980s have seen almost every type of business, large and small, embrace the microcomputer as an important piece of equipment.

A Brief History of Microcomputers

The first microcomputer was a kit computer called the Mark-8, which was designed by Ed Roberts in 1974. He followed the Mark-8 with a machine called the Altair, named for the destination of the starship Enterprise on a *Star Trek* episode. The Altair sold for $397 in 1975. The bank that had financed Roberts' company, MITS, hoped he could sell 200 computers. In April of 1976, MITS reported at a meeting of the

APPLICATION

"THE 32-BIT DASH."

The microprocessor market reached $700 million last year, and 32-bit chips accounted for 4 percent of it, according to researchers at Electronic Trend Publications. By 1990, the market is expected to grow to $2.9 billion, with 32-bit chips taking 23 percent.

It is simplest to think of a microprocessor as the brain of a computer. However, its functions are limited to quickly doing simple calculations and moving data from one location to another inside the computer.

The most recently developed microprocessors are dramatically faster than their predecessors—able to process 32 bits of information at a time instead of 16 or eight. This means that inexpensive desktop computers based on chips of silicon that fit comfortably on a fingertip can, for the first time, compete in processing power with multimillion-dollar mainframe computers that require specialists to operate.

Although there are dozens of microprocessors, most of today's popular desktop computers and workstations use chips designed by either Intel, based in Santa Clara, or Motorola, based in Schaumburg, Ill.

Intel, until last year, did not have a true 32-bit chip—first introduced by Motorola in 1981. As a result, Intel lagged in the performance race until it announced the 80386, which the company claims will run PC software as much as 17 times faster than the 8-bit chip in a standard desktop IBM PC. It also can simultaneously run the AT&T UNIX operating system widely used by engineers and scientists.

Before the end of the year, as many as 20 to 30 computer makers will introduce new desktop computers based on the new Intel chip, led by Compaq Computer Corp.

Homebrew Computer Club (a pioneering microcomputer club) that 4000 Altairs had been ordered.

Two computer programmers in Boston, Paul Allen and Bill Gates (then a Harvard freshman), learned about the Altair and convinced Roberts to adopt their BASIC interpreter. Allen and Gates subsequently established Microsoft, now one of the world's largest software publishers.

The Tandy Corporation began as a leather business in 1927. In 1962 the owner's son suggested buying a chain of mail-order electronics stores in Boston called Radio Shack, which was losing four million dollars a year. By August 1977 the TRS-80 microcomputer was announced. Within a month the Tandy Corporation had sold 100,000 units.

The story of the Apple computer is an interesting one. Stephen G. Wozniack built an addition-subtraction machine for a local service firm in 1962. By 1971 he had built his own computer from spare electronic parts. Wozniack knew about the Altair computer, but he couldn't afford one at the time. So he and a high-school friend named Steve Jobs (pronounced "jobes" with a long "o"), another electronics buff, decided to develop a BASIC interpreter to run on the 6502 chip, and to build a computer to run it. Wozniack dubbed the result the Apple. (Some say he named it after the Beatles' record label, others say the inspiration came from visiting Steve Jobs in Oregon, a state famous for apple orchards.)

In February 1977, the Apple Computer Company opened its doors in Cupertino, California. The Apple II computer was unveiled a few months later at the first West Coast Computer Faire.

IBM entered the microcomputer market on August 12, 1981, with its announcement of the IBM Personal Computer, or IBM PC. IBM's computer was built from parts available to the general public. Other computer manufacturers scrambled to build their own "IBM look-alike" computers. An entire industry has grown up around the IBM PC and compatible computers.

Recognizing IBM's importance in the microcomputer field, the Apple Computer Company took out a full-page advertisement in the *Wall Street Journal*. "Welcome IBM," the ad said. "Welcome to the most exciting and important marketplace since the computer revolution began 35 years ago."

That advertisement says it all. As you can see, the history of the microcomputer has been brief, but very exciting. Now let us consider the impact the microcomputer explosion has had on us.

The Impact of the Microcomputer

One immediate effect of the microcomputer proliferation is that people who once could not, as the saying goes, recognize a computer in a room full of sewing machines, had to become computer literate almost overnight. Business people from chief executive officers to financial analysts to warehouse managers to clerks and salespeople had to learn how to work with a computer. In 1986 over 9.6 million microcomputers were in use in the United States. The vast majority of current PC users did not know how to turn on a computer, load the system, or start an application four years ago. They learned how because they had to. Introductory computer courses, like the one you are now taking, either did not exist five years ago or were taken only by computer science or data processing majors. Now it is unusual to find college students in any major who have not taken at least one computer course.

Another significant effect that the microcomputer explosion has had is in creating entire lines of business that did not exist until recently. Although early PCs were marketed through large department store chains, such as Sears, Roebuck & Co., nowadays every major city has at least one computer store. Computer stores distribute computer systems and peripherals; software from dozens, sometimes hundreds of software publishers; computer supplies and accessories; even gimmicks such as t-shirts and baseball caps. It is fashionable to own a computer and advertise that fact with clothing.

APPLICATION

"THOSE USERS SIMPLY WANT TO GET THE JOB DONE."

One of the prevailing myths associated with personal computers is that everybody who gets a machine is destined to become a power user, crunching data and devising formulas with dazzling speed and efficiency. In the real world, however, power users are a minority, far outnumbered by the klutzes and the merely functional.

One company, Software Publishing Corporation (SPC) of Mountain View, California, has made its reputation and based its considerable success on producing programs for the adequate majority — those users who are not looking for the ultimate whiz-bang from their software but *simply* want to get a job done. The company's products are not designed to dazzle or to include every feature imaginable. Instead, Software Publishing operates, according to cofounder John Page, on the "principle of least astonishment."

Software Publishing has been profitable since its first year in business (1980), and sales revenues for its fifth fiscal year, which ended last September, hit the $37 million mark. The company is ranked among the top four in the software industry, along with Lotus, Ashton-Tate, and Microsoft. And as if to underscore Software Publishing's success, it has recently begun to attract a number of imitators — and to take steps down the acquisitions road.

Software Publishing achieved its stature in the industry with its highly regarded *pfs:* series — *pfs:file*, *pfs:report*, *pfs:access*, *pfs:write*, *pfs: graph*, and *pfs:plan* — which is often described as "low-end" software. Company president Fred Gibbons doesn't like the characterization, suggesting that it has led to misunderstanding. "We build easy-to-use products, but that doesn't mean they're not powerful," he asserts. "We tackle complex problems with simple software."

Software Publishing's first office was the proverbial garage — Janelle Bedke's garage. There, Bedke wrote the first manual, handled sales negotiations, and generally kept things running. She still does, although Software Publishing's office, which is company-owned, is now 50,000 square feet, houses 185 employees, and markets a growing product line to more than 3500 customers, which include distributors, independent sales representatives, dealers, and original equipment manufacturers (OEMs).

Gibbons believes that a significant portion of the software market remains unserved. And that, he affirms, means business. He says that in this market, the computer industry in general has concentrated on power users who want the PC to perform increasingly sophisticated tricks, because "that's where the big bucks were. The reason we haven't yet tapped the available business market is that there's a prejudice against 'easy-to-use' in large corporations.

"MIS managers think everyone in the company is a power user. But when I was addressing an MIS user group recently and asked how many in the audience felt they weren't getting their money's worth out of their personal computers, a third raised their hands. The MIS managers just aren't segmenting their market."

Too often, Page believes, major figures in the computer industry focus on "hot" new products and technologies, ignoring the established products preferred by a large proportion of users. The industry "is inbred and listens to its own lies," he maintains. "Key industry influences don't necessarily influence the customer."

Still, Gibbons concedes that his company's growth is tied directly to the unit growth of the personal computer market, which he claims is far from moribund. In fact, he predicts that market growth will exceed 35 percent as PCs become more integrated into office automation strategies, displacing dedicated word processors and dumb terminals tied to minicomputers or mainframes.

Bookstores and publishers have felt the impact of the microcomputer explosion. When the microcomputer hit Main Street, people suddenly needed to know how to use one, how to select one, how to make it do things. Hundreds of "how-to" books have been written in an attempt to answer some of the public's questions about the microcomputer. Go to a local bookstore and count the number of titles in the computer section.

Until the 1980s, software houses dealt primarily with applications for large mainframes. Now there is a tremendous demand for software for the PC (see module B for an overview of three of the most popular types of PC software). People who were not necessarily computer professionals have designed and built relatively inexpensive software packages for microcomputers, and hundreds of millions of dollars are spent on these programs every year. In fact, one reason microcomputers have been so readily accepted is that there is an abundance of good software available for them; consequently, people do not have to learn how to program in order to use their PCs.

Actually, it is difficult to say whether abundant software made the microcomputer feasible, or if the acceptance of the microcomputer resulted in the development of so much good software. If the microcomputer had not become so popular, few people would have bothered to put the time and effort into developing good software — the way to make money in PC software is to sell many copies of a program. If there were little good software from which to choose, then ordinary business people would be reluctant to buy PCs — they have neither the skills nor the interest required to program them. If people do not have computers, they will not buy software for them. Although it may not be clear whether the availability of good software helped the microcomputer to catch on or if the popularity of the PC resulted in the development of good software, it certainly is clear that both together have created a whole new business.

Another factor in the burgeoning interest in PC software is the fact that microcomputer **hardware architecture** has become almost standardized. To appreciate this you must realize that programs written for use on one line of computers do not necessarily run on another line. Thus, until recently, a publisher of computer software who wanted to reach as large a market as possible had to design several versions of a package, one for each line of computers. This, of course, drove up the cost of software development, resulting in higher consumer prices or in software packages that could run on only one computer.

Not surprisingly, the accepted standard for microcomputer architecture is the one developed by the International Business Machines (IBM) Corporation. A quick perusal of microcomputer magazines will testify to this fact: Notice how many times the phrase "IBM compatible" appears. This is significant because programs designed to run on the IBM PC can also run on another manufacturer's IBM-compatible computer. Consequently, software designed for the IBM PC can be readily used by the largest segment of the microcomputer market, making it economically worthwhile to publish high-quality software. Naturally, this is good for the consumer.

Still another significant development in microcomputers is the emergence of local area network (LAN) technology (see chapter 10). LANs allow several geographically close microcomputers to communicate with each other and to share central resources, such as databases. Although this capability has long been available for mainframe computers, it is now feasible for even small businesses to acquire the networking capabilities they need—and at a cost of only a few thousand dollars.

In addition to creating entire new businesses, the microcomputer has also changed the way some businesses operate. One example is book publishing.

Preparing a manuscript on a microcomputer with word processing software (see module B) is easier than it would be using a typewriter. Typing, editing, retyping, proofreading, and typesetting are all very time-consuming tasks without the aid of a computer. With a microcomputer, the process is streamlined.

This text was prepared on a microcomputer (a Compaq Deskpro) using a word processing package called MultiMate, a product of Ashton-Tate. The only truly manual task was proofreading. After the final manuscript was prepared, it was copied onto diskettes and mailed from Connecticut to California, where the compositor electronically inserted special typesetting codes (for example, to tell the computer to boldface a word) and then used another computer to set the type.

How does this effect you? Because book production is less expensive than it used to be, publishers are able to produce higher quality books for the same amount of money. Also, it is now easy (relatively speaking) to publish a book. Whereas a few years ago only the large publishing houses had the resources necessary to publish, nowadays a far smaller investment is required. This could result in the emergence of smaller, more specialized publishing companies, reducing the control large publishing houses have traditionally had on what makes it into print.

The ease with which ordinary people can now use a computer would startle the business person of the 1960s or 1970s. It is difficult to imagine any field of business (or education or politics) that has not been changed by the microcomputer. Almost every field has profited from the use of the computer. It is likely that the microcomputer explosion has only just begun, that we are now experiencing only the early rumblings. We do not know for sure. However, one does not have to be clairvoyant to see that the microcomputer, which is already changing the way we do business, is bound to have an even more profound effect on our lives in the future.

APPLICATION

"WELCOME TO THE WORLD OF DESKTOP PUBLISHING."

Welcome to the world of desktop publishing. Sophisticated software and cheaper hardware have made publishing everything from résumés to full-length books the fastest-growing use for personal computers since the spreadsheet. The new technology makes fancy typefaces and elegant layouts available to a wide range of customers, from carwashes to church groups. Corporate print shops are saving millions of dollars. And desktop publishing may provide the computer industry with the most convincing answer yet to that vexing customer question: "I'd like to buy a computer, but what would I use it for?"

The key development is the plummeting cost of laser printers, which use laser beams, rather than mechanical print heads, to etch characters on a piece of paper. These printers can produce anything from a plain typewriter character to elaborate magazine and advertising typefaces. They once sold for $20,000 or more, but some now sell for $2,000. With the printer, electronic Gutenbergs also need a fairly high-powered personal computer and one of a half-dozen new software packages bearing names like PageMaker or MacPublisher (after Apple's Macintosh, the current favorite for desktop publishing).

Computer owners can now produce dramatically designed pages on screen, changing layouts and typefaces at the touch of a key. The demanding, timeconsuming tasks of typesetting and pasteup are done entirely by the computer. When Linda Foust and Tony Husch wrote their first marketing book "That's a Great Idea!" last spring, they decided to act as their own publisher and typesetter. They used their Apple computer to lay out the book in neat Times Roman, then rented a laser printer to produce one copy of each page, at a cost of about 30 cents a page. (Professional typesetting would have cost them $10 to $30 a page.) They took those pages to a conventional printer, who ran off thousands of copies on an offset press. Foust and Husch have already sold enough copies to finance their next book.

For corporations which spent $200 billion publishing 2.5 trillion pages of manuals, reports and other material in 1984, the savings can be even more dramatic. Switching from conventional typesetting to desktop publishing can cut a corporation's printing bill almost in half, providing one of the quickest "paybacks" of any computer investment. At Steelcase, an office-furniture manufacturer headquartered in Grand Rapids, Mich., design manager Justin Corby estimates he has saved $10,000 in printing costs since March by producing forms and manuals in-house; the saving equals the cost of his computer and laser printer. Laser-printed documents also look better than typical in-house materials; "Now you've got the power to be creative," says Laurel Brunner, an analyst with the Seybold Report on Publishing Systems. "How you design a report could affect the presentation as much as the words do."

Full-scale typesetting

For now, however, desktop publishing still cannot offer the quality and flexibility of traditional typesetting. A laser printer can't produce images quite as sharply, and even the most sophisticated software can't provide as many typefaces. But when extremely high-quality type is required do-it-yourself typesetters can use a personal computer to drive full-scale phototypesetting machines. Krishna has what may be the first self-service phototypesetting machine in the country: customers can sit down at a computer and set type on a $30,000 Allied Linotronic 100, paying less than the cost of the cheapest professional typesetter.

▥ SUMMARY

Although the history of computation began thousands of years ago, the development of computers is a recent phenomenon. In the early 1800s, Charles Babbage developed many of the design concepts used in today's computers. However, these concepts were not implemented at that time. Many of the mistakes that Babbage made are still being made today.

In the late 1800s, the U.S. Census Bureau had a problem. They hired Herman Hollerith to develop automated ways of computing census data. This led to the development of punched-card equipment and the beginning of the punched-card industry.

Computers were not actually developed until the mid 1940s. Early computers were produced through the cooperation of universities, government, and industry. There have been four generations of computers so far. First-generation computers had vacuum tubes, and main storage was a magnetic drum. These computers were huge and very hard to maintain. Programs were written in machine code.

Computers in the second generation used transistors and had main memory made of magnetic core. They were smaller and still very expensive. High-level languages were developed for programming, and rudimentary operating systems were invented.

The third-generation computers have integrated circuits on silicon chips. These chips are used both for the arithmetic and logic unit and for main memory. Third-generation computers are much smaller and cheaper than first- or second-generation computers.

Today computers are in their fourth generation. They have become significantly cheaper and more powerful. In the near future, the cost of a CPU will be essentially zero. We may see the development of supercomputers that are banks of microprocessors.

Unfortunately, the costs of developing programs has increased during this same time period. To compensate for these increases, businesses have turned to packaged programs and fourth generation languages. It is possible that users will one day be able to do all of their own programming using 4GLs.

Microcomputers have had a profound impact on business in the 1980s. They are widely accepted as an important piece of business equipment, and millions of people have learned how to use them in only a few years.

The availability of high-quality software has helped the microcomputer gain popularity. Other developments, such as local area networking, continue to make the microcomputer an indispensible feature of business.

QUESTIONS

A.1 Explain what people can learn today from the experiences of Charles Babbage.

A.2 What role did the U. S. Census Bureau play in the development of computers?

A.3 Explain the contribution to the development of computers made by each of the following individuals:
Charles Babbage
Herman Hollerith
Howard Aiken
John Mauchly
J. Presper Eckert
John V. Atanasoff
John von Neumann
Rear Admiral Grace Hopper

A.4 How did Herman Hollerith set the pace for computer entrepreneurs?

A.5 What was the IBM marketing philosophy in the early days of computing? How did it help the company?

A.6 Characterize the machines and programs of each of the four generations of computers.

A.7 Explain why computers are becoming inexpensive.

A.8 Why has the cost of developing computer programs not decreased as the cost of hardware has?

A.9 Name and describe two ways businesses have found to decrease the cost of acquiring programs.

WORD LIST

Abacus	Grace Hopper	Minicomputers
Charles Babbage	Adele Goldstine	Fourth-generation computers
Difference engine	UNIVAC I	Very large-scale integrated
Analytical engine	First-generation computers	(VLSI) circuits
Ada Augusta Lovelace	Vacuum tubes	Microprocessor
Herman Hollerith	Transistors	Microcomputer
Howard G. Aiken	Second-generation computers	Supercomputer
Mark I	Core memory	Off-the-shelf programs
John W. Mauchly	Machine code	Prototyping
J. Presper Eckert	Assembly language	Fourth-generation language
ENIAC	High-level languages	(4GL)
John V. Atanasoff	Offline input/output	Hardware architecture
John von Neumann	Third-generation computers	Local area network (LAN)
EDVAC	Integrated circuits	
EDSAC	Online processing	

QUESTIONS TO CHALLENGE YOUR THINKING

A. The rate of computer technology development has been astronomical in the last thirty years. What impact do you think this growth has had on industry? How do you think a company can best cope with this type of growth if it continues in the future?

B. What impact do you think the rapid change in technology has had on education? How do you think education will change as computers become less and less expensive?

C. Judging from the past, what do you think is going to happen in computing? What impact will computers of the future have on business? How will the business of the year 2000 use computer technology?

PERSONAL COMPUTER APPLICATIONS

MODULE B

When computers were first used for commercial purposes in the early 1950s they were so big, expensive, unreliable, and difficult to use that experts dismissed the notion that more than 100 computers would ever be installed in U.S. companies. How wrong they were. In the 25 years that followed, computers proved to be so valuable in business that they became established as standard equipment. As technology forced both the size and the price of computers down, their use became even more widespread. The mid-70s saw the advent of **personal computers (PCs),** affordable computers fast enough and powerful enough to satisfy the needs of individuals and even small companies.

▥ INCREASING PERSONAL PRODUCTIVITY WITH A COMPUTER

Although most software until the mid 1970s had been developed for large mainframe computers, personal computers opened up a whole new market: software designed especially for personal computers to serve individuals rather than groups of users. Suddenly software engineers, computer hackers, even business professionals turned amateur programmers were creating programs to solve problems from home budgets to stock market analyses to managing the family dairy herd. Visit a computer store and you will find shelves full of software for PCs.

Personal computer software packages share some common characteristics. First, they are relatively inexpensive, at least when compared to the equivalent package for a mainframe. For example, software for a mainframe database management system might cost $200,000, while a high-quality DBMS for a personal computer might cost only $1,000. Of course, you get what you pay for. One is a fully-equipped Rolls Royce, and the other is a fuel-efficient subcompact.

Second, personal computer software is designed for microcomputers, and therefore it is somewhat restricted by the limitations of the hardware. The most notable limitations are on file size, record size, and data-access speed.

Third, most PC software is designed for use by noncomputer professionals. In theory such software is supposed to be user friendly, but in reality some programs are more friendly, or easy to use, than others. Before you purchase PC software, try using several similar programs at a computer store. Also compare user and operating procedures and supporting documentation for similar programs before selecting the one that is best for you.

Despite some limitations, personal computer systems offer many benefits. As the sole user of the system, an individual has no problems interfacing with other people or other systems. He or she has control over system functions, data, and security. Once mastered, many soft-

PROFILE

U.S. Personal Computer Sales Growth

(in millions of units)

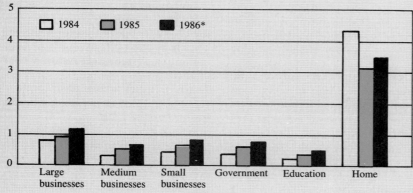

☐ 1984   ▨ 1985   ■ 1986*

Large businesses   Medium businesses   Small businesses   Government   Education   Home

*Projected

The PC Market

U.S. retail sales, in billions of dollars

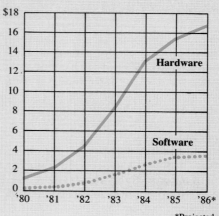

Hardware

Software

'80   '81   '82   '83   '84   '85   '86*

*Projected

PC Peripherals

Domestic shipments, by units and by dollar value (in millions of dollars)

		1981	1982	1983	1984	1985	1986*
Modem	UNITS	41,860	210,975	528,480	658,600	682,680	795,960
	AMOUNT	$13	$74	$185	$244	$259	$310
Floppies	UNITS	721,000	3,061,000	7,568,000	9,145,000	10,897,000	12,704,000
	AMOUNT	$257	$1,071	$2,649	$3,035	$3,619	$4,219
Hard disk	UNITS	54,000	286,000	675,000	1,566,000	2,201,000	2,912,000
	AMOUNT	$70	$372	$878	$1,793	$2,481	$3,195
Printers	UNITS	211,000	1,100,000	2,019,000	3,521,000	4,000,000	4,562,000
	AMOUNT	$223	$1,058	$1,925	$2,864	$3,180	$3,602

*Projected

APPLICATION

"TIPS FOR THE ENTERPRISING SALESPERSON."

Keep meaningful records. Use data base software to help you keep track of customer information, trigger follow-ups, and produce analytical reports. Experienced salespeople who use computers aggressively report a 20 to 50 percent productivity improvement from data base use alone.

Get maximum mileage from your data. Look for new ways to use the information you collect and the applications software you have. Your data base on sales calls, for example, may help you realize a relationship between time spent with a client and sales results. Or data that you run through specialized software may show revealing trends when viewed with a spreadsheet or graphics package.

Go graphic. Enhance presentations, correspondence and reports with charts. Everyone is more receptive to numerical or comparative data in graphics form. Charting and drawing software is reasonably priced and easy to use.

Follow up. Write more personal letters with computer word processing software. In this age of heavy telephone use and photocopied forms, people respond favorably to personalized letters. If you're still using a typewriter, you can improve productivity three to five times with a personal computer for word processing.

Communicate. Your personal computer is a potential window to the world. Use it to send bulletin messages to colleagues and clients. Take advantage of the best electronic mail services. Research your prospects and markets — even your competition — with on-line services.

Get Organized. Utility programs that offer calendar functions, note-taking and telephone-list dialing capabilities may be just the thing for your harried work pace.

Close the sale. Don't limit your computing expertise to preparation and follow-up; when possible, take the computer along on the sales call. On-the-spot analysis, information

gathering and order checking can do more than impress your clients — it may convince them.

Go beyond the obvious. There is a widespread tendency to become comfortable with one or two applications. This limits the effectiveness of your computer system and reduces your chances for exceptional sales success. Learn as much about each application you employ as possible; don't be hesitant to use additional software as you need it.

Pay attention to detail. One of the wry jokes in business is "It was a computer error." Computer errors ultimately translate to people errors, and that will reflect you in the worst light. For example, a word processing error that addresses letters to one person and makes the salutation to someone else makes you look unprofessional and careless. Proofread everything you send out to make sure it is as complete and professional as you can make it.

ware packages can help a person be more productive. Consequently, a personal computer and some good software is a sound investment for many people. Furthermore, there are many powerful portable PCs, so many business people can now take their computers with them wherever they go.

A personal application is usually something that needs to be done by the individual, with or without a computer. A computer and appropriate software merely amplify the person's ability to do the task. Three personal applications are addressed in this module: document handling, financial modeling, and data storage and retrieval. There are reasonably priced, high-quality software packages available for each application. **Word processing programs** are used for document handling, **electronic spreadsheet programs** are used for financial modeling, and **personal database management systems** are used for data storage and retrieval.

There are so many programs available for each application — over fifty word processing programs for the IBM PC, for example — that exhaustive coverage of all of them would fill several volumes. Thus, instead of presenting unique details of only one of the many good products available, we will present a generic discussion of each application and the software that addresses it.

WORD PROCESSING SYSTEMS

Preparing, editing, retyping, copying, and filing documents have always accounted for much of the work done in an office. Although computers were recognized early on for their accounting abilities (see chapter 4), it was not until much later that they began to have an impact on document processing and, consequently, on office paperwork. **Word processing** is the manipulation of text material to produce printed documents. Word processing systems grew out of a need for a faster, more efficient way to create, store, and retrieve documents.

Word processing programs allow students, business people, consultants, attorneys, and anyone else who might otherwise use a typewriter to quickly and easily create, edit, print, and file documents. A good word processing package for a personal computer might cost up to $500.

Word processing, whether manual or computerized, includes four related functions: document handling, document editing, document formatting, and document printing. Document handling deals with creating and storing a document. Document editing means changing the document after the first draft. Document formatting means changing the appearance of a document, but not its contents. Document printing means producing one or more hard copies of the document. In a manual system, documents are "printed" as they are typed. In a computerized system, printing a document can be delayed until after the entire document has been created and edited.

Document Handling

The unit of work for a word processor is called a **document.** A document can be one page long or hundreds of pages long (some word processors limit the number of pages in a document). And although standard typing paper is 8 1/2 by 11 inches, you can specify your own page dimensions to a word processor, as we will discuss under document formatting.

FIGURE B–1
Menu of word processing functions

```
                    M u l t i M a t e
                     Version 3.31

      1) Edit an Old Document
      2) Create a New Document

      3) Print Document Utility
      4) Printer Control Utilities
      5) Merge Print Utility

      6) Document Handling Utilities
      7) Other Utilities
      8) Spell Check a Document
      9) Return to DOS


         DESIRED FUNCTION:   ▮

  Enter the number of the function; press RETURN
    Hold down Shift and press F1 for HELP menu
```

All documents are stored on the personal computer's disks, either floppies or hard disks. The word processing program is also stored on disk, which is why you have to enter the appropriate instructions at your computer keyboard to **load** the word processing software into the computer.

A word processing program usually presents a **menu** of functions (figure B–1) from which you select the one you want performed. The first document handling function we will examine is *create* (the second option on the menu in figure B–1). Though the specifics vary from one program to the next, every word processor asks you to give a *name* to the document you are creating. It checks its directory of documents to be sure there is not already a document with that name because each document must have a unique name.

Having named the document, you are now free to enter the text. A computer keyboard looks almost like a typewriter keyboard, and you enter words as if you were typing. As you type, the **cursor** indicates the position you are about to type in. The cursor is usually a box or a flashing underline. Word processors have a feature called **wrap around,** which lets you type past the end of a line. The program automatically drops the cursor down to the next line, so you need not hit the carriage return until you reach the end of a paragraph.

Once you have created a document you must *save* it on disk. Up until now, you have typed text into the computer's main memory, and it has been displayed on the screen so you can see what you've typed. But if you were to turn off the computer or load another program without saving the document, you would have no record of it — it would be erased from the computer's memory.

Creating and saving documents are the two most frequently invoked document handling functions. Others allow you to *rename* a document that you have already created, *delete* a document you no longer need to save on disk, *list* the names of all of your documents, and *copy* a document. The copy function is used to make backups. Disks, especially floppy diskettes, are sometimes damaged, making the data on them irretrievable. Backup copies of your word processing files are insurance against that loss.

Document Retrieval and Editing

The second category of word processing functions that we will examine allows you to *retrieve* and *edit* documents you have already *created* (edit is the first menu selection in figure B–1). After you select the edit function from the menu, name the document you wish to edit. The word processing program retrieves the document from disk and displays it on the screen.

There are only a few kinds of changes you can make to a document: You can *insert* letters or whole blocks of text, you can *delete* letters or blocks, you can *replace* letters or whole blocks with other text, and you can *rearrange* text (sometimes known as **cut and paste).**

The first editing function allows you to insert letters or blocks into existing text. The word processing program needs to know where you want to insert new text. When you type the new text and then indicate that you are finished the program automatically inserts the new text, moving everything else on the page over and down to make room for it.

The second editing function is deleting text. Deleting is very simple with a word processor. You indicate what you want to delete, and the program erases those characters, automatically moving all the remaining text up and over, filling in the space left by the deleted text.

The third editing function is replacing text, either characters or entire blocks. Replacing individual characters, or even short strings of characters, is easy. You simply type over the unwanted text. The new text will overlay the old, and when you save the document only the new version will be stored.

Replacing blocks of text requires you to indicate the text you wish to replace. When you type in the new text the word processing program automatically exchanges the old block for the new one, even if they are different lengths.

The fourth editing function allows you to move blocks of text to different locations in the document. Rearranging what you have typed on paper means retyping it. But electronically rearranging text with a word processor couldn't be easier. You simply indicate the block of text you want moved, and then indicate the location you want it moved to. The program automatically deletes the block from its original location, moving up all the following text to fill in the gap, and automatically inserts the block where you want it to be, pushing text over and down to make room for it.

Document Formatting

The **format** of a document refers to its physical appearance. This includes the *length of each line* (or the width of the margins, if you prefer to think of it that way), the number of *lines on a page*, and the location of one or more *tabs*. You need to format a document whether you use a typewriter or a word processor. One of the marvelous features of word processors, though, is that you can change one or several format characteristics, and the program electronically shifts everything around to fit the new format. For example, increasing the size of your right margin by half an inch can be done by pressing a few keys on the computer keyboard. The next time you print that document, every line will have been shortened and the text moved down and over, resulting in the desired margin size.

Standard typing paper is 8 1/2 by 11 inches. Standard pitch is 10 characters per inch, and standard line spacing is 6 lines per inch. So the dimensions for filling up an entire sheet of typing paper, with no margins, is 85 characters per line and 66 lines per page. Of course, we seldom want to do that. More often we leave a one-and-one-half-inch left margin and a one-inch right margin, resulting in a line containing 60 characters. We also leave an inch at the top of each page and another at the bottom, resulting in a page containing 46 lines. How you indicate your page format details depends on the word processor you are using. But all of them need to know those details.

Most word processors include a feature that automatically centers text for you — a feature that is useful for report titles and page headers, for instance. Most also include a feature that allows you to indent an entire block of text with one or two keystrokes. Using a typewriter, you would have to tab every line.

One feature available with word processors that is almost nonexistent in typewriting is right-justification. As you know, typed text is aligned, or justified, along the left margin. However, text along the right margin is ragged. Most word processors allow you to align text on the right side of the page as well (figure B–2). They do this either by varying the amount of space between letters or by varying the amount of space between words.

Other formatting features allow you to underscore, double underscore, and print in boldface. A very useful and time-saving feature is repagination. The repagination feature automatically moves lines of

```
This paragraph illustrates a feature        This paragraph illustrates a feature of
of many word processing programs            many word processing programs called
called right-justification. Without         right-justification. Without right-
right-justification, the right edge of      justification, the right edge of this
this paragraph is ragged. However,          paragraph is ragged. However, with
with right-justification, all printed       right-justification, all printed lines
lines are aligned with both the right       are aligned with both the right and left
and left margins. Compare the two           margins. Compare the two versions of this
versions of this paragraph to see the       paragraph to see the difference.
difference.


a. Without right-justification the          b. With right-justification both the left
   right edge is ragged.                        and right sides have even margins.
```

text so that every page has the same number of lines, which is handy if you have inserted blocks on some pages (so they exceed the number you can fit on one sheet of paper) and deleted blocks on others, leaving large gaps at the bottoms of some pages. Repagination cleans up everything before you print.

FIGURE B–2
Right-justification feature

Document Printing

Almost all documents eventually are printed. However, some documents that are prepared on word processors are transmitted electronically to another computer terminal through an **electronic mail system.** A copy of the document is stored in the recipient's "mail box." Once the recipient retrieves and reads it, he or she might file it or destroy it — electronically, of course, because it was never printed on paper. Except for electronic mail, most word processing documents are printed. Some very powerful, time-saving features are available, including ones that print only selected pages of a document (you tell the program which ones), print more than one "original" copy (you tell the program how many), adjust the type font, and number pages automatically.

Type font refers to the size and style of printed characters. Many word processing programs allow the user to determine type font for a document. Elite and pica are the type fonts used most frequently in business, although many styles are available. Some word processors allow the user to vary fonts within the document. For example, you might want to italicize one word in a sentence. This is usually done with control characters imbedded in the document.

You should know that many printing features are dependent on the printer attached to the personal computer. For example, impact printers (see chapter 3) use a daisy wheel or Selectric ball — therefore, type fonts are not electronically adjustable. To change the font you must change the print element. Dot matrix printers are more versatile in this area. However, impact printers produce **letter quality** images, meaning that the type is crisp, dark, and clear, while dot-matrix printer quality is not quite as good. Which feature is more important? A smart consumer will know what printing features are important for his or her system *before* buying a printer (or any other hardware or software, for that matter). See the photo essay on selecting a microcomputer system.

The last printing feature we will mention is automatic page numbering. When used in conjunction with the repagination feature, automatic page numbering saves a lot of retyping time. You simply type a few special keys to indicate automatic page numbering, and the page numbers appear as the document is printed.

Printing a document is usually very simple, requiring only a few keystrokes. Once you enter the name of the document you want to print, the word processing program fetches that document and offers various options, such as the ones mentioned above. After responding to the questions, you simply ready the printer (turn it on, load paper into it and so forth) and let the word processor do its job.

The four categories of word processing system features are document handling, document retrieval and editing, document formatting, and document printing. These features are incorporated into even the most basic, inexpensive word processing software. Many other sophisticated features are included in some word processors. Recall from chapter 1 that Mary Forsythe's word processing program interfaced with her database system. She stored names and addresses using the DBMS, and then her word processor *imported*, or accessed, them for personalized letters and mailing labels. All word processing programs and DBMSs do not have this feature. Of course, a smart shopper will carefully define system requirements before purchasing software.

Costs and Benefits of a Personal Word Processor

This module is devoted to personal productivity tools, so you should consider what a personal word processing system will and will not do for you. First, remember that a word processing system (hardware, software, documentation, diskettes for storage, and so forth) is likely to cost more than a really good typewriter (a few thousand dollars versus a few hundred). If you type only a little bit — a few letters a year or three or four papers each term — investing in a word processing system might be frivolous. Of course, if you use your computer for other things as well, like Mary Forsythe did, then the word processing cost drops to a fraction of the overall cost, making this function more reasonable. The bottom line is that everybody does not need a word processor to be successful, either in school or in business.

A standard marketing ploy for word processors is that they can "make writing easier." Do not be fooled by this strategy. Writing,

PROFILE

TOP PC PURCHASERS

	COMPANY	INSTALLED MICROCOMPUTERS		COMPANY	INSTALLED MICROCOMPUTERS
1.	GENERAL MOTORS	31,000	24.	INTEL	4,000
2.	GENERAL ELECTRIC	18,000	25.	SECURITY PACIFIC	3,000
3.	WESTINGHOUSE	12,000	26.	LOCKHEED	3,000
4.	CITICORP	10,000	27.	ALLIED PRODUCTS	2,500
5.	DU PONT	10,000	28.	CHEVRON	2,400
6.	FORD MOTOR CO.	9,000	29.	UNION CARBIDE	2,200
7.	PACIFIC BELL	7,000	30.	MOBIL	2,000
8.	CHASE MANHATTAN BANK	6,700	31.	PG&E	2,000
9.	EXXON	6,000	32.	CHEMICAL BANK	1,700
10.	PEAT, MARWICK, MITCHELL	5,600	33.	TIME	1,700
11.	UNITED TECHNOLOGIES	5,000	34.	J. P. MORGAN & CO.	1,600
12.	McDONNELL DOUGLAS	5,000	35.	AMERICAN CAN	1,500
13.	HUGHES AIRCRAFT	5,000	36.	WELLS FARGO	1,400
14.	AETNA LIFE & CASUALTY	5,000	37.	UPJOHN	1,400
15.	TRW	5,000	38.	NORTHWESTERN MUTUAL	1,400
16.	BOEING	5,000	39.	LTV STEEL	1,200
17.	SPERRY	4,700	40.	PILLSBURY	1,000
18.	GENERAL DYNAMICS	4,700	41.	GENERAL MILLS	1,000
19.	TRAVELERS	4,500	42.	NABISCO	1,000
20.	MERRILL LYNCH	4,400	43.	FEDERAL EXPRESS	1,000
21.	DUN & BRADSTREET	4,300	44.	R. J. REYNOLDS	1,000
22.	TOUCHE ROSS & CO.	4,100	45.	BECHTEL	1,000
23.	3M	4,000	46.	TELEDYNE	1,000

whether a letter, a report, a thesis, or a textbook, involves much more than punching some keys on a computer. If you have nothing to say, a word processor will not say it for you. Do not expect more from the tool than it can deliver. Well, you might ask, just what will it deliver?

Because words are recorded electronically rather then permanently on paper, many people are more willing to produce several drafts of a document, making each version a little better than the previous one. Because editing is so easy, typing skills are not essential. It is more important to master the functions of the word processor than to type perfectly.

Cutting and pasting are easy to do with a word processor, so you are more likely to rearrange a document until it is as good as you can make it. The ease with which you can make document changes will make

QUESTIONS

B.1   Name four functions of a word processing program.

B.2   Name three things that are easy to do with a word processor but difficult to do with a typewriter.

B.3   Define these terms: cursor, wrap around, cut and paste, repagination, type font.

B.4   Do you believe that using a word processor can make someone a better writer? Why or why not?

B.5   What impact do you think the word processor has had on clerical workers in large companies? What about in small companies?

B.6   Did Mary Forsythe (chapter 1) make a wise investment in buying a PC and a word processing program? Compare the costs of preparing a letter with and without the aid of a word processor.

you less reluctant to incorporate them. Some people think that students who use word processors, especially at the elementary school level, will write more because doing so is easier, and that writing more will make them better writers. Some time will be needed to determine if there is anything to that theory.

All in all, if you write a lot, a word processor is a must. If you have access to a word processor at your school you should learn how to use it. But beware — once you have used a word processor you may never want to use a typewriter again.

▦ ELECTRONIC SPREADSHEETS

The first electronic spreadsheet program, VisiCalc, was sold in 1979. Since then, over 5 million electronic spreadsheet programs, including bestsellers like VisiCalc, Multiplan, Symphony, and Lotus 1-2-3, have been purchased by business people for use on their PCs. With prices ranging from $150 to $500, hundreds of millions of dollars already have been spent on electronic spreadsheets. Most corporate financial officers can no longer get along without them. The importance of these software packages in business is evidenced by the fact that students at many business schools are required to become proficient in their use. Some analysts say that the electronic spreadsheet is not merely a tool that has helped business people — it has actually *changed* business. What are electronic spreadsheets, and why are they so popular?

An electronic spreadsheet is a program (it is not a system by itself) that enables a user to quickly and easily manipulate numerical data. The electronic spreadsheet is an automated version of the ledger paper used by accountants (figure B–3). The paper spreadsheet is simple in its concept and in its design. The electronic spreadsheet is equally simple, both in concept and design, but it is far more powerful than the paper version. Let's first examine spreadsheets and compare paper ones to electronic ones.

Paper Spreadsheets versus Electronic Spreadsheets

The **spreadsheet** illustrated in figure B–3 is a typical one. It organizes and presents numerical data in a structured format that allows a user to answer many questions. Notice that the document is organized in columns and rows. Each column represents a time period, in this case one month. Each row represents a source of income or an expense. Every row is totaled (these totals appear on the right side of the page), and every column is totaled (these totals appear at the bottom of the page). Thus, many details about this company's financial status have been captured on a single page: The income from each source for each month, the expenses for each month, the total income for the entire

Elliot Bay Electronics
First Quarter Summary

	JAN	FEB	MAR	1ST QTR TOTAL	
SALES					
St. Louis	18000	7605	12953	38558	
Portland	21600	14900	6500	43000	
Appleton	11750	8800	17040	37590	
TOTAL SALES	51350	31305	36493	119148	
EXPENSES					
Advertising	5000	2000	2000	9000	
Salaries	11200	11200	11200	33600	
Bonuses	650	1000	1300	2950	
Travel & Entertain.	8400	8000	8600	25000	
TOTAL EXPENSES	25250	22200	23100	70550	
NET BEFORE TAXES	26100	9105	13393	48598	

time period, the total expenses for the entire time period, the net income (income minus expenses) for each month, and the net income for the entire time period.

Business people need to know this kind of financial information about their businesses. The need is no different for a huge corporation than it is for a self-employed business person. The serious drawback of paper spreadsheets is that business people who want to play "what if" games with a company's finances face tedious hours with a calculator or

FIGURE B–3
Paper spreadsheet

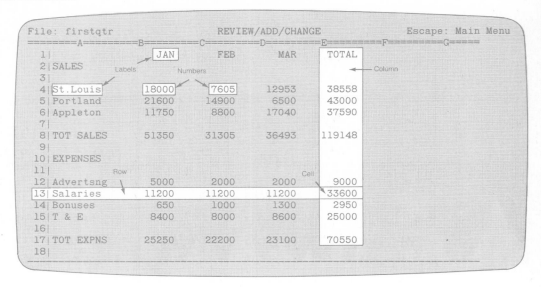

FIGURE B–4
Electronic spreadsheet

run up a large bill from their accounting firm. For example, a person might want to know what effect cutting travel and entertainment expenses, or increasing advertising by 10 percent, or building a new plant in Atlanta would have on the "bottom line." Because many figures (such as totals) on a spreadsheet are dependent on other figures, much recalculating must be done when even one figure is changed. Because business people knew that answering those questions was difficult and costly (accountants are not cheap), they tended not to ask them unless the answers were very important. It simply is not cost-effective to pay a staff of accountants to fiddle around with figures just because someone is mildly curious. And then the electronic spreadsheet was developed.

Perhaps the most powerful aspect of the electronic spreadsheet is that all calculations are performed by the computer, and any time a figure on the spreadsheet is changed ("Let's see what would happen if I hire one more salesperson at $50,000 a year"), all recalculations involving that figure are performed automatically.

The implications of this for business are enormous. For one thing, financial officers and other business people no longer need to depend on accountants or clerks to get answers to financial questions — they are instantly available at their fingertips. Questions that once took days to answer can be answered in minutes. And questions that went unasked because answering them was too difficult can now be routinely asked.

Whereas some business decisions were once made on instinct alone, the electronic spreadsheet has enabled business people to rely more on financial facts. Building even very complex financial models is relatively easy, and comparing many different scenarios can help businesses make sound decisions. In fact, you will recall from chapter 11 that an electronic spreadsheet is one of the cornerstones of a DSS.

Using an Electronic Spreadsheet Program

The spreadsheet in figure B–4 is the electronic version of the one in figure B–3. As you can see, they contain exactly the same data and present it in exactly the same format. What you cannot see is what goes on behind the scenes in an electronic spreadsheet. In this section we will examine some of the fundamental functions a user performs when working with an electronic spreadsheet package, including creating, saving, and printing a spreadsheet. (The material presented here is generic. If you are interested in the details of a specific spreadsheet package you can refer to documentation available from an electronic spreadsheet publisher.)

Creating a Spreadsheet

Prior to sitting down at the PC and loading the electronic spreadsheet program, it is wise to prepare the material you are going to enter. In fact, sketching a paper spreadsheet is usually a good way to start. Once you have a clear picture of what you want to do, then you can load the electronic spreadsheet program and work with it.

An electronic spreadsheet, like a paper one, is a standard form of rows and columns. Most electronic spreadsheets, however, are over 250 columns wide and at least 250 rows long (one is 8192 rows long), so their capacity far exceeds that of a single sheet of paper. Obviously, the entire spreadsheet cannot fit onto a computer screen at once, so at any time you see only a piece of the entire form. This piece is called a **window** (figure B–5), and you can move it around on the form anytime

FIGURE B–5

A computer screen is a window to the spreadsheet

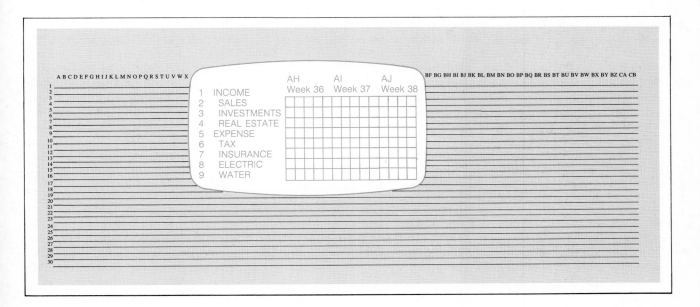

APPLICATION

"WHY NOT CREATE SPREADSHEETS ON A MICROCOMPUTER?"

As Dan Bricklin remembers it, the idea first came to him in the spring of 1978 while he was sitting in a classroom at the Harvard Business School. It was the kind of idea — so obvious, so right — that made him immediately wonder why no one else had thought of it. And yet it was no accident that this breakthrough should have been his.

Bricklin had graduated from the Massachusetts Institute of Technology, where — and this is crucial to the idea he would have that afternoon in 1978 — he had worked intimately with computers. Before deciding to go to graduate school, he had worked for two major computer companies — first for Wang, then for the Digital Equipment Corporation, for whom he helped design a word-processing program. Like most Harvard MBA candidates, he wanted to be a businessman; but more often than not, his thoughts strayed to the technological.

The question Bricklin was pondering that day concerned how he might use what he knew about computers to help him in his finance course. This was the assignment: He and several other students had been asked to project the complicated financial implications — the shift in numbers and dollars, and the shifts resulting from those shifts — of one company's acquisition of another.

Bricklin and his classmates would need ledger sheets, often called spreadsheets. Only by painstakingly filling in the pale green grids of the spreadsheets would they get an accurate picture of the merger and its consequences. A row of the ledger might represent an expense or a category of revenue; a column might represent a specific period of time — a day, a month, a year. Run your finger across, say, a row of figures representing mortgage payments for a certain property, and the number in each "cell" of the horizontal row would be the figure paid in the time period represented by that particular vertical column. Somewhere on the sheet the columns and rows would be tallied, and that information would be entered on even larger sheets.

The problem with ledger sheets was that if one monthly expense went up or down, everything — *everything* — had to be recalculated. It occurred to him: why not create the spreadsheets on a microcomputer? Why not design a program that would produce on a computer screen a green, glowing ledger, so that the calculations, as well as the final tabulations, would be visible to the person "crunching" the numbers? With a computer-programmer friend from MIT named Bob Frankston, he set to work developing the first electronic spreadsheet program. It would be contained on a floppy disk and run on the then-brand-new Apple personal computer. Bricklin and Frankston released VisiCalc (the name was derived from Visible Calculation) in late 1979.

FINGERTIP FLEXIBILITY

Today, VisiCalc and its newer rivals — most notably, a more powerful spreadsheet program designed by the Lotus Development Corporation called 1-2-3 — are making fundamental changes in the way American businesses work. For the first time, businessmen have at their fingertips sophisticated and flexible means of charting all the variables — from interest rates to warehouse space — that make (and break) businesses. The biggest firms, the most diversified corporations, can be neatly translated into spreadsheet "models" — each box of the grid a window onto once overlooked facts or relationships. These models can be used not only to keep track of transactions but also to analyze the nature of a business itself. They allow businessmen to calculate the effects of sudden changes in the corporate environment (a decrease in the prime rate, for example) and to experiment with scenarios (anything from the expansion of a product line to a merger) — all with an ease inconceivable five years ago.

Mitch Kapor, 34, a former teacher of transcendental meditation, is chairman of the board of the Lotus Development Corporation. In 1983, less than a year after selling its first 1-2-3 package, Lotus went public, a move that brought Kapor's personal net worth to more than $75 million. "Compare the expansion of business today to the conquering of the continent in the 19th century," Kapor said during an interview in his modest office in the old iron-casting factory in Cambridge, Massachusetts, that is now Lotus's headquarters. "The spreadsheet in that comparison is like the transcontinental railroad. It accelerated the movement, made it possible, and changed the course of the nation."

COSTLY MISTAKES

People tend to forget that even the most elegantly crafted spreadsheet is a house of cards, ready to collapse at the first erroneous assumption. The spreadsheet that looks good but turns out to be tragically wrong is becoming a familiar phenomenon. Sometimes the erring model-makers themselves pay the price. Last August, *The Wall Street Journal* reported that a Texas-based oil and gas company had fired several executives after the firm lost millions of dollars in an acquisition deal because of "errors traced to a faulty financial-analysis spreadsheet model."

An often-repeated truism about computers is "garbage in, garbage out." Any computer program, no matter how costly, sophisticated, or popular, will yield worthless results if the data fed into it are faulty. With spreadsheets, the danger is not so much that incorrect figures can be fed into them as that "garbage" can be embedded in the models themselves. The accuracy of a spreadsheet model is dependent on the accuracy of the formulas that govern the relationships between various figures. These formulas are based on assumptions made by the model-maker. An assumption might be an educated guess about a complicated cause-and-effect relationship. It might also be a wild guess, or a dishonestly optimistic view.

you want to. It is as if you have a magnifying glass that can take in only so much of an object at a time; to see another part of the object, you move the magnifying glass.

Each intersection of column and row is called a **cell** (figure B–6), and each cell is addressed in terms of its coordinates. The columns are identified with letters (A-Z for the first 26 columns, then AA, AB, and

FIGURE B–6

Cells, labels, and numeric entries on a spreadsheet

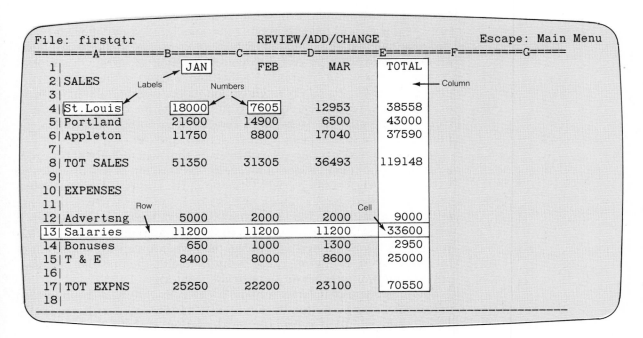

so forth), and the rows are numbered. Thus, A1 is the address of the cell in the upper left corner of the form, and D16 is the name of the cell in the fourth column (D) and the sixteenth row.

You can enter values (labels or numbers) or formulas into any cell. You simply move the cell pointer (a flashing line or box) to the appropriate cell and begin typing. **Labels** (see figure B–6) are used across the top of the page to identify each column and down the left side of the page to identify each row.

Numbers (see figure B–6) are entered into the form as easily as an accountant writes with a number 2 pencil. Simply position the cell pointer at the correct cell and type the number. Entering labels and numbers is exactly what is done with a paper spreadsheet. But the one thing you can do with an electronic spreadsheet that you cannot do with a paper one is enter formulas.

Formulas specify the calculations that must be done to determine the number to place in a cell. Remember that some numbers are simply entered (such as the figure for January's telephone bill), and other numbers are derived (such as the total expenses for the month of January). By specifying a formula, you tell the spreadsheet program to derive the number to be placed in this cell. The calculation identifies the arithmetic operations to be performed and the variables to be used. These variables are actually the contents of other cells, so their names are coordinates such as J12 and AH95.

All spreadsheet programs allow the arithmetic functions (add, subtract, multiply, divide, exponentiate), some offer statistical functions (mean, standard deviation), some include built-in mathematical functions (square root, trigonometric functions), and some offer standard business calculations (rate of return, regular payment on a loan). They all offer some other powerful calculations, such as SUM, which totals columns or rows of figures; AVG, which calculates the average of a group of numbers; and CNT, which counts the number of entries in an area of the spreadsheet. Although the formats for calculations differ from one spreadsheet program to another, a sampling of formulas you might find in a spreadsheet is illustrated in figure B–7.

One quirk of electronic spreadsheets is that when you enter data or a formula into a cell, it doesn't appear there as you type. Instead, you work on a sort of scratch pad at the top of the computer screen. When you are satisfied that the label, number or formula is correct, then you strike the return key, and the entry appears in the appropriate cell. If you entered a label or a number, then what appears is exactly what you typed. If you entered a formula, then what appears is the result of the calculation. Remember, the formula itself is behind the scenes— only the answer appears on the spreadsheet form.

Each time you enter new numbers into cells that have been named in formulas, the computer automatically updates all the affected cells. This feature is called **automatic recalculation,** and it accounts for the great success of electronic spreadsheets.

```
┌─────────────────────────────────────────────────────────────────────────┐
│  File: firstqtr            REVIEW/ADD/CHANGE        Escape: Main Menu      │
│  ==========A==============B=============C============D=============E====== │
│    1|              JAN           FEB           MAR          TOTAL          │
│    2| SALES                                                               │
│    3|                                                                     │
│    4| St.Louis     18000         7605         12953        aSUM(B4...D4)   │
│    5| Portland     21600        14900          6500        aSUM(B5...D5)   │
│    6| Appleton     11750         8800         17040        aSUM(B6...D6)   │
│    7|                                                                     │
│    8| TOT SALES  aSUM(B4...B6) aSUM(C4...C6) aSUM(D4...D6) aSUM(B8...D8)    │
│    9|                                                                     │
│   10| EXPENSES                                                            │
│   11|                                                                     │
│   12| Advertsng     5000         2000          2000        aSUM(B12...D12) │
│   13| Salaries     11200        11200         11200        aSUM(B13...D13) │
│   14| Bonuses        650         1000          1300        aSUM(B14...D14) │
│   15| T & E         8400         8000          8600        aSUM(B15...D15) │
│   16|                                                                     │
│   17| TOT EXPNS  aSUM(B12...B15)aSUM(C12...C15)aSUM(D12...D15)aSUM(B17...D17)│
│   18|                                                                     │
│   19| PRE-TAX     (B8-B17)      (C8-C17)      (D8-D17)      (E8-E17)        │
│   20|                                                                     │
└─────────────────────────────────────────────────────────────────────────┘
```

Saving a Spreadsheet

An electronic spreadsheet program can work on only one spreadsheet at a time. When you have finished working on one, you must *save* it on the computer's disk for future reference. The command you use to do this depends on your spreadsheet program, but it certainly will require you to assign this spreadsheet a unique name. After you have saved a spreadsheet, you can *load* another one from disk and work on it. Most spreadsheet packages also allow you to *delete* unwanted spreadsheets, *rename* a spreadsheet, *copy* a spreadsheet, and *list the directory* of spreadsheets. Since most spreadsheet names are limited to a few characters (usually eight), it is wise to keep a separate list of names and descriptions so you can remember which spreadsheet is which.

Printing a Spreadsheet

Although manipulating the figures on a spreadsheet is important, equally important is using the results of that manipulation in the decision-making process. This means that copies of the spreadsheet must be made available to people other than the spreadsheet's author. All spreadsheet programs allow you to print the spreadsheet, but the technique you employ to do this varies from one program to another.

Keep in mind that the dimensions of an electronic spreadsheet are far larger than the paper version. Also keep in mind that computer

FIGURE B-7
Sample of formulas used in electronic spreadsheets

paper has limited dimensions. All of this means that it is entirely possible that your electronic spreadsheet cannot be easily transferred to paper. If there are many columns, then you may have to print the spreadsheet on several pages and tape them together, side by side. If there are more rows than can fit on a sheet of paper, then you may have to tape several sheets together top to bottom.

Of course, you could plan for this when you design your spreadsheet. If possible, break your spreadsheet into page-sized sections and include subtotals on each page. Then incorporate a summary page to total the subtotals. For more information on business graphics, see the photo essay on that topic.

Costs and Benefits of a Personal Electronic Spreadsheet Program

Is a spreadsheet program worth buying? Should you spend $500 on an electronic spreadsheet? The answer is yes— and no. If your job calls for the manipulation of numbers, then a spreadsheet program must be part of your tool kit. Keep in mind that you will need a microcomputer, and the hardware alone might cost $2,000 or more. You will also need to invest time in learning how to use a spreadsheet program, although they are very easy to use.

Do all business people need electronic spreadsheets? No, certainly not. But few managers and financial people would be unwilling to invest a few hundred dollars in a program that could save them large amounts of money and countless hours of tedious calculations. Almost anyone who works with budgets or financial projections can benefit from the electronic spreadsheet.

Keep in mind that electronic spreadsheets are intended for business use. Although some would have you believe that it is smart to buy an electronic spreadsheet to handle the household budget, such an investment would probably not be very cost effective.

Hidden Dangers

Electronic spreadsheets are powerful tools that offer business people tremendous opportunities to see what business might be like by allowing them to create financial models and play out many scenarios with just a few keystrokes. But there are some hidden risks in the use of electronic spreadsheets. For one thing, users can easily lose sight of the fact that they are working with a make-believe company when they manipulate a financial model: Those are just numbers inside a computer, merely an electronic image of a real company or even of a fictitious one. Spurred by the excitement of playing with the numbers, users can forget that a company is more than figures — it also includes people, a corporate image and mission, corporate and individual values and ethics, and many other intangibles. Decisions that affect a company certainly should be supported by facts from a computer, but not exclusively. In some cases other factors must also be considered.

Second, computers have a tendency to legitimize things. You realize after taking this course that the output from electronic spreadsheet programs is only as accurate and realistic as the formulas and input figures a user enters. But some people do not realize that. If it is easy to manipulate figures with an electronic spreadsheet, it is just as easy to present incorrect, incomplete or misleading information with one. The problem here is a societal one—we tend to believe what the computer tells us is true. It is perhaps more important than ever to question the author of a spreadsheet program about the source of his or her input, the formulas used, the assumptions that were made, and so forth. Computer printouts look so authoritative that we often accept them with complacency. We must instead question their authority.

PERSONAL DATABASE MANAGEMENT SYSTEMS

You learned in chapter 9 that a database management system is a system (hardware, programs, data, procedures, and people) that allows rapid access to integrated collections of data. All of the early DBMSs were designed for mainframes. But when it became apparent that personal computers would be a valuable business tool, the need for microcomputer database management systems was recognized and addressed. Like the electronic spreadsheet, the personal DBMS changed the way people do business.

Users of personal DBMSs are able to control their own data storage and access. They no longer need to depend on a large, often bureaucratic and slow corporate data processing department to satisfy all of their information needs. Certainly, data processing must remain the caretaker for the bulk of a company's corporate data; but in instances where an individual has his or her own data, a personal database management system can be invaluable. For example, salespeople can maintain data on customers, sales calls, prospective buyers, pending sales and so forth. Managers can maintain data on the people in their units. They might track personal and professional goals, training received, special contributions made by individuals, and other data important to the manager but not part of the corporate database.

Personal database management systems are not used exclusively by employees of large companies. They also can be powerful enough to be the primary data processing system for a small company. Perhaps the term *personal* is misleading—in this section we are including any database management system that runs on a microcomputer. You will recall from chapter 3 that as microcomputers become more and more powerful, it is becoming difficult to distinguish them from larger

QUESTIONS

B.7 What is an electronic spreadsheet?

B.8 What do columns on a spreadsheet usually identify? What do rows on a spreadsheet usually identify?

B.9 Is an electronic spreadsheet larger or smaller than a paper one?

B.10 Define the following terms: *cell, window, formula, recalculation.*

B.11 Why is an electronic spreadsheet part of a decision-support system?

B.12 What is the most powerful feature of an electronic spreadsheet?

B.13 How has the electronic spreadsheet changed business in the United States? What has it enabled managers to do that they couldn't do before?

B.14 Describe two risks involved in the use of electronic spreadsheets in business.

B.15 Should every household have an electronic spreadsheet?

APPLICATION

"FEATURES HANDLE ALMOST ANY OF YOUR DATA STORAGE AND RETRIEVAL TASKS."

Brian Kerns keenly appreciates the way his data base manager organizes his work. As project development engineer for Phillips 66 Natural Gas Co., a subsidiary of Phillips Petroleum, Kerns coordinates the collection of natural gas throughout Phillips's network of oil wells in the Midwest. (The gas comes from well-drilling operations.) Kerns' job entails tracking voluminous amounts of data on each well, including well location and dimension (depth and volume), gas quality, gas volume, gas composition and the length of pipe needed to link the well to a central collection site. By weighing these factors against each other, Kerns develops a way to efficiently bring gas from scattered independent wells to a central gathering station. The result is a collection process that yields the most gas for the least amount of money.

Kerns' information storage and retrieval requirements put heavy demand on his data base software.

Fortunately, Kerns is equipped for the task. His program, like other sophisticated data base programs available only in the last year or so, exemplifies a new functionality in data bases, one that gives users greater data-handling flexibility than was available before. It includes improved data entry procedures, extended report flexibility; greater processing speed; added programming commands; applications generators; file import and export functions; and savings in time due to improved menus, help screens and better user interfaces. This new functionality shows up not only in new features themselves, but in features upgraded from earlier programs.

Kerns values these features as effective means to an end. A former R:base 4000 user, Kerns needs R:base 5000's increased functions, namely a greater number of report variables, improved data retrieval options, new programming commands, and more flexible access to **MS-DOS** functions

from within R:base, to get his job done.

For example, in entering data, Kerns found R:base 4000 limited him to writing data to a single file (table). He had to put as much well information in each table as he could, to make data retrieval as easy as possible by opening as few tables as necessary. The result was forced compactness. "In R:base 4000, when you create a form, it can be used with a single table [only]," says Kerns. R:base 5000 changed that. "In R:base 5000, you can create multi-screen input tables, and then extract data using multiple forms as well." Kerns now uses a single form to enter and extract data to and from several tables at once, reducing the amount of information crammed into the report and the time required to enter and retrieve data. By decreasing the number of operations he performs, he spends less time and effort manipulating data.

computers. Many small businesses are supported by a single powerful PC; some use local area network (LAN) technology (see chapter 10) to link together several microcomputers and allow all of them to access the same central microcomputer database.

Personal DBMSs evolved; they did not suddenly appear on the scene. In fact, early attempts to satisfy data storage and retrieval needs for PC users resulted not in database management systems, but in **file management systems.** File management systems, as you recall from chapters 7 and 8, suffer problems that DBMSs do not. Some of the problems include redundant data, slow retrieval of specific records, and an inability to integrate data in separate files. However, many business people need to maintain only one or two files — for them, file management systems work just fine. Other users have more complex needs, and for them only a true database management system will do.

All of the characteristics of a DBMS described in chapter 9 are also true for a microcomputer DBMS. You should review that chapter now. However, there is a difference between the amount of time the user of a corporate database and the user of a personal database needs to devote to the design and creation of the database. The user of a corporate database usually participates only in the requirements definition of the database, along with all the other users. Then highly skilled database technicians take over. They design the physical layout of the database, build it, and usually load the initial data into the database. After that, the DBA (see chapter 9), not the user, is responsible for backup, recovery, security, and any modification of the database structure necessary.

In contrast, the user of a personal database often *is* the DBA. Usually not a skilled database professional, the user still is expected to design, build, load, use, back up, protect, and modify the database. Fortunately, many PC database management systems are "user friendly." In this text we cannot show you how to use every DBMS package. We will examine the basic steps the user of any personal DBMS can expect to take.

Building the Database

Before you can access data you must first build the database. You need to decide what data you want to store, define the database structure to the DBMS, and load the data. The first step is preparation, and it is done without the help of a computer.

Step 1: *Preparation*

Begin by writing a list of the **objects,** or things in the real world, you want to keep track of. In a small retail company you might want to track customers, salespeople, and sales .

Next, identify the associations between any of the objects. For example, a sale involves both a customer and a salesperson (figure. B – 8). These associations, or **relationships,** will need to be represented in the database later on.

Now, for each object, write a list of the facts you want to keep:

Customer
   <u>Account number</u>
   Name
   Address
   Telephone number

FIGURE B—8
Identifying relationships among objects

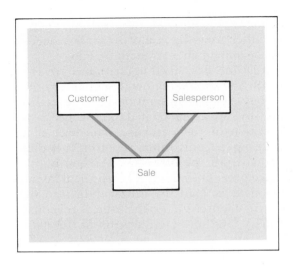

• **Salesperson**
    <u>Social security number</u>
    Name
    Salary
    Commission rate

• **Sale**
    <u>Sale number</u>
    Date
    Amount
    Customer name
    Salesperson name

For example, you might want to keep a customer's account number, name, address, telephone number, and account balance. You might want to keep a salesperson's social security number, name, salary, and commission rate. For a sale you might need to store the number of the sale, date, amount of the sale, and the names of the customer and salesperson involved. Be sure there is a unique **key field** for each object. In this example, Customer Account Number is the key field for Customer, Social Security Number is the key field for Salesperson, and Sale Number is the key for Sale. The key fields are underlined above.

The next step is to **link** related objects together by using the key fields you identified. In this example, the fields for Customer and Salesperson remain the same. However, for a sale you will replace the name of the customer with the customer's account number, and you will replace the name of the salesperson with the salesperson's social security number, as shown below:

• **Customer**
    <u>Account number</u>
    Name
    Address
    Telephone number

- **Salesperson**
    Social security number
    Name
    Salary
    Commission rate

- **Sale**
    Sale number
    Date
    Amount
    Account number
    Social security number

The final preparation step is to decide on the *length* of each field and the **type of data** you want the computer to store in it (figure B–9). If you will use the field for arithmetic, then it must be defined as numeric. Some DBMSs ask you to further define numeric fields as integer, decimal, dollar, or scientific. If you will not use the field for arithmetic, then you can define it as a field for character data. Some DBMSs also allow you to select special formats such as date formats (mm/dd/yy).

Notice the number of details the user of a personal DBMS has to know about stored data. It is unlikely that the user of a corporate DBMS would need to decide on the length of fields or their data types. But remember: When you use a personal DBMS, you often are your own DBA.

OBJECT/FIELD	LENGTH	DATA TYPE
Customer		
Account number	3	integer
Name	38	character
Address	55	character
Telephone number	8	character
Balance	9	dollar
Salesperson		
Social security number	11	character
Name	38	character
Salary	7	dollar
Commission rate	3	decimal
Sale		
Sale number	5	integer
Date	8	date
Amount	7	dollar
Account number	—	—
Social security number	—	—

FIGURE B–9
Defining field lengths and data types

Step 2: *Creating the Database Structure*

After completing the preparation step, the rest of the job is relatively easy. Now you can begin to work with the DBMS software. Load the DBMS into your computer's memory. You will probably be presented with a menu of options (figure B–10) from which you select the function you wish to perform. You should select the one that allows you to create a new database.

The DBMS will ask you to name the database. A DBMS can work with only one database at a time, so all databases must be stored on disk when not in use. Therefore, each database name must be unique. After naming the database, you must define the **database structure.** This is often referred to as building the data dictionary. You must enter the name of each object (some DBMSs call them files, some call them tables, some call them relations) and then the name, length, and data type of each field. If you have done your preparation well, this part is very easy. After you finish with one object, you repeat the steps for each of the remaining objects. Finally, you indicate to the DBMS that you are finished with the creation step. When the menu appears, you should select the option that allows you to enter data.

Step 3: *Entering Data*

At this point the DBMS knows the file and field formats, but the files are completely empty. You must now enter the data. This step is often called *loading* the database. (The word "load" is also used to mean place a program into memory. Don't be confused.) Once again, preparation is important. The data you are entering should be organized and

FIGURE B–10

Menu of options for one microcomputer DBMS product

```
                    Application EXPRESS
        Copyright (c) 1985 by Microrim, Inc. (Ver. 1.01 PC-DOS)

              Select option - [F10] for help
          (1)  Define a new database
          (2)  Change an existing database definition
          (3)  Define a new application
          (4)  Change an existing application
          (5)  Display file directory
          (6)  Exit
```

legible. If you are copying data from manual files, then you should pull from the files those sheets of paper containing the data you need. Many users do not perform this step themselves, because it requires a lot of typing. Instead, they organize the data and then hire professional typists or data-entry personnel to load the database. In fact, that is what Mary Forsythe did in chapter 1.

Individuals who are tracking their own personal data, such as a salesperson tracking his or her own contacts and sales, often use the DBMS as a tool for organizing. They sit in front of the computer with a briefcase full of scraps of paper and enter the data, bit by bit. Other users of personal DBMSs track information captured by other people and must be more organized. For example, a sales manager might want to enter data about each salesperson at the end of each week. This is done more quickly and accurately if the salespeople complete forms that match the computer screen layout. Most DBMSs prompt the user with the name of each field. This is one good reason for using meaningful field names (*name* rather than *n* or *addr* rather than *fld#4*).

When you have entered all of your initial data (you will probably add more data later) you must be sure to *save* it. At that point you will have created your database. Now you must learn how to back it up and how to access the data in it.

Backing Up the Database

Microcomputer users must be especially aware of the necessity for backup and recovery procedures. **Backing up** files means making copies (on diskette or cassette tape) of them and storing the copies in a safe place off site. **Recovery** means reloading the files after some disaster makes the current file copies unusable.

To back up your database you probably will have to exit from the DBMS and invoke a system utility program (see module E) that copies files. Follow the procedures defined by the computer manufacturer. Then carefully label the diskettes or tape, being sure to include the date the backup was made. Store backup copies away from the computer site. What good would backups do if they burned in the same fire that destroyed the computer?

The frequency with which the database needs to be backed up depends on how often it is updated and how costly it would be to reenter all the changes that have occurred since you last made a backup copy. Because backing up microcomputer files is often tedious and time consuming (although high-speed tape backup systems exist), users tend not to do it often enough. It is better to be on the safe side and back up your database more frequently than you think you have to.

Accessing the Database

There are two functions you will want to perform on your database: maintaining the data and retrieving data. **Maintenance** means keeping your database current, modifying it to reflect changes in the real world. There are three changes you can make to a database: you can *insert* new records, *delete* unwanted records, and *update* existing records. All three are accomplished with simple database commands. You will need to select the menu option that allows you to change the database and then make the change. When you wish to delete or update an existing record, you must first identify the record so the DBMS can locate it. When you wish to insert a new record, the DBMS first checks to be sure that a record with that key does not already exist.

The other important database function is **data retrieval.** Data retrieval can be done with a DBMS query language or with an application program. Using a DBMS **query language,** you can select data from the database to be displayed on the computer screen, to be copied to a file (for use in another program such as an electronic spreadsheet), or to be printed. The commands that you use to do this vary from one DBMS to another, but all of them allow you to perform three basic operations: projection, selection, and join. We will use the IBM relational database language called SQL to illustrate each of the three query language operations.

A file is referred to as a table in SQL. A table contains rows, each of which can be thought of as a record. Table columns represent data fields within records.

FIGURE B–11
Data for customer and sale relations

CUSTOMER Table

Account number	Name	Address	Phone number	Balance
100	JONES	CLINTON	669-2555	250.00
200	RODRIGUEZ	MADISON	245-3621	100.00
300	CHANG	MADISON	245-0000	0.00
400	HOFFBERG	CLINTON	669-4197	100.00
500	KELLY	CLINTON	669-2544	200.00
600	NGUYEN	MADISON	245-7777	0.00

SALE Table

Sale number	Date	Amount	Account number	SS number
63295	10/15/87	50.00	200	049-22-1111
63296	10/15/87	25.00	500	621-94-7297
63299	10/15/87	100.00	200	621-94-7297
64011	10/18/87	20.00	500	049-22-1111
64023	10/18/87	35.00	300	049-22-1111

Examine the tables in figure B–11. There are 6 customers in the Customer table, and 5 sales in the Sale table. There are 5 fields in each customer record (5 columns in the Customer table) and 5 fields in each sales record (5 columns in the Sale table). The formats of these tables match the data formats described in figure B–9.

Notice that the underscore character (–) is used to "hyphenate" words in SQL. A different character might be used in other DBMS query languages.

Using the data in figure B–11 for illustration, we will look at each of the three fundamental DBMS query operations — projection, selection, and join.

When you use **projection,** you are telling the DBMS to retrieve all of the records in a file, but only certain fields. You might use this operation if you wanted to extract a list of customer names and telephone numbers, but you were not interested in their account numbers and addresses. Thus, projection retrieves only specific fields for all the records in a file. The SQL language statement that retrieves all customers' names and telephone numbers from the Customer table is as follows:

```
SELECT          NAME, PHONE_NUMBER
FROM            CUSTOMER
```

The results of this projection on the data in figure B–11 are as follows:

```
JONES           669-2555
RODRIGUEZ       245-3621
CHANG           245-0000
HOFFBERG        669-4197
KELLY           669-2544
NGUYEN          245-7777
```

When you use **selection**, you tell the DBMS to retrieve only certain records from a file. Selection will get you entire records, but only the ones you want. This operation would be useful if you needed complete data about all customers whose accounts were overdue. The SQL selection command to produce such a list is as follows:

```
SELECT          ACCOUNT_NUMBER, NAME, ADDRESS,
                PHONE_NUMBER, BALANCE
FROM            CUSTOMER
WHERE           BALANCE > 0
```

The results of this selection on the data in figure B–11 are as follows:

```
100    JONES        CLINTON     669-2555   250.00
200    RODRIGUEZ    MADISON     245-3621   100.00
400    HOFFBERG     CLINTON     669-4197   100.00
500    KELLY        CLINTON     669-2544   200.00
```

When you use the **join** operation, you are telling the DBMS to build records from two or more files by matching the values in a particular field. This operation enables the DBMS to link one file to another. For example, consider the customers table and the sale transactions table in figure B–11. Both tables contain the customer account number field (Account_number), because that is what links a particular sale to a particular customer. When you print customer invoices at the end of the month, you might use the join operation to build records that contain customer data and sale transaction data for all customers who made purchases this month. (Sending bills to overdue accounts is done separately.) The join operation will not extract customers who do not have at least one matching sale transaction — consequently, you send bills only to people who bought something this month. Using SQL to do this join operation we would write:

```
SELECT              ACCOUNT_NUMBER, NAME, ADDRESS,
                    SALE_NUMBER, DATE, AMOUNT
FROM                CUSTOMER, SALE
WHERE               CUSTOMER.ACCOUNT_NUMBER
                    = SALE.ACCOUNT_NUMBER
```

The results of this join operation on the data in figure B–11 are as follows:

```
200    RODRIGUEZ    MADISON    63295    10/15/87     50.00
200    RODRIGUEZ    MADISON    63299    10/15/87    100.00
300    CHANG        MADISON    64023    10/18/87     35.00
500    KELLY        CLINTON    63296    10/15/87     25.00
500    KELLY        CLINTON    64011    10/18/87     20.00
```

Combinations of the three fundamental operations — projection, selection, and join — can be used to instruct the DBMS to retrieve the exact data you need for any application.

Use of a DBMS query language enables a user to reference data in the database. But we often need to process that data — summarize it, do arithmetic with it, compare it with other data from other sources, and so forth. As you can see, query languages, though powerful, do not by themselves satisfy all user needs. Instead we may have to write **application programs** that process the database data. In these cases, the application programs regard the database simply as a source of input. Because most programming languages do not include database commands — they are restricted to file processing commands — a programmer using a microcomputer database must write code in the special programming language provided by the DBMS manufacturer.

Do you understand the ramifications of this? Using a query language is easy enough for almost all users to master quickly. But query languages are not powerful enough to process data. Therefore, programs must be written. But most microcomputer database users have neither the skills to do this nor the interest in learning how to do it. The user might feel trapped. However, there are some reasonable options from which the nonprogramming user can choose.

First, many hundreds of application programs already have been developed. The needs of users of most small computers are not really unique. A little research can reveal many programs that can be purchased, installed and used with few or no alterations.

An entire market has been created by microcomputer database management systems and is being filled by **value-added resellers (VARs)**. These are people who develop DBMS applications for specific database packages in specific niches. An example of such an application is a software package designed for use in a dentist's office using dBASE III Plus (one of many microcomputer database management systems). An interested dentist would simply purchase the DBMS and the off-the-shelf application software.

DBMS publishers usually can provide you with a catalog of application software developed for their DBMS. For instance, a catalog called *Microrim Applied* lists almost 500 programs that have been developed for the R:Base family of DBMSs published by Microrim. You can get catalogs like this one through your DBMS publisher or through a knowledgeable microcomputer dealer.

A second option, and the one Mary Forsythe chose in chapter 1, is to hire a consultant to write the application programs for you. Although this may seem like an expensive way to develop applications, applications are almost always cheaper and more reliable when they are developed by an expert than when you develop them yourself. A word of caution, though: Be sure to state your system requirements clearly and unambiguously to the consultant before development begins. System development as described in chapter 5 should follow the same steps for small systems as for large ones. Also, keep in mind the warnings about using a consultant described in a box in chapter 5.

Costs and Benefits of a Personal DBMS

A personal DBMS is not a must for every household nor for every business person. But a personal DBMS can be very useful to anyone who needs to maintain several files of data, particularly if those files need to be integrated.

Even a few years ago, people who could have benefited from a personal DBMS had to do without, either because DBMSs were too expensive or too difficult to use. Now, however, powerful, user-friendly DBMSs are available for only a few hundred dollars. Some microcomputer databases can even be accessed through natural language commands making them even more user-friendly. It is tempting to predict that very soon all microcomputer file processing systems will

APPLICATION

"USERS HAVE COME TO EXPECT CERTAIN FEATURES."

Sophisticated data base software has become so powerful in the last year that certain advanced capabilities have come to be regarded as standard. Most data base programs put no limits on file or record size. Others set limits you'll probably never reach; dBase III, for instance, allows over 2 billion records per data base. A menu-driven user interface and on-line help are the norm, as is a sophisticated report generator that produces subtotals.

dBase III Plus offers all these features, plus the capability to open up to 10 files at once, pull-down menus and an Assist mode to help you learn command language syntax. You choose commands from menus and dBase displays the proper command syntax at the bottom of the screen (you can turn this feature on or off). III Plus also offers networking and a screen painter and application generator.

The real power of Plus, however, is its support of over 50 new programming commands. Some of these provide additional programming capabilities while others help reduce the number of lines of program code.

Just over a year ago R:base 5000, a product with a new twist, was introduced. While it, too, offers a strong programming language, a screen painter, the ability to open up to 40 files at once and a menu-driven interface, it also includes the Application Express, which helps you build basic applications by writing the application code as you select menu options. This feature can save you the expense of hiring a consultant or the time involved in learning a language just to produce simple applications.

Paradox is comparable to dBase and R:base in features and functionality. It takes advantage of a Lotus-like interface and arranges data in tables. Paradox also incorporates safety features that make it nearly impossible to lose data in restructuring a file. When you change a file, Paradox warns you about possible data losses. You can then cancel the change, save endangered data in a temporary file or invoke the change anyway.

The latest release of Paradox contains an application generator and eliminates copy protection. Paradox' biggest plus, however, is its ease of use, especially when you are creating complex queries. Based on query-by-

example, Paradox lets you display all the fields in all the files you want to query. You simply check off fields you want included in the report; you can even set up specific search conditions using operators such as 'and' or 'greater than.' The program searches for inexact matches, too. For example, if you know how someone's name is pronounced but not their spelling, you can have Paradox search for a name "like Tomson."

Another product, KnowledgeMan, has been upgraded within the last year. Most of the changes are in the user interface. KnowledgeMan/2 supports seven modules, menu-driven implementations of the program's command language. It includes modules for designing screens, editing text and program code, and creating charts and graphs.

Reflex offers some complex capabilities in a straightforward manner. The program's strong point is its ability to provide five different data displays, ranging from the full details of a single record to graphed information. This makes Reflex well-suited to applications that require a lot of data analysis.

be replaced by their more powerful successors, database management systems.

What is the cost of a personal DBMS? Several costs have been mentioned, including hardware, software, and the time it takes to learn how to use the system. Is a personal DBMS worth the cost? The answer to that question depends on your own needs, but for most small businesses and for small business units within larger corporations, the answer is more frequently becoming yes.

▓ SUMMARY

The continued proliferation of microcomputers is influenced by many factors, but two of the more significant ones are: (1) microcomputers are becoming less expensive, and (2) many excellent software packages are available for microcomputers. Three of the most important types of personal computer software are word processing programs, electronic spreadsheets, and personal database management systems. All three have proven to be very popular with individuals and businesses alike.

Word processing programs have helped to streamline document preparation and filing. Electronic spreadsheet programs have made financial modeling easy. And personal DBMSs have enabled individuals to easily store and retrieve data and have allowed employees of large corporations to reduce their dependence on the corporate data processing department.

It is evident that these three tools have already had a great impact on business. Other programs are also available for microcomputers, and still more are being developed and released all the time. You should frequently scan both business and microcomputer periodicals to find out what new personal productivity tools are available for microcomputers.

QUESTIONS

B.16 Name two advantages users of a personal DBMS have over users of a corporate DBMS.

B.17 Name four responsibilities users of a personal DBMS have that users of a corporate DBMS do not have.

B.18 List the steps a user should complete before attempting to create a database.

B.19 What is the difference between the structure of a database and database data?

B.20 How frequently should a personal database be backed up?

B.21 Name three maintenance functions performed on a database.

B.22 Name two ways of accessing the data in a personal database.

B.23 What are three data-retrieval operations you can perform on a database? Give an example, other than one mentioned in this text, of the use of each one.

B.24 Describe three ways a user can acquire application programs for his or her database.

B.25 What is a value-added reseller?

WORD LIST

Personal computer (PC)
Word processing program
Electronic spreadsheet program
Personal database management
  system
Word processing
Document
Load
Menu
Cursor
Wrap around
Cut and paste
Function key
Document format

Electronic mail system
Letter-quality print
Spreadsheet
Window
Cell
Label
Formula
Automatic recalculation
File management system
Object
Relationship
Key field
Link
Data type

Database structure
Backup
Recovery
Maintenance of a database
Data retrieval
Query language
SQL
Projection
Selection
Join
Application program
Value-added reseller (VAR)

QUESTIONS TO CHALLENGE YOUR THINKING

A. Determine the cost of purchasing a microcomputer with a word processing program, an electronic spreadsheet, and a personal database management system. Do this by visiting your local computer store or by examining computer catalogs. Be sure that your hardware configuration will support the software you select. Indicate the cost for each of the *five* components of your system.

B. Contact a DBMS publisher and acquire a copy of its VAR catalog. If it is too expensive for you to buy, then ask to use the reference copy in your local computer store. How many programs are already available for that DBMS? What areas of business are included? What businesses are *not* included?

C. Investigate "integrated packages" such as Lotus 1-2-3 and Symphony by researching the literature or by interviewing a knowledgeable computer dealer or consultant. What applications do they include? What are the advantages of using an integrated package? What are the disadvantages?

D. In a survey of high-level corporate executives, this question was asked: "What personal database management system (DBMS) do you use?" A significant number of executives listed the name of their electronic spreadsheet program, not a DBMS. Explain the difference between the two in terms an executive would understand. Why do you suppose so many executives answered the question the way they did?

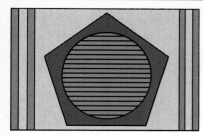

PHOTO ESSAY

COMPUTERS AND SOCIETY

More Uses, More Users, More Questions

Textile design is a timely example of computer use today.

▓ ROBOT MYTHS AND REALITIES

R2D2 and C3PO are fiction. At this time, state-of-the-art robotics does not even include voice recognition and communication in one language, let alone C3PO's claim to over six million forms of communication. Today's mobile robots can do little more than avoid objects, utter a few canned phrases, and wave an arm or two around in the air. Such robots are toys.

Industrial robots, on the other hand, are very much a reality. Although they are unexciting to see, industrial robots are quite useful, performing repetitive, sometimes dangerous, tasks with a high degree of reliability. Industrial robots cut airplane parts, pack candy, drill holes, and remove parts from hot ovens. Further, such robots are cost effective. In 1981, a robot could be operated at $5.50 an hour; during that same year, the average wage and benefit expense for a comparable laborer was $18.10.

Industrial robots have the potential to eliminate drudgery and meaningless labor. They can replace humans in unpleasant environments, such as mines or hot factories. Industrial robots can also work in dangerous environments, such as the bowels of nuclear reactors or in the presence of highly contagious and dangerous diseases.

The robots are here! Is this Star Wars setting a myth or reality?

Robots are tireless and uncomplaining workers, while 24 million industrial workers are worried about increasing automation.

Japan is the leader in the practical application of industrial robots.

This 'Apprentice' robot produces uniform, reproducible aluminum coatings.

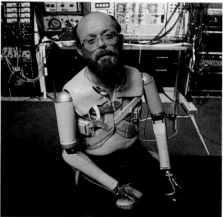

A victim of a power-line accident tries out his new electronic arms, activated by motion sensors and electrical signals from the skin.

But what are the social consequences? If robots take over spot welding, what will happen to the world's spot welders? If robots take over auto painting, what will happen to the world's auto painters? Although robots will create some new jobs, the ratio of lost jobs to new jobs will not be one to one. Further, today's spot welders are unlikely to be tomorrow's robot mechanics. What will the response of the labor unions be? What *should* the response of the labor unions be?

Furthermore, the use of robots means a loss of control. Who is responsible if a robot accidentally kills someone? If robots can be programmed to produce useful work, they can also be programmed to commit crimes. Who is responsible if a robot intentionally kills someone?

Less dramatically, considering that robots follow standardized procedures, will products become so similar that our environment becomes uniform, sterile, and bland? Will craftsmanship and creativity in workmanship disappear? Does today's laborer have only three choices — to become a technologist, an artisan, or unemployed?

▥ HEALTH AND MEDICINE

Computers prolong life and reduce pain and suffering. Computers help doctors to detect diseases; they improve diagnoses; they enable surgeons to operate more precisely; they monitor critically ill patients. Computer systems analyze the occurrence of disease and help determine causes and means of prevention.

Computer technology also helps people to compensate for or overcome handicaps. Hearing can be improved; artificial limbs can be made more useful; optical sensors can detect eye movements, thus enabling paraplegics to turn pages or cause other action to occur by moving their eyes.

All of these benefits are possible, but not without social cost. People are confronted with new ethical dilemmas. When is someone really dead? At what point should life-sustaining equipment be removed to allow a person to die? At what point is life no longer worth living? Who pays the cost of maintaining a person who cannot afford to be maintained? Such questions necessitate a new morality. Meanwhile, physicians, relatives, and friends are forced to make life-and-death decisions.

Imaging systems help doctors at Duke University to examine electronically enhanced images, such as X-rays, from the next room or from thousands of miles away.

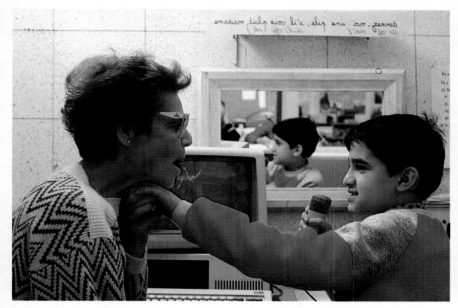

Computer-assisted speech training works for this therapist and child.

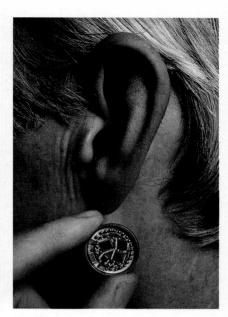

Small hearing devices continue to decrease in size, with medical research producing circuitry as tiny as nerves and neurons.

Furthermore, what are the biological consequences of introducing technology into medicine? If the evolution of the human race is governed by the law of the survival of the fittest, what happens when the unfit are maintained? Should people with certain diseases or medical conditions be prohibited from procreating?

By controlling the processes of aging and by using artificial organs, doctors may extend life expectancy to 100 years or more. When it becomes possible, should it be allowed?

Delicate eye cornea surgery is aided by computers.

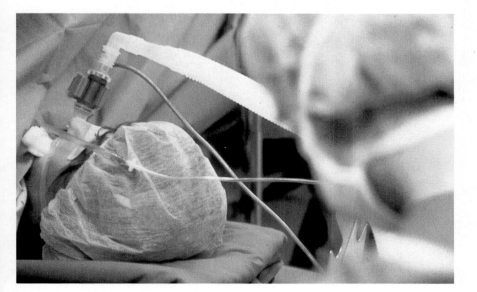

▦ BUSINESS

The computer has revolutionized the way we do business. Credit checking, order processing, travel reservations, automated manufacturing, typing, communications—all have been changed by computers. In fact, many services we take for granted would be impossible without computer technology.

Computers improve productivity and operating efficiency. Product quality can increase, costs can decrease, or both. Consider the telephone: Because of the computer, long distance service has improved, while costs have decreased. Computer technology can substantially improve our material well-being.

At the same time, however, computers can create standardized, sterile, and inflexible environments. With computers, warm and friendly offices can become cold and hostile. Decision making can be constrained, and people can lose freedom of action. Computer systems provide new opportunities for crime. Privacy can be invaded, and sometimes the victim is unaware of the invasion.

Worst of all, computer systems contribute to the acceleration of our pace of life. With computers, we can acquire better and cheaper things more and more rapidly. But do we want better and cheaper things, more and more rapidly? Computers do not help us answer that question.

Harwood K. Smith & Partners employs 25 computer-aided design (CAD) systems to increase productivity in its architectural, interior design, and health facilities departments.

ATMs, or automatic teller machines, have helped take the "wait" out of banking.

Stockbrokers and investment houses use computers to provide customers with current and accurate information about stocks and markets.

Lap-top computers help professionals on the road retain and communicate information.

Warehouses throughout the world use computerized inventory control systems to make decisions regarding shipments, stock, and billing.

Business people today are expected to master the latest advances in microcomputer applications.

Many teachers find that microcomputers stimulate curiosity and learning.

▥ EDUCATION AND TRAINING

Educational games and drill and practice programs can improve the quality of education and increase teacher productivity. Educational software can make learning easier and more fun, and it can respond to individual differences. For example, computer-assisted instruction (CAI) can respond to each student's level of knowledge. Students who answer all questions correctly can be introduced to new and more difficult material. Students who consistently answer incorrectly can be presented with more basic material or with tutorial discussions.

Even more exciting, computers offer opportunities to teach subjects in entirely new ways. Computer graphics can be used to present mathematical principles, such as the concept of a limit. Students who are exposed to mathematical concepts from a graphical point of view appear to gain improved intuition into mathematical concepts.

Simulation provides another educational possibility. Students can perform chemistry or physics experiments on the computer. For example, students can instruct the computer to combine chemical compounds, and the computer will simulate a chemical reaction. Such simulation can reduce laboratory expenses, as well as allow students to learn from experiments that would be too dangerous to do in reality.

Computer-assisted instruction (CAI) can be useful as a learning tool for many subjects.

Hands-on training helps the user learn quickly about Tele-Video products.

High school geometry has been taught in the same fashion for centuries. With the computer language LOGO, however, geometry can be taught using entirely new methods.

Unfortunately, there are not enough computers to go around. According to one estimate, there are more than 200 students for every microcomputer. (In contrast, IBM has one computer terminal for every two employees.) The benefits of computer-based education will have little impact until this ratio is drastically reduced.

Even then, what are the social costs? Will computers take the humanness out of teaching? Will students feel more isolated and alone when using computer-based systems? A classroom may be slow and inefficient, but it is social. Will the cost of computer-assisted instruction be less well-developed social skills?

▦ COMMUNICATIONS

Computer-aided publishing material can be prepared and printed from many, many miles away.

The world gets smaller and smaller. Reporters at remote sites write stories on word processing systems and submit their stories over communications lines to a computer at the newspaper's headquarters. The paper is composed in electronic form and sent via satellite to distributed printing plants. Finally, near the point of sale, the paper is printed.

Using teleconferencing, businesspeople in different locations meet face-to-face without travel. Air traffic controllers instruct pilots whom they never meet to fly airplanes that they never see, except electronically. Airplanes are kept on the ground in Seattle because of crowded airspace in Chicago. A shopper at home in Milwaukee buys a TV from a store located in Phoenix using a credit card from a bank in Memphis. In less than five seconds, computers in Milwaukee, Phoenix, and Memphis communicate to verify credit and inventory levels, to generate the shipping invoice, and to record the sale.

It becomes easier and easier to "reach out, reach out and touch someone," whether that someone is a friend, a business associate, a business, or a computer. What are the consequences of all this reaching out? Closer communication, better understanding among people, a world view instead of a neighborhood view are some consequences. Others are a furious pace of life, confusion and complexity, and more information than we are capable of handling. According to Bell Laboratories, the weekday edition of *The New York Times* contains more information than a person in the sixteenth century received in an entire lifetime. How can we cope? Do we need a computer to say "no thanks" when someone reaches out?

The USA Today newsroom reporters enter their stories for the next day on computer terminals.

USA Today provides a practical example of today's telecommunications technology.

Some systems can be interconnected through a local area network to accommodate more than 1000 workstations.

Teleconferencing is used by large companies for face-to-face communication without the cost of travel.

Switchboard operator using a computer to track guests for calls.

Electronic mail provides a timely method of communication.

Communications control at the Bell Telephone network center.

Shuttle launch used computers for communication and control and employed a robotic arm to deploy and retrieve the space platform.

▥ COMMUNICATIONS AND CONTROL

Computers control processes. They run machinery, regulate the speed of production lines, monitor power plants and refineries, and control space probes. Computers instructed a robot on Mars to perform experiments—experiments that, ironically, were concerned with searching for signs of life. Computers assimilate more data than human beings, make decisions in split seconds, and work tirelessly at boring and repetitive jobs. They are ideal for industrial control.

But should we trust computer control? If surgeons avoid surgery and lawyers avoid lawsuits, will computer programmers avoid automated airplanes? Who is responsible for mishaps? Computers introduce possibilities for crime, sabotage, and blackmail. Are these possibilities being examined, discussed, and controlled?

Control of electricity and water is essential to our society and impossible without the aid of computers, such as those shown here at the Bonneville Power Authority.

GENERAL ELECTRIC COMPANY
ADVANCED TERRAIN REPRESENTATION
MILITARY TACTICAL SCENE WITH OVERLAY SHOWING DEPLOYMENT
OF FORCES (KEY CULTURE FEATURES CUED WITH SYMBOLS)

Military use of computers can combine computer graphics and computer communications to provide commanders with realistic representations of troop movements as they are occurring.

Today's sheriff with today's gold: recovering $150,000 worth of computer chips.

Many congressional representatives use local communication networks for status information on legislation.

▥ GOVERNMENT AND LAW ENFORCEMENT

Computers facilitate the making, the keeping, and the breaking of the law. Computer systems control the massive flow of paperwork through the U.S. Congress. Computer systems keep congressional schedules, record ballots, send and receive electronic mail, maintain records of correspondence, and help to produce the *Congressional Record*.

Computers assist law enforcement by keeping records of crimes and criminals. Using computers and communications, police can check records on a suspected stolen automobile without stopping the vehicle. More information for law enforcement means greater safety for police and less disruption for law-abiding citizens. Computer systems also increase the efficiency of policy operations, producing lower costs and better law enforcement.

Unfortunately, computer systems provide new opportunities for crime, necessitating new laws and new law enforcement techniques. If money in a French bank is stolen in the United States through communications with a computer located in Switzerland, which country's laws pertain? Suppose such a crime is suspected. Who investigates it? Where and how?

Suppose someone steals software by copying it. How should the investigating officer proceed? Since no object was stolen, what evidence should be gathered? Clearly, the investigation of computer crime requires special training. Who has this training?

Law enforcement agencies, such as this one, use computerized consoles to monitor locations of and dispatch calls to police vehicles.

Computers in a police car can access information on people and automobiles immediately.

▥ SUMMARY

Computer systems are tools; as such, they are instruments for accomplishing jobs or solving problems. Tools have no conscience. They can be used for good or evil, for creation or destruction, for benefit or harm. Whether a tool is beneficial, on balance, depends on the people who use it.

In the preceding pages, you have seen some of the ways computer systems benefit society. Each of these applications is, in itself, good. The tool behind these applications, however, is ethically neutral. Computers are powerful tools, and the more powerful the tool, the greater the potential danger. To avoid such danger, human beings need to gain awareness and to maintain control.

Street-map navigation displays help for visitors so that they can find their way around town.

QUESTIONS

1. Describe the benefits and dangers of robotics. What can you, as a citizen, do to reduce the dangers?

2. Summarize the ethical problems caused by the introduction of computers into the medical field.

3. Consider the consequences of obtaining better and cheaper goods, more and more rapidly. At what point does the acquisition of material goods lose value to you?

4. Describe the advantages and disadvantages of computers in education. Do you think the impact of computers on education is positive?

5. Summarize the ways in which computer technology has made the world smaller and smaller. Has this change been beneficial? What changes do you expect to see in the future?

NUMERIC REPRESENTATION AND COMPUTER ARITHMETIC

MODULE C

In this module, we discuss how computers represent numbers and perform arithmetic. This information supplements material in chapter 2, so be sure to read chapter 2 before continuing with this section.

Computers represent two basic types of data: **numeric** and **alphanumeric**. Numeric data consists of numbers that can be processed arithmetically, and alphanumeric data consists of numbers, letters, and special symbols such as #, $, and %. Alphanumeric data is not processed arithmetically. Even if alphanumeric data consists entirely of numbers, the computer represents it in such a way that arithmetic cannot be performed on it.

Alphanumeric data is represented by character codes such as EBCDIC. This type of representation was discussed in chapter 2, and we will not repeat that discussion here. Instead, we will discuss the format and processing of numeric data.

DECIMAL AND BINARY NUMBERS

To understand how numbers are represented in the computer, try to recall your second-grade math. Remember Mrs. Gazernenplatz, your second-grade teacher? When she wrote a number such as 5437 on the board, she said that the 7 is in the ones place, the 3 is in the tens place, the 4 is in the hundreds place, and the 5 is in the thousands place. The number can thus be defined as 5 times 1000, plus 4 times 100, plus 3 times 10, plus 7 times 1.

Later, in algebra, you learned that you also can write 1000 as 10^3 ($10 \times 10 \times 10$), 100 as 10^2, 10 as 10^1, and 1 as 10^0. Thus, each place is a power of 10. The power value starts with 0 and increases by 1 for each place to the left of the decimal point. (See figure C−1).

In the computer, numeric data often is represented in binary form. The binary number system has only two digits (or symbols): 0 and 1. Each binary place is assigned a binary digit, or **bit.** Examples of binary numbers are 110110, 01110, 11111, and 00000. The number 0121 is not a binary number, because the symbol *2* is not defined in the binary system. As explained in chapter 2, computers use the binary system because the symbols 0 and 1 are easy to represent electronically.

FIGURE C−1
Decimal-place notation

5437 DECIMAL		
5 × 1000		5 × 10^3 (thousands place)
+4 × 100	or	+4 × 10^2 (hundreds place)
+3 × 10		+3 × 10^1 (tens place)
+7 × 1		+7 × 10^0 (ones place)

1010 BINARY IS 10 IN DECIMAL FORM

FIGURE C–2
Binary-place notation

1×8		1×2^3 (eights place)
$+0 \times 4$	or	$+0 \times 2^2$ (fours place)
$+1 \times 2$		$+1 \times 2^1$ (twos place)
$+0 \times 1$		$+0 \times 2^0$ (ones place)

Binary numbers are constructed the same way as decimal numbers, but, instead of powers of 10 in the places, powers of 2 are used. Thus, there is the ones place 2^0, the twos place 2^1, the fours place 2^2, the eights place 2^3, and so forth, as shown in figure C–2. The binary number 1010 is interpreted as 1 times 8, plus 0 times 4, plus 1 times 2, plus 0 times 1, or 10 in decimal. Figure C–3 shows the first 16 binary numbers.

Humans like to work with decimal numbers, but computers are more efficient when working with binary numbers. Therefore, when many calculations are to be performed, the computer converts decimal numbers to binary form and makes the calculations using binary, arithmetic. Results are then reconverted to decimal format before they are printed. We will discuss how these conversions are performed after we discuss binary arithmetic.

Binary Arithmetic

Binary numbers can be added much the way decimal numbers are added. You add one column at a time and carry when necessary. In binary format,

$$0 + 0 = 0$$
$$0 + 1 = 1$$
$$1 + 0 = 1$$
$$1 + 1 = 10$$

BINARY	DECIMAL	BINARY	DECIMAL
0000	0	1000	8
0001	1	1001	9
0010	2	1010	10
0011	3	1011	11
0100	4	1100	12
0101	5	1101	13
0110	6	1110	14
0111	7	1111	15

FIGURE C–3
The first 16 numbers in binary and decimal formats

Thus, when two 1's are added, a 1 is carried into the next place. The following are examples of binary addition:

```
                              1  ←—(Carries)—→1111
       0010                 1010              1111
     + 0101               + 0010            + 0001
       0111                 1100             10000
```

Although subtraction can be done in binary arithmetic just as it is done in decimal, computers usually do not do this. In fact (here's an amazing fact), *most computers cannot subtract*! Instead, they find the result of a subtraction by adding in a special way. This technique is called **complement addition**.

Suppose that you want to compute 8 minus 3 in decimal arithmetic. To do this subtraction using complements, you add 8 to the **tens complement** of 3 and throw away the carry. The tens complement of a number is the value you add to the number to get 10. Thus, the tens complement of 3 is 7 because 3 plus 7 is 10. The tens complement of 6 is 4 (6 + 4 = 10), and the tens complement of 2 is 8 (2 + 8 = 10).

Now, to compute 8 minus 3, you add 8 to the tens complement of 3 and throw away the carry. Thus, 8 plus 7 (the tens complement of 3) is 15. Throwing away the carry, you get 5, which, equals 8 minus 3 (see figure C–4). Now you try subtraction. Compute 9 minus 2. The tens complement of 2 is 8. Add 9 and 8 to get 17. Throw away the 1 and you have 7, which is the result of 9 minus 2.

Try another computation. Compute 9 minus 5. The tens complement of 5 is 5 (5 + 5 = 10). Adding 9 and 5 gives you 14. Throw away the carry to get 4, which is the same as 9 minus 5.

What happens if the answer should be a negative number? Suppose that you compute 3 minus 6? The answer should be –3. Using complements, we add 3 to the tens complement of 6. Thus, we add 3 to 4 and get 7, which is not –3.

What happened? Complement addition has one more rule: If the result of the addition leaves no carry to throw away, the answer is negative. When this occurs, take the tens complement of the answer and add a minus sign to get the correct result.

Thus, 3 minus 6 is computed by adding 3 to 4 (the tens complement of 6), which yields 7. There is no carry, so the answer is negative; take

FIGURE C–4
Subtraction using complement addition

To compute 8–3,
   a. Find the tens complement of 3, which is 7.
   b. Add 8 to the complement of 3 to obtain 15.
   c. Throw away the carry to obtain 5, the difference of 8 and 3.

To compute 9–5,
   a. Find the tens complement of 5, which is 5.
   b. Add 9 to the complement of 5 to obtain 14.
   c. Throw away the carry to obtain 4, the answer.

FIGURE C–5
Subtraction using complement addition
to obtain negative answers

To compute 3−6,
   a. Find the tens complement of 6, which is 4.
   b. Add 3 to the complement of 6 to obtain 7.
   c. There is no carry, therefore the answer is negative. Take the tens complement of 7, which is 3, and add a minus sign. The answer is −3.

To compute 7−9,
   a. Find the tens complement of 9, which is 1.
   b. Add 7 to the complement of 9 to obtain 8.
   c. There is no carry, therefore the answer is negative. Take the tens complement of 8, which is 2, and add a minus sign. The answer is −2.

the tens complement of 7 and add a minus sign. The answer is −3, as it should be (see figure C−5).

Try 7 minus 9. The answer should be −2. Take the tens complement of 9, which is 1. Add 7 and 1 to get 8. There is no carry, so the answer is negative. Take the tens complement of 8 and add a minus sign. The answer is −2. It works!

Computers do the same thing in binary arithmetic. To form the **twos complement** of a binary number, the computer just turns all the 1's to 0's and all the 0's to 1's; then it adds 1. Thus, the twos complement of 0110 is 1001 plus 1, or 1010.

Suppose that we want to compute 1111 minus 0110. The answer should be 1001. To compute this subtraction, we add 1111 and the twos complement of 0110. The twos complement of 0110 is 1001; thus, we add 1111 to 1010.

```
(Carry) ⟶   111
              1111
           +  1010
             ‾‾‾‾‾‾
             11001
```

We throw away the carry, and the answer is 1001, as it should be. If there is no carry, the number is negative. Complement the answer by switching 1's and 0's and adding 1.

Thus, computers subtract by adding complements. Forming twos complements is easy, and adding also is easy, so computers can work very fast.

Computers multiply by successive additions. Thus, to multiply 7 times 8, the computer adds eight 7's together. To multiply 1234 times 438, the computer adds 438 1234's together. Division is performed by successive subtractions.

OCTAL AND HEXADECIMAL NUMBER SYSTEMS

Working with binary numbers is easy and convenient for computers, but it is not so easy for people. Adding the binary number 11010101110100 to the binary number 110100100001111110100110101 is a chore. It's also very easy to drop a bit and get the wrong answer.

FIGURE C – 6
Binary numbers and their abbreviations
(octal equivalents)

BINARY NUMBER	OCTAL EQUIVALENT	BINARY NUMBER	OCTAL EQUIVALENT
000	0	100	4
001	1	101	5
010	2	110	6
011	3	111	7

To make errors less likely, people have found a way to shorten binary numbers.

One way is to group the binary symbols into threesomes and to represent each threesome by a number. The table in figure C – 6 shows how to represent three binary digits with a single number. The first column lists all the possible three-place binary numbers, and the second column lists the symbols used to represent them.

Let's use this table to shorten some binary numbers. Group the binary symbols into threes and substitute the corresponding single digit from figure C – 6.

111011 becomes 111 011, or 73
011010 becomes 011 010, or 32
111000 becomes 111 000, or 70
111111 becomes 111 111, or 77

Notice that the symbols 8 and 9 are not used in this abbreviation scheme. The largest symbol is 7. We have created a number system that has only has eight symbols: 0, 1, 2, 3, 4, 5, 6, and 7. This system is called the **octal number system** because it uses eight symbols.

Figure C – 7 shows the decimal equivalents of some octal numbers. In the decimal system, we have the ones place, the tens place, the hundreds place, and so forth. In the binary system we have the ones place, the twos place, the fours place, the eights place, and so forth. In the octal system, we have places for the ones, the eights, the sixty-fours, and other powers of eight. The octal number 3456 is equal to 3 times 512 ($8 \times 8 \times 8$), plus 4 times 64 (8×8), plus 5 times 8 (8×1), plus 6 times 1, or 1838 in decimal format.

As mentioned, octal format is used primarily as a shorthand for binary format. Converting from octal to binary format is very easy. We just replace each octal symbol with the three binary symbols that it

FIGURE C – 7
Octal numbers and their decimal
equivalents

OCTAL NUMBER	DECIMAL FORM
47	$4 \times 8 + 7 \times 1$ or 39
312	$3 \times 64 + 1 \times 8 + 2 \times 1$ or 202
4057	$3 \times 512 + 0 \times 64 + 5 \times 8 + 7 \times 1$ or 1583

represents. Thus, 234 in octal format equals 010 011 100 in binary format.

Several manufacturers produce computers that abbreviate binary numbers with octal numbers. Control Data Corporation (CDC), for instance, makes computers that have 60 bits per word. When the binary value of a word is printed by these machines, it is usually shown in octal format. So, instead of printing 60 binary symbols thus:

111111111111111111111111111111111111111111111111111111111111

they print the octal number 7777777777. Such a number is much easier for humans to understand and manipulate.

Sometimes computers print a **dump** at the end of a run that terminated abnormally. This dump shows the values in certain critical areas of main memory. The values in these critical areas will be in binary format, but the computer will print them in octal format so humans can understand them more easily.

Some computers, such as some IBM machines, have 32 bits per word. In these computers, the octal number system cannot readily be used to abbreviate the stored values, because 32 bits cannot be broken into equal groups of three. Thus, the word is divided instead into eight groups of 4 bits each. This division presents a problem, however.

Four bits can represent the decimal values 0 through 15. To abbreviate 4 bits by one character we need 16 symbols. We can use the symbols 0 through 9 to represent the first 10 numbers, but we need other symbols to represent the last 6. Figure C–8 shows a scheme for solving this problem.

The binary values 0 through 1001 are represented by the decimal characters 0 through 9. The binary value 1010 equals decimal 10. However, we need a single symbol to represent 1010. Hence, we use the letter A. The letter B represents 1011, C represents 1100, and so forth.

This scheme creates a number system with 16 symbols: 0 through 9 and A through F. It is called the **hexadecimal number system**. The places in this system are powers of 16. The places are the 1's place, the

BINARY NUMBER	HEXADECIMAL EQUIVALENT	BINARY NUMBER	HEXADECIMAL EQUIVALENT
0000	0	1000	8
0001	1	1001	9
0010	2	1010	A
0011	3	1011	B
0100	4	1100	C
0101	5	1101	D
0110	6	1110	E
0111	7	1111	F

FIGURE C–8
Binary numbers and their hexadecimal equivalents

FIGURE C – 9
Hexadecimal numbers and their decimal equivalents

HEXADECIMAL NUMBER	DECIMAL FORM	
79	$7 \times 16 + 9 \times 1$ or	121
E4	$14 \times 16 + 4 \times 1$ or	228
A1C	$10 \times 256 + 1 \times 16 + 12 \times 1$ or	2588
A14E	$10 \times 4096 + 1 \times 256 + 4 \times 16 + 14 \times 1$ or	41,294
1F7C8	$1 \times 65,536 + 15 \times 4096 + 7 \times 256 + 12 \times 16 + 8 \times 1$ or	128,968

16's place, the 256's place, the 4096's place, and so forth, increasing by powers of 16. As shown in figure C – 9, the hexadecimal number A14E represents 10 times 4096, plus 1 times 256, plus 4 times 16, plus 14, or 41,294 in decimal format.

On computers that use 16- or 32-bit words, the dumps and other binary printouts are produced in hexadecimal format. To convert from hexadecimal to binary format, just substitute the bit pattern for each character from figure C – 8. Thus, A14E in hexadecimal format represents 1010000101001110 in binary.

So far, we have discussed four number systems. Decimal numbers are traditionally used by people. Binary numbers are used by computers, mostly because the binary symbols 0 and 1 are easy to represent electronically. However, working with binary numbers is troublesome for people. Therefore, binary numbers sometimes are abbreviated using either octal or hexadecimal numbers.

CONVERTING BETWEEN NUMBER SYSTEMS

Sometimes people and computers need to convert a number from one system to another. For example, we may need to know what the hexadecimal number A1A equals in decimal format, what the decimal number 789 equals in octal format, and so forth.

Converting from binary, octal, or hexadecimal format to decimal format is easy. In fact, we have already seen how. Just multiply each symbol by its place value. In the binary system, the place values are powers of 2, in the octal system they are powers of 8, and in the hexadecimal system they are powers of 16.

Converting from binary to octal or from binary to hexadecimal format also is easy. Just use the table in figure C – 6 or in figure C – 8. To convert from decimal to binary, octal, or hexadecimal format, however, is not so easy.

Such conversions can be done by the **division/remainder method**. This method uses successive divisions by the base number. For example, to convert from decimal to binary format, the decimal number is successively divided by 2. To convert from decimal to octal format, the decimal number is successively divided by 8. As the divisions are done, the remainders are saved; they become the transformed number.

Examine figure C−10. Three conversions are shown. In the first, the decimal number 37 is converted to binary format; 37 is repeatedly divided by 2 until the quotient is 0. As the division is done, the remainders are written on the right-hand side. The equivalent binary number is read from these remainders, from the bottom up. Thus, 37 in decimal format equals 100101 in binary format.

In the second example, the decimal number 92 is converted to octal format; 92 is repeatedly divided by 8 until no whole division is possible. Then the number is read from the remainders. Thus, 92 decimal equals 134 octal.

In the third example, 489 is converted to hexadecimal format; 489 is repeatedly divided by 16 until no whole division is possible. The remainders are kept on the right-hand side. Note that the remainder of 14 is represented by the hexadecimal symbol E, not by 14. The number 489 decimal equals 1E9 hexadecimal. In practice, such conversions are done by special hand calculators.

FLOATING-POINT NUMBERS

The binary format just described is only one of the ways that computers represent arithmetic numbers. Another format is called **floating point**. This term is used because the decimal point of the number is allowed to move, or float. The same form can represent 0.45 or 4500. The advantage of this form is its flexibility. It can represent very large and very small numbers, including fractions.

Floating-point numbers are represented in **exponential** or **scientific form**. The decimal number 1257 is represented in exponential form as

FIGURE C−10
Converting from decimal format to binary, octal, and hexadecimal formats

Division	Remainder	Division	Remainder	Division	Remainder
2⌊37		8⌊92		16⌊489	
	1		4		9
2⌊18		8⌊11		16⌊ 30	
	0		3		E
2⌊ 9		8⌊ 1		16⌊ 1	
	1		1		1
2⌊ 4					
	0				
2⌊ 2					
	0				
2⌊ 1					
	1				

Answer: 100101 binary   Answer: 134 octal   Answer: 1E9 hexadecimal

a. Decimal 37 Converted to Binary   **b.** Decimal 92 Converted to Octal   **c.** Decimal 489 Converted to Hexadecimal

FIGURE C–11
Floating-point word formats

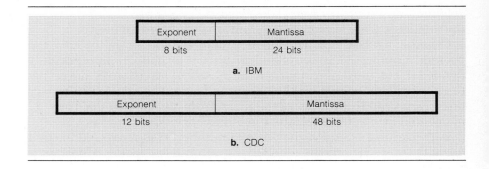

0.1257 times 10^4. This notation means that 1257 equals 0.1257 times 10,000 (0.1257 × 10 × 10 × 10 × 10). Numbers from other number systems can be represented similarly. Thus, the binary number 1011 equals 0.1011 times 2^4 (0.1011 × 2 × 2 × 2 × 2). Similarly, the octal number 765 equals 0.765 times 512 (0.765 × 8 × 8 × 8).

In each of these cases, the fractional number is called the **mantissa** and the power of the base is called the **exponent**. The mantissa of 0.1257 times 10^4 is 0.1257, and the exponent is 4.

Scientific notation can represent fractions as well as whole numbers. The decimal number 0.0123 is 0.123 times 10^1. The number 0.000345 is 0.345 times 10^3. In this latter case, the mantissa is 0.345 and the exponent is -3.

Floating-point numbers use exponential notation. Each computer word has two sections: One section holds the exponent, and the other holds the mantissa. On IBM computers, for example, the first 8 bits of a word hold the exponent (a power of 16), and the remaining 24 bits hold the mantissa (see figure C–11).

On Control Data computers, the first 12 bits hold the exponent (a power of 8), and the remaining 48 bits hold the mantissa. Because more bits are used to represent the mantissa on CDC computers than on IBM computers, greater precision is possible. The mantissa can have a larger number of characters.

Both the mantissa and the exponent have a sign. The sign of the mantissa indicates whether the number is positive or negative. The sign of the exponent indicates whether the number is greater or less than 1.

The particular method of representing floating-point numbers is beyond the scope of this book. You should know that they exist and that they are represented in a special way in the computer. You should also be aware that, because of the special format, extra instructions (and time) are required to process floating-point numbers.

Some small computers use only one type of number. Some microcomputers use only integer numbers and integer instructions; others have only floating-point numbers and instructions. Make sure that your computer has floating-point capability if you need it. Otherwise, you will have to program your own floating-point capability, and that is a chore.

FRACTIONS AND ROUND-OFF ERRORS

Fractions can be represented in two ways. The first is floating-point format, as just described. The second way is **fixed-point binary format**. For this format, numbers are represented in binary format, but a binary point is assumed to exist. (A binary point, like a decimal point, separates the integer part of a number from the fractional part.) For example, a binary point could be defined as being to the left of the third bit in a word. Then the binary number 110111 would be interpreted as 110.111 (see figure C–12 for other examples). When using this format, the program defines where it wants the point to be, and all operations are based on that definition. Note that in this case the binary point cannot float; every number has the same number of places to the right of the point.

There is a curious fact about fractions. Exactly representing a fraction that can be represented exactly in one number system may not be possible in another system. For example, the decimal fraction 0.1 cannot be evenly represented in the hexadecimal (or binary) system. It is slightly more than hexadecimal 0.199.

The fact that 0.1 cannot be evenly represented in the binary system is very important in business. For instance, the dollar value $12.10 does not have an even binary representation, nor does $1.1 trillion.

Assume that you ask the computer to add the value $0.01 one hundred times. If 0.01 is represented in binary format, you may not get $1.00. Instead you may get $0.99999999999999. This problem, called the **round-off error**, can be inconvenient and embarrassing to computer personnel. Sometimes it makes the computer appear unable to add.

FIXED-POINT FORMAT	BINARY NUMBER	IS INTERPRETED AS
XXX.XX	11101	111.01
	10011	100.11
	10001	100.01
X.XXXX	11101	1.1101
	10011	1.0011
	10001	1.0001
.XXXXX	11101	.11101
	10011	.10011
	10001	.10001

FIGURE C–12
Examples of fixed-point binary numbers

QUESTIONS

C.1 Which of the following are valid binary numbers?
    a. 1101
    b. 1200
    c. 9812
    d. 0000

C.2 Decimal places have values of ones, tens, hundreds, and so forth.
    a. What are the values of binary places?
    b. What are the values of octal places?
    c. What are the values of hexadecimal places?

C.3 Add the following binary numbers:
    a. 110 + 001
    b. 110001 + 001110
    c. 111111 + 0000001
    d. 11101 + 00011

C.4 How do most computers perform subtraction?

C.5 Perform the following subtractions using complements:
    a. 9−4 (decimal)
    b. 1101−0001 (binary)
    c. 1111−0101 (binary)
    d. 4−9 (decimal)
    e. 0011−0100 (binary)

C.6 What are octal numbers used for?

(continued)

▦ DECIMAL NUMBERS

Because of this problem (and for other reasons as well), some computers have the ability to perform arithmetic in decimal format. With these computers, the inputs are never converted to binary format, and the round-off error does not occur. Unfortunately, decimal arithmetic is slower than binary arithmetic. Therefore, decimal arithmetic is only done when calculations are simple and few. In business, such calculations often are required. Many business systems need only perform simple additions or multiplications. Therefore, the decimal form of data often is used in business.

Figure C−13 shows decimal digits represented in the EBCDIC code. Two hexidecimal, or "hex," characters are used to represent each decimal digit: F1 represents 1, F2 represents 2, and so forth. Note how inefficient this scheme is. Two hex characters, or 8 bits, are needed for each decimal character. In binary form, these 8 bits can represent all of the numbers from 0 to 255. In decimal form, they can represent only the numbers from 0 to 9.

Using the code shown in figure C−13, the decimal number 287 is represented by F2F8F7. Other examples are shown in figure C−14. This format is sometimes called **unpacked** (or **zoned**) **decimal format**.

In figure C−13, the first hex character for each of the digits is F. To reduce the storage space consumed by decimal numbers, all but one of the F's can be removed. This is called **packed decimal format**. Thus, in figure C−14, the decimal number 287, which has unpacked decimal notation F2F8F7, has the packed decimal notation 287F. All but one of the F's has been removed, and the remaining F is put at the end of the number.

In many applications, numbers must have signs. These can be positive or negative. In packed decimal notation, the last hex position is used to denote a sign. This format is called **signed decimal format**. If the last character is a hex C, the number is positive. If the last character is a D, the number is negative. Thus, 287C represents +287. 287D represents −287. The notation 287F is still valid. It just means that the number 287 is unsigned. Figure C−14 provides other examples.

FIGURE C−13
EBCDIC code for decimal numbers

DECIMAL NUMBER	EBCDIC CODE (HEXADECIMAL)	DECIMAL NUMBER	EBCDIC CODE (HEXADECIMAL)
0	F0	5	F5
1	F1	6	F6
2	F2	7	F7
3	F3	8	F8
4	F4	9	F9

DECIMAL NUMBER	DECIMAL FORM		
	UNPACKED	**PACKED**	**SIGNED**
287	F2F8F7	287F	287C (+287)
			287D (−287)
1492	F1F4F9F2	1492F	1492C (+1492)
			1492D (−1492)
77	F7F7	77F	77C (+77)
			77D (−77)

FIGURE C–14
Unpacked, packed, and signed decimal data formats

▥ SUMMARY

Computers represent two types of data: numeric and alphanumeric. This module described the representation and processing of numeric data. The binary number system is most often used to represent numeric data. The binary system uses only two symbols: 0 and 1. In the decimal system, the place values of a number are ones, tens, hundreds, thousands, and so forth. In the binary system they are ones, twos, fours, eights, sixteens, and so forth.

Binary numbers are added just like decimal numbers are. However, instead of carrying when the sum of two numbers exceeds nine, we carry when the sum exceeds one. Subtraction is usually done by computers in complement form. The complement of the number to be subtracted is added to determine the answer.

Two other number systems are used to abbreviate binary numbers. The octal number system has eight symbols; each octal symbol represents three bits. The hexadecimal number system has 16 symbols; each hex symbol represents four bits. Octal format is used when the computer's word size is a multiple of three bits. Hexadecimal is used when the word size is a multiple of four bits.

Floating-point numbers allow the decimal point to shift. They represent both very large and very small numbers. They can also represent fractions. In addition to floating-point format, fractions can be represented in fixed-point binary format. In this format, a fixed location of the binary point is assumed.

Decimal fractions are not necessarily represented evenly in binary format; for example, 0.1 does not have an even representation in binary format. This means that computers can make round-off errors. To eliminate this problem, some computers can perform decimal arithmetic. With these computers, decimal numbers are not converted to binary format, and arithmetic is done in decimal form. Data is carried in packed decimal format.

C.7 Convert the following numbers to decimal format:
  a. 1101 binary
  b. 1110101 binary
  c. 453 octal
  d. 7671 octal
  e. A21 hexadecimal
  f. ABC hexadecimal

C.8 What are hexadecimal numbers used for?

C.9 Convert the following numbers to binary format:
  a. 789 decimal
  b. 1234 decimal
  c. 643 octal
  d. 77777 octal
  e. CE4 hexadecimal
  f. FEBCAD hexadecimal

C.10 What causes the round-off error? Why is it important in business?

C.11 How can the round-off error be eliminated?

C.12 What are the unpacked and packed decimal formats of each of the following numbers:
  a. 12345
  b. 484930
  c. 23
  d. 1

C.13 What is the signed decimal format of each of the following numbers:
  a. −19   c. −78965
  b. 7345   d. 0

WORD LIST

(In order of appearance in text)

Numeric data	Dump	Exponent
Alphanumeric data	Hexadecimal number system	Fixed-point binary number
Bit	Division/remainder method	Round-off error
Complement addition	Floating-point number	Unpacked decimal format
Tens complement	Exponential form	Zoned decimal format
Twos complement	Scientific form	Packed decimal format
Octal number system	Mantissa	Signed decimal format

COMPUTER CRIME, SECURITY, AND CONTROL

MODULE D

HAROLD JOHNSON, COMPUTER CRIMINAL

Harold Johnson applied for a systems analysis/programming job at Modern Record Distributing Company (MODREC). Harold was young, only 25, but he had an impressive background. He had had major responsibility in the development of three different computer systems at his prior place of employment. His reason for leaving was that he believed the major challenges were over, and he wanted something new.

In fact, Harold was very bright and eager for new opportunities to apply his problem-solving skills. He was highly motivated and willing to spend many hours solving difficult problems. Furthermore, he was courageous and would stand up to anybody when his ideas were disputed. He was also creative and adventurous, and he enjoyed challenges. In short, he had all the skills and traits needed to be a superior systems developer.

MODREC was a spinoff company. It had been a division of a large, traditional record manufacturer. The separate company was created when MODREC's sales exceeded $5 million, and the directors of the parent company thought forming a subsidiary made sense. MODREC specialized in distributing rock music of interest to people under 30.

MODREC's first president was the son of one of the parent company's directors. He was promoted to his position through influence and not ability. Consequently, MODREC's sales began to slip, personnel morale fell, and MODREC lost many opportunities in the marketplace.

MODREC's small data processing department was managed by the chief accountant. The accountant meant well, but he was uneducated about data processing. When Harold Johnson applied for the systems analysis/programming job, the chief accountant was delighted. He made Harold an excellent offer, and Harold came to work for MODREC.

In his first year, Harold made many contributions to data processing. There was a vast improvement in the level of service. Salespeople were given better information about their customers. The time required to deliver an order was cut in half. Sales went up. Further, the accounting systems were improved, and the chief accountant had better information than ever.

Unfortunately, Harold began to feel discontented. Nobody paid attention to him. He felt that no one recognized the contributions he made. He probably would have gone to another company, but after a year, MODREC gave him a substantial pay increase. He thought that he would have trouble earning as much money elsewhere.

As Harold worked with the accounting systems, he began to notice MODREC'S large profits. These profits were possible in spite of ineffective management, because MODREC's products had a very high markup. Harold concluded that MODREC was "ripping off" its customers.

One day Harold mentioned this to Joan Everest, the manager of a neighborhood record store that

ordered from MODREC (see figure D–1).

"Harold," said Joan, almost in jest, "why don't you reprogram one of those computers to offer special discounts to my store? Perhaps I could share the savings with you."

Harold was never quite the same. He was bored at work, and the technical challenge of programming such "special discounts" excited him. Additionally, he was angry with the way MODREC had treated him, and he believed that it was unfair for the company to make so much profit. Joan needed the financial help, and MODREC could easily afford to lose $40,000 to $50,000 per year. In some ways he felt he was playing Robin Hood— stealing from the rich and giving to the poor.

Once Harold decided to cooperate, the technical aspects of his task were easy. In fact, Harold was disappointed at the lack of challenge. He changed the pricing program to look for Joan's customer number and to reduce her prices by 85 percent. He was the only one to see the special copy of the program. The unchanged version was kept in the program documentation library for appearances.

FIGURE D–1
Harold and Joan plotting a computer crime

Harold Johnson is a typical computer criminal. He also was caught. We will explain how as this module progresses.

▦ WHAT IS COMPUTER CRIME?

No one knows for sure how many **computer crimes** have occurred or what the total losses have been. Computer crime statistics are difficult to obtain, and most sources claim their statistics are unreliable. One expert estimates that $300 million is lost per year through computer crime. He estimates the average loss per crime at $450,000. Compare this to the $10,000 that is typically lost in a full-service bank robbery, or the $19,000 that is lost in the average conventional bank embezzlement.

Figure D–2 presents computer crime data published by the Bureau of Justice Statistics [73]. From 1958, the year of the first reported computer crime, to 1979, a total of 669 cases were reported. In many of those cases, the amount of the loss was undetermined (companies are reluctant to state their losses). The average of the known losses was $1.685 million per crime. According to the National Institute of Justice

FIGURE D–2
Computer crime statistics

YEAR	TOTAL CASES	TOTAL KNOWN LOSSES	AVERAGE KNOWN LOSS
1958	1		
1959	1	$ 278	$ 278
1962	2		
1963	2	2,081	1,040
1964	6	2,600	1,300
1965	8	126	63
1966	3	28	9
1967	4	10	5
1968	12	12,454	2,075
1969	20	3,011	376
1970	38	19,353	967
1971	59	16,137	849
1972	73	14,524	518
1973	75	233,066	6,474
1974	73	8,162	247
1975	84	98,312	2,006
1976	59	52,601	1,461
1977	87	67,853	1,330
1978	42	15,207	633
1979	20	200	200
Totals	669	$546,001	$1,685

(Losses in thousands of dollars)
Source: *Criminal Justice Resource Manual*

APPLICATION

"PERPETRATORS WERE INSIDERS."

WASHINGTON, D.C. — Perpetrators of computer crimes against the U.S. government typically steal money in response to stress or a crisis, such as a financial problem or disgruntlement on the job, according to a government study based on confidential interviews with 46 computer criminals.

"Connie," for example, was a terminal operator for a state program who enjoyed exploring the computer system. She discovered there were no security screens for making emergency payments under $1,000. "When it started I was playing on the terminal on a break. I typed in my friend's name and then I hit return; it was processed. I could have canceled it, but I didn't," she reported.

Not surprisingly, most perpetrators said computer security and internal controls in their offices were weak and did not pose significant barriers to their crimes. "They described identification numbers and passwords as simplistic, edits and screens as known and therefore avoidable and supervision as lax or naive regarding automated systems," the study said.

According to a state claims examiner, "Everyone had an ID number, and there was a password to bring the system up. But the codes and ID numbers were [posted] on the wall, so everyone and anyone could see them. No one cared."

HHS Inspector General Richard P. Kusserow reported that the average loss per computer crime was $45,000, and about one-fifth of the cases exceeded $100,000 in losses.

A key finding of the study was that the perpetrators were insiders — federal employees or employees of state or private agencies administering federal programs — and not outside hackers. In general, they were considered good employees, it said.

Kusserow reported that one-fifth of the perpetrators had a prior criminal record. He recommended that government managers reevaluate personnel security policies for persons in positions of trust, including all jobs with access to payroll and payment data.

(NIJ), the theft of *information* — usually done with the aid of a computer — costs business as much as $20 billion a year. NIJ estimates that the average computer theft nets $400,000 and can be committed in less than three milliseconds. In 1983 alone, somewhere between $70 million and $100 million were stolen from the nation's banks by automated teller machine fraud.

Unfortunately, computer crime is a very slippery subject: Companies that have been victimized are reluctant to publicize it. And computer crime can be extremely difficult to detect, let alone investigate and prosecute. There are many stories of computer crimes, and some of them seem downright ludicrous; it's hard to tell what's fact and what's fiction. The following three cases, however, have been well documented.

Pacific Telephone

Jerry Schneider was a child prodigy who developed his own telecommunication system at the age of 10. By the time he was in high school, he had started his own electronics company. While he was a part-time college student, he found a way to steal electronic equipment from the Pacific Telephone Company. He used a terminal in his home to order parts without being charged for them. He learned the correct account numbers, passwords, and procedures by taking old computer printouts and other documentation from a telephone company trash container.

Jerry had expensive telephone components delivered to his home and other locations. He got bored with the project and, to add more excitement, had the company deliver a $25,000 switchboard to a manhole cover at the intersection of two streets. The company delivered, and he picked up the switchboard in the telephone truck that he had bought at a telephone company surplus auction.

Much of the equipment that he stole in this way he resold to Pacific Telephone. In fact, he used their own information system to determine what they were low on so he could know what to steal.

Schneider was caught when one of his own employees informed on him. The employee wanted a pay raise, and Jerry refused. When he was apprehended, Pacific Telephone refused to believe that he had stolen as much inventory as he claimed. He said he had stolen $800,000 to $900,000 worth; they said $70,000.

Penn Central Railroad

Another famous computer crime concerned the Penn Central Railroad. In the early 1970s, someone modified a freight-flow system to send boxcars to a small railroad company outside Chicago. There, the box cars disappeared. Apparently, they were repainted and sold to or used by other railroads. Estimates vary, but somewhere in the vicinity of 400 boxcars disappeared. Somehow, the computer system was modified so that it would not notice that railroad cars were missing.

The Penn Central case is mysterious. Although a Philadelphia grand jury was convened to investigate the case, and although some stolen boxcars were found, Penn Central refused to acknowledge the affair. For some reason, it was in Penn Central's interest to minimize attention to the crime. No criminal action was ever taken. There were rumors that organized crime was involved.

Equity Funding Corporation

A third famous case occurred in 1973. This large fraud involved the Equity Funding Corporation. Over 20 people were convicted on federal charges. Estimates of loss are as high as $2 *billion*.

Equity Funding was a conglomerate of companies that specialized in investments and insurance. Top-level management distorted the company's financial situation to lure investors. They also created artificial insurance policies.

Although the media described this crime as a modern computer fraud, there is some debate about whether it can be blamed on the computer. Most of the criminal activity did not involve the computer. All of the phony accounting was done manually.

The Equity Funding case is very complex. Over 50 major lawsuits were filed. Basically, the fraud was accomplished by inflating the company's reported income. This misrepresentation was done in two ways. First, the company's officers declared income and assets that didn't exist, simply by writing them into financial statements. The firm's auditors were severely criticized for not detecting this activity.

The second way income was inflated did involve the computer. Massive numbers of phony documents were generated by a computer system. These documents were supposed to be valid insurance policies. In fact, they were computer fabrications. The phony policies were sold to other insurance companies for cash.

In retrospect, it is amazing that these documents were accepted at face value. The system was audited, but it was designed to print only valid policies at the times audits were being done. Further, insurance industry personnel believed in computer-generated documents. It didn't occur to them that the computer could produce phony data.

Types of Computer Crime

These three short stories represent only a few of the ingenious ways that people have found to commit crimes with computer help. Most computer crimes fall into one of the five categories shown in figure D–3. Sometimes, the *input to the computer is manipulated*, as was done in the Pacific Telephone case. Other crimes are perpetrated by *changing computer programs*, as Harold Johnson did.

A third type of computer crime is to *steal data*. Such data might be the names and addresses of a company's customers. It might be proprietary designs or plans. Fourth, *computer time can be stolen*. The criminal either uses the time or sells it to others who may not be aware that the time is stolen. For example, a computer communications system may be used to transmit unauthorized data. In one case, a company's message-switching system was used daily to broadcast racing results.

TYPE OF CRIME

Manipulating computer input
Changing computer programs
Stealing data
Stealing computer time
Stealing computer programs

FIGURE D–3

Types of computer crime committed

APPLICATION

"THE MOST INSIDIOUS VERSION OF COMPUTER CRIME IS DATA INTERCEPTION".

Computer crime can be divided into five different categories: playpen, input fraud, data manipulation, program manipulation and data interception. These categories are not mutually exclusive, but each instance of computer crime fits comfortably into only one.

Playpen computer crime is the misuse of computers primarily to "have fun," to beat the system or to gain full access to computer resources.

The usual access method for outsiders is via telephone ports. Any system that can be accessed by telephone is potentially vulnerable to this type of abuse. If the system is not protected with passwords or other similar types of protection, it becomes even more vulnerable.

The method of protecting your organization against playpen abuse by outsiders consists of using an effective password control system that includes:

- the use of non-English word alpha numeric sequences of at least six characters.
- the secure distribution of passwords.
- the frequent changing of passwords.
- the assignment of passwords to a single individual.
- the development of an accountability system that makes all users responsible for all events that are done 'by' their password.

For people inside an organization, the reason for this type of crime is to have access to some normally off-limits computer facility. For example, a programmer might want to do his budget on the spread sheet package that runs on a mainframe, or he may want to create an index of his library. The potential inside abuser is anyone who has access.

The crime must lie in the intent and effect. A company would not prosecute an individual for copying a recipe on a company copier, but would prosecute an employee for copying and selling a customer list or proprietary manufacturing process on the same copier. The organization should not be offended by minor personal use of computer resources by employees. In fact, it may be a good idea that organizations with computers allow free usage by employees on a controlled basis.

The perpetrators of *input fraud* seek to misallocate money or merchandise, or to cover up management problems. With this kind of crime, the organization risks losing cash or other assets and control. The criminal uses the techniques of modifying or adding transactions to the normal processing stream of the organization. Sometimes the system or batch control totals are also modified.

The most effective techniques for the prevention of this type of computer crime are the time-proven methods recommended by auditors and others interested in internal control. These include: separation of responsibilities, batch totaling, input and output review by supervisory personnel, attention to error conditions and refunds, review of returned checks, and so on.

Data manipulation is true computer crime, because the perpetrator uses the computer as an active weapon. The goal of the criminal and the risks to an organization are the same as in input fraud: misallocating money or merchandise or covering up management problems. At risk is the loss of cash or assets and control. Techniques include modifying data, which is resident in the system.

In the previous category denoted, data was modified before it entered into the system. In this type of computer crime, data already in the system is modified.

Employees that most frequently commit this crime are computer operators, programmers or others with access to the operating system.

The techniques that can be most effectively used to prevent this type of computer crime include:

- having adequate system control procedures in effect so that control totals, especially record counts, are maintained throughout the system.
- maintaining control totals not only on items such as dollar balances, but also on elements such as account numbers and other fields which will indicate tampering with data.
- review of console logs.
- review of file accesses by unusual people at unusual times.

- installation of security packages that restrict file access

The fourth type of computer crime is **program manipulation.** In addition to the goals listed above, the computer violator may be trying to gain access to sensitive information. And along with the usual risks, an organization's security stands to be weakened by the loss or disclosure of sensitive information. A typical method used to effect this crime is to modify and put into "production" a program that illicitly manipulates organizational data.

Barriers to this category of crime consist of having and enforcing program library procedures, including the use of program library systems such as Panvalet, use of a program librarian who has the exclusive authority to update production libraries, the review of programmer's code by supervisory personnel before the program is put into production, review of program output, and review of transactions for unusual data such as large amounts of money or repeated transactions at specific times to specific accounts.

The most insidious version of computer crime is **data interception**, the goal of which is almost always intelligence, or information. Potential techniques include phone taps, microwave transmission interception, electronic monitoring of computer rooms, or other sophisticated techniques. Potential abusers are almost anyone. A criminal using data interception, does not necessarily need any type of access to the target computer.

Depending on the type of information your organization transmits, this type is potentially the largest risk of all. The risk to an organization is the loss or disclosure of sensitive information.

Finally, *computer programs can be stolen.* Computer programs are very expensive and time consuming to produce. They can give a company a competitive edge in its marketplace. Therefore, stealing programs is a criminal act.

The theft of computer data and computer programs is very hard to detect. It can be done simply by copying the computer files that hold the data or programs. Since the original copy is not missing, companies have difficulty knowing a crime was committed.

Many computer crime experts think the cases we know about are only the tip of the iceberg. Some companies have been victims of crimes and have not acknowledged it because they want to avoid adverse publicity. A bank that lost money by computer crime will not want its customers to know it. Further, businesses do not want to advertise their vulnerability. They may not know how to prevent similar crimes in the future, and they certainly do not want the crime advertised in the newspapers. Therefore, they do not prosecute suspected computer criminals.

For this reason, computer criminals often are not penalized. Further, when they are, they typically receive light sentences. Jerry Schneider spent only 40 days in jail and lost just $8500 in a court battle.

Here are 12 warning signals indicating that the potential for computer crime exists:

1. The computer seems to run the company; management just reacts.
2. Management expects computers to solve major existing problems.
3. Management does not (cannot) communicate with the EDP staff.
4. Users are told how their systems will be designed.
5. There are no documented standards for the development of new applications or the maintenance of existing ones.

6. Technical management is actively involved in programming and troubleshooting.
7. Programmers are uncontrolled; they can do what they want with the computer.
8. EDP staff has easy access to data and to program libraries.
9. Errors occur so frequently that adequate investigation is not possible.
10. Auditors treat the computer like a mysterious black box.
11. Management fails to implement audit recommendations.
12. No EDP audits are performed.

These signals are characteristics of companies in which crimes have occurred. Let's hope that, in the course of your business career, you will not work for a company that demonstrates many of these signs. However, if you do, you should be aware of the possibility of computer crime.

Most of the characteristics listed above indicate poor data processing management. Except for the items concerning audits, every one of these characteristics is a violation of a principle discussed in this book. Thus, good data processing management is needed to build and use systems that are less susceptible to computer crime.

PREVENTING COMPUTER CRIME

Unfortunately, there is no such thing as a completely secure data processing installation. First, computer manufacturers do not provide completely secure computers. An ingenious programmer can find a way to modify the operating system. Once such a modification is made, computer security features such as passwords and account numbers are ineffective.

Second, many, if not most, data processing departments are so busy just keeping up with the business and with changes in computer technology that they do not take the time to consider computer security adequately. Inputs to the computer are not as well controlled as they should be. Outputs are not checked for accuracy and completeness. Furthermore, security issues often are only superficially considered when systems are designed or when programs are written. Most companies have the attitude that computer crime "won't happen here."

Finally, effective security can be costly. Building a secure system takes time and resources. Additionally, the system may be more expensive to operate because of security features. If a user must spend half of each working day verifying output, then in a year half of the person's salary is spent for security. Good computer security also means that programs operate more slowly. More instructions must be processed for security functions. Thus, more computer power is required.

Most companies must strike a balance between no security at all and as near-perfect security as possible. How much security is needed depends on the potential loss and the level of threat. An accounts payable system probably needs more security than a system that produces company telephone lists.

One aspect of computer crime is both surprising and distressing: Most computer crimes are caught by accident. In some cases, the computer failed, and irregularities were discovered while someone was fixing it. In other cases, people consistently spent more money than they were earning, and the source of the additional money was traced back to a computer system. The Internal Revenue Service (IRS) has caught some of these people for not paying taxes on their criminal earnings. In other cases, the Federal Bureau of Investigation (FBI) caught them in illegal gambling activities.

The distressing part of this statement is that few crimes are caught as a result of controls in the business computer system. Apparently, few systems provide protection against computer crime. However, this vulnerability need not exist; systems can be designed to thwart unauthorized activity. We will see how in the next section.

COMPUTER AUDITING AND CONTROLS

The American Institute of Certified Public Accountants has recognized the possiblity of computer crime or other unauthorized activity. This organization has issued an official statement (called SAS-3) directing certified public accountants (CPAs) to pay special attention to business computer systems. As a result of this statement, auditors are paying more and more attention to data processing departments and personnel.

Further, groups of auditors and data processing personnel have worked together to develop recommended procedures or *controls* over data processing operations. In the remainder of this module, we will discuss these controls. To show the usefulness of them, we will relate each control to the MODREC case introduced at the start of this module.

The term **EDP controls** originated with the accountants and auditors. **EDP** is an accounting term that means *electronic data processing*. EDP controls are features of any of the five components of a business computer system that reduce the likelihood of unauthorized activity. Here is a list of the basic categories of EDP controls:

- Management
- Organizational structure
- Data center resource
- Input/processing/output
- Data administration
- Systems development

APPLICATION

"THE GREATEST THREAT TO DATA SECURITY IS THE CORRUPTION OF DATA BY THE USERS."

Large-scale computer systems traditionally use a variety of access control measures to protect data from unauthorized access. When microcomputers are viewed within an organization as stand-alone, single-user units, such measures usually are not considered necessary or practical.

But when microcomputers are more widely used, and when they link into existing system networks, the need for adequate access control exists.

When microcomputers are linked together in a local-area network, relatively simple procedures for access control should ensure the following:

- All users are identifiable.
- Adequate user verification is performed by passwords and IDs.
- Network access points are not left unattended once verification of a user has been completed.

THE USER THREAT

Perhaps the greatest threat to data security in a local-area network is the corruption of data by the users themselves. Controls must be in place to guard against access to sensitive data by people who are not authorized or from simultaneous update by two different users. Confidential memos and data that were once hand carried between offices or delivered in sealed envelopes can now be sent via electronic mail and may be read by anyone on the network unless adequate security controls are in place.

Microcomputers with access to mainframe data should be required to use the same access control procedures as any other dumb terminal. Standard procedures should include user identification with verification via password or key.

Users, however, should not store

Microcomputer Access Control

General Controls

1. Have individuals authorized to use the microcomputer been identified?
2. Have procedures been established for authorizing new users?
   a. Are training programs for equipment use available?
   b. Are training programs for software applications available?
   c. Is proficiency testing part of the authorization procedure?
   d. Does someone have adminstrative responsibility for access authorization?
3. Have critical or sensitive data files been identified?
4. Are they protected from unauthorized access (by password)?
5. Are they protected from unauthorized update?
6. Are they encrypted?
7. Are deleted or erased files destroyed or overwritten so they cannot be recovered by utility programs?

Stand-alone units

1. Is the unit protected from unauthorized access?
   a. Locked cover or cabinet?
   b. Locked room?
   c. Locked power supply?
2. Is the unit password protected (such as with an installed chip)?

Networked units

1. Are all accesses logged?
   a. Is the user identified?
   b. Are the date and time of access identified?
   c. Are the functions performed identified?
   d. Is the microcomputer identified?
2. Are all users and all microcomputers uniquely identified (password/card access)?
3. Are invalid access attempts reported?
4. Are access attempts verifiable (for example, a user ID/password combination)?
5. Are both public and private files maintained?
   a. Are private files secure from browsing by unauthorized network users?
6. Are unattended units logged off or turned off when not in use?

Public networks/dial-up services

1. Are customer files protected from unauthorized access by other customers?
2. Does the service bureau provide adequate security measures for user IDs and passwords?
3. Does the service bureau provide adequate backup and recovery for customer files?

their identification and passwords on the microcomputer as a convenience measure to perform an automatic log on — this will negate any security facilities in place on the mainframe since the microcomputer itself may not be totally secure. As with other terminals connected to the network, microcomputers should never be left logged on and unattended so that unauthorized individ-

uals can use the computer resource and gain access to sensitive data.

DIAL-UP ACCESS

Dial-up access for microcomputers has become an attractive service for users with occasional needs to access mainframe files. But a dial-up port waiting for a phone call can be a tempting target for an information

thief.

Access to dial-up telephone numbers should be restricted, and individuals who do have dial-up privileges should be aware of the security implications of distributing the access number. It's expected that once a dial-up link has been established, some type of verification of the intended user will take place.

Harold Johnson was dissatisfied with the management at MODREC. He felt underappreciated. Because his boss was only the chief accountant, Harold was buried in the finance department. Consequently, neither he nor anyone else in data processing had access to top management.

Top management did not have access to Harold or data process-

ing either. They knew little of what he was doing, and they had only a limited idea of how data processing operated. They spent considerable money on data processing operations, but they did not know how the money was spent. In short, there was a large gulf between top-level management and data processing.

Management Controls

Over the years, professionals have learned that management situations like the one at MODREC are an invitation to trouble. Senior managers of a company should take an active part in the management of the data processing function. They do not have to be walking the machine floor, mounting tapes. However, they should recognize the importance of data processing to the company, and they should set the direction for, and be actively involved in, data processing plans. In other words, **management controls** need to exist.

It may seem surprising that this statement even needs to be made. However, in the past, too many managers have washed their hands of data processing. They have stayed as far away from the computer as possible. Perhaps they didn't understand computing, perhaps they were afraid of it, or perhaps the data processing personnel used a strange language. In any event, data processing went its own way. In some cases (like Harold's), data processing personnel felt disassociated from the company. They felt rejected and unappreciated, and computer crime was the result.

Senior managers can handle data processing in several ways. First, they can demonstrate an appreciation for and an interest in the data processing function. Occasional visits to the computer staff, recognition of them in the company newsletter, and references to data processing in the year-end report are examples of showing their interest.

Senior managers can recognize data processing in another significant way as well. They can place the data processing function high in the organizational structure. Instead of burying data processing somewhere in accounting or finance where none of the senior managers ever see or hear of it, they can make it a department on a par with other business departments. Figure D–4 shows two ways that data processing can be raised from the company bilges to gain the attention it deserves.

Next, senior managers can understand the company's vulnerability to computer crime. Once they do, they can communicate the importance of controls to the entire organization. As we will see, controls on the data processing function involve more than just the data processing department. To encourage other departments to cooperate, management needs to be very positive about the need for controls.

Another responsibility for management is to form a steering committee. As stated in chapter 5, such a committee controls data processing development efforts. The committee receives reports about project status and makes go/no-go decisions as appropriate. Refer to chapter 5 for more information about the steering committee.

Finally, management can take a role in data processing by requesting and paying attention to periodic operations reports. Management should know how well the computing resources are being used, how happy or unhappy the users are with the data processing function, and what the major data processing problems are. These reports increase the amount of communication between data processing and senior management. Management control responsibilities are summarized below:

1. Data processing is placed at high organizational level.
2. Senior management demonstrates knowledge and good attitude toward data processing.
3. Data processing steering committee takes active role in DP.
4. Management requests and reviews periodic reports.

Harold Johnson had free access to the computer and all of its resources. When Harold needed a tape file to determine Joan's account number, he walked into the tape library and got it. When he wanted to obtain the pricing program, he instructed the computer to print a copy of it. After he made the changes, Harold put the changed program into the standard program library. No one checked Harold's authority to do these things.

Organizational Controls

Organizational controls concern the organizational structure of the company. We have already mentioned that data processing should be organizationally on a par with other functions of the company. In addition, the company should be structured so that authorization and duties are separate.

The MODREC case is a good example of what can happen when no separation exists. Data processing employees had unlimited access to the computer. MODREC should have at least two categories of data processing personnel: operations and development. These groups should provide checks and balances on each other. The operations group should control the equipment and the production program library. The development group should develop new programs in accordance with requirements. They should not have access to the tape library or to the production programs.

If this were the case, authorization and duties would be separated. Only the programmers could develop program changes, and only the operations department could change the production library. Further, making changes to the program library would require a supervisor's authorization.

Separating authorization and duties provides checks and balances in the system. In general, the more people and the more levels of management that are involved in authorizing and performing duties, the less susceptible the system is to unauthorized activity.

After Harold Johnson changed the pricing program to give Joan special discounts, he wanted to test it. After all, he didn't want to make a mistake and give the discounts to the wrong customer. However, to test the change, he needed to mount the customer and price files on the tape drives. To avoid suspicion, Harold stayed at work after hours the next week. Since none of the managers paid any attention to data processing, they didn't ask what Harold was doing. In fact, nobody asked Harold what he was up to. Harold took his time, and after three short nights, he had fully tested his program. Not only was he sure it would work, he was also sure no one could trace the changes to him.

Data Center Resource Controls

Data center resources controls also should be implemented. Use of computer equipment should be restricted to authorized personnel. Processing should be controlled by schedules, and records of use should be reviewed. Therefore, access to the computer must be controlled. Only authorized personnel should be allowed in the computer room. This restriction not only protects the equipment from damage, but also helps to ensure that outputs are delivered only to the right people. Furthermore, limiting access to the machine room allows a quieter working environment and helps eliminate operator errors.

Computer operations should be controlled as well. Procedures and job schedules should be documented and followed. A supervisor should examine operations to ensure that the procedures are followed, and records of all computer activity should be kept. These records should be reviewed. It should be very difficult for operators to deviate from the established schedule and procedures.

In addition to protecting computing resources during normal operations, plans and procedures should exist to recover from problems. All files and libraries should be backed up by copies stored in secure, off-premise locations. Further, recovery procedures should be well documented, and the staff should be trained in their use.

The company also should have a disaster recovery plan that explains what to do in case of fire, flood, earthquake, or other disaster. The company should consider having backup hardware and programs available in other locations. The procedures and data necessary to use the hardware should be available in the backup location. Resource controls are summarized below:

1. Access to computer center is controlled.
2. Operating procedures are documented.
3. Program libraries are secure.
4. Backup and recovery procedures exist.
5. There is protection from natural hazards.
6. There are documented emergency procedures.

Harold Johnson did not have to modify program inputs. He found a way to provide special discounts by changing the processing. This process changed the outputs. If anyone had ever examined the in-voices generated by the pricing program, they would have seen that something was amiss. Luckily for Harold, MODREC did not have a policy of examining outputs.

Input, Processing, and Output Controls

In general, **input, processing, and output controls** should be used. First, the authorized form of input data should be documented. The operations personnel should be trained not to accept improper input data. Second, data processing personnel should be trained not to make changes to input data. Such changes should be made by the system users.

Where appropriate, control totals should be used. For example, when the users send the weekly payroll to data processing, they should calculate (independently) the sum of the hours worked or a similar total. The payroll program should be written to calculate the total number of hours worked and to print this total on a summary report. The report should be examined by the payroll department after the payroll run to ensure that the manually prepared total and the computer-generated total match.

Similar totals can be kept on changes to master files, number of accounts payable checks to be issued, and so forth. Users must be trained to compute these totals and to treat them seriously. Often they are the most important control in the business computer system.

Input to teleprocessing applications are harder to control. A program can be coded to accept only certain input from certain users or certain locations. However, it is possible to fool such a program. Therefore, the use of terminals must be limited to certain individuals and to specified times. Further, the supervisors of these individuals need to be trained to review their subordinates' terminal activities.

There must also be controls over the processing of data. As stated earlier, all operations procedures should be documented and followed. The performance of the operators should be monitored periodically. The operations department should keep records of all errors and system failures. The corrections for each of these should be documented. These records should be reviewed periodically by data processing supervisory personnel to determine whether or not the failures are related to unauthorized activity. The records can also be used to determine whether or not there is a need for additional training, as well as to assess employee performance.

Finally, the output of all data processing activities should be controlled. Procedures for disseminating output should be documented and followed. Output should be given only to authorized users, and these users should examine the output for completeness and accuracy. Control totals produced by programs should be reconciled against input control totals.

Output from online systems is hard to control. Where data is changed online, tracing the sequence of activities can be very difficult. For example, a price might be changed several times with no written record generated. The absence of records can make the job of the auditor impossible. Consequently, online programs often are programmed to log transactions on computer tape or disks. These logs are saved and used for error correction or audits. Figure D–5 summarizes input, processing, and output controls.

FIGURE D–5
Input/processing/output controls

CATEGORY	TYPE OF CONTROL
Input	Documentation of authorized input format
	Separation of duties and authorities
	Verification of control totals
	Online system input controls
Processing	Documented operating procedures
	Reviews of processing logs
	Adequate program testing
Output	Documented output procedures
	Control over disposition of output
	Users trained to examine output

APPLICATION

"A PSYCHOLOGICAL PROFILE OF THE HACKER."

GAITHERSBURG, Md.— Tracking a hacker? Look for a boy who eats junk food or Chinese food from 24-hour restaurants.

That is one of the characteristics described by Julie A. Smith, an analyst for the government's National Computer Security Center, at the recent National Computer Security Conference.

Because it is easiest to work on computers undetected during the wee hours of the night, and because many hackers are in school during the day, Smith explained, a hacker's meals tend to be take-out junk food eaten at the computer terminal or food eaten at 24-hour restaurants. "In fact, Chinese food tends to be a favorite among college hackers," Smith said.

This was just one of the characteristics Smith reported in a research paper that provides a psychological profile of the hacker. She said the late hours and self-imposed confinement to computer rooms tend to reinforce the "environmental isolation" of most computer hackers.

She said hackers tend to lose interest in schoolwork that is not related to computer science, and thus, their school grades plummet. College-age hackers tend practically to live in the computer buildings on campus.

Smith's research provided additional characteristics of hackers:

- They are almost 100% male.
- Like computer programmers, hackers are extremely bright, investigative and logical thinkers, competitive and prefer structured but creative activities.
- With every successful action at the keyboard, hackers see themselves as asserting authority over the machine and whoever is connected to it, giving them a sense of power and control. Thus, they are more concerned with gaining this sensation of power than they are with the effects of their actions on others.

- Hackers tend to dabble at computer projects with no long-term goal and do not plan ahead.
- Hackers have little respect for those who know nothing about their favorite subject, computers.

One way to investigate hackers engaged in criminal activity is to catch them bragging about their exploits on electronic bulletin board networks.

If school is more challenging, teenagers with hacker personality traits may develop interests in subjects like music.

Developing young hackers' interests in noncomputer fields would further develop their intellectual abilities, give them exposure to different environments and enhance their social skills, Smith said. She praised a special Duke University program for talented students that features a balance of challenging academic work and well-planned extracuricular activities.

Other EDP Controls

Some EDP controls are not oriented toward preventing criminal activity. Instead, their purpose is to encourage effective use of EDP systems. Data administration controls are one example. Controls over systems development are another. We will not discuss these controls in this module. They are important to systems designers and auditors, and if you make either of these professions your career, you should learn more about them.

Harold Johnson and Joan Everest were able to continue their crime for eighteen months. During that   *period, they obtained $150,000 worth of records for $22,500. The crime would have gone on longer,*   MODREC — THE REST OF THE STORY *except for a change of management at MODREC.*

A new president was hired, and he expected better performance from the entire company. As part of his improvement program, he required the sales force to increase sales. When one of the new sales managers reviewed the performance of the region containing Joan's store, he detected something suspicious. It seemed that the volume of sales should have netted larger income. He examined the sales invoices for the past year and saw what had been going on. He contacted the new president, and the game was up.

Harold was actually relieved. The strain of perpetrating the crime had begun to wear on him.

Furthermore, he was frustrated. He liked to brag about his creations, and he wanted to tell his friends about the crime. He thought it was clever, and he wanted credit for it.

MODREC threatened to sue for damages, but a settlement was made out of court. Harold and Joan paid MODREC $50,000, and Joan turned over a sizable part of her record inventory. Surprisingly, Harold had saved all but a few hundred dollars of the money Joan had paid him. He really didn't participate for the money.

Criminal action was taken. Since both Harold and Joan were first-time criminals, they received light sentences. They each spent 60 days in jail and were fined $5000.

QUESTIONS

D.1 How much money is lost due to computer crimes every year?

D.2 Describe five types of computer crime.

D.3 List 12 indications that an organization is vulnerable to computer crime.

D.4 How have most computer crimes been discovered?

D.5 What are EDP controls?

D.6 List the categories of EDP controls described in this module.

D.7 Describe management controls.

D.8 Describe organizational controls.

D.9 Describe data center resource controls.

D.10 Describe input/processing/output controls.

▓ SUMMARY

Computer crime is an important issue. Millions of dollars are lost each year. There are five types of computer crime: manipulating input, changing programs, stealing data, stealing computer time, and stealing programs.

The characteristics of companies that are vulnerable to computer crime are known. Most of these characteristics reflect bad data processing management and violate the principles of effective data processing discussed in this book.

To prevent crime, companies need to develop better controls within their business computer systems. These controls involve several areas: management, organizational structure, data center resources, input/ processing/output, data administration, and systems development. EDP controls will not guarantee that crime is eliminated, but they will reduce the likelihood of crime.

WORD LIST

(In order of appearance in text)

Computer crime
EDP controls
EDP
Management controls
Organizational controls
Data center resource controls
Input/processing/output controls

QUESTIONS TO CHALLENGE YOUR THINKING

A. What organizations or industries do you believe are particularly vulnerable to computer crime? If you worked for one of these companies, what would you do to reduce the likelihood of computer crime?

B. What would you do if you believed computer crime was happening at a company for which you worked? Would you report it? If so, to whom? Suppose you didn't report it, but later someone found out that you knew about it all along? What might happen? Could the company hold you accountable because you never reported the crime?

C. How can computer crime be detected? What role do you think accountants and auditors have in the detection of computer crime?

D. Find out more about SAS-3. (Ask an accounting professor.) What does it mean to public auditors? What does it mean to data processing professionals? How do you think you should respond to an EDP auditor?

E. Are existing laws sufficient for prosecuting computer crimes? Are special laws needed? What laws are currently in effect at the federal level? What laws are being considered by Congress concerning computer crime? What are the strengths and weaknesses of the laws being considered?

SYSTEM PROGRAMS, OPERATING SYSTEMS, AND PROGRAMMING LANGUAGES

MODULE E

System programs manage the computer's resources and provide services that improve the productivity of the computer. Programming languages enable people to take advantage of the problem-solving capabilities of the computer. In this module we will define major categories of system programs and discuss their functions. Then we will examine several programming languages in use today.

APPLICATION VERSUS SYSTEM PROGRAMS

Application programs satisfy a particular user need. For example, there are application programs to do financial analysis, to keep the general ledger, to account for goods in inventory, to analyze laboratory data, and so forth. Such programs have a specific purpose that relates directly to the needs of the company that uses them. Sources of application programs were discussed in chapter 5. To review, application programs can be obtained *off the shelf*, they can be *purchased and altered*, or they can be *custom developed*. When programming is required, it can be done by in-house personnel, or it can be done by personnel who are employed by an outside company. Application programs are generally neither as large nor as complex as system programs.

System programs are more general than application programs. They do not satisfy a particular need such as inventory accounting. Rather, they provide an environment in which application programs can be executed; they also make the computer more usable. System programs are normally provided by the manufacturer of the computer. They are acquired off the shelf, although in rare circumstances an organization alters a system program. Because system programs are complex, and because their development requires in-depth knowledge of hardware, they are almost never custom developed. System programs for mainframe computers are normally leased from the computer vendor. System programs for microcomputers can be purchased at a computer store. The characteristics of system and application programs are summarized in figure E–1.

FIGURE E–1

Characteristics of application and system programs

APPLICATION PROGRAMS	SYSTEMS PROGRAMS
Solve a particular problem	Are general purpose

Acquired:
  Off-the-shelf
  Altered
  Custom-tailored
	Usually acquired off-the-shelf

Sometimes written in-house	Usually obtained from CPU vendor
Purchased or leased	Usually leased

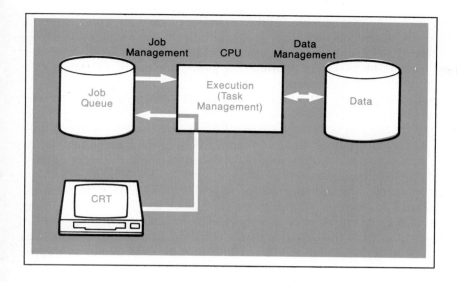

System programs can be divided into three broad categories. The **operating system** (or **supervisor**, or **executive**) manages the computer's resources. **Utilities** are the second category of system programs. Utilities provide commonly needed services. For example, there are utilities to copy a file, to make a duplicate diskette, and to sort a file of data. Utilities save an organization the work of having to write its own programs for these services. The third category of system programs is the **language processors**. These programs translate instructions coded in languages such as BASIC into machine instructions, and they prepare the translated instructions for execution. We will consider the operating system first, then the utilities, and finally the language translators.

THE OPERATING SYSTEM

The three basic functions of the operating system are job management, task management, and data management. Figure E–2 shows the relationships of these three functions. Work to be done is kept on a job queue. The job management portion of the operating system selects jobs from the queue and starts them. Once started, a job is controlled by the task management portion of the operating system. Task management assigns CPU time and main memory to jobs and controls the flow of jobs residing in main memory. Data management provides data access services to programs during processing.

Job Management

A **job** is a sequence of one or more units of work that accomplishes a user task. For example, the job to produce payroll checks might have three units of work, or steps. In the first step, payroll amounts are computed, and a new master file is generated. In the second step, a payroll register (list of checks) is printed. Finally, in the third step, the paychecks themselves are printed. Normally, one program (executable load module) is run per step.

The function of the **job management** portion of the operating system is to schedule jobs and to allocate computer resources to them. There may be many jobs waiting for execution at one time. These jobs will need different types of computer equipment. Job management allocates resources and starts jobs so as to maximize throughput and avoid resource conflicts.

For example, the job to produce payroll checks may require three tape drives for its first step and one tape drive for the two remaining steps. If the computer only has three tape drives, this job cannot be started until all of the drives are free. Once the first step is completed, however, other jobs can be started that require only one or two tape drives. Similar conflicts can occur with disk drives, printers, main memory, and other resources.

The function of job management is even more complex because jobs may have different priorities. Processing order entries is probably more important than producing a summary of last year's sales. If so, the order entry job should receive resources before the sales summary. Balancing the needs of jobs and recognizing priorities is difficult. Job management functions are summarized below:

- Select jobs from job queue
- Allocate resources
- Avoid resource conflicts
- Recognize priorities

If you have run programs only on a microcomputer, you may not realize the need for job management. Most micros are single-user systems; only one person can use them at a time. However, there are many computers that run dozens of jobs concurrently. For these computers, job management is critical.

Task Management

Task management begins when a job is scheduled for execution. The job is loaded into main memory, and the CPU begins to execute the job's instructions. At this point, the job is referred to as a **task**. A task is a unit of work that competes in its own right for CPU time. As soon as the job is started, it may create additional tasks to perform work concurrently. In a sense, the primary task of the job gives birth to additional tasks.

Each task requires CPU time and main memory. Usually, the CPU is allocated to tasks in round-robin fashion. For example, each task may be allocated one-tenth of a second of CPU time. This one-tenth is given to the first task, then to the second, then to the third, and so forth. If

APPLICATION

"THE 'QUICK-AND-DIRTY OPERATING SYSTEM' WOULD BE THE FOUNDATION."

Tim Paterson might be the guy you've been griping about. He's the anonymous one you've growled at when an unexpected "A" prompt appears or when a microcomputer's memory just isn't what you wish it could be.

Hindsight is 20-20, of course, but Paterson admits he would do a few things differently if he had known five years ago that the "Quick-and-Dirty Operating System" (internally known appropriately as QDOS) he was piecing together would be the foundation for millions of microcomputers today.

The project became, of course, MS-DOS, which Paterson, as an employee of Seattle Computer Products, Inc., wrote in 1980 on a contract for Microsoft Corporation, which had a job with an unnamed "major OEM."

"The thing was they needed to get something really quick," Paterson recalls. "I figured later I'd go back and work out the finished operating system with multitasking and all that."

As to eventual memory limitations, well, "in 1980, who would've thought that 64 megabytes was going to be considered not big enough?"

And, admittedly, the so-called 86 DOS he churned out in just two months is the ancestor of the MS-DOS or PC-DOS in use today.

Both Microsoft's and IBM's own programmers had a hand in developing the version eventually released with the IBM Personal Computer in August 1981, as well as in spearheading subsequent revisions of the product.

Paterson wrote DOS in 8080 assembly language on a Zilog, Inc., Z80 machine and translated it to the 8086 system. Microsoft paid $50,000 for it in 1981.

Last year alone, Microsoft's systems software sales (including MS-DOS) were $75 million, just over half of the company's total revenue.

---

there are 10 tasks, one second is required to complete the entire cycle. If there are 20 tasks, two seconds are required for a cycle. Sharing the CPU in this way is sometimes called **time slicing**.

CPU time allocation is complex for two reasons. First, the tasks may have different priorities. A task that is doing work for order entry will likely have a higher priority than a task doing work for the sales history report. Thus, the round-robin strategy may have to be modified to give more time to high-priority tasks.

The second reason that time allocation is complex is that tasks may be unable to use all of their allocated time. For example, suppose that the highest-priority task needs data before it can continue. If so, data management will be called upon to transfer the data. Data retrieval, however, takes a long time (relative to the speed of the CPU). Therefore, the CPU will go on to other tasks while the data is being transferred. Once the data arrives, however, the CPU should be assigned to the waiting task (because it has the highest priority).

This reassignment is accomplished via **interrupts**. Whenever events of importance occur within the computer, an interrupt message is sent to task management. Task management can choose to respond to the interrupt or not. In general, task management will respond to interrupts that involve work at a higher priority than the CPU is currently doing. If the interrupt involves work at a lower priority, the interrupt message is saved and processed later.

Let us return to the example where the highest-priority task is waiting for data: When the data transfer is complete, an I/O-complete interrupt message will be generated. Task management routines will examine this message and determine that the highest-priority task is now ready to continue. The CPU will be reassigned from whatever work it is doing to process the highest-priority task.

Interrupts are used for other purposes as well. For example, on some computers, when power fails, a power-failure interrupt is generated. This interrupt has a very high priority. When it is detected, task management sends a death message to every active task. Essentially, this message says, "We're dying—you have 100 milliseconds (or whatever) of CPU time to tidy up your affairs. Write your will and generate whatever messages you will need in your next life." When power is restored, the tasks are restarted, and they read the messages written at the end of their previous lives. Most likely, these messages will tell them how to resume processing.

Another task management function is providing **supervisor services**. There are many activities that are too complex or too risky for user

FIGURE E–3a
A virtual-memory system

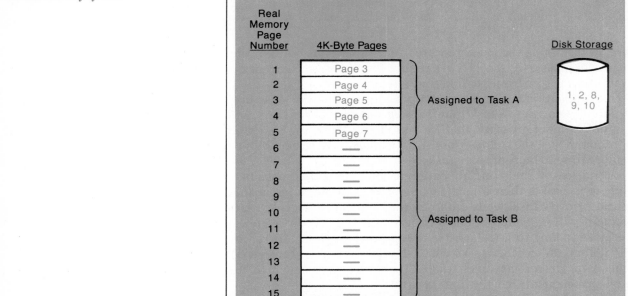

a. Task A Using Pages 3, 4, 5, 6, and 7

tasks to do for themselves. For example, a task may want to send a message to another task. To do so, the task will need to write in the memory space assigned to the other task. In general, however, this activity cannot be allowed; if one task were able to write in another task's memory whenever it wanted, havoc could result. Thus, to send a message to another task, the task must ask task management to send the message. In response, the operating system will send the message, but it will coordinate the message with other processing in the task, and it will be certain to write the message only in the correct memory location. In this way, the message will be safely delivered.

The **allocation of main memory** is the last function of task management that we will discuss. When tasks are initiated, a certain amount of memory is allocated to the task. As the task progresses, more or less memory may be needed. When the task wishes to change the amount of memory it has, it requests the change from task management (changing memory allocation is another supervisor service).

Some computers have **virtual memory**. This term means that the task thinks it has more memory than it actually has. To understand this concept, consider figure E–3, which illustrates the scheme used by one popular virtual-memory system. In this figure, memory has been

FIGURE E–3b

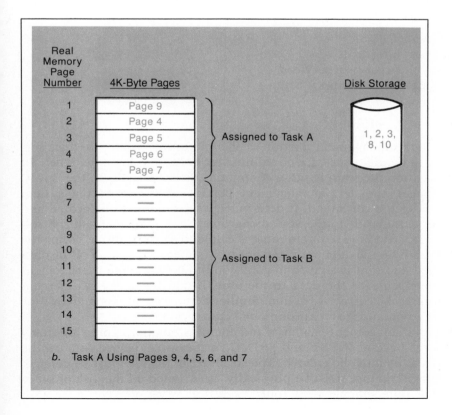

b.   Task A Using Pages 9, 4, 5, 6, and 7

divided into 4K-byte pages (K = 1024). Task A has been assigned pages 1 through 5, and task B has been assigned pages 6 through 15.

In actuality, task A has been assigned only five real pages of memory. When task A is running, any five of the pages 1 through 10 can be in main memory at a time. In figure E–3a, pages 3, 4, 5, 6, and 7 reside in memory. The remaining pages (1, 2, 8, 9, and 10) have been stored temporarily on disk. If the task needs an instruction or data located on one of the pages on disk, the operating system will remove one of the pages in memory and replace it with the needed page. Thus, in figure E–3b, page 9 was needed. The operating system removed page 3 and copied page 9 into the place that was held by page 3.

Thus, it appears to task A that it has 10 pages of memory. However, only five of those are resident in memory at once. The task is unaware of the real situation, because whenever it needs data, the operating system provides it. The operating system makes it appear to task A that 10 consecutive pages of memory are available.

Using virtual memory, programs can be much larger than the actual main memory size. This is an advantage because main memory is expensive, and in many large programs, much of the code is unused for long periods of time. With a virtual system, the unused code will be stored on disk until it is needed. Task management functions are summarized below:

- Allocate CPU
- Process interrupts
- Provide supervisor services
- Allocate main memory

Data Management

The **data management** portion of the operating system provides services to create, process, and administer data. For example, when an application program issues a command such as INPUT (in the BASIC language), the data management portion of the operating system processes the command. It determines where the data is located and issues commands to the various hardware components (disk controller, disk drive, and so on) to cause the data to be transmitted. When the data arrives, the data management routines ensure that all of the data arrived and that it arrived in good condition. If so, data management routines transfer the data to the user. If not, the data management routines take corrective action. Similar actions occur when PRINT (or other commands to create or modify data) is issued.

Data management is a large and complex function. There are many services beyond INPUT and PRINT. For example, before data can be input, a file must be created. The structure of the file must be defined, and the structure must be physically constructed on the disk or other media. Data management routines do this work in accordance with instructions from the program or other source. The situation is even more complicated when you consider that files can have sequential, indexed sequential, and random organizations. Data management must be able to support all three.

In addition to creation and processing, data management provides services to facilitate **data administration**. In some systems, data management routines maintain a catalog of data. This catalog records who created the data, when it was created, when it was last processed, and so forth.

Data catalogs are useful for managing libraries of data. Consider the problem of a tape library containing thousands of tape volumes. How can operations know which of the tape volumes are needed? If there are tapes that have not been used in several years, are they still needed? To determine this, operations needs to know who created the data and when. In one large data center, the operations staff did a manual inventory of all tapes. They called the person responsible for the creation of every tape in their library. Among other surprises, they found 107 tapes that had been issued to someone who had died two years previously.

Some computers have a set of programs that perform **database management**. These programs are called the *database management system (DBMS)*. Database processing is discussed in more detail in chapter 9. For now, realize that the DBMS, if used, is part of the operating system data management function. With some computers, a DBMS is built into the operating system. With others, the DBMS is an optional item. With still others, the DBMS is provided by a completely different vendor. Data management functions are summarized below:

- Provide facilities to:
    Create data
    Process data
        For sequential, indexed sequential, and direct files
    Administer data
- Support database processing

▐▐▐ POPULAR OPERATING SYSTEMS

The performance, reliability, and capabilities of a computer system are at least partially dictated by the operating system under which the hardware is running. Consequently, many operating systems have been developed in the past three decades, each one providing (supposedly) improvements over the others available at the time. Operating systems for large mainframe computers usually have evolved; that is, a large manufacturer such as IBM has enhanced existing operating systems with new features. Normally, all the old features of the system being replaced continue to be supported by the new one. This is called

upward compatibility. One notable exception to the evolutionary approach to operating system development was IBM's revolutionary introduction of its Operating System/360 (OS/360), a replacement of its predecessor, the Disk Operating System (DOS) that was currently being used on IBM's family of System/360 mainframe computers. Far from being upwardly compatible, OS was dramatically different from DOS, and the conversion from DOS to OS was so difficult and costly that many users refused to change, instead pressing IBM to incorporate some of OS's features into new releases of DOS. That has now been done to a certain extent, but in the meantime IBM developed two more operating systems that have become the operating systems of IBM's System/370 and similar mainframe computers: MVS and VM.

MVS

MVS (which stands for *multiple virtual storage*) was designed to provide performance, reliability, availability, and compatibility for the large System/370 environment. To appreciate the size of a large computer environment, you should understand that the large S/370 computers have over 16 million bytes of main memory. Of that, 8 million bytes are reserved for programmer use, and the rest is used by the operating system. When the computer is run under MVS, however, the illusion of much more main memory is created because the operating system carefully manages main memory and loads only fragments of programs into it at a time. Using this concept of virtual memory, MVS provides each user with 16 million bytes of memory. In fact, some MVS systems have increased this to 2 billion bytes. That is a *big* computer system.

In addition to the size of memory, another notable aspect of MVS is the number of users that it can support at once. The practical limit is said to be around 300 or 400 concurrent users, each with an individual address space. Within an address space, between 500 and 700 users can be using the computer at one time. It is mind boggling to consider the complexity of an operating system that manages the resources of one computer system among so many thousand users.

MVS is IBM's top-of-the-line batch processing operating system, and thousands of IBM users have made a commitment to it. This means that a drastic change in operating system would require hundreds of thousands of programs to be modified, retested, and reinstalled. Consequently, MVS will probably continue to be IBM's big-machine batch processor. However, another IBM operating system, called *VM*, provides attractive features not offered by MVS.

VM

VM (which stands for *virtual machine*) is an IBM operating system that allows each user to operate as if the user were using a separate dedicated System/370 computer and its input/output devices. Of course, in reality there is only one machine, but the VM operating system creates the illusion that everyone has a private computer.

VM includes a component called the *Conversational Monitor System (CMS)*, which includes powerful features for interactive program development on a mainframe computer. This is very important to companies whose programmers are developing hundreds of application programs each year. Interactive program development is much faster than batch program development.

The most significant feature of VM is that each user can select a different operating system for his or her own virtual computer. VM can actually run several different operating systems at a time. Why is this so significant? Because users who are committed to another operating system, say DOS or MVS, can still run those programs under VM — they simply run one virtual machine under DOS or MVS while they take advantage of other more powerful features of VM on other virtual machines. The point is that VM is so powerful that it sees another operating system as simply another application program. It coordinates many application programs at once, allocating the real computer's memory and resources as they are needed. And a user organization can keep its old programs, upgrade to VM, and not spend a fortune on conversions.

UNIX

The **UNIX** operating system was developed at Bell Laboratories as a convenient system for supporting program development. It has a simple and powerful command language and is popular in academic environments and in industry. UNIX, or versions of it, are also available for use on personal computers.

UNIX was designed for the DEC PDP-11 family of computers for multiuser time-sharing. However, UNIX has been successfully implemented on many other systems, including the DEC VAX computer as well as computers by other manufacturers. Unlike the operating systems considered previously, which were designed specifically for large IBM mainframe computers, several versions of UNIX are available for microcomputers, minicomputers, and mainframes.

An interesting aspect of UNIX is that it is written in a high-level programming language called **C**. Until recently, most operating systems were written in a computer's assembly language, which is one step above the computer's machine code. Because each computer family has its own machine code, an operating system written for one can not be run on another. By writing UNIX in C, the developers made the program more portable and understandable, thereby increasing its marketability.

Unlike IBM's MVS, VM, or dozens of other operating systems developed by teams of systems programmers employed by computer manufacturers, UNIX was actually developed by only two people, and they

APPLICATION

"UNIX IS FAR FROM BEING A FAILURE."

Developed at Bell Laboratories, Unix is a de facto standard for engineering workstations, but it has yet to be widely adopted for business applications. A lack of good business application software, incompatibilities between Unix versions from different vendors, and the complexity of Unix itself are among the reasons commonly cited by users and developers for the operating system's cool reception by corporations.

Despite its problems, Unix is far from being a failure. According to AT&T Information Systems, about 250,000 Unix systems are in use and, according to analysts, that number is growing at the rate of 30 percent to 40 percent per year. Because it is in-

herently a multiuser, multitasking operating system, Unix offers solutions to several business problems, including networking.

For sophisticated microcomputer and minicomputer users, the promises of hardware independence and software portability are Unix's greatest advantages. But Unix is still hampered by a lack of standardization. Most of the 30 or so Unix variants available are descended from three versions: Bell Labs' System III and System V, and BSD Unix, developed at the University of California at Berkeley. Most versions of Unix are fairly similar in basic functions, but they vary enough to make software portability a concern for

corporate users.

Having the same product available on both Unix and MS-DOS is particularly popular in offices in which micros co-exist with Unix terminals. At the Philip Morris Research Center in Richmond, VA, a division of Philip Morris Inc., about 200 employees use Wordmarc word processing software from Marc Software on micros and several minis, including a VAX/11 785 from Digital Equipment Corp., running DEC's Ultrix version of Unix, and a Gould 9000 running Gould's UTX version. "Users have all the functionality of the MS-DOS version — they just have to hit different keys," says Jack Stimler, project leader for applications development.

were both users of the system. The result was a coherent and simple operating system that can be learned by a skilled systems programmer in a few weeks, whereas other operating systems might take years to comprehend.

Also, UNIX was intended from the start to be simple and to provide only the minimum amount of function — all sophistication in application programs was left to the application programmer. Another design goal was to enable programmers to accomplish large tasks by combining many small programs rather than develop new ones from scratch — a modular approach to program development.

To achieve device independence, UNIX treats all input and output as continuous streams of data, rather than as records and files. Consequently, any difference between a punched card, a tape, or a disk is effectively ignored by the operating system. A disadvantage of this is that the user must write some data management code.

UNIX was intended for use in program development, not in large-scale business production processing. It is very useful for the purpose for which it was created, but it does not compete with the operating systems of the large mainframes. UNIX simply does not address hardware performance, security, reliability, and other issues vital in large-scale commercial systems.

XENIX

XENIX is an operating system developed by Microsoft for the microcomputer industry. It is based on the UNIX operating system and has become very popular for several reasons. For one, XENIX provides microcomputer users with powerful multiuser time-sharing capabilities. For another, Microsoft also developed compatible versions of popular microcomputer languages, including BASIC, COBOL, FORTRAN, and Pascal. Finally, IBM selected Microsoft to develop a scaled-down version of XENIX called *IBM Personal Computer DOS* (*PC DOS*) for its line of personal computers. That move alone greatly enhanced Microsoft's popularity.

There are many more operating systems available today for large mainframes, for minicomputers, and for microcomputers. All of them are intended to make the computer's resources available to the user. Some emphasize batch processing, some interactive processing. Some operating systems support many computers at a time, some only one. Some operating systems allow a single user, some allow a few dozen users, and others can support several thousand users at once. Which operating system is the best? Of course, that is a question without an answer. No one operating system is the best for every application. Like so many other things in business computer systems, the operating system that satisfies an organization's particular needs is the one that should be chosen.

UTILITIES

The second category of system programs that we will discuss is utilities. These programs provide commonly needed services such as sorting data, copying data from one diskette to another, and initializing files.

The list below shows the menu of utilities available on a WANG word processing system:

- Copy document to archive diskette
- File document to archive diskette
- Retrieve document from archive diskette
- Delete document from system diskette
- Delete document from archive diskette
- Prepare archive diskette for processing

When the user selects one of the items on this menu, one of six utility programs is executed. This word processing system has two floppy diskettes. One is called the **system diskette**, and the other is called the **archive**. The first utility copies a document from the system diskette to the archive diskette. The original copy remains unchanged. The second utility files a document (when it is filed, a document is copied from the system diskette to the archive diskette, and the original is deleted from the system diskette). The third utility retrieves documents from the archive diskette. The fourth and fifth utilities delete documents, and the last utility prepares a new diskette for processing and storing data. During preparation, the diskette is labeled, and the basic structure is recorded.

The utilities listed previously are typical. Larger systems have more utilities, but they are essentially the same. The point to remember is that utilities are provided with computer systems, and that system evaluations should include consideration of whether necessary utilities are available.

LANGUAGE PROCESSORS

The third category of system programs that we will consider is the language processors. Any computer understands only one language, and that is called **machine code**. Figure E – 4 shows a few **binary instruction codes** for large IBM computer systems. Multiply is represented by the code 10011100; divide is represented by the code 10011101. The memory locations of the operands is also represented in binary format, but that representation is beyond the scope of this discussion.

In the early days of computing, programmers had to memorize binary instruction codes. Thus, someone might spend an hour or two to produce the following program:

```
110010001000111110101010101011101010111010001111101001
110110010101011110010101010101000000010111101111000110
110101010111001001001000101111101001110010101010001010
101010001010101001011111100010101011000011100101001110
001001010111001010101010100100101010111110101101000101
```

Writing such gibberish might be fun for a few hours, but clearly it is no way to spend a lifetime. Further, programs produced by this

FIGURE E – 4
Examples of IBM binary instruction codes

INSTRUCTION	BINARY CODE
Add	10011010
Divide	10011101
Multiply	10011100
Subtract	10011011
Move	10010010

method often had errors, and the errors were very hard to find and fix. Consequently, people looked for a better way to produce programs.

Program Compilation

The early developers of what eventually became known as **high-level programming languages** were trying to make things easy on themselves. They needed to use the computer, but they wanted to spend their time solving problems, not writing strings of 1's and 0's. They decided to write a program that could translate certain words and symbols into the binary instruction code the computer understood. That would enable people to write computer instructions using familiar symbols and words. The program, or **source code**, would then be read by the translator program, called a **compiler**, and the compiler would generate the machine code for the program. This required an extra step, compilation, but solving problems was much faster.

There was not just one programming language invented — in fact, over a thousand programming languages have been developed in the past 35 years. Fortunately, only a few have survived. And you will be not be expected to learn all of these.

Why were so many developed? One reason was that computer scientists were working somewhat in isolation. Another reason was that different people had different needs. Later in this module you will learn about various programming languages.

As a result of this need for an easier way to write programs, language translators, or compilers, were developed. There is a separate translator for each language: a COBOL compiler for COBOL programs, a FORTRAN compiler for FORTRAN programs, a Pascal compiler for Pascal programs, and so forth. Remember that a compiler is simply a program. When an organization installs a computer, it must select an operating system (described previously), and it must choose the compilers it will need. If you decide to purchase a microcomputer, you are almost sure to get BASIC with it; BASIC has become a standard piece of microcomputer software. You might also buy a COBOL compiler, a Pascal compiler, a FORTRAN compiler, or many others.

All compilers do essentially the same thing: They translate source code into machine language. For example, a programmer might write a program such as this:

```
INPUT A, B
C = A + B
PRINT C
```

These English-like statements are translated into a sequence of 0's and 1's that cause the computer to read two numbers, add them together, and print the result.

Figure E–5 illustrates program compilation. The English-like source code statements are entered into the compiler, or translator program.

FIGURE E–5
Example of program compilation and
load process

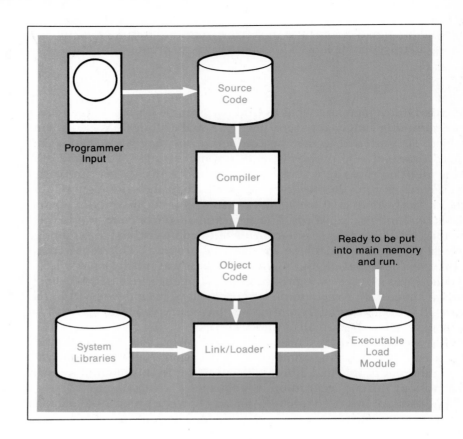

The compiler produces a binary (0's and 1's) version of the program called **object code**.

Keep in mind that the compiler is a program. It is *not* a piece of hardware or a special machine. It is a program that resides in main memory, and it accepts other programs as its data. Compilers, like all other programs, are written by people.

In figure E–5, the object code generated by the compiler is stored in a file. Even though it has been translated, it may not be ready for execution. The program may contain references to other programs. For example, a programmer may write an application program that requires the current time of day to be printed on a report. Although the programmer can write his or her own routine to determine the time, there is probably a routine that determines the time in a **system library**. When the programmer needs the time routine, he or she will consult the library documentation to determine the name of such a routine. Suppose the name of this routine is TIME, and it is specified as follows:

$$X = TIME$$

This statement sets the variable *X* to the current time of day.

When the application program is translated, the compiler will recognize TIME as the name of an external routine. Since the compiler does not have the source code of the TIME routine, it cannot translate it. Instead, the compiler inserts a note into the object code indicating that TIME is an **external reference**. This note means that the time routine should be taken from a library.

Before the application program object code can be executed, the object code of TIME must be appended to it. This action is done by a program called a **link/loader**, a **linkage editor**, or some other name. The link/loader searches the libraries for the TIME routine, or for any other external programs. These programs are then appended to the object code. The output of this process is an **executable load module**. This module is ready to be read into main memory and executed.

If the program is to be used over and over again, the executable load module is saved. This way, the program need not be compiled and link/loaded every time it is run. For example, a weekly payroll program is not compiled each week. Instead, its load module is saved from week to week. It is only compiled when changes are made to the program.

Thus, every program has three versions or formats. It is written by a person in *source form*, it is compiled (translated) into *object form*, and it is merged with other routines to form an *executable load module*.

Program Interpretation

Figure E–5 shows program compilation. An alternative form of translation is program **interpretation**. The difference between the two processes is that, whereas in compilation, the entire program is translated before execution begins, in interpretation, the program is translated and executed one line at a time. When interpretation is used, a line is translated and executed, then the next line is translated and executed, and so forth. External references such as the TIME routine are resolved as they are encountered.

Interpretation is more common with small and simple programs, like the ones you are writing in this class. In fact, most BASIC systems use interpretation. In the commercial world, however, compilation is far more commonly used.

POPULAR COMPUTER PROGRAMMING LANGUAGES

Programming languages are developed for use in one field of application or another. This has led to families of computer languages, each family focusing on one particular field. There are languages that are used for business applications, for scientific applications, and for systems programming. There are also special-purpose languages used for operations research, process control, computer simulation, and so forth. A chart listing several popular programming languages appears

APPLICATION

in figure E–6. We will examine four programming languages used for business applications: BASIC, COBOL, PL/I, and RPG. Other applications and languages are summarized in subsequent sections. If you pursue a field other than business, you may need to learn some other programming languages.

Business Applications and Languages

Business applications typically involve transferring large amounts of data, and business programs often execute many input/output instructions. However, once the data is in main memory, business programs usually perform few mathematical operations on it. Instead, data items are compared to one another, decisions are made, and changes are made to stored data. Structured reports are frequently produced.

Additionally, business applications are often online. Many users may operate concurrently at many terminals, and users often want to access the same files of data, so program coordination is important. This topic is discussed further in chapter 10.

Business is a dynamic activity, and business programs change frequently. Because the person who wrote a program is often not available to change it, business programs need to be easy to read and understand.

Order entry is a typical business application. When an order is processed, customer, inventory, and production records must be accessed. Data about customer credit, items on hand or in production, shipping addresses, and so forth is processed to make order approval and shipping decisions.

Hundreds of orders may be processed in a day, so a tremendous volume of data may be transferred to and from the files. However, the processing of this data involves simple arithmetic; there is no need for sophisticated mathematics.

LANGUAGE	PRIMARY USES	COMMENTS
ADA	Systems, Scientific	Derivative of Pascal; developed for U. S. Dept. of Defense
ALGOL	Scientific	Popular in Europe, not in North America
APL	Scientific	Requires special keyboard; primarily available on IBM computers
Assembler	Systems	Highly efficient; system dependent; difficult to read and understand
BASIC	Education, Simple programs	Simple to learn; limited functions
COBOL	Business	Old language; wordy; extensive file-handling capability; durable
FORTRAN	Scientific	Old language; has limitations, but very popular in science
Pascal	Education, Systems, Scientific	Excellent structured language; limited I/O
PL/I	General purpose	Rich language, but complex
RPG	Business report writing	Parameter driven; quick way to generate reports

FIGURE E–6
Comparison of programming languages

Generally, several order entry clerks process the same files. If their access is not carefully controlled, they can interfere with one another.

These characteristics of business programs mean that a business programming language should have extensive input/output capability. Performing I/O operations should be easy, and data should be transferred efficiently. Further, the language should have a rich vocabulary for describing records, fields, data types, and so forth, but sophisticated mathematical vocabulary and notation are unimportant.

Because online, concurrent processing is prevalent, the language should have commands for locking and unlocking records and for performing other types of program coordination.

The characteristics of business applications are summarized in figure E–7. This figure also lists four languages commonly used for business programming. We will briefly describe each of these.

BASIC

The acronym **BASIC** stands for **Beginners' All-purpose Symbolic Instruction Code**. BASIC was designed in the late 1960s at Dartmouth College and was intended to introduce students to programming. As its name implies, it is an all-purpose language for beginners.

A simple BASIC program is shown in figure E–8. This program reads accounts receivable records and computes the number of accounts with a zero balance, the number with a positive balance, and the total of the balances. After all records have been entered, the results are printed. BASIC's primary virtue is that it is simple and therefore easy to learn and use. BASIC has very primitive input/output capabilities, and its vocabulary for alternation (decision making within a program, which usually takes the form If-Then-Else) is clumsy. Loops, or iteration structures, can be awkward to implement in BASIC.

BASIC is popular because it is simple, and it works well for small problems, such as computing the interest on a mortgage. However, because of its limitations, BASIC is not good for all business applications. When complex programs are written in BASIC, the code is usually hard to read and understand, and therefore it is hard to change.

FIGURE E–7
Summary of business application programs

CHARACTERISTICS OF BUSINESS APPLICATIONS	LANGUAGES COMMONLY USED
Frequent input and output of large amounts of data	BASIC
Little mathematical manipulation of data	COBOL
Frequent online processing	PL/I
Concurrent processing control important	RPG
Programs often need to be changed	
Programs need to be easy to read	

```
010 REM       THIS PROGRAM PROCESSES ACCOUNTS RECEIVABLE DATA
020 REM       VARIABLE ASSIGNMENTS ARE:
030 REM       N1 = NUMBER OF ACCOUNTS WITH ZERO BALANCES
040 REM       N2 = NUMBER OF ACCOUNTS WITH POSITIVE BALANCES
050 REM       T = TOTAL OF BALANCES
060 REM       N$ = NAME OF CUSTOMER
070 REM       B = AMOUNT OF CUSTOMER BALANCE
100    N1 = 0
150    N2 = 0
200    T  = 0
225 REM        PROCESSING LOOP STARTS HERE
250    INPUT N$, B
300    IF N$ = "END" THEN 650
350    IF B = 0 THEN 550
400    N2 = N2 + 1
450    T = T + B
500    GOTO 250
550    N1 = N1 + 1
600    GOTO 250
625 REM        TERMINATION SECTION
650    PRINT "NUMBER OF ACCOUNTS WITH ZERO BALANCE IS", N1
700    PRINT "NUMBER OF ACCOUNTS WITH POSITIVE BALANCE IS", N2
750    PRINT "TOTAL OF BALANCES IS", T
800    END
```

Actually, BASIC's simplicity has turned out to be a disadvantage. BASIC has been applied to problems for which it is not suited. Beginners have learned BASIC and then never graduated to a language that is harder to learn but more powerful. As beginners' programming skills improve, they may take on more complex tasks, but still use BASIC, eventually using a beginner's language to accomplish complex tasks. The resulting code is hard to read and generally undesirable.

BASIC is offered with many small business computers and microcomputers. Often the computer vendor extends the capabilities of BASIC to allow for the sophisticated input/output needed for business data processing. Such extension of capabilities, however, is a trap. Once a company develops programs using the language extensions, they find it hard to switch to another vendor's computer. If they switched, all of their programs would have to be rewritten to remove the special commands. This modification can be very expensive.

To summarize, BASIC is an easy language for beginners to use when they are learning about programming, and it is often used with microcomputers. The standard language can result in programs that are hard to read and excessively complex. Vendors have augmented the language to give it more power.

FIGURE E–8
Sample BASIC program

COBOL

The acronym **COBOL** stands for **COmmon Business-Oriented Language**. COBOL was designed by a committee of users and computer manufacturers in the late 1950s. The users wanted a language that would be suited to business problems and that would support sophisticated input and output processing.

COBOL is an old and established language. It is nationally standardized and supported by all major computer manufacturers. Between 60 and 80 percent of all business application programs are written in COBOL.

FIGURE E–9

Procedure division of a COBOL program

Note: A COBOL program has four parts, called *divisions*. The IDENTIFICATION DIVISION names the program. The ENVIRONMENT DIVISION describes the files to be used; the DATA DIVISION describes the format of the data. Finally, the PROCEDURE DIVISION describes actions for the computer to take. For simplicity, only the PROCEDURE DIVISION is shown here.

```
PROCEDURE DIVISION.
    PERFORM A10-INITIALIZE.
    PERFORM A20-PROCESS UNTIL EOF-FLAG = 1.
    PERFORM A30-WRAPUP.
    STOP RUN.
A10-INITIALIZE.
    OPEN INPUT DATA-FILE
        OUTPUT PRINT-FILE.
    MOVE 0 TO EOF-FLAG.
    MOVE 0 TO NUM-ZERO-BAL.
    MOVE 0 TO NUM-POS-BAL.
    MOVE 0 TO TOTAL-BAL.
    READ DATA-FILE AT END MOVE 1 TO EOF-FLAG.
A20-PROCESS.
    IF BAL IS GREATER THAN 0
        ADD 1 TO NUM-POS-BAL
        ADD BAL TO TOTAL-BAL
    ELSE
        ADD 1 TO NUM-ZERO-BAL.
    READ DATA-FILE AT END MOVE 1 TO EOF-FLAG.
A30-WRAPUP.
    WRITE PRINT-REC FROM HEADER1.
    WRITE PRINT-REC FROM SUMMARY-DATA.
    CLOSE DATA-FILE PRINT-FILE.
```

Figure E–9 shows the accounts receivable problem coded in COBOL. This problem is the same one used to demonstrate BASIC in figure E–8.

Because COBOL was designed with business applications in mind, it has been very successful in the business environment. It has an extensive vocabulary for defining files, records, and fields. Its alternation and iteration constructs are much better than BASIC's.

Unfortunately, COBOL has disadvantages, too. It is a large language with many features. Like any committee project, everyone's good ideas were incorporated. Consequently, COBOL is easily misused, and it takes most people a year or so of programming to learn the language well.

Further, COBOL was designed to be **self-documenting**. Many lines of code must be written even for simple problems. A few years ago, when programmers wrote programs on punched cards, someone said that when the weight of the cards containing the COBOL statements exceeds the weight of the computer, then the program is ready to run. Actually, COBOL was designed to solve medium- and large-sized business problems. It is time consuming and frustrating to write small COBOL programs.

COBOL was designed before online processing existed. Therefore, the standardized language does not have any special commands to coordinate concurrent processing. Most manufacturers of computers with online capability have expanded their versions of COBOL to include such commands.

If there is *one* business programming language, COBOL is it. Over the years, COBOL has proven to be amazingly durable. It has the features necessary to handle most business processing problems. You probably do not go one day without handling a document or form that was generated by a COBOL program.

PL/I

Programming Language I, or **PL/I**, was developed by IBM in the mid 1960s as a general-purpose language that could be used for all types of computer processing — business, scientific, and systems.

Figure E–10 shows the accounts receivable problem coded in PL/I. Compare this to the BASIC and COBOL programs shown in figures E–8 and E–9.

PL/I is in many ways similar to COBOL. The vocabulary for defining files, records, and data items is rich. A wide variety of input/output techniques is available. The constructs for alternation and iteration are excellent. PL/I has all the features necessary for business application programming. Additionally, PL/I has features for scientific and systems programming that make it truly a general-purpose language.

```
ACCT_REC: PROCEDURE OPTIONS(MAIN);
```
Note: Definitions of variables go here. For simplicity, they are not
shown in this example.
```
    ON ENDFILE (AR_FILE) EOF_FLAG = 1;
    EOF_FLAG = 0;
    NUM_ZERO_BAL = 0;
    NUM_POS_BAL = 0;
    TOTAL_BAL = 0;
    GET LIST (CUST_NAME, AMOUNT);
    DO WHILE EOF_FLAG = 0;
        IF AMOUNT GT 0
            THEN DO;
                NUM_POS = NUM_POS + 1;
                TOTAL_BAL = TOTAL_BAL + AMOUNT;
                END;
            ELSE NUM_ZERO_BAL = NUM_ZERO_BAL + 1;
        GET LIST (CUST_NAME, AMOUNT);
    END;
    PUT PAGE LIST ('NUMBER OF ZERO BALANCES IS ', NUM_ZERO_BAL);
    PUT SKIP(2) LIST ('NUMBER OF POSITIVE BALANCES IS ',
                    NUM_POS_BAL, 'TOTAL OF BALANCES IS ',
                    TOTAL_BAL);
    STOP;
    END;
```

FIGURE E–10
Portion of a PL/I program

Unfortunately, all of these features mean that PL/I is complex. The learning period required for PL/I is lengthy. The designers of PL/I attempted to reduce the impact of this complexity by defining levels of the language. The idea was that beginners could easily use a subset of PL/I and never know that other features were available. The implementation of this idea has been only partially successful.

In spite of its excellent features, PL/I has not been readily accepted in the business community. There are several reasons for this rejection. First, for many years, PL/I was only available on IBM computers. Companies that developed programs in PL/I were in effect committing themselves to the use of IBM equipment now and in the future. This commitment was more than most companies wanted to make.

Second, the existing PL/I compilers do not generate efficient object code. Programs written in PL/I occupy more main storage than equivalent programs written in another language. They take more machine time to run.

Finally, although PL/I is an excellent language, it does not appear to have substantial advantages over COBOL for business applications. Therefore, it is not sufficiently better to justify switching languages and possibly becoming dependent on IBM. Consequently, most companies have stayed with COBOL.

RPG

The acronym **RPG** stands for **Report Program Generator**. RPG is not a programming language like BASIC, COBOL, or PL/I, but it is sometimes called a programming language. Many business reports are generated using RPG, so you should know about it.

To use RPG, a programmer defines the format of input files by naming fields and specifying their lengths and types (numeric, character, and so on). Then the programmer defines simple operations on fields, such as "add all order amounts together." The programmer then specifies that this total is to be printed in a report.

RPG is well named. It is useful for reading files and producing reports. However, when complex logic is involved, many experienced programmers choose a programming language like COBOL or PL/I. An example of RPG is shown in figure E–11.

FIGURE E–11

Sample RPG program

```
010F* THIS PROGRAM CALCULATES THE NUMBER OF ACCOUNTS WITH ZERO
020F* BALANCES, THE NUMBER WITH POSITIVE BALANCES,
030F* AND THE SUM OF THE BALANCES
040FPAYROLL IP   F 80  80             READ40
050FREPORT  O    F 133 133       OF   PRINTER
010IPAYROLL AA    01
020I                                         1 20 NAME
030I                                        21 262AMT
010C      01        AMT     COMP  0                 10  20
020C      10        TPOS    ADD   1       TPOS      30
030C      10        TBAL    ADD   AMT     TBAL      82
040C      20        TNEG    ADD   1       TNEG      30
010OREPORT   H    201  OF
020O          OR       1P
030O                            56 'RECEIVABLE REPORT'
040O          H    2  OF
050O          OR       1P
060O                            26 'NUMBER OF ZERO BALANCES'
070O                            61 'NUMBER OF POSITIVE BALANCES'
080O                            90 'TOTAL OF BALANCES'
090O          T    1  LR
100O                      TNEG  15
110O                      TPOS  48
120O                      TBAL  86 '  ,    $0.  '
```

Scientific Applications and Languages

A second category of languages includes those used for **scientific applications**. These applications differ from business applications in that they involve considerably less input/output. Although scientific applications do access stored data, this access is much less frequent and the volume of data transferred is much smaller than for business systems. However, the data that is transferred is heavily processed using complex mathematical and logical algorithms.

Scientific applications are usually batch oriented. Sometimes online processing is used to enter data to start a scientific program, but then the program executes autonomously. Few scientific programs are interactive, and few involve concurrent processing.

Statistical analysis is a typical scientific application. To estimate the impact of smoking on cancer, doctors may gather data about the health and smoking habits of 1000 people. This data will be entered into programs that compute statistics such as the average rates of cancer among smokers and nonsmokers, the correlation of smoking with cancer, and other more sophisticated indicators.

The amount of data read into the program will be small, at least in comparison to a business system like order entry. However, the data will be manipulated in mathematically sophisticated ways. The CPU will be very busy squaring and summing numbers, integrating probability functions, and so forth.

Further, there will be no need for several users to access the data concurrently. The researchers will be content to receive reports one at a time.

Finally, scientific programs are not changed as frequently as business programs are. When changes do occur, they are usually additions to programs and not rewrites. For example, it is unlikely that a new method will be defined to compute the average or standard deviation of a sample of data. However, changes in business order processing procedures can and do occur frequently.

Note that we have not defined scientific programs as programs used by scientists. Sometimes scientists use programs from the business

FIGURE E–12
Summary of scientific application programs

CHARACTERISTICS OF SCIENTIFIC APPLICATIONS	LANGUAGES COMMONLY USED
Less input/output than business	ADA
Heavy mathematical processing	ALGOL
Primarily batch applications	APL
Little concurrent processing	BASIC
Change less frequent than with business programs	FORTRAN
	Pascal
	PL/I

CHARACTERISTICS OF SYSTEM APPLICATIONS	LANGUAGES COMMONLY USED
Sophisticated and complex logic	Assembler
Extensive input and output	ADA
Concurrent processing frequent	Pascal
Very large programs	PL/I and its derivatives
Extensive use — efficiency important	

FIGURE E–13
Summary of system application programs

category. For example, when scientists have applications involving a great deal of data, they use the computer as a business person would. In this case, the scientist is using business data processing techniques.

Figure E–12 summarizes the characteristics of scientific application programs and lists several languages commonly used.

System Applications and Languages

The third category of programming applications is **system programs.** These programs belong to the computer itself. The operating system, including compilers and utilities, is one example, and a database management system is another. Programs in this category can be very sophisticated. They contain complex logic, are often executed concurrently, and tend to be very large. Further, system programs run almost continuously, so efficiency is very important.

The **operating system** is primarily involved with logical operations. These operations include such tasks as selecting the next job; allocating files, main memory, and CPU time; and coordinating input/output operations. Relatively little I/O or mathematical processing is involved, so these functions are not so important. The major requirement for a system programming language, therefore, is that it easily represent complex logic. The structures used to represent alternation and iteration should be clear and straightforward. System programming languages also need to be very efficient.

Figure E–13 lists the characteristics of system applications. Although four languages are listed, the language still used most frequently in system programming is **assembly language.** Assembly language is very efficient, but it is also difficult to learn and to maintain. In fact, assembly language is closer to machine language than to any of the others discussed here — it is not considered a high-level programming language. Other languages have enjoyed some success as languages for system programs (recall that the UNIX operating system was written in C, a high-level language), but it will be some time before another language is used as extensively as assembly language for system programs.

If you pursue a career in business, the programming languages you are most likely to encounter are COBOL, BASIC, RPG, and PL/I. Keep

QUESTIONS

E.1 Name and briefly describe the three primary categories of system programs.

E.2 Name the three functions of an operating system.

E.3 Describe the functions of job management.

E.4 Describe the functions of task management.

(continued)

E.5 Describe the functions of data management.

E.6 Explain the term *virtual memory*. Why is virtual memory useful?

E.7 What does *upward compatibility* mean? Why is it important in operating system development?

E.8 What is the purpose of a compiler? Is the compiler a machine? a person? What is it?

E.9 Explain the purpose of a link/loader. How does it integrate programs from a system library with a compiled program?

E.10 Explain the difference between compilation and interpretation.

E.11 Name five characteristics of business applications.

E.12 Give two advantages and two disadvantages of each of the following languages. Assume these languages will be used for business processing.
   a. BASIC
   b. COBOL
   c. PL/I

E.13 Is BASIC a good business programming language? Explain why or why not.

E.14 Is COBOL a good business programming language? Explain why or why not.

E.15 What is the significance of COBOL's being a standardized language?

E.16 Approximately what percentage of all business application programs are written in COBOL?

E.17 Describe four characteristics of scientific applications.

E.18 Describe four characteristics of system applications.

in mind that other languages are being developed all the time. In fact, the fourth generation languages, or 4GLs, described in module A will undoubtedly change the nature of programming in the near future.

▦ SUMMARY

In this module we discussed the operating system, system utilities, program translators, and programming languages. Application programs solve specific problems, while system programs allow a general-purpose computer to be used for many applications by providing computer resources to any application program.

The operating system is a set of programs that controls the use of the computer. These large and complex programs control the computer's resources and manage computer jobs. The operating system has three major parts, each with a different role: job management, task management, and data management. Job management allocates resources and starts jobs. Task management supervises jobs being executed and allocates the CPU and main memory. Data management provides facilities to create, process, and administer data. Some popular operating systems are MVS, VM, UNIX, and XENIX. Operating systems are usually purchased from the computer manufacturer.

Utilities are programs that provide commonly needed services. Examples are programs to copy a diskette and programs to sort a file of data.

Programs are written in source code, translated into object code by a compiler, and then formed into executable load modules by the link/loader. A compiler is a program that translates other programs. It is not a piece of hardware or a special machine. There is a separate compiler or compilers for each computer language. When interpretation is used rather than compilation, programs are translated and executed a line at a time.

Since the advent of the computer, over 1000 different programming languages have been developed. Of these, only about 10 are in popular use today. There are four categories of language applications: business, scientific, system, and special-purpose applications. Business applications typically involve large amounts of data with little mathematical processing. Popular business languages are COBOL, BASIC, PL/I, and RPG. Scientific applications usually involve far less data than business applications, but the data is heavily processed. Common scientific languages are ALGOL, APL, FORTRAN, PL/I, and Pascal. System applications involve large programs that contain complex logic and often execute concurrently. Assembly language, Pascal, ADA, or a PL/I derivative are used for system programming.

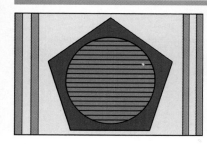

THE CHIP

The Heart of the Computer

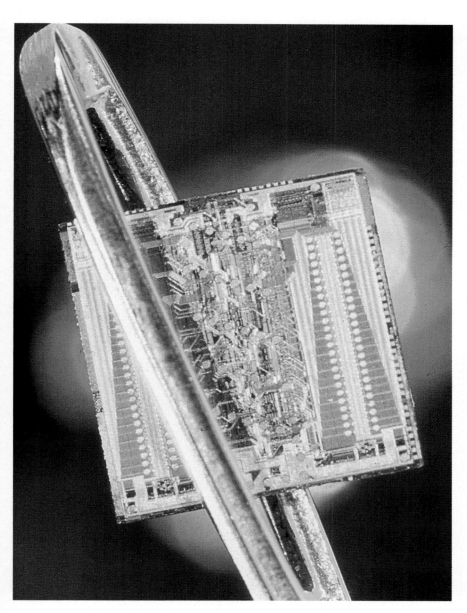

At the heart of the computer is the tiny silicon chip, still shrinking in size. It has reduced the cost of computers as well as their size.

THE CHIP: A BRIEF HISTORY

In 1959, Jack Kilby of Texas Instruments and Robert Noyce of Fairchild Semiconductor simultaneously developed the first integrated circuit (IC). Noyce left Fairchild in 1968 to form Intel Corporation, which is an important part of the chip industry today. The IC was marketed commercially in the early 1960s, and in 1971 the first true microprocessor chip was developed by Intel.

The production of silicon chips starts with rocks in the southeastern United States, not from sand as popularly believed.

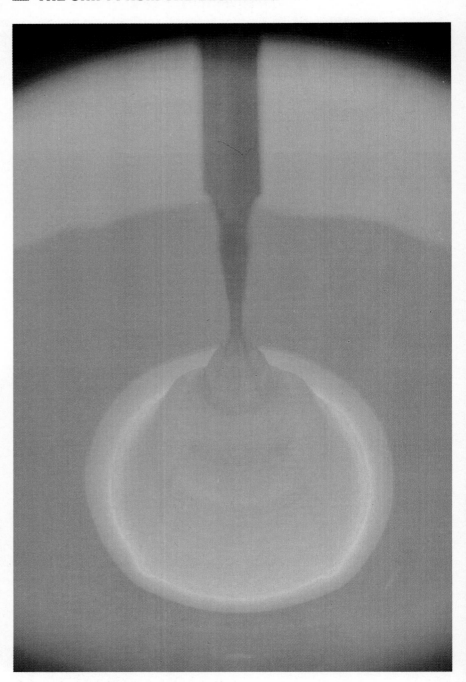

These rocks are melted into nearly pure silicon.

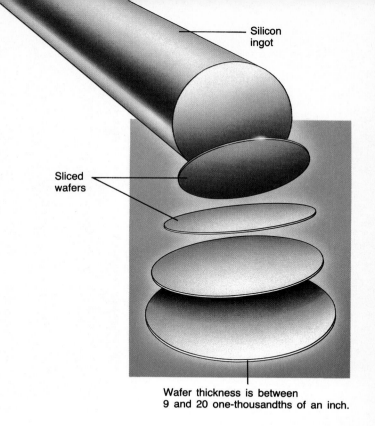

Silicon ingot

Sliced wafers

Wafer thickness is between 9 and 20 one-thousandths of an inch.

Ingots, or silicon crystals 2–6 inches in diameter, are created from the melt.

Wafers are sliced from the ingot and polished.

Until recently, it was necessary to draw and check all the circuits on a chip manually. Today, detailed "blueprints" can be designed on a CRT screen.

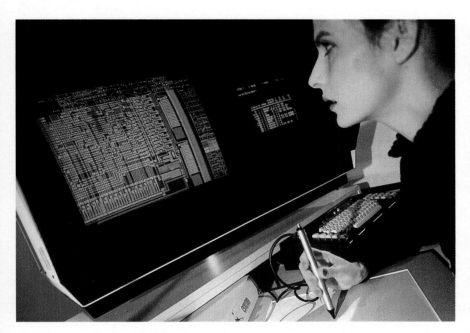

These enlarged circuit designs are used to determine the circuitry to be reduced onto the chip. Their detailed rendering also ensures the necessary precision.

The diagram is photographically reduced as many as 500 times to chip size and is then reproduced onto a glass plate, which becomes a mask and can be as small as 1/2000 of a square inch. This mask is only one of 10 or more that are necessary to manufacture a chip. Each mask will characterize a layer of the multilayer chip structure.

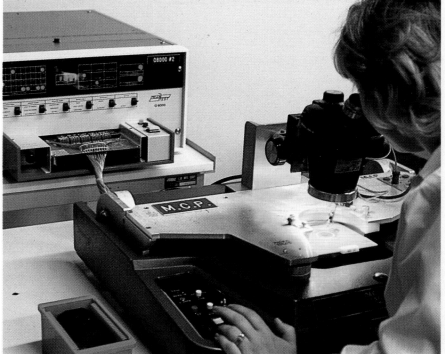

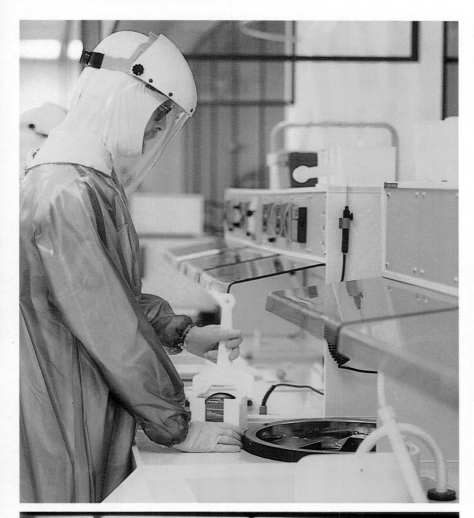

Silicon wafers 3–5 inches in diameter are fabricated in "clean rooms," where any particle, no matter how small, could disrupt the circuitry of the chip to be transferred onto the wafer.

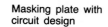

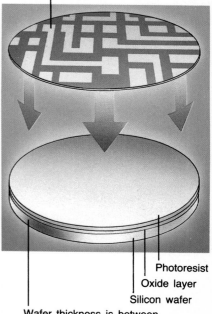

Masking plate with circuit design

Photoresist
Oxide layer
Silicon wafer

Wafer thickness is between 9 and 20 one-thousandths of an inch.

A light-sensitive plastic, called "photoresist," is applied to the wafer.

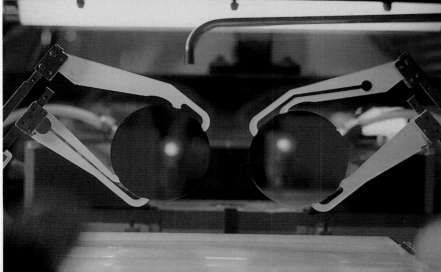

A masking plate is placed on top of the wafer.

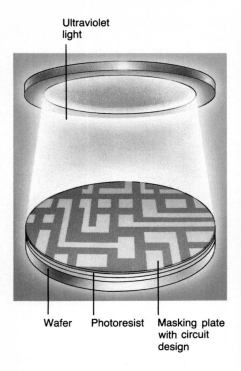

Ultraviolet light

Wafer   Photoresist   Masking plate with circuit design

The wafer is flooded with ultraviolet light, which etches the mask pattern on the exposed photoresist. The areas of the wafer covered by the mask remain hardened after the exposure.

The wafer is dipped into an acid bath that precisely erodes the resist from the exposed areas, leaving the intricate patterns of the circuitry, or blueprint, exposed. The pattern transfer and dipping process is repeated for each required layer.

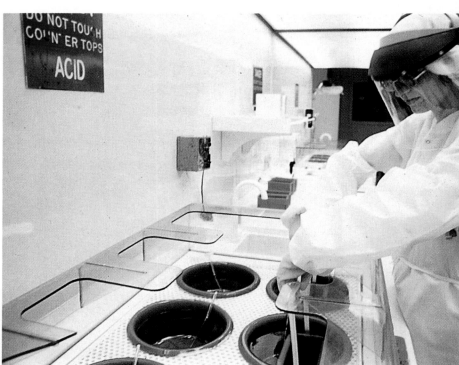

Mask blueprint imprints on photoresist

Chemical doplants are embedded to create positive and negative zones

To create the necessary negative and positive zones, chemicals called doplants are embedded in the circuitry.

The wafers are loaded into oxygen furnaces where they are baked at temperatures of 1,400 degrees Celsius.

The wafers are carefully inspected under a microscope and tested. Photoresist, masked ultraviolet-light exposure, acid bath, oxygen furnace diffusion, and inspection must normally be repeated many times before they are complete.

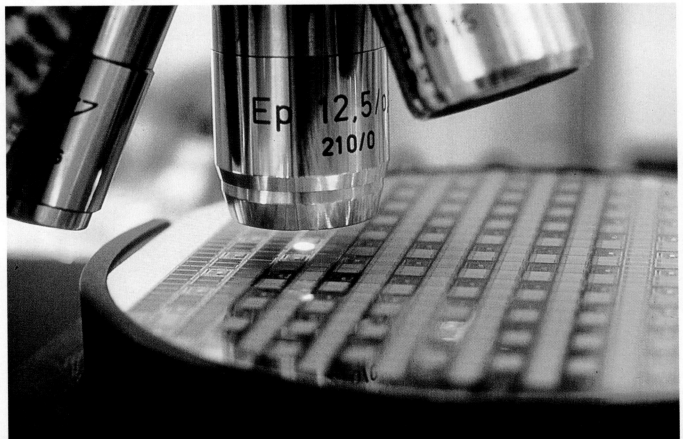

THE WAFER BECOMES A MICROPROCESSOR

The wafer is sawed, with fine diamond saws, into the individual chips.

A single wafer contains several hundred chips, each chip now a microprocessor.

Each chip is soldered and mounted on carriers, which provide the necessary connection to the electronic signal sources of the computer system.

ANATOMY OF INTEL'S 80286

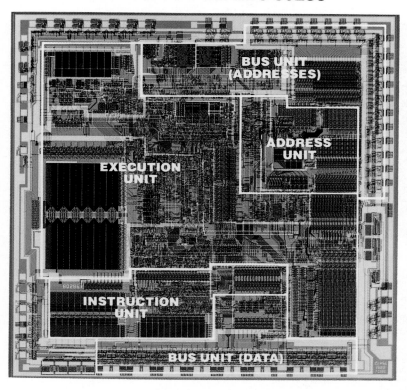

BUS UNIT (ADDRESSES)

ADDRESS UNIT

EXECUTION UNIT

INSTRUCTION UNIT

BUS UNIT (DATA)

The components of a popular Intel chip are labeled.

▦ THE CHIP: ITS BLUEPRINTS

Reflected light can produce a colorful mosaic of the wafer's chips and individual circuitry.

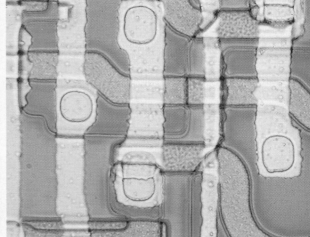

▥ THE CHIP BECOMES A "BOARD"

Finally, the chip passes its last inspection.

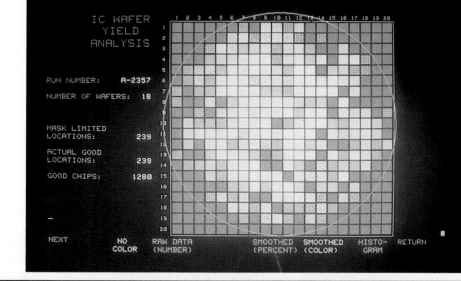

AT&T's new megabit chip is smaller than a pen point, yet it can store more than a million bits of information.

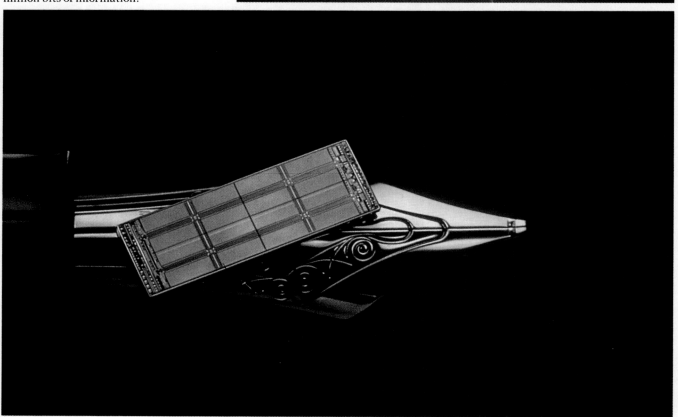

It is packaged for sale and installation in a computer system.

A board with its microprocessor packages is loaded into a computer.

Microprocessors are often used to help grocery stores to maintain inventory.

A computer-controlled machine prepares a model for television faceplate; superimposed is a computer-aided design.

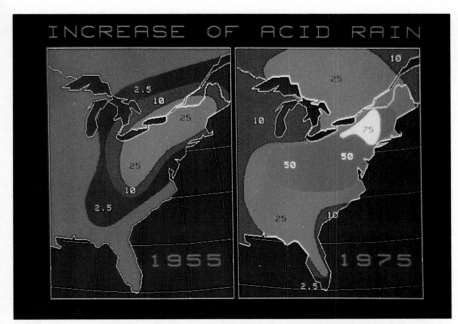

Scientists can use weather graphics' displays for both examination and explanation. This graph presents a tremendous amount of data, yet it can be quickly understood.

Guest registration at a Sheraton hotel.

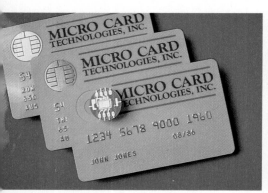

"Smart Cards" that contain their own memory and logic will be used for electronic payment, individual portable files, or access to data banks.

Computerized keys are growing in popularity.

Computerized phones handle inquiries at Occidental College.

The chip is an increasingly important component in the automobile industry.

The watch has been revolutionized by the size, dependability, and decreasing cost of the chip.

New technology: the bubble chip.

1. Why are computer memories that are embedded on chips smaller and cheaper than first-generation computer vacuum tubes?
2. Why are "clean rooms" used in chip manufacturing?
3. List ten common applications of microprocessors.
4. What damage to a country's defense could be effected by EMP?
5. Distinguish between a microprocessor and a microcomputer.
6. Name a possible new application for cheaper and more powerful chips.

BUBBLES

- Mass Storage — UP to one million bits per chip
- Nonvolatile
- Replacement for mechanical, rotating disk memories
- Excellent for harsh environments (military applications)
- Applications range from small portable data-gathering equipment to crash recorders in aircraft.
- Naturally radiation resistant

WORD LIST

(In order of appearance in text)

Application programs	Database management	Link/loader
System programs	Upward compatibility	Linkage editor
Operating system	MVS	Executable load module
Supervisor	VM	Interpretation
Executive	UNIX	Business applications
Utilities	C	BASIC (Beginners' All-purpose
Language processors	XENIX	Symbolic Instruction Code)
Job	System diskette	COBOL (COmmon
Job management	Archive diskette	Business-Oriented Language)
Task management	Machine code	Self-documenting
Task	Binary instruction code	PL/I (Programming Language I)
Time slicing	High-level programming	RPG (Report Program
Interrupts	language	Generator)
Supervisor services	Source code	Scientific applications
Allocation of main memory	Compiler	System applications
Virtual memory	Object code	Operating system
Data management	System library	Assembly language
Data administration	External reference	

QUESTIONS TO CHALLENGE YOUR THINKING

A. Consider the problem of initiating computer jobs. Suppose that a system supports low-, medium-, and high-priority jobs. Further, suppose that the only constraints on jobs are the amount of memory and the number of tape drives. For each job in the job queue, the priority, the amount of memory needed, the number of tape drives needed, and the expected length of the job are recorded. Specify an algorithm for selecting jobs to be executed. Assume that M bytes of memory and T number of tape drives are available.

B. If the complier is a program, what compiles the compiler?

C. Interview the operations manager of a data center. List and describe the utilities used in operations. Interview a systems and programming manager. List and describe the utilities used for systems development.

D. Suppose a company is using a language that is inappropriate for its needs. What are the likely results of this situation? Is the company even likely to know that it is using the wrong language? How could a company find out if its application programming language is appropriate?

E. Some people claim that the language that we use limits or constrains the thoughts we have. For example, Sanskrit (an ancient human language) had more than 15 different words for love. Consequently, it is possible to describe nuances of love more specifically in Sanskrit than in English. How does this situation pertain to programming? How does the choice of language affect programmers? Can an inappropriate language constrain programmers? Can an appropriate language liberate them? What impact does language choice have on companies?

PROGRAMMING

PART FIVE

In this part we present three modules: program design, an introduction to BASIC, and using BASIC to solve some common business problems. You can study modules F and G alone, or F, G, and H together.

The approach taken in these modules is different from that of most introductory computer texts. The emphasis here is on problem-solving, not simply on the BASIC program language.

Module F is an introduction to program design. As any professional programmer will tell you, design takes time, but the time taken also ensures that the final program will be correct. A common saying in programming runs like this: "If you don't have time to do it right, you don't have time to do it over."

Module G consists of a subset of BASIC instructions in the context of a sample program. This program is written in Microsoft BASIC, although modified instructions for DEC computers are also included where practical.

The sample program might appear somewhat lengthy for a "first" program. In reality the sample program, like most programs in business and industry, is made up of several mini-programs, or modules. Each module is presented and explained as if it were a program in itself. Thus, when all the modules are joined together to form a whole program, you will have become familiar with each of the program parts. As a result, you will see at the outset that all programs, regardless of their size and complexity, can be broken down into small, easily understandable modules.

In Module H you will learn three of the most important and fundamental programming functions: creating a disk file, reading a disk file, and writing a report. By combining your knowledge of these three functions together with the BASIC language subset presented in Module G, you will be able to solve a very large number of business problems in BASIC — and again, problem-solving is what these three modules are all about.

DESIGNING COMPUTER PROGRAMS

MODULE F

Most computer professionals agree that there are steps in problem solving:

- Understand the problem.
- Break the problem into small, manageable segments.
- Solve each small problem.
- Join the small solutions together to solve the overall problem.

Those four steps are used in developing a computer program to solve a problem. Breaking the problem into pieces and planning how to solve each one is called **program design**. In this module you will learn how to design a computer program.

Program designs are language independent; that is, they can be implemented using almost any programming language. Although you will probably write only BASIC programs in this course, the principles of program design presented here work equally well when implemented in any language.

THE IMPORTANCE OF DESIGN

Some computer programs are easier then others for programmers to read, understand, and modify. Certain characteristics have long been recognized as marks of a good program. Not long ago, companies began insisting that programming standards be established within their data processing departments to ensure that all programs were good ones. What is a *good* program?

A good program is easy to develop; solves the problem at hand; and can be easily read, understood, and modified by another programmer. These are the hallmarks of a good program:

- It works.
- It solves one and only one well-defined problem.
- It is composed of many subroutines, each one of which performs a single, well-defined function in the program.
- Each subroutine is relatively small (50 or fewer instructions).
- The first subroutine in the program controls all the others. With the exception of the first subroutine, no subroutines are executed unless called on by another one.
- Meaningful names are used for all data items and subroutines.
- Meaningful and useful remarks are placed where appropriate.

Good program design is good business: A well-designed program takes less time (and therefore less cost) to develop than one that is hastily thrown together. Well-designed programs typically have fewer bugs, or program errors, and the few there are more easily identified and fixed. Once in production, a well-designed program is easier (and therefore less expensive) to modify. Easier modification means that changes can be done faster, thereby satisfying the user's needs sooner. In all, a well-designed program is much cheaper to a company than one that is constructed piecemeal. Designing a program well takes time, but it is time well spent.

There are two fundamental principles of program design:

- A problem should be *decomposed* into its component parts, and the corresponding program should be assembled from single-function modules that solve the small problems.
- *Program flow should be limited* to only three control constructs: sequence, iteration, and alternation.

Let's look at each of these principles.

DECOMPOSITION

When we decompose a problem, we break it into its components, which are actually smaller problems. When we design programs, we identify the functions the program has to accomplish. Each function solves one of the small problems.

Program Functions

The concept of **program functions** is a slippery one. When a U.S. Supreme Court Justice was struggling to come up with a definition of pornography, he said, "Even though I can't define it, I'll recognize it when I see it." The same can be said for a program function—though it is difficult to define, a function usually can be recognized.

A rule of thumb is that a program function should solve a problem directly related to the business problem being solved. Thus, computing a monthly mortgage payment probably is a true program function, but opening a computer file probably is not. In fact, opening a computer file probably is merely one of the many steps involved in the function of getting input data for the program. Here are some examples of program functions:

- Get mortgage data from users.
- Display monthly payments.
- Issue purchase order.
- Calculate employee deductions.
- Determine the bin location of items to be picked from stock.
- Adjust inventory with today's receipts.
- Convert date from Gregorian format to Julian format.
- Compute new customer balance.
- Find sales tax rate.

Notice that each of these functions (taken from many different, unrelated programs) falls into one of three general categories: Some of them get input data for the program (*get, find*); some produce output (*display, issue*); and others manipulate data (*calculate, determine, adjust, convert, compute*). Almost all functions fall into one of these three categories.

When you design a program, begin by writing a list of all the tasks your program will need to do. Try to name each of these tasks with an action verb (such as *issue, compute, find*) and a specific direct object. Thus, "calculate gross pay" is clearly a function, while "get some data" is not specific enough to be one. Each function you identify will become a program module, or subroutine.

Modules

A **module** is a group of computer instructions that collectively perform a program function. With one exception, a module can run only when called upon by another module. The exception is the opening module of a program that is actually called upon by the operating system. Every programming language has a mechanism for invoking a module, or subroutine. The actual command varies from one language to another, so we will use the generic term *call*. (In **BASIC** we use GOSUB, in COBOL we use PERFORM or CALL, in Pascal we use CALL, in assembler we use BAL.)

When you design programs, you should be sure that each module performs a single, well-defined function. This is easy to do if you begin by listing all the program tasks first and giving each one a specific name. If a task is called "Calculate optimum payment date," then the corresponding program module will be called "Calculate optimum payment date." Naming modules carefully is important, because the module name specifies what the program instructions inside the module accomplish.

Many programmers make the mistake of putting instructions for more than one function in a single module. To be sure you are not doing this, confirm that every instruction in each program module is needed to accomplish the function the module name says it accomplishes.

The *structure chart* is frequently used to illustrate modules in a program. Let's take a close look at a structure chart.

The Structure Chart

The **structure chart** is a simple document that is easy to read and interpret. There are several types of structure charts, although they all divide a program into functional components. Some people call the structure chart a **hierarchy chart** or **VTOC** (pronounced vee-tock). VTOC is an acronym for visual table of contents.

A structure chart reveals several aspects of a program. It identifies the purpose of the program, all of the major functions of the program, and the hierarchy of subroutines in the program. The structure chart in figure F–1 represents the design for a program that is used to maintain the videotape inventory at a rental store. The purpose of the program — to rent videotapes — is revealed by the name of the top module. The major functions of the program can be determined from the names of the other modules. These functions are

- Find out what tape the customer wants to rent and get the customer's membership number (Get Tape Name and Membership Number).
- Check the inventory records to see if the tape is available (Determine Availability).
- See if the customer is a member of the tape rental club (Verify Membership).
- Change the inventory records to indicate that the tape has been rented (Check Out Tape).
- Print the customer's bill (Issue Invoice).

A module's name, as you can see, is a terse statement of the module's function. Creating an accurate name that will fit into a small rectangle on the structure chart is an art in itself.

The third thing you can tell from a structure chart is the hierarchy of the program. *Hierarchy* refers to the fact that modules (except for the one at the top) can be executed *only* when called by other modules. We use the terms **boss** and **worker** to describe the relationship between a calling module and a called one. In the example in figure F–1, there is only one boss module. The others are workers. In structure charts for more complex programs, there are usually several levels of modules. Any module that is called is a worker; if it calls another lower-level module, then it also plays the role of a boss.

FIGURE F–1
Structure chart for Rent Videotape program

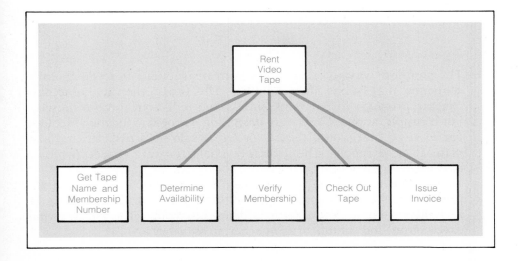

QUESTIONS

F.1 List the four steps in problem solving.

F.2 List four characteristics of a good program.

F.3 What are the two fundamental principles of program design?

F.4 What is the term for breaking a problem into its component parts?

F.5 What is a subroutine?

F.6 What are three categories of subroutines?

F.7 What is a module?

F.8 How many modules are there on a structure chart?

F.9 What does a structure chart reveal about a program?

F.10 What does *hierarchy* mean?

F.11 How is the top module in a structure chart invoked?

F.12 How are all of the other modules on a structure chart executed?

F.13 What is the difference between a boss module and a worker module?

F.14 Can a single module be both a worker and a boss?

To develop a structure chart, then, you must first break the problem into small parts, list each of the functions in the program (one function for each small problem to be solved), and then draw a structure chart that shows a controlling, or boss, module at the top and worker modules below.

When organizing the modules on the page, we usually place the modules that perform input functions at the left of the page, the modules that manipulate data in the middle of the page, and the modules that produce output at the right. This is only a convention; it is not a hard and fast rule. The purpose of a structure chart is simply to show program functions and module hierarchy. A structure chart does not show program flow. That is the second part of program design. Program logic is the next topic in this module.

PROGRAM LOGIC

Having established the functions of the program, you must then join them together in such a way that the problem is solved. This is called designing the **program logic**. The module at the top of the structure chart is responsible for invoking each of the other modules in the correct sequence and under the correct circumstances. When we talk about program logic, then, we are focusing on the instructions inside the highest-level module.

When developing the logic of a program (or in this case, a module) we need to control the execution of program functions. It has long been recognized that all programs can be written using only three basic **control constructs**: sequence, iteration, and alternation. In the next three sections we will examine each of these and show how to illustrate program logic using two popular tools: pseudocode and program flowcharts.

Sequence

The simplest way to execute program instructions is to do them in **sequence**, that is, one after the other. This is also the way computers execute program instructions, unless you tell them to do otherwise. For example, suppose you were designing a program for the videotape rental store that would record (or *log*) a sale on a diskette and also print it in a report. The structure chart for this simple program appears in figure F–2.

The logic for the top module, Log Sale, is very simple: First the program gets a sale record, then it logs the sale record onto a diskette, and then it copies the sale record onto a report. The module thus executes one instruction after another, in *sequence*.

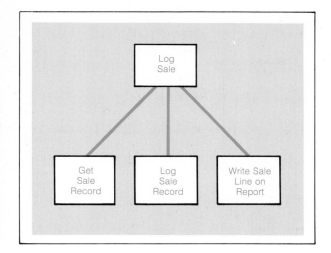

FIGURE F–2
Structure chart for program that logs one sale

Illustrating Sequence with Pseudocode

One tool for describing the logic of the top module is called **pseudo-code**. Pseudocode resembles real program code, but is not as restrictive as a real programming language. Pseudocode is intended to be flexible and more English-like than programming languages. In pseudocode, we indicate the beginning and end of a module with BEGIN and END statements; in between, we write simple sentences, one per line, that indicate what we want the program to do. Here is the pseudocode for the module called Log Sale:

```
BEGIN LOG SALE
     CALL GET SALE RECORD
     CALL LOG SALE RECORD
     CALL WRITE SALE LINE ON REPORT
END LOG SALE
```

Illustrating Sequence with a Program Flowchart

Another technique for describing program logic is the **program flow-chart**. Like pseudocode, a flowchart describes program logic. The major difference between flowcharts and pseudocode is that flow-charts are graphic. This is both an advantage and a disadvantage. Pictures often speak louder than words, and some flowcharts are easier to grasp because they are pictorial. On the other hand, pictures are more difficult to draw and to change than pseudocode is to write. Many businesses have abandoned flowcharts because programmers now use wordprocessors to write and maintain pseudocode quickly.

The basic building block of the flowchart is the rectangle. Each rectangle contains an instruction, just as each line of pseudocode

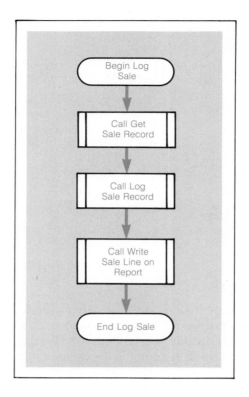

contains an instruction. Rectangles that contain vertical stripes down the sides indicate subroutine calls. In addition to the rectangle, we also use an oval shape to indicate the beginning and the end of a module. Figure F–3 shows a flowchart for the module called Log Sale.

Iteration

The second control construct is called **iteration**. Iteration means that a group of instructions will be executed in a loop until a defined terminating condition is met.

Let's modify the program whose structure chart appears in figure F–2 so it can log all of the store's daily sales. The revised structure chart is shown in figure F–4. Notice that the only change is the name of the boss module. The logic in the boss module must be modified so the instructions are repeated until there are no more sale records to log. We don't know how many that will be. Of necessity, the terminating condition is a general one: when there are no more sale records.

An oddity of computer logic is this: A computer does not realize that all of the records are gone until it tries to get the next one and comes up empty. Consequently, files are set up with one extra, dummy record at the end, following all of the data records. This dummy record is called the **end-of-file (EOF)** marker. The format of the EOF record depends on the computer system (and sometimes the programming language) you are using, and it is not important for understanding program logic. What is important is this: In order to take into account the fact that the very first record might be the end-of-file marker (suppose there were no sales at the videotape store one day), we must get the first input record and *then* go into the loop. In the loop we first test for the end-of-file condition and if it is found, exit from the loop (that takes care of the unusual situation of hitting the end-of-file marker the first time through). If the first record is actually a data record (as it usually is), then we process the record and then replace it (get the next record) before returning to the beginning of the loop where we test for the end-of-file condition again. The following illustrations show how this is done.

Illustrating Iteration with Pseudocode

There are two phrases we use in pseudocode to indicate iteration: "Repeat until" and "Repeat while." Both have the same effect, and both will be illustrated here. Notice that the condition is stated differently, depending on which form you use.

```
BEGIN LOG DAILY SALES
     CALL GET SALE RECORD
     REPEAT UNTIL END OF FILE IS ENCOUNTERED
          CALL LOG SALE RECORD
          CALL WRITE SALE LINE ON REPORT
          CALL GET SALE RECORD
     END REPEAT
END LOG DAILY SALES
```

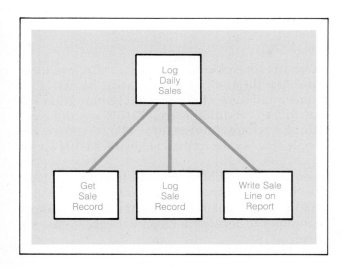

FIGURE F – 4
Structure chart for program that logs all daily sales

Compare this pseudocode to the pseudocode for the program that processed only one record. The next illustration uses the "Repeat while" phrase for controlling the loop.

```
BEGIN LOG DAILY SALES
      CALL GET SALE RECORD
      REPEAT WHILE THERE ARE MORE SALE RECORDS
            CALL LOG SALE RECORD
            CALL WRITE SALE LINE ON REPORT
            CALL GET SALE RECORD
      END REPEAT
END LOG DAILY SALES
```

Notice that the difference between these two versions of pseudocode is the condition used to control the loop. In one case it is a **terminating condition** (when the condition becomes true, stop executing the loop), and in the other case it is a **continuing condition** (as long as the condition is still true, execute the instructions in the loop).

Illustrating Iteration in a Program Flowchart

The symbols we use to illustrate iteration in a flowchart are the diamond and flow arrows. The condition that controls the loop is written inside the diamond. Two flow arrows emerge from the diamond: One of them indicates the logic path to take when the condition is met (true), and the other one indicates the logic path to take when the condition is not met (false). Figure F–5 shows the logic for the module called Log Daily Sales. It is exactly equivalent to the preceding pseudocode examples.

Alternation

The third and final program control construct is called **alternation**. Alternation allows us to give the computer alternative blocks of instructions to execute under different circumstances. Alternation follows the general format: IF the condition is true THEN execute some block of instructions ELSE execute a different block of instructions. Consequently, some people refer to alternation as the **IF-THEN-ELSE** construct.

Alternation always includes a condition that is tested. One logic path is taken when the condition is true, and the other logic path is taken when the condition is false. This is also called **decision making** because we allow the computer to decide which path to take (following our instructions, of course).

Three options are available to us:

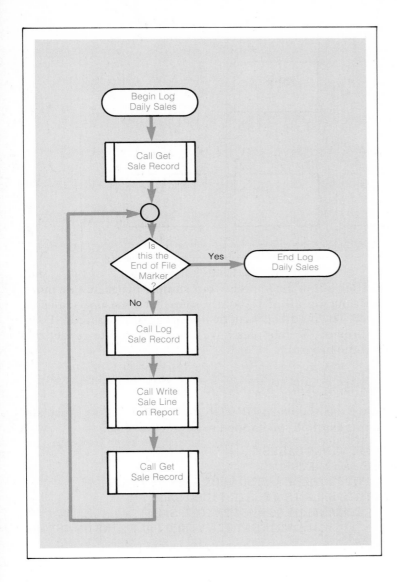

- We can define two mutually exclusive blocks of instructions: one block to be executed only when the condition is true, and the other block to be executed only when the condition is false.
- We can define a block of instructions to be executed only when the condition is true. When the condition is false nothing special happens. This is called a **null else**.
- We can define a block of instructions to be executed only when the condition is false. When the condition is true, nothing special happens. This is called a **null then**. It is used less frequently than the null else.

Structure chart for Log Daily Music
Video Sales program

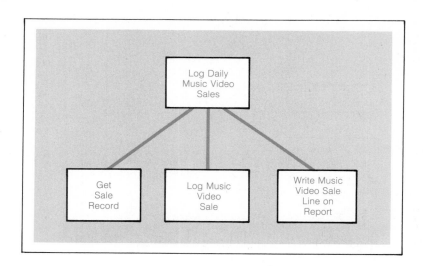

To illustrate alternation, let's modify our sample program one more time. Instead of logging all of the daily sales, let's log only sales of music videotapes. The modified structure chart appears in figure F—6. The names of three of the modules have been changed to reflect the new functions of the program.

Illustrating Alternation with Pseudocode

In pseudocode we use the words **IF-THEN-ELSE-ENDIF** to illustrate alternation. In this example we happen to have a null else:

```
BEGIN LOG MUSIC VIDEO SALES
     CALL GET SALE RECORD
     REPEAT UNTIL THERE ARE NO MORE SALE RECORDS
          IF THIS SALE IS A MUSIC VIDEO SALE
               THEN CALL LOG MUSIC VIDEO SALE
                    CALL WRITE MUSIC VIDEO SALE LINE ON REPORT
          ENDIF
          CALL GET SALE RECORD
     END REPEAT
END LOG MUSIC VIDEO SALES
```

Notice in this and other pseudocode examples how indentation is used to identify blocks of instructions.

Now suppose that we modified the program one more time to log music video sales only to diskette and to write all sales *except* music video sales on the report. The modification to the structure chart would be minor (we would change the name of the top module to Record Daily Sales and the name of the rightmost module to Write Non-Music Video Sale Line on Report). Here is the pseudocode for the new boss module:

```
BEGIN RECORD DAILY SALES
      CALL GET SALE RECORD
      REPEAT UNTIL THERE ARE NO MORE SALE RECORDS
            IF THIS SALE IS A MUSIC VIDEO SALE
                  THEN CALL LOG MUSIC VIDEO SALE
                  ELSE CALL WRITE NON—MUSIC VIDEO SALE LINE ON REPORT
            ENDIF
            CALL GET SALE RECORD
      END REPEAT
END RECORD DAILY SALES
```

Illustrating Alternation with Program Flowcharts

The symbols we use to illustrate alternation in program flowcharts are, again, the diamond and logic flow arrows. Inside the diamond we write the condition being tested. Then we label each of the two outgoing flow arrows, one for the path taken when the condition is true, and the other for the path to be taken when the condition is false. Figure F–7 illustrates the logic for the module called Log Daily Music Video Sales, and it is equivalent to the first pseudocode example. Figure F–8 illustrates the logic for the modified program that logs only music video sales and writes all others on the report.

Nesting

The three control constructs can appear within one another. This is called **nesting**. Figure F–7, for example, shows an alternation construct inside an iteration construct. This sort of nesting occurs frequently. You can also design program logic with loops inside other loops and decisions inside other decisions. Because nesting makes program logic more difficult to understand, your instructor (or company) might place restrictions on the number of levels of nesting allowed.

▦ MODEL PROGRAM DESIGNS

The purpose of this section is to show you the completed designs of three programs. You can refer to these models when you are designing programs, not only in modules G and H, but also in other programming courses. The programs presented here deal with three common programming problems: data validation, counting and accumulating, and control level breaks.

Data Validation

When data comes into a program from the world around it, there is no guarantee that it is formatted properly or that it is the correct type

QUESTIONS

F.15 Name the three program control constructs.

F.16 Give an example of each of the three control constructs.

F.17 What are two techniques for illustrating program logic?

F.18 What is the difference between pseudocode and program flowcharts?

F.19 How do you indicate a loop in pseudocode? How do you indicate a loop in a flowchart?

F.20 What is a terminating condition?

F.21 How do you indicate alternation in pseudocode? How do you indicate alternation in a flowchart?

F.22 What is a null else?

F.23 For which module on a structure chart are you most likely to write pseudocode or draw a flowchart?

F.24 What is nesting?

Program flowchart for Log Daily Music
Video Sales module

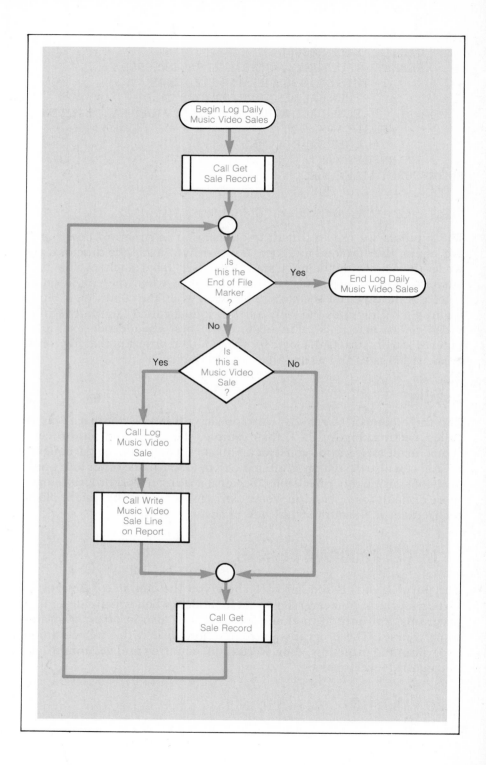

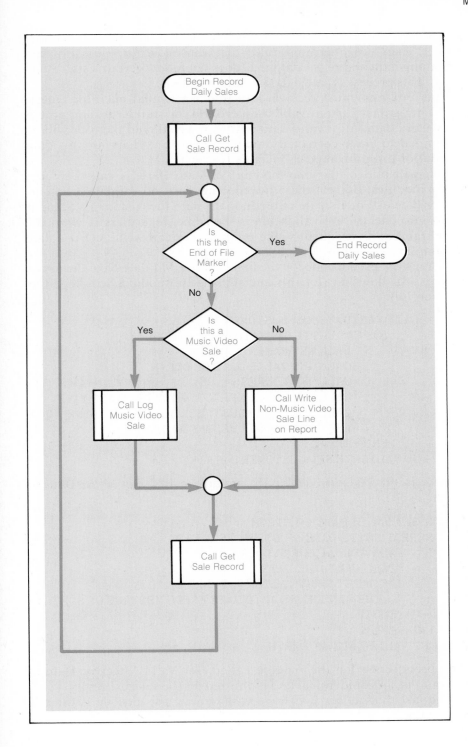

(numeric versus alphanumeric, or string) or that it contains allowable values. Therefore, programs are written whose sole purpose is to screen incoming data and reject data that does not follow certain established rules. This process is called **data validation**.

This program must receive data that a terminal operator enters, check it against certain **validation criteria,** or standards, and accept only valid data. All invalid data will be rejected, and the user will be prompted to enter corrected data. The structure chart for this data validation program appears in figure F—9.

You will notice that one module, Validate Date, is called by two other modules. Both of the other modules need to validate a date—either the customer's date of birth or the date the customer's account went into effect. Date validation is the same, regardless of what the date signifies. Consequently, the programmer can write just one date validation routine and use it in both cases.

Here is the pseudocode for the first module, Validate New Customer Details (the flowchart for this and subsequent modules will be left as an exercise):

```
BEGIN VALIDATE NEW CUSTOMER DETAILS
      REPEAT UNTIL OPERATOR WANTS TO QUIT
            CALL GET NAME
            CALL GET VALID DATE OF BIRTH
            CALL GET ADDRESS
            CALL GET VALID EFFECTIVE DATE OF ACCOUNT
            CALL STORE NEW CUSTOMER DETAILS ON DISK
            ASK OPERATOR IF HE/SHE WANTS TO QUIT
      END REPEAT
END VALIDATE NEW CUSTOMER DETAILS
```

Here is the pseudocode for the module called Get Valid Date of Birth:

```
BEGIN GET VALID DATE OF BIRTH
     REPEAT UNTIL DATE OF BIRTH IS VALID
          ASK OPERATOR FOR DATE OF BIRTH
          CALL VALIDATE DATE
          IF DATE IS NOT VALID
             THEN ISSUE INVALID DATE ERROR MESSAGE ON SCREEN
          ENDIF
     END REPEAT
END GET VALID DATE OF BIRTH
```

The pseudocode for the module called Get Valid Effective Date of Account is almost identical and is omitted for the sake of brevity.

The last module for which we will provide pseudocode is the one called Validate Date.

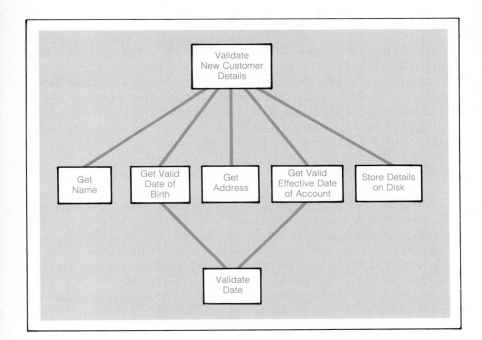

Structure chart for Data Validation
program

```
BEGIN VALIDATE DATE
     IF MONTH IS NOT NUMERIC
          OR MONTH IS NOT BETWEEN 1 AND 12
       THEN DATE IS INVALID
     ENDIF
     IF DAY IS NOT NUMERIC
          OR DAY IS LESS THAN 1
          OR DAY IS GREATER THAN THE HIGHEST DATE ALLOWED FOR
          THAT MONTH
        THEN DATE IS INVALID
     ENDIF
     IF YEAR IS NOT NUMERIC
        THEN DATE IS INVALID
     ENDIF
END VALIDATE DATE
```

The modules called Get Name, Get Address, and Store Details on
Disk are very simple and have been omitted for the sake of brevity.

This program is an interactive one; that is, it prompts the user to
enter data and issues error messages to which the user responds. In
contrast, the next program is a file processing program. Rather than
getting its input from a user at a terminal, the next program reads data
from an input file.

Counting and Accumulating

A common feature of many computer programs is the ability to issue a summary at the end of a report that indicates the number of records that were processed by the program as well as totals of various fields. This feature is often used with file processing programs (as opposed to online programs such as the previous example of online data validation). Before we examine our next model program, let us first consider computer files and how they are processed.

File Processing

The basic unit of a computer file is called a **record.** A record is a collection of data about some person, thing, event, or transaction. For example, a videotape store might maintain a **file** that contains one record for each tape sale that was made during the day. One or several **fields** are included in each record. A field is simply one small piece of data. For instance, the tape sale record might contain five fields: the account number of the customer who bought a tape, the catalog number of the tape, the date of the sale, the amount of the sale, and the initials of the sales clerk who made the sale (see figure F–10).

When computer files are processed, certain steps need to be included in the program. For example, a file must be designated as either as *input file* or an *output file*. An input file contains data the program needs; an output file is created by the program. Also, a file must be *opened* before any data can be read from it or written onto it. Opening an input file causes the operating system programs to locate the desired file on disk, make sure it can be accessed (some of them are protected by passwords — see module D), and prepare the file to be read. Opening an output file causes the operating system programs to check the disk for a file with the same name (each file must have a unique name), and prepare the new file to be written.

When reading data from an input file, a program must check to see if it has processed all of the records in the file. Files can have any number of records (usually limited only by the capacity of the disk

FIGURE F–10

Sample sales records sorted on date field

CUSTOMER #	TAPE #	SALE DATE	SALE AMOUNT	CLERK
6994	AQ97	03/08/87	29.95	JKN
5341	BJ21	03/08/87	29.95	JKN
3108	MD63	03/10/87	35.50	BTD
5341	LG14	03/10/87	24.50	JKN
1067	XP55	04/01/87	29.95	BTD
3508	EY78	04/15/87	35.50	BTD
5341	AQ97	04/22/87	29.95	BTD
EOF				

VIDEO TAPE SALES SUMMARY

CUSTOMER #	TAPE #	DATE	CLERK	SALE AMOUNT
6994	AQ97	03/08/87	JKN	29.95
5341	BJ21	03/08/87	JKN	29.95
3108	MD63	03/10/87	BTD	35.50
5341	LG14	03/10/87	JKN	24.50
1067	XP55	04/01/87	BTD	29.95
3508	EY78	04/15/87	BTD	35.50
5341	AQ97	04/22/87	BTD	29.95

7 SALES TOTALLING 215.30

FIGURE F–11
Sales Summary Report

and the size of the records). Consequently, we seldom know how many records there are. We depend on the end-of-file marker to signal the end of the data records in the file. Programming languages usually have a built-in function to check for the end-of-file marker, but the program still needs to test to see if the end-of-file has been reached. Attempting to read another input record after all records have been processed causes a program to terminate abnormally (also called *abend,* for *ab*normal *end*ing, or *crash*).

Finally, after a file has been processed, the program must *close* the file. Closing a file releases it so other programs can use it. Closing an output file places an end-of-file marker after the final data record.

To review, files contain records made up of fields. File processing programs must identify a file as input or output, they must open a file before attempting to input data from it or output data to it, they must test for EOF when reading an input file, and they must close files when they are finished with them.

Sales Summary Program

In this program we will read an input disk file and produce a report. The disk file is shown in figure F–10, a sales file for a videotape store. We need to produce the report shown in figure F–11. Notice that there are three groups of lines being printed: There is a *report header group* (two lines) at the top of the page, followed by several *detail lines* (one line for each input record), followed by one *summary line* at the bottom of the report. The numbers in the summary line are of special interest to us.

The problem with learning how a computer program produces this kind of a report is that a computer does it very differently from the way you would produce the report manually. If you were to produce the report manually, you would probably begin by typing the report header lines, then you would copy each of the sale records onto the report. When you were finished with the bulk of the report, you would count the number of detail lines (seven). Next, armed with a calculator, you would add up all of the sales figures — probably twice to be sure you were correct — and finally you would type the last line of the report. A computer does not produce the report that way.

A computer is unable to go back over records it has already processed. Therefore, it could not print most of the report and then go back and count the records and add up the sales total. Instead, a computer must process each record completely before it reads the next one. This program needs to do three things to each input record before it reads the next one: 1) it must print the record; 2) it must count the record; and 3) it must add the sale amount on the record to a running total. When all three tasks are complete, the program can move on to the next input record.

The structure chart for this program appears in figure F–12. Each of the lower level modules deals with either input or output. The controlling module at the top, Issue Sales Summary Report, calls each of the lower level modules when they have to perform a function. The pseudocode for the controlling module follows:

```
BEGIN ISSUE SALES SUMMARY REPORT
      CALL ISSUE REPORT HEADER
      OPEN SALES FILE AS INPUT
      CALL GET SALES RECORD
      REPEAT UNTIL EOF IS REACHED
            CALL ISSUE DETAIL LINE
            ADD 1 TO RECORD COUNTER
            ADD SALE AMOUNT TO SALE TOTAL
            CALL GET SALES RECORD
      END REPEAT
      CALL ISSUE SUMMARY LINE
      CLOSE SALES FILE
END ISSUE SALES SUMMARY REPORT
```

Notice that the program begins by writing report headers, opening the input file, and getting the first record from the file. Then the loop that processes each record in the file is executed until the end-of-file marker is detected. By the time that happens, RECORD COUNTER contains the number of records that were processed. RECORD COUNTER is known as a *counter*. At end-of-file SALE TOTAL contains the total of the sale amounts. SALE TOTAL is known as an *accumulator*. Upon exiting from the loop, the program has both the numbers it needs to write the summary line at the end of the report. Finally, the program releases the sales file by closing it.

This program introduced you to file processing, counters, and accumulators. The next model design is for a more complex program. It also processes an input file but this time, in addition to a grand total at the end of the report, summary totals need to be accumulated for groups of records within the file.

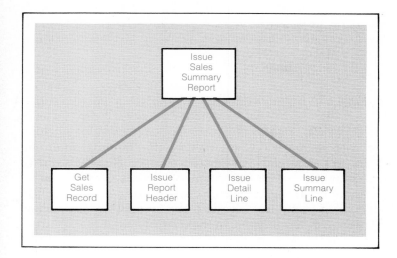

FIGURE F–12
Structure chart for Issue Sales Summary
Report program

Control Level Break

Many programs use a logic pattern called the **control level break.** In a control level break program, the records in the input file are arranged, or sorted, into sequence on some field. Unlike a key field, which must be unique, this **control field** is not unique. In fact, the point of a control level break program is to cluster together records with the same value in the control field and process them as a group.

We will use the following program to illustrate a control level break. The program produces a report (almost all control level break programs produce reports) summarizing sales at the videotape rental store. It uses an input file of daily sales records that have been sorted by sale date. The report indicates the total sales for each month, as well as the total sales for the entire period. Obviously the control field, month, is not unique. There will be many sales during any month. The point of a control level break program is to treat the sales records for a single month as a unit.

An example of a sales file appears in figure F–10. Notice that all of the sales for the month of March are together, and all of the sales for the month of April are together. EOF simply indicates the end-of-file marker.

Using that input file, the program will produce the report seen in figure F–13. The report is aptly called a *summary* report: The details about any individual sale have been ignored. Only the totals are printed. Other reports might show both.

The structure chart for this program appears in figure F–14. There are very few functions, and they are primarily input and output functions. The complexity of a control level break program lies in the logic of the controlling module, in this case Write Sales Summary.

As already mentioned, a computer does not know that it has processed all of the records in a file until it reads the next record and

FIGURE F–13
Sample monthly sales summary report

SALES SUMMARY BY MONTH

Total Sales for March 119.90
Total Sales for April 95.40

Total Sales for Period $215.30

discovers the end-of-file marker. Consequently, the computer finds out after the fact that it has already processed an entire file. The same is true when the computer processes groups of records with the same value in the control field: the computer doesn't know it has reached the end of one control group until it reads the first record of the next group and discovers a different value in the control field.

When the value in the control field changes we say a control level break has occurred. The control level break signals to the computer that it has reached the end of the previous group. If there are any subtotals to be printed or other processing to be done for the previous group, the computer must do it before it processes the first record of the next group.

Recognizing a control level break is done by saving the control field value for a record and then comparing control field values in subsequent records to the saved one. So long as they are equal, the records are in the same group. When they are not equal, then a level break has occurred. Subtotals must be printed, and the new value of the control field (the one that tripped the level break) must be saved — it becomes the standard against which subsequent records will be compared until another break occurs. This process continues until the input file is exhausted.

FIGURE F–14
Structure chart for control level break program

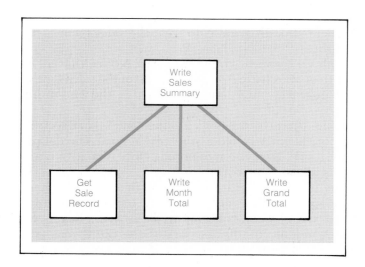

Because subtotals are printed only when there is a change in the value of the control field, the very last group in the file creates a problem. There is no "next group" to trip a level break for the last group in the file. Therefore, encountering the end-of-file marker indicates the very last level break.

Here is the pseudocode for the module called Write Sales Summary:

```
BEGIN WRITE SALES SUMMARY
        WRITE REPORT TITLE
        CALL GET SALE RECORD
        SAVE NEW MONTH FIELD

        REPEAT UNTIL EOF

                REPEAT UNTIL CONTROL BREAK OR EOF OCCURS
                        ADD SALE AMOUNT TO MONTH TOTAL
                        CALL GET SALE RECORD
                END REPEAT

                CALL WRITE MONTH TOTAL
                ADD MONTH TOTAL TO GRAND TOTAL
                ZERO OUT MONTH TOTAL
                SAVE NEW MONTH FIELD

        END REPEAT

        CALL WRITE GRAND TOTAL
END WRITE SALES SUMMARY
```

Trace the logic of this program using the sample data shown in figure F–10. Write the values of various fields, such as the saved month field, subtotal and grand total, as you follow the program logic. You should get the same results as the report in figure F–13.

The important points to remember about a control level break program are

- Read the first record and save the value of the control field before entering the main program loop.
- Once you are in the main program loop, enter another loop that processes a control group until a level break occurs — either because the control field value changed or EOF was encountered.
- When a level break occurs, reset the subtotals to zero before starting to process the next group; also save the new value of the control field.
- When EOF occurs, issue the final summary (or grand total) line.

The three programs presented here are models. There are hundreds of variations on them. There are also many more complex program patterns that are beyond the scope of this text. The purpose of this

QUESTIONS

F.25 Why must input data be validated?

F.26 What are validation criteria?

F.27 Can one module in a program be called by more than one boss?

F.28 How is the situation in question F.27 illustrated on a structure chart?

F.29 What advantage is there, if any, to worker modules that are called by more than one boss?

F.30 When processing an input file, how does the computer know it has read the entire file?

F.31 What is a counter? What is an accumulator?

F.32 In a control level break program, what is the significance of the control field?

F.33 Are the values in the control field unique for each record?

F.34 How does the computer know it has finished processing all of the records in one control group?

F.35 Why do you have to save the control field of the first input record before entering the main program loop?

F.36 How does the computer know it has processed the last control group in the input file?

module, however, is not to make you a professional programmer. The purpose of this module is to offer you a foundation in program design. If you need to write programs one day (because there is no off-the-shelf software available for the problem you are trying to solve), then this foundation will help you use the computer to solve problems.

SUMMARY

Most companies are turning to purchased software rather than developing programs in house. However, in those instances where there is not adequate software available, custom programs must be written. In this case, program design is a vital part of system development. Although it takes time to design a program well, it is time well spent, because a well-designed program is easy to read, understand, and modify. The same cannot be said for programs that are thrown together at the terminal.

Program design is based on two fundamental principles: A program is made up of several single-function modules; and the flow, or logic, of a program is restricted to three control constructs — sequence, iteration, and alternation.

The structure chart is a diagram that shows the modules, or functions, of a program, and the organization, or hierarchy, of the program. It shows one controlling module at the top; all other modules are subordinate to this one. The controlling module is invoked by the operating system. All other modules can run only when they are called upon by another module. Calling modules are known as bosses, and called modules are known as workers.

The two tools used most frequently to represent program logic are pseudocode and program flowcharts. Pseudocode resembles program instructions, but it is not an actual programming language. Flowcharts are more pictorial than pseudocode. Flowcharts are sometimes easier to read than the equivalent pseudocode, but they are more difficult to draw and to maintain.

Both techniques can be used to represent sequence, iteration, and alternation. Nesting of one construct inside another can also be illustrated using either tool.

WORD LIST

Program design
Program function
Module
Structure chart
Hierarchy chart
VTOC
Boss
Worker
Program logic
Control construct
Sequence
Pseudocode
Program flowchart

Iteration
End-of-file (EOF) marker
Terminating condition
Continuing condition
Alternation
IF-THEN-ELSE
Decision making
Null else
Null then
Nesting
Data validation
Validation criteria
Input file

Output file
Open
Abend
Crash
Close
Report header
Detail line
Summary line
Counter
Accumulator
Control level break
Control field

EXERCISES TO CHALLENGE YOUR THINKING

A. Using the structure chart in figure F–1, write the pseudocode for the controlling module, Rent Video Tape. A tape cannot be rented if it is not available. One-day rentals cost $5.00, two-day rentals cost $8.00, and one-week rentals cost $17.00. Members get a 20 percent discount on tape rentals.

B. Design a program that can be used at the video-tape rental store to add new tapes to its inventory. The program should be interactive—a clerk will enter the new data at a terminal. The following data should be entered for a new video-tape:

- Tape number: The first two characters must be alphabetic, and the next two must be numeric.
- Tape name.
- Selling price: This must be numeric.
- Type of tape: music video, movie, cartoon, documentary.

The inventory file is stored on disk.

C. Modify the model control level break program in this module so it produces a summary report containing sales clerk subtotals each month in addition to overall monthly totals and a grand total. You can assume that the input file is sorted so all the records for each month are together and within each month all the records for each sales clerk are together.

INTRODUCTION TO PROBLEM SOLVING USING BASIC

MODULE G

One of the five components of a business computer system is programs. There are three ways a business can acquire programs: buy them off the shelf from a software vendor or computer store, buy them and then hire someone to alter them, or write them from scratch. In this module and in module H you will learn how to develop programs from scratch. You might wonder why you should learn how to write programs when it is usually easier, faster, and more cost-effective to buy programs rather than develop them.

It is important for you to know something about the process of programming or, more specifically, the process of using a computer to help you solve business problems. In a few years, every businessperson will likely use a computer on the job. And although it is unlikely that every businessperson will wind up writing programs, you will almost surely have something to do with programs. You may find yourself selecting software, installing a system, buying a computer system, explaining your requirements to a programmer who will alter software packages for you, and so forth. Therefore you should know what goes on behind the scenes.

The language chosen by most colleges (and high schools and elementary schools) as an introduction to computer programming is **BASIC**. BASIC, which stands for Beginners' All-purpose Symbolic Instruction Code, was developed at Dartmouth University specifically for teaching purposes. Since then, it has been enhanced with enough instructions to make it moderately useful in the business world. Almost every microcomputer system comes with a BASIC interpreter, and BASIC is easy to learn.

The BASIC instructions you will learn in this module and in module H are a *subset* of BASIC instructions. When you master this subset, you will have the tools necessary to use the computer to solve many problems. After completing these modules you may want to learn more. In that case, you should refer to the BASIC reference manual available at your school.

▥ REVIEW OF APPLICATION PROGRAMMING

The two types of programs in a business computer system are system programs and application programs. **System programs** "belong" to the computer. They provide useful services to all users of the system, solving problems of a general, and system-wide nature.

Application programs solve specific problems for users. Application programs perform functions such as accounting, payroll, and inventory control. They have less to do with the computer system and more to do with the real business problems at hand. The programs you will write in this course, and probably all the programs you will ever write, are application programs.

In every case, a program solves a problem. In fact, problem solving is what this module and the next one are all about. We happen to use BASIC as a vehicle for solving problems, but we could just as easily use some other programming language.

Writing a program is not as simple as sitting down in front of a computer and tapping keys. There are several steps involved, and following them will help you to quickly develop correct solutions to the problems you are trying to solve. These are the steps:

- Study and understand the problem.
- Break the large problem into small pieces.
- Develop a miniprogram to solve each of the small problems.
- Join the small solutions together into a solution to the original problem.

This divide-and-conquer approach works equally well for program development, systems development (see chapter 5), and almost any other problem-solving activity.

AN ILLUSTRATION OF PROBLEM SOLVING

In this section, you will see an example of how the steps listed here are done.

Problem Statement

One important aspect of an individual's financial plan is knowing the value of investments at their maturity. We will develop a BASIC program that answers the very important question, "How much will this investment be worth when it matures?" The user must provide the following input parameters: the principal, interest rate, and number of years until maturity. The program determines interest compounded annually. For example, $2,000.00 invested at 15 percent for three years would be computed as follows:

After year 1: Balance = $2,000 + $2,000 × .15 or $2,300.00
After year 2: Balance = $2,300 + $2,300 × .15 or $2,645.00
After year 3: Balance = $2,645 + $2,645 × .15 or $3,041.75

Understanding the Problem

Most programmers begin their study of a problem by determining the output to be produced by the program. The only thing needed in the example is one line that says something like "The value of your investment at maturity will be $xxxxx.xx." Other problems require more output than this one. Can you understand how to solve the problem manually? If not, study the preceding example before continuing.

Breaking the Problem into Small Pieces

This program actually has four separate parts, although you would not be expected to know this. After you have written several programs, breaking them into functional pieces gets easier. The four parts are these: Display on the computer screen instructions for using the program; accept the input parameters — principal, rate, duration — from the user; compute the value of the investment; display the answer on the computer screen.

Figure G−1 shows a **structure chart** of this problem. The box at the top, Compute Investment Balance, is a **module** that represents the entire program (the name of this module should state the problem the program solves). Each of the other four modules represents a small part of the overall problem — each one solves a miniproblem. The first one, Display Instructions, solves the problem of the user not knowing what to do. The second one, Accept Input Parameters, solves the problem of getting data for the computer to process. The third one, Compute Investment Value, solves the problem of predicting how much money the investment will be worth at maturity. The fourth module, Display Results, solves the problem of the user needing to know the answer to the question. Collectively, these four modules solve the overall problem.

Notice that each of the modules on the structure chart has a number written in the corner. That number indicates the line number within the BASIC program on which each module begins.

FIGURE G−1
Structure chart for Compute Investment Balance program

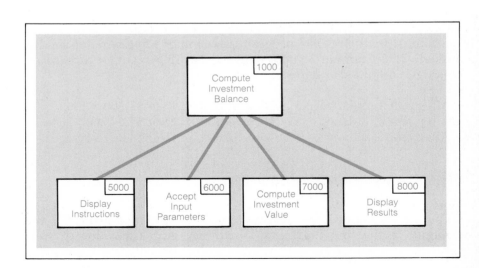

Solving Each Problem Separately

Within the program there will be one group of instructions for each module on the structure chart. The first group we will examine starts with the number 5000. (This number is arbitrary. You will learn about line numbers later.) The entire module follows:

```
5000 REM ******************************************************
5001 REM *           DISPLAY INSTRUCTIONS FOR USING THIS PROGRAM    *
5002 REM ******************************************************
5003 REM
5010 CLS
5020 PRINT "This program will calculate the value of an investment"
5030 PRINT "compounding interest annually.  You will be prompted"
5040 PRINT "to enter the principal, interest rate, and number of years"
5050 PRINT "until maturity.  When you enter the interest rate,"
5060 PRINT "be careful to enter it in decimal format.  A rate of 10%"
5070 PRINT "is entered as .10 and a rate of 15 1/2% is entered"
5080 PRINT "as .155"
5090 PRINT
5130 PRINT "When you are ready to begin, press the carriage return"
5140 PRINT "or enter key."
5150 INPUT RESPONSE$
5999 RETURN
```

This group of instructions clears the computer screen, positions the cursor in the upper-left corner, prints several lines for the user to read, and then pauses until the user indicates he or she is ready to begin by pressing the Return key. This may look like a lot of instructions, but the function of this module is very simple.

The next module, Accept Input Parameters, was solved with program lines 6000 through 6999.

```
6000 REM ******************************************************
6001 REM *           ACCEPT INPUT PARAMETERS FROM USER             *
6002 REM ******************************************************
6003 REM
6010 CLS
6020 PRINT "Enter principal.  You may use a decimal point. ";
6030 INPUT PRINCIPAL
6040 PRINT "Enter interest rate.  Use a decimal point (eg, 12% = .12) ";
6050 INPUT INTEREST.RATE
6060 PRINT "In how many years will this investment mature ";
6070 INPUT YEARS.REMAINING
6999 RETURN
```

This group of instructions clears the computer screen, positions the cursor in the upper-left corner, prompts the user to enter the principal amount, waits until this amount is entered, prompts the user to enter the interest rate, waits until this amount is entered, prompts the user to enter the number of years until maturity, and waits until the user enters this number. Like the previous module, this one is very short, very simple, and very single-minded. It solves one small problem.

The next module, Compute Investment Value, starts on line 7000. The BASIC instructions follow.

```
7000 REM ****************************************************************
7001 REM *     COMPUTE TOTAL INVESTMENT BY CALCULATING BALANCE       *
7002 REM *     (PRINCIPAL PLUS INTEREST) EACH YEAR.   CONTROL        *
7003 REM *     LOOP BY DECREMENTING NUMBER OF YEARS REMAINING        *
7004 REM *     BY 1 EACH TIME THROUGH THE LOOP.                      *
7005 REM ****************************************************************
7006 REM
7010 WHILE YEARS. REMAINING > 0
7020    PRINCIPAL = PRINCIPAL + (PRINCIPAL * INTEREST.RATE)
7030    YEARS.REMAINING = YEARS.REMAINING - 1
7040 WEND
7999 RETURN
```

This module is deceptively small, and yet it is the heart of the program. This module contains a **loop**, a group of instructions that are repeated until some condition is detected that causes the loop to stop. In this case, the instruction to calculate this year's interest and add it to the principal is performed once for each year for the life of the investment. The number of years remaining until the investment matures is reduced by one each time through the loop. If the investment were for 10 years, the loop would be repeated 10 times; if it were for 45 years, the loop would be repeated 45 times.

Like the previous modules, this one is very simple and focuses on one part of the overall problem.

The fourth module we will look at starts on line 8000.

```
8000 REM ****************************************************************
8001 REM *              DISPLAY RESULTS                              *
8002 REM ****************************************************************
8003 REM
8010 PRINT
8020 PRINT "When fully matured, your investment will be worth "; PRINCIPA
8999 RETURN
```

The function of this module is to display the answer on the computer screen. It is only a few lines long.

These four modules solve the miniproblems we saw in the structure chart in figure G–1. The next step is to join these solutions together into a coherent program to solve the user's problem.

Joining the Small Solutions Together

To join the small modules together we must write a module that governs their execution. Each of the modules must perform its job only when it is needed. Figuring out how to do this is called developing the **program logic**. Several tools are available to program designers to help them develop program logic, including flowcharts and **pseudocode**. Pseudocode rather than flowcharts will be used here and in other examples in this module and in module H.

As you learned in module F, pseudocode enables the programmer to write the module without worrying about language restrictions or program syntax rules. A pseudocoded module is a *model* of the real thing. Here is the pseudocode for the module called Compute Investment Balance:

```
BEGIN COMPUTE INVESTMENT BALANCE
    IF USER NEEDS INSTRUCTIONS
    THEN CALL DISPLAY INSTRUCTIONS
    ENDIF
    CALL ACCEPT INPUT
    CALL COMPUTE INVESTMENT VALUE
    CALL DISPLAY RESULTS
END COMPUTE INVESTMENT BALANCE
```

By writing pseudocode, the program designer can quickly see if anything has been left out and if the routines are being performed in the correct order. Any problems then can be quickly corrected before any actual program code has been written.

Having established the logic for Compute Investment Balance, the programmer can code the module. This module, though brief, is more complex than the others because it controls the execution of all the other modules. The code follows.

```
1000 REM *******************************************************************
1001 REM *                                                                 *
1002 REM *                 COMPUTE INVESTMENT BALANCE                      *
1003 REM *                                                                 *
1004 REM *******************************************************************
1005 REM
1080 CLS
1090 PRINT "Do you want to see the instructions for this program?"
1100 INPUT RESPONSE$
1110 IF RESPONSE$ = "Y" OR RESPONSE$ = "y"
        THEN GOSUB 5000: REM Call display instructions module
1120 GOSUB 6000:   REM Call accept input module
1130 GOSUB 7000:   REM Call compute investment module
1140 GOSUB 8000:   REM Call display results module
1999 END
```

When the program runs, this module first clears the computer screen and positions the cursor in the upper-left corner. Then it displays instructions for using the program, but only if the user wants to see them—most users do not want to be bothered with the instructions after they have used the program once.

Whether or not the instructions are displayed, this module next invokes the module that accepts the input parameters; then it calls on the module that figures the investment, and finally it calls on the module that prints the answer. When all three of these **subroutines** have been executed, the program stops.

Unlike the other four modules, which were very simple and single-minded, this **controlling module** is more complex. It does some work itself, such as asking the user whether it should display the instructions, but it also calls on the other four modules to do their jobs when they are needed (for example, GOSUB 5000). This module *joins* the other four modules in such a way that all five of them together solve the overall problem.

The BASIC Program

This sample program was presented in pieces because that is the most effective way of solving a problem: Break it into pieces and then solve each one separately. However, seeing the big picture is equally important. Therefore, the entire BASIC program is presented in Figure G–2. Notice that although the program might at first glance look threatening because of its size, each part of it is easy to read and understand.

FIGURE G–2
BASIC program for Compute Investment Balance

```
1000 REM ******************************************************
1001 REM *                                                    *
1002 REM *              COMPUTE INVESTMENT BALANCE            *
1003 REM *                                                    *
1004 REM ******************************************************
1005 REM
1080 CLS
1090 PRINT "Do you want to see the instructions for this program?"
1100 INPUT RESPONSE$
1110 IF RESPONSE$ = "Y" OR RESPONSE$ = "y"
        THEN GOSUB 5000: REM Call display instructions module
1120 GOSUB 6000:   REM Call accept input module
1130 GOSUB 7000:   REM Call compute investment module
1140 GOSUB 8000:   REM Call display results module
1999 END
5000 REM ******************************************************
5001 REM *          DISPLAY INSTRUCTIONS FOR USING THIS PROGRAM      *
5002 REM ******************************************************
5003 REM
5010 CLS
5020 PRINT "This program will calculate the value of an investment"
5030 PRINT "compounding interest annually.  You will be prompted"
5040 PRINT "to enter the principal, interest rate, and number of years"
```

(continued)

```
5050 PRINT "until maturity.  When you enter the interest rate,"
5060 PRINT "be careful to enter it in decimal format.  A rate of 10%"
5070 PRINT "is entered as .10 and a rate of 15 1/2% is entered"
5080 PRINT "as .155"
5090 PRINT
5130 PRINT "When you are ready to begin, press the carriage return"
5140 PRINT "or enter key."
5150 INPUT RESPONSE$
5999 RETURN
6000 REM ****************************************************************
6001 REM *             ACCEPT INPUT PARAMETERS FROM USER               *
6002 REM ****************************************************************
6003 REM
6010 CLS
6020 PRINT "Enter principal.  You may use a decimal point. ";
6030 INPUT PRINCIPAL
6040 PRINT "Enter interest rate.  Use a decimal point (eg, 12% = .12) ";
6050 INPUT INTEREST.RATE
6060 PRINT "In how many years will this investment mature ";
6070 INPUT YEARS.REMAINING
6999 RETURN
7000 REM ****************************************************************
7001 REM *     COMPUTE TOTAL INVESTMENT BY CALCULATING BALANCE         *
7002 REM *     (PRINCIPAL PLUS INTEREST) EACH YEAR. CONTROL            *
7003 REM *     LOOP BY DECREMENTING NUMBER OF YEARS REMAINING          *
7004 REM *     BY 1 EACH TIME THROUGH THE LOOP.                        *
7005 REM ****************************************************************
7006 REM
7010 WHILE YEARS.REMAINING > 0
7020    PRINCIPAL = PRINCIPAL + (PRINCIPAL * INTEREST.RATE)
7030    YEARS.REMAINING = YEARS.REMAINING - 1
7040 WEND
7999 RETURN
8000 REM ****************************************************************
8001 REM *                DISPLAY RESULTS                              *
8002 REM ****************************************************************
8003 REM
8010 PRINT
8020 PRINT "When fully matured, your investment will be worth "; PRINCIPAL
8999 RETURN
```

Do not be concerned if you do not understand every line of the sample program. Later in this module you will study various **BASIC** statements. For now, you need only understand that

- We can use a computer to solve problems.
- Sometimes we need to *write* (rather than buy) programs to solve problems.

FIGURE G-2
BASIC program for Compute Investment Balance *(continued)*

• When we write programs, we follow certain steps: understand the problem we are trying to solve; break the big problem into small, manageable ones; solve each small problem separately; join all the small solutions together to form a cohesive whole.

In the next section you will learn about your computer system, how to run the BASIC translator program, and some fundamental BASIC commands. In the section following that one you will study several BASIC program instructions, many of which were used in the sample program.

GETTING STARTED

Colleges use many different computers, including personal computers (IBM, Kaypro, Apple, Compaq, and many others) and larger minis and mainframes (DEC VAX, IBM 4300, Burroughs, and so forth). Each computer's operating system can be different from all the others. Likewise, each **version** of BASIC can be different. The result of this is that your computer may not do things exactly the same way as the one used to develop examples for this textbook. When you find variations between your school's system and the illustrations in this text, note them in the margins. All of the programs in this module and in module H were written in Microsoft BASIC and were executed under MS-DOS. These programs can be run on any IBM PC or IBM-compatible PC.

Signing on or Loading BASIC

To use the BASIC programming language you must power on or log onto a computer, and you must load the BASIC language translator into your computer's memory. The steps needed to do this vary widely from one computer system to another, so write the sequence of instructions your instructor gives you for getting started on your school's computer system in the box provided here.

Signing On

Some Fundamental Commands

BASIC **commands** perform various kinds of program maintenance, such as loading and saving programs. Commands usually are executed as soon as you enter them. The commands you will use most often are NEW, LIST, LLIST, RUN, SAVE, and LOAD.

BASIC instructions, which you will learn about later in this module, must follow certain rules of **syntax**; that is, they must be written a certain way using particular words, punctuation, and format. The notation used in this module and in module H is illustrated in figure G – 3.

NEW

The function of the **NEW** command is to clear the computer's memory when you want to enter a new program. If you do not issue this command, your new program statements may be interspersed with whatever garbage was in the computer's memory at the time you enter the program. The format of the NEW command is

NEW

LIST

As you enter a BASIC program into the computer, you should be able to review what you have done. The function of the **LIST** command is to list all or part of a program on the computer screen. The format of the LIST command is

LIST [*line number*][*–line number*]

If you do not specify a **line number**, the entire program will be listed on the computer screen. Sometimes a program is too long to fit on one

FIGURE G – 3
Syntax notation for BASIC commands and statements

[ ]	*Italics*	...	CAPS	Punctuation	Spaces
Square brackets indicate that the entry inside is optional.	*Italics* indicate that you must enter the data. For example, RUN *program-name* means you have to enter the name of the program you want to run.	Ellipses indicate that an entry may be repeated.	Capital letters indicate parts of a BASIC statement that must be entered exactly as shown.	All punctuation, such as commas, quotation marks, parentheses, and equal signs, must be entered exactly as shown.	Spaces are used to separate words, items in a list, and other entries. Wherever one space is required several may be entered.

screen, so the computer **scrolls** it, that is, fills the screen and then adds a new line to the bottom, moving one line off the top of the screen (as with movie credits). Find out from your instructor how to stop the scrolling and restart it, so you can read the code before it whizzes by. Record how to do this in the box provided here.

Controlling Scrolling

If you specify a line number in the LIST command, then only that line will be displayed on the computer screen. Two line numbers tell the computer to list a **range** of lines. This is especially useful when you are interested in a particular subroutine.

LLIST

The function of the **LLIST** command is to list your program to a line printer. Some people find it easier to work on programs that are printed out, called **hard copy**. You always should print your program occasionally as a backup. The format of the LLIST command is

$$\text{LLIST } [\textit{line number}][\textit{-line number}]$$

The line numbers specify ranges, just as they do in the LIST command.

RUN

The function of the **RUN** command is to execute all or part of a program. The formats of the RUN command are:

$$\text{RUN } [\textit{line number}]$$
$$\text{RUN } \textit{"program name"}$$

The first format is used when you are in the process of writing a BASIC program. If you specify a line number, the program in the computer's memory will be executed starting with that line. Otherwise the entire program will be run. The second format is used when you want to execute a program stored on disk. When you specify a **program name**, the computer system will find that program on disk, load it into the computer's memory, and then begin executing it.

SAVE

The function of the **SAVE** command is to store a BASIC program on a disk or diskette. Every program must have a unique name. If you are working on a program that you already saved once, then using the same program name will replace the old version of your program with the new one. But be careful. Most computer systems do not warn you if you are using a program name that already exists—you could inadvertently erase a good program. Most programmers keep a list of program names and a brief description of each one. The format of the SAVE command is

SAVE "*program name*"

Find out from your instructor what the maximum length of a program name is on your computer system. Note this in the margin.

LOAD

The function of the **LOAD** command is to place into the computer's memory a copy of a BASIC program stored on disk. This is useful when you want to work on a program, but do not want to RUN it. The format of the LOAD command is

LOAD "*program name*"

In summary, there are six BASIC commands that you will use frequently. They are NEW, LIST, LLIST, RUN, SAVE, and LOAD. BASIC commands are usually executed as soon as you enter them. The formats of some of these commands may be different for your computer system. If so, you should note them in your textbook.

▓ PROGRAMMING WITH A SUBSET OF BASIC INSTRUCTIONS

In this section, you will learn the format and structure of a BASIC program, some fundamentals about storing data in a program, and a subset of BASIC instructions. In all, there are about 150 BASIC instructions. In this module you will learn the most useful ones, instructions that will enable you to write programs to solve many different business problems.

Program Readability

BASIC instructions can be executed in two modes, **direct** and **indirect**. In the direct mode (also called immediate mode), BASIC commands and statements are not preceded by line numbers. They are executed as soon as they are entered. This can be useful for **debugging**, or determining if a program instruction is functioning the way you expect it to. The other mode, indirect mode, is the one in which programs are written.

In the **indirect mode**, program instructions are preceded by line numbers. The computer stores the instructions in order by line number, no matter what order they happened to be entered. When the RUN command is issued, the program in memory is executed.

Line numbers are integers in the range 0 to 64000 (or so — the upper limit varies from one computer system to another). You can number your program statements any way you wish, but most people leave gaps between numbers to make inserting instructions easier later on. For example, in the sample program in figure G–2, most of the lines are numbered by tens (6010, 6020, 6030, 6040, and so forth). This way, if the programmer decides to insert an instruction between lines 6030 and 6040, he or she can number the new instruction 6035 (or any number between 6030 and 6040). The BASIC interpreter places that new line in sequence, between the other two. Had the original lines been numbered 6031 and 6032, then at least one of them would have to be renumbered to insert another instruction in between.

Notice in the sample program that the lines in each subroutine are numbered within a *range*, in this case in the thousands. The first module is in the one thousands, the next one is in the five thousands, and so forth. The choice of numbers was strictly arbitrary, although selecting line numbers carefully can make matching the program to the structure chart (see figure G–1), and identifying subroutines easier.

Another way to make a program more readable is to use the BASIC **REM**, or REMarks, statement. The REM statement allows you to include comments in your program. The BASIC interpreter ignores anything you write in a REM statement. The format for the REM statement is

REM [*comment*]

Placing meaningful remarks in a program can be helpful not only to other people reading your program listing, but also to you, especially when your program is a long one. Notice that in the sample program, each module is clearly identified with a box of asterisks constructed from several REM statements. Other remarks are also interspersed throughout the program. Lines 1110 through 1140 contain remarks. Notice that on each of those lines a colon (:) follows the first statement on the line. The colon indicates that another statement is going to occupy the same line number. The technique of placing two or more program instructions on a single line is dangerous and should be used *only* to include remarks.

Data Types

The purpose of programs is to process data: to get input from the business world, manipulate it, sometimes store it, and produce data for the user. In BASIC you need to distinguish between *numeric data* and *string data*. You also need to know the difference between *variables* and *constants*.

Numeric data can be integers (whole numbers), such as 123, −87, and 64232. Numeric data can also be decimals (fractions), such as 98.6, .075, and −3.14159. Numbers are entered using any combination of the 10 digits (0−9), the decimal point (.), and the minus sign (−). Do not use commas, dollar signs, or any other symbol. If you use a minus sign, it must precede the number.

String data is sometimes called *alphanumeric data*. It includes any combination of letters, digits, punctuation, and special characters. String data is enclosed in quotation marks. Some examples follow:

```
"Do you want to see the instructions for this program?"
"Y"
"Time flies? You cannot! They fly too fast!"
"15786"
```

A **constant** is a data item whose value cannot change. Any string or number can be a constant. All of the preceding examples of numeric data and string data are constants.

In contrast, a **variable** is a data item whose value *can* change during program execution. When you write a program, you create variables, or locations in the computer's memory where data you need is stored during program execution. You need to do two things to define a variable: You must name it, and you must indicate whether it will contain numeric or string data.

The variable name accomplishes both tasks. All versions of BASIC accept one- or two-character variable names, and the rules for creating them are simple:

- A numeric variable name can be one alphabetic character (for example, K), or one alphabetic character followed by a digit (for example, K9).
- A string variable name is one alphabetic character followed by a dollar sign (for example, K$, pronounced "K string").

Most versions of BASIC allow many more characters in variable names, and the examples throughout these modules take advantage of the improved readability of longer, more descriptive variable names. Determine the limits that your school's version of BASIC imposes on variable names before you begin to write a program.

Examine the sample program and identify the variable names. Is RESPONSE$ a variable name (line 1100)? Is it a numeric variable or a string variable? What about PRINCIPAL (line 6030)? Is PRINCIPAL a numeric or a string variable?

Keywords are words such as RUN, LLIST, INPUT, and PRINT that have a special meaning to the BASIC translator program. Keywords cannot be used as variable names.

Now that you know something about the format of a BASIC program and some fundamentals about the way BASIC names and handles data, you can learn some BASIC program statements. These statements are presented in groups. First we will look at how to get input and then how to manipulate data, how to control the sequence of instructions in the program, and finally how to issue output.

Getting Input

The BASIC statement we use to get input from the person at the computer keyboard is the **INPUT** statement. Its format is

INPUT [*"prompt string"* ;] *variable*

The prompt string is a message that will be displayed on the computer screen to tell the user what to do. Notice that it is optional. You can also tell the user what to enter by preceding the INPUT statement with a PRINT statement — you can then eliminate the prompt string (as was done in the sample program; see lines 1090 through 1100 and lines 6020 through 6070 for examples).

The variable may be either numeric or string data. When the INPUT statement is encountered during program execution, the computer displays the prompt string, if any exists, and then pauses for the user to type a response. When the user presses the carriage return or Enter key, the data is placed in the variable, and program execution resumes with the next statement.

The data type the user enters must match the variable type. If it does not, the program will wait until the correct type of data is entered. For example, if the program instruction is

INPUT PRINCIPAL

and the user types $2000.00, the program cannot continue. The dollar sign makes the entry string data rather than numeric data. PRINCIPAL, however, is a numeric variable. The data types do not match, so the program will wait for the user to try again.

Because what kind of data is to be entered is not always clear to the user, you always should tell the user. This can be done with a PRINT statement or by using the *"prompt string"* option of the INPUT statement.

Manipulating Data

Once data is in the program we need to process it. This usually means performing arithmetic operations on it or moving it around from one place in the computer's memory to another. Both of these functions are accomplished in BASIC by the **LET**, or **assignment**, statement.

The function of the LET statement is to assign the value of an expression to a variable. An **expression** can be a string or numeric constant; a variable; or a combination of constants, variables, and arithmetic operators. This last option is used for performing arithmetic operations.

The format of the LET statement is

$$[\text{LET}] \; \textit{variable} = \textit{expression}$$

Notice that the word *LET* is optional. Some older versions of BASIC require it, but this is becoming rare. The equal sign indicates that the statement is a LET statement.

When a LET statement is encountered during program execution, the computer evaluates the expression on the *right* side of the equal sign and then places its value in the variable named on the *left* side of the equal sign. If the expression is a constant, then the computer simply sets the variable to that constant. For example, LET DELI.ORDER$ = "TUNA ON RYE" replaces whatever used to be in the variable DELI.ORDER$ with the letters "TUNA ON RYE". (See figure G–4.) Similarly, LET PI = 3.14159 replaces whatever was in the variable PI with the numeric value 3.14159.

The expression can also be another variable. This causes the value in the variable on the right of the equal sign to be copied into the variable on the left of the equal sign, replacing whatever was there before. Some examples follow on the next page.

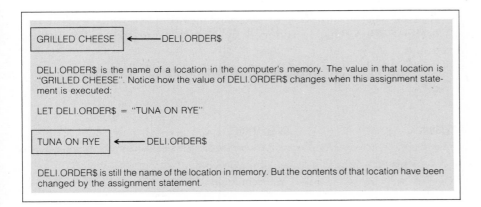

FIGURE G–4
Assignment statement changes the value of a variable

```
STARTING.NUMBER = AGE
X = Y
ITEM.ORDERED$ = STOCK.DESCRIPTION$
```

In every case, the value of the variable on the left is changed to match the value of the variable on the right.

Finally, the expression in a LET statement can be an **arithmetic expression**, a combination of numeric variables, numeric constants, arithmetic operators, and parentheses. The **arithmetic operators** are symbols we use to indicate which operations we want performed on the data. The operations are addition ($+$), subtraction ($-$), multiplication ($*$), division ($/$), and exponentiation ($\wedge$ or $\uparrow$).

When an expression contains more than one operation, the order in which the operations are executed is significant. This order is called a **hierarchy**, and in BASIC the hierarchy is as follows: Operations enclosed in parentheses are evaluated first, followed by all exponentiation, followed by multiplication and division (which one happens first is not significant), followed by addition and subtraction (which one happens first is not significant). See figure G–5 for a summary.

The **operands** in an arithmetic expression must be either numeric constants or numeric variables. The computer cannot perform arithmetic on string data. Examples of arithmetic operations follow:

```
AVERAGE = GRADE.POINTS / CREDITS
TOTAL.DUE = SUBTOTAL + TAX + SHIPPING + PAST.DUE - CREDIT
BATTING.AVERAGE = HITS / AT.BATS * 1000
AREA = 3.14159 * RADIUS ^ 2
PROJECTED.INCOME = (MONTHLY.SALARY + MONTHLY.BONUS) * 12
```

In the sample program there are two lines that contain arithmetic operations: line 7020 and line 7030. In line 7020, the value of PRINCIPAL is increased by adding this year's interest to it.

```
7020 PRINCIPAL = PRINCIPAL + (PRINCIPAL * INTEREST.RATE)
```

In line 7030, the number of years remaining for the investment, YEARS.REMAINING, is reduced by 1 each time the instruction is executed.

```
7030 YEARS.REMAINING = YEARS.REMAINING - 1
```

FIGURE G–5
Arithmetic operators listed in hierarchy

SYMBOL	OPERATION
( )	Parentheses
$\wedge$ or $\uparrow$	Exponentiation
$*$ and $/$	Multiplication and division
$+$ and $-$	Addition and subtraction

Notice that all of the operands are numeric. Also notice that parentheses were used in line 7020 for clarity, not because they were necessary.

In summary, the LET statement allows you to manipulate data in the computer. Use it to set the value of a variable to a constant, to the value of another variable, or to the value of an arithmetic expression.

Controlling Program Sequence

If you do not specify otherwise, the instructions in your BASIC program are executed in the order in which they are stored, that is, by line number. Program control falls through from one statement to the next. There are three important statements, or pairs of statements, that allow you to alter the sequence of events. They are IF, GOSUB-RETURN, and WHILE-WEND. A fourth instruction, END, marks the end of the program. Be sure to learn whether your school's version of BASIC supports these instructions and if the rules of syntax are different for your version of BASIC than for the Microsoft BASIC.

IF

The function of the IF, or **IF-THEN-ELSE**, statement is to make a decision regarding program flow based on the result of a test condition. The format is

```
IF condition THEN statement(s) [ELSE statement(s)]
```

When an IF statement is encountered during program execution, a condition is tested. If the condition exists, or is true, then the statement or statements following the word *THEN* are executed, but not the ones following the word *ELSE*. If the condition is false, then the statement or statements following the word *ELSE* are executed, but not the ones following the word *THEN*. No matter which path is taken, the computer then continues with the next sequential instruction following the IF statement.

Notice that the ELSE part of the IF statement is optional. Leaving out the ELSE simply indicates that something will be done only if the condition is true. Nothing special happens when the condition is false. This is sometimes referred to as a null ELSE.

A **condition** is a logical expression composed of variables, constants, and relational operators. **Relational operators** are used to compare two values. Figure G–6 shows the relational operators and their meanings.

The statement(s) in the IF statement can be other IF statements, LET statements, GOSUB statements (explained in the next section), or any other BASIC statement. Here are some examples of IF statements:

```
IF SALARY > 30000
      THEN BONUS = SALARY * .05
      ELSE BONUS = 500
IF STATE$ = "CT"
      THEN TAX.RATE = .075
IF PARENT.AGE < = CHILD.AGE
      THEN PRINT "Age error. Re-enter."
```

Another example may be found in the sample program in line 1110.

```
1110 IF RESPONSE$ = "Y" OR "y" THEN GOSUB 5000
```

Notice that the IF statement on line 1110 includes a **compound condition**—actually two conditions connected by a **logical operator**. Two of the logical operators are **AND** and **OR**. Building a compound condition using the logical operator OR means that the condition will be true as long as at least one of the subconditions is true. That is what is happening in the sample program. As long as there is either an uppercase *Y* or a lowercase *y* in the variable RESPONSE$, the condition is considered true, and GOSUB 5000 will be executed.

If the logical operator AND is used, then *both* subconditions must be true for the condition to be considered true. For example, if we wanted to count the number of customers in Chicago whose balances exceed $500, then we would write this IF statement:

```
IF CUSTOMER.CITY$ = "CHICAGO" AND CUSTOMER.BALANCE > 500
      THEN COUNT = COUNT + 1
```

In summary, the IF statement is used to direct the flow of a program based on the results of a test condition. One set of statements can be performed when the condition is true, another set when the condition is false. After the IF statement is executed, program control resumes with the next instruction following the IF statement.

GOSUB-RETURN

Perhaps the most useful pair of statements in many versions of BASIC are the **GOSUB-RETURN** statements. The purpose of the GOSUB-RETURN statements is to branch to, and return from, a subroutine.

FIGURE G–6

Relational operators

OPERATOR	RELATION TESTED	EXAMPLE
=	Equality	SALARY = 30000
<>	Inequality	SALARY <> 30000
<	Less than	SALARY < 30000
>	Greater than	SALARY > 30000
< =	Less than or equal to	SALARY < = 30000
> =	Greater than or equal to	SALARY > = 30000

Recall that one of the first steps in good program design is to break the large problem into smaller, manageable ones and then write a subroutine to solve each of the smaller problems. The GOSUB-RETURN statements make the implementation of such a design relatively easy.

The format of GOSUB-RETURN is

```
GOSUB line number
    :
    :
RETURN
```

Line number is the first line number of the subroutine. When a GOSUB statement is encountered during program execution, control passes to the subroutine starting at that line number. When the RETURN statement is encountered, control returns to the statement following the GOSUB. Here is an example:

```
1000 INPUT "Enter volume in liters"; LITERS
1010 GOSUB 6000 : REM Subroutine performs conversions
1030 PRINT CUBIC.INCHES; " Cubic inches, "; DRY.QUARTS; " Dry quarts"
1040 END
6000 REM Convert liters to cubic inches and dry quarts
6010 CUBIC.INCHES = LITERS * 61.02
6020 DRY.QUARTS = LITERS * .908
6999 RETURN
```

The sequence of instructions is line 1000, line 1010, line 6000, line 6010, line 6020, line 6999, line 1030, line 1040.

Notice that the GOSUB-RETURN statements always return control to the instruction following the GOSUB statement.

Several examples of GOSUB-RETURN can be found in the sample program, at lines 1110, 1120, 1130, and 1140. Figure G–7 shows how GOSUB-RETURN statements control program flow in the sample program.

WHILE-WEND

A third BASIC statement pair, **WHILE-WEND**, enables you to easily build a loop into your program. A loop, you will recall, is an instruction group that is executed again and again *as long as some condition is being met*. (Another way to describe a loop is to say that it is repeated *until some terminating condition is met*. This perception is also true — you can think of it either way. For example, maybe you will play baseball *while it is light outside*. Or you might prefer to say that you will play baseball *until it gets dark*. The statements are essentially the same.)

The function of the WHILE-WEND statements is to execute a series of statements in a loop as long as a given condition is true. Their format is

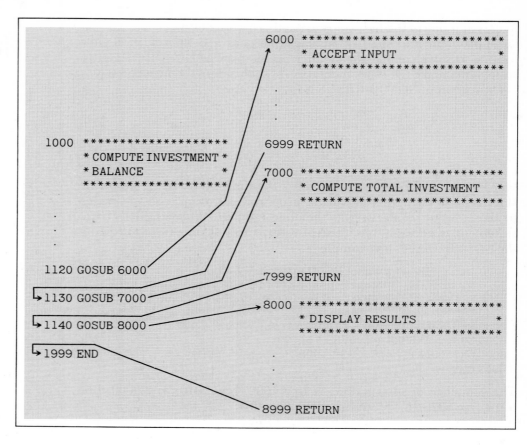

```
                                        6000 ******************************
                                             * ACCEPT INPUT               *
                                             ******************************
                                              .
                                              .
                                              .
1000  ********************              6999 RETURN
      * COMPUTE INVESTMENT *            7000 ******************************
      * BALANCE            *                 * COMPUTE TOTAL INVESTMENT   *
      ********************                    ******************************
      .
      .
      .
1120 GOSUB 6000                         7999 RETURN
1130 GOSUB 7000                         8000 ******************************
                                             * DISPLAY RESULTS            *
1140 GOSUB 8000                              ******************************
1999 END
                                              .
                                              .
                                              .
                                        8999 RETURN
```

```
WHILE condition
  .
  .
  .
[Instructions you want to execute in the loop]
  .
  .
  .
WEND
```

   When a **WHILE** statement is encountered during program execution, the condition is tested. If it is true, the instructions following the **WHILE** are executed until the **WEND** is encountered. When the **WEND** is encountered, BASIC passes control back to the **WHILE** statement, and the condition is tested again. If the condition still is true, the process is repeated. If the condition is not true any time it is tested, program control passes to the instruction following the **WEND**.

Here is an example of WHILE-WEND statements that allow a user to run a program over and over until he or she types "QUIT":

```
1000 INPUT "IF YOU WANT TO STOP, TYPE <QUIT>";RESPONSE$
1010 WHILE RESPONSE$ <> "QUIT"
1020    INPUT "NAME";NAME$
1030    INPUT "SALARY";SALARY
1040    TAX = SALARY * .1667
1050    PRINT "TAX FOR";NAME$;" IS";TAX
1060    INPUT "IF YOU WANT TO STOP, TYPE <QUIT>";RESPONSE$
1070 WEND
1080 END
```

Notice that the operand in the **terminating condition**, RESPONSE$, is altered by an instruction inside the loop, the INPUT statement on line 1060. It is important to ensure that the terminating condition is eventually met—otherwise the instructions will be repeated forever (or until you interrupt the program). This situation is called an **endless loop**. Find out from your instructor how to interrupt a program (for example, some computers use Control-C) and write the instructions in the box provided here.

Interrupting Program Execution

The loop in the sample program is found in the subroutine COMPUTE TOTAL INVESTMENT (lines 7000 through 7999). This loop repeats an arithmetic operation once for every year in the life of the investment.

END

The purpose of the **END** statement is to terminate program execution. When an END statement is encountered during program execution, the program ceases to execute. The END statement is sometimes referred to as the **logical** end of the program (as opposed to the **physical** end of the program, which is simply the instruction with the highest line number). The format for the END statement is

END

The END statement can appear anywhere in the program, but it *should* be placed at the end of the controlling module. In the sample program, for example, the controlling module is in lines 1000 through 1999; the END statement is on line 1999, the last line of that module. Placing the END statement here ensures that none of the subsequent modules (Display Instructions, Accept Input Parameters, and so forth) are accidentally executed. Program control should be passed to those modules only by means of a GOSUB statement, not by falling through to them accidentally.

Issuing Output

The final group of BASIC instructions presented in this module are the ones you use to produce output.

CLS

The purpose of the **CLS** statement is to clear the computer screen. When it is encountered during program execution, everything displayed on the computer screen is erased, and the cursor is positioned in the upper left corner of the screen. Its format is

```
CLS
```

The CLS statement is used three times in the sample program, in lines 1080, 5010, and 6010. Some BASIC versions use the word HOME.

PRINT

The function of the **PRINT** statement is to display output on the computer screen. Its format is

```
PRINT [expression][...expression]
```

A PRINT statement with no expressions displays a blank line on the computer screen. A PRINT statement with one expression displays the value of the expression. An expression can be a numeric or string variable, a numeric or string constant, or an arithmetic expression. In the following examples, assume that NAME$ contains MURPHY, and AGE contains 7 (note: the symbol ⌿ means a blank is displayed):

PRINT statement	Displayed on screen
PRINT 1234	⌿1234
PRINT "ACME PAINT"	ACME PAINT
PRINT NAME$	MURPHY
PRINT AGE	⌿7
PRINT AGE * 3	⌿21

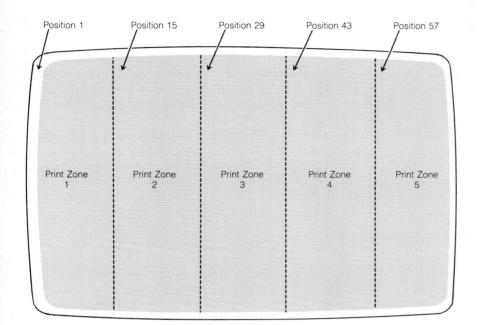

You can also display several items on the same line. This is accomplished by listing more than one expression in the PRINT statement. Where the items will appear on the computer screen depends on the **delimeter** you use to separate the expressions in the list. You can use a semicolon (;) or a comma.

BASIC divides a line on the computer screen into **print zones**. (The Microsoft **BASIC** used in this text uses print zones of 14 positions each; your version of **BASIC** may be different. If so, note the width of your **BASIC**'s print zones in the margin of this book for quick reference.) If you use a comma between two expressions, the second expression will be printed in the next print zone on the screen (see figure G – 8).

In contrast, a semicolon causes the next value to be printed immediately after the previous one. Here are some examples:

```
PRINT Statement              Displayed on screen

PRINT "DATE"                 DATE
PRINT "DATE", "NAME"         DATE        NAME
PRINT "DATE" ; "NAME"        DATENAME
PRINT "DATE " ; "NAME"       DATE NAME
```

There are many **PRINT** statements in the sample program. Most of them display only one expression. The **PRINT** statement on line 8020 displays both a string constant and the value of a numeric variable.

```
8020 PRINT "When fully matured your investment will be worth "; PRINCIPAL
```

QUESTIONS

G.1 Why is BASIC a popular language in schools? Why is its popularity growing in the business field?

G.2 List the four steps taken to develop a computer program to solve a problem.

G.3 What do the boxes on a structure chart represent? What relationship, if any, is there between the boxes on a structure chart and the corresponding BASIC program?

G.4 What is the purpose of pseudocode? Which module on a structure chart is usually defined with pseudocode? What makes that module different from the others on the structure chart?

G.5 What is the difference between a constant and a variable? Give three examples of each.

G.6 What is the difference between a numeric constant and a string constant? Give three examples of each.

G.7 What is the advantage of placing many REM (remark) statements in a BASIC program? What is the disadvantage?

G.8 What is a loop? How is a loop implemented in BASIC? What is a terminating condition? What happens if the terminating condition is never met?

G.9 Examine the loop in the sample program (lines 7010-7040). What is the terminating condition? How did the programmer ensure that the loop eventually terminates?

(continued)

In summary, the CLS and PRINT statements are used to display output on the computer screen.

Let's review the problem we solved in this chapter. We needed to write a program that would calculate the value of an investment at its maturity. We began by breaking the problem down into small pieces, and then we drew a structure chart to illustrate the program that would solve the problem.

Next, we used a subset of BASIC instructions to code each of the lower level modules on the structure chart. Finally, we wrote the instructions for the controlling module at the top of the structure chart. In doing this, we joined all the small solutions together to form a cohesive program that solved the overall problem.

SUMMARY

More and more businesses are turning to ready-made software rather than developing programs themselves. This virtually eliminates the need for business people to become skilled computer programmers. However, because many business people will have some contact with programs or programmers, it is useful to have a fundamental knowledge of computer programming. The language chosen most frequently as an introducion to programming is BASIC, primarily because it is easy to learn.

Developing a program involves several steps:

- Understanding the problem.
- Breaking the problem into small ones.
- Solving each small problem separately.
- Joining the small solutions together into one program.

Several tools are available to aid the program designer. Two of them are the structure chart, which is a pictorial description of the program broken down into small modules, or subroutines; and pseudocode, which looks like a programming language, but is not restricted by strict rules of syntax like a programming language is. Both a structure chart and pseudocode describing the logic of a program are developed *before* code is written.

BASIC commands are usually executed as soon as they are entered. Commands usually perform program maintenance functions. The commands presented in this module are NEW, SAVE, LIST, LLIST, RUN, and LOAD.

BASIC programs are made up of numbered statements. Execution of a program is deferred until the programmer issues the RUN command. The BASIC statements presented in this module are REM, INPUT, LET, IF, GOSUB-RETURN, WHILE-WEND, END, CLS, and PRINT.

These statements and commands are a *subset* of the ones available. You can write programs to solve many business problems using just these instructions. More BASIC instructions will be presented in module H. The BASIC reference manuals at your school contain a comprehensive listing and description of all the BASIC instructions available on your system.

Refer to the sample program in this module to do the following exercises.

G.10 Change the program so the final output includes the original principal amount. The final message should be: "When fully matured, your investment of xxxxx will be worth xxxxx."

G.11 Change the program so the final output states the length of the investment. The sentence should say: "After xx years, your investment of xxxxx will be worth xxxxx."

G.12 Change the program so it computes the profit made on the investment at maturity (the difference between the original principal and the final balance). In addition to its present output, the program should also print: "The profit on your investment is " followed by the amount.

G.13 Change the controlling module in the program so the user can rerun the program until he or she wants to quit.

WORD LIST

BASIC	RUN	IF-THEN-ELSE
System program	Program name	Null ELSE
Application program	SAVE	Condition
Structure chart	LOAD	Relational operator
Module	Direct mode	Compound condition
Loop	Indirect mode	Logical operator
Program logic	Debugging	AND
Pseudocode	REM	OR
Subroutine	Numeric data	GOSUB-RETURN
Controlling module	String data	WHILE-WEND
Version	Constant	Terminating condition
Command	Variable	Endless loop
Statement	Keyword	END
Syntax	INPUT	Logical end
NEW	LET	Physical end
LIST	Assignment	CLS
Line number	Expression	PRINT
Scroll	Arithmetic expression	Delimeter
Range	Arithmetic operator	Print zone
LLIST	Hierarchy	
Hard copy	Operand	

EXERCISES TO CHALLENGE YOUR THINKING

A. Develop a program that calculates sales averages. The user will enter four sales figures for a sales representative. The program will respond with the average sale amount. The user should be able to run the program again for a different sales representative.

B. Develop a program that calculates sales commission totals. The user will enter several sales commission values for a sales representative, but we do not know how many values will be entered. Therefore the program must tell the user how to indicate that all the sales commissions for a representative have been entered. The user should be able to run this program again for a different sales representative.

C. Using as a starting point the program you developed for exercise B, develop a program that calculates the sales commission total and average sale commission for a sales representative.

In order to find the average sale commission value you need to count the number of commission values entered. When all the values have been entered you will divide that number into the sales commission total.

D. Develop a program to calculate the monthly payment on a mortgage. The formula is

$$PAYMENT = PRINCIPAL \times \frac{IR}{(1 - (1 + IR)^{-N})}$$

where

PRINCIPAL = Original loan amount
IR = Monthly interest rate (annual interest rate/12)
N = Number of payments on the loan (12 × number of years of the loan)

The user will need to enter the original loan amount, the annual interest rate, and the number of years of the loan.

APPLYING BASIC
TO COMMON BUSINESS
PROBLEMS

MODULE H

You learned a small subset of BASIC instructions in module G. In this module you will add to your knowledge of BASIC and of problem solving. We will examine three very common program functions: storing data on a disk file, retrieving data from a disk file, and producing printed reports. Each program function is illustrated with a program that might be used at a videotape store. As in the previous module, all programs were written in Microsoft BASIC and executed under MS-DOS. They will run on any IBM PC or PC-compatible computer. If some of the BASIC instructions at your school are different, then you should note them in the margins of this text.

Three popular techniques to improve program readability are incorporated into the sample programs in this module. First, some versions of BASIC (including Microsoft BASIC and IBM BASIC) allow a single quotation mark (') to replace the BASIC keyword REM (for remarks). This option helps reduce the cluttered look of some program listings. Second, some versions of BASIC allow a remark to appear on a line of code without using the colon (:) to indicate multiple statements. Third, many programmers find listing all of a program's variables in a remarks section at the beginning of the program helpful. You are encouraged to do the same.

Keep in mind as you study this module that you are learning a subset of BASIC instructions that can be used to solve many programming problems. If you discover that you want to learn more about BASIC, then you are encouraged to use the BASIC reference manuals at your school.

CREATING A DISK FILE

Magnetic disks are by far the most popular storage media for microcomputers. It thus makes sense to know how to record data on a disk (create a disk file) and retrieve data from a disk (read a disk file). Processing disk files is the topic of the next two sections.

Figure H–1 shows data as it is stored on a disk (for more information about disk files, see chapter 8). Notice that each record contains several fields. One record simply follows the previous one on the disk.

When a program creates a disk file, we must perform certain tasks. First, because many files are usually stored on the same disk, each file must have a *unique file name*. This is sometimes called an **external file name**, because it actually is recorded on the disk directory and so is external to the program.

Second, the file management routines for input files (files that already contain data) are different from the routines used for output files (files that are being created). Therefore, the program must distinguish between an **input file** and an **output file.**

Third, a file must be **opened** before it can be written to or read from. Opening a file causes the operating system's data management routines to search the disk directory for a file by that name. When a

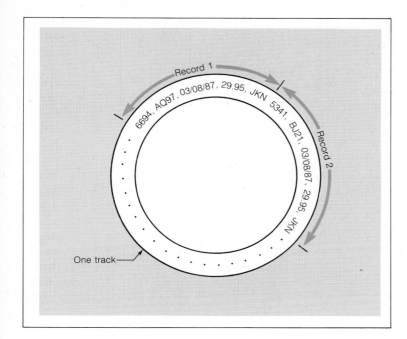

program attempts to open an input file, the file must be on the disk or an error occurs. When a program opens an output file, if a file with the same name already exists on the disk, the new data will write over the data that is already there; if no file with the same name is on the disk, the data management routine finds space for the new file somewhere on the disk.

Fourth, because several files can be used by a single program, each one must be assigned a different number within the program. The *number* — not the external file *name* — is used by the program whenever the file is referenced. This number can be thought of as the file's **internal name**, that is, the one used inside the program.

Fifth, when a program is finished with a file, the program must release the file back to the system, because other programs may be waiting to process it. In most cases, once a file is opened by a program, that program is the only one that can use the file. Releasing a file is accomplished by **closing** it. For an output file, the end-of-file marker (see module F) is written when the file is closed. Clearly, closing an output file is very important. If the end-of-file marker were not written, then subsequent programs would have difficulty processing the file. These tasks are summarized here.

- Assign a unique external file name.
- Identify a file as an input or output file.
- Assign an internal file number.
- Open the file before reading it or writing to it.
- Close the file when you are finished with it.

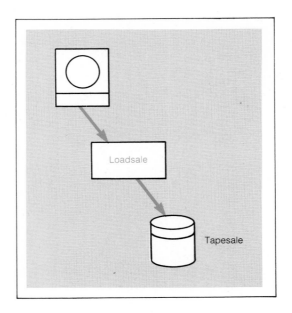

Designing the Program

Suppose the videotape store referred to in module F needs to store sales transactions on disk. A sales clerk periodically enters into the computer system details about videotape sales. The data entered for each sale is the customer number, tape number, date of sale, sale amount, and the initials of the clerk who made the sale. These five fields make up a tape sale record, which is stored in a disk file called TAPESALE.

The system flowchart in figure H–2 shows that the input for this program is data from the computer keyboard, and the output is a disk file.

This program contains only three modules, which are illustrated in the structure chart in figure H–3. The lower-level module called Get Input Data prompts the user to enter the sale data. The other lower-level module, Write Record on Disk, actually records the tape sale record in a disk file.

The controlling module, Load Sales File, enables the user to enter data until all of the tape sales are in. It begins by opening the disk file and then enters a loop to get input data and write a disk record. The loop is terminated when the user quits.

Pseudocode for the controlling module and for Get Input Data follow. Because the remaining module contains only one instruction, no pseudocode is needed.

```
BEGIN LOAD SALES FILE
      OPEN TAPE SALES FILE AS OUTPUT
      REPEAT WHILE USER WANTS TO ENTER DATA
            CALL GET INPUT DATA
            CALL WRITE RECORD ON DISK
            ASK USER IF HE/SHE WANTS TO QUIT
      END REPEAT
      CLOSE TAPE SALES FILE
END LOAD SALES FILE

BEGIN GET INPUT DATA
      PROMPT USER TO ENTER EACH FIELD
END GET INPUT DATA
```

Key BASIC Statements

This program contains three new **BASIC** statements. They are **OPEN**, **WRITE #**, and **CLOSE**. First we will look at the format of each statement. Then we will study the sample program.

OPEN

The purpose of the **OPEN** statement is to establish a file as an input or output file and to make it available to the program for processing. The format of the OPEN statement is

OPEN "*file name*" FOR *mode* AS *#file number*

The *file name* is the external file name recorded in the disk directory. Rules governing the format of the file name vary from one system to

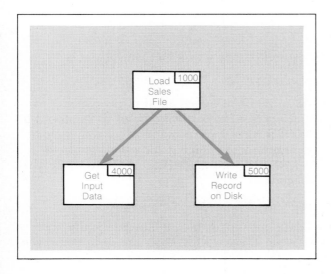

FIGURE H–3
Structure chart for program to create disk file

another. Find out from your instructor what the conventions are for naming files at your school and write them here:

```
Rules For Naming Disk Files
```

The *mode* is either INPUT or OUTPUT. Because this program is creating a file, the mode is OUTPUT. In the next sample program, the file will be read into the program, so the mode will be INPUT.

Keep in mind that if you open an output file and a file by that name already exists on disk, the old file is automatically destroyed. You should keep a list of all of your filenames to be sure you do not inadvertently destroy any of them.

The *file number* is a number from 1 up to the maximum number of files that the system allows to be open at once. Note here the maximum number of files your system allows at a time:

If we were to open one output file named New Order and another output file named Work Log, then the BASIC instructions would be

```
OPEN "NEWORDER" FOR OUTPUT AS #1
OPEN "WORKLOG" FOR OUTPUT AS #2
```

WRITE

The **WRITE #** statement stores data in a disk file. The format is

```
WRITE #file number, list of expressions
```

The *file number* is the number assigned to the file when it was opened. The *list of expressions* is a list of all the fields to be stored in one record. For example, if a record were made up of four fields — name, address, telephone number, and age — then the list of expressions might be NAME\$, ADDRESS\$, PHONE\$, AGE. To write this record on a file you would code

```
WRITE #1, NAME$, ADDRESS$, PHONE$, AGE
```

When BASIC writes data in a disk file, it automatically inserts delimiters (commas) between the data fields on the disk; some versions of BASIC put quotation marks around each string field. Thus, data recorded by the preceding write statement might look like this:

```
"HENRY KNOX","OSHKOSH","555-7932",21
"ELENA CONTERRON","SAN FRANCISCO","555-1000",36
"FREDERICK KLINE","APPLETON","555-8294",42
```

CLOSE

The function of the **CLOSE** statement is to disassociate a file from a program and, in the case of an output file, to write the end-of-file marker. After a file is closed, it cannot be accessed by the program until it is again opened.

The format of the CLOSE statement is:

```
CLOSE  #file number
```

The *file number* is the number under which the file was opened.

The sample program in figure H–4 uses the three new BASIC statements, as well as several you already know. Study this program carefully. Trace the flow of the program using the structure chart in figure H–3 and pseudocode on page 603 as guides.

▓ READING A DISK FILE

Data stored on a disk must be read into a program to be processed. Such a disk file is called an *input file* because it provides input data to the program. In this section you will learn how to read data from a BASIC input file.

Designing the Program

The program we will develop here reads the data about videotape sales that is stored in a disk file and displays the file contents on the computer screen. The system flowchart in figure H–5 shows this program's input and output. The external name of the disk file is TAPESALE.

You learned in module F about program design for processing files. This program is so brief that a structure chart is not necessary — it would have only one module. The pseudocode for the single program module follows.

```
BEGIN READ SALES
      WRITE COLUMN HEADERS ON SCREEN
      OPEN INPUT FILE
      REPEAT UNTIL EOF IS ENCOUNTERED
            GET A RECORD FROM THE FILE
            DISPLAY RECORD CONTENTS ON SCREEN
      END REPEAT
      CLOSE INPUT FILE
END READ SALES
```

QUESTIONS AND EXERCISES

H.1 What function does the OPEN statement perform? Why is it needed when processing a disk file?

H.2 What function does the WRITE statement perform?

H.3 What is the WRITE statement that records TAPE.NUMBER\$ and PRICE on output file #3?

H.4 What is the function of the CLOSE statement?

H.5 In addition to the function named in your answer to question H.4, what else does the CLOSE statement do when it is used with an output file?

H.6 When you put data into a new file, is the file opened as an input or an output file?

H.7 When you retrieve data from a file, is the file an input file or an output file?

H.8 Develop a BASIC program that creates a disk file containing names and phone numbers. The user should be allowed to enter as many names and phone numbers as he or she wants to.

H.9 Develop a BASIC program that creates a disk file containing the following data:

Tape Number	% Discount
BJ21	10
MD63	12
XP55	15
EY78	25
LG14	10

BASIC program that creates disk file

```
1000 '*********************************************************************
1010 '*  PROGRAM NAME = "LOADSALE"                                       *
1020 '*  CREATES DISK FILE CALLED "TAPESALE"                             *
1030 '*********************************************************************
1040 '
1041 '
1042 'Format of TAPESALE file:
1043 '    CUSTOMER.NUMBER$
1044 '    TAPE.NUMBER$
1045 '    SALE.DATE$
1046 '    SALE.AMOUNT
1047 '    CLERK$
1048 '
1049 'User modified control fields:
1050 '    QUIT$   Initialized to N; user changes it to Y to quit program
1053 '
1100 OPEN "TAPESALE" FOR OUTPUT AS #1
1105 QUIT$ = "N"
1110 WHILE QUIT$ <> "Y" AND QUIT$ <> "y"
1120     GOSUB 4000          ' Get input data
1130     GOSUB 5000          ' Write record
1140     PRINT
1150     INPUT "DO YOU WANT TO QUIT < Y or N >"; QUIT$
1160 WEND
1170 CLOSE  #1
1999 END
4000 '*********************************************************************
4010 '*  PROMPT USER FOR INPUT DATA                                      *
4020 '*********************************************************************
4030 '
4040 CLS
4070     INPUT "CUSTOMER NUMBER"; CUSTOMER.NUMBER$
4080     INPUT "TAPE NUMBER"; TAPE.NUMBER$
4090     INPUT "DATE OF SALE"; SALE.DATE$
4100     INPUT "SALE.AMOUNT"; SALE.AMOUNT
4110     INPUT "INITIALS OF CLERK"; CLERK$
4999 RETURN
5000 '*********************************************************************
5010 '*  WRITE RECORD ON DISK FILE                                       *
5020 '*********************************************************************
5030 '
5110 WRITE #1, CUSTOMER.NUMBER$, TAPE.NUMBER$, SALE.DATE$,
              SALE.AMOUNT, CLERK$

5999 RETURN
```

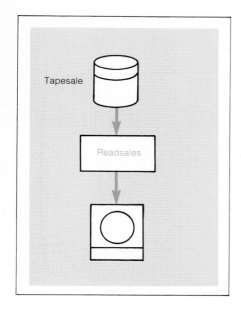

Notice the instruction "Write column headers on screen." *Column headers* are words displayed at the top of the screen so the user knows what the data is (see figure H – 6). Without column headers, how would a user know whether 23.99 were the price of a tape, the markup on a music video, the weight of a VCR, or something else? Name your columns carefully, giving the user as much information in as little space as possible — after all, a computer screen is rather small.

This program needs to open the input file. Then it reads and displays each record until the end-of-file marker is detected. When the file has been completely processed, the file must be closed to release it back to the system.

Key BASIC Statements

The key BASIC statements for input file processing are OPEN, INPUT #, the EOF function, and CLOSE. We will examine the function and format of each of these, and then we will put them together into a BASIC program that solves the problem of reading the tape sales file.

OPEN

We noted earlier that the function of the OPEN statement is to prepare a file for processing. The format of an OPEN statement is

OPEN "*file name*" FOR *mode* AS #*file number*

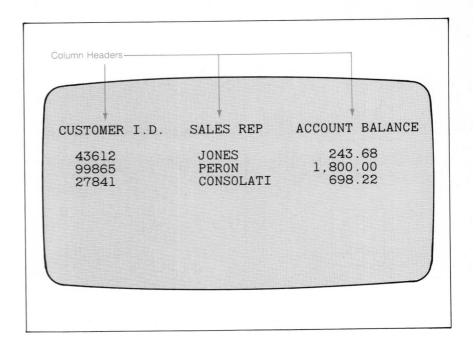

The *file name* is the external file name that was used when the file was created. The *mode* for an input file is INPUT. The *file number* is the file's internal file identification; it can be any integer from 1 to the maximum specified for your system. Thus, the only difference between an OPEN statement for an input file and an OPEN statement for an output file is the value of the mode parameter.

These **BASIC** instructions would open three input files:

```
OPEN "NAMES" FOR INPUT AS #1
OPEN "GRADES" FOR INPUT AS #2
OPEN "AWARDS" FOR INPUT AS #3
```

INPUT

The next key **BASIC** statement for input file processing is the **INPUT #** statement. This statement is not the same as the INPUT statement that gets data the user enters via the keyboard. This statement gets data from an input file. Its format is

```
INPUT #file number, list of expressions
```

The *file number* is the number under which the file was opened. The *list of expressions* is a list of the data fields that make up one record in the file. The data fields in the record will be read, one by one, into the fields named in the list. For this to be done correctly, you must know how many fields there were when the file was created, and you must know which fields are string and which are numeric — the data types must match.

For example, suppose a file were created with the following record format: Account number (numeric), Name (string), Age (numeric), Eye color (string), Weight (numeric). If the file were opened as file #1, then the INPUT # statement might look like this:

```
INPUT #1, ACCOUNT.NUM, NAME$, AGE, EYE.COLOR$, WEIGHT
```

Notice that the list of expressions defines the fields in the order used when the file was created and uses the same data types.

EOF Function

When you read an input file, you must not read past the last data record, or a program error will occur. To prevent this, you can test for the end-of-file condition in the WHILE statement that controls the program loop.

The purpose of the **EOF function** is to signal when the last data record in an input file has been processed. EOF is false when records remain in the file and is true when all the records have been read. The format of the WHILE statement that tests for the end of a file is

```
WHILE NOT EOF (file number)
```

The *file number* is the number assigned to a file when it was opened. Thus, if the program were looping through file #3, the WHILE statement controlling the loop might be

```
WHILE NOT EOF (3)
```

Here is a program that counts the number of records in an account file:

```
05  COUNT = 0
10  OPEN "ACCOUNTS" FOR INPUT AS #1
20  WHILE  NOT EOF (1)
30      INPUT#1, NAME$, ADDRESS$, BALANCE
40      COUNT = COUNT + 1
50  WEND
60  PRINT "NUMBER OF ACCOUNTS IS"; COUNT
70  CLOSE #1
80  END
```

You can think of the WHILE NOT EOF statement as peeking ahead into the file to see if the next record is the end-of-file marker. So long as the next record is *not* the end-of-file marker, the loop will be executed one more time.

```
1000 ' ******************************************************
1010 ' * PROGRAM NAME: READSALES                            *
1020 ' * READS DISK FILE CALLED "TAPESALE"                  *
1030 ' ******************************************************
1040 '
1041 '
1042 'Format of TAPESALE file:
1043 '   CUSTOMER.NUMBER$
1044 '   TAPE.NUMBER$
1045 '   SALE.DATE$
1046 '   SALE.AMOUNT
1047 '   CLERK$
1048 '
1110 CLS
1120 PRINT "CUST#", "TAPE", "DATE", "AMOUNT", "CLERK"
1130 OPEN "TAPESALE" FOR INPUT AS #1
1200 WHILE NOT EOF (1)
1210    INPUT #1, CUSTOMER.NUMBER$, TAPE.NUMBER$, SALE.DATE$,
                  SALE.AMOUNT, CLERK$
1220    PRINT CUSTOMER.NUMBER$, TAPE.NUMBER$, SALE.DATE$, SALE.AMOUNT, CLERK$
1250 WEND
1260 CLOSE #1
1999 END
```

FIGURE H–7
BASIC program that reads a disk file

CLOSE

The last key **BASIC** statement used in file processing is the **CLOSE** statement. You learned about the **CLOSE** statement when studying output files. The format of the **CLOSE** statement is identical for input and output files:

CLOSE #*file number*

In the previous example statement 70 closes the file:

70   CLOSE #1

The program presented in figure H–7 reads the video tape sales file described previously. It is a very short program, but it uses some new statements. Study it carefully.

▥ PRINTING A REPORT

The type of output most frequently produced by business computer systems is printed output. Computers print invoices, purchase orders, theater tickets, inventory summaries, bank deposit receipts, and thousands of other documents. In this section you will learn how to design a report and develop a program to issue it.

Designing the Report

Reports must be easy to read and interpret. Producing such a report takes careful planning. You must determine what information should be printed, where information should be printed, and how information should be labeled. Look at the report in figure H – 8.

This report is easy to read. Each column of data is clearly labeled. The summary figures at the bottom of the page are separated from the body of the report. The report is carefully laid out so the columns are close enough together to be easily read but are not crowded. The report itself is centered on the page.

There are four types of lines in this report, and they are labeled in figure H – 8. **Header lines** appear at the beginning of a report (and at the top of each new page, if the report is several pages long). Header lines can be report headers or column headers. **Report headers** usually include the title of the report and the time period the report covers. **Column headers** identify the columns of data.

Detail lines comprise the body of the report. There is often (but not always) one detail line for each input record.

Summary lines often include accumulated subtotals, grand totals, averages, and counts. In the sample report summary lines show the number of sales made as well as a grand total of all sales.

Trailer lines are printed at the end of the report. A trailer line simply indicates that the report is complete. Trailers can be useful to a user reading a report several pages long. Trailers can also be helpful to data-control clerks who separate reports printed on continuous-form paper. A highly visible trailer — say, several lines of asterisks — can make finding the end of a report easier.

QUESTIONS AND EXERCISES

H.10 What is the function of the OPEN statement with respect to an input file?

H.11 Why must you test for end-of-file when processing an input file?

H.12 Is EOF true or false when data records remain in a file to be read?

H.13 Why must the number of fields in an INPUT # statement match the number of fields used when the file was created?

H.14 Besides the number of fields, what else must match between the INPUT # statement and the file as it was created?

H.15 Develop a program that reads the file you created in your answer to exercise H.8. This program should display all the records in the file on the computer screen.

H.16 Develop a program that reads the file you created in your answer to exercise H.9. Your program should display all the records on the screen. It should also count the number of records in the file and display that number.

FIGURE H – 8
Tape Sales summary report

```
Report headers                TAPE SALES SUMMARY
                               MARCH — APRIL 1987      Column headers
         TAPE NUMBER           SALE DATE      AMOUNT        CLERK

Detail    AQ97                 03/08/87       29.95         JKN
lines     BJ21                 03/08/87       29.95         JKN
          MD63                 03/10/87       35.50         BTD
          LG14                 03/10/87       24.50         JKN
          XP55                 04/01/87       29.95         BTD
          EY78                 04/15/87       35.50         BTD
          AQ97                 04/22/87       29.95         BTD

                           NUMBER OF SALES...    7         Summary
                           TOTAL SALES...    $215.30       lines

END OF REPORT          Trailer
```

FIGURE H–9
Printer spacing chart

FIGURE H–10
Design of Tape Sales Summary Report

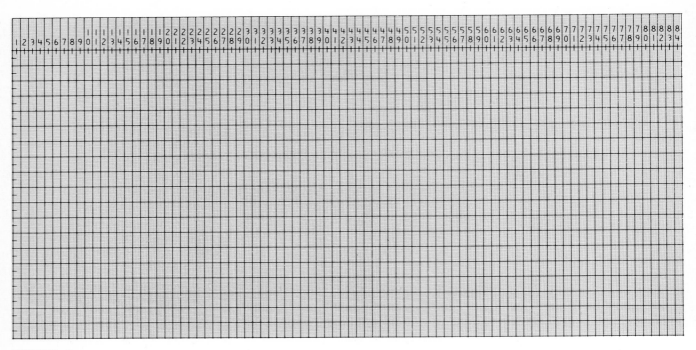

```
                          TAPE SALES SUMMARY

                          MARCH - APRIL 1987

        TAPE NUMBER        SALE DATE        AMOUNT        CLERK

            XXXX           XXXXXXXX         XXX.XX         XXX
            XXXX           XXXXXXXX         XXX.XX         XXX
            XXXX           XXXXXXXX         XXX.XX         XXX
            XXXX           XXXXXXXX         XXX.XX         XXX


                          NUMBER OF SALES...XXX
                          TOTAL SALES...XXXX.XX


  END OF REPORT
```

A special grid paper, called a **printer spacing chart** (see figure H – 9), is used to design a printed report (a slightly different one can be used for screen design). Printer spacing charts, or *print charts* as they are sometimes called, are usually 144 columns wide to accommodate the very wide paper used in some computer printers. Most microcomputer printers print 80 or 132 characters on one line. You thus need to use only the first 80 or 132 boxes on the chart when you use a microcomputer printer. In this section, we will design a report to be issued by an 80-character printer.

The report design for the report in figure H – 8 appears in figure H – 10. Notice that some of the boxes contain X's. X's indicate where *variable data* will be printed. Contrast that to the header and trailer lines, which contain *constant data*, characters that are the same no matter how often or with what data the program is run. Designing the report format should be done prior to designing the program. In many cases, user approval of the report format is needed before programming can begin.

Designing the Program

Having established what is to be printed and where it will appear, we can now design the BASIC program. Input for this program will be the tape sales file we have used previously. Notice that we are printing only four of the five fields from each input record. Also, note that we need to count the number of sales to be printed at the end, and we need to accumulate a grand total of sales. The structure chart for this program is illustrated in figure H – 11.

FIGURE H – 11
Structure chart for program that issues report

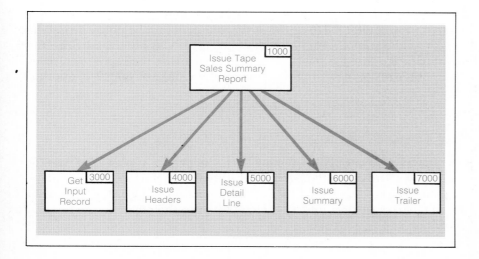

Each of the lower-level modules requires only a few lines of code, because each one is so simple. The controlling module, Issue Tape Sales Summary Report, contains most of the program logic. The pseudocode for that module and for Issue Headers follows. The other modules are simple, and their pseudocode is not included here.

```
BEGIN ISSUE TAPE SALES SUMMARY REPORT
     CALL ISSUE HEADERS
     OPEN INPUT TAPE SALES FILE

     REPEAT WHILE THERE ARE MORE INPUT RECORDS
          CALL GET INPUT RECORD
          CALL ISSUE DETAIL LINE
          ADD 1 TO NUMBER OF SALES
          ADD SALE AMOUNT TO GRAND TOTAL
     END REPEAT

     CLOSE TAPE SALES FILE
     CALL ISSUE SUMMARY
     CALL ISSUE TRAILER
END ISSUE TAPE SALES SUMMARY REPORT

BEGIN ISSUE HEADERS
     ADVANCE TO TOP OF PAGE
     WRITE HEADER LINES
END ISSUE HEADERS
```

The logic in the controlling module is straightforward. Notice that the headers, summary, and trailers are issued outside of the main program loop. This ensures that they are printed only once. Conversely, detail lines are issued from within the loop. There will be one detail line for every input record.

In the module called Issue Headers we find the instruction "Advance to top of page." This ensures that the program begins printing the report at the top of a blank sheet of paper. If you do not advance the printer to the top of a page, it will begin printing the report wherever the printer rests, including the middle of the page or on top of another report.

Key BASIC Statements

You need to learn only a few new topics to print a report. You need to learn how to advance the paper in the printer to the top of a new page, and you need to learn the LPRINT statement with the TAB and USING options. First we will look at how to advance the paper to the top of a page.

ASCII Code for Form Feed

Most printers can be controlled by commands sent from a program. Some commands control the type size; some control the density of the printed characters; some move the printer carriage forward for single, double, or triple spacing. One command tells the printer to eject whatever paper is currently available for printing and to prepare to print at the top of a new page. This means either rolling continuous form paper past the next perforation or waiting for a new sheet of paper to be inserted.

Printers are designed to interpret certain one-byte ASCII codes as carriage-control instructions. The ASCII code for advancing to the top of a new page is 00001100. Thus, when that particular one-byte code is sent from the program to the printer, the printer advances to the top of the next page.

Unfortunately, there is no easy way to send that one-byte code, because no key on the computer keyboard matches it. (There are 256 unique ASCII codes, but far fewer keys. As a result, some codes are not easily represented.) The only way to access the code is to copy it from a special list of ASCII codes, or **control characters** (it happens to be the twelfth one in the list), into a variable. Then you can send the value in the variable to the printer, and the printer will know what to do. Here's how it works:

```
10  FORM.FEED$ = CHR$(12)
20  LPRINT FORM.FEED$
```

The variable is called FORM.FEED$. Into FORM.FEED$ we place the twelfth control character in the list of ASCII codes: **CHR$(12)**. Had the form-feed character been number 15 in the list, we would have used CHR$(15); had it been number 236 in the list, we would have used CHR$(236). As it happens, the form-feed character is number 12, so we use CHR$(12).

Now FORM.FEED$ contains 00001100, the code that tells the printer what to do. The next step is to send the code to the printer. All data and control characters are sent to the printer with the **LPRINT** statement. LPRINT stands for *line print*. Thus, the next instruction, LPRINT FORM.FEED$, sends the one-byte code to the printer, which receives the character and then does exactly what it is supposed to. After the LPRINT instruction is executed, there is a clean sheet of paper in the printer.

LPRINT

The function of the LPRINT statement is to print data on a line printer. The format of the LPRINT statement is the same as the PRINT statement. Refer to module G for a review of the PRINT statement.

One option of the LPRINT (and PRINT) statement writes data at specific print positions. This option is the TAB option. The format of **LPRINT TAB** is

LPRINT TAB(*print position*); *expression*

The *print position* is the number of the print position in which you want the value of expression to begin. For our purposes, TAB can be between 1 and 80. On other printers you might be able to print in up to 132 positions.

If you have carefully designed your report on a printer spacing chart, then coding the LPRINT statement is easy. You can tell at a glance the print position in which every constant and variable begins. The following examples print the words "Pepperidge Farm" beginning at position 41 and the value of a name field beginning at position 6:

LPRINT TAB(41); "PEPPERIDGE FARM"
LPRINT TAB(6); NAME$

LPRINT USING

The purpose of the **LPRINT USING** (and PRINT USING) statement is to print numbers using a special format. The format you specify determines the placement of the decimal point, commas, and dollar sign. Thus, instead of printing a number like this—56674.32—you can print it like this: $56,674.32. The format of the LPRINT USING statement is

LPRINT USING "*print format*"; *list of expressions*

The *list of expressions* can be numeric variables or numeric constants. If several numbers are printed, all of them are formatted with the same **print format**.

The *print format* is a series of characters that you build to format the number when it is printed. Some of the characters you can use in the print format are the number sign (#), the decimal point (.), the comma (,), and the dollar sign ($). Let's look at each one.

The number sign is used to indicate a digit position. Digit positions are always printed, except for leading nonsignificant digits. A decimal point may appear anywhere in the format. If all of the digits to the left of the decimal point are zeros, then only one zero will be printed—the rest of the positions will be filled with blanks. If there are more digits to the right of the decimal point than your print format can accommodate, the number will be **rounded** when it is printed. Figure H-12 contains several examples of formatted numbers.

Include a comma to the left of the decimal point to cause a comma to be inserted to the left of every third digit to the left of the decimal point (between the hundreds and thousands columns, between the hundred thousands and millions columns, and so forth).

QUESTIONS AND EXERCISES

H.17 Name four types of lines on a printed report.

H.18 What is the difference between a report header and a column header?

H.19 What is the purpose of a printer spacing chart?

H.20 Why must you advance paper to the top of a page before printing a report?

H.21 What BASIC instruction sends the form-feed character to the printer? Write the entire statement.

H.22 What is the function of the LPRINT statement?

H.23 What does the TAB option of the LPRINT statement accomplish?

(continued)

PRINT FORMAT	DATA	DISPLAYED RESULTS
"##.##"	15.78	15.78
"##.##"	.78	⌿0.78
"##.##"	.786	⌿0.79
"#,###.##"	2365.86	2,365.86
"#,###.##"	2365.8	2,365.80
"#,###.##"	.892	⌿⌿⌿⌿0.89
"$$###.##"	56.32	⌿⌿$56.32
"$$###.##"	56.328	⌿⌿$56.33

Note: ⌿ indicates a blank print position.

FIGURE H–12
Formatted numeric data

A double dollar sign ($$) at the beginning of the print format causes a dollar sign to be printed to the left of the first significant digit. This is sometimes referred to as a **floating dollar sign**, because its position depends on the number of digits being printed.

With these new topics—advancing paper to the top of a page, LPRINT TAB, and LPRINT USING—in mind, examine the program listed in figure H–13. This program produces the report in figure H–8, following the design we developed previously. As you can see, the program gets its input from a disk file, and it produces a report with header, detail, summary, and trailer lines. Study it carefully, until you understand every instruction.

▦ SUMMARY

Many business programs read data from disk files, create disk files, or produce reports—in fact, most do all three. File processing and report writing can be done in BASIC, and there are special statements for these functions.

Disk files must be opened as input or output files; they must be identified with an external file name and an internal file number, and when the program finishes processing disk files, it must close them. The key BASIC instructions for an output disk file are OPEN, WRITE #, and CLOSE.

The key BASIC statements for an input disk file are OPEN, INPUT #, and CLOSE. In addition, a program must test for the end of the input file. A special built-in BASIC function, called *EOF*, enables the program to check for the end-of-file condition. EOF is false when data records remain in the input file.

The number of fields named in an INPUT # statement and the data types of those fields must match those of the data stored in the file. That is, the list of fields in an INPUT # statement must correspond to the list of fields in the WRITE # statement that created the file.

H.24 Write the BASIC instruction to print your name centered on an 80-column report line.

H.25 What is the function of the # symbol in a numeric print format? What is the function of the comma? What is the function of the decimal point? The double dollar sign?

H.26 Modify the sample program in figure H–13 to leave a blank line between the first and second lines of report headers (between TAPE SALES SUMMARY and MARCH–APRIL 1987).

H.27 Modify the sample program to calculate and print the average sale. (Hint: Average sale = Total sales ÷ Number of sales).

H.28 Modify the same sample program as in exercise H.27, but this time center the report trailer (END OF REPORT) on the last line.

H.29 Develop a program that produces a report listing the data in the file you created in your answer to exercise H.8. Include report headers and column headers.

H.30 Develop a program that produces a report listing the data in the file you created in your answer to exercise H.9. Count the number of records and print that number at the end of the report.

BASIC program that issues Tape Sales
Summary Report

```
1000 ' ****************************************************
1010 ' *  PROGRAM NAME: "SALESRPT"                        *
1020 ' *  ISSUE SALES SUMMARY REPORT                      *
1030 ' *  READS DISK FILE CALLED "TAPESALE"               *
1040 ' ****************************************************
1041 '
1042 ' Format of TAPESALE file:
1043 '    CUSTOMER.NUMBER$
1044 '    TAPE.NUMBER$
1045 '    SALE.DATE$
1046 '    SALE.AMOUNT
1047 '    CLERK$
1049 ' Accumulators:
1050 '    NUMBER.OF.SALES Count of all sales
1052 '    GRAND.TOTAL Total sales for all clerks
1053 '
1054 ' Special control characters:
1055 '    NEW.PAGE$   Set to ASCII code for top of page—CHR$(12)
1056 '
1100 NUMBER.OF.SALES = 0            'Initialize counter
1101 GRAND.TOTAL = 0                'Initialize accumulator
1103 GOSUB 4000                     'Call Issue Headers module
1105 OPEN "TAPESALE" FOR INPUT AS #1
1110 WHILE NOT EOF (1)
1120    GOSUB 3000                  'Call Get Input Record
1130    GOSUB 5000                  'Call Issue Detail Line
1140    NUMBER.OF.SALES = NUMBER.OF.SALES + 1
1150    GRAND.TOTAL = GRAND.TOTAL + SALE.AMOUNT
1160 WEND
1170 '
1180 GOSUB 6000                     'Call Issue Summary Lines
1190 GOSUB 7000                     'Call Issue Report Trailer
1200 CLOSE #1
1999 END
3000 ' ****************************************************
3010 ' *  GET INPUT RECORD                                *
3020 ' ****************************************************
3030 '
3110 INPUT #1, CUSTOMER.NUMBER$, TAPE.NUMBER$, SALE.DATE$,
               SALE.AMOUNT, CLERK$
3999 RETURN
4000 ' ****************************************************
4010 ' *  ISSUE HEADERS                                   *
4020 ' ****************************************************
4030 '
4100 NEW.PAGE$ = CHR$(12)     'Control character for form feed
4110 LPRINT NEW.PAGE$
```

```
4120 LPRINT TAB(31); "TAPE SALES SUMMARY"
4130 LPRINT TAB(31); "MARCH - APRIL 1987"
4135 LPRINT
4140 LPRINT TAB(18); "TAPE NUMBER";
4150 LPRINT TAB(34); "SALE DATE";
4160 LPRINT TAB(48); "AMOUNT";
4170 LPRINT TAB(59); "CLERK"
4180 LPRINT
4999 RETURN
5000 ' ************************************************
5010 ' *  ISSUE DETAIL LINE                          *
5020 ' ************************************************
5030 '
5100 LPRINT TAB(21); TAPE.NUMBER$;
5110 LPRINT TAB(34); SALE.DATE$;
5120 LPRINT TAB(48); USING "###.##"; SALE.AMOUNT;
5130 LPRINT TAB(60); CLERK$
5999 RETURN
6000 ' ************************************************
6010 ' *  ISSUE SUMMARY LINES                        *
6020 ' ************************************************
6030 '
6100 LPRINT
6110 LPRINT
6120 LPRINT TAB(33); "NUMBER OF SALES...";
6130 LPRINT TAB(51); USING "###"; NUMBER.OF.SALES
6170 LPRINT TAB(33); "TOTAL SALES...";
6180 LPRINT TAB(47); USING "$$#,###.##"; GRAND.TOTAL
6999 RETURN
7000 ' ************************************************
7010 ' *  ISSUE REPORT TRAILER MESSAGE               *
7020 ' ************************************************
7030 '
7100 LPRINT
7105 LPRINT
7110 LPRINT TAB(5); "END OF REPORT"
7999 RETURN
```

Report writing is a two-step process: First you design the report, and then you develop the program to produce the report. Report design is performed with the aid of a printer spacing chart. Reports can have as many as four different line types: header lines, detail lines, summary lines, and trailer lines.

Several BASIC statements are used for report writing. The **LPRINT** statement sends data and control information to the printer. One such control character is the ASCII code that tells the printer to feed another sheet of paper or move continuous-form paper to the top of the next page.

The LPRINT statement also sends data to the printer. The TAB option of the LPRINT statement allows the programmer to specify the starting print position for each field.

The LPRINT USING statement is used to format numeric data to make it more readable. This includes suppressing leading zeros, inserting decimal points and commas, and including a dollar sign. Special symbols in a format string indicate the particular formatting wanted.

The BASIC programming language includes dozens of other instructions, and it can be used to write astonishingly complex programs. If you are interested in mastering the BASIC language, you should get one of the many fine books about the language available today — and you should practice. Writing programs is one way to use a computer to help you solve business problems.

WORD LIST

External file name	EOF function	Control character
Input file	Header line	CHR$(12)
Output file	Report header	LPRINT
Opening a file	Column header	LPRINT TAB
Internal file name	Detail line	LPRINT USING
Closing a file	Summary line	Print format
OPEN	Trailer line	Rounding
WRITE #	Printer spacing chart	Floating dollar sign
CLOSE	Variable data	
INPUT #	Constant data	

EXERCISES TO CHALLENGE YOUR THINKING

A. Refer to the model program design for data validation presented in module F. Write a BASIC program for that model design.

B. Refer to the model program design for counting records and accumulating totals presented in module F. Write a BASIC program for that model design.

C. Refer to the sample program design for the control level break presented in module F. Write a BASIC program for that model design.

CREDITS

Table of Contents

Apple Computer, Inc., Hewlett-Packard, Cullinet Software, Inc., Apple Computer, Inc., Hewlett Packard, Anacomp, Inc., Gannett Company, ISSCO, The Computer Museum, Apple Computer, Inc., Hewlett-Packard, Interleaf, Inc., Calcomp Company, Apple Computer, Inc., Apple Computer, Inc.

Hardware

Page 1: Anacomp, Inc. Pages 2–3: Universal Data Systems, Hewlett-Packard. Pages 4–5: Prime Computer, Inc., American Airlines, Apple Computer, Inc., IBM Corporation, American Airlines. Pages 6–7: Ramteck Corporation, Hewlett-Packard, IBM Corporation, Apple Computer, Inc. Pages 8–9: Apple Computer, Inc., Apple Computer, Inc., Digital Equipment Corporation, Sun Microsystems. Pages 10–11: Digital Equipment Corporation, CRAY Research, Inc., Sun Microsystems. Pages 12–13: Anacomp, Inc., Xerox Corporation, Xerox Corporation, Hewlett-Packard. Pages 14–15: L.A. Schwaber-Barziley, AT&T Company, Hewlett-Packard.

The Chip

Opener: IBM. Pages 2–3: Chuck O'Rear, Chuck O'Rear, Chuck O'Rear, Ramtek Corporation. Pages 4–5: Chuck O'Rear, Intel Corporation, Intel Corporation, Chuck O'Rear. Pages 6–7: Chuck O'Rear, Intel Corporation, Intel Corporation, Intel Corporation. Pages 8–9: Intel Corporation, AT&T Company, Intel Corporation, Intel Corporation, Intel Corporation, Chuck O'Rear, Hewlett-Packard. Pages 10–11: Hewlett-Packard, AT&T Company, Intel Corporation, Hewlett-Packard. Pages 12–13: RCA, National Semiconductor Corporation, Intel Corporation. Pages 14–15: Motorola, Hewlett-Packard, Hewlett-Packard. Page 16: National Semiconductor Corporation.

Computers and Society

Page 1: IBM Corporation. Pages 2–3: Chuck O'Rear, McDonnell Douglas Corporation, Chuck O'Rear, Battelle Memorial Institute. Pages 4–5: IBM, AT&T Company, Chuck O'Rear. Pages 6–7: IBM Corporation, Anacomp, Inc., IBM, Hewlett-Packard. Pages 8–9: Hewlett-Packard, Apple Computer, Inc., Televideo Systems, Inc., Universal Data Systems. Pages 10–11: Gannett Company, Gannett Company, Gannett Company, Fairchild, L. A. Schwaber-Barziley, Fairchild, AT&T Corporation. Pages 12–13: NASA, Ramtek Corporation, Chuck O'Rear. Pages 14–15: Apple Computer, Inc., Chuck O'Rear, Chuck O'Rear, IBM Corporation. Page 16: Chuck O'Rear.

Graphics

Page 1: Ramtek Corporation. Pages 2–3: Ramtek Corporation, Decision Resources, Inc., Ramtek Corporation, 3M. Pages 4–5: Tektronic, Inc., ISSCO. Pages 6–7: 3M,

Cullinet Software, Inc., IBM Corporation, Honeywell, Inc., Hewlett-Packard. Pages 8–9: ISSCO, Decision Resources, Inc., Decision Resources, Inc., Decision Resources, Inc., ISSCO, ISSCO. Pages 10–11: 3M, ISSCO, ISSCO, ISSCO, ISSCO. Pages 12–13: Decision Resources, Inc., 3M, ISSCO, Cullinet Software, Inc. Pages 14–15: Apple Computer, Inc., ISSCO, 3M. Page 16: Decision Resources, Inc.

Chapter 1: Why Study Business Computing?

Profile: Use of Computer Technologies to Develop More Selective and Profitable Mailing Programs, p. 7. © *Marketing and Media Decisions*, April 1986. Application: The Graphic Representation Makes Information Easily Digestible and Easier to Remember, p. 12. Reprinted with permission from *Working Woman Magazine*. © 1986 by HAL Publications, Inc. Profile: A Computer System for an Expanding Small Business, p. 15. Reprinted with permission from *Working Woman Magazine*. © 1986 by HAL Publications, Inc. Profile: The Sales Force Is an Extension of the Marketing Research Department, p. 25. © *Sales and Marketing Management*, January 1986. Profile: IBM Marches Steadily Onward in the Vanguard, p. 29. *Fortune*, © 1985 Time, Inc. All rights reserved.

Chapter 2: Introduction to Business Computer Systems: Data

Microcomputers: A Strategic Tool that Gives Powerful Leverage in Manipulating Information, p. 36. © 1986 by *CW Communications, Inc.*, Framingham, MA. 01701. Reprinted from *Computerworld*. Profile: Accessing Words and Numbers by Computer Is Becoming an Increasingly Efficient Way to Do Business, p. 38. Reprinted with permission from *Working Woman Magazine*. © 1986 by HAL Publications, Inc. Application: The Smart Card Is Becoming a Fixture in Europe, p. 41. Fortune. © 1986 *Time Inc.* All rights reserved. Application: A Home Shopping Software Package Has Changed the Way to Purchase Supermarket Goods, p. 43. Reprinted by permission from *Chain Store Age Executive*, April, 1986. © Lebhar-Friedman, 425 Park Ave., NYC 10022. Application: Corporations Achieving Major Financial Advantage from Strategic Uses of Computerized Data, p. 45. © 1984, James Martin, *An Information Systems Manifesto*, pp. 8–9. Reprinted by permission of Prentice Hall, Inc., Englewood Cliffs, NJ.

Chapter 3: Introduction to Business Computer Systems: Hardware, Programs, Procedures, and Trained Personnel

Profile: Technology Driven When Market Driven Is The Management Rage, p. 70. © *Electronic Business*, April 1986. Profile: Open Systems Make their Machines Adaptable to the Industry's Evolving Technology, p. 75. © *Business Week*, February 1986. Application: Voice Response Equipment Is Beginning to Transform the Way Businesses Conduct Daily Affairs, p. 80. Reprinted by permission of the *Wall Street Journal*, © Dow Jones and Company, Inc. 1985. All rights reserved. Profile: Edgar Will Revolutionize both the Dissemination and Creation of Corporate Information, p. 93. Condensed by permission from *Nation's Business*, December, 1985. © 1985, U.S. Chamber of Commerce.

Chapter 4: Survey of Business Computer Systems Applications

Application: Ten Ways to Get Ahead with Information Technology, p. 97. © *Business Week*, November 1985. Application: Information is a Valuable Asset that Needs to be Managed, p. 102. Reprinted by permission of the *Wall Street Journal*. © Dow Jones and Company, Inc. 1985. All rights reserved. Application: Expensive Executive Toys or Productivity Tools?, p. 105. Excerpted from *Administrative Management*, © 1986, by Dalton Communications, Inc., NYC. Application: Retail Chains Make Strategic Use of Computers, p. 115. Reprinted by permission of the *Wall Street Journal*, © Dow Jones and Company, Inc. 1985. All rights reserved. Profile: Soviet Industry is in Big Trouble with Computers, p. 127. Seligman, *FORTUNE*, © 1985 — Time Inc. All rights reserved.

Chapter 5: The Systems Development Process

Application: A Properly Planned Interview Can Be an Analyst's Best Tool, p. 149. © *Data Management*, April 1986. Data Processing Management Association. Application: Prototyping Has many Advantages over Traditional Methods, p. 157. © *Data Management*, March 1986. Data Processing Management Association. Application: Yourdon, Inc. p. 163.

Chapter 6: A Case Application

Profile: Are Structured Methods for Systems Analysis and Design Being Used? p. 178. © *Journal of Systems Management*, June 1985. Cleveland, Ohio. Profile: Intech, p. 188. Application: You Can Cut Development Time By Up To 70%, p. 199. © *Computer Decisions*, March, 1986.

Chapter 7: Sequential File Processing Systems

Profile: A Sequential File System that Would Be User Friendly, p. 217. Reprinted by permission from *Chain Store Age Executive*, January, 1986. © Lebhar-Friedman, 425 Park Ave., NY 10022. Profile: A Service to Provide Businesses with Timely, Accurate, and Inexpensive Payroll Processing, p. 240. © *Business Computer Systems*, January 1986. Cahners Publishing.

Chapter 8: Direct Access File Processing Systems

Profile: TRW's Product Is Information, p. 248. Reprinted from *Computer Decisions*, October, 1985. © 1985, Haydon Pub. Co. Profile: The System Handled 45% Of All Airline Reservations Made In The U. S., p. 251. © 1986 by *CW Communications, Inc.*, Framingham, MA 01701. Reprinted from *Computerworld*. Profile: TWA Uses a Computer to Track Training, p. 267. © *Data Management*, 1986. Data Processing Management Association. Application: How Can They Back Up Files That Are Continuously Being Updated, p. 277. Reprinted with permission of *Datamation*® magazine, © by Technical Publishing Company. A Dun and Bradstreet Company, 1986.

Chapter 9: Database Processing

Application: Identify all Information Requirements of a User, p. 300. Reprinted from *Infosystems*, June 1986. © Hitchcock Publishing Company. Application: What Database Technology will Offer During the next Five to Ten Years, p. 318. Reprinted with permission of *Datamation*® magazine. © Technical Publishing Company. A Dun and Bradstreet Company, 1985. Profile: Database Professionals Have Suddenly Been Elevated to a Unique Level of Power, Respect and Visibility, p. 324. © *Data Management*, July 1985. Data Processing Management Association.

Chapter 10: Teleprocessing and Distributed Processing Systems

Application: Digital Signals Used by Computers and Printers Are Sent Long Distances, p. 342. © 1986 by CW Communications, Inc., Framingham, MA. 01701. Reprinted from *Computerworld*. Application: Innovations in LANs and Micro Networks Are Emerging, p. 363. © 1986 by CW Communications, Inc., Framingham, MA. 01701. Reprinted from *Computerworld*. Application: In Search of Datacomm Expertise, p. 368. Reprinted from *Infosystems*, March 1986. © Hitchcock Publishing Company.

Chapter 11: Management Information and Decision-Support Systems

Application: Computer Anxiety in Management: The Problem is neither Extensive nor Severe, p. 377. © *Communications* of ACM, July 1986. ACM, NY 10036. Application: Information Officers Bridge the Gap Between the Techies and Management, p. 380. Application: Decision Support Systems (DSS) for Marketing Mean Different Things to Different People, p. 383. © *Marketing Communications*, March 1986. New York, 10010. Application: Organizations Are Already Making DSS a Reality, p. 395. © 1986 by CW Communications, Inc., Framingham, MA. 01701. Reprinted from *Computerworld*. Application: Provide Expert Advice and Knowledge Support to Company Management, p. 400. © 1986 by CW Communications, Inc., Framingham, MA. 01701. Reprinted from *Computerworld*. Profile: Sperry Corp. Has Invested Heavily in Expert Systems, p. 403. © *Electronic Business*, February 1986.

Module A: History of Data Processing

Application: The Ultimate Factory Technology: Computer-Integrated Manufacturing, p. 432. © *Business Week*, March 1986. Application: The Key to Success in the Microcomputer Software Business, p. 434. © *Computer Decisions*, June 1986. Application: The 32-Bit Dash, p. 435. © *San Francisco Examiner and Chronicle*, 9/21/86. Application: Those Users Simply Want to Get the Job Done, p. 437. Excerpt from "Nothing Succeeds Like Simplicity" from *PC World*, May 1986. Application: Welcome to the World of Desktop Publishing, p. 440. © *Newsweek*, July 1986.

Module B: Personal Computer Applications

Application: Tips for the Enterprising Salesperson, p. 446. © *Personal Computing*, July 1986. Profile: Top PC Purchasers, p. 453. Reprinted by permission of the *Wall Street Journal*, Dow Jones and Company, Inc., 1985. All rights reserved. Application: Why Not Create Spreadsheets on a Microcomputer? p. 458. © *Harpers Magazine*, November 1984. Application: Features Handle almost any of Your Data Storage and Retrieval Tasks, p. 464. © *Personal Computing*, June 1986. Application: Users Have Come to Expect Certain Features, p. 474. © *Personal Computing*, June 1986.

Module D: Computer Crime, Security, and Control

Application: Perpetrators Were Insiders, p. 495. © 1986 by, CW Communications, Inc., Framingham, MA. 01701. Reprinted from *Computerworld*. Application: The Most Insidious Version of Computer Crime Is Data Interception, p. 498. © *The Office*, March 1986. Application: The Greatest Threat to Data Security Is the Corruption of Data by the Users, p. 502. © 1985 by CW Communications, Inc., Framingham, MA. 01701. Reprinted from *Computerworld*. Application: A Psychological Profile of the Hacker, p. 509. © 1985 by CW Communications, Inc., Framingham, MA. 01701. Reprinted from *Computerworld*.

Module E: System Programs, Operating Systems, and Programming Languages

Application: The Quick-and-Dirty Operating System Would Be the Foundation, p. 517. © 1986 by CW Communications, Inc., Framingham, MA. 01701. Reprinted from *Computerworld*. Application: Unix Barters for Business. © July, 1986. *Computer Decisions*. Application: One of the Hottest Software Developments of the 80s, p. 530. © *Direct Link*, June 1986.

INDEX